WITHDRAWN

MARKETING

2nd Edition

Rosalind Masterson & David Pickton

MARKETING
an introduction

© Rosalind Masterson and David Pickton 2010

This edition first published 2010
First edition first published by McGraw-Hill 2004

SAGE Publications Ltd
1 Oliver's Yard
55 City Road
London EC1Y 1SP

SAGE Publications Inc.
2455 Teller Road
Thousand Oaks, California 91320

SAGE Publications India Pvt Ltd
B 1/I 1 Mohan Cooperative Industrial Area
Mathura Road, Post Bag 7
New Delhi 110 044

SAGE Publications Asia-Pacific Pte Ltd
33 Pekin Street #02-01
Far East Square
Singapore 048763

Library of Congress Control Number: 2010929950

British Library Cataloguing in Publication data

A catalogue record for this book is available from the British Library

ISBN 978-1-84920-570-2
ISBN 978-1-84920-571-9 (pbk)

Typeset by C&M Digitals (P) Ltd, Chennai, India
Printed and bound in Great Britain by Ashford Colour Press Ltd
Printed on paper from sustainable resources

Brief contents

Part one   This is marketing 1

1   Marketing today   3

2   The marketing environment   37

Part two   Making sense of markets 81

3   Buyer behaviour   83

4   Market segmentation, targeting and positioning   119

5   Marketing research   161

Part three   The marketing mix 199

6   Product   201

7   Service products   239

8   Promotion (marketing communications)   269

9   Place   317

10   Price   355

Part four   Managing marketing 393

11   Building brands using the marketing mix   395

12   Marketing planning   435

v

Contents

Acknowledgements ix
Introduction to the focus themes x
Guided tour xvi

1 Marketing today 3

Introduction 4
What is marketing? 4
What marketing is not 9
Before marketing 10
Marketing beginnings 11
Demand and supply 12
Exchanges 14
Markets 15
Strategic orientations 15
Focusing on customers 23
Customers or consumers? 23
Marketing's changing emphasis 24
Retaining valuable customers 25
Twenty-first-century marketing 26
Summary 32
Challenges reviewed 32
Reading around 33
Self-review questions 33
Mini case study 34
References 35

2 The marketing environment 37

Introduction 38
Market dynamics 38
Environmental information 41
Marketing environment models 44
The organisational environment
   (the internal environment) 46
The external environment 48
The international marketing environment 68
Situation analysis 71
Stakeholders 74
Summary 76
Challenges reviewed 76
Reading around 77
Self-review questions 77
Mini case study 78
References 79

3 Buyer behaviour 83

Introduction 84
The consumer buyer decision process 84
Types of consumer buying decision 91
Levels of involvement 92
Influences on consumer buyer
   behaviour 95
The consumer buyer decision process
   for new products 104
Types of organisation and the products
   they purchase 106
Characteristics of organisational
   markets 107
Organisational buying situations 109
The buying centre 109
The organisational buying process 110
Organisational purchase criteria 112
Summary 114
Challenges reviewed 114
Reading around 114
Self-review questions 115
Mini case study 116
References 117

4   Market segmentation, targeting and positioning 119

Introduction   120
Market attractiveness   120
Why segment and target markets?   122
Segmentation approaches   125
Target marketing   142
Positioning   147
The five-stage process from market
    segmentation to positioning   154
Summary   157
Challenges reviewed   157
Reading around   158
Self-review questions   158
Mini case study   159
References   159

5   Marketing research 161

Introduction   162
 The use and value of marketing
    research   163
The marketing research process   164
Ethics in marketing research   166
Areas of marketing research   167
Secondary (desk) research   171
Commercially available research   173
Primary (field) research   175
Primary research methods and
    techniques   179
Sampling   187
Questionnaire design   189
Quality of marketing information   192
Forecasting and trend spotting   194
Summary   195
Challenges reviewed   195
Reading around   195
Self-review questions   196
Mini case study   197
References   197

6   Product 201

Introduction   202
What is a product?   202
The total product offering   204
Product types   208
Branding   212
Product development   217
The product life cycle   223
Product portfolio management   229
Summary   235
Challenges reviewed   235
Reading around   235
Self-review questions   236
Mini case study   237
References   238

7   Service products 239

Introduction   240
The importance of services   241
The nature of services   245
Different types of service   254
The services marketing mix   256
Service quality   261
Branding services   262
Service recovery   263
Summary   265
Challenges reviewed   265
Reading around   266
Self-review questions   266
Mini case study   267
References   268

8   Promotion (marketing communications) 269

Introduction   270
Managing promotion   271
Marketing communications objectives   272
Promotional strategy   273
The marketing communications process   276
Influencing customers   278
The marketing communications mix   281
Advertising   281
Public relations (PR)   293
Sales promotion   297
Personal selling   301
Direct marketing   304
Regulations   307

Part three

THE MARKETING MIX

Setting the marketing budget   308
Summary   311
Challenges reviewed   311
Reading around   312
Self-review questions   313
Mini case study   314
References   315

9 Place   317

Introduction   318
The importance of distribution   318
Channel members   319
The right space and time   324
Differing views of place   329
Place management   332
Designing the supply chain   334
Overseas operations and market
    entry options   339
Sources of power and conflict in the
    supply chain   342
Marketing functions in the supply chain   344
e-channels   346
Summary   350
Challenges reviewed   351
Reading around   351
Self-review questions   351
Mini case study   353
References   354

10 Price   355

Introduction   356
Why it is so important to get the
    price right   356
Pricing viewpoints   358
Pricing in the mix   361
Pricing objectives   361
Pricing techniques   362
Pricing methods   362
Pricing strategies   372
International pricing   376
Pricing tactics   378
Changing the price   380
Price elasticity of demand   382
Pricing on the Internet   385
Summary   388
Challenges reviewed   388
Reading around   389
Self-review questions   389
Mini case study   390
References   390
Appendix: additional cost-based
    pricing activity   391

Part four

MANAGING MARKETING

**11 Building brands: using the
marketing mix**   395

Introduction   396
Marketing mix objectives   396
The marketing mix: a reprise   398
Packaging – the fifth P?   407
The extended marketing mix: 7Ps   409
Mixing it (integrating the marketing mix)   412
Varying the mix through a product's life   413
Criticisms of the marketing mix   415
Branding   416
Brand equity   419
Brand types   420
Brand names   420
Branding strategies   422
Global branding   424
Brand loyalty   425
Summary   429
Challenges reviewed   429
Reading around   429
Self-review questions   430
Mini case study   431
References   432

12 Marketing planning   435

Introduction   436
Organising for marketing   436
Top-down or bottom-up planning?   440
The marketing planning process   444
Situation analysis   452
Business mission and marketing objectives   460
Marketing strategy   463
Marketing operations and implementation:
    tactics, resources and action   473
Contingency plans   475
Marketing evaluation and control   476
Summary   482
Challenges reviewed   482
Reading around   482
Self-review questions   483
Mini case study   484
References   484

Glossary   487
Index   499

Acknowledgements

The authors would like to extend their warmest thanks to the contributors to chapters in the first edition of this book:

Tony Garry
Len Tiu Wright
Kit Jackson
Phil Garton
Lynn Stainsby
Tracy Harwood

and also to case contributors:

Lynn Stainsby for *British Airways strike wrecks holidays and honeymoon*
Tracy Harwood for *All change!*

Introduction to the focus themes

Throughout this book there are focus boxes that relate the chapter's subject matter to certain key marketing themes. The boxes are:

- e-focus
- global focus
- B2B (business-to-business) focus
- ethical focus
- CRM (customer relationship management) focus
- expand your knowledge.

The themes have been chosen to reflect marketing's current major preoccupations. Marketing is a broad subject that overlaps with many other business functions: corporate strategy, human resource management, operations management, research and development, design and corporate communications. It also draws on many other academic disciplines, for example: psychology, economics, management strategy, intercultural relationships, media studies and sociology.

e-focus

The Internet has changed the way many businesses operate. It has far-reaching effects throughout the business world, affecting the ways that businesses communicate with their customers, their suppliers, their own staff. The Internet has shortened supply chains by cutting out trade intermediaries such as wholesalers and retailers, and allowing manufacturers to deal directly with their end customers. It has broadened the geographic reach of companies by providing a fast, cheap way to communicate with customers in other countries. It has increased the levels of competition in many industries, and the ways in which firms compete, by making it easier for companies to get into new markets and for smaller companies to compete with larger ones for business. For example, Amazon did not exist pre-Internet but it is now a serious global competitor in book selling. It has taken enormous amounts of trade away from the more established bookshops, and is rapidly branching out into other areas too.

Web pages provide a shop front to the world. Many companies now do very well without a high-street presence. Online, everyone looks the same size so there is no immediately obvious disadvantage for a smaller firm like there is for a smaller shop. It still has to deliver the goods of course, as only a few businesses manage to do that online (e.g. software and music downloads, and some services such as banking).

The influence of the Internet has been so great that many have declared it a new economy or a new market. Few marketers now take that position, referring to it instead as new media or a new marketing channel (i.e. way to sell to customers). The confusion arises because of the differing definitions of 'market'. Traditionally, a market is a place where buyers and sellers meet – in which case the Internet is a new place. However, increasingly, the term 'market' is used to refer to customers *en masse*. In this case, the Internet is not a new market; Internet buyers just buy online rather than offline, they are not necessarily new customers. If a firm finds new customers in another country via the Internet, then that is a new market – but the old way of describing them as a new geographic territory is still valid, indeed necessary, if their needs and wants are to be met effectively.

E-marketing does not stop at the Internet. Further new communications technologies are being developed all the time. Mobile phones are becoming a marketing tool – and are particularly useful for reaching the young. Digital television is in its infancy but interactive TV (iTV) may radically change the way we watch TV – and do TV advertising.

Throughout this book we will take the opportunity to reflect on the impact of new technologies and how they can be used to market goods and services.

global focus

There seems to be a general consensus that all marketing today is international. If this is not quite universally true now, it is certainly the way the trend is going. Almost all large firms have to deal with foreign competitors either in their home markets or abroad or both. Foreign rivals may not be much in evidence in the local shop, but foreign products are, and it may be foreign-owned supermarkets that are taking away its customers.

However, there are a large number of small to medium-sized businesses that have little or no dealings outside their own country. Many services businesses (e.g. cleaning, consultancy, law, accountancy, hairdressing and plumbing) have no significant international dimension. Will they all be crushed by the march of the multinationals? It seems unlikely that everyone will desert their regular hairdresser (especially those that make home visits and therefore have very low costs and, consequently, low prices), or that individuals and small business people will prefer to hand over their tax returns to an anonymous corporation or Internet service rather than the accountant round the corner.

All businesses, however small, need to be aware of the forces of globalisation though. They need to look out for new competition, new products and services and new opportunities. (See Chapter 2 for more about monitoring changes in the organisation's environment.)

The patterns of trade are changing. The twentieth century was the era of free trade, with richer countries pushing for the lowering, or abolition, of barriers to trade between nations, such as import duties, quotas (specified maximum amounts of imported goods), embargoes (bans on certain imported products) and subsidies (grants to producers that make home-produced goods cheaper). The twenty-first century may well prove, at least in its early part, to be a time of reconsolidation, but along new lines. Countries are clamouring to join trading blocs such as the European Union (EU), the North American Free Trade Association (NAFTA), the Association of South East Asian Nations (ASEAN) and Mercosur (an alliance of South American nations). Between them, the EU and NAFTA account for the bulk of world trade. Within their borders, member countries conduct trade on preferential terms. For example, within the EU, there are no import taxes and EU citizens can move to any country to work without obtaining work permits.

B2B (business-to-business) focus

Marketing grew from a start in consumer goods – in particular, FMCG (fast moving consumer goods). The term FMCG describes products that move off the shelves fast, i.e. they are bought frequently and so shops need to restock them regularly. These are everyday products such as soap, washing-up liquid, toothpaste, shampoo, breakfast cereal and bread – low-cost, kept in the cupboard all the time, items. Because of this heritage, modern marketing techniques favour the selling of these kinds of items to individuals for their own use. It is also the type of shopping that most people are more familiar with, so they usually relate to it better than B2B.

ACTIVITY

Look around your room. What items can you see that both a business and an individual might buy? How might their uses of the items differ? Where would they go to buy them?

When you want to buy something, the decision is usually yours although you may consult other people, particularly if you are not paying the whole cost yourself. Within organisations, it is rarely just one person who makes the decision on any significant purchase. There is a group of people who are referred to as the decision-making unit (DMU).

Take the example of a new car. There may be the fleet manager (who will specify which cars may be bought), the buyer (who will choose a supplier and negotiate terms), the finance department (which will set the budget and pay the invoice) and, of course, the person who is actually going to drive the car: the user. A potential supplier may have to deal with all these people and more. (See Chapter 3 for more on decision-making units.)

With all these people involved, purchasing decisions can become long and complicated. There are often forms that must be filled in, committee meetings called, procedures that must be followed. The organisation is likely to have rules about how many suppliers must be invited to bid for a contract. All of them must get a fair chance, and so there are more rules and procedures to ensure that this happens. It is a lot more complex than when you decide to buy a new printer for your PC.

However, just consider how much more money businesses have to spend than individuals. Large companies spend millions every year. When they do buy the everyday items that we do (pens, paper, sticky tape, etc.), they buy them by the crate. This is a good market to be in.

ethical focus

Different businesses operate according to different ethical codes. There was a time when it was considered perfectly acceptable for an employer to own his workers and their children, yet now such a practice would cause outrage. Ethics change with the times. There are a number of different ethical models under which an organisation can operate.

There are different views on who should be the main beneficiaries of business activities. Many companies are ostensibly run for the sole benefit of their owners or shareholders, whose primary requirement is likely to be profit. In practice, though, a business cannot run without workers, and so they must benefit too, usually through wages or salaries. Then again, if the firm's products and/or services do not benefit anyone, why would customers buy them? So perhaps a firm is run primarily for the benefit of customers?

The stakeholder view of business ethics takes all of these interests, and more, into account. The argument is that the benefits to all of an organisation's stakeholders should be considered by the management team.

When an ethical position is generally accepted within a country, it is likely to be formalised by the passing of a law. Regulations and codes of practice are watered-down laws. They still reflect what is generally accepted as right or wrong. There are many laws governing marketing, e.g. product liability, consumer protection, trades descriptions, pricing, anti-competitive practices. There are regulations and codes of conduct covering advertising, sponsorship, sales promotion, Internet trading, tel-esales, data protection and many other marketing activities. For example, the UK Sale of Goods Act requires goods that are delivered to be the same as the ones that

Does his face ring a bell?

ethical focus

Continued deregulation in the UK telecommunications market meant that, in 2003, directory enquiry services were opened up to competition. A new operator, The Number, quickly gained an impressive 50 per cent market share thanks to its unusual advertising campaign featuring two athletes who appeared to have run straight out of the 1970s.

However, former world record holder David Bedford felt that they looked all too familiar and consulted lawyers. The Number denied basing their characters on him, saying that the look was typical of 1970s sportsmen.

He wasn't the only famous runner to appear in adverts around that time. Prince Charles (or rather, what appeared to be Prince Charles) made it on to Belgian billboards, in lycra shorts and looking surprisingly fit, to advertise tours to Britain. The Queen also appeared in that campaign – skirt flying just like Marilyn Monroe's. Clearly the royal appearances were the construct of modern imaging technology. Advertisers can also place dead stars with products they could never have seen (e.g. Steve McQueen driving a modern Ford). They can change a photo's background and a subject's appearance. Racing driver Eddie Irvine successfully sued a radio station that had used a digitally altered picture of him in promotional material without his permission.

We are used to seeing famous faces in adverts and assume that these people are paid for the use of their image. If people are in the public eye, or even actively seek out publicity, should it be OK to use their image without their permission? If not, then how close must the resemblance be for us to say that it really is that famous face?

were shown to the customer. This is particularly important for mail order where the pictures and descriptions must be accurate. In many European countries, a code of practice prevents overt product placement on television (although the practice is considered acceptable in the USA).

Products can be unethical. There are a number of products that are banned in most countries (e.g. recreational drugs). Many would argue that cigarettes should not be on sale either. Sales of some products are severely restricted (e.g. guns, alcohol – which is banned in some countries – and strong medicines).

Unethical pricing practices include fixing prices so that consumers are forced to pay too much. This usually involves collusion between competitors (e.g. as a cartel) or the existence of a monopoly or a severe shortage of goods. In wartime, there are people who exploit other people's misery by charging dearly for essential goods, and so they become rich.

Too low a price may be considered unethical too. The outlawing of **dumping** is called for at meetings of the WTO (World Trade Organisation) and there are now severe restrictions on its legality. Dumping is an anti-competitive practice whereby a company exports its products at a very low price and so undercuts competitors in the target country. These competitors are then unable to compete and eventually go out of business, and so jobs and wealth are lost in that country. The low price is, of course, unsustainable. The company that has dumped the products will either raise its prices or will stop exporting, so the residents of the dumped-on country end up with either no products of that type or more expensive ones.

dumping
when a company exports its products at a very low price and so undercuts competitors in the target country

Professional marketers, and marketing associations such as the Chartered Institute of Marketing, strive to behave ethically towards all their organisation's stakeholders. There are still those who doubt their motives, however, and consider their caring stance to be enlightened self-interest or just good PR.

CRM (customer relationship management) focus

One of the trickiest things about CRM is getting people to agree on what it is. In this textbook, we have taken the acronym to stand for customer relationship *management*, but you may see it used in other places as customer relationship marketing. The two terms are used interchangeably by some, and to add further to the confusion, the initials CRM are often used to refer to cause-related marketing, which is a form of sponsorship and therefore a different thing altogether.

The term 'management' is preferred here because it has more scope. If you are managing a relationship, then you are nurturing it, progressing it – perhaps in the end terminating it. If you are using a relationship for marketing purposes only, then you are using your knowledge of someone to further marketing aims: to woo them into loyalty, persuade them that the brand's image is right for them, sell them more products and over a longer time period. Both sets of activities are valid and both go on. However, the management of customer relationships is more likely to contribute to the long-term health of the company. Some even claim that it is more important to manage the life cycles of these customer relationships than it is to manage the life cycles of products; that this is the route to strategic advantage (Wilson, 1996).

So there is some confusion over what CRM stands for, and further differences of opinion surface over what it actually means in practice. There is a school of thought that takes CRM as a set of technological tools that capture customer information and enable an organisation to use it to market its products more effectively: 'the application of technology to learning more about each customer and being able to respond to them one-to-one' (Kotler, 2003). This is really just a sophisticated modern form of **database marketing**. It enables a company to cross-sell (i.e. sell existing customers additional, different products) and up-sell (i.e. sell customers a more expensive version of the product) and it is not the way the term CRM will be used here. Customer relationship management is more than just technologically enhanced customer service. It is the use of procedures and management techniques that enhance the customer's experience of the organisation, build loyalty and contribute to long-term profitability.

database marketing use of computerised customer data to communicate with customers and promote further sales

---

An expanded definition

CRM is about:

- finding the right customers – i.e. those with an acceptable current and future net value
- getting to know them – as individuals or groups
- growing their value as customers (if appropriate)

- retaining their business – in the most efficient and effective way.

It is achieved by companies enabling their people, processes, policies, suppliers and customer-facing technologies to manage all customer interactions proactively during each stage of the customer life cycle in a way that enhances each customer's experience of dealing with the company.

SOURCE: Woodcock et al. (2000)

It is all about attracting and keeping the right customers. Technology is an enabler and not a main driver, i.e. if you have a lousy value proposition you are not going to gain or keep too many customers. (Woodcock et al., 2000)

It is as important to be skilled in ending relationships as it is to be able to maintain them. A customer will end a relationship that no longer has value. The organisation must be prepared to be similarly ruthless. Some customers, particularly long-standing ones, can in fact cost the firm money.

EXPAND YOUR KNOWLEDGE

These boxes contain references to further reading to help you understand better the points raised in the book. Many of the references are well accepted articles that have shaped and often changed marketing thinking over the years; they are *marketing classics* that have been influential in developing marketing thought. These are informative and insightful articles written by some of the leading and most prestigeous authors in the fields of marketing and strategy. The considerations contained within them are still relevant today and still shape our thoughts and understanding and are especially useful for students first learning about marketing. Marketing has travelled a long way from its early beginnings, but a far richer appreciation of marketing is gleaned by understanding its roots and how it has branched into the discipline it is today. While significant changes have occured in marketing over the years, such as the move away from transactional to relationship marketing and greater emphasis placed on customer loyalty and lifetime value, internal marketing, marketing of services and marketing effectiveness and metrics, we would contend that these are natural developments that refocus marketing rather than deny its origins.

Other articles in the expand your knowledge boxes are of more recent publication. Their inclusion allows readers to delve more deeply into specific areas and into some of the latest thinking that has influenced or is influencing marketing thinking now.

REFERENCES

Kotler, P. (2003) *Marketing Insights from A to Z*. New York: John Wiley & Sons.
Wilson, K. (1996) 'Managing the industrial sales force of the 1990s', in B. Hartley and M. Starkey *The Management of Sales and Customer Relations*. London: International Thomson Business Press.
Woodcock, N., Starkey, M. and Stone, M. (2000) *The Customer Management Scorecard: A Strategic Framework for Benchmarking Performance Against Best Practice*. London: Business Intelligence.

Guided tour

Part opening page each part opens with a summary of the area of marketing under study and with an outline of the chapters that make up the part.

Chapter opening page each chapter opens with a set of 'Marketing Challenges'. These are real-life challenges that you could face as a marketing professional. As you read the chapter, think about how you would tackle each challenge.

Margin notes to help you to spot the important terms you will need for revision purposes, each new concept appears in coloured text and defined in the margin where it first appears in the text.

Glossary terms key terms highlighted in the text are defined in the glossary at the end of the book.

insight boxes insight boxes encourage you to pause from your reading and take time to think about the topic in more detail.

Activity boxes each chapter contains a number of marketing–related activities, that you can try out on your own or in class.

ethical focus a closer look at marketing and social responsibility.

global focus cases of international marketing in a global economy.

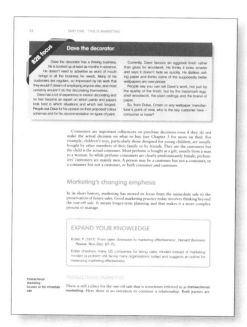

B2B focus business-to-business marketing examples.

e-focus examples of how technology impacts marketing.
expand your knowledge further reading to help increase your understanding.

CRM focus illustrations that demonstrate customer relationship management in practice.

Summary recaps the key topics for review at the end of each chapter.

Challenges reviewed hints are given to help provide further guidance to answer the challenges posed at the beginning of the chapter.

Reading around suggested titles for further reading to enhance your background knowledge.

Self-review questions test your understanding of the key marketing ideas in the chapter.

Case study with questions apply your marketing knowledge by reading a case example and working through the case questions.

Companion website

Be sure to visit the companion website (www.sagepub.co.uk/masterson) to find a range of teaching and learning material for both lecturers and students.

For lecturers:

- Instructor's manual: Helpful notes for lecturers including exercises, activities and discussion questions for every chapter.
- PowerPoint slides: Slides are provided for each chapter and can be edited as required for use in lectures and in seminars.
- Case studies: Lecturers and tutors can supplement their classes by giving students extra case studies.
- Multiple choice questions: Test students' knowledge with downloadable MCQs available for every chapter.

For students:

- Links to relevant websites: Save time by using these useful links to helpful websites.
- Self-test questions: Test yourself before exams with these questions from each chapter.
- Flashcard glossary: Learn key terms and definitions using this online glossary.

Homepage

About the Book
Description
Author Details
Table of Contents

Resources for students
Links to relevant websites
Self-test questions
Flashcard glossary

Resources for lecturers
Instructor's manual
PowerPoint slides
Case studies
Multiple choice questions

Book Details

Author
Ros Masterson and David Pickton

Pub Date: Sep 2010

Pages: 528

Click here for more information.

Rosalind Masterson & David Pickton

MARKETING
2nd Edition
an introduction

Rosalind Masterson and David Pickton

Welcome to the Companion Website for *Marketing: An Introduction (2nd edition)*.

About the Book

This section contains details on the new edition and its authors.

Lecturer Resources

This section contains a variety of resources which are available free of charge to to teaching staff in higher and further education institutions who adopt *Marketing: An Introduction (2nd edition)*. The material within the Lecturer Resources sections includes:

- Tutor's Guide

- PowerPoint Slides

- Multiple Choice Question Testbank

- Additional Case Studies

This area of the site is password-protected. To request an inspection copy please contact mailto:inspectioncopies@sagepub.co.ukYou will be sent a password on adoption.

For lecturers based inside North America, please contact books.marketing@sagepub.com to request a complimentary copy and password.

Student Resources

This section contains self test questions, a flashcard glossary of key terms, links to useful websites and study skills and career advice.

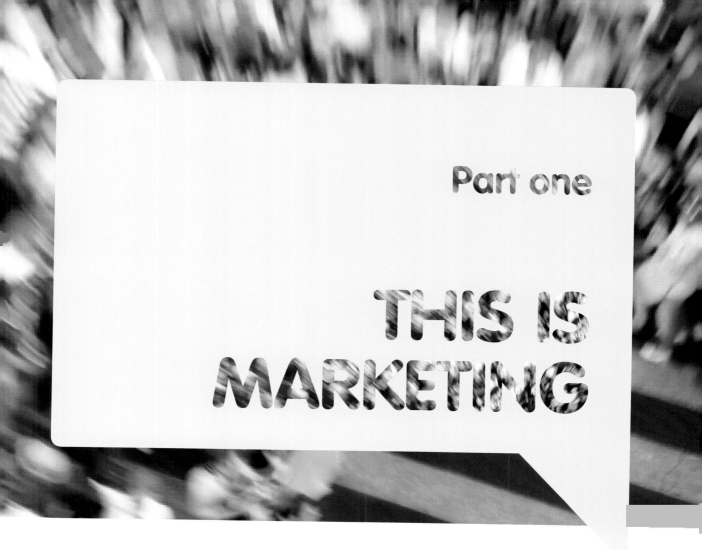

Part one

THIS IS MARKETING

THIS PART CONTAINS:

1 Marketing today
2 The marketing environment

WHAT THIS PART IS ABOUT:

The term 'marketing' comes literally from market: a place where traders go to sell and customers come to buy. Sellers have always tried to show their products to advantage, and buyers have always looked for good value. This has not changed. However, marketing has come a long way since the days when traders travelled around the market towns with their goods packed in a wagon.

The first part of this book looks back at marketing history to show where the marketing discipline has come from in order to shed light on its strengths and limitations. It explains why marketing is more important today than it was in earlier times. It looks at how marketing has evolved into such a sophisticated business discipline and also briefly considers the key aspects of modern marketing.

All business organisations, and most non-commercial organisations too, are built around four main business functions: marketing, finance, operations (or manufacturing) and human resources (HR). Marketers must work with their colleagues from other disciplines in order to make the best use of the resources available. However, no organisation exists in isolation. It has to interact with other organisations and with individuals. Successful marketing depends upon a thorough understanding of the context in which the organisation is operating. Good marketers will be prepared for changes in their world and so they are constantly scanning their marketing environment and making changes to their plans.

Marketing today

CHAPTER CONTENTS

Introduction
What is marketing?
What marketing is not
Before marketing
Marketing beginnings
Demand and supply
Exchanges
Markets
Strategic orientations
Focusing on customers
Customers or consumers?
Marketing's changing emphasis
Retaining valuable customers
Twenty-first-century marketing
Summary
Challenges reviewed
Reading around
Self-review questions
Mini case study
References

MARKETING CHALLENGES

At the start of each chapter in this book, you will find several challenges. They are there to help you see the significance of the chapter you are about to read. *You aren't expected to know how to deal with the challenges now*; just bear them in mind as you read the chapter and see what you can find that helps.

- You tell friends who are studying sciences that you are doing a marketing course. One says, 'You're studying advertising, what fun.' Is he right? Is marketing just another name for advertising?

- You are the marketing manager for a large university. Funds are always short. A local bar owner has offered the university Registry a substantial amount of money for its list of student names and addresses so that he can text them with a very tempting offer to visit the bar. The Registry wants your advice.

- You are a sales assistant in an electronics store. The shop is in a quite poor area and business is slow. You have a lot of DVD recorders that are getting harder to sell now that there are newer technologies available. The manager tells you to sell them hard and offers the sales staff bonuses for every recorder sold. Other salespeople are selling more than you are but they are not telling customers that the sets won't work as well when the analogue signal is switched off. What will you do?

- Winston Smith installs CCTV systems for a living. He is self-employed and all his jobs are one-offs. Today he's very annoyed because he's just seen someone else adding to one of his systems. The customer was pleased with the work Winston did but couldn't remember his name, so he got someone else in when the system needed enlarging. How could Winston have got that job himself?

Introduction

A market is a place where things are bought and sold. It is often defined as a place where buyers and sellers meet.

Marketers are the sellers. They set out their stalls, displaying goods to their best advantage, and then try to attract buyers. Of course, modern marketing is rather more complex than a street market, but it is still about attracting customers, serving them well, competing with others and making a profit (usually). Marketing is a customer-focused discipline centred on an exchange between two (or more) parties. That exchange is at the centre of marketing activity and is usually of products for money. Good marketing brings about fair exchanges where both sides feel that they got good value.

In this chapter, marketing is introduced through a brief look at how it evolved to become what it is today. We will consider current marketing issues and where marketing might be tomorrow.

Some organisations see themselves as marketing companies, while others see themselves as primarily manufacturers, or as financially excellent, or perhaps as innovators. They may have different strategic orientations but all businesses need customers, ideally loyal ones. Customer retention and brand loyalty will be introduced here.

Towards the end of this chapter, there are overviews of the five focus themes that run throughout the book: e-focus, ethical focus, global focus, B2B (business to business) and CRM (customer relationship management) focus. These are key areas in modern marketing and so each one has been singled out for extensive commentary.

What is marketing?

The two most commonly quoted definitions of marketing come from the Chartered Institute of Marketing (CIM) and the American Marketing Association (AMA).

The first definition of marketing is:

Traditional markets are the origin of the term *marketing*

The management process which identifies, anticipates and satisfies customer requirements efficiently and profitably. (Chartered Institute of Marketing, n.d.)

This definition stresses the need for management action to understand what customers really want from products. A product must meet customer needs physically (e.g. it should work), psychologically (e.g. they should feel good about owning it), financially (e.g. they should be able to afford it) and time-wise (e.g. it should not take too long to actually get it). For the company, this may involve considerable market research and analysis. (The words in **colour** can be found in the glossary at the back of the book.)

Take a moment to think about what people really want from a pair of shoes. Clearly, they need to fit and they need to be affordable, but what else? They may also need to be comfortable, although how comfortable will depend on whether they are high-fashion shoes or walking boots or something in between. It is unlikely that customers will be prepared to travel too far to buy a pair of shoes; they need to be easily purchased. As a final act before purchase, customers usually walk up and down in the shop, look in the mirror, see if the shoes suit them. Do they feel right? Do they look good? Do they make the wearer feel good? With today's plethora of choice, this may be the most important consideration.

The second definition of marketing is:

Marketing is the activity, set of institutions, and processes for creating, communicating, delivering, and exchanging offerings that have value for customers, clients, partners, and society at large. (The American Marketing Association, 2007)

The American Marketing Association's (AMA) definition was revised in 2007 and looks for balance between the needs of the firm, the needs of the customer and the needs of other **stakeholders**. There are a number of ways in which marketing can create value, most obviously through good products and prices, but also through good service, convenience and any number of imaginative other ways. The AMA's previous definition (AMA, 2004) referred to 'the organisation and its stakeholders', however the new one makes more specific reference to 'society at large' and therefore embraces societal marketing for the first time.

> **stakeholders**
> individuals or groups who are involved in, or affected by, the organisation's actions and/or performance

EXPAND YOUR KNOWLEDGE

Kotler, P. and Levy, S. (1969) 'Broadening the scope of marketing', *Journal of Marketing*, 33 (Jan): 10–15.

This early article argued against focusing marketing too narrowly and asserted that organisations of all types undertake marketing activities. As the authors conclude, '... no organisation can avoid marketing. The choice is whether to do it well or poorly.'

MIXED TERMINOLOGY: CONCEPT, PHILOSOPHY OR FUNCTION?

Marketing can be viewed in many different ways. It is:

- a function
- a department
- a discipline
- a concept
- a philosophy
- an orientation.

First, let's distinguish between the marketing 'function' and the marketing 'department'. Function is a wider concept. It embraces all marketing activity within the organisation – whether or not it is carried out by members of the marketing department. The department is a defined part of the organisation in which specialist marketers work. They report to marketing managers and directors who lead

Cars for the people

A car is often the single most valuable item that a person owns. Great thought and effort goes into the selection and purchase of a car: it is not just transport, it is a statement, a status symbol, an outward representation of its owner's inner self. In the developed world, the make and style of a car says a lot about its driver, especially about their wealth. Then again, in some other parts of the world, just owning a car, any car, speaks of affluence. Imagine the joy of buying your first, brand new car in a society where fewer than eight people in a thousand own one.

This is the dream that the Tata motor company hoped to make come true for thousands of Indians when it proudly launched the world's cheapest car. With a price of just 100,000 rupees (approx. £1,447/€1,596), the Nano was less than half the price of the next cheapest car already available in India and only slightly more expensive than an upmarket motor bike. It was aimed at those who wanted quick and convenient transport but could not afford any of the cars then on the market.

The idea for this radical new product came from observing whole families piled on to one motorbike (quite a common sight on Indian roads), father driving with a child standing between his knees while mother sits behind with the smallest child on her lap. Tata's designers felt that the practice demonstrated a clear customer need for safer, more comfortable transport.

The Nano was promoted as the latest in a distinguished tradition of people's cars that started with the Model T Ford and included the Volkswagen Beetle and the Mini. The Nano had no radio, no boot, no airbag, no passenger side mirror and only one windscreen wiper. It was light and simple, held five adults (just), had more plastic than steel and was held together by hi-tech glue. Questions were raised about its ability to pass the stringent safety tests required by markets such as the European Union (EU) but Tata claimed that the design allowed for further strengthening with metal plates should they decide to sell it in such markets – at a cost of course.

Analysts were predicting that India would soon be the fastest-growing car market in the world but still not everyone wanted to celebrate the launch of this new wonder car. Environmental campaigners were concerned about the pollutant effect of so many extra cars on the road. They made the point that if just 10 per cent of Indian motorcyclists bought Nanos instead, there would be an extra 1 million cars in the country. Many major Indian cities already suffered from smog and the traffic in Delhi crawled along at an average of nine miles an hour. Delhi's Centre for Science and Environment argued that people needed better public transport rather than more affordable private cars.

The Indian motoring lobby remained positive in the face of the criticism and pointed out that Indians owned very few cars compared to Western consumers who had been able to afford cars for many years. Would the highly affordable Nano be able to do for the Indian car market what Ford's Model T did for the USA?

the department. The distinction is important because, in a truly market-orientated organisation (see below for an explanation of market orientation), everyone will think marketing and, at least some of the time, carry out marketing-related activities.

For example, reception staff could be said to play a key role in the maintenance of a company's image and the building of relationships with customers; they do not report to the marketing manager, are not part of marketing staff, but they do perform a marketing function as part of their job. See Exhibit 1.1 for the most common marketing activities.

The 'discipline' of marketing is of primary interest to students and their tutors. Discipline means 'field of study' (Allen, 2000). Organisations are more likely to consider marketing as a function or a department.

Academic researchers are more concerned with the marketing 'concept', marketing 'philosophy' and market 'orientation'. The distinction between these terms is sometimes unclear. They are used differently within different texts and journal articles. Sometimes they are even used interchangeably with no real distinction drawn between the terms, for example Dibb et al. (2006: 17) define the marketing concept as:

the philosophy that an organisation should try to provide products that satisfy customers' needs through a co-ordinated set of activities that also allows the organisation to achieve its goals.

However, Hooley et al. (1990) suggest that the marketing concept is a process, rather than a philosophy (or way of thinking) and Jobber also sees the marketing concept as a process, i.e. something that organisations do, defining it as:

the achievement of corporate goals through meeting and exceeding customer needs better than the competition. (Jobber, 2006: 5)

These differences in definition are less important than the principles behind marketing – and are not something to be too concerned about at this stage. An awareness that such terms are often substituted for each other, without there being any great significance to the way they are used, is all that is required.

Market orientation is another term that gets thrown into this mix. An organisation's strategic orientation provides 'the guiding principles that influence a firm's marketing and strategy making activities' (Noble et al., 2002) and so determines how it will interact with its marketplace. Orientation literally means the way a person, or organisation, faces. Market-orientated firms, then, look to markets and markets are made up of buyers and sellers, so a truly market-orientated organisation ought to be both customer and competition facing. (Strategic orientations are covered in more detail below.)

For the purposes of this textbook, the terms 'marketing concept' and 'marketing philosophy' will be used in a similar way. Market orientation will be used to describe those firms that have embraced the marketing philosophy (or concept) and use it to inform all their activities and strategies. So a true market orientation requires marketing actions, not just thoughts or intentions.

EXPAND YOUR KNOWLEDGE

McDonald M. (2009) 'The future of marketing: brightest star in the firmament, or a fading meteor? Some hypotheses and a research agenda', *Journal of Marketing Management*, 25 (5/6): 431–450.

Good marketing has always come from a deep understanding of consumer needs and expectations, however in the early twenty-first century 'marketing' is often seen as 'mis-marketing' in practice. The blame rests largely with the use of disreputable tactics such as spamming, misleading advertising and hard selling. A few bad marketers are in danger of giving the whole discipline a bad name. In his article, Malcolm McDonald makes some suggestions for possible new initiatives/directions for marketing including some ideas about the name 'marketing' itself.

Exhibit 1.1   Marketing activities

Marketing research and analysis – *where and who we are now*

Market research – who are our customers and what do they want?

Competitive research – who are our competitors and what do they do?

What is our position in the market? (market share, customer views)

Organisational research – what are we good at? (organisational strengths)

What are we bad at? (organisational weaknesses)

What have we done that worked well in the past? (e.g. promotions)

Are we risk takers?

Objective setting – *where and who we want to be*

Targets – e.g. market share, profits, sales, brand image, brand awareness, numbers of sales outlets, locations where products are available (at home and abroad), new product launches, product updates, customer satisfaction levels...

Marketing tasks – *how we are going to make it happen*

Planning – selecting and scheduling marketing tasks

Staff – suitably selecting and training

Budgets – allocating to activities

Promotional activities – advertising, PR, sales promotions, sales force support, direct marketing, packaging, website, etc.

Sales – finding new customers, getting repeat business

Pricing – setting prices, discounts, credit terms, etc.

Distribution – stock holding, packaging, shipping, order handling, etc.

Product management – development, dropping old products, standardisation, adaptation to suit different customers, etc.

Branding – branding strategy, maintaining brand image, logos, colours, etc.

Market entry – selling in new markets (directly or through a third party)

Customer service – loyalty schemes, complaints handling, after-sales service, warranties and guarantees

Customer management – customer database, events/actions designed to build relationships

Collecting feedback and controlling activities – *how we will keep track of things*

Objectives – have they been achieved? Are they likely to be achieved?

Customer feedback – complaints, compliments, recommendations, repeat buys, satisfaction surveys

Checklists and deadlines – have things happened on time?

Market position – are we doing better/worse than our competitors?

What marketing is not

The world, even the business world, has some erroneous ideas about what marketing is. It is worth being aware of these (it may save you some confusion) as it is important to be clear that marketing is not just selling, **advertising**, promotion or **marketing communications**. Let's take selling first. Although the idea of selling pre-dates that of marketing, for some years now selling has generally been viewed as a part of marketing, an important part. The underlying aim of most marketing activity is to make sales. However, this could be said to be the underlying aim of most business activities. After all, where is the profit without sales? The clear importance of commercial organisations making sales has led to a counter-movement where sales is held to be a discrete function worthy of a sales director on the Board – though this may be a consequence of a more limited view of the nature of marketing.

Selling is about persuading customers to buy and this may involve either a hard sell or a soft sell. Hard selling is pushy, an aggressive stance that is usually resented by customers and is therefore not a good tactic if you want them to come back again. It is often used in selling items that people are reluctant to buy, such as replacement windows. A soft sell, just as it sounds, is a gentler approach – more persuasive.

Peter Drucker, a world renowned marketer, once famously said that: 'The aim of marketing is to make selling superfluous.' If the product is something that the customer actively wants to buy, then a hard sell is unnecessary.

So selling is a part of marketing, but not all of it. In fact, it would be more accurate to say that selling is a part of marketing communications or promotion (these

---

ACTIVITY   What does BOGOF stand for?

If you don't know, look it up in the glossary at the back of the book. (All terms in **purple text** can be found in the glossary and terms are defined in the margins when first used in each chapter.)

The hard sell

global focus

It may seem obvious that the soft sell is the better sales technique, but it depends. In many countries, and some situations, a hard sell is needed. It may even be part of the local culture. If you have ever been a tourist anywhere, but particularly in a less-developed country, then you will almost certainly have been subjected to a hard sell. Trinkets, local crafts, postcards, boat tickets, even accommodation, are thrust at tourists as soon as they arrive anywhere. Many sales are made (and many are later regretted by the new owner of a stuffed donkey or undrinkable local liqueur).

© iStockphoto.com/Brett Charlton

Holiday souvenirs are typical one-off transactions

The right relationship

Think back to the earlier example of hard selling to tourists. Tourists are, by their very nature, not in a place for very long. They are often actively seeking mementoes and gifts on which to spend their money. Is it better for vendors to build a relationship with the tourists or to make a quick sale?

Many of those souvenirs are made in factories and workshops in other parts of the country (or even in other countries altogether). Think about the craftsperson hundreds of miles away. Should he or she be selling hard to the street vendor or would it be better to develop a relationship so that he or she can rely on selling more products next month?

are alternative terms for the same thing), and that marketing communications is part of marketing. Marketing communications (promotion) will be covered in more depth in Chapter 8. It is a collective term for all the activities that an organisation undertakes to promote its products to its customers. Such activities may include holding press conferences, designing appealing packaging, making promotional offers such as prize draws and BOGOFs, supporting websites, sponsoring sports teams and advertising, which means that advertising is only part of marketing communications, which in turn is part of marketing. Clearly, there must be more to marketing too than just advertising. So what is included in marketing besides promotional activities?

One of the biggest areas of marketing is market research (see Chapter 5). Research is vital in understanding customer needs, buyer behaviour (see Chapter 3) and how to design goods and services to meet those needs. Without new product development (see Chapter 6) a company will die. Marketing is also concerned with getting the right products to the right place at the right time, and so distribution (place) is key (see Chapter 9). Those products also need to be at the right price (Chapter 10) or they will not sell.

Although marketing definitions tend to be centred on customers, marketing is also about understanding your competitors (competitive intelligence) and devising strategies to beat them. Strong branding is a competitive strategy that is often used today. Think of the sportswear market; it has some of the strongest, most valuable brands – Nike, Adidas, Reebok, Sergio Tachini, Umbro, Head. There are many of them but some are stronger than others and therefore have a **competitive advantage** over their rivals. Yet how much is there to choose in terms of quality, value for money, even style, between Nike shorts and those made by Adidas?

Marketing, then, encompasses a large number of business activities. An examination of Exhibit 1.1 will give you more detail on its scope.

competitive advantage something about an organisation or its products that is perceived as being better than rival offerings

Before marketing

In a subsistence economy, such as the poorest in the world today, there is very little trade. Only when people have a surplus of goods do they swap them with other people for different things. So if farmers have an abundance of apples, say, they may go to market and try to trade them for something else. If they have only enough to feed their own families, there will be no apples left over for others to buy. So markets, and marketing, are only found where the economy has developed beyond these very early stages.

In Europe, before industrialisation, the emphasis was on making enough goods to supply people's needs, not on persuading them to buy them. There is no need to be persuasive when there are not enough shoes, soap or sugar to go round anyway. There was a time when goods were produced in small quantities, sold locally and farmers or craftspeople could sell everything they could make. There were enough local buyers and no need for the expense, and risk, of travelling to find more custom. So marketing is a relatively new discipline.

Those markets were **supply led**, not **demand driven**. That is, the challenge lay in producing enough to meet customers' needs rather than in persuading customers to choose your products. However, as factories opened and towns developed, there were more goods available and the city workers became more reliant on buying things from others to meet their needs. They did not have land on which to grow their own vegetables or keep animals. They needed to buy food with the wages they earned. Farms became larger and so produced surpluses that could be sold at market. Smaller farmers sold their surplus food to intermediaries, who would take it to market for them, where it would be sold alongside other products from other parts of the country, or even overseas.

This represented a major change in the way that goods were sold. Sellers no longer had direct contact with their buyers; there were agents and shopkeepers in between. This had two effects: first, it meant that they were not as aware of customers' requirements, relying as they did upon these intermediaries, and, second, it meant that customers no longer knew their suppliers – they only knew the shopkeepers or stallholders.

So the smarter producers made conscious efforts to find out what customers wanted – i.e. they began to conduct rudimentary **market research** (largely through those same intermediaries). Some also badged their products so that customers could recognise them. These makers' marks were an early form of **branding**.

The new factories brought with them an even more significant change. Their new mass-production techniques meant that there was a greater supply of products and that they were cheaper. Initially, the focus was still on finding more efficient ways to produce larger quantities as people queued up to buy all these new cheap products. There was more than enough demand to keep the early factories going. However, technology continued to improve and the volume of products available grew until there was no longer a shortage but a surfeit of almost everything. These days suppliers cannot rely on people to buy everything they produce. They have to compete for customers. In such a situation, they need good marketing skills.

Marketing beginnings

Before mass production, value for money, pleasant service, a shop sign, a maker's mark and a reputation built by word of mouth were enough to keep a business afloat. Modern marketing is clearly more

supply led
shortages of goods mean that suppliers can dictate terms of business

demand driven
a surplus, or potential surplus, of goods to be sold gives buyers more power

Manufacturing before modern mass production techniques

© iStockphoto.com/Grafissimo

complex than that, although those early good-business principles are still valid today. More sophisticated marketing techniques were originally developed for the everyday, high-volume products of the new mass-production techniques: washing powder, toothpaste, shoe polish, soap, foodstuffs, etc. They were easier to make and so there were more companies making them. At the same time, transport improved. There were roads, railways and canals available to ship goods to other parts of the country. Consumers had lots of choice and competition became an issue.

These mass-produced products acquired brand names, had posters and press advertisements, were sold on special offer, and were adjusted to suit customer tastes and to be better than rival products. Manufacturers clearly could not sell such large volumes to so many customers directly and so the intermediaries, the shopkeepers and **wholesalers** became more significant. They were persuaded to stock products (and perhaps not to stock rivals' products), to display them more prominently, to recommend them to customers. So a number of factors led to the birth of modern marketing, the main ones being:

- breakthroughs in production technology
- advances in the technology for transporting goods (particularly railways)
- social changes such as the move away from the countryside and into towns
- increased competition.

These forces still drive marketing today. Modern technological breakthroughs (such as the Internet) still have the power to change the way we sell goods and services. Air freight has made it possible to have fresh foods from around the world. It means we can have tropical fruits in northern Europe all year round. The changing age profile of our population means more products are developed for, and aimed at, older age groups. In many parts of the world, people are leaving rural areas and heading for the towns to find work. They have to buy food that they might previously have grown for themselves. They need housing and transport, etc. Competition now is global; it is no longer limited to rivals based in the same town, or even the same country. European Union (EU) companies compete fiercely with each other across the region – and across the world. The wealth of Europe attracts American, Canadian, Japanese, Chinese, African and Asian competitors. Almost all countries across the world are home to at least some internationally competitive companies.

You will learn more about how these forces shape marketing – and indeed our world – in later chapters, particularly Chapter 2 which looks at the marketing environment. 'Global focus' boxes throughout the text will provide further insights into the nature of global competition.

Demand and supply

The concepts of **demand** and **supply** are fundamental in business – and in marketing. The word 'demand' causes some confusion. It is being used here in its economic sense, i.e. it means what people will buy, not just what they would like if only they could afford it, find it, etc.

Today, most markets are **demand-driven**. This means that the amount of goods made available for sale is dependent upon the customers and how much they will buy. In a **supply-led** market, the amount of goods available would depend on how much could be produced.

In a **supply-led** market, the most successful companies will be those that are the most efficient producers. Everything they can make will be bought. However, in a

---

wholesaler
a reseller, buying products in bulk to sell on to other businesses in smaller quantities

demand
quantity of goods that customers actually buy at a certain price, i.e. sales

supply
quantity of goods that sellers are prepared to put on the market at a certain price

insight   Modern markets

Although most modern markets are demand driven, there are still some that are supply led. Some products are in short supply just by their nature (e.g. precious stones or antiques), others by design (e.g. limited-edition prints or collectibles).

Have you ever struggled to buy a concert or football match ticket? Perhaps you have even paid more than the marked price? These are modern-day, supply-led markets.

demand-driven market, companies have to compete for custom, hence the modern-day importance of marketing. It is the job of marketers to stimulate demand, to provide the goods and services that people want, and to persuade them to buy.

Ideally, demand should equal supply exactly. At this point firms maximise sales without having anything left over. The point where the supply curve and the demand curve cross (see Exhibit 1.2) is called the equilibrium point. At this price, customers will want to buy just exactly the amount that suppliers want to sell. Take the example of a book publisher. The easiest way to make sure that all its books are sold would be to produce fewer books than demanded. However, this would mean that some customers will be unable to get copies and the publishing firm will miss out on potential sales and so make less profit. It would be in its interest to print more books.

Exhibit 1.2   Demand and supply

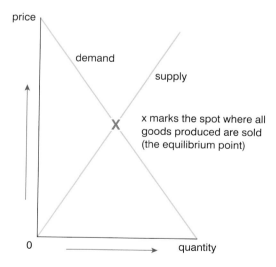

If the publisher wants be sure that it makes all the sales it possibly can, satisfying all potential customers, then it will print more books than could ever be required. The problem with this is that it will have books left over. It will probably end up selling these at a reduced price, maybe even at a loss. (For more on how demand and supply affect prices, see Chapter 10.)

Exhibit 1.3   Equilibrium

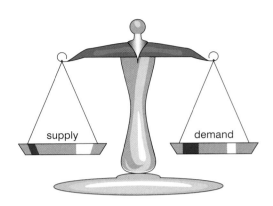

supply   demand

Exchanges

exchange
when two parties swap
items perceived to be of
approximately equal value

It is often said that marketing is about managing the **exchange** process. If you exchange something, you part with something of value (e.g. a product or an idea) in return for something else of value. The 'something else of value' is, of course, usually money, though it could be another product.

Clearly, there must be two parties to an exchange: the seller and the buyer. Each wants to exchange something for something else that they value more. So the car that the customer is buying must be a car that he or she wants more than the money he or she will part with in order to obtain it, and the car dealer would rather have the money than the car standing on the forecourt. This may sound obvious, but it is a concept worth remembering as you move on to more complex marketing ideas. This valued exchange is at the heart of marketing. If we cannot offer customers goods and services that are worth more to them than whatever they have to give up to obtain them, then we will not sell much.

Good marketing will create and maintain mutually beneficial exchange relationships. They may be very short-term relationships, if the sale is a one-off, or ongoing ones if a company is looking for repeat business. To be sure of repeat business, a company needs to make its customers loyal and loyalty should, of course, be a two-way street. The company needs to be consistent in its good treatment of its customers if it wants the same in return. (See below and Chapter 11 for more on customer loyalty.) This idea of ongoing relationships with customers will be revisited many times

Exhibit 1.4   An exchange of value

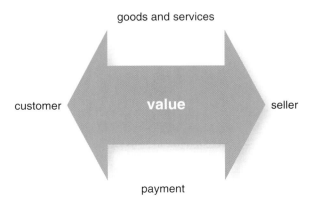

goods and services

customer   **value**   seller

payment

throughout this book, particularly in the CRM (customer relationship management) focus boxes and below, under the subheading 'Relationship marketing'.

EXPAND YOUR KNOWLEDGE

Bagozzi, R.P. (1975) 'Marketing as exchange', *Journal of Marketing*, 39 (Oct): 32–39.

The article highlights exchange as a fundamental aspect of marketing.

Customers give up more than just money. They give up time: the time taken to check out the other options, to test drive other cars, for example. They put in effort that could have been expended doing something else. They have to weigh up the pros and cons of each possible car in order to make their decision. Sometimes customers will pay more for something just because it is less hassle, or quicker, or safer, or for any number of other good reasons. For example, train tickets are cheaper if booked in advance, but it is often just not convenient to book ahead. Many products can be bought more cheaply on the Internet, but many people do not yet trust Internet sales. Vegetables are usually much cheaper when bought from a market stall than from supermarkets, but still you see lots of people with supermarket carrier bags full of them.

Customers take a risk when they hand over their money for a product. The product may not do the job it is being bought for, or may not work at all. It may go out of fashion. It may not suit them or other people may not like it. A good salesperson recognises this and tries to reassure customers that the risk is minimal and worth taking.

Markets

A **market** is a place where buyers and sellers meet. The term is often made more complex, but it is worth hanging on to that simple definition.

There are lots of different markets (e.g. consumer markets, industrial markets, B2B markets, overseas markets). These are broad groups of buyers and sellers, and they can be narrowed down into smaller groupings such as product type (e.g. **white goods** market) or customer type (e.g. youth market) or a combination (e.g. children's clothing market). Often, when people refer to 'markets' they are using the term interchangeably with 'customers'. However, a market needs sellers too and so any thorough study of a market should also include the seller – and its competitors. Exhibit 1.5 provides a framework for categorising markets.

market
a composite of individuals or organisations that have a willingness and ability to purchase products; a market can consist of a single or multiple segments

white goods
large electrical household appliances such as fridges and washing machines (traditionally coloured white)

Strategic orientations

Different organisations take different approaches when it comes to achieving their objectives. Almost all (the successful ones anyway) will have a strategy to guide their future actions but there are many ways to achieve success. The strategies themselves, and the thinking behind them, vary. If an organisation has embraced a marketing philosophy, then the needs and wants of its customers, coupled with a recognition of what competitors offer them, will be the driving force behind its thinking. That organisation will be market-orientated.

Exhibit 1.5   Market classifications

Market	Typical purchase descriptions	Purchase
B2C (business to consumer) markets	Personal purchases	E.g. household weekly shop
Industrial markets	Things that will be used in the making of other things	E.g. glass to go into headlights for cars, cooling fluids for machinery
B2B (business to business) markets	Things for use in the course of another business	E.g. delivery vans
Not-for-profit markets	Purchases and marketing activities by charities, government organisations, trades unions, clubs and associations, etc.	E.g. as other organisations
Government markets	Purchases by central government, local government, health services, schools, public libraries, armed forces, police, etc.	E.g. office supplies
Reseller markets	Goods to be sold on, e.g. by retailers, wholesalers, distributors, dealers, etc.	E.g. anything found for sale in a shop
Overseas markets	All above categories – but in other countries or outside the home country's trading bloc (e.g. EU)	Could be anything at all
Internal markets	Other divisions, subsidiaries or employees of the organisation itself	E.g. own product sales (usually at discounted prices), services provided by one division for another in the same organisation

corporate social responsibility (CSR)
'the continuing commitment by business to behave ethically and contribute to economic development while improving the quality of life of the workforce and their families as well as of the local community and society at large' (World Business Council for Sustainable Development 1999)

However, 'market' is not the only strategic orientation an organisation could adopt. Exhibit 1.6 shows some of the other options.

Many textbooks ascribe these orientation strategies to specific eras, usually making production the earliest and 'market' the most recent. However, there are still organisations that are product or production orientated, even though market orientation is widely accepted as better in terms of business performance.

Cooperative and financial orientations are beyond the scope of this book. The next section goes into detail on the other, more marketing-related orientations. Production is included as it often appears in marketing texts, though it is out of favour with modern-day management thinkers. Societal orientation is included because of its links with **corporate social responsibility (CSR)** and positive corporate image.

Exhibit 1.6 Strategic orientations

Orientation	Focuses on	Typical objectives
Production	Production efficiency	Higher profits through reduced costs
Product	Product quality and features	Increased sales through product improvements
Sales	Sales techniques and advertising	Sales volume – often short-term
Customer	Customers' needs	Increased long-term sales through customer loyalty, positive image
Marketing	Customers' needs and competitors' strategies	Long-term profits through good customer relations and a sustainable competitive advantage
Cooperative	Workers' needs	Long-term job security, good working conditions
Financial	Financial ratios and other measures	Return on investment (ROI), higher share prices and dividend payments
Societal	Society's well-being	Environmental regeneration, community welfare

PRODUCTION ORIENTATION – PUTTING THE FACTORY FIRST

Firms that have a production orientation focus on production efficiency. They try to make their products and services as quickly as possible and at the lowest possible cost. A production-orientated firm will take great pride in its production facilities, which may well be state of the art.

Such firms place great emphasis on **economies of scale** and so are likely to be large-scale producers. It is usually most cost-effective to produce a large amount of a product because it makes it worthwhile to have the largest, fastest machinery or specialist tools, gains bulk discounts on component parts, and enables workers to concentrate on certain tasks and so become expert in them. This efficiency often comes at the cost of product range. If a firm is making a huge quantity of one product, then it cannot also make others. In fact, it is in the interest of such a firm to offer its customers limited product choice. The most famous example of a production orientation is the original Ford car, the Model T, of which Henry Ford is alleged to have said, 'They can have any colour they like, so long as it's black.' This lack of consideration for customer requirements means that a production orientation is not in keeping with the marketing philosophy. However, today, technological developments are making it possible to achieve production efficiency and lower production costs without the need to go into large mass-production quantities.

PRODUCT ORIENTATION – PUTTING THE PRODUCT FIRST

Firms with a product orientation are concerned with making the best possible product. They put great effort into product development and improvements, adding new features, expanding ranges, improving quality, etc. Their view is nicely summed up by the nineteenth-century American philosopher and poet Ralph Waldo Emerson, who asserted that if someone can build a better mousetrap than anyone else can, the world will beat a path to their door. This is often used as an indictment of marketing communications – showing it to be unnecessary. However, there are a number of flaws in this product-orientated view, not least that the world can only beat that path to your door if it knows about the mousetrap and where to get one. So communication in some form is required. If you build a better mousetrap, chances are that someone will steal your idea – or build an even better one, or make a cheaper one. Technology moves on and it is hard to keep ahead of the competition even with groundbreaking new ideas. Also, sometimes the mice just get smarter.

EXPAND YOUR KNOWLEDGE

Levitt, T. (1960) 'Marketing myopia', *Harvard Business Review*, 38 (Jul/Aug): 45–56.
Levitt, T. (1975) 'Marketing myopia: a retrospective commentary', *Harvard Business Review*, Sept/Aug: 1–14.

The first of these two articles has been one of the most widely read and quoted articles in marketing. In it, Levitt argued that companies needed to define the nature of their business in a wide sense if they were to best highlight the competitive forces that surrounded them and avoid demise. He warned about the dangers of marketing short-sightedness. In the second article, written some 15 years later, he revisits the issues and considers the use and misuse that has been made of marketing myopia, describing its many interpretations and hypothesising about its success.

In his famous article 'Marketing myopia', Levitt (1960) stated that product-orientated industries inevitably died. The example he used was that of the North American railways, which believed themselves to be in the railroad business and were therefore surprised when they lost all their customers to airlines. They had not appreciated that they were all in the transport market.

Product-orientated firms believe that, if they provide a good quality product, at a reasonable price, then people will buy it without much further effort on the firm's part. This concentration on product improvement has its advantages. For example, it may well produce groundbreaking new products. Many technology companies are product orientated; they produce new computers, machinery, gadgets and gizmos believing that other people will be as caught up in the invention and its cleverness as its designers are.

Sometimes this works. Vacuum cleaner manufacturer Dyson is a modern example of a successful product-orientated firm. After all, people find it hard to imagine products or services that do not currently exist. Someone, often someone with technical expertise, has to come up with the ideas before they can run them past potential customers to check their likely popularity. Imagine a world without DVDs. Would you have come up with such an idea? How about recorded music generally? That is only a twentieth-century invention. Before that, if you wanted to hear music, you had to learn to play an instrument, or befriend others who could. If you had only ever known communication over distance by letter, would you have asked for a mobile phone? (See Chapter 6 for more on product innovation.)

Of course there are some basic needs that we know we want fulfilled, even without imagining new technology. For example, we want cures for a number of diseases, from cancer and HIV through to the common cold. We want to be able to get to places faster and more reliably. Many of us want to be slimmer. Often, it is more useful to ask people what they want to be able to do, what desires they have, rather than what new products they would like.

Technological breakthrough products, then, usually require a leap of imagination, and faith, on the part of their providers. Most such products fail in the marketplace. The ones that do succeed tap into a real customer need, either a pre-existing one that was being met less well (or not at all) previously, or a need not previously recognised (e.g. to be able to talk on the phone, hands-free of course, while driving a car).

Other situations where product orientation may be effective are when there is little effective competition or a shortage of that type of product. For example, where a company has a patent, as Dyson had on its vacuum cleaner technology, or a monopoly, as many train operators have in their designated areas or under the terms of their franchises. Product-orientated companies that do not have these advantages may need to do some very hard selling.

SALES ORIENTATION – SAYING THAT THE CUSTOMER COMES FIRST

Firms that are sales orientated spend a lot on sales training, sales aids and support materials (brochures, presentations, etc.). They do a lot of **sales promotion** (short-term special offers such as 'buy one get one free', coupons, competitions) and often use hard-sell advertising ('amazing special offer', 'this week only', 'never before available to the public', etc.). They are likely to have a large salesforce that may be quite pushy. Such firms seem to believe that customers will not want to buy their products unless they are pushed into doing so. They are trying to overcome customers' reluctance to buy. Double-glazing firms and timeshare sellers are often sales orientated.

The emphasis here is on the seller's need to shift stock or to make the targets, rather than on customers' needs. However, as part of the heavy sales drive, the salespeople may pay lip-service to marketing – perhaps by calling sales managers 'marketing managers' (as IBM used to do) and by taking an interest in the customer's requirements (so they can sell them other products). This may really just be part of their sales technique, a way of generating rapport with a prospect. Sales-orientated firms are far more interested in their own needs than those of their customers and their salespeople often have high quotas of products to sell with the prospect of large commissions if they succeed. So the success of a sales-orientated firm depends largely upon the skill of its salesforce.

Sales-orientated companies are stuck in the old transaction exchange way of thinking (see above). Pushing a customer to buy something that they may not really want or need, and may later regret, is no way to build a relationship.

CUSTOMER ORIENTATION – ACTUALLY PUTTING THE CUSTOMER FIRST

Many writers do not distinguish between customer orientation and market orientation – but there is a key difference. A market is made up of buyers and sellers so, within this text anyway, a market orientation will be taken to include serious consideration of the competition.

A customer orientation is held by most to be essential to long-term success. How strange, then, that so few organisations are customer-orientated. Many pay lip-service to the idea but fail to gear their systems to satisfying customers, focusing too much on the needs of the organisation itself instead.

An organisation has a number of types of customer. A company that focuses on end customers, without considering trade customers, may find that its products are not actually available for sale (trade customers include **retailers**, **wholesalers**, distributors, and import and export agents).

The timeshare scam

ethical focus

Not so long ago, timesharing was a popular way to own a holiday home. You could buy a share in your very own villa or apartment for a fraction of the cost of owning it outright. Your share effectively made you the owner of the property for a specified two weeks or so every year. Holidays sorted!

Timeshare-sales companies employed attractive young people in holiday resorts, dressed them in beachwear and trained them to persuade relaxed holidaymakers to sign up for another holiday next year, or to attend a party (at which they would hear all the benefits of timeshare). They offered inducements like cheaper rates for those who signed up before they went home (and got their feet back on the ground). They told people that there were only a couple of apartments left; the others had all been snapped up.

Back home, they lured prospects with amazing deals and promises: 'Just attend our presentation,' they said, 'with absolutely no obligation to buy, and we'll give you a fine lunch, unlimited champagne and a free gift.' They sent out invitations telling the lucky recipients that they had definitely won a prize. Soon people wised up to the way that the prize always turned out to be the cheapest thing on the list (a pen, a scarf – often with the company's name emblazoned on it), so the companies upped the offer. The prize would be nothing less than a television or a stereo. After two hours or so of hard selling, during which people found it almost impossible to leave (and if they did they didn't get a prize at all), many caved in and signed up.

One of the main objections that potential purchasers raised was that it tied them to the same time and the same place every year. While some people liked this, others thought it might become dull and would prefer a change. 'No problem,' said the timeshare sellers (who were well versed in objection handling), 'you can swap with someone else and go during their timeslot. You can even sell your two weeks if you want to and, if you get tired of the place altogether, there's a waiting list of people who want to buy. This is an investment. Sell in five or ten years at a nice fat profit.'

For many it hasn't worked out like that, though. There are now thousands of timeshare holiday homes across Europe standing empty and unwanted.

The move to a true customer orientation is not easy and takes a long time. Organisations typically experience considerable resistance from individual departments and employees. Any organisational change has to be managed carefully to ensure that it is accepted and works, but turning an organisation around, so that all its processes are geared towards the customer, can be particularly gruelling and may cause major conflict. An organisation's orientation is a feature of its culture. Organisational culture can loosely be described as 'the way we do things around here'. The procedures an organisation follows are evidence of its culture. The culture may be formal (as in many banks) or informal (as in many software companies). It may be traditional (like Harrods) or contemporary (like, say, Virgin radio). The tone of it is often set by the chief executive or founder and their lead influences the behaviour of all members of the organisation – all successful members that is.

An organisation's culture is possibly the hardest thing about it to change. It can be a source of great strength but, if it is too rigid, it can hold an organisation back and prevent it from moving with the times (as happened with IBM in the late 1980s). Changing an organisation's culture is rather like asking you to become another nationality – and to behave appropriately, forgetting all of your original beliefs and behavioural patterns. You would have to learn to like different food, support a different football team (possibly a whole new sport), maybe wear different clothes, talk another language, etc. Very few firms have yet managed to adopt a true customer orientation that permeates their whole organisation. Do not underestimate the obstacles in their way.

MARKET ORIENTATION – PUTTING THE CUSTOMER FIRST, WHILE WATCHING THE COMPETITION

A true market orientation requires a focus on both customers and competitors. Marketing is about providing products and services that meet customers' needs, but it is also important to do that better than your competitors. Many marketers believe that there is a third, vital, component of a true market orientation, and this is coordination between the different functions of the business. Kohli et al. (1993) defined market orientation as:

the organisation-wide generation of market intelligence pertaining to current and future needs of customers, dissemination of intelligence horizontally and vertically within the organisation, and organisation-wide action or responsiveness to market intelligence.

Much recent evidence suggests that organisations that are market orientated enjoy better overall performance than those with other orientations and marketing practitioners see clear-cut benefits from the adoption of this orientation. This is in no small part due to these organisations' emphasis on marketing research. They use their superior market information to find new marketing opportunities in advance of the competition.

Market-orientated organisations take marketing research seriously. Research is essential to an understanding of customers and their needs. It may not be formal marketing research; many smaller companies are able to maintain personal contact with their customers which is by far the best way to get to know them. Larger companies have to find more cost-effective ways to understand their much larger customer base. These may include customer satisfaction surveys, websites, loyalty schemes, owners' clubs, helplines and customer service desks.

Market-orientated firms take a long-term view of their markets and the products and brands they develop to serve them. Not for them the quick fix that will make this year's sales targets at the expense of next year's – that's a tactic more likely to be employed by a sales-orientated company. For example, if you were an industrial machinery salesperson with a quota of sales to make before the year end, achievement of which would gain you a large bonus, then you would want a customer to order sooner rather than later. However, suppose the customer said they could only afford the smaller machine this year, but if you wait until their next financial year they would buy the larger, newer model. Might you offer them discounts and other incentives to order early so that you get your bonus and your company makes its targets (and makes you a hero)? Then, next year, when the new, improved model comes out, how welcome is that customer going to make you? Will they buy any more from you? Probably not.

The advantages of a market orientation are:

- better understanding of customer needs and wants
- better customer relations
- a better reputation in the marketplace
- more new customers
- more repeat purchases
- improved customer loyalty
- more motivated staff
- competitive edge.

However, the other orientations should not all be dismissed out of hand – they may work for specific organisations in particular circumstances (Noble et al., 2002).

Technology companies, such as Apple Inc, can become market leaders through their product focus while others, such as The Body Shop, are successful thanks to their societal marketing orientation (see below).

SOCIETAL MARKETING ORIENTATION – PUTTING CONSUMERS AND THEIR SOCIETY FIRST

consumer
the individual end user of a product or service

Societal marketing involves meeting customers' needs and wants in a way that enhances the long-term well-being of **consumers** and the society in which they live. Some of the products and services on sale today (e.g. cigarettes) are known to be bad for consumers. Some are damaging to our environment, either in use or in production (e.g. cars). Organisations that adopt a societal marketing orientation recognise the wider implications and responsibilities of marketing and take them into account when formulating strategies. For example, they may design packaging that is minimal, made from recycled materials and biodegradable. Their product design may take into account how the product can be disposed of at the end of its life. Their advertising will encourage responsible product use, for example, they would not encourage children to over-indulge in high-sugar treats. The Co-operative Bank's mission statement commits it to being 'a responsible member of society by promoting an environment where the needs of local communities can be met now and in the future' (Co-operative Bank, n.d.).

EXPAND YOUR KNOWLEDGE

Kohli, A.J. and Jaworski, B. (1990) 'Market orientation: the construct, research propositions and managerial implications', *Journal of Marketing*, 54 (April): 1–18.

Narver, J. and Slater, S. (1990) 'The effect of a market orientation on business profitability', *Journal of Marketing*, 54 (Oct): 20–35.

Both of these pairs of authors are the early researchers of market-orientation. Each has taken a slightly different perspective to the elements which best characterise market-orientation and that may be used in its evaluation. Much of the work that has followed, both by these authors and others, has taken its directions from these early works.

Know when to stop

ethical focus

Diageo (the company that makes Guinness and Smirnoff vodka) ran an unusual ad campaign. Titled 'Know when to stop', the TV campaign encouraged people to drink less. Diageo claimed it was part of its corporate social responsibility programme.

The drinks industry has been heavily criticised in recent years for not doing enough to tackle problems caused by drink, particularly drunk-driving and under-age, excessive drinking. Anti-drinking charities welcomed the campaign as a step in the right direction but pointed out that it didn't amount to much when set against the £200 million (€280 million) or so that is spent each year on alcohol advertising in the UK.

Whose responsibility do you think it is to promote sensible drinking – if anyone's?

Cynics would say that societal marketing is just another marketing ploy: responding to a current trend. Societally-orientated companies may be motivated by enlightened self-interest or they may have a genuine desire to do good. Consumers are beginning to choose organic foods and other green products, and these are proving lucrative niche markets as customers seem prepared to pay a little more for them (not too much more, though).

Focusing on customers

'The customer is king!'

This is a rather sexist and hackneyed phrase, but it has a serious point: companies cannot exist without customers. It would therefore seem to make sense to design the company around the customer, gearing everything to serve the customer better. This focus on the customer is at the heart of good marketing and is one of the hallmarks of a market or customer orientation (see above).

It is important that employees recognise that they are there to meet customers' needs and wants rather than their own. It is no good a delivery person standing on the doorstep and saying 'But this is the best time for me to deliver' if it is not a good time for the customer. It is equally important that investors recognise that without the customer there is no company. A few years ago, Gerald Ratner was widely reported as saying that his firm's products were of poor quality and not what he would buy. The firm's share price, and Mr Ratner's standing, plummeted.

Not all customers are of equal value. In fact, it is possible for some customers to actually cost the company money. This is the reason behind the closure of uneconomic shops, bus services and post offices in some rural areas. There are customers but they do not use these services frequently enough, or pay enough for them, to cover the company's costs.

Sometimes there are good reasons for continuing to support loss-making customers, either temporarily or as part of a customer group that includes more profitable customers that can support the losses made. Perhaps:

● this is a new customer and the company wants to nurture them, hoping that they will become a good customer in the future
● the company is trying to break into a new market, perhaps in a different country, and can afford to sustain losses for a while
● there are considerable social benefits (often in the case of rural services) that outweigh the financial considerations.

Customers or consumers?

There is a distinction between customers and consumers, both of whom are vital to business success. A customer is someone who buys the firm's products. However, they may not actually use the products themselves. The eventual user of the product is called the consumer.

ACTIVITY

Think about paper. Who buys it? What for?
How many different types of customers and consumers can you list? What do they want from paper?

B2B focus

Dave the decorator

Dave the decorator has a thriving business. He is booked up at least six months in advance. He doesn't need to advertise as word of mouth brings in all the business he needs. Many of his customers are regulars, so impressed by his work that they wouldn't dream of employing anyone else, and most certainly wouldn't do the decorating themselves.

Dave has a lot of experience in interior decorating and so has become an expert on which paints and papers look best in which situations and which last longest. People ask Dave for his opinion on their proposed colour schemes and for his recommendation on types of paint.

Currently, Dave favours an eggshell finish rather than gloss for woodwork. He thinks it looks smarter and says it doesn't fade as quickly. He dislikes ceiling paper and thinks some of the supposedly better wallpapers are over-priced.

People say you can tell Dave's work, not just by the quality of the finish, but by the trademark eggshell woodwork, the plain ceilings and the brand of paper.

So, from Dulux, Crown or any wallpaper manufacturer's point of view, who is the key customer here – consumer or trade?

Consumers are important influencers on purchase decisions even if they do not make the actual decision on what to buy (see Chapter 3 for more on this). For example, children's toys, particularly those designed for young children, are usually bought by other members of their family or by friends. They are the customers but the child is the actual consumer. Most perfume is bought as a gift, usually from a man to a woman. So while perfume consumers are clearly predominantly female, perfumiers' customers are mainly men. A person may be a customer but not a consumer, or a consumer but not a customer, or both consumer *and* customer.

Marketing's changing emphasis

In its short history, marketing has moved its focus from the immediate sale to the preservation of future sales. Good marketing practice today involves thinking beyond the one-off sale. It means longer-term planning and that makes it a more complex process to manage.

EXPAND YOUR KNOWLEDGE

Kotler, P. (1977) 'From sales obsession to marketing effectiveness', *Harvard Business Review*, Nov–Dec: 67–75.

Kotler chastises many US companies for being sales minded instead of marketing minded (a problem still facing many organisations today) and suggests an outline for measuring marketing effectiveness.

transactional marketing
focuses on the immediate sale

TRANSACTIONAL MARKETING

There is still a place for the one-off sale that is sometimes referred to as **transactional marketing**. Here there is no intention to continue a relationship. Both parties are satisfied by that one sale and they go their separate ways. A **transactional exchange** is likely to be appropriate where the product is a basic commodity, such as salt, or an occasional purchase, such as a house. Alternatively, the circumstances of the exchange may dictate that it be transactional. For example, the buyer may just be passing through, a visitor to the area. The seller may only have one thing to sell, perhaps a private sale of a car or furniture that is no longer wanted, or they may be winding a business down.

transactional exchange
a one-off sale or a sale that is conducted as if it were a one-off

RELATIONSHIP MARKETING

Relationship marketing is a long-term, continuous series of transactions between parties. (Doyle, 2002)

When it was first proposed, **relationship marketing** was a revolutionary idea that turned sales and marketing on their heads. No longer were end-of-year sales figures the prime measure of success, companies wanted to look ahead to next year and the year after that. Could they count on repeat business from this year's customers?

relationship marketing
a long-term approach that nurtures customers, employees and business partners

The other new and exciting thing about relationship marketing was that these long-term relationships were to be built not just with customers, but with all members of the supply chain, both upwards and downwards. The key to maximising long-term profitability was seen to lie not just with loyal customers, but also in ongoing relationships with suppliers. Keeping the same suppliers not only makes for more pleasant, comfortable working relationships, but also saves the time and risk involved in finding new ones. It can have more direct benefits as well. A supplier who is secure and has a good working relationship with the buyers is more likely to be flexible and to try harder.

Although the term 'relationship marketing' can be traced back to Berry (1983), the importance of building long-term customer relationships really became apparent from some groundbreaking studies in the 1990s. Researchers found that retaining customers for just a little longer increased a company's profitability significantly and also that it was much cheaper to hold on to existing customers than to find new ones. Loyal customers may prove a company's best form of promotion: they tell their friends about their good experiences with the company and so word of mouth spreads. Who would you be more likely to believe when they recommend a product, a friend or the company's salesperson?

EXPAND YOUR KNOWLEDGE

Payne, A. and Frow, P. (2005) 'A strategic framework for customer relationship management', *Journal of Marketing*, 69 (4): 167–176.

In this article, the authors develop a conceptual framework for customer relationship management (CRM) that helps broaden the understanding of CRM and its role in enhancing customer value and, as a result, shareholder value. The authors explore definitional aspects of CRM, and they identify three alternative perspectives of CRM.

Retaining valuable customers

Long-standing, regular customers can be valuable assets. They buy more products, tell their friends good things about the company (word of mouth advertising), are less time-consuming (because they already know how to handle orders with the company and they trust its products) and less likely to be put off by a price increase. It costs approximately five times more to attract a new customer than it does to keep an existing one happy. **Customer relationship management (CRM)** has evolved in response to this need to retain customers and increase their value to the company.

It is often said that 20 per cent of a firm's customers generate 80 per cent of its profits (the Pareto principle). The other 80 per cent of customers only account for 20 per cent of profits and so may not justify the time and money spent on servicing their needs. This is not a hard-and-fast rule, of course, for example, new customers take up a lot more time than older ones who know the ropes, but a firm must still have new customers if it wants to grow and thrive. They may well turn into profitable customers in time.

If the relationship is good enough, then some of those regulars may become loyal or even brand ambassadors, i.e. people who feel strongly enough about the brand to recommend it highly, and frequently, and without even being asked. Exhibit 1.7 illustrates these different stages.

Exhibit 1.7   Customer loyalty

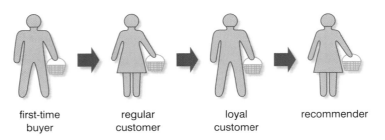

first-time   regular   loyal   recommender
buyer   customer   customer

Loyalty is an emotional attachment. Not all regular customers are loyal, and a strong brand is not enough to create loyalty on its own (although it helps). For example, customers may buy products regularly just because they are cheap or convenient, and when something else becomes available, either more cheaply or more conveniently, then they may switch. Someone who usually buys milk from their local petrol station is unlikely to be a loyal customer, just a rather disorganised person who runs out of milk a lot. They could be lured away quite easily by milk delivery or another, more convenient, retail outlet.

See Chapter 11 for more detail on **branding** and brand loyalty.

Twenty-first-century marketing

E MARKETING

The end of the twentieth century saw what many claimed was a revolution in the way we communicate, work and live. The Internet was heralded as a new economy that would change the world. Whether or not that is so is a debate for another book, but what is certainly true is that the Internet has had a significant impact on the lifestyles of many and on the way that many companies market their products. Firms seek technological edge and cost savings through increased use of the Internet and call centres. Some organisations, e.g. Amazon, eBay and Google, only deal through the Internet, while most follow a more flexible business model that incorporates both online and offline customer contacts – so-called bricks and clicks operations.

Call centres, which are often located in countries such as India, where wages are lower than they are in Western nations, have huge cost-saving potential but are unpopular with many customers. Automated call handling is an even cheaper alternative, but that is even less popular. As companies have tried to drive down costs in search of higher profits, both ideas have become widely used, but at what price for customer relationships? Other companies are returning to a more old-fashioned idea of service. The HSBC subsidiary bank First Direct boasts that customers always get through to a real person – no automated call-handling systems there. For First Direct, this is a key competitive difference from other banking services, although it should be noted that they have no branches so their customers do not actually receive personal, face-to-face service.

This important area of online marketing is considered throughout the book in the inset e-focus boxes.

COMMUNICATIONS OVERLOAD

Advancing technology has brought some additional problems with it. As the costs of reaching people have fallen, thanks largely to electronic (especially digital) communication technologies, so everyone seems to want to talk to as many people as possible. This desire to communicate is not limited to marketers. Organisations and individuals are sending and receiving more messages than ever before. Take the phenomenon of personal web pages and blogs, for example. Never before have so many people broadcast their lives and views so generally.

One consequence of this is that we are all sent many more messages than we can possibly deal with. The average Briton or American gets approximately 3,000 marketing messages a day and the majority feel overwhelmed and are becoming increasingly negative towards advertising messages in particular (Benedictus, 2007). Consumers have to block out the majority of this bombardment in their own self-defence and that presents an additional challenge to marketers who have to find ways to cut through the clutter and be heard.

Marketers have responded to this difficulty in getting heard in a number of ways. Some try to get closer to their customers either through strategic use of CRM or through integrating their brands into consumers' lifestyles (see lifestyle branding below). Others look for more original media through which to convey their marketing messages. Anything that is capable of carrying a message to an audience can be construed as a marketing communications medium and so marketers have lots to choose from and vie with each other to dream up unique media (Pickton and Broderick, 2004). Advertising messages have been written on bus tickets, on the edge of steps, on web pages, in the sky, on the sides of buildings (by laser), and on people's heads, cars and houses.

It is generally recognised that the best media of all is **word of mouth**; people pass on the message to each other. The snowball effect of this method reaches many people quickly and, because the message is relayed by someone you know, a friend, relative or colleague, then its content is more credible. It is a personal recommendation of a product. **Viral marketing** is a modern variant of word of mouth. Instead of speaking personally to friends and passing messages on that way, the information, or picture, or joke, is texted or emailed on.

Buzz marketing

Have you heard the buzz? Did you recognise it or did you think that stranger who so kindly recommended a drink, a club or a place to eat was on the level? Perhaps they were, but then again they may have been part of a buzz marketing campaign.

Buzz marketing is a variant of word-of-mouth marketing, but instead of friends and relatives recommending products to you, people are paid to do it. They seem like one of the crowd but they have infiltrated it deliberately in order to sell products.

For example, when a Premiership football club launched a text message service, it was struggling to persuade fans to sign up. They advertised the service in programmes and on the website, and employed a troop of attractive young women to hand out leaflets on match days, but still fans were resistant to parting with 25p a message to find out the latest club news. So the club decided it was time to hire professionals in the form of a local marketing agency.

'We got a group of 14 or 16 actors, who were all football fans,' explained Graham Goodkind, founder and chairman of the Sneeze Marketing Agency. 'And they went round bars and clubs around the ground, in groups of two, saying that one of their mates had been sacked from work because he kept on getting these text messages and talking to everyone about it, and his boss had had enough and given him the boot. So they were going round with this petition trying to get his job back – kind of a vaguely plausible story.

'And then the actors would pull out of their pocket some crumpled-up leaflet, which was for the text subscription service. They'd have a mobile phone in their pocket, and they'd show them how it worked. "What's the harm in that?" they'd say. And they could have these conversations with lots of people – that was the beauty of it. Two people could spend maybe 20 minutes or half an hour in each pub, working the whole pub. We did it at two home games and reckon we got about 4,000 people on the petition in total.'

Subscriptions to the club's texting service soared – though the petitions went straight in the bin.

In the USA, marketers have been paying people to spread marketing messages by word of mouth for some years. A little known sausage brand became much better known after a holiday weekend when hundreds of people arrived at barbecues with packets of sausages and enthusiasm for their low fat recipe. They were invited guests at the parties, but paid agents for the sausages.

Buzz marketing, which is sometimes known as stealth marketing, is often criticised as unethical, although its professional proponents usually stop short of breaking any laws. The buzz marketers themselves defend it as a necessary tactic to reach increasingly cynical and media-literate consumers in these over-communicated times. They also say that there are few, if any, complaints. But then if the marketing is stealthy enough, people just don't realise that it's marketing at all.

SOURCES: Benedictus, 2007; Walker, 2004

FAST-CHANGING MEDIA

The many electronic technologies and software packages now available have, of course, changed the way people communicate. They have also changed the way the marketers communicate. One of the rules of good marketing is that it should put the customer at its heart. So marketers study the way that consumers behave and try to ensure that their brands become a valuable part of their lives.

It used to be that media owners (e.g. television companies, newspapers, cinemas) controlled all the significant means of communication, but that is no longer true. Modern electronic technologies have given birth to a host of consumer-controlled communications possibilities: emails, blogs, SMS messages, tweets, chat rooms, discussion boards, wikis, etc. Numerous social networking sites allow people to say almost anything, instantly to the world (or their approved friends' list). A significant portion of communications power has shifted from corporations to individuals who do not even need to be particularly computer literate thanks to *Facebook*, *MySpace*, *YouTube*, *Friends Reunited*, *Twitter* and other social networking sites. These have now become mainstream leisure activities enjoyed by all ages and social classes and, as their parents and businesses join, so the younger generation are deserting such sites and moving on to the next thing.

Twenty-first-century communications technology is likely to be even more dynamic than that of the late twentieth century. (For more on the use of electronic media and social networking in marketing communications, see Chapter 8.)

THE RISE OF CONSUMERISM – AND ANTI CONSUMERISM

In the Western world, we have more material wealth, more stuff, than any society has ever had before. The amassing of goods is seen as a sign of success. Expensive, desirable possessions confer status. **Consumerists** believe that it is economically desirable to consume (i.e. eat, drink, use) more and more. Modern production techniques mean that we have more than enough of everything. Every day, Western businesses and households throw away millions of excess goods. In the meantime, there are parts of the world that are so poor that they are short of basic necessities: food, water, clothing, shelter. This disparity provokes envy and conflict, yet still, even where governments have the will to do so, it is difficult to even things out.

consumerism
the belief that increasing consumption is economically desirable

With this surplus of goods, the power has shifted to consumers. Today, most producers of goods and services are more reliant on their customers than the other way around. A customer can usually go to another supplier but, for the supplier, a replacement customer is harder to find. This would suggest that customers have the upper hand but this is not always true. Large customers, which are usually big companies, can indeed dictate terms to their suppliers. UK supermarkets have such dominance in the food market that they can demand low prices, specially packed products and frequent (often several times a day) deliveries. However, it is harder for an individual consumer to make demands on a large corporation. Even with the current levels of competition for customers, just one customer among thousands is not so significant a loss.

As a consequence, just as workers formed trades unions in the early twentieth century, consumers in the latter half of that century got together and formed pressure groups. The power of numbers can make large corporations listen. Organisations such as the Consumers' Association have significant influence. The media can make an impression too – even the largest of multinationals wants to protect its reputation. Most newspapers have consumer advice columns and are prepared to take on any size of organisation, as are television programmes such as the BBC's *Watchdog*.

Consumer protection

In the West, consumers have rights. In 1962, US President John Kennedy proclaimed four basic consumer rights. These were the right to:

- be safe
- have information
- choose
- be heard.

There are laws to protect consumers. In the UK, for example:

- all loans and other credit agreements have to display their true costs in a way that consumers can compare with other offerings

- there must be no hidden product costs (e.g. it must be clear whether or not VAT is included)
- many purchases (e.g. insurance policies, timeshare holidays) have a cooling-off period during which customers can change their minds and cancel with no penalty
- direct debits (automatic bank payments) have a guarantee of immediate refund if a customer complains
- adverts must be truthful
- consumer information should not be used for any purpose other than that agreed to by the consumer (Data Protection Act 1998)
- descriptions in mail-order catalogues and other direct mail items must be accurate (Sale of Goods Act 1979 amended 1994).

Other countries have similar laws, although there are, of course, some differences in detail. For example, data protection laws across the EU are much stricter than they are in the USA.

The fall of consumerism?

Despite all these protective measures, there are consumers who still feel exploited and who believe that consumerism is wrong. Their concern is that we are using up the Earth's resources, in effect destroying our world. They feel that there is an over-emphasis on materialism and that its main point is to make a few fat cats richer. The anti-globalisation protesters who make the news every time the World Trade Organisation (WTO) or some other such body meets are part of this anti-consumerism movement. They champion the rights of the underdog: the less-developed countries (LDCs), the poorer workers and consumers. Unfortunately, a small but significant number of more aggressive protesters often turn their demonstrations into vandalism and clashes with the police. Bricks may be aimed at symbols of Western (most commonly US) domination, such as McDonald's. This is a clash of views that will continue for some time. You can follow its progress through TV news and documentaries, newspapers and magazines. Look out for new consumer protection laws, changing government attitudes on green issues and trading with LDCs. Many of the protesters hold marketers as much to blame as governments. This is an interesting time to be studying marketing – and thinking of a marketing career.

LIFESTYLE BRANDING

In the twentieth century, many organisations moved from a product focus to a customer focus (see strategic orientations above), even public sector organisations started to regard the people who received their services as customers, although there is a considerable backlash against this now. For example, it really may not be helpful for Probation Officers to regard their charges as customers or teachers to treat schoolchildren as such. Towards the end of the century, the term 'brand' became more commonly used than 'product'. Now almost everything is branded. Even public services have logos, mottoes and are endowed with brand values.

Traditional brands, with their values based on the organisation's and the product category's, are being overtaken by lifestyle brands. This can be seen as the next step in the goal of true customer orientation. Brands are developed with the values of a particular consumer group in mind and the resultant products slot into, and enhance, those consumers' lifestyles. Lifestyle brands usually have loyal customers who use the brand to declare their identity, or membership of a group. Abercrombie and Fitch,

Mini, Harley Davidson, Nike and Virgin are all lifestyle brands and their consumers are generally proud to be associated with them. If consumers identify closely with a brand, it becomes easier to launch new products, even those in a different category. For example, designers such as Calvin Klein have made successful inroads into perfumery. Youth culture has particularly strong, though changeable, values that are shared the world over, making global youth lifestyle brands, such as Adidas, possible. Not all global products aimed at the youth market are by any means lifestyle products though, much as the brand owners might like to think that they were. McDonald's has tried hard to achieve this status but it just does not have the appeal that makes people want to be identified with it (Kiley, 2005). Would you wear their clothes, carry their logo with pride?

It is not yet clear what, if anything, will replace branding as the competitive weapon of choice for twenty-first-century companies. There is a trend towards more socially responsible marketing (though for many organisations this is currently no more than a token gesture, a chance to be seen as doing the right thing), and cynics would say that this is merely another positive image projection for competitive effect. It may be that firms seek to build even stronger relationships with their customers (see relationship marketing above), though, again, there is evidence that customers do not always want to have relationships with their suppliers. In fact, increasing numbers choose the anonymity of the Internet marketplace in order to avoid personal contact with sellers (O'Connor and Galvin, 2001).

ACTIVITY

Visit The Body Shop's website at www.thebodyshop.com. In what ways is the company trying to improve our well-being? Why do you think it does that?

EXPAND YOUR KNOWLEDGE

Kaur, G. and Sharma, R.D. (2009) 'Voyage of marketing thought from a barter system to a customer centric one', *Marketing Intelligence and Planning*, 27 (5): 567–614.

This article charts the developments that have taken place in marketing thinking and provides an extensive review of much of the relevant literature.

SUMMARY

This chapter has been an introduction to the marketing concept and its development as well as to this textbook. We have looked at what marketing is, and what it is not. Marketing has been defined and the modern marketing concept explained. The origins of marketing should be helpful in understanding how the discipline has developed and why.

An organisation's strategic orientation has a huge influence on how, and what, decisions it makes. Some organisations put their products at their heart, others focus on customers. Those with a market orientation put their customers first, while keeping a close eye on the competition, but this does not mean that firms must be market-orientated in order to do any marketing at all. Almost all organisations, even those that are clearly production-orientated, must do some marketing in order to survive.

Some basic economics, notably the theory of demand and supply, has been considered. Economic theory is highly relevant to marketing and informs much of what marketing managers do. Marketing is based on the idea of an exchange of equal value – usually an exchange of products for money, but rarely for money alone. Customers give up their time and the opportunity to buy other things when they buy something. They also take risks. The product may not work, it may not be good value, others may think them foolish for buying it, it may not suit them after all. Marketing can help reassure customers and reduce their perceptions of the risks inherent in a product purchase.

Customer relationship management (CRM) is one of the focus themes of this book and this chapter introduced it through the concept of relationship marketing. Relationship marketing takes a long-term view of both customers and suppliers. This contrasts with transactional marketing, which sees sales as one-off events.

This book has been carefully designed to help those new to marketing as a subject. As well as the questions and case studies that you would expect to find in a textbook of this type, we have included challenges, activities and focus boxes. The focus themes are key marketing issues and they, along with the Insight boxes you will see throughout the text, should help build a bridge from your academic studies to the marketing practitioner's world – and your future marketing career.

CHALLENGES REVIEWED

Now that you have finished reading the chapter, look back at the challenges you were set at the beginning. Do you have a clearer idea of what's involved?

Hints:

- see 'definitions' and 'what marketing is not'
- good marketers always act ethically; also, check the Data Protection Act 1998
- this is an ethical challenge: is it right to sell outdated technology? Would it be taking advantage of a vulnerable group? What would be a better strategy?
- customer retention and CRM, database marketing; if he had kept in touch, then they would have known how to find him; also, a simple sticker on the cameras might have helped!

READING AROUND

Books

Silk, Alvin J. (2006) *What is Marketing?* Boston: Harvard Business School Press.
Evan Davis, Duncan Bannatyne, Deborah Meaden, Peter Jones, Richard
    Farleigh, Theo Paphitis and James Caan (2007) *Dragons' Den: Success, from Pitch to Profit*. London: Collins.

Book chapters

Michael J. Baker (2008) (ed) *The Marketing Book* (6th edn). Oxford: Butterworth Heinemann/
    Chartered Institute of Marketing. Chapter 1, 'One more time – what is marketing?'

Journals

Journal of Marketing
European Journal of Marketing
Journal of Marketing Management

Magazines

Marketing Week
Marketing
The Marketer (Chartered Institute of Marketing magazine)
(Most libraries will have these magazines – possibly online – ask your librarian.)

Websites

www.cim.co.uk – website for the Chartered Institute of Marketing, including lots of
    information and articles and an excellent glossary.
www.brandrepublic.co.uk
www.mad.co.uk

SELF-REVIEW QUESTIONS

1. Define a market. (see page 4)
2. Is marketing an alternative term for advertising? (see page 9)
3. What is another term for marketing communications? (see page 9)
4. Why is marketing less important when there is a shortage of goods? (see page 9)
5. Give five examples of FMCG items. (see page xi (in the Introduction))
6. Why is it desirable for a product's demand and supply to be in equilibrium? (see page 13)
7. Why is value such an important part of an exchange? (see page 14)
8. List five advantages of a market-orientation. (see page 21)
9. What is relationship marketing? (see page 25)
10. What are the five focus themes that run through this book? (see pages x-xv (in the Introduction))

Liverpool relaunched

mini case study

Read the questions, then the case material, and then answer the questions.

Questions

1. What problems did Liverpool face in attracting tourists? (Use the information in the case study, but you may also want to look up Liverpool, and rival cities, on the Internet.)
2. How could good marketing help to overcome these problems?
3. Write a short piece (approx. 200 words) on Liverpool for inclusion in a tourist guide. You should identify different aspects of the city that will appeal to different types of visitor.
4. How could relationship marketing help Liverpool to attract more visitors?

In its heyday, as England's busiest port, Liverpool saw the launching of many fine ships but, with those glory days long gone, the city was in need of a relaunch itself.

For years Liverpool had suffered from jokes and abuse and for being more famous for its sense of humour than its work ethic. TV programmes such as *Bread*, *Brookside* and *The Fast Show* built a picture of Liverpool as a city of lazy benefit fraudsters and chancers. As a result, most tourists, shoppers and business travellers avoided it, fearing for their wallets and their safety. Yet locals always claimed that the Northern city's poor image was invented by London-based media and that the truth was very different.

Liverpool's waterfront

Image provided by The Merseyside Partnership (TMP)

A golden opportunity to put things right came in 2008 when Liverpool became the European Capital of Culture. Over £2 billion was invested in the city to fund such ambitious plans as reinventing rundown Paradise Street as a suitable venue for a variety of entertainments, including street theatre and music. The rejuvenation of Liverpool was one of Europe's biggest regeneration projects. The impressive waterfront and the city's fabulous architecture were cleaned up and shown off. New facilities were provided. New hotels were built. This was Liverpool's chance to show the world what a great place it really was.

Liverpool has always had a lot to boast about. As well as writers such as Beryl Bainbridge, Willy Russell, Alan Bleasdale, Catherine Cookson and Roger McGough, Liverpool has produced many pop-cultural icons. More artists with number-one hits were born in Liverpool than in any other British city. Its most famous sons are, of course, The Beatles. These symbols of the 1960s first played at the Cavern club – now redeveloped as a Beatles museum. The National Trust now owns John Lennon's childhood home (a gift from his widow, Yoko Ono-Lennon) and opened it to public view. Liverpool Football Club has been one of the country's premier clubs for decades. Comedians as diverse as Ken Dodd, Jimmy Tarbuck and Lily Savage all hail from the city. Cilla Black started her days (as Priscilla White) singing in Liverpool, and more recent music exports include Atomic Kitten, Space, the Lightning Seeds, the Coral and Cast.

Unusually for a city, Liverpool has been abroad itself. Its wealth of architectural styles and the grandeur of its buildings have made it an ideal film double for a number of European cities, including Moscow, Dublin, Paris and, most surprisingly, Venice. The most dramatic aspect of Liverpool has always been best viewed from the Mersey. It is, of course, the UNESCO listed waterfront with its 'three graces': the Royal Liver Building, the Cunard Building and the Port of Liverpool Building which together form one of the world's most well-recognised skylines. Liverpool's docks were once among the busiest anywhere and the Albert Dock remains so, though now it is home to thriving bars, restaurants and shops, upmarket apartments and the Tate art gallery rather than ocean-going ships.

Even with all these advantages, if the city was to make it on to every tourist's must-see list, it had a lot of image rebuilding to do. A spokesperson for the

(Continued)

(Continued)

City Council said, 'People just haven't been listening. Unemployment is reducing and it is one of the safest cities in the country. Liverpool has art galleries, shopping centres and trendy bars. We are also close to becoming the film capital of Britain with the number of films shot here. I don't see why it should be a problem marketing ourselves to the UK and abroad.'

Liverpool was a smash hit as Capital of Culture in 2008 and has managed to build on that success. It has been named in the top three UK city break destinations for the second successive year by readers of travel bible, *Condé Nast Traveller Magazine*, and was recently voted the best loved of Britain's non-capital cities.

SOURCES: BBCi, n.d. Liverpool City Council, n.d.; Liverpool 08 n.d.; Singh, 2003; Visit Liverpool, n.d.

REFERENCES

Allen, R. (ed.) (2000) *New Penguin English Dictionary*. Harmondsworth: Penguin.

American Marketing Association (AMA) (2007) *Community* 'AMA definition of marketing', American Marketing Association. Available at: **www.marketingpower.com/Community/ARC/Pages/Additional/Definition** (accessed 06/11/2009).

Bagozzi, R.P. (1975) 'Marketing as exchange', *Journal of Marketing*, 39 (Oct): 32–39.

BBCi (n.d.) Capital of Culture (web page). Available at: **www.bbc.co.uk/capitalofculture** (accessed 10/08/2003).

Benedictus, L. (2007) 'Psst! Have you heard?', *The Guardian,* 30 January.

Berry, L.L. (1983) 'Relationship marketing', in L.L. Berry, G. Shostack and G. Upah (eds), *Emerging Perspectives on Services Marketing*. Utah: American Marketing Association.

Chartered Institute of Marketing (CIM) (n.d.) *Marketing Glossary*. London: Chartered Institute of Marketing. Available at: **www.cim.co.uk/cim/ser/html/infQuiGlo.cfm?letter=M** (accessed 11/06/2007).

Co-operative Bank (n.d.) *Social Responsibility.* Available at: **www.co-operativebank.co.uk/partnership1997/97_local_social.html** (accessed 30/10/2009).

Dibb, S., Simkin, L., Pride, W.M. and Ferrell, O. (2006) *Marketing Concepts and Strategies* (5th European edn). Boston, MA: Houghton Mifflin Company.

Doyle, P. (2002) *Marketing Management and Strategy*. Harlow: FT/Prentice Hall.

Hooley, G.J., Lynch, J.E. and Shepherd, J. (1990) 'The marketing concept: putting theory into practice', *European Journal of Marketing*, 24 (9): 7–24.

Jobber, D. (2006) *Principles and Practice of Marketing* (4th edn). New York: McGraw-Hill.

Kaur, G. and Sharma, R.D. (2009) 'Voyage of marketing thought from a barter system to a customer centric one', *Marketing Intelligence and Planning*, 27 (5): 567–614.

Kiley, D. (2005) 'Not every brand is a lifestyle brand', *Business Week*, 5 July.

Kohli, A.J. and Jaworski, B. (1990) 'Market orientation: the construct, research propositions and managerial implications', *Journal of Marketing*, 54 (April): 1–18.

Kohli, A.K., Jaworski, B.J. and Kumar, A. (1993) 'MARKOR: a measure of market orientation', *Journal of Marketing Research*, November: 467–77.

Kotler, P. (1977) 'From sales obsession to marketing effectiveness', *Harvard Business Review*, Nov–Dec: 67–75.

Kotler, P. and Levy, S. (1969) 'Broadening the scope of marketing', *Journal of Marketing*, 33 (Jan): 10–15.

Levitt, T. (1960) 'Marketing myopia', *Harvard Business Review*, July–August.

Levitt, T. (1975) 'Marketing myopia: a retrospective commentary', *Harvard Business Review*, Sept/Aug: 1–14.

Liverpool City Council (n.d.) *Liverpool, European Capital of Culture*. Available at: **www.liverpool.gov.uk** (accessed 10/08/2003).

Liverpool 08 (n.d.) *2008 Highlights*. The Liverpool Culture Company. Available at: **www. liverpool08.com/Events/2008Highlights/index.asp** (accessed 12/06/2007).

McDonald M. (2009) 'The future of marketing: brightest star in the firmament, or a fading meteor? Some hypotheses and a research agenda', *Journal of Marketing Management*, 25 (5/6): 431–450.

Narver, J. and Slater, S. (1990) 'The effect of a market orientation on business profitability', *Journal of Marketing*, 54 (Oct): 20–35.

Noble, C.H., Sinha, R.K. and Kumar, A. (2002) 'Market orientation and alternative strategic orientations: a longitudinal assessment of performance implications', *Journal of Marketing*, 66 (4): 25–39.

O'Connor, J. and Galvin, E. (2001) *Marketing in the Digital Age*. Harlow: FT/Prentice Hall.

Payne, A. and Frow, P. (2005) 'A strategic framework for customer relationship management', *Journal of Marketing*, 69 (4): 167–176.

Pickton, D. and Broderick, A. (2004) *Integrated Marketing Communications* (2nd edn). Harlow: FT/Prentice Hall.

Ramesh, R. (2008) 'India gears up for mass motoring revolution with £1,260 car', *The Guardian*, 11 January: 29.

Singh, S. (2003) 'Can Liverpool set the record straight?', *Marketing Week*, 12 June.

Visit Liverpool (n.d.) 'Liverpool Tourist Information'. Available at: **www.visitliverpool.com/** (accessed 05/12/2009).

Walker, R. (2004) 'The hidden (in plain sight) persuaders', *The New York Times*, 5 December.

Wilson, K. (1996) 'Managing the industrial sales force of the 1990s', in B. Hartley and M. Starkey (eds) *The Management of Sales and Customer Relations*. London: International Thomson Business Press.

Wookcock, N., Starkey, M. and Stone, M. (2000) *The Customer Management Scorecard: A Strategic Framework for Benchmarking Performance Against Best Practice*. London: Business Intelligence.

2

The marketing environment

CHAPTER CONTENTS

Introduction
Market dynamics
Environmental information
Marketing environment models
The organisational environment (the
    internal environment)
The external environment
The international marketing environment
Situation analysis
Stakeholders
Summary
Challenges reviewed
Reading around
Self-review questions
Mini case study
References

ENVIRONMENTAL CHALLENGES

The following are illustrations of the types of decision that marketers have to take or issues they face. *You aren't expected to know how to deal with the challenges now*; just bear them in mind as you read the chapter and see what you can find that helps.

- You work in the marketing department of a multinational which has a large investment in the Middle East. Your company often considers pulling out. Can you devise a system for monitoring the often volatile situation there?

- You are the manager of a small chain of cafés. Business has been a bit slower this year than it was last, but you are better off than many of your competitors, some of whom have gone out of business. Do you know why that happened to them? Are you in danger too?

- You run a mail-order business and have been piloting selling over the Internet. You've heard rumours that the EU may introduce laws that will make e-commerce more difficult. You do not know whether this will affect your business and nothing is definite yet. Is there anything you could be doing to prepare?

- You work for an oil company and Greenpeace protesters are currently camped outside the refinery. They are protesting over a proposed new pipeline and no one at the oil company seems surprised that they are there. In fact, the counter-arguments were prepared in advance and the press release has gone to all the newspapers. Greenpeace kept its intentions a secret, so how was this possible?

- You work in banking and a colleague has just come up with a new service idea that has got the whole bank talking and will probably get him a promotion. It takes advantage of a new IT product that IBM has just announced. Why didn't you come up with that idea?

Introduction

The word 'environment' has come to be associated with conservation, with the green movement. However, that is not the sense in which the word is used in this chapter. The *New Penguin English Dictionary* (Allen, 2000) defines environment as 'the circumstances, objects, or conditions by which somebody or something is surrounded', and this is closer to the way the term is used in marketing.

Organisations do not operate in isolation. They have to take account of other organisations and individuals in their plans and in their day-to-day dealings. They operate within a specific marketing environment which is changing all the time. Managers always need to be aware of what is going on in the world around them. They have to identify trends within their organisation's environment and make plans. To do this, they will need good information gained from sound marketing research (see Chapter 5). They will need to have a clear idea of exactly who their market is both currently and potentially (see Chapter 4) and what potential their product has. They need to have a solid understanding of their customers, the ways in which they use products, how they relate to brands, and how they choose what to buy (see Chapter 3). If a company is to be successful, then it is vital that it understands its competitive environment well. Without current knowledge of what competitors are doing, and of how well that is working, how can a company make its own marketing plans? All this information feeds into the setting of prices, the design of distribution networks and choice of retailers, the development of promotional campaigns and the development of a distinctive, desirable **brand**.

This chapter will consider the nature of the marketing environment and explain how to monitor changes within it. There are a number of frameworks available to help with the organisation of this environmental information and this chapter will introduce the PRESTCOM analysis tool (see below for an explanation). The analysis of an organisation's current situation forms the basis for strategic planning and we will touch on that – though it is covered in more depth in Chapter 12. The analysis tool used here is one of the best known in management: the SWOT analysis (see below).

Market dynamics

MARKET LEADER OR MARKET LED?

Some companies are said to be market-led, others to be market leaders. Strictly, the market leader is the company that sells the most. It is important to be clear which market you are referring to when talking of a market leader. Cadbury's may well be the market leader in chocolate in the UK but not in the USA, where it is more likely to be Hershey's, or in any other European country, each of which has its own favourites.

The term 'market leader' is often used more loosely, however, to refer to a firm that leads the way in a market. This may be in terms of setting prices, releasing innovative products, devising new forms of promotion, moving into different market segments, or any number of other ways of starting an industry trend. Such leaders are not necessarily large organisations. Often the recognised market leader is a smaller firm that is more innovative (e.g. Dyson and its vacuum cleaners), or that has more expertise (e.g. some specialised consultancy and accountancy firms), or has exceptional talent (e.g. fashion designers such as Stella McCartney).

If a company is said to be market-led, then it follows other firms within that market. Such firms are often termed market followers. Market followers take their lead from competitors and copy their successful ideas and strategies. This does not mean that they produce only me-too designs or campaigns, only that they wait for more radical ideas to be tested by others first and cash in on their research. Throughout the 1990s, many fast-food chains waited for McDonald's to set up a new store and then set up their own stores nearby. They assumed that McDonald's had done the research and found an area with good potential.

The disadvantage of this is that the followers are, by definition, second (or third, fourth, etc.) into the market and therefore do not usually get the benefit of **first mover advantage**. Often, the first significant company to move into a market becomes the leader. It can be hard to dislodge as it is the brand people know, the one they tried first and presumably liked – or there would be no market.

Coca-Cola was the first company to make a cola drink and it still outsells all others in most countries. The Body Shop was the first to build a retailing chain around the idea of more ethically produced toiletries. Amazon was the first company to sell books online with a view to making a large business of it, and it had the resources and skills to make that dream a reality. All these firms have first mover advantage.

However, being first into the market does not guarantee success as many IT and Internet companies have found. Sometimes the first in is a very small company which is unable to exploit the market to the full, or which may make mistakes, thus letting another, larger or more able company steal the high ground. Peter Doyle (2002) lists the four most common mistakes made by market pioneers, i.e. the first in:

- marketing mistakes, e.g. misjudging who will want to buy the product and so targeting it at the wrong market segment
- product mistakes, e.g. technical or design flaws and limitations that challengers can exploit
- first-generation technology, e.g. market challengers can incorporate the very latest technology into their products, perhaps leaving the pioneer behind
- resource limitations, e.g. the pioneer may be a smaller company whose resources are therefore limited and who can be outgunned by a larger challenger.

The first company bears the brunt of the risks and so may fail where later companies succeed. If it is successful, it is likely to attract the attention of larger competitors. A highly praised Internet browser called Netscape pre-dates Microsoft Internet Explorer. Which one do you use? Market leaders are constantly challenged by the other firms who wish to supplant them. These market challengers employ a number of strategies, and adopt a number of positions, in order to achieve their goal of market leadership. Some challengers are small, but they can be very large. Pepsico is a market challenger, constantly harrying Coca-Cola and trying to steal some of Coke's **market share**. Most market leaders are large, although it is possible to be a small market leader. It just depends on how you define the market. Niche brands sell into small, well-defined **market segments** so it is common to find a small brand leading the way. For example, Bentley by no means lead the car market, but they are certainly one of the leaders of the prestige car market.

It is easier to challenge a market leader in the early stages of a market's development before the leader has built significant **economies of scale** which bring their costs down and make it very hard for others to compete on price. Internet Explorer does have viable competition, e.g. Firefox, but despite the efforts of enthusiatic Firefox users and of people who are anti-Microsoft on principle, Internet Explorer still dominates the market.

first mover advantage
The first significant company to move to into market often becomes the market leader and can be hard to dislodge from that position

market segment
a group of buyers and users/consumers that share similar characteristics and who are distinct from the rest of the market for a product

insight   Game on

The world market in computer games is worth about $27 billion a year and it's a fast-moving one. In a highly competitive market such as this one, it is important to get your product innovations out ahead of the competition as the first company into a market often builds the highest share and commands the greatest loyalty. Those early market leaders cannot afford to relax though. There is always someone snapping at their heels, just waiting for the smallest chink to appear in the leader's defences. Then they nip in and grab market share.

The must-have Christmas present of 2006 was Sony's new PS3. At least, that was the plan – Sony's plan. The machine was originally scheduled for launch in the UK in spring. Then it was put back to November, apparently due to a lack of parts. British children had nagged and their parents had given in and were prepared to pay the considerable price required to secure a PS3. Then Sony scuppered plans for a festive bonanza by confirming that it was pushing the European launch date back to March.

Not all Sony's potential customers were affected equally though. The PS3 launched in the USA and Japan, the biggest games markets, in November. The delay in the UK launch handed a golden opportunity to one of Sony's smaller rivals – Nintendo. With its new Wii product, Nintendo set out to steal Sony's share in the world's third largest games market.

The Nintendo machine was cheaper, it was available and, with its unique remote control, which allowed players to take a swing at their virtual golf or tennis balls, or boxing opponent, it had wider appeal. TV presenters almost queued up to demonstrate the Wii. Wii games were more inclusive (as the name was meant to suggest – it is pronounced 'we') – families could play them together. Gamers were no longer isolated couch potatoes, they could get up and move around, making Nintendo's games actually look like fun to non-game-playing observers. Never before had gaming been telegenic. The PR coup was massive and, despite having a few supply problems of its own, in the UK the Wii outsold the PS3 by more than two to one.

According to Van Baker from Gartner market analysts, the big challenge for Sony was that PS3s were hard to get and so many people bought something else. Sony lost valuable market share and gave 'a two Christmas advantage to Microsoft, and a one Christmas advantage to Nintendo'.

The number of games consoles in use is extremely important because that determines the volume of the more lucrative sales of the software games themselves. Christmas 2006 saw Sony and Microsoft lose both market share and profit on console sales, while Nintendo won all round.

SOURCES: Durman, 2006; Johnson, 2006

ASSET LED OR MARKETING LED?

asset-led marketing
basing marketing strategy on the organisation's strengths rather than on customer needs and wants

Not all organisations are marketing focused, so they cannot be said to be either led by the market or driven by it. For example, some companies are said to be **asset led**. These companies concentrate on doing what they already have the resources and skills to do, rather than looking for market opportunities and adapting to fit them. The asset in question might be equipment, people, contacts, a distribution network, shops – almost anything. In the UK, many shoe repairers also cut keys, and frequently now take in dry cleaning. They have suitable shop premises to do this. Their shops are major assets to be exploited. Many universities rent out rooms in their halls of residence to tourists in the summer months, using an asset that would otherwise stand empty. Theatres, museums and art galleries rent out their foyers for upmarket parties. Did any of these organisations conduct research to discover people's needs and then design their offerings to fit? No, they realised they had spare space and came up with something profitable to do with it.

It is not just spare space that can be exploited profitably. Mars started making ice cream versions of its products, trading on the considerable asset that is its brand name. IBM realised it had hundreds of highly trained management and computing personnel whose skills could be offered to clients as consultants. Many years ago, when textile production was dying in the UK, the factory owners realised that the same machines could be used to knit tea bags.

So, is it best to build your strategy around what your customers want, or around the assets you already have? This is an occasion where companies look for the best of both worlds. The ideal is to meet your customers' needs while making the best possible use of all your assets.

Sometimes circumstances allow you to be more proactive about this, e.g. when moving or building new premises. When Leicester City Football Club had its new stadium built, for instance, it incorporated private rooms of various sizes into the design so that it could develop its business of hiring out space for meetings, lunches and other functions.

Environmental information

Organisations build up information on what is happening in the world around them so that they are better able to deal with any threats to their business or to take advantage of any new opportunities before their competitors do. For example, Western companies that do business in the Middle East or parts of Africa, notably Zimbabwe, should have been monitoring the political situations there carefully over the last decade. Those that did were ready to pull their people out before the invasion of Iraq and before the situation in Zimbabwe became too dangerous.

A firm's environment is commonly split into two parts: its external environment and its internal environment. Things that happen in the external environment are largely outside the firm's control and so are referred to as

Picture courtesy of Leicester City Football Club

Leicester City Football Club making full use of its assets

---

insight   Minarik

Andrew Minarik runs a hairdressing salon. It is a family business, passed down from mother to son. The business thrives, thanks to its well-established (and largely well-off) clientele and a prime position on a busy road. There was no absolute need to diversify, but the salon had spare rooms and bored clients sitting around. As anyone who has had their hair coloured knows, it's a long and tedious business. So, if you've got the premises and a regular, captive audience, why not find more things for those customers to buy?

So now there's a beauty salon upstairs. You can have your nails painted at the same time as your hair changes colour. Regular hair clients become regulars at the beauty salon too – making separate appointments for facials and massages – and walking past the handmade jewellery display on the way to each. Sometimes there are gifts and knick-knacks for sale too. In another room, you can get an all-over tan in 10 minutes or so. The machine is looked after by another company which maintains and services it and takes a cut of the proceeds.

Some people do still go there just to get a good haircut.

insight   Not so sweet

Tate and Lyle is one of the oldest brands in the UK. It dates back to 1921 when Mr Tate merged his sugar cube business with Mr Lyle's business, best known for the golden syrup that is still a favourite flavour for pancakes today. By 1939, Tate and Lyle's Thames factory was the largest sugar cane refinery in the world and the brand has gone from strength to strength ever since. By 2007, the company operated 65 production plants in 29 countries, but profits were sliding and the company seemed about to lose its blue-chip status.

Tate and Lyle were no longer just sugar refiners. Over the years, the company had diversified into food additives, such as citric acid, starches, and animal and fish feed. Their research and development division had been highly productive and had made a number of major breakthroughs, including, in 1976, the invention of a superior, zero calorie, sugar substitute called *Sucralose*. This revolutionary product has since been renamed *Splenda* but is still solely manufactured and sold by Tate and Lyle.

Despite such diversification, sugar remains at the heart of Tate and Lyle's business and therein lies its problem. Governments and researchers throughout the world say that too much sugar is not good for hearts, nor for health generally. Obesity is at crisis levels in many Western countries – notably the USA and the UK, which are key Tate and Lyle markets. Consumers generally are watching their weight – and therefore their sugar intake. These trends in the political and social environments are proving costly for Tate and Lyle. *Splenda* should have saved the company but apparently it just tastes too good – too much like the real thing. Consumers expect their diet and lite drinks to taste more artificial. Then there's the consumer backlash against additives and artificial flavourings – poor *Splenda* just cannot win.

There have been issues in the international environment too. Much of Tate and Lyle's business is conducted in the USA and the weakness of the dollar has meant that US profits translated into fewer pounds than in previous years. A further problem with the company's US connections has arisen in the regulatory environment. The European Union has banned imports of US corn gluten (a by-product of maize that is used as animal feed) after some was found to have come from a genetically modified source. The problem gluten was not actually supplied by Tate and Lyle, but they are suffering from the fall-out anyway as they are unable to import their gluten into the EU and, because of the resultant glut of the product in the USA, prices there have fallen dramatically. Meanwhile, in Europe, the price of maize (a key raw ingredient for Tate and Lyle) has shot up and so, with higher costs to deal with, profits are being further squeezed.

So Tate and Lyle's current marketing environment is not a sweet one.

SOURCE: Finch, 2007

---

uncontrollables
events, issues, trends, etc. within the external environment

uncontrollables (or 'uncontrollable variables'), e.g. wars, crop failures, a change of government, new technology. The internal environment ought to be more easily controlled and so occurrences within it are often referred to as controllables (or 'controllable variables'), e.g. skill levels of employees, finance available, product range.

Environmental information is used in two main ways:

1 As input to the planning process
2 As part of ongoing analysis of marketing opportunities and threats (environmental scanning).

INPUT TO THE PLANNING PROCESS

Particularly during the planning process, it is useful for a firm to have a framework in which to place its environmental data. It can then assess the data's impact and what to do about it. For example, a firm would wish to identify its key competitors and investigate their strategies; it is then in a position to develop counter-strategies if necessary. It would want to know about the lives of its customers, and then it can develop products and services to meet their needs.

Planners do not stop at identifying relevant trends or competitors. They take the environmental data, feed it into a situation analysis and so arrive at a fuller understanding of the organisation's current situation on which they can build their plans.

ENVIRONMENTAL SCANNING

Wise organisations continuously scan their environments so that they can keep up with changes and are ready to deal with market developments, be they good or bad. This is an ongoing research exercise. The collected data helps build a better picture of their world. Perhaps they will find that a new law or regulation is being proposed and that it will affect their interests adversely. Take, for example, the recent proposals by various government organisations to increase taxes on 4×4 vehicles, the so-called 'gas guzzlers'. These are highly profitable products for many car companies and so they have been **lobbying** to get the proposals scrapped or watered down, while at the same time taking account of a likely fall in sales (or a total ban) when making their plans. Some firms have research departments, or employ outside research consultants, to scan their environment. However, most do this on a more ad hoc basis.

Most managers rely on personal contacts for their environmental knowledge, possibly because it can be difficult to get hard facts on external environmental trends (economics, for example, has never been an exact science). These personal sources are supplemented by, or cross-checked in, newspapers, magazines, trade journals and other secondary sources (for sources of **secondary data**, see Chapter 5). The approach that academic commentators recommend, however, is to analyse the external environment as a team, i.e. to consult a range of employees from senior managers to the most junior staff. This way the firm benefits from a wide range of viewpoints and is more likely to identify key things that will affect it in the future (Mercer, 1995).

How do managers decide what is, and what is not, relevant?

Taken to its extreme, the whole world and everything in it can be considered as having an impact upon the organisation – particularly if it is a very large organisation such as IBM or ICI. Clearly it is not practical to study absolutely everything and so the management team must initially decide what sorts of things to include. There are a number of models to help them do this, but again academia and management practice do not always agree. Most firms rely upon judgement. The insight box on the following page provides an example process.

Unfortunately, this sometimes means that pressing matters take precedence over long-term thinking. Many organisations have come unstuck by not looking beyond the requirements of current decision-making. The firm's most immediate operating environment (customers, suppliers, distributors, etc.) is likely to change rapidly and to receive more management attention than its wider environment (Brownlie, 2000). For example, sales of red meat have been falling for some time. There have, of course, been a number of health scares associated with the eating of meat (high cholesterol, BSE, foot and mouth disease, excess growth hormones, etc.). It would be easy for farmers to blame their troubles on these scare stories. At the same time, however, many people are eating more chicken or fish, rather than red meat, for more general health reasons and, in many countries, significant numbers of people

---

insight   **Environmental scanning process**

The environmental scanning process involves the following stages:

Monitor – broad trends, issues and events. In addition, develop a list of relevant publications, which should be checked regularly.

Identify – trends, issues, events that are significant to the organisation. It is helpful if the management team

sets, and regularly reviews, criteria to determine what is likely to be significant and what is not.

Evaluate – the impact of the trends etc. upon the organisation's operation in its current markets.

Forecast – where the trends are heading, and examine the threats or opportunities they are likely to bring in the future.

Evaluate – the impact of those threats and opportunities on the firm's long-term strategies.

SOURCE: Brownlie, 2000

---

are becoming vegetarian. These people are unlikely to return to their meat-eating habits when the latest scare dies down.

Marketing environment models

The data that an organisation collects through its environmental research must then be analysed. This process involves sorting the data, categorising it and then looking for trends, changes in trends, patterns, dangers and opportunities. There are a number of models of the marketing environment that an organisation can use to help it to analyse environmental data.

Probably the best-known environmental model is PEST:

Political
Economic
Social
Technological.

Common variants are STEP, SLEPT and PESTEL. The L in the last two acronyms stands for legal. The extra E in PESTEL can be environmental or ecological. All of these models are ways of looking at a firm's external environment. The **macroenvironment** is the term favoured by economists and refers to the broadest, external environment in which a firm operates.

macroenvironment
the broad, external influences that affect all organisations in a market, e.g. the political situation in a country

Many textbooks, e.g. Dibb et al. (2006) and Jobber (2004), eschew these environmental acronyms, which might seem to suggest that PEST and its variants have had their day. However, they are a useful *aide-mémoire*. Perhaps their current lack of favour can be attributed to the fact that most omit so much that is important (e.g. the microenvironment) along with a tendency to follow them too slavishly rather than use them as prompts. There is no need to invent things in order to fill every box. If there is nothing of significance happening in one of the categories, then it should be passed over. The important thing is to have thought everything through.

What is commonly referred to outside business theory as 'environmentalism' causes commentators some problems of classification. First, there is the issue of what to call it: Jobber (2004) uses 'ecological/physical forces', Kotler et al. (2001) 'the natural environment', while Dibb et al. (2006) use the term 'societal/green forces'. In this text, the term 'natural environment' will be favoured (with due acknowledgement to Professor Kotler).

Second, there is the question of whether the natural environment even requires its own heading in an environmental analysis, or fits under some, or all, of the others. Certainly there are political aspects to environmentalism, especially when lobbyists such as Greenpeace, Friends of the Earth or (perhaps at the other end of the political spectrum) the Countryside Alliance are involved (the Countryside Alliance is an organisation that campaigns to preserve certain traditional aspects of British country life, such as hunting). Regulation is relevant in terms of laws and codes governing issues such as pollution or recycling. The using, or spoiling, of irreplaceable natural resources has economic implications. Social attitudes towards green issues are changing. Technology has the power to harm or heal the natural world. Being seen to be more green than rival firms can give a company a valuable competitive edge – there is a significant minority of customers who choose environmentally friendly products.

The natural environment affects an organisation in numerous ways. Whether this means it should be treated separately or within the context of other forces is a choice the analyst must make. It will probably depend upon the nature of the organisation, its products and the rest of its operating environment. In the cause of flexibility, this book will follow both courses, considering the natural environment where it is relevant within other categories, but then pulling its key elements together separately as well.

PEST, and its variants, only cover *part* of the organisation's external environment. Marketers must consider all of the external environment and the internal environment as well. This more immediate environment is what economists refer to as the microenvironment. It comprises competitors, distributors, suppliers and the organisation's own internal resources.

The macroenvironment refers to broad influences that affect all organisations in a market, whereas the microenvironment contains influences specific to the nature of the business, its suppliers, marketing intermediaries, customers and competitors.

So PEST does not give the whole picture: it only covers the macroenvironment. In order to complete the picture, Wright and Pickton (cited in Pickton and Broderick, 2001) proposed a more comprehensive, environmental model: PRESTCOM. PRESTCOM provides a framework for the analysis of both the internal and the external environments (see Exhibit 2.1).

Exhibit 2.1 PRESTCOM

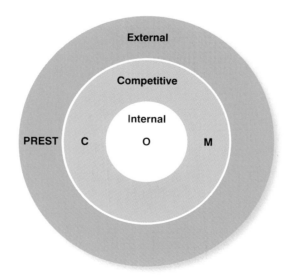

> ## EXPAND YOUR KNOWLEDGE
>
> Oxenfeldt, A.R. and Moore, W.L. (1978) 'Customer or competitor: which guideline for marketing', *Management Review*, Aug: 43–48.
>
> Much increased emphasis has been placed by some on the need to recognise the significance of competitors as well as customers to effective marketing. Many naïve views have been developed about marketing by placing too much emphasis on the importance of customers alone. Even though customers are clearly important, there are other factors that have to be balanced for marketing to be carried out well. This is an early article which highlights the need for companies to tune into the competition and balance this with a customer-orientated approach.

PRESTCOM

PRESTCOM is an acronym that stands for:

Political
Regulatory
Economic
Social
Technological
Competitive
Organisational
Market.

Over the following pages, each of these categories will be considered in turn, commencing with the one so often ignored: the organisation itself. We will start with organisation as this is the one category that is internal – all the others are in the external environment.

The organisational environment (the internal environment)

The organisational heading in the PRESTCOM analysis is the only one that concerns internal factors, i.e. things that are particular to the company in question. This includes the organisation's structure as well as its assets (people and their skills, money, brands, buildings and machinery, etc.).

There are five basic functions within a business (see Exhibit 2.2), of which marketing is one. It is important that these functions work well together and support each other. This requires good communication between staff and a culture that encourages interaction and mutual support. If all functions display a **customer orientation** (see Chapter 1), then this harmony will be easier to achieve. One of the key things that the company wishes to achieve from this cooperation is a consistent image.

The following are examples of how these functions interact.

The human resources department (HR) is primarily responsible for ensuring that there are suitable staff, both in terms of quantity and quality, in place in order to carry out all the activities of the business. Their duties include various administrative

customer orientation
the whole organisation is focused on the satisfaction of its customers' needs

Exhibit 2.2   The internal environment

functions such as hiring, firing and paying, as well as more strategic activities such as training, career management and succession planning. HR and marketing may liaise over the writing and production of communications such as staff newsletters and recruitment advertising. HR should also be kept appraised of product development and future growth plans to ensure that staff with appropriate skills are hired or trained.

The finance function includes accounting and also strategic financial planning. These departments will be heavily involved in the setting of marketing budgets and will also require regular reports on sales and forecasts of future incomes. Finance is often involved in aspects of costing, pricing and the collection of overdue customer accounts, all of which require close liaison with marketing/sales.

Operations is often called 'production' in manufacturing industries. Operations personnel actually make the goods or deliver the service. For example, in a cleaning company, the cleaners are operations personnel. Clearly it is important for marketing and operations to work together closely to ensure sufficient supply of goods and services – but not oversupply, which would be wasteful and cost the firm money. Getting the balance right requires accurate demand forecasting. This is particularly difficult with new products but, if stocks run out, this could scupper the product's launch. Marketing also needs to make sure operations are consulted in advance before any sizeable promotional campaign is undertaken. Sales will (hopefully) rise and production will need to increase to match.

Research and development (R&D) is where new ideas are uncovered and tested. This is a crucial function for any firm that operates in an innovative market, where new products are key to competitive advantage. The marketing function has a part to play in the introduction of new ideas as well as in the dissemination of them. Marketers, particularly salespeople, are more in tune with customers and their needs. There should be a process in place for this vital information to be passed on to R&D (see Chapter 6 for new product development).

In analysing an organisation's internal resources, the analyst is looking for sources of advantage and disadvantage. For the purposes of marketing planning, these should be of relevance to the marketing function (although that does not mean that they will always be contained within the marketing department). Examples include skilled product researchers, large capital reserves, innovative products, leading-edge production technology, strong brand name, good location, or, on the other hand, high staff turnover (people do not stay long), poor reputation in the industry, a dreary shop, no cash.

Building an international business

global focus

When they begin as international marketers, most companies try to maintain a minimal level of involvement in the new, unknown, foreign markets. That is, they try to keep their risks low by investing the minimum time, money and other resources in the project. Most start as exporters which means that they make the goods at home as they have always done, and then ship them out. Exporters employ other organisations, or individuals, to handle their business in the foreign country. Initially, the employment of such intermediaries, or agents, may be the limit of the company's involvement in its export markets. However, as the export business grows, they are likely to need more staff at the home end to organise things.

If exporting is a success and the company finds that it is making regular sales, then it will feel more comfortable investing more in this new market. It will seem less of a risk. At this point the company may set up an export department. The main function of most export departments is sales and marketing, although there will be some administration as well, notably keeping track of orders and shipments.

As the company's foreign sales build up, so its structure will evolve. International divisions tend to handle all business functions (i.e. not just sales and marketing) and are really essential for managing branches or manufacturing facilities overseas. Such divisions are commonly organised by area (e.g. Europe, the Middle East and Africa, Australasia), by product (e.g. home electronics and computing, office equipment, consultancy services), or by function (e.g. HR, finance, marketing).

When the company's international business becomes as important (or almost as important) as its domestic business, it is commonly reintegrated into the organisation. This is a prelude to a truly global structure, where all countries are fully involved.

agents

↓

export department

↓

international division

↓

reintegration into organisation

The external environment

The external environment (or macroenvironment) is represented graphically in Exhibit 2.3.

Exhibit 2.3   The macroenvironment

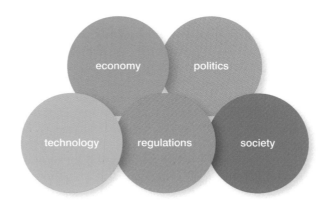

THE POLITICAL ENVIRONMENT

Players in the political environment include:

- government – i.e. domestic government bodies (central, regional and local, and government-appointed committees), supranational government bodies (e.g. the EU) and foreign governments
- special interest and pressure groups – i.e. political organisations that exist to further a cause (e.g. Friends of the Earth) or the interests of a particular group of people (e.g. trades unions)
- political parties.

These groups affect an organisation and its operations in a number of ways. The philosophy of the government in power sets the business climate. Government policy has a direct effect on the way in which businesses are allowed to operate. For example, some governments are characterised as interventionist and others as non-interventionist. The interventionists are far more likely to interfere in the running of businesses, by introducing laws, setting up watchdog committees, levying new taxes, imposing new bureaucratic rules, even by nationalising an industry. Nationalisation is when a government takes over a business or part of a business – often without consultation or adequate compensation. The Bolivian government has been pursuing a re-nationalisation policy and in 2008 took back control of telephone company Entel from its foreign owners. They had already seized control of a BP oil pipeline and other foreign-owned gas and oil fields. The Bolivian government believes that all basic services should be publicly owned (BBC News, 2008). On the other hand, a non-interventionist government may scale down all of these things, and even privatise previously nationalised industries. Right-wing governments tend to be less interventionist than more left-wing, or socialist, governments. Generally speaking, communist governments exert the most control of all.

Some countries have arrangements that favour certain other countries by allowing goods to be imported at reduced **tariffs**. These were originally most likely to be arrangements between neighbouring countries, but now there is an increasing number of trading blocs across the world. These blocs of countries have reciprocal arrangements on the movement of goods across their borders. The largest trading bloc in the world is the European Union (EU) which generates approximately 20 per cent of global exports and imports while being home to only 7 per cent of the world's population (European Commission, 2009a). Additionally, the members of the EU have a common tariff, i.e. they all charge the same amount of duty on goods imported from outside the EU. This prevents other countries from shipping goods into a country with lower taxes and then taking advantage of the lack of barriers within the EU to move the goods on.

International marketers will also need to take account of any export restrictions imposed by their own home government or import restrictions imposed by the other government. For example, many governments very sensibly ban the sale of weapons to countries that they are concerned might use them against them. Some countries have exchange control restrictions, preventing their currency from leaving the country. India had such restrictions for many years. It may be possible to get an import licence from the government in question, which is effectively a permit to exchange the local currency for another. In some cases it may still be impossible to exchange the currency. In that case the firm may have to arrange a **countertrade** or spend their profits in the country in which they were made – on supplies or wages perhaps. This is, of course, the foreign government's intention. They are trying to keep as much wealth in their own country as possible and, in the case of a large multinational

countertrade
exchanging goods for other goods rather than for money, there are various forms of countertrade, the best known of which is barter

insight   European union members

In 2009, there were 27 member states in the EU. The dates in brackets show when the country joined:

Austria (1995)
Belgium (founding member, 1957)
Bulgaria (2007)
Cyprus (2004)
Czech Republic (2004)
Denmark (1973)
Estonia (2004)
Finland (1995)
France (founding member, 1957)
Germany (founding member, 1957)
Greece (1981)
Hungary (2004)
Ireland (1973)
Italy (founding member, 1957)
Latvia (2004)
Lithuania (2004)
Luxembourg (founding member, 1957)
Malta (2004)
Netherlands (founding member, 1957)
Poland (2004)
Portugal (1986)
Romania (2007)
Slovakia (2004)
Slovenia (2004)

Spain (1986)
Sweden (1995)
UK (1973)

The following are candidate countries who have started, or will soon start, accession negotiations:

Croatia
Macedonia
Turkey

The European Union

SOURCE: European Commission, 2009b

trading with a relatively poor nation, this would indeed be a more ethical course of action.

A country's tax regime is important to businesses. Taxes are the government's primary means of raising income, which it can then spend on public works such as road building, or on health and education services, defence, etc. However, taxes can also be used to encourage, or deter, businesses and consumers from certain actions. For example, the British government reduced tax on diesel and unleaded petrol while increasing it on traditional, leaded fuel in order to encourage motorists to switch and so reduce pollutants. In a government attempt to deter smoking, and to help pay smokers' medical bills, cigarettes in Britain are taxed at a rate that would horrify the French. This has been a somewhat less than successful strategy. Cigarettes are, of course, addictive and therefore not very price sensitive (they have **price inelastic demand** – see Chapter 10). Also, France is easily reached from England, and therefore French cigarettes, with their lower taxes, are easily acquired.

price inelastic demand product sales are not very sensitive to price changes

The government of a country may also exert influence through its commercial dealings. Most governments have enormous spending power and can therefore be lucrative, if demanding, customers. Many national governments have at some point followed a policy of giving their own country's suppliers preference when placing orders. Many more have imposed taxes, or **quotas**, on foreign imports.

The relationship between two governments may act as a help or a hindrance to trade. Some Middle Eastern governments are reluctant to trade with the USA and Britain because of their foreign policies. At the time of writing, the British are also unwelcome in Zimbabwe.

A country's political stability has a huge bearing on its attractiveness to investors, especially to foreign investors. For example, foreign-owned **multinationals** were reluctant to invest in Britain during the late 1970s and early 1980s because of the large number of strikes that were called at that time. Today, many firms are unprepared to risk investments in parts of the Middle East; Iraq and Afghanistan are only for the extreme risk takers. On the other hand, foreign investment in China is now booming – a situation that would have looked very unlikely when the tanks rolled into Tiananmen Square in 1989. That incident not only deterred investment in China, but also in the neighbouring countries of Hong Kong and Taiwan, which were well within the range of China's military might.

Demonstrations are a common form of political protest

Overseas governments

global focus

Governments, and the ways in which they deal with business, vary enormously across the world. The political affiliation of a government suggests how it might approach business but this is not a hard-and-fast rule. One would expect that left-wing governments, such as those in Cuba and in China, would be more interventionist, i.e. impose more strict controls, but right-wing governments may have strict rules too, particularly governing overseas businesses. For example, the US government comes under pressure from US organisations to protect their interests. Democratically elected governments, such as those in the USA or in European countries, are answerable to the people and dependant upon them and upon business organisations for party funds.

They therefore have to court popularity – sometimes even at the expense of their own political beliefs – and this may mean making populist, rather than politically motivated, decisions.

The people of the West tend to take democracy for granted, but in many countries there are no elections, or the elections are skewed in favour of the ruling party. Nor is freedom of speech by any means a universal right. In China, for example, Google built censorship controls into its search engine, blocking references to events such as the killings in Tiananmen Square, the campaign to free Tibet and Taiwan's independence claims, in order to make it acceptable to the Chinese government. Indian Internet users are blocked from viewing blogs hosted by the online service *Blogger*, and for many years the British people were not allowed to hear the voice of Gerry Adams, leader of Sinn Fein.

SOURCES: adapted from BBC News, 2006; Guardian Unlimited, 2007

Watch me!

In the summer of 2003, Mexican security forces drew up a list of 80 anti-globalisation activists who were thought to be intending to disrupt the World Trade Organisation (WTO) meeting due to be held in their country. Their intention was to make it easier to keep those people under surveillance. They wanted to avoid a repeat of the riots at the Seattle summit in 1999. It was expected that this would provoke an angry response from the human rights-conscious activists. And it did – from those who were missed off the list!

Hundreds of activists signed a letter addressed to 'government agents bent on restricting civil liberties'. It read:

I recently found out about the 'watch list' prepared by Mexican authorities, purportedly to quell the voice of civil society at the upcoming WTO Ministerial [sic] in Cancun. Despite heavy expenditures of tax money on intelligence gathering ... we are concerned that you were only able to find 60 internationals and 30 Mexicans who are opposed to the World Trade Organisation. Haven't you noticed that the tide of public opinion is turning decidedly against the WTO? ... Please add my name to your 'watch list' immediately!

The authorities feared that hundreds, possibly thousands, of demonstrators would turn up to make their points. While most restrict themselves to carrying placards and shouting, there are those who prefer to make their protests more forcefully. In Seattle, hundreds of thousands of pounds worth of damage was done.

SOURCE: Campbell, 2003

Western Europe is currently a relatively stable political environment. However, a change of government can cause firms some problems. Policies change to match the political persuasion of the new government. Just the holding of an election affects sales. The feel-good factor kicks in as election promises of tax cuts and other benefits are fulfilled. Often disposable income rises, as does employment. This does not always last the full term of the government, of course.

The most extreme political risk a firm will encounter is the outbreak of war, and there are usually clear signs that this is a possibility. More common risks include being subjected to pressure group activity. This is a frequent occurrence for a number of large, high-profile firms such as McDonald's and Shell. Nike has suffered too as protestors voiced their objections to its manufacturing methods, particularly the use of child labour in developing countries.

THE REGULATORY ENVIRONMENT

The actions that an organisation can take are constrained by the rules imposed upon it and by the duties it owes to other organisations or individuals. These rules and duties may be formalised as laws (e.g. the Human Rights Act 1998) or as codes of practice (e.g. those governing what is, and what is not, acceptable in advertising) or they may be merely accepted behaviour (e.g. an advertising agency not handling competing clients).

Laws and regulations vary from country to country. There are very few laws that span borders and, contrary to popular belief, there is no international body of law or international court that covers all trading agreements between companies. Increasingly, there are supranational laws and bodies within trading blocs, e.g. the European Union, but in the main, individual countries' laws still apply and so it is vital that companies from different countries agree which country's rules should apply to a contract at the outset. This variety of laws in countries is one of the things that makes international marketing additionally complicated. Take sales promotion laws as an example: in some countries, such as Britain, it is perfectly acceptable to entice customers to buy your product by giving them a money-off voucher. In other countries, such as Germany, this is not allowed.

Although the parties to the contract can choose which country's law applies to an international contract, they cannot opt out of another country's laws and regulations concerning the product itself and its sale within that country. It is important to understand the laws and business regulations of any country with which you hope to trade. Ignorance is rarely a defence in law and unwary companies who assume that judicial systems and laws in all countries are the same are likely to earn themselves hefty fines – or even find their employees imprisoned.

A law is the formalisation of a moral code that is generally accepted by the community. Laws cover the most serious business transgressions (fraud, theft, sale by deception, etc.) and must not be broken. Less serious rules are articulated in a less formal way – often as a code of practice. The UK Advertising Standards Authority (ASA) administers a code of practice for advertisers. It is based on four principles. Advertising must be:

- legal – it must not break any law
- decent – it must not cause widespread, or serious, offence
- honest – it must not exploit the audience's credulity or ignorance
- truthful – it must not mislead by inaccuracy, omission, ambiguity or exaggeration.

Advertisers who fail to live up to these standards are censured and asked to withdraw the offending advertisement. They have not broken a law, no one is going to prison (as they might for fraud), but they have broken the code. Just as the punishment for not complying with a code of practice is less severe than the punishment for breaking the law, so the consequence of simply failing to behave in an acceptable manner is relatively mild. A firm that fails to deliver when promised will find itself with a bad reputation and, eventually, less custom.

Laws are developed by governments, or the judiciary, and usually take a long time to come into force. This gives organisations (or at least those that have identified the proposed laws through their environmental scanning) an opportunity to try to influence the content of laws during their development. This activity is called **lobbying**.

Lobbying is a means of influencing the politicians. It is often employed by pressure or interest groups (e.g. trade associations) rather than by individual firms. The tobacco industry and farmers both have strong lobbies in many EU countries. Trained lobbyists will identify the key members of committees that are debating the proposed changes in law, and put their arguments to them. They hope to persuade the committees to make favourable changes or to drop any harmful proposals altogether. In Britain, the tobacco lobby has been particularly effective: even when it had been agreed that cigarette companies should no longer be allowed to sponsor sports, it managed to get motor racing and snooker exempted for some years. More recently, alcohol producers lobbied to try and prevent stricter rules on the advertising of alcoholic drinks being imposed and the UK TV industry successfully lobbied advertising regulators and the UK government to get **product placement** rules relaxed.

lobbying
a means of influencing those with power, particularly politicians and legislators

product placement
arranging for products to be seen, or referred to, in entertainment media, e.g. during TV or radio programmes, films, plays, video games

THE ECONOMIC ENVIRONMENT

The E in PRESTCOM refers to the macroeconomic environment – *not* to the internal costs of firms. All firms are affected by changes in their macroeconomic

Friends of the Earth

ethical focus

Friends of the Earth is an environmental pressure group that lobbies governments to get them to introduce laws that will protect the environment.

One recent effort was the 'Real Food' campaign, which aimed to raise the public's awareness of the levels of pesticides in food as well as the danger posed by modern farming practices such as the introduction of GM (genetically modified) crops.

As part of the campaign, FoE sent pre-printed postcards to its supporters, asking them to sign them and send them on to politicians.

It also put pressure on supermarkets by publishing a league table ranking them in order of which ones were the best at trying to eliminate pesticides from their products. Website visitors could take advantage of a direct link to email the stores and tell them what they thought of their performance on green issues. There were also email links to relevant central government and EU ministers, as well as the opportunity to vote on whether farmers should be given subsidies to protect the environment.

Farmers have their own lobby and in the EU they are very strong. They try to persuade governments to protect their industry – often by providing subsidies.

The activities of these two powerful, but often opposing, groups are a key part of the environment of food manufacturers and retailers.

Visit the Friends of the Earth website (www.foe.co.uk) and see what campaigns the group is running now.

---

environment. The macroeconomic environment is what is commonly referred to in newspapers as 'the economy'. It is made up of all the buying and selling that goes on in a country (the national economy) or in the world (the global economy). Economic trends today are increasingly global rather than affecting a country in isolation, and this makes it harder for countries to manage their own economies. Most Western governments publish data on economic trends, as do professional organisations such as the Chartered Institute of Marketing (CIM) and international bodies such as the Organisation for Economic Cooperation and Development (OECD).

A country's wealth is normally measured in terms of gross domestic product (GDP), which can be calculated in a number of ways (none of them is 100 per cent accurate) and is an estimation of the value of everything produced within that country in the space of one year. Of more interest to marketers is the GDP per capita (i.e. the average income of individuals), which can give an indication of whether or not the population can afford the product. In 2004, Luxembourg had the highest per capita GDP in the world at just under US$58,000. The USA came next (just under $48,000) closely followed by Norway (OECD, n.d.). Nowadays a country's GDP is usually considered alongside its Human Development Index (HDI), which attempts to measure the population's life expectancy, literacy, education and standard of living.

Most governments set targets for economic growth – sometimes very high targets. In theory, this would mean that everyone within that country would be better off, but there are many today who argue that high growth rates are not sustainable in the longer term. They come at too high a price – and that price is the health of the planet.

A more immediate problem with rapid economic growth stems from the old adage 'What goes up, must come down'. Many Western economies suffer from recurring cycles of boom and slump. Booms are the good times, characterised by high consumer spending and business profits, and low unemployment. Unfortunately, this increase in demand for goods and services may lead to shortages and so to raised

Exhibit 2.4   The trade cycle

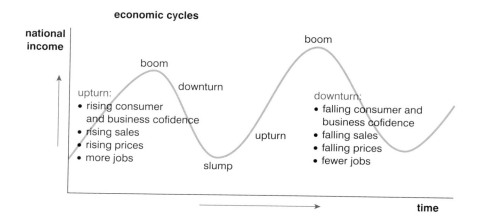

prices (inflation) and the need to import more while exporting less (balance of payments deficit). A slump is likely to follow. Consumers cannot afford the high prices and so demand falls. Businesses find they have surplus capacity and cut back, so unemployment rises, and consumers have even less money to spend. It is a vicious circle (see Exhibit 2.4).

So what is the impact of all this on marketing? Clearly, booms and upturns (as an economy moves from slump to boom) are good times to sell more products. With high consumer demand for products, this might be the time to introduce new, higher-specification models more often – as customers are likely to replace products sooner. With more money to spend, companies are likely to have higher marketing communications budgets. Those that do not, risk being left behind. It is a good time to break into new areas, perhaps by setting up new sales outlets. Prices are likely to rise, but pushing prices up without good reason is a dangerous strategy. That is the path to inflation, which is likely to spell the end of the boom. It is also likely to be very unpopular with customers, of course, and they may desert the firm at the earliest opportunity.

A slump, or downturn in the economy, brings with it a lot of marketing headaches for most businesses. There are a few businesses that are said to be recession proof (**recession** is another term for a downturn). These are companies involved in making and selling essentials, such as food, power, health products and services. However, most companies will see falling sales and reducing profits. They may need to reorganise because of cutbacks in the workforce or the loss of distributors. It is likely that budgets will be cut. Often, promotional activity is one of the first things to go.

Stopping **promotion** is a mistake for at least three good reasons. First, other firms may be cutting back on advertising and so this is a good time to make a real impression – there will be fewer other ads to distract your audience. Second, if brand recognition is lost, then it costs much more to build it up again once the good times return. Third, competition will be cut-throat and advertising is needed to protect **market share**. Price cutting and special offers are popular tactics during the hard times, but these are not image enhancing and should be treated with care by those who have invested heavily in brand building. Many businesses will fail during a slump.

Most firms will hold off new product launches during a slump and it is almost certainly not the time to launch the latest luxury model. It may, however, prove a good time to launch cut-down, budget versions of products, e.g. the no-frills version

recession
when an economy experiences reducing sales and investment; if this continues, it may go into a depression

promotion
another name for marketing communications, communication designed and implemented to persuade others to accept ideas, concepts or things; to motivate consumers to action

market share
a firm's sales expressed as a percentage of the total sales of that type of product in a defined market

of a mass-market car. Prices are likely to need careful monitoring and may need to be changed more often than in better economic times. It is important to remember the negative implications of reducing prices though. For example, a low price may be associated with lower quality (see Chapter 10).

Just as some companies are said to be recession-proof, so are some individuals (i.e. the very rich). Businesses that target wealthy consumers, e.g. top designers such as Christian Dior and luxury goods makers such as Rolex, are less likely to suffer significant drops in sales because of changes in the world economy. Income distribution is as important as average income. In some counties (e.g. Saudi Arabia) a small proportion of the population controls the bulk of the country's considerable wealth.

Firms that trade internationally will have to take account of the economies of all the countries in which they trade. They will also need to take account of import duties (taxes) and other import barriers when devising their marketing plans. This is not such an issue for EU countries trading with each other as a large part of the point of the EU is to remove such barriers. Exports to many other countries are more complicated though.

A firm that understands the economic environment in which it operates is far better placed to take advantage of changes in income and spending. Even a slump can be turned to competitive advantage by well-informed and talented marketers.

THE SOCIAL ENVIRONMENT

Population changes, demographic trends (including age profiles and gender balance), the switch to urban living, lifestyle changes, cultural considerations – all of these come under the heading of the social environment.

Next to the technological environment, this is the area that has perhaps seen the most changes over the last century. Populations have exploded in some parts of the world (notably China and India), while declining in others (notably the Western nations). This has led to a significant shift in the world's population and put a massive strain on the resources of some countries, while the richer nations try to close their doors to a potential flood of immigrants.

In many Western countries, the average age of the population is rising. This has major implications for product developers. We are seeing an increasing number of products, even whole companies, that are aimed at this seniors market, e.g. Saga holidays, *The Oldie* magazine.

This is partly a result of the increased birth rate in the years after the Second World War. Baby boomers, as they are called, were the teenagers of the 1960s, the parents of the 1970s and 1980s and are looking forward to their retirement within the next ten years or so. These people have had a major impact on demand for goods and services throughout their lives. Take housing as an example: when they were young adults they would have wanted flats; as young parents in the 1970s, they would have bought small family houses and then moved up to larger, more expensive ones when their incomes, and families, grew. Now their children are leaving home and many are looking for smaller houses again – perhaps (for the higher income brackets) with a second home in Spain or France. Soon, there should be a boom in retirement homes. At every stage of their lives, these baby boomers have created high demand for the products relevant to them.

The baby boomers' influence does not stop with them. Their children form a baby boom in themselves. Born in the late 1960s through to the 1970s, this is Generation X. A privileged group, born in a time of wealth and peace, Generation Xers have high expectations, especially of brands that they have given their allegiance to. They have grown up during the rise of consumerism. They are cynical and advertising literate. They will not accept shoddy products and they see through insubstantial campaigns. Because they know the advertisers and their tricks so well, they like clever campaigns with insider jokes.

This cycle of population booms continues of course, as each baby boomer becomes a parent, until enough time has passed for the effects to even out. The children of Generation X form a smaller population peak themselves: Generation Y.

insight   Gender trends

Men's and women's roles are changing. Women's earnings are increasing and this seems to have left some brands distinctly confused about how to sell to the new female market. Some have found a new approach that works: the motor industry has succeeded in marketing car brands, e.g. the Fiat Punto, the Renault Clio, and the Ford Fiesta and Focus, to women; pubs have catered for the female market with more female-friendly bars; and drinks manufacturers have spent much of the past decade dreaming up new alcoholic drinks that appeal to women.

Women do not seem to mind taking up brands that were previously aimed at men. Examples of this are numerous. Apart from the car brands, such as Audi, Saab and MG, there are beers such as Stella Artois and Hoegaarden that appeal to today's women. Even shaving products, such as Gillette, which has the

Venus shaving system for women, are getting in on the sister act.

Men, on the other hand, are sensitive about adopting brands that may appear feminine. They are wary, for instance, of many personal care and alcopops brands, which they perceive as having a female bias.

Knowledge of such trends and attitude changes enables marketers to develop brands that suit today's, and tomorrow's, consumers and to position them accordingly.

Nestlé, which makes Yorkie bars, aims its advertising at men, even turning the 'o' in Yorkie on the packaging into a street-sign image of a woman with a red line across. Its posters and print ads have included lines like 'Not available in pink' and 'King size, not queen size'. Clearly, Nestlé wants men to buy the bars but, if it has judged the trends well, its advertising shouldn't put women off either.

SOURCE: Benady and Charles, 2002

Population and demographic trends vary from country to country. For example, while the more developed countries (MDCs) are experiencing rapid rises in the average age of their citizens, in some African countries the bulk of the population are under 35 due to the devastating effects of disease. In developing countries, rural populations often try to migrate to cities, whereas in some of the MDCs the reverse is true, as inner cities empty out. A further example of differences between countries can be found in levels of education. In some countries, products may have to be adapted for a largely illiterate population. Some products, e.g. advanced domestic appliances or cars with onboard computers, will just not be suitable for lesser developed countries (LDCs) because of a lack of skilled personnel to service them.

The very way we live our lives is changing all the time and products, and marketers, must keep up. It is not so long ago that most women were housewives. Now nearly 70 per cent of UK women are in employment (Goodridge, 2006). In the past, marketers could just target all women's products and household items at housewives. It is not so easy now. They have to address a variety of different types of women, with different lifestyles and different requirements. Take a look at 1950s adverts for cleaning products or foodstuffs; they are comically patronising to today's eyes.

> *According to David Nichols, managing director of brand consultancy Added Value: even the women who stay at home and don't work have very different lives from 50 years ago and a variety of things to focus on. Now people want quick solutions from products so that they can either spend time with their families or get on with the things that they like doing. Everything that used to be the housewife's life has been shrunk to as small a job as possible. (Mortimer, 2002)*

The result of this has been a boom in **convenience goods,** such as cleaning wipes and ready meals. It has also led a retail revolution as shoppers seek convenience through home delivery services, mail order, Internet shopping and personal shoppers.

It is not just women's lives that have changed. Men's have too. The 1990s saw the birth of the new man – just as able as a woman to change a nappy or cook a meal. New man is a caring, sharing sort of bloke, much beloved by women in adverts but less apparent in real life, where surveys consistently show that women still take responsibility for, and do the lion's share of, domestic chores.

THE TECHNOLOGICAL ENVIRONMENT

In the last two centuries, technology has changed at an unprecedented rate. In the life spans of just three generations, people in the UK have moved *en masse* from a way of life based on agriculture to industry with its mass production, and on

---

insight   Tipping your hat

Attitudes and what constitutes acceptable behaviour change all the time. A hospital consultant was interviewed on BBC Radio 4 in 2002, where he complained about the rudeness of a number of patients who never removed their baseball caps when in hospital. The wearing of baseball caps off the baseball field, and the attitudes of non-wearers to the fashion, would make an interesting sociological study in itself. A number of people expressed views in support of the consultant, and of the patient. It was clear that many people just would never have considered the patient's behaviour to be rude, and really did not understand why the consultant was offended. Revealingly, the consultant explained that part of the offence came from not being able to see the baseball cap wearer's eyes. Not being able to look the patient in the eye made it harder to communicate with him/her and to establish whether there was a need to probe further into their symptoms. Yet looking directly into someone's eyes is considered offensive in some cultures. So rules of courtesy are by no means universal. They differ between social classes, ages, nationalities – it is so easy to offend and so difficult to retrieve the situation. It is far better for marketers to ensure that they understand their market well in the first place.

to jobs in a microprocessor-based service economy. The more developed countries are now becoming post-industrial information- and communication-based societies.

Rates of technological advancement vary across the world. It would be expected that the MDCs would have all the latest technology while LDCs lagged behind – and this is generally speaking true. However, international marketers must be careful about making assumptions about countries' readiness to accept types of goods based on their level of development alone. It is not uncommon to see colour televisions and satellite dishes in rudimentary homes in poorer countries. Such luxuries can be status symbols that people are prepared to go without basics in order to obtain. There is also the phenomenon of technology skipping, where a developing country misses a whole generation of technology and jumps in at the next level. For example, in parts of Africa mobile phones are common while there are no landlines – the distances are too great to make it viable to install telephone wires. Never make assumptions about other countries – always check.

Recent significant technological advances include:

- more sophisticated information technology
- the convergence of computer and telecommunications technologies (as in Blackberry phones)
- the large numbers of people with access to PCs, digital television, mobile phones
- the development of high-speed, unifying communications networks (e.g. broadband)
- high credit card ownership and use
- personal webpages, e.g. *MySpace*, and blogs.

Technology has made parts of the world much richer but, from the nineteenth-century factory wreckers to the twentieth-century print workers (who went on strike against the introduction of computerised printing equipment in the 1980s), technological change has always been resisted.

ACTIVITY

Look around your room. Are there any items in it that wouldn't have existed 20 years ago? What about ten years ago? And of the things that did exist, would you have been likely to own them?

It is not just our working lives that change with technology, our whole lives would be radically different if technology had not progressed at the pace it has. Houses would be colder and a lot less convenient. The kitchen would be a very different place in which to cook. Hygiene standards would be lower as hot water would be a more complicated treat. There would be fewer home offices if the recent advances in communications and personal computing had not happened.

Technological change has far-reaching effects. Its impact can be felt right across the external environment. Technological innovation is a key driver of economic growth and a major determinant of a company's competitiveness (Baker, 1998). The technological environment has to be watched very carefully. Most environmental changes happen quite slowly, over a considerable period of time, but a technological breakthrough can change an organisation's prospects overnight. Long-established businesses often lose their market leadership to younger rivals with better technology.

Swiss watches used to be reckoned to be the best in the world, until the Japanese put microprocessors in theirs. IBM, once the undisputed leader in almost all forms of computing, lost out to Microsoft's more user-friendly Windows operating system. Cars and planes harmed the railway industry and vinyl has become a niche market thanks to the invention of CDs, which have in turn lost out to downloads and MP3 players. How long will DVDs hold out against HDD recorders?

Some industries (e.g. telecommunications, computing, video gaming and aerospace) exist solely to provide technology to others, but all industries, no matter how low-tech, will be affected by technological change in some way.

Some of the ways in which technology affects marketing are:

lead time
the time it takes for an order to reach the customer

- the invention of new products and services (see 'Innovation', below)
- marketing research is easier thanks to database systems, CD-ROMs, the Internet
- CAD (computer-aided design) has radically changed the way products are designed; designers can try out alternatives and run simulations without building prototypes
- more responsive manufacturing operations mean shorter customer **lead times**
- automated warehousing gets goods to the customer faster
- computerised order taking and online order tracking speed up the ordering process and provide better customer service
- point-of-sale systems (computerised tills) automatically reorder items, avoiding stockouts and so increasing sales
- email and other communications technologies cut down travel times and help firms keep in touch with their customers
- laptops and mobile phones mean salespeople can spend more time with customers and less time in the office
- the Internet has changed the way many services are delivered, e.g. banking, book retailing.

EXPAND YOUR KNOWLEDGE

Arnott, D.C. and Bridgewater, S. (2002) 'Internet, interaction and implications for marketing', *Marketing Intelligence and Planning*, 20 (2): 86–95.

The implications for marketing of the Internet and the interactions it facilitates is explored. The paper examines the extent to which the Internet is used for informational purposes or to facilitate relationship building.

Innovation

Some industries compete largely on the strength of their new ideas (e.g. computer games, mobile phones, convenience foods), and for firms in these industries it is particularly important to invest in research and development. They need original, well-researched product ideas in order to stay competitive. Just how innovative an organisation and its products are depends on a number of things, including:

- how old the product, or the technology the product is based on, is – the older the technology, the more likely it is to be replaced; younger technologies may be able to be refined
- the size of the organisation – small firms are often more inventive, it is easier for new ideas to get heard; unfortunately, they often lack the resources to develop an idea fully and so may lose out to a larger firm
- how competitive the market is – lots of competitors may drive a firm to innovate; however, monopolies are more likely to have the money, if they see the need
- how quickly **consumer** tastes change – anything that could be considered a fashion item will change frequently; anything that customers will tire of (films?) will be replaced regularly.

Technology is a catalyst for change. Once a breakthrough has been made, there is no going back, only further development. Technology spreads, leaping across boundaries to areas where it was never intended to go. The Internet was originally designed as a means for academics and scientists to share their research – look at it now.

(For further discussion of innovative products, see Chapter 6.)

NATURAL ENVIRONMENT

There is increasing concern about the way we have exploited the planet on which we live. Any responsible analysis must take into account the impact that a firm's marketing will have on the world around us – the Earth is rich in resources but these are not limitless. There is a growing trend towards only harvesting things that can be replaced or regrown. Wooden and paper goods proudly declare it if they are made from sustainable sources. Organic food has become big business in the UK, where consumers are worried about pesticides and genetically modified (GM) products. However, the natural environment is not just about green issues. It is not just a way to make manufacturers feel guilty. Nature provides a wealth of opportunities for marketers too.

Economists have long since recognised that a firm's costs are not limited to the things that it buys and pays for. A manufacturer's activities may cause pollution, and someone has to pay to clean it up. It may appear cheaper to run extra-large lorries rather than use rail transport, but the lorries will put a heavy load on the roads, are noisy and potentially polluting, and eventually someone else will have to pay for these things. These **social costs** often end up the responsibility of the government, or, to be more precise, the taxpayer.

The natural environment is something that marketers particularly need to take account of when designing products and packaging, and organising distribution.

The end of the line for plastic packaging may be a previously beautiful beach such as this one

© iStockphoto.com/syagci

Product design

How will products be disposed of when they are obsolete? Britain has a mountain of old fridges awaiting safe disposal. Products such as washing machines used to be designed with built-in obsolescence – they would not last more than about ten years. This was a marketing idea, not a technological limitation. Is this a responsible use of resources? The late twentieth century was a throwaway society: convenience was all, things were not mended, it was cheaper to buy new ones. However, is it really cheaper? It may cost an individual less in the short term to buy a new vacuum cleaner rather than to get the old one fixed, but the new one is using valuable resources in its manufacture, while the old one is adding to a rubbish tip somewhere. In the very long term, it could cost us the ability to make such things at all.

Packaging design

It is increasingly common to see a symbol on packaging that indicates that it can be recycled, although the facilities are not always available to do this. Much twentieth-century packaging was not biodegradable so it can hang around in landfill sites, potentially forever.

ACTIVITY

Take a look at the grocery shopping that comes into your house. *Before it is unpacked*, identify any superfluous or unnecessarily elaborate packaging. Why do you think the product was packaged that way? Can you find a product whose packaging seems to you to be an example of good practice?

Distribution

As companies have got larger, and marketing has become global, so warehouses and distribution networks have grown. It may appear to be cheaper (thanks to economies of scale) to put one huge warehouse in the Netherlands and use it to send goods all over Europe, but this will use more petrol (a scarce resource) and cause more pollution. Bigger is not always better.

Some governments have introduced laws to make firms responsible for these costs. For example, Germany has laws governing the recycling of packaging. The producer is responsible for disposing of packaging. If companies do not take action soon (and some now do perform green audits), then it is likely that more such laws will follow.

ACTIVITY

What are some of the (probably) unforeseen consequences of the invention of:
- cars
- PCs
- credit cards
- mobile phones
- email
- laser printers
- the World Wide Web?

THE COMPETITIVE ENVIRONMENT

The competitive environment is part of the external environment (see Exhibit 2.5).

Exhibit 2.5   The competitive environment

competitors
- direct
- close
- substitute
- indirect

Many companies devote considerable time and effort to competition watching. Some industries are more competitive than others. For example, the rivalry between UK supermarkets is high, with frequent price undercutting and heavy promotional activity. Supermarkets have even been known to offer to accept the loyalty points that customers have built up at rival stores. Some firms are arch-rivals. Often these companies are vying for each other's **market share** – perhaps to take over as the **market leader**. PepsiCo and Coca-Cola, for instance, compete fiercely, as do Nike and Adidas.

Firms analyse the competitive environment to see how they compare with rivals, and to try to understand their competitors' strategies – what they are doing now and what they intend to do in the future. This is essential if the firm is to develop counter-strategies and maintain, or improve, its market position.

The first thing to work out is: who are the competition? Competitive products can be categorised as:

- direct
- close
- substitute
- indirect.

Direct competition

A direct competitor offers a product or service that is similar to the company's own. For example, Heineken is a direct competitor to Carlsberg, just as Coca-Cola is to Pepsi.

Close competition

A close competitor offers a similar product – one that satisfies the same need. Other soft drinks, such as Tango, can be said to be close competitors to Coca-Cola and Pepsi. Close competition might be said to extend to any drink, in fact.

Substitutes for a cross-channel trip: plane, ferry and Eurostar

Substitute competition

These are products that are different from the company's own, but might be bought instead. Again, they satisfy the same or similar needs. An ice cream is a substitute product for a chocolate bar – either can be eaten as a sweet snack.

Indirect competition

This is competition in its widest sense. People have limited amounts of money to spend and so all products compete for that spending ability. A woman may go out to buy a jacket but then see an irresistible pair of shoes. If she does not have the money for both, the jacket and shoes are in competition.

The competitive environment of countries differs greatly – often as a result of the political regime. In the old communist countries, there are still state-owned enterprises that control much of the country's natural resources and are significantly favoured by the government when it awards contracts.

Despite the growing internationalisation of business, a company entering a new market is likely to find itself facing at least some new competitors. For example, Coca-Cola and Pepsi Cola lead the market in most countries across the globe, except in India. In India, the favoured cola drink was Thums Up. Coca-Cola was finding it unusually hard to compete against Thums Up and Pepsi at the same time. The strategy they eventually settled on was to buy the Thums Up company.

EXPAND YOUR KNOWLEDGE

Slater, S. and Narver, J. (1994) 'Does competitive environment moderate the market orientation-performance relationship?', *Journal of Marketing*, 58 (Jan): 46–55.

These authors have been instrumental in maintaining a research interest on issues related to market-orientation. In this paper, they address issues pertaining to the effect of competitive environment on the adoption of orientation.

Exhibit 2.6   Markets

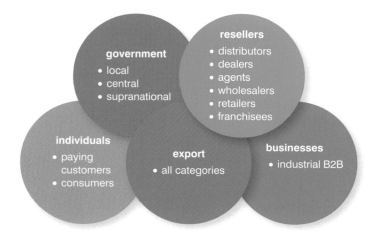

THE MARKET ENVIRONMENT

The market environment is part of the external environment (see Exhibit 2.6). A market is a place where buyers and sellers meet. However, in modern marketing terms, the word 'market' is most often used to refer to the buyers or the consumers. Where would an organisation be without customers? Increasingly, the recipients of goods or services are referred to as customers even when they are not paying, as in the case of charities and other not-for-profit organisations. This is an attempt to improve the effectiveness of organisations by focusing their attention on the people they exist to serve (see the section on customer orientation in Chapter 1).

Markets can be classified according to the customers within them. The major customer groups are described below:

- Individuals, i.e. consumer markets: where private individuals buy goods for their own use, or perhaps to give to someone else. For some purchases, a distinction can be made between customers (who pay for products) and consumers (who use the products). For example, children's clothes are bought by adults (customers) but worn by children (consumers) – both groups are important.
- Businesses, which may be either industrial or B2B (business to business).

  - Industrial buyers use the products they buy as an ingredient, or component, in the making of something else (e.g. Peugeot buying tyres to fit on to new cars) or to contribute directly to the manufacturing process (e.g. oil for machinery). Those tyres could, of course, have been bought by an individual to replace the worn-out tyres on their own car, and that would be a consumer purchase, and from a different source (and almost certainly more expensive).
  - Organisations also need general supplies, office stationery, etc., which they use rather than make something with it. The sale of such goods is a B2B market.

- Government/public sector – governments are extremely large customers, spending millions on goods and services annually.
- Resellers, i.e. those who sell on the products they buy to someone else, such as wholesalers, distributors, dealers, franchisees (see Chapter 9).
- Overseas markets, i.e. all the above, but in other countries.

When a firm's customers are abroad, there are special difficulties in maintaining good relations with them. These difficulties arise from the distances involved and from the language and other cultural barriers (see section on culture below). Many firms have no contact with their overseas customers at all because all their foreign business is handled by **agents**. It is always important to stay close to customers and to ensure that there is good mutual understanding no matter where those customers are. So there is a management challenge here. Market research can help identify different needs. Good analysis, which takes into account local market conditions, can help to formulate solutions and ensure that the product offering is suited to the market. It is harder to maintain good relations with customers in another country, but with the right personnel dealing with them, and good management and control procedures, it is possible to do.

Market fragmentation

The invention of mass-production techniques brought in the era of **mass marketing**. Now we are moving into an era of customised marketing, which is really at the opposite end of the spectrum. Mass marketing sold one design of product to a wide range of people. This was fine when there were only limited products available but, as production techniques improved, it became possible to vary the designs to build

insight   Consumer choice

Toothpaste was once considered a basic product – not any more. At one time, people used soda to clean their teeth, now that's just a nostalgic option. Here are just some of the varieties of toothpaste that can be found in the shops today:

- anti-plaque
- whitening
- breath freshening
- tartar control
- 'total', i.e. all (or most) of the above

- with fluoride
- without fluoride
- for sensitive teeth (in various flavours, whitening)
- smokers'
- bicarbonate of soda
- peppermint
- spearmint
- chocolate
- strawberry
- striped.

On top of that, there are various packaging and size options, and you can probably add many more varieties.

a range of products. Rather than all cars being black (as decreed by Henry Ford's famous edict), cars could be many colours and have different features.

Customers became more demanding. They had more choices and they exercised them. It became desirable for companies to make products that were different from the rest. Marketers recognised that customers were not all the same, that they had different needs and preferences, and wanted different things from the products they bought. Some people like plain burgers, some want cheese, some want blue cheese. Some like mayonnaise, some do not. The same applies to pickle and salad. Today there are almost endless variations on a hamburger – even curry burgers (in the UK at least) and burgers made of fish, beans, even lamb (in India).

ACTIVITY

See how many variants on the following basic products you can think of:

- milk
- household cleaning products
- margarine.

Visit Sainsbury's or Tesco's online shopping site, search for 'milk' and see if there are any you missed. Why do you think all these different products exist?

So end-user markets could no longer be treated as one undifferentiated mass; they had to be split up. People with similar tastes could be sold to as groups. This is called **market segmentation** (see Chapter 4). Companies can select (**target**) certain segments with specific products from their range. The trend today is towards **mass customisation**, which is an attempt to treat all customers as individuals and tailor the company's products, and their marketing efforts, specifically to each one. It is, again, a technological advance that has made this possible, although this time it has more to do with computing than it does with manufacturing. The power of microprocessing, the sophistication of database programs and the communications abilities of the Internet are making personalisation so much easier.

As consumer markets are fragmenting, many industries are reconsolidating. A fragmented industry is one in which there are a lot of players, few of whom have any sizeable market power. At its extreme, this is similar to what economists would refer to as perfect competition. Design agencies formed a fragmented industry in the 1980s and 1990s, and there are still a large number of small agencies in that field.

There has been a recent trend (notably in retailing and among advertising agencies) towards consolidation, i.e. companies are becoming larger and smaller ones are being pushed out. The advertising agencies have been achieving this mainly through mergers and takeovers of other agencies. Retailers employ a number of growth strategies. Franchising has been a particularly successful one for many (e.g. The Body Shop, McDonald's).

So this is a turbulent part of the organisation's external environment and one that needs careful monitoring.

EXPAND YOUR KNOWLEDGE

Goldsmith, R.E. (1999) 'Personalised marketplace: beyond the 4Ps', *Marketing Intelligence and Planning*, 17 (4): 178–185.

The author argues, as many have before, of the need for marketing management and strategy to adapt to changes in the marketing environment and the marketplace and the need for increased 'personalisation' or 'mass-customisation'.

---

cross-selling
persuading a customer to buy extra products

A computer with a personal touch

e-focus

Probably the most significant influence on marketing in the last decade of the twentieth century came from the technological environment. The Internet has had a huge effect on the way we market goods and services. A debate has raged over whether the Internet is a whole new marketplace or just another channel to market or new medium. That debate seems to have settled down now in favour of new channel/new medium, but still the impact of this technology has been greater than that of previous innovations, such as telemarketing.

The power of the computing technology behind the Internet has allowed companies to collect enormous amounts of information on visitors to their sites.

What's more, they can use this information to address customers on an individual basis. This personalised, one-to-one marketing is far more subtle and effective than the old direct mail techniques ever were. Where *Reader's Digest*'s mailers would address you by name throughout the text, Amazon's website knows who your favourite authors are and what kind of music you like. You get personal recommendations, your own page showing which items you've looked at – even an invitation to sell your past purchases online, with an estimate of their worth.

Cross-selling is so much easier with all that computer power behind you. Before a visitor checks out of Amazon's site, a list pops up: 'Other customers who bought books in your basket, also bought. . .'

The international marketing environment

The PRESTCOM model can be adapted for use in international situations, along with the addition of three Cs.

Political
Regulatory
Economic
Social
Technological
Competitive
Organisational
Market
+
Country
Currency
Culture

PRESTCOM

The international marketing environment is very much more complex than the domestic one – not least because no two countries are alike and researchers therefore need to conduct PRESTCOM analyses for each and every country in which the company trades (see Exhibit 2.7).

Exhibit 2.7   International environments

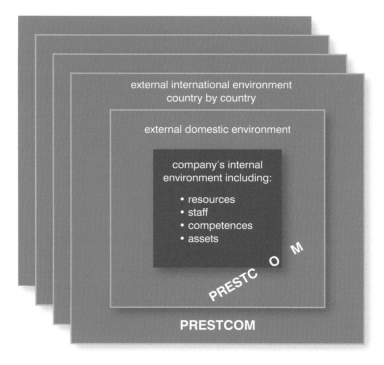

THE THREE CS

Country

A country's history and geography should be taken into account when designing and implementing plans. How good is the relationship between the two countries involved? Britain has very good relations with a number of its ex-colonies (many of which belong to the Commonwealth), but not with all. For example, Zimbabwe is currently a difficult, if not impossible, place for British firms to trade, despite the fact that the two countries once had very good relations and a lot of British people remained there after independence was gained.

Geography and climate strongly affect the suitability of some countries for certain products and the ease, or otherwise, with which they can be distributed. Some countries are remote and inaccessible, e.g. Tibet, which is politically inaccessible as well as being surrounded by the Himalayan mountains. Many landlocked African countries have roads that are too poor to carry trucks of goods safely to their destinations. There is a limited market for warm clothes in equatorial countries and for air conditioning in the UK, where it is rarely hot enough to make the expense worthwhile. On the other hand, the market for conservatories is thriving in the UK where they allow residents to make the most of limited sunshine. In Mediterranean countries, these would mostly be too hot.

Currency

Most countries have their own currencies and products will normally have to be sold in that currency. Some currencies are unconvertible (i.e. they are not generally recognised outside the country in question and therefore cannot be changed into another currency) and so are unattractive to international marketers, but these are rare. Normally, international marketers will wish to convert at least some of the profits made in other countries into their own currency or another hard (i.e. stable and easy to change) currency in order to spend them at home. Rates of exchange vary and so will need to be watched closely. A large drop in the value of the foreign currency could wipe out a company's profits. For this reason, companies may be reluctant to trade in countries with unstable currencies.

Culture

Culture is a key contributor to the kind of person that you are and it is not solely determined by where you were born or who your parents are. As well as ethnic or geographic cultures, there are youth cultures, organisational cultures and religious cultures.

The *Oxford Dictionary of English* (2005) defines culture as 'the ideas, customs, and social behaviour of a particular people or society'. An understanding of a person's cultural background helps marketers to anticipate their responses to products and to tailor campaigns to appeal to them.

International marketers are primarily concerned with the culture shared by the people of a specific country, but it is important to remember that even within a country there are going to be a variety of cultures. Just take a walk down London's Oxford Street and see if you think all the people there share the same cultural background – well, perhaps they are all part of a consumer culture at least.

ACTIVITY

Visit a place that is popular with tourists or, if that's not possible, watch one on television or just imagine one. How do the people there differ from each other? How do you know that they are from different countries? Can you tell (without actually asking them) where they are from?

high-context culture
one where communication must be interpreted according to the situation; much of the message is in the context rather than being explicitly expressed in the words

low-context culture
the information to be communicated is put into words explicitly; there is little need to take account of the surrounding circumstances

Language is clearly a major distinguishing feature of national cultures and can provide a serious obstacle to international communication. Translation may not be good enough, especially for culturally sensitive communications where nuances and the tone may not translate accurately. There are also concepts that just do not translate, e.g. three is really not an adequate translation of a 'hat trick'.

Although it is important to provide instructions, packaging, etc. in people's own language, that is not enough to tailor a product to another culture in itself. Marketers need to take account of different beliefs, attitudes, customs, uses for products and the way the people of a country live.

insight   High- and Low-context cultures

The noted anthropologist Edward Hall (cited in Usiner and Lee, 2005) is responsible for the introduction of the concepts of **high-context and low-context cultures** into the study of international exchanges. In a high-context culture, such as Japan, it is important to take account of the situation in which something is said. The words alone may not convey the true meaning of the speaker. It is difficult for most Northern Europeans to decode this, but it is important to be aware that 'first we must do x' or 'I'll let you know next week' might well actually mean 'no' depending on the circumstances in which it is said, who is saying it and where they come from. On the other hand, a North American (low context) will have no compunction in saying 'no' if they do not want to make the deal, and will see that as commendable honesty and straight-dealing rather than as shocking discourtesy. The use of language in extreme low- and high-context cultures can be as different as its use in technical manuals and in poetry: the first tries to make the meaning as clear as possible through words alone; the second works on a number of different levels and requires interpretation by someone familiar with the poetic form.

The following are usually considered low-context cultures:

- USA
- Canada
- Germany
- Switzerland
- Austria
- Scandinavian countries
- Australia
- New Zealand.

The following countries are considered to be high-context:

- Latin American countries
- Middle Eastern countries
- Japan.

The British are the source of some confusion, especially to Americans, who assume a greater similarity between these two peoples than there really is. (There is an old saying: two peoples divided by a common language.) Britain fits into the middle of the high/low-context spectrum thanks to the British tendency towards understatement and euphemism as well as the demands of courtesy which make some statements too bold.

Another country that causes problems in categorisation is France. The French language has long been considered the ideal diplomatic language because it can be precise or vague according to the speaker's wish (Usiner and Lee, 2005).

When language lets us down, we often try sign language, or gestures instead, but there is no more a universal understanding of gestures than there is of words. In many countries it is extremely rude to point, whereas in others it is just a normal way to indicate something. On the Indian subcontinent, people shake their head for yes and nod for no; in Europe, it is the other way around. The holding up of the index and middle fingers (or even just the index finger) is very rude in the UK, but a sign that is not readily understood elsewhere. It can make it quite dangerous for foreigners to count on their fingers in Britain. Even in the UK, it makes a huge difference if you hold the hand the other way, palm out, as the two fingers then symbolise peace. And, if we go back to the end of the Second World War, when British Prime Minister Winston Churchill first used the gesture, he was not being rude – his two fingers symbolised victory.

© Reg Speller/Hulton Archive/Getty Images

Winston Churchill's V for Victory

ACTIVITY

Choose three countries (one can be your own) and investigate their most popular sporting event(s). You can do this either through an Internet search or by discussing sport with people who have been involved, either as players or spectators, in other countries. What happens around the match/race/contest? What do spectators do? Does anything happen on the pitch/court/track etc. that is extraneous to the sporting action (e.g. cheerleading)? What does this tell you about the similarities and differences between the peoples of those countries?

These cultural differences make the world a more interesting place but are a minefield for unwary international marketers.

Situation analysis

It is very hard (and usually spectacularly unsuccessful) to plan a route ahead without an understanding of the starting point. Take the example of a journey to London. The travel agent is going to need to know the journey's starting point before they can possibly recommend a method of travel. It makes a big difference whether the traveller is currently in Paris, New York or Leicester.

Similarly, a company needs to know where it stands at the moment before it can make plans to improve its position. Acquisition of another chain might well be a suitable way for a large chain of stores with a dominant market position to grow, but a smaller chain, with fewer resources, is unlikely to be able to do this.

An analysis of the current situation is the starting point for most plans. It tells a firm where it is now.

The basic planning process looks like this:

Where are we now?

(situation analysis)

↓

Where do we want to be?

(objectives)

↓

How will we get there?

(the plan)

↓

How will we know when we've arrived?

(evaluation and control)

There are a number of techniques and models that the organisation can use to analyse its situation, the most widely used of which is a SWOT analysis. This analysis is based on organising environmental data gleaned from a PRESTCOM environmental analysis.

ACTIVITY

Pick a company that is in the news. What has been going on in its environment that has helped put it there?

SWOT

A **SWOT analysis** is a general management tool rather than being peculiar to marketing. However, it is widely used as a basis for marketing planning. Selected environmental variables from the PRESTCOM analysis (see page 46) are placed under one of the four SWOT headings:

Strengths	internal, i.e. under the organisation's control, e.g. well-developed brand
Weaknesses	internal, i.e. under the organisation's control, e.g. small budget
Opportunities	external, i.e. not under the organisation's control, e.g. favourable fashion trend
Threats	external, i.e. not under the organisation's control, e.g. unfavourable fashion trend

Strengths and weaknesses are internal factors, while opportunities and threats are external. So, only organisational factors go into strengths or weaknesses; the rest of the PRESTCOM analysis is external and so feeds into opportunities or threats.

A strength is something that the firm has, or something that it does, that is better than its competitors. For example, a stronger brand name would be a strength.

A weakness is the opposite of a strength: something that the firm has (or does not have), or does, that is worse than the competition. For example, an outdated product range would be a weakness.

Threats and opportunities are part of the external environment and therefore an organisation will have far less (if any) control over them.

A threat is something that is going on in the firm's external environment that is likely to cause it problems. The drinks industry is threatened by proposed regulations that will make it much more difficult to promote alcohol.

An opportunity is the opposite of a threat: it is something that is going on in the external environment that is likely to be good for the organisation. For example, an upturn in the economy is an opportunity for many firms.

Opportunities have deliberately been left until last as they seem to be the cause of much student confusion. It is important to realise that the word 'opportunity' is being used in a very particular way here: *an opportunity is not an action*. It is not something that the firm could *do*. It is just something good that is happening outside that the firm might be able to take advantage of – somehow.

Further examples of possible opportunities are:

- the election of a government that is pro-foreign trade in one of the firm's export markets
- the relaxation of rules governing what can and what cannot be **sponsored**
- a drop in interest rates
- a baby boom
- digital iTV
- a competitor goes out of business
- a new store opens locally.

Not all of these opportunities will apply to all organisations. For example, the last one (the new local store) may only be of relevance to local suppliers – but, to them, it is clearly a great opportunity. They may be able to sell more. How they go about persuading the store to stock their products (if indeed they decide that they want to do that) comes further along in the planning process. The SWOT analysis just identifies that an opportunity exists.

ACTIVITY

Pick one of the following companies and make a list of relevant PRESTCOM trends, issues, events (i.e. environmental variables). Then categorise them under the SWOT headings. Companies to choose from:

- Microsoft
- Virgin
- Gap
- Vodafone
  or choose your own company.

When you've completed the exercise, check the following points:

- do all your strengths/weaknesses come from the 'organisation' heading? Are they all particular to the firm and (mainly) its responsibility?
- do all your opportunities/threats come from the external environment (the other PRESTCOM headings)? Do they all affect other companies too?
- are any of your opportunities actions or things the company can do? If so, then they are strategies or tactics, *not* opportunities!

Ranking

SWOT analysis does not stop at listing the relevant variables under their correct headings – that is just the start. The next task is to rank the variables in order of their importance to the company.

Matching

The really interesting bit of the SWOT analysis comes during a process called matching. The firm looks for opportunities that play to its strengths (that match them). If there is an opportunity that matches a strength, then these will be key to the company, and objectives and strategies will be built upon them. For example, AOL merged with Time Warner and so gained access to its cable pipes. This coincided with increased interest from customers in broadband services (such cable pipes are needed to deliver broadband). The pipes were an AOL strength, while broadband presented the company with an opportunity. The two matched. The exploitation of this opportunity became a key part of its marketing strategy.

It is also important to watch out for threats that prey upon weaknesses. These are significant threats, and action needs to be taken to reduce their effect. Let's take the example of AOL again. AOL grew into one of the biggest Internet service providers (ISPs) by offering a standard, suits everyone, style of service. As the Internet market matured, people wanted different types of product, e.g. home users wanted something simpler and with more support. AOL did not have this. The standardised service was a weakness that was matched by the market's new demand for different types of service.

EXPAND YOUR KNOWLEDGE

Pickton, D.W. and Wright, S. (1998) 'What's SWOT in strategic analysis', *Strategic Change*, 7 (2): 101–109.

This article takes a critical look at the use of SWOT analysis as a second, deeper and more detailed level of analysis following on from PRESTCOM and encourages a more insightful use of this tool which, if used too simplistically, could result in poor strategic development.

Stakeholders

There are a large number of individuals and groups that exist within a company's environments and that have an interest in the company and its activities. These are its **stakeholders.** Freeman (1984) defined stakeholders as 'any group or individual who can affect or is affected by the achievement of an organisation's activities'. All organisations have a large number of stakeholder groups and they will be different for each one.

Typically, stakeholder groups include:

- customers (who buy goods and services)
- consumers (who use the goods and services – for further discussion of this distinction see Chapter 1)

- employees, including directors
- pensioners, i.e. ex-employees who receive their pension income from the firm
- suppliers of goods and services, e.g. advertising agencies, raw materials providers
- distributors, e.g. **wholesalers, retailers, agents**
- government (local and central)
- local community, from whom customers, employees and pressure group members (e.g. local residents' organisations) may be drawn
- shareholders, who own the company
- pressure groups, e.g. trades unions, consumer groups
- bankers, who may have lent the company money
- other investors, e.g. venture capitalists
- professional bodies, e.g. the Chartered Institute of Marketing.

These groupings are very like the audiences that **PR** people sometimes refer to as publics.

Stakeholder groups will want different things from the firm, and often their objectives for the firm conflict. For example, customers usually want the best quality but at the lowest possible price. Shareholders, on the other hand, will want the company to make high profits so that their dividends are higher and their shares are worth more. Pressure groups such as Greenpeace will want the company to spend money on protecting the environment and will consider any resulting increase in prices, or decrease in profits, as perfectly acceptable. Trades unions may want higher wages and better working conditions. This will, again, push up the company's costs and so it may have to raise its prices (which the customers will not like) or cut its profits (which the shareholders will not like). Setting objectives, developing strategies and managing situations in a way that resolves the conflicts between these differing stakeholder groups is a key management task and one that can use up much time and effort.

The idea of a firm having a responsibility towards its stakeholders is relatively new in management thinking. Previously, a company's prime duty was thought to be to its shareholders, or owners, alone. This led to many organisations' main objective being short-term profit maximisation, which was often not in its best interests in the longer term. Current managerial thinking takes account of other stakeholder groups when setting the organisation's direction. Just how far to take this has become a moral question that has prompted significant debate.

SUMMARY

No organisation exists in isolation. What is happening in and around it largely determines its ability to succeed in achieving its goals. Monitoring changes in the environment helps a company to spot key opportunities and threats, and forms the basis for sound marketing planning. Some firms do have formal processes for the collection of environmental data but many gather their information in a more ad hoc manner, relying on the judgement and contacts of managers.

There are a number of acronyms that can be used as frameworks for the analysis of the external environment. The one proposed here is PRESTCOM, which encompasses not just the macroenvironment, but the competitive and internal environments as well.

The key environments to be monitored are: political, regulatory (or legal), economic, social, natural, technological, competitive, the organisation itself (internal), distribution and customers (market). When an organisation is trading internationally, it will have to assess these environments in its home country and in all the others in which it trades.

For many firms, the technological environment is a key determinant of competitive edge. Technological change may speed economic growth, provide a means for innovation, change the way people work, spend their leisure time, even how they think. It can also make an organisation more efficient. Often, technologies, such as production and transport, have an impact upon the natural environment that may need to be watched out for.

Environmental data can be input into a situation analysis using a framework such as SWOT. This categorises and prioritises the information, and so identifies the key opportunities and threats that the organisation should address. That situation analysis then becomes the base upon which the organisation's marketing plans are built.

CHALLENGES REVIEWED

Now that you have finished reading the chapter, look back at the challenges you were set at the beginning. Do you have a clearer idea of what's involved?

Hints:

- think about PRESTCOM and environmental scanning
- again think about environmental scanning and SWOT and whether the demise of some cafés presents your business with an opportunity
- you should be carefully monitoring the regulatory environment, and be ready to take action should new laws transpire; even better, you will know when and who to lobby to try to get the laws amended
- such a company should have been monitoring groups like Greenpeace, and could therefore have predicted such action and contingency plans would be put in place
- there are any number of reasons why you might not have been as creative as your colleague, but one of them may be that you were not keeping up with relevant changes in the technological environment.

READING AROUND

Books

Stephen Croall (2000) *Introducing Environmental Politics*. Cambridge: Icon Books.
Ian Worthington and Chris Britton (2009) *The Business Environment* (6th edn). Harlow: Prentice Hall.
For further reading on SWOT, the following texts are recommended:
Gerry Johnson and Kevan Scholes (1993) *Exploring Corporate Strategy* (3rd edn). Harlow: Prentice Hall.
Richard M.S. Wilson and Colin Gilligan (1997) *Strategic Marketing Management* (2nd edn). London: Butterworth Heinemann.

Articles

A critical commentary of SWOT analysis can be found in:
David Pickton and Sheila Wright (1998) 'What's SWOT in strategic analysis?', *Strategic Change*, 7 (2): 101–109.

Websites

www.statistics.gov.uk – check out the latest UK social trends.
www.wto.org – the World Trade Organisation's website.

SELF-REVIEW QUESTIONS

1. Define marketing environment. (see page 38)
2. What are uncontrollables? (see page 42)
3. What are the two ways in which environmental information is used? (see page 42)
4. How is environmental data gathered? (see page 43)
5. What does PRESTCOM stand for? (see page 46)
6. Name three ways in which the political environment can impact upon a firm's marketing operations. (see pages 49–52)
7. List four characteristics of a downturn that would adversely affect a firm's ability to sell its goods. Why is that? (see page 55)
8. What are social costs? Why do some people think that companies should account for them? (see page 61)
9. Why is innovation important? (see page 60)
10. List and describe four types of competition. (see pages 63–4)
11. What are the five main internal functions of a business? (see page 47)
12. Define an opportunity. What is the key difference between opportunities and threats, and strengths and weaknesses in a SWOT analysis? (see page 73)

Haircare: hygiene or high fashion?

Read the questions, then the case material, and then answer the questions.

Questions

1. Do a PRESTCOM analysis for L'Oreal, drawing on the information given below.
2. Now do a SWOT analysis.
3. If you were a marketing consultant, what advice would you give to a haircare company? Your suggestions should be based on your analysis of the case and they should all be *explained* and *justified*.

For some, choosing haircare products is simple. After all, the point is to end up with clean hair, isn't it? So the cheapest shampoo will do. Other people spend significant amounts of time and money on their haircare. They don't just buy shampoo, but look for the very best in conditioners, styling products and dyes. After all, you wear your hair every day, don't you? So why wouldn't you take at least as much time with it as you do in choosing your clothes.

Fashions in hairstyles change as often as those in clothing styles. Celebrity hairstyles can make the news and attract as much comment as their clothes, bags and shoes do. The film and pop stars who make the trends often have their own personal hairdressers on hand, but most people cannot afford such luxury and so they need help from gels, mousses and other miracle products to make their curly hair poker straight or to coax their straight hair into curls. Then, thanks to all that frequent washing and blow-drying, their heat-damaged hair needs yet more products to make it shine.

The fashionistas have added value to the haircare sector but this market has been adversely affected by changes in the economy. The first decade of the twenty-first century has seen one of the deepest recessions in living memory. Many jobs have been lost, pay packets have shrunk and people have had to give up some of their luxuries, e.g. trips to the hairdresser. Shampoo is an essential purchase for most people but shoppers have been buying own labels and cheaper brands or value packs, or looking out for price promotions. Clever shoppers wait for the promotions and then stock up with their preferred brands.

Western Europe's ageing population is another problem for the haircare brands because older consumers tend to wash their hair less frequently and use fewer products. Conditioner sales have been even worse hit than shampoos; some consumers have cut conditioning from their haircare routine altogether. Women are still far more likely to buy conditioner than men; just over one-third of men use this type of product, compared with three-quarters of women.

Manufacturers have also had to deal with increasing consumer concern about the negative environmental impact of haircare products which find their way into oceans and water supplies. Recycling of packaging is also an issue.

Global demand for L'Oreal's premium brands, which include Lancôme and Kiehl's, has fallen sharply. Retailers have cut their orders and some manufacturers have responded with lower prices to try to stimulate sales. In an attempt to revitalise the market, L'Oreal's scientists are developing new products for mass-market brands, such as Maybelline New York and L'Oreal Paris.

In 2007, retail sales of shampoo and conditioner reached £706 million, dropping to £700 million in 2008 and Mintel predicts they will fall further. Shampoo has the biggest share of the market with sales of £391 million in 2009.

Hairdressers have also been hit hard as women visit them less often. Some of the premium haircare brands have responded to this trend by launching products with salon-finish quality or longer colour maintenance benefits.

This is a highly segmented market presenting marketing opportunities for a variety of differentiated products. Shampoos are available for different hair types, hair colours and hair lengths. Frizzy hair can be tamed or thin hair volumised. Older hair can be rejuvenated or children's sensitive eyes protected from accidental contact with shampoo. Combined shampoo and conditioner products such as Elvive 2 in 1 were in decline before the recession hit and manufacturers seem to be phasing them out. L'Oreal still markets these products to children and men, but has dropped them from most of its adult women's ranges. They tend to be more popular among men who want convenience rather than the more exotic benefits promised by so

(Continued)

(Continued)

many female brands. Nivea have responded to this need with Men Active 3: a combined shower gel, shampoo and shaving foam.

Procter & Gamble is very strong in this sector with a 36 per cent market share. Brands such as Head & Shoulders and Herbal Essences are long-time favourites with customers and P&G has continued to innovate through the recession and has kept up its advertising. It launched a new range of men's haircare products under its Gillette brand name and these are building market share. Although women still spend far more on haircare, there is a growing trend among men, especially younger men, to purchase more grooming products.

Johnson & Johnson is another key competitor. Its strong brand positioning in babycare makes it ideally placed to take advantage of opportunities presented by the rising number of under 4-year-olds in the UK.

Unilever has been pushing its Timotei brand, launching variants including Golden Highlights, Soft & Smooth and Strengthen & Shine. It also extended its Dove brand with the addition of the Therapy range, offering colour protection and intensive conditioning.

Meanwhile L'Oreal cut its ad budget for the Garnier Fructis brand and focused its attention instead on its Elvive brand, possibly because of its purchase of The Body Shop in 2006. Sales have dropped by almost 54 per cent since 2007, according to Mintel.

SOURCES: Keynote, 2008; Mintel, 2009; WARC, 2009; Wood, 2009

REFERENCES

Allen, R. (ed.) (2000) *New Penguin English Dictionary*. Harmondsworth: Penguin.

Arnott, D.C. and Bridgewater, S. (2002) 'Internet, interaction and implications for marketing', *Marketing Intelligence and Planning*, 20 (2): 86–95.

Baker, M.J. (1998) *The Marketing Manual*. London: Butterworth Heinemann.

BBC News (2006) 'Google censors itself for China', 25 January. Available at: **news.bbc.co.uk/1/hi/technology/4645596.stm** (accessed 30/01/2007).

BBC News (2008) 'Bolivia nationalises energy firms'. Available at: **news.bbc.co.uk/1/hi/business/7378803.stm** (accessed 28/02/2010).

Benady, D. and Charles, G. (2002) 'The battle for the sexes', *Marketing Week*, 4 April.

Brownlie, D. (2000) 'Environmental scanning', in M.J. Baker (ed.), *The Marketing Book* (4th edn). London: Butterworth Heinemann, pp. 81–107.

Campbell, D. (2003) 'Indignant activists demand names go on police list', *The Guardian*, 1 September.

Dibb, S., Simkin, L., Pride, W.M. and Ferrell, O. (2006) *Marketing Concepts and Strategies* (5th European edn). Boston: Houghton Mifflin.

Doyle, P. (2002) *Marketing Management and Strategy* (3rd edn). Harlow: FT Prentice Hall.

Goldsmith, R.E. (1999) 'Personalised marketplace: beyond the 4Ps', *Marketing Intelligence and Planning*, 17 (4): 178–185.

Durman, P. (2006) 'Nintendo Wii steals the Christmas show', *The Sunday Times*, 24 December.

European Commission (2009a) 'Key facts and figures about Europe and the Europeans'. Available at: **europa.eu/abc/keyfigures/tradeandeconomy/index_en.htm** (accessed 21/11/2009).

European Commission (2009b) 'Member states of the EU'. Available at: **europa.eu/abc/european_countries/eu_members/index_en.htm** (accessed 21/11/2009).

Finch, J. (2007) 'How Tate and Lyle went sour', *The Guardian*, 29 September, p. 41.

Freeman, R. (1984) *Strategic Management: A Stakeholder Approach*. London: Pitman.

Goodridge, P. (2006) 'Labour market analysis and summary'. London: HMSO. Also available at: **www.statistics.gov.uk/downloads/theme_labour/LMT_Dec06.pdf** (accessed 20/07/2007).

Guardian Unlimited (2007) 'Indian bloggers fight government censorship', *The Guardian*, 19 July. Also available at: **blogs.guardian.co.uk/news/archives/2006/07/19/indian_bloggers_fight_government_censorship.html** (accessed 20/07/2007).

Jobber, D. (2004) *Principles and Practice of Marketing* (4th edn). New York: McGraw-Hill.

Johnson, B. (2006) 'From must-have to can't have', *The Guardian*, 7 September.

Keynote (2008) *Marketing Assessment Clothing and Personal Goods, Men's and Women's Buying Habits*. London: Keynote.

Kotler, P., Armstrong, G., Saunders, J. and Wong, V. (2001) *Principles of Marketing* (3rd European edn). Harlow: Pearson Education Ltd.

Mercer, D. (1995) 'Simpler scenarios', *Management Decision*, 33 (4): 32–40.

Mintel (2009) *Shampoos and Conditioners – 2009 – UK*. London: Mintel.

Mortimer, R. (2002) 'Consumer life made easy', *Brand Strategy*, 12 June.

OECD (n.d.) 'OECD Factbook: Macroeconomic Trends, GDP per capita'. Available at: **miranda.sourceoecd.org/vl=585457/cl=23/nw=1/rpsv/factbook/data/02-01-01-t02.xls** (accessed 05/01/2007).

Oxenfeldt, A.R. and Moore, W.L. (1978) 'Customer or competitor: which Guideline for marketing', *Management Review*, Aug: 43–48.

Pickton, D. and Broderick, A. (2001) *Integrated Marketing Communications*. Harlow: FT Prentice Hall.

Pickton, D.W. and Wright, S. (1998) 'What's SWOT in strategic analysis', *Strategic Change*, 7 (2): 101–109.

Slater, S. and Narver, J. (1994) 'Does competitive environment moderate the market orientation-performance relationship?', *Journal of Marketing*, 58 (Jan): 46–55.

Usiner, J.C. and Lee, J.A. (2005) *Marketing Across Cultures* (4th edn). Harlow: FT Prentice Hall.

WARC (2009) 'FMCG giants target male consumers', *WARC News*, 09 September. Available at: **www.warc.com/News/TopNews.asp?ID=25645** (accessed 10/09/2009).

Wood, Z. (2009) 'L'Oreal shares jump 10% after firm beats profit forecast', *The Guardian*, 28 August.

Part two

MAKING SENSE OF MARKETS

THIS PART CONTAINS:

3 Buyer behaviour

4 Market segmentation, targeting and positioning

5 Marketing research

WHAT THIS PART IS ABOUT:

Part 2 goes behind the scenes and looks at the forces that shape an organisation's marketing activities.

Successful marketing depends upon a thorough understanding of customers, their worlds and their needs. Consequently, marketers spend much time, effort and money on research and analysis. They draw on other social science disciplines to shed further light on their customers' behaviour: economics, psychology and sociology in particular. Such in-depth market understanding confers a valuable competitive advantage.

3

Buyer behaviour

CHAPTER CONTENTS

Introduction
The consumer buyer decision process
Types of consumer buying decision
Levels of involvement
Influences on consumer buyer
    behaviour
The consumer buyer decision process
    for new products
Types of organisation and the products
    they purchase
Characteristics of organisational
    markets
Organisational buying situations
The buying centre
The organisational buying process
Organisational purchase criteria
Summary
Challenges reviewed
Reading around
Self-review questions
Mini case study
References

BUYER BEHAVIOUR CHALLENGES

The following are illustrations of the types of decision that marketers have to take or issues they face. *You aren't expected to know how to deal with the challenges now*; just bear them in mind as you read the chapter and see what you can find that helps.

●   You are the marketing manager for a toy manufacturer. The company is planning to produce a range of toys for children under 3 years old. How do people decide to buy such toys? Who purchases these types of toy? Who influences the purchase and what do they consider when purchasing such toys?

●   You have developed a brand new product that is a technological break-through: a teleporter. It reduces people to their component atoms and transports them almost instantly to wherever in the world they want to go. Eventually, it will make most other forms of transport redundant. Which type of person is most likely to be the first to use such a product and how would you persuade them to do so?

●   Tony was brought up in a quiet village in the north-west of Scotland. As a child he loved the Scottish countryside. However, he subsequently went to university and now has a highly paid, stressful job with a blue-chip company in the City. He misses Scotland and frequently visits home. You are product development manager for a brewery. What type of drink would appeal to him and why?

●   You are attempting to sell a computer system to a large governmental department. You have to give a presentation to the end users of the computer system, the head of department, the IT manager and an accountant. What criteria do you think they will use to assess the suitability of your computer? Who else should you target within the organisation and who do you think has the most influence?

●   *The Apprentice* is a BBC television programme in which young business people compete for a job with Sir Alan Sugar, Chairman of Amstrad. In one episode, the teams were asked to sell expensive lollipops at a zoo. One contestant's approach was to hand a lollipop to a small child, ask if the child liked it/wanted it – and then charge the parents. What do you think of that idea?

Introduction

There are a number of well-known sayings about customers, e.g. 'The customer is king' and 'The customer is always right', and it should hardly come as a surprise that marketers invest a great deal of money and effort into finding out about their customers. A company that understands its customers well is far more likely to bring successful products to the market than one that operates on false assumptions.

In an ideal world, marketers could treat each customer as a unique individual. However, that is hardly practical. It would involve making too many product variants and would be unlikely to be profitable. So marketers group similar individuals together and design their marketing programmes for these groups. The next chapter will consider markets as groups, or segments, consisting of buyers or users who share similar characteristics.

The first part of this chapter focuses on consumers as individuals within a market. It explores how consumers purchase products in terms of the decisions they make and the various stages they may go through in reaching a purchase decision. It subsequently examines what influences them in terms of internal factors (such as their personality) and external factors (such as friends and family – see Exhibit 3.1).

However, most purchases are made by organisations rather than individuals. The way organisations make decisions is considerably more complex, not least because there are likely to be a number of people involved. The second part of the chapter will look at buying behaviour from an organisational perspective.

The consumer buyer decision process

consumer models
representations of consumer buying behaviour, usually as diagrams

Marketers spend large amounts of time and money attempting to find out how consumers respond to different elements of the **marketing mix**. There have been many attempts to portray these responses through the creation of **consumer models** of

Exhibit 3.1   Chapter structure

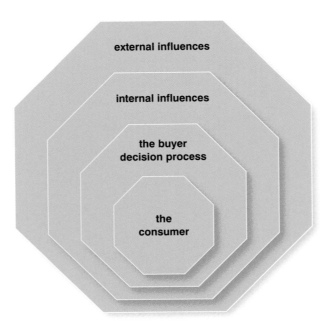

buyer behaviour. These aim to provide frameworks for explaining the stages that consumers pass through in their decisions on whether or not to purchase a product or service.

Engel et al.'s (2006) model (see Exhibit 3.2) is a well-known example.

Exhibit 3.2 shows the key stages that a consumer passes through in deciding whether or not to buy a product. Although it is more relevant to new or difficult purchases, the model is useful as an aid to understanding all purchases because it shows all the factors facing a consumer when deciding what to buy. The next part of this chapter will look at these stages in more detail.

EXPAND YOUR KNOWLEDGE

Howard, J.A. and Sheth, J.N. (1967) 'A theory of buyer behavior', in R. Moyer (ed.) *Changing Marketing Systems ... Consumer, Corporate and Government Interfaces: Proceedings of the 1967 Winter Conference of the American Marketing Association*. Washington, DC: AMA.

Howard and Sheth are the architects of one of the early comprehensive marketing buyer behaviour models. In this article they outline the elements used in their model of buyer behaviour in consumer markets. This model is one amongst others used in their more extensive textbooks on buyer behaviour.

Need/problem recognition

The buyer decision process begins with a potential customer recognising that they have a problem or an unfulfilled need. The person realises that there is a difference between their current, or actual, state and their desired state (see Exhibit 3.3). In other words, they want something. The trigger for this need may be an internal factor, such as being hungry or thirsty and therefore needing food or drink, or it may come from an external source, such as a suggestion from a friend (e.g. 'let's have a drink'), an advert or the display in a shop window.

Exhibit 3.2   The buyer decision process

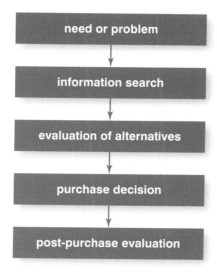

SOURCE: (Engel et al., 2006)

In this model, and in most other need or problem recognition models, the problem does not have to be serious or life-threatening. For example, imagine you are watching TV and an advert for crisps appears. This may stimulate a desire for a snack even though you are not hungry. There is no serious problem here, you are not even really hungry, but there is a discrepancy between your actual state (snack-less) and your desired state (eating crisps). You have recognised a problem that could be solved by a packet of crisps.

Sometimes the recognition of a need or problem is not as obvious as this. It may be based on vague feelings. For example, students who do not do as well in an exam as they had hoped may well treat themselves to large bars of chocolate or ice creams on the way home. The trigger was the feeling of disappointment, the need was to feel better and the treat was the means – but clearly something else was going on in their heads between the recognition that they were feeling low and the decision to make themselves feel better by buying something. Then yet another thought pattern kicked in, which made the decision on what kind of treat to buy. These decisions are much harder to understand, and to predict, than the simple 'I am thirsty so I will drink' type.

Sweets at a supermarket checkout are designed to be external triggers to stimulate **impulse purchase**

impulse purchase
buyer behaviour, made on the spur of the moment

level of involvement
the extent to which the purchase is important to the purchaser

The amount of effort that **consumers** are prepared to make to solve the need or problem depends on how large the difference is between their current and their desired state, and the relative importance of that need to the individual consumer. This is known as the **level of involvement** and is discussed in more detail later in this chapter.

Marketers must be aware of consumers' needs so that they can be in a position to offer goods or services that will satisfy these. Marketers must also be aware of what is likely to generate and influence those needs so they are able to develop the appropriate marketing mix.

Exhibit 3.3   The process of problem recognition

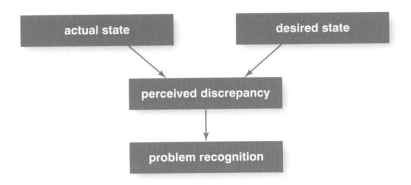

SOURCE: Wilkie, 1990

INFORMATION SEARCH

Once consumers have recognised that they have a need, or a problem, the next stage of the buyer decision process begins: the information search. Information search involves identifying the ways that need can be satisfied or problem can be solved. This required information may be found internally or externally.

An internal search involves accessing memory and using previous experience. So, for example, if the consumer had had a craving for crisps before, and a particular brand of crisps had proved satisfying and so solved the problem, then they might buy them again. However, if no satisfactory solution is found within the consumer's memory, then they may have to look for new information elsewhere. External sources of information include, but are not limited to:

● personal sources, such as family, friends and other students
● commercial sources, such as shop assistants, websites and adverts (interestingly, someone who is considering buying for example a new laptop PC, tends to notice laptops and adverts for laptops when they might never have registered them before)
● third-party reports, such as magazine comments, newspaper editorials, Watchdog reports, blogs or webpages.

The information gathered through information searches is used to build up the consumer's **awareness set**. An awareness set is a range of products or brands that may satisfy a need or provide a solution to a consumer's problem, i.e. it is a mental list of all the known possibilities.

awareness set
range of products or brands that may satisfy the need or provide a solution to the problem

ACTIVITY

Choose a product from the list below and write out a list of all the brands you know of, i.e. build up your own awareness set for that product:

● football boots
● holiday companies
● mascara
● PCs
● tennis racquets
● razors.

Marketers design their **marketing mixes** in order to make consumers aware of their products (i.e. to get them in the consumer's **awareness set**) and to provide consumers with the information they need to make a decision. A product cannot be in the consumer's **awareness set** if the consumer does not know it exists. Marketers need to be aware of the various information sources that consumers within their target market use, and their relative importance to the consumer. From this, marketers are in a position to target their own resources more effectively.

EVALUATION OF ALTERNATIVES

Once a consumer has built up their **awareness set**, the next stage in the process is to assess the products within it in order to see which would best solve the problem, i.e. to evaluate the alternative options. Consumers do this in a number of ways. Because the consumer is attempting to satisfy a need, they will be examining the benefits that can be derived from the product's features (product attributes). For example, a drink

e-disinformation: Kentucky Fried Monster

The Internet has changed the way many of us decide what to buy and when and where to buy it. Users can browse the web looking for information, and can also share the information they have with others. Potential customers are able to access not only the official company websites, but also impartial consumer watchdog websites (such as www.which.co.uk), Internet chat rooms, blogs, discussion boards and personal webpages where information and opinions are available from people who have bought, or at least have opinions about, products and the organisations which supply them. Potential buyers are no longer reliant upon company-controlled sources.

However, the Internet has no official, central controlling body. Anyone can set up a website and post almost anything on to it. While reputable host organisations have rules governing the content within their own sites, no one checks up on all the myriad blogs, boards and emails that have blossomed across the Net. People can say pretty much anything about anyone with little risk of being taken to task about it. This has caused problems for some organisations who have been the subject of hoaxes. These untrue stories may be malicious, but they are usually just mischievous.

One such hoax is the famous chicken-less KFC story which was widely circulated by email. It appeared in a number of variants, one of which is reproduced below. Please do note that the University of New Hampshire denies that any such study ever took place.

> Many people, day in and day out, eat at KFC religiously. Do they really know what they are eating? During a recent study of KFC done at the University of New Hampshire, they found some very upsetting facts.
>
> First of all, has anybody noticed that just recently, the company has changed their name? Kentucky Fried Chicken has become KFC. Does anybody know why? We thought the real reason was because of the 'FRIED' food issue. It's not. The reason why they call it KFC is because they can not use the word chicken anymore. Why? KFC does not use real chickens. They actually use genetically manipulated organisms. These so called 'chickens' are kept alive by tubes inserted into their bodies to pump blood and nutrients throughout their structure. They have no beaks, no feathers, and no feet. Their bone structure is dramatically shrunk to get more meat out of them. This is great for KFC because they do not have to pay so much for their production costs. There is no more plucking of the feathers or the removal of the beaks and feet.
>
> The government has told them to change all of their menus so they do not say chicken anywhere. If you look closely you will notice this. Listen to their commercials, I guarantee you will not see or hear the word chicken. I find this matter to be very disturbing. I hope people will start to realise this and let other people know.
>
> Please forward this message to as many people as you can. Together we [can] make KFC start using real chicken again. (University of New Hampshire, n.d.)

Such hoaxes can cause severe damage to a business and it is hard to get the refutation published as widely as the original story.

For more information on how to spot a hoax, and to see further examples, visit hoaxbusters.org/.

---

with a high sugar content has the benefit of providing quick energy and tasting good. The downside is, of course, potentially rotten teeth and excess weight. Different consumers will attach different degrees of importance to different attributes, e.g. a person's view of the high sugar content may depend upon their propensity to put on weight. Salient attributes are those attributes a consumer considers are important and associates with a product when they think of it.

ACTIVITY

List the attributes you consider important when you are deciding which film to see at the cinema. Get a friend to do the same. Would you be choosing the same film?

The way consumers evaluate the products in their **awareness set** depends upon the individual consumer and the specific buying situation. The consumer narrows down the number of products in the **awareness set** by assessing the products' salient features (i.e. their distinguishing features) against their choice criteria (i.e. the things the product must have if it is to solve their problem). The consumer's shortlist of remaining products is known as their **evoked set** and they will make a final choice from this shortlist. A number of formal and informal criteria may be used in the final choice. These may include price, reliability and service, as well as more subjective criteria, such as status and image (see Exhibit 3.4).

Having evaluated the alternatives, the buyer should be ready to decide what to buy – if anything at all.

Exhibit 3.4 Criteria for evaluating alternatives

Criteria	Includes
Performance related	Reliability Quality Longevity Specification Style Comfort Taste
Financial	Actual price Price of extras Value for money Credit terms Running costs Depreciation
Social	Status Reputation Perceived image Social acceptability
Personal	Self-image Level of risk Ethics Emotional appeal

PURCHASE DECISION

Consumers next rank the products in their **evoked sets** in order of preference (according to their choice criteria). They are then ready to make a **purchase decision**, i.e. they select their preferred product or brand. The surroundings in which the purchase decision are made may vary, for example, buyers may be in a shop, on the Internet

purchase decision
the selection of the preferred product to buy

or on the telephone. There are, however, a number of influences that may affect consumers' purchase decisions wherever they are (see Exhibit 3.5):

● The attitude of friends, family, partners etc. may influence the purchase intention: consider a situation where a young teenager goes shopping for new clothes with his or her parents. They may consider price and reliability to be more important criteria than the teenager's status or self-image.
● When a consumer is about to make the purchase, unexpected situational factors may intervene, e.g. a particular product size or colour may be sold out and so the consumer is forced to make a re-evaluation.

Exhibit 3.5   From evaluation of alternatives to purchase decision

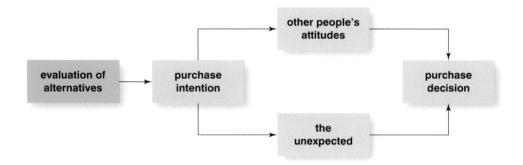

POST-PURCHASE EVALUATION

The post-purchase stage of the decision process is particularly important to marketers as it determines whether or not the consumer will purchase the product again and how they will influence other people in terms of purchasing the product. Smith and Taylor (2004) suggest that consumers tell up to 11 people of a bad experience but only three or four of a good one. This **word of mouth** is extremely important to organisations, which try and harness its positive power as effective **advertising**. Unfortunately, it is even more difficult to counteract bad **word of mouth** than it is to encourage the good. (See Chapter 8 for more on word of mouth.)

Consumers evaluate the product they purchase in terms of what was promised (e.g. in the adverts or by sales assistants in shops) before they purchased it, and how it actually performed after they purchased it. There are three common outcomes of this:

● disappointment – the consumer is unlikely to repurchase the product
● satisfaction
● delight – the consumer is likely to repurchase the product, will talk favourably to others about the product, and will pay less attention to competing brands when watching adverts (and will not feel the need to try them).

Sometimes, when a consumer has invested a lot of time, effort and money into the purchase decision, or when there are many similar alternatives available, they may experience feelings of doubt about whether they have made the right decision. You can probably think of examples where you have purchased a product and your friends have questioned your decision: 'How much did you pay for that? I could have got you it for half the price.'

This is called **post-purchase dissonance** (Festinger, 1957) and means that the consumer may be psychologically uncomfortable with their purchase. Consumers attempt to reduce this feeling of doubt in a number of ways:

- ignoring information that undermines their choice
- paying more attention to information that supports their choice.

post-purchase dissonance
when a consumer is psychologically uncomfortable about their purchase

So a marketer's job does not end when a customer makes a purchase. They need to reinforce that purchase decision in order to reduce any cognitive (or post-purchase) dissonance and to stimulate positive **word of mouth** and encourage repeat purchases. Marketers can minimise cognitive dissonance in a number of ways. First, they must set expectations correctly prior to purchase, then they must provide reassurance afterwards. Some of the ways they do this are by:

- ensuring salespeople and other means of promotion (e.g. **advertising**) do not exaggerate the product features (over-promise)
- allowing consumers to sample or test the goods prior to purchase so that they know what to expect from the product
- helping customers in the early stages of product use, e.g. with installation, training, etc.
- providing reassurance through advertising, good **public relations** and community building (e.g. owners clubs)
- offering excellent after-sales support, advice lines, etc.

Clearly, the appropriateness of these techniques depends upon the category of product. Firms are unlikely to offer much in the way of after-sales service for small items like chocolate bars – nor do consumers need it. This sort of service is traditionally offered for larger items, with higher **levels of involvement** (see below), such as computers, DVD recorders, cars.

EXPAND YOUR KNOWLEDGE

Schewe, C.D. (1973) 'Selected social psychological models for analyzing buyers', *Journal of Marketing*, 37 (Jul): 31–39.

Charles Schewe briefly and concisely overviews selected bases that influence buyer behaviour. Four models are outlined: McClelland's achievement motivation; Goffman's role theory; Festinger's cognitive dissonance; and Riesman's inner versus other-directed individual.

Types of consumer buying decision

So far, the buyer decision model suggests that consumers unvaryingly pass through all these purchase decision stages for everything that they purchase, but this is clearly not the case. Sometimes some stages are missed out or they may be worked through in a different order. A major factor affecting the flow and the formality of the decision-making process is the situation in which the purchase is being made. There are three main types of buying situation (see Exhibit 3.6).

Routine problem solving is where a consumer buys a product on a regular basis and there is no lengthy decision-making process. Packets of crisps and bars of chocolate

Exhibit 3.6   Types of buying situation

are routine purchases. There is very little financial (or any other) risk associated with the purchase of these products and so the consumer does not usually think too much about them.

With *limited problem solving*, the product is purchased less frequently and is likely to be more expensive and expected to last longer. Typical examples of limited problem solving products are electrical products such as TVs. These types of product usually involve more deliberate decision-making.

Infrequently purchased expensive items, such as houses and cars, call for *extended problem solving*. It is important to the consumer to make the right choice and so there is a high level of information search and evaluation of alternatives.

Levels of involvement

The consumer's **level of involvement** in a purchase decision has a direct bearing on how they make that decision and how much time they spend on it. People get more involved in (i.e. think harder about and spend more time on) significant purchases. When the purchase is a high-involvement one, consumers are more likely to follow a lengthier, more complex decision-making process. However, when the purchase is of a low involvement, or is of no or limited interest, consumers will often use short-cuts, or choice tactics, to reduce the time and effort they expend in their decision-making process (see Exhibit 3.7).

Research suggests there are four factors that affect a consumer's level of involvement with a product (see Exhibit 3.8):

1 *Self-image*: where the consumer thinks that a product will affect their self-image (e.g. cars and clothes), then involvement levels are likely to be higher.
2 *Perceived risk*: where the consumer thinks there are risks in making a wrong choice (usually financial risks because the product is expensive, but it may be physical risk if the product is potentially dangerous or a number of other risks), then involvement levels are likely to be higher.
3 *Social factors*: where the consumer thinks that a purchase may affect their social acceptability to others (e.g. being seen in the right (or wrong) nightclub), then involvement levels are likely to be higher.
4 *Hedonism*: where the consumer thinks that the purchase may be capable of delivering a high degree of pleasure (e.g. a holiday), then involvement levels are likely to be higher.

Exhibit 3.7   Purchase decisions and levels of involvement

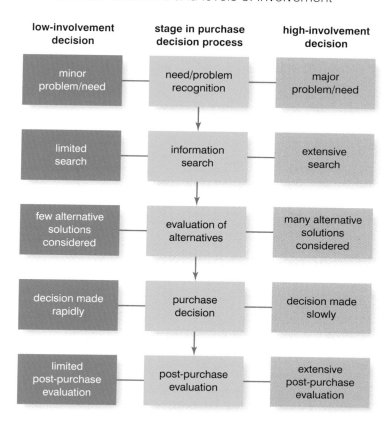

Exhibit 3.8   Factors affecting level of involvement

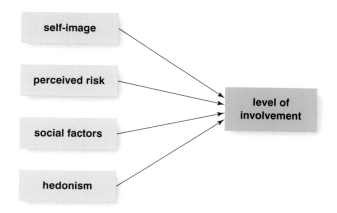

SOURCE: Laurent and Kapferer, 1985

EXPAND YOUR KNOWLEDGE

Zaichkowsky, J.L. (1985) 'Measuring the involvement construct', *Journal of Consumer Research*, 12 (3): 341–352.

The levels of involvement in the product being purchased has been recognised as a distinguishing feature of purchase behaviour. This article explores the measurement of involvement.

The buying situation, **level of involvement** and perceived differences between products will all affect the buyer's behaviour. Four major types of buyer behaviour can be seen in Exhibit 3.9.

Exhibit 3.9   Four types of buyer behaviour

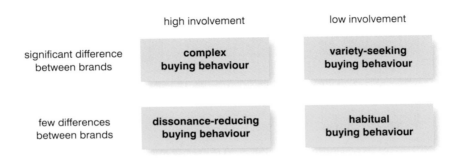

1 *Complex buying behaviour*: consumers will move through the complex decision-making process by collecting knowledge and learning (covered later in the chapter) about the product category. From this, they develop beliefs, and then attitudes, about the product type before making a decision to purchase.
2 *Dissonance-reducing buying behaviour*: because the consumer thinks there is little difference between brands, consumers will collect information about a product category by shopping around to reduce **post-purchase dissonance**, but are likely to make a decision to purchase relatively quickly.
3 *Variety-seeking buying behaviour*: marketers attempt to encourage variety seeking in terms of attempting to get the consumer to switch to their product through lower prices and **sales promotion** (e.g. free samples through your letterbox).
4 *Habitual buying behaviour*: market leaders will try to stimulate consistent repeat purchases by dominating shelf space in supermarkets and avoiding substitution (i.e. consumers buying alternatives) because of stockouts (e.g. salt, pepper, sugar).

Marketers need to be aware of the **level of involvement** that consumers generally have in relation to their products. With high-involvement products, marketers need to understand how consumers gather and evaluate information. Consumers will be actively searching for lots of information and marketers need to provide it in a format that these consumers can study at their own pace (e.g. newspapers, magazine adverts).

When selecting low-involvement products, consumers are often passive in their information search. They do not actively search for information in these types of situations so marketers attempt to create, and increase, awareness of their product and to reinforce its positive attributes. Television is often used to advertise low-involvement products because of the opportunity this provides for repetition and reinforcement, and because of the large amount of people who, potentially, will see the advert (think about how many people watch, say, *Coronation Street*).

ACTIVITY

Think of three items from each of the following categories that you have purchased, or used, recently:

- a food or snack item that you purchase regularly
- an expensive item such as a TV or CD player
- an emergency or distress purchase.

For each of these, make notes on the following:

- How did the need arise?
- How long did it take to make a decision?
- How many alternatives did you consider?
- How did you choose between them?
- Was it the sort of purchase or consumption your friends would make?
- Would you say the purchase was a high- or low-involvement product? Why?

Influences on consumer buyer behaviour

Having looked at the consumer buyer decision process, and the different types of consumer buying decision, the next section of this chapter will look at the internal and external factors that may influence these.

INTERNAL INFLUENCES

Marketers recognise that, although there are discernible segments, or groups, of customers with common features (see Chapter 4), these groups are nonetheless made up of individuals with their own, unique characteristics. The next section of this chapter looks at what these characteristics are and how they affect individuals' buying behaviour.

Personality

The term **personality** describes a person's distinguishing psychological characteristics, which lead them to respond to situations in particular ways. **Personality** consists of all the features, behaviours and experience that make individuals unique and distinctive. It is often described in terms of personality traits, such as dominant, sociable, introvert or extrovert.

Marketers attempt to identify and define the personality traits of **market segments** through lifestyle or psychographic segmentation. For example, personality is often related to self-image or the concept of self. One of the fundamentals of self-image is that a person's possessions (e.g. clothes, books, CDs) reflect their identity. For example, new acquaintances commonly check out each other's CD collections or books in order to form an opinion of that individual.

Perception

Two people seeing the same advertisement may react to it differently because they perceive the situation differently. Even the same individual may perceive the same advertisement differently at different times. Imagine how you would react to an advert for a snack when you are hungry and compare that to when you have just eaten.

perception
the process by which people select, organise and interpret sensory stimulation (sounds, visions, smell, touch) into a meaningful picture of the world

Perception, therefore, is the process by which people select, organise and interpret sensory stimulation (sounds, visions, smell, touch) into a meaningful picture of the world. There are three main processes that lead to the formation of individual perceptions.

Selective attention is the process by which stimuli are assessed and non-meaningful stimuli, or those that are inconsistent with our beliefs or experiences, are screened out. This has major implications from a marketing perspective. For example, it is estimated that the average person is exposed to 1,500 advertisements per day. Only 5–25 per cent of these advertisements catch the attention of the individual, the rest are screened out. Marketers use various techniques (such as colours, contrasting backgrounds and foregrounds, centre of vision) to ensure their advertisements are given attention.

These people almost certainly share certain personality traits and belong to a particular reference group

Selective distortion occurs when consumers distort or change the information they receive to suit their beliefs and attitudes. Information framing refers to the ways in which information is presented to people to ensure **selective distortion** does, or does not, happen. For example, in most of Europe we associate blue with cool and red with hot. Packaging takes advantage of our selective distortion in its use of these colours (e.g. in the packaging for different flavours of tortilla chips). A famous cat food advert stated that 8 out of 10 cat owners preferred a particular brand. The impact of this is greater than the statement that 2 out of 10 cat owners did not prefer it.

Selective retention refers to the way consumers retain only a small number of messages in their memory. Consumers tend to remember messages that support their existing beliefs and attitudes.

Thus **perception** and memory are closely associated with learning.

Learning

learning
changes in an individual's behaviour arising from their experiences

stimulus
something that provokes a reaction, activity, interest or enthusiasm

response
a reaction to a stimulus

Learning describes changes in an individual's behaviour that arise from their experiences. Marketers are keen for consumers to learn from promotion so that they know which product to buy and why. Learning can take place in a number of ways (see Exhibit 3.10).

CLASSICAL CONDITIONING

Classical conditioning is the process of using an established relationship between a **stimulus** and a **response** to evoke or teach the same response to a different stimulus. The most famous example is that of Pavlov's dogs. At the dogs' mealtimes, Pavlov

Exhibit 3.10 Types of learning

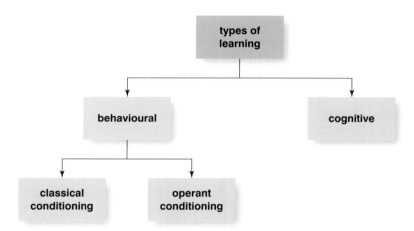

(a renowned nineteenth-century psychologist) rang a bell. The dogs learnt to associate the bell (the stimulus) with food and their response was to salivate. After a
while, they always salivated on hearing the bell – even if no food was forthcoming.
At a more sophisticated level, marketers often use humour in advertising as humour
evokes pleasure and the advertisers are hoping this will be associated with their products. An example of this would be the 'Lynx Effect'. See Exhibit 3.11.

Exhibit 3.11 The classical conditioning approach to influencing product
attitudes

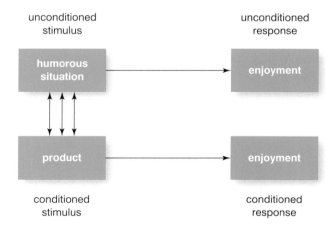

SOURCE: Engel et al.,
2006

OPERANT OR INSTRUMENTAL CONDITIONING

Operant conditioning also requires a link between a stimulus and a response.
However, with operant conditioning, the stimulus that results in the highest reward
is the stimulus that is learnt. There are ways to increase the likelihood of a specific
response (positive reinforcement).

  While classical conditioning is useful in explaining how consumers may learn simple kinds of behaviour, operant conditioning is much more useful in determining
more complex, goal-desired behaviour.

**operant conditioning
(instrumental
conditioning)**
the learner's response
produces a reinforcing
stimulus

For example, the *Financial Times* (*FT*) sells its paper to students for 20p instead of 85p. The reduced-rate *FTs* are distributed on campus and, because it is at a reduced rate, students purchase it (desired response) and because it has desirable properties (i.e. may help with their studies) it is thought useful (positive reinforcement) and the likelihood of it being purchased again increases (Exhibit 3.12) even without the initial stimulus of the discount. Likewise, negative reinforcement and punishment may also be used.

Exhibit 3.12   Operant conditioning over time

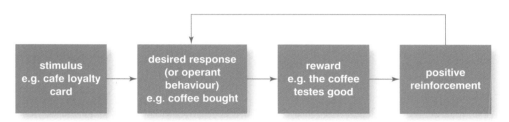

cognitive learning
active learning using complex mental processing of information

Cognitive learning involves the complex mental processing of information rather than emphasising the importance of external reward and repetition. It may include rote learning, where two concepts are associated with each other without conditioning, or vicarious learning, which involves learning from others without direct experiences or reward.

Motivation and values

Motivation involves a complex relationship between needs, drives and goals. A motive is a need that is sufficiently pressing that the person is driven to seek satisfaction of that need. According to Maslow, these needs can be placed in a hierarchy in terms of their relative importance (see Exhibit 3.13).

Exhibit 3.13   Maslow's hierarchy of needs

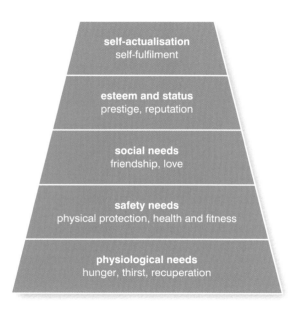

SOURCE: Maslow, 1943

An individual will try to satisfy the most important needs of survival first (the bottom row). When these needs are met, they will stop being motivators and the individual will then try to satisfy the next most important need, i.e. the one at the next level up in the hierarchy. For example, an individual who is starving will have no interest in anything else until their hunger is satisfied. Someone in danger of dying of thirst will drink from a dirty pool – and only later worry about whether that was a safe thing to do. Once a person has satisfied their basic physical and safety needs, then, and only then, will they look for the company of others. Human beings are social animals and so socialising with others is important – but not as important as staying alive. Not satisfied with having friends, a decent social life, romance, people next look for esteem, for the approval and even admiration of others. Typically we do this through our work, or our wealth, but certain products also fulfil this need. Sports cars are not bought just because their drivers want to break speed limits; they are objects of desire and provoke envy in others. They enhance the status of the driver. The final level, self-actualisation, is the hardest to reach. It involves the fulfilment of dreams and ambitions. This is a general model of motivation. It was not created with marketing in mind and Maslow did not envisage its use as a marketing tool. However, many modern ads have dream fulfilment at their heart, positioning their product as the answer to prayers – and not always with tongue in cheek. Many car (and holiday) ads appear to fall into this category. For example, the 'Volvo C70 feel' campaign where the car takes them above the clouds (this advert, and many others, can be viewed at www.visit4info.com).

ACTIVITY

Work through Maslow's hierarchy of needs one level at a time (see Exhibit 3.13) and associate products with each level. For example, bread is clearly aimed at the bottom level, 'physiological needs', as it is designed to satisfy hunger, but what about a restaurant meal?

It is clearly important that marketers should understand the motives that drive consumers to purchase products. Those motives determine how consumers choose products and such knowledge enables marketers to design product offerings that have the best chance of being chosen. Consumer motives can also be used to group potential customers together and so to segment markets (see Chapter 4). For example, consider the purchase of a mobile phone. While some people's primary motive may be to be contactable in an emergency, others may consider it an important tool for socialising or a status symbol. The phone's advertising would need to take this into account.

Attitudes and beliefs

Attitudes and **beliefs** are acquired through the experience of doing things and the resultant learning process. A belief is a thought that a person holds about something, usually based on knowledge, opinion or faith. Beliefs are important to marketers because beliefs about certain products or brands may affect a consumer's choice criteria.

An attitude describes a person's consistently favourable or unfavourable evaluation, feelings and tendencies towards an object or idea. From a marketing perspective, this attitude may be directed at a product or brand (i.e. the object) and thus will be reflected in their behaviour (i.e. whether they purchase the product or not). Attitudes can be discovered by asking the person how they feel about the brand.

attitude
describes a person's consistently favourable or unfavourable evaluation, feelings and tendencies towards an object or idea

belief
how or what a person thinks about something, usually based on knowledge, opinion or faith

Williams (1981) suggests that attitude comprises three components: cognitive, affective and conative. The cognitive attitude relates to beliefs about a product; the affective attitude relates to positive and negative feelings associated with the product; the conative attitude relates to the link with behaviour (thus attitude X is likely to lead to behaviour Y). It is this link between attitude and behaviour that is of prime interest to the marketer.

EXTERNAL INFLUENCES

The previous section looked at how the consumer buyer decision process might be influenced by internal factors, there are also many external influences on this process.

Culture

culture
the set of basic values, perceptions, wants and behaviour learnt by a member of society from family and other institutions

Culture manifests itself through art, language, literature, music and religion. As children grow up, society provides them with a framework within which they are able to develop acceptable beliefs, value systems and cultural norms (see Exhibit 3.14).

Within any culture, there will be subcultures. A subculture is a group of people with shared value systems based on common life experiences and situations. These shared value systems may be based on ethnic origin, geographic areas and religion. Subcultures often form very important market segments. For example, MTV has a global format that appeals to youth culture, whether the station is watched in the UK, Hong Kong, India or the USA.

Exhibit 3.14   Elements of culture

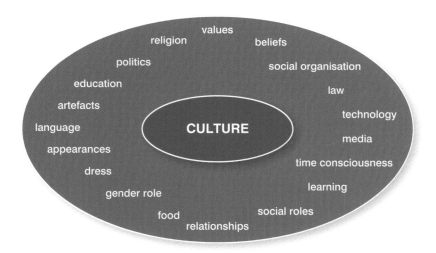

Reference groups

Reference groups are the groups that an individual belongs to or aspires to. These may be formal or informal groupings, and may influence the consumer's attitudes and behaviour. Examples of reference groups include sporting clubs, work colleagues and professional bodies.

There are three main types of reference group that may affect a consumer's attitude and purchasing behaviour:

1 Membership groups are groups that an individual already belongs to and therefore have a direct influence on their behaviour.
2 Aspirant (aspirational) groups are those groups to which an individual would like to belong; they identify with them but there is no face-to-face contact – an amateur footballer may aspire to be a professional footballer, a young female may aspire to be a professional singer (reflected in the popularity of programmes such as *Pop Idol* and *Fame Academy*).
3 Disassociative groups are groups to which the individual does not want to belong or be seen to belong. For example, an upmarket shopper may not wish to be part of a discount club.

Talent show contestants form an aspirant group for many

Reference groups may influence consumers in at least three ways:

1 They expose the consumer to new behaviours and lifestyles.
2 They may influence the consumer's self-concept (e.g. they want to be accepted and fit in with a particular group).
3 They may create pressures to conform that may impact on product or brand choice.

CRM focus   Harley riders

A Harley-Davidson is perhaps the most distinctive motorcycle in the world – and it inspires extreme devotion. If you own a Harley, you are a member of an elite club and this is a feeling the company recognises and fosters.

Visit its website (www.harley-davidson.com or www.harley-davidson.co.uk) or one of its other international sites, and see how it builds that community feeling. The first page is the 'Harley-Davidson experience', which includes welcoming information and tips for new riders. There are sections where you can post your own photos – even build up an online photo album of you, your friends and, of course, your bikes. You can join HOG (the Harley Owners Group) and so get access to special information and invitations to join in at special events.

Harley owners, and would-be owners, are a privileged, membership, group.

How important a reference group is to a consumer will vary depending on the nature of the product. It tends to be most important for conspicuous purchases. A product is conspicuous if:

- it is exclusive and therefore noticeable; many designer brands will fall into this product category (e.g. Rolex, Lacoste)
- it is consumed in the public domain and other consumers may see it, e.g. drinking a particular brand of bottled beer in a nightclub.

Exhibit 3.15 shows how group influence may affect brand choice for four types of product.

Exhibit 3.15　Group influence on brand choices

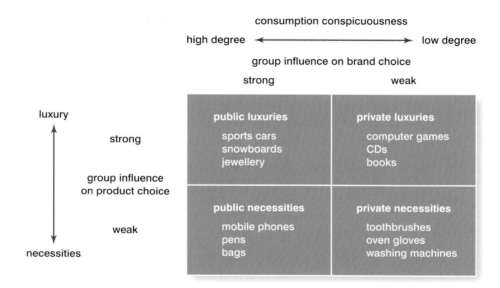

SOURCE: Bearden and Etzel, 1982

Family

The influence of family members – whether the family is nuclear or extended, single-parent or two-parent – may strongly influence a buyer's behaviour over their whole lifetime, i.e. not just during the time they live in the family home. Family influence can generally be divided into one of two categories: family orientation influence and family procreation influence.

Family orientation influence is the influence parents exert over their children, even when there is no longer any interaction. This may be at a general level in terms of values and attitudes towards product types (e.g. whether you view a car as a status symbol or as a functional product to get you from A to B), or at a more specific level (e.g. continuing to purchase the same brand of coffee as your parents did).

Family procreation influence consists of the more direct influences on daily buying behaviour that family members exert upon one another. This is continually changing with changing social conditions and working patterns. For example, the increase in the number of working mothers has meant the evolution of latchkey kids – i.e. children who arrive home from school before their parents arrive home from work and who prepare a snack or tea for themselves. Such consumers have particular requirements for food products, e.g. ease of preparation.

Pester power

The pre-school market is estimated to be worth around £4.3 billion a year and, if you add those areas where children influence their parents' purchases the most (areas such as clothing, food, leisure activities, holidays, etc.) that estimate rises to up to £30 billion a year. The Advertising Code of Practice has been tightened in an attempt to prevent advertisers from directly encouraging children to ask for things. However, think about the number of collectable toys, usually based on cartoon films, that are offered by fast-food restaurants, or tins of spaghetti in the shape of children's favourite characters, such as the Tweenies or Postman Pat. The Market Research Panel suggests that the five biggest causes of pester power are:

1 TV advertising
2 Free promotional gifts
3 Attractive packaging
4 Licensed characters (e.g. Postman Pat)
5 In-store samples.

Consumer buying roles

Within groups such as families, or even student households, there is a combination of individuals and roles that make up the **decision-making unit** (DMU) (see Exhibit 3.16). A consumer may fulfil one or more roles in making a purchase decision and their role may vary depending upon what is being purchased. For example, parents may pay for the children's clothes but leave it to them to decide what to buy. Whereas the children may pay for their own sweets but within rules set by their parents.

decision-making unit (DMU)
all the individuals who participate in and influence the customer's purchase decision

Exhibit 3.16   The decision-making unit

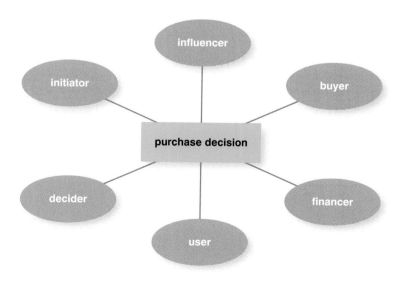

The DMU may be defined as all the individuals who participate in and influence a consumer's purchase decision. The individual roles (although an individual may have one or more roles) may be identified as follows.

The *initiator* is the person who initially suggests, or thinks of, the idea of buying a particular product. It may be a friend, parent or work colleague. For example, a child may suggest a trip to Disneyland, Paris.

The *influencer* is the person who influences the buyer by offering advice or an opinion. Again, it may be a friend or relative or it may be a salesperson. For example, Dad's feelings about France may influence the trip.

The *decider* is the person who actually makes the decision whether to buy the product. Mum's vacation time may be limited by her schedule as a lawyer so she decides when, and where, the family goes.

The *financer* is the person who provides the money for the purchase. For example, perhaps the grandparents are paying for everyone to go.

The *user* is the person who actually uses or consumes the product. For example, the whole family would consume the Disneyland, Paris experience.

The *buyer* is the person who actually makes the purchase. For example, Dad may telephone the reservations office at Disneyland, Paris.

ACTIVITY

Using the example of a Friday night out, who carries out the roles of initiator, influencer, decider, buyer and user?

EXPAND YOUR KNOWLEDGE

Kotler, P. (1965) 'Behavioural models for analyzing buyers', *Journal of Marketing,* 29 (4): 37–45.

Kotler offers five approaches/models to analysing and understanding buyer behaviour from Marshellian economics to Veblen social constructs (Veblen originated the term 'conspicuous consumption' so beloved of marketers) and organisational buying behaviour.

Sheth, J.N. (1967) 'A review of buyer behaviour', *Management Science,* 13: 718–756.

In this survey article, the author reviews all the important approaches to understanding buying behaviour and provides a bibliography.

The consumer buyer decision process for new products

Having already examined the stages buyers go through when purchasing products generally, and who and what may influence them, this section will explore how consumers approach the purchase of *new* products.

A new product may be defined as a good, service or idea that is *perceived* by potential customers as being new (see also Chapter 6). Consumers go through a mental process (see Exhibit 3.17) in deciding whether to adopt, or use, a new product.

- *Awareness*: the consumer becomes aware of the product but does not have any information about it.
- *Interest*: the consumer actively seeks information about the new product if they think it may be of use to them.
- *Evaluation*: the consumer decides whether or not they should try the new product.
- *Trial*: the consumer tries the new product on a small scale to judge its value.
- *Adoption*: the consumer decides to make full and regular use of the new product.

Marketers need to plan how they can aid potential consumers to move through the various steps by, for example, providing information or having a trial or testing plan.

Exhibit 3.17   The stages of buyer readiness

SOURCE: Strong, 2007

INDIVIDUAL DIFFERENCES AND NEW PRODUCTS

Individuals differ in their willingness to try new products. How willing individuals are to try new products also varies according to the nature of the new product. For example, while some people may be willing to try new food, they may not be so willing to adopt broadband or book a space shuttle flight. This has led marketers to classify consumers into a number of product adoption categories according to a product adopters model (see Exhibit 3.18), as follows:

- *Innovators* (2.5 per cent) are consumption pioneers who are prepared to try new ideas.
- *Early adopters* (13.5 per cent) are often opinion leaders within their reference groups. Opinion leaders are those individuals who have special skills, knowledge, personality or other characteristics, and exert influence on others (e.g. DJs).

- The *early majority* (34 per cent) are quite adventurous in their decision-making and, as a result, adopt new ideas before the average person.
- The *late majority* (34 per cent) are more sceptical. They adopt new products only after most have tried them.
- *Laggards* (16 per cent) are conservative and suspicious of change. They adopt a new product only when it has become something of a tradition in itself.

Exhibit 3.18   The product adoption categories

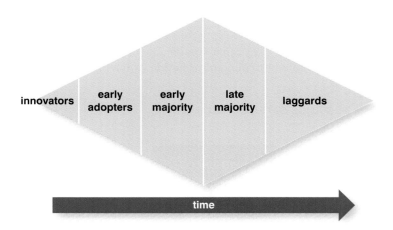

SOURCE: Rogers, 1995

Marketers need to research and identify the characteristics of the various groups and tailor their marketing mix and, in particular, the message accordingly.

The models looked at so far relate to consumer purchases. The next section will look at the way organisations purchase products.

EXPAND YOUR KNOWLEDGE

Rogers, E.M. (1976) 'New product adoption and diffusion', *Journal of Consumer Behaviour,* 2: 290–301.

Rogers is the recognised proponent of this important marketing concept and model that is sometimes referred to as *innovation diffusion* and which has widespread application in marketing practice.

Types of organisation and the products they purchase

The business to business (B2B) market is far larger than the business to consumer (B2C) market. Consider the purchase of a car: the B2C transaction is only the final stage of a number of B2B purchases that make up the supply chain involved in producing and distributing the product (see Chapter 9 for examples).

Although there are many similarities between the B2C and B2B markets, there are also a number of key differences. This section of the chapter looks at organisational customers and how their buying decisions are made, who may be involved and what criteria they may use.

Organisations purchase a diverse and complex range of goods and services. These include:

- utility services (such as water, electricity, gas)
- raw materials
- component parts
- capital items (such as buildings and machines)
- MRO goods (maintenance, repair and operations materials)
- professional services (such as legal and financial advice).

Characteristics of organisational markets

There are many similarities between business markets and consumer markets but there are also a number of key differences between these two types of market. They typically differ in terms of:

- market structure
- nature of demand
- complexity of the buying process.

MARKET STRUCTURE

Industrial concentration

In B2B markets, there are normally fewer buyers but they are far larger in terms of purchasing power. Compare the selling of computers to the consumer market with selling dedicated computer systems to car manufacturers. There are fewer customers and they are more easily identifiable.

Geographical concentration

Some industries have a strong geographical concentration. This may have arisen because of the availability of resources (e.g. steel manufacturing in Sheffield), because of political incentives (e.g. EU grants) or for historical reasons (e.g. financial services in London).

NATURE OF DEMAND

Derived demand

All business demand is derived demand, i.e. demand that ultimately comes from (or is derived from) the demand for the final product. The demand for steel panels is derived from the demand for cars, which ultimately comes from the end consumer.

Joint demand

Joint demand is demand that is linked with the demand for other organisational products. So, the demand for tyres is linked to the demand for cars.

Inelastic demand

Many organisations have price inelastic demand. Inelastic demand is where the total demand for a product is largely unaffected by price changes, especially in the short run. For example, the tyres on a jumbo jet's wheels are one small component of the overall cost of the finished product. A fall in the price of tyres will not affect the overall demand for jumbo jets. (See Chapter 10 for a fuller explanation of inelasticity of demand.)

Fluctuating demand

Demand for goods and services tends to fluctuate more rapidly in B2B markets.

COMPLEXITY OF THE BUYING PROCESS

The purchasing habits of organisations are rather different from those of individuals. Typically, businesses:

- buy in larger quantities
- negotiate harder on delivery terms
- expect reduced prices for bulk buying
- may require tailored products
- are harder to please
- have more people involved in making the decision to buy
- have longer, more complex decision-making processes.

Businesses buy in larger quantities just because they are buying goods and services for more people. An individual may buy one or two biros; a company would need several boxes just so that each employee can have one. If the goods they are buying are actually for use in their production process (e.g. Birds Eye buying rice as an ingredient for its ready meals) or for selling on (as shops do), then they will have to buy enough for all their customers.

If a consumer orders something, such as a new CD or a new computer add-on, then usually they want it to arrive quickly, just because they cannot wait to play it or plug it in. Businesses have a more pressing need to know that their orders will arrive on time. A company's whole production process may well depend on having sufficient rice to make its paella, or there may be just one time slot, say a national holiday, when it can install its new computer hardware without too much disruption. So businesses tend to insist on particular delivery times and, if their orders are large enough, suppliers will comply.

Organisations are well aware that they are more valuable customers than individual purchasers. Often they expect something in return. They may settle for superior customer service, or they may insist on a discount as an incentive to place a large order.

Some business customers will ask for their own version of a supplier's products. For example, Zanussi has made special washing machine models for UK high-street stores such as Dixons. There are a number of reasons why businesses may want this. In the case of Dixons, it would almost certainly be to confer a competitive advantage by offering a model that other stores do not have. Businesses may want cars in the company colours or pens with their name on. They may want the rice they buy to be of uniform quality so that they can be sure it will all cook through when they cook it in a large batch. It would not usually be worth the supplier's while to customise its products for an individual customer, but for a large organisation? Well, that's a different matter.

The business buying process therefore tends to be more formal and often involves professional purchasers who adopt sophisticated purchasing systems. Very often, organisations will have policies and guidelines (e.g. a purchasing policy) as to whether purchasing should be centralised or decentralised, and from a single supplier (single sourcing) or a number of suppliers (multiple sourcing). All these policies have advantages and disadvantages.

Organisational buying situations

There are three main types of organisational buying situation. These may be viewed on a continuum ranging from a straight rebuy, through modified rebuy, to new task at the other end of the scale (see Exhibit 3.19).

- Straight rebuy is where the buyer routinely reorders a product without any change to the order whatsoever to the extent that, in some cases, there may be an automatic (perhaps computerised) reordering system. These products are usually low risk, frequently purchased and inexpensive items (e.g. products such as electricity or gas).
- Modified rebuy is where the buyer wants to modify an element of the rebuy. This may be the product specification (such as colour, size or technical specification) or the price or the terms (such as delivery time) of the purchase.
- New task is where the buyer purchases a product for the first time. This is the most complex category of purchase. Examples of this may include infrequently purchased, high-risk, expensive products such as computer systems or the sourcing of a new raw material supplier.

Exhibit 3.19   Types of organisational buying situations

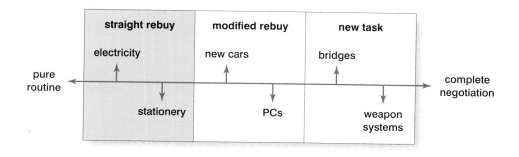

SOURCE: Adapted from Enis, 1980

The buying centre

Similarly to the consumer DMU (**decision-making unit**), the **buying centre** comprises all the individuals that participate in the business buying decision process. The buying centre will vary depending on the nature of the purchase.

Individuals within a buying centre still fulfil one or more of the roles as outlined in Exhibit 3.16 above, although their roles are often more formal, e.g. part of their jobs, and they may behave differently to typical consumers. The organisational DMU (or buying centre) also has an added role: gatekeeper.

buying centre
comprises all the individuals that participate in the business buying decision process

Initiators: people who first identify the need for the product and communicate it to the others, e.g. a dissatisfied canteen customer who complains that there are no healthy choices on the menu.

Users: members of the organisation who will actually use the purchase, e.g. administrators using computers.

Influencers: individuals whose opinions may contribute to the final choice of purchase. Their influence may be related to their expertise (e.g. an IT specialist) or it could be of a more informal and/or personal nature.

Buyers: the individuals who actually make the purchase, or select and approve suppliers, and negotiate the terms of the purchase.

Deciders: individuals (e.g. the boss) who have formal or informal powers to select or approve the final suppliers.

Financiers: the individual or department who holds the budget which will fund the purchase.

In business buying decisions there is also an additional role:

Gatekeepers: individuals who have some control over the flow of information into the organisation. These may include buyers, technical personnel (e.g. IT experts) or receptionists.

The organisational buying process

Individuals within the organisational buying process have their own personal agendas, motives and dynamics. It is important to remember that they are individuals and that each must be understood and treated as such. Organisations do not make decisions – people do. The organisational buying process is longer and more complex than the consumer one (see Exhibit 3.20).

Problem recognition

An individual, or group, within an organisation identifies a problem that may be solved by acquiring a specific good or service. This may be an entirely routine operation, such as reordering stationery, or a much more complex operation, such as purchasing a capital item (e.g. a fork lift truck).

For example, if an organisation is to launch a new product, then to do so it may need new manufacturing systems or new component parts for it. External factors that influence the choice of product and supplier may be trade press, exhibitions or sales representatives.

General need description

Having identified a need, the organisation describes the general characteristics and qualities of the required product in terms of what it is required to do, e.g. the manufacturing equipment must be capable of making six varieties of cake, all the same size but with different ingredients, and must be ready to start production within the year.

Product specification

The organisation has to select and specify the attributes that the product should have. This is very different from the situation in consumer markets, where much of

Exhibit 3.20   A model of the organisational buying process

problem recognition

↓

general need description

↓

product specification

↓

supplier search

↓

proposal solicitation

↓

supplier(s) selection
and commitment

↓

order routine specification

↓

performance review

the enjoyment of shopping is not knowing exactly what is required, but seeing what is available. The product specification will often incorporate aspects such as colour, material quality, performance levels and its compatibility with other components. This may require external assistance from, for example, consultants if the product is of a technical nature.

Supplier search

The buyer organisation then searches for the best vendor (selling organisation) to supply the product to the specification requested. This may be done using trade directories or brochures kept on file, exhibitions or, increasingly, the Internet.

Proposal solicitation

The next stage is for the organisation's specialist buyer to invite suitable prospective suppliers to submit proposals. These proposals may range from catalogues to formal presentations and substantial written proposals dependent upon the value and importance of the potential order.

Many business customers visit trade exhibitions to find new products or suppliers

Courtesy of ExCel London

Developing a relationship

In recent years, much emphasis has been placed on the importance of buyer–seller relationships and how these may be a source of competitive advantage. The emphasis is on long-term, collaborative relationships between a small number of suppliers and customers. Building trust between organisations is essential to maintaining such relationships.

Ford (1980) proposed the following model of relationship development:

Pre-relationship stage: this stage involves the buyer evaluating potential new suppliers.

Early stage: potential suppliers are in contact with buyers to negotiate trial deliveries.

Development stage: deliveries of the product increase as trust and understanding develops between the buyer and the seller.

Long-term stage: the buyer and seller are mutually dependent.

Final stage: the relationship has become institutionalised.

Decisions need to be made as to the level of relational development required, since it is clearly a waste of valuable resources to invest in unwanted or unprofitable relationships. Technical support, increased access to expertise, better service levels and risk reduction are some of the benefits to the two organisations that need to be considered.

Supplier(s) selection and commitment

The buying organisation then reviews the proposals from the prospective vendors and, based on prespecified criteria, selects one. The selection criteria usually revolve around attributes such as delivery times, product quality, prices, and possibly even honest corporate behaviour. Companies have, historically, used a number of suppliers as this enables them to obtain price concessions. However, increasingly, companies are working more closely with a smaller number of suppliers and, as a result, expecting preferential treatment (see the section on relationship marketing in Chapter 1).

Order routine specification

The buying organisation finalises the order in terms of product specification, quantities, delivery times, price, etc., and forwards it to the supplying organisation(s).

Performance review

The final stage is performance review. The buying organisation assesses the performance of the supplying organisation and its products, and decides whether to use them as a supplier in the future.

Organisational purchase criteria

Organisational purchase criteria are usually much more rational, functional and objective than consumer criteria. Criteria such as price, conformity to product specification, quality, reliability and customer service levels, and continuity of supply are likely to be used. However, organisations are composed of individuals who have their own personal goals and motives. Therefore, more intangible, or implicit, criteria may be important. Such criteria may include preferential treatment, which in turn may lead to useful professional relationships between individuals within, and between, organisations.

EXPAND YOUR KNOWLEDGE

Webster, F.E. and Wind, Y. (1972) 'A general model for understanding organizational buying behaviour', *Journal of Marketing*, 36 (Apr): 12–19.
Sheth, J.N. (1973) 'A model of industrial buyer behaviour', *Journal of Marketing*, 37 (Oct): 50–56.

Both of these articles focus on organisational buying behaviour in contrast to consumer market behaviour. The significant factors that influence the eventual buying decision are explored.

SUMMARY

Markets are made up of individual people and organisations. In consumer markets (B2C), these people vary enormously in terms of gender, age, income, education, personality, perceptions, attitudes, and many other factors. Marketers need to understand the processes that consumers go through when making purchase decisions: the stages they go through and the criteria they may use. These purchase decisions are influenced by internal factors, such as motivation, attitude and perception, as well as external factors such as family, friends and culture.

Organisational (B2B) buying is much larger and more complex than B2C buying. Organisations vary in terms of size, culture, purchasing policy and many other factors. Organisational buying tends to be much more objective and rational than consumer decision-making, to the extent that it may be over-bureaucratic. It is important for marketers to understand the processes that businesses go through and who is involved in purchase decisions.

Before developing a marketing strategy, all these factors must be understood and taken into account. Without this understanding, the marketing organisation is unlikely to exert as much influence as it might have during its customers' decision-making processes.

CHALLENGES REVIEWED

Now that you have finished reading the chapter, look back at the challenges you were set at the beginning. Do you have a clearer idea of what's involved?

Hints:

- roles within the decision-making unit (DMU)
- product adoption categories
- influences on consumer buying behaviour
- organisational decision-making unit (buying centre) and organisational buying process
- thinking about the roles the child and its parents play in the decision-making unit here, what reaction would you expect from the parents whose roles have been usurped? What is the likely impact on future business? Is the sales technique used ethical?

READING AROUND

Books

Nessim Hanna, Ricahrd Wozniak and Margaret Hanna (2009) *Consumer Behaviour: An Applied Approach*. Dubuque, IA: Kendall Hunt Publishing Company.
For more on B2B, see:
David Ford, Lars-Erik Gadde, Håkan Håkansson and Ivan Snehota (2006) *The Business Marketing Course: Managing in Complex Networks* (2nd edn). New York: John Wiley & Sons.
Allissa Quant (2003) *Branded: The Buying and Selling of Teenagers*. London: Arrow.

Journals

Journal of Consumer Research
Advances in Consumer Research

Journal articles

Russell Belk (1988) 'Possessions and the extended self', *Journal of Consumer Research*, 15 (2): 139–68.

Gordon Foxall (1984) 'Consumers' intentions and behaviour', *Journal of Market Research Society*, 26 (3): 231–41.

Abraham Maslow (1943) 'A theory of human motivation', *Psychological Review*, 50 (4): 370–96 – this is a classic!

Magazines

Ethical Consumer (Ethical Consumer Research Association)
Which? (The Consumer Association)

Websites

www.acrwebsite.org – the Association of Consumer Research, which has an interesting section for marketers.

www.mintel.co.uk – Mintel provides a range of market research reports, to which many libraries subscribe.

Video

The Money Programme (December 2005) 'Primark: King of No Frills Fashion'. London: BBC.

SELF-REVIEW QUESTIONS

1. What are the main stages of the consumer decision-making process? (see page 85)
2. List the three main types of buying situation and the types of product that might be included in each of them. (see page 92)
3. What are the four main types of consumer buyer behaviour? (see page 94)
4. What are the major internal influences on consumer buying behaviour? (see pages 95–100)
5. What are the main types of learning process? (see page 97)
6. Name the stages of Maslow's hierarchy of needs. (see page 98)
7. What is the difference between an attitude and a belief? (see page 99)
8. List the key roles in the decision-making unit. (see page 103)
9. What are the main stages of the product adoption process? (see page 106)
10. What are the main organisational buying situations? (see page 109)
11. What are the main characteristics of organisational markets? (see pages 107–8)
12. What are the main stages of the organisational buying process? (see page 111)

Getting there

Read the questions, then the case material, and then answer the questions.

Questions

1. Identify the decision-making units for the two decisions outlined in the case study: Duncan's Paris journeys and the couple's holiday plans. Explain and justify your answer.
2. What factors, internal and external, are likely to influence Duncan's decision about Paris? How?
3. Apply the decision-making framework to Annie and Duncan's holiday decision, picking relevant information out of the case and adding to it from your own knowledge (e.g. of information sources) if you can. What is likely to influence the outcome of each stage? How can marketing techniques assist them in their decision-making?

© Eurostar ID Brand Library

Boarding the Eurostar

Technological breakthroughs in transport have had an even more dramatic impact on the way we live our lives than those in communication. Mass air travel is perhaps the biggest contributor to the changes, opening up possibilities that were impractical, or at least extremely time consuming, in the past. Before the advent of commercial airlines, a trip from Europe to South Africa or Australia took months.

For some time, the emphasis in our hectic and stressed-out world, has been on getting from A to B as quickly as possible. Travellers have tended to favour the plane and the car as the speediest modes of transport. Cars were also preferred to public transport as they were considered more comfortable, more convenient and of higher status. Ex UK Prime Minister Margaret Thatcher famously remarked in a 1986 government debate that; 'A man who, beyond the age of 26, finds himself on a bus can count himself as a failure' yet today governments are encouraging the use of public transport rather than cars while environmental pressure groups advocate trains and boats rather than planes. Whether or not such green policies will prevail, will depend upon consumer attitudes and behaviour.

Many people are switching from plane to train in order to reduce their carbon dioxide emissions. Eurostar's Business Premier class which has a 10-minute check-in facility and a work-friendly environment on board, has become increasingly popular with busy executives. In 2009, Eurostar's daily ticket sales were approximately £1.85m and rising, the growth coming mainly from business travel.

Richard Brown, Chief Executive of Eurostar, commented: 'The growth in traveller numbers clearly indicates that concerns about the environmental impact of short-haul air travel, combined with the worsening experience of flying, are prompting more people to look for a greener and easier way of travelling to the Continent.'

Eurostar is leading the way in an image change for train travel generally. Its excellent punctuality record, with 95% of trains arriving on time in 2009 (before the Christmas crisis), has been a key factor in changing attitudes towards train travel generally.

The service has got even better since the new terminus at St Pancras opened. Journeys from St Pancras International are at least 20 minutes quicker than before. Passengers are whisked from London to Paris in just two hours 15 minutes and London to Brussels in only one hour 51 minutes. When compared to the time it takes just to get to the departure gate at a UK airport (upwards of two hours), the train looks even more attractive.

Duncan Scott travels from London to Paris on business at least once a week. He has always taken a taxi

(Continued)

(Continued)

to Heathrow airport (a journey of about 10 miles) and then flown from there. At Charles de Gaulle airport, he gets another taxi to his destination in Paris. However, his friends are starting to harass him about his carbon footprint – some seriously, some light-heartedly. His girlfriend, Annie, has done the research and found that he could walk to his local tube station, catch a tube to Kings Cross Railway Station, stroll through the smart shops and cafes of St Pancras International and from there take the Eurostar to Paris Nord in the heart of the French capital. Then he could take the Metro, though it would mean two changes and would take about three quarters of an hour, or he could take a taxi which would be quicker. Annie thinks he should take the Metro but Duncan dislikes being underground and is worried about getting lost.

He is also concerned that the train may actually cost more and that his firm will be reluctant to pay for it. The travel department, who book everything, are notoriously inflexible and cost conscious. However, he is playing golf with his boss and the Finance Director soon and has promised Annie that he will raise the issue. He hasn't dared tell her about the Finance Director's attitude to trains. According to him, train travel is for other people. He flies, drives his Bentley or is driven by someone else – usually someone wearing a peaked cap.

As well as trying to reorganise Duncan's travel arrangements, Annie is worried about Duncan who seems stressed and in need of a good holiday (they haven't had one for nearly a year). She can only take one week off work so they need to spend as little time travelling as possible so that they have enough time at their destination. Duncan thinks they should fly but is leaving the decision to Annie. She is worried about what her friends will say if she flies, given the fuss she has been making about Duncan flying to Paris. One of her friends, Irene, is a travel agent and she is trying to find suitable ferries and trains for them to get to their first-choice destination, Austria, where they had planned to hike. So far it is not looking hopeful. Irene has suggested they go to France or Holland instead. There is the possibility of hiring a barge in Holland, which really appeals to Duncan. Annie would prefer horse riding in the Camargue, although her mother is absolutely against it, claiming that it is far too dangerous. She suspects that they will end up cycling somewhere as a compromise and she is content with that – as long as they don't have to fly.

Travel decisions have been dominating Annie and Duncan's lives. Their flat is liberally scattered with brochures, the PC seems to be permanently linked to travel sites and they get at least two messages a day from travel agents. When Duncan gets home from a long day, made longer by a security alert at Heathrow, he finds Annie excitedly waving two tickets to Amsterdam (ferry and train). Her mother has decided to treat them to a Dutch canal trip.

SOURCE: Eurostar (2007)

REFERENCES

Bearden, O. and Etzel, M. (1982) 'Reference group influence on product and purchase decisions', *Journal of Consumer Research*, 9 (2): 183–94.

Engel, J., Blackwell, R. and Miniard, P. (2006) *Consumer Behaviour* (9th edn). Fort Worth, TX: The Dryden Press.

Enis, B.M. (1980) *Marketing Principles* (3rd edn). Santa Monica, CA: Goodyear.

Eurostar (2007) 'Press release: Eurostar revenues rise as travellers go for high speed rail'. Available at: **www.eurostar.com/UK/uk/leisure/about_eurostar/press_release/2007_07_18_greener.jsp** (accessed 23/07/2007).

Festinger, L. (1957) 'A theory of cognitive dissonance', in J. Sheth, B. Mittal and B. Newman (1999) *Customer Behavior: Consumer Behavior and Beyond*. Fortworth, TX: The Dryden Press.

Ford, D. (1980) 'The development of buyer–seller relationships in industrial markets', *European Journal of Marketing*, 14 (516): 339–54.

Howard, J.A. and Sheth, J.N. (1967) 'A theory of buyer behavior', in R. Moyer (ed.) *Changing Marketing Systems … Consumer, Corporate and Government Interfaces: Proceedings of the 1967 Winter Conference of the American Marketing Association*. Washington, DC: AMA.

Kotler, P. (1965) 'Behavioural models for analyzing buyers', *Journal of Marketing,* 29 (4): 37–45.

Laurent, G. and Kapferer, J. (1985) 'Measuring consumer involvement profiles', *Journal of Marketing Research*, 22 (Feb.): 41–53.

Maslow, A.H. (1943) 'A theory of human motivation', *Psychological Review*, 50 (4): 370–96.

Rogers, E.M. (1976) 'New product adoption and diffusion', *Journal of Consumer Behaviour,* 2: 290–301.

Rogers, E.M. (2003) *Diffusion of Innovations* (5th edn). New York: The Free Press.

Schewe, C.D. (1973) 'Selected social psychological models for analyzing buyers', *Journal of Marketing*, 37 (Jul): 31–39.

Sheth, J.N. (1967) 'A review of buyer behaviour', *Management Science*, 13: 718–756.

Sheth, J.N. (1973) 'A model of industrial buyer behaviour', *Journal of Marketing*, 37 (Oct): 50–56.

Smith, P.R. and Taylor, J. (2004) *Marketing Communications: An Integrated Approach* (4th edn). London: Kogan Page.

Strong, E.K. (2007) *The Psychology of Selling*. New York: McGraw-Hill.

University of New Hampshire (n.d.) 'Kentucky Fried Chicken Hoax'. Available at: **www.unh. edu/BoilerPlate/kfc.html** (accessed 22/07/2007).

Webster, F.E. and Wind, Y. (1972) 'A general model for understanding organizational buying behaviour', *Journal of Marketing*, 36 (Apr): 12–19.

Wilkie, W. (1990) *Consumer Behavior*. New York: John Wiley & Sons.

Williams, K.C. (1981) *Behavioural Aspects of Marketing*. London: Heinemann Professional Publishing.

Zaichkowsky, J.L. (1985) 'Measuring the involvement construct', *Journal of Consumer Research*, 12 (3): 341–352.

Market segmentation, targeting and positioning

CHAPTER CONTENTS

Introduction
Market attractiveness
Why segment and target markets?
Segmentation approaches
Target marketing
Positioning
The five-stage process from market
   segmentation to positioning
Summary
Challenges reviewed
Reading around
Self-review questions
Mini case study
References

MARKET SEGMENTATION CHALLENGES

The following are illustrations of the types of decisions that marketers have to take about market segmentation. *You aren't expected to know how to deal with the challenges now*; just bear them in mind as you read the chapter and see what you can find that helps.

- You are the marketing director of a loss-making brewery. You need to develop new products to revitalise the business but you do not have the resources to launch a full range. How will you choose what type of beer to sell and to whom?

- You have just joined the marketing department of a car company. Your managing director has asked your advice about the launch of a new product. The investment to date on product development has been large and high sales targets have been set. Should you try to appeal to as wide a market as possible, aiming to attract as broad a cross-section of customers as possible?

- You are a marketing manager for a firm of solicitors. Research has indicated that you are operating in a marketplace where people see little difference between rival solicitors' services. How could a deeper understanding of the customers help you to find profitable opportunities?

- You work in a travel agency. Recently published market research has revealed the existence of a variety of different types of customer who book package holidays. What criteria will you use to select one or more to concentrate your marketing efforts on?

Introduction

Marketers are interested in satisfying the wants and needs of customers and consumers but not everybody wants the same things. This poses a problem for marketers. If they try to market the same goods or services to everybody, they are unlikely to be successful except under some special circumstances. If they try to provide something unique for each individual, it would not be cost-effective unless, again, there are some special circumstances. There has to be a compromise, and fortunately, there is. Marketers can take advantage of the fact that some people share similar wants and needs. They can be grouped according to these similarities. Market segmentation is about breaking up a market into sections or segments so that marketing effort can be focused better towards particular segments. This is efficient and effective marketing.

The process of market segmentation requires accurate information on customers and potential customers and this is found through market research (see Chapter 5). It is also important to understand which buyer characteristics (see Chapter 3) are important in the purchase of the product in question. For example, it is quite common to split markets into male and female, but this is not likely to be the best way to do it if you are selling PC supplies.

In practice, there are different ways of segmenting a market and the particular approach taken will depend on the nature of the market and the way in which a company wishes to deal with it. The way a company segments a B2B market will be different from the way a company segments a consumer market.

This is not where the process ends, though. It is the starting point. Having identified the different segments in a market, decisions have to be made about which ones to target and how many to target. This is referred to as target marketing (or may be referred to as market targeting or simply targeting). These decisions lie at the very heart of marketing decision-making as they will affect the range of marketing activities undertaken. In choosing targets, marketers will need to consider competing brands and position their brands accordingly in order to reduce unnecessary direct competition. This is called brand, or competitive, positioning.

This chapter emphasises the need to determine which markets are attractive, and explores different approaches to the important process of segmentation, targeting and positioning.

Market attractiveness

market attractiveness
an assessment of how desirable a particular market or market segment is to an organisation

Choosing which markets to focus on, based on their **market attractiveness** to the organisation, is one of the most fundamental aspects of marketing. It involves a matching process based on an assessment of:

- market opportunity – to identify what is possible
- competitive advantage – to determine the degree of challenge
- the objectives of the organisation – to confirm what the organisation wishes to achieve.

These aspects will allow organisations to decide on their marketing strategies and tactics. How many opportunities are selected will depend on the thinking of top management and the objectives of the firm. Some will want to be innovators and will be keen to search out new opportunities; some will be followers and quickly imitate the leaders. Others will consider themselves to be low risk takers and will be slow to adopt change, even if this, ironically, may create risk because they are failing to move with the times.

To stand the best chance of achieving marketing success, a thorough understanding of the market is absolutely necessary. It is unusual for an organisation to attempt to capture an entire market. What is more likely is that one or more sections, or 'segments', of the market will be deemed to be attractive. For profit-making organisations, whose objectives will be based around financial gain, this will typically revolve around such issues as sales volume, sales value, profits and projected growth rates, and these will usually vary from segment to segment. For both profit-making and for not-for-profit organisations, segmenting and targeting their efforts will result in the more effective use of resources and will increase their chances of achieving successful outcomes.

WHAT ARE MARKETS?

Markets are people. Or, more accurately, a market is a composite of individuals or organisations that have a willingness and ability to purchase products. A market can consist of a single segment or multiple **segments**.

Even though markets may be described in terms of products, such as the 'drinks market', 'car market' or 'market for nuclear power stations', it is important that marketers never forget that markets are composed of people.

In basic marketing terms, markets are composed of **customers** (buyers) and **consumers** (users) but will also include other groupings as well, such as sellers and

market
a composite of individuals or organisations that have a willingness and ability to purchase products; a market can consist of a single or multiple segments

segments
distinct parts of a larger market; customers and consumers in each segment share similar characteristics

customer
buyer of a product or service

consumer
the individual end user of a product or service

---

insight   Yes, customers are important … but!

All marketing texts highlight the importance of customers and we do here, but this, in so many ways, is an over-simplification. Beware placing all your marketing focus on customers (to the exclusion of other parties), even though this is emphasised as part of the marketing concept. Marketing does, indeed, try to satisfy customers and, through this process, the organisation achieves its objectives, such as making sales and profits, or achieving donations if it is a charity, or improving attendance if it is an art gallery or museum, etc. First, not all customers are the same or want the same things; we must choose between potential customer groups. Consumers are not necessarily the same as customers; they are the users of goods and services and may not be the actual customers (buyers). This applies to many household products and toys for children, for example, and certainly applies to many industrial goods and services. Other members of the distribution chain, such as agents, wholesalers and

retailers, are important too, and they may be the first link in the chain of customer groups even though they are not the final customer or consumer. In short, there are a range of groups who become important if marketing is to be successful. Final customers are just part of a bigger picture of stakeholders and audience groups. Yes, they are an important part, but only a part nevertheless.

© iStockphoto.com/sculpies

These typical shoppers may be part of a consumer market but their needs and wants are likely to vary significantly

competitors (see Chapter 1). In terms of segmentation, targeting and positioning (all of which will be explained in this chapter), we are particularly concerned with understanding customers (actual and potential) and consumers (actual and potential). Markets are, without doubt, very complex environments, as was highlighted in Chapter 2, but identifying markets only in terms of customers can overlook one other important dimension: that of the role of consumers. While customers are strictly the purchasers of products, consumers are the users. Recognition of the respective roles of both in the marketplace is important to marketers.

Why segment and target markets?

One of the most profound realisations to strike any marketer is that there is a great diversity among customers. (Louden and Della Bitta, 1993: 30)

mass marketing
delivering the same marketing programme to everybody without making any distinction between them

Until fairly recently, marketers would speak in terms of **mass marketing**. This was generally founded on the belief that if large numbers of customers/consumers shared sufficiently common needs and wants, the same marketing programme could be delivered to everybody. It is easy to presume that this has always been the way marketing is carried out, but this is certainly no longer the case in the vast majority of circumstances in today's markets and probably was not the approach adopted in the past. As pointed out by Lindgren and Shimp (1996), mass marketing is a very recent phenomenon. Up until the early 1900s, most goods were produced to meet the needs of specific customers, but as populations and demand grew, this became an inefficient process. Henry Ford, founder of the Ford Motor Company, is frequently attributed with developing and popularising the concept of mass production, in which he standardised his production techniques to achieve **economies of scale**. The consequence was that he could produce more cars at lower prices and thereby satisfy the demands of the market for cheaper and more easily available vehicles. This mass-marketing strategy, however, meant that Ford offered just one product (the Model T), in one colour (black), at one price ($360) to the entire market.

economies of scale
unit costs fall as larger quantities are produced; a cost advantage associated with large organisations

In times of scarce supply of products, customers will make do with whatever is available. In many countries, we now live in times of oversupply of most products. We are demand-driven, rather than supply-driven (see Chapter 1). As a consequence, markets are fragmenting and we are moving away from mass marketing to more targeted approaches. Under such circumstances, trying to apply mass-marketing techniques, offering a single product and single marketing programme across the total market, while achieving economies of scale, runs the risk that few customers will be adequately satisfied (Dibb and Simkin, 1996). In contrast to mass marketing, some now talk of **mass customisation** to refer to the way in which, even in very large markets, organisations are being challenged to tailor their product offerings almost to meet individual needs. Once again, technology is being harnessed to provide solutions.

mass customisation
tailoring product offerings almost to meet individual needs

Marketers need to recognise that potential customers/consumers want different things, and that this creates opportunities to develop different markets and sub-markets *and* to develop different marketing programmes for each. So numerous and diverse are people's requirements that it would be impossible for any single organisation to satisfy everybody. This creates competitive opportunity and the potential for competitive advantage.

Although everybody is different, we have the advantage that people do at least share similarities and it is this feature that allows companies to direct their efforts with greatest effectiveness, efficiency and economy.

Technology provides the means to market one-to-one

Fortunately, at a time when there is greater need for marketers to be able to cope with an increasingly complex marketplace, technology comes to the rescue.

Today it is a thousand times cheaper to hold a customer's details on a computer than it was 20 years ago. Media and markets are fragmenting. Marketing budgets are being squeezed. The ability for marketers to identify key customers and prospects is no longer a 'nice to have' but a necessity. This is achieved through the use of databases for segmentation and targeting.

Over the last ten years, companies have embraced database marketing and now know who are the best customers. Over the next ten years, leading companies will move to one-to-one marketing by developing customer relationship management (CRM) capabilities so that they can give the right offer, to the right person, at the right time and through the right channel.

One-to-one marketing requires changing the business focus from share of market to share of customer. CRM and a good segmentation strategy, particularly if it is based on share of customer, can make one-to-one marketing technically and administratively more practical and achievable. (Mark Patron, Executive Vice President, Claritas (Europe) BV, quoted in Pickton and Broderick, 2004: 372)

WHAT IS MARKET SEGMENTATION?

Market segmentation is the splitting of a market into smaller groups (segments) so that marketers can better direct or focus their efforts. Segmentation can be defined as:

> *the process of dividing a total market into subgroups (segments) such that each segment consists of buyers and users who share similar characteristics but are different from those in the other segments.*

Ideally, from the marketing point of view, a segment would be those people who share the same buying behaviour and practices in every respect, but this is not possible. Instead, marketers make use of a variety of measures or techniques that approximate this. It is possible, therefore, to segment according to such things as age, where people live, their interests and lifestyles, and so on. In the case of business-to-business (B2B) marketing, organisations can be segmented according to their location, industry grouping, etc. These segmentation approaches or variables give an indication of likely similarities and behaviour between members of the segment. They could be described as surrogate or substitute measures for the real thing, which would be to measure and model actual buyer and usage behaviour. A fuller description of the variables used as bases for segmentation follows after the next section, which briefly highlights the main factors that make for a good segment to target.

market segmentation
the process of dividing a total market into subgroups (segments) such that each segment consists of buyers and users who share similar characteristics but are different from those in other segments

CRITERIA FOR DETERMINING GOOD MARKET SEGMENTS

Today there is a veritable wealth of information available to marketers to help them segment markets. But good segmentation should meet particular criteria. Segments should have the features outlined below:

- *Measurable* – without being measurable, a segment cannot be assessed for its size and profit potential. Marketers need to know the characteristics of who is in each segment, how many potential customers are in each segment, and what their buying and usage behaviour is like (as well as other environmental and competitor factors).
- *Homogeneous* (similar) within – the customers/consumers in a market segment should be as similar as possible with respect to their likely responses to marketing mix variables (i.e. they should display similar behavioural responses).
- *Heterogeneous* (different) between – the customers/consumers in different segments should be as different as possible with respect to their likely responses to marketing mix variables (i.e. they should display different behavioural responses). Ideally, the less segments overlap each other, the better.
- *Substantial* – the segment should be big enough to be profitable (or otherwise be capable of meeting the objectives of the organisation).
- *Accessible* – segments need to be reached and served effectively, not only in terms of delivery of product but also in terms of being able to communicate with the members of the segment. It is in this area that some of the most intractable implementation difficulties can apply. It may not be possible, for instance, to arrange new, or rearrange existing, distribution systems cost-efficiently to reach a chosen segment (Dibb and Simkin, 1996).
- *Operational* – the segmentation approach adopted should be useful for identifying and distinguishing between customers/consumers and deciding on marketing mix variables. In this context, the stability of the segment in the short, medium or long term may also be important.

While the above factors may be applied to evaluate whether or not a segment is likely to be suitable for targeting marketing effort, Dibb and Wensley (2002) make the point that other important considerations also have to be borne in mind if market segmentation is to be effective. Quoting the research of other authors, they identify the need for additional criteria to be met. Such factors are about turning segmentation analysis into effective marketing action:

- the commitment and involvement of senior managers within the organisation
- the readiness of the company to respond to market change
- inter-functional/departmental coordination
- the need for well-designed planning.

insight   Even the biggest companies can't do it all

Although described as appealing to wide and mass markets, major world brands such as KFC and McDonald's have their limitations. Strong branding helps to focus products into particular market segments and for this reason they can become very successful. But their brand associations mean they cannot take advantage of other segment opportunities. It would be virtually impossible for such fast-food chains to expand into upmarket, high-quality, gourmet restaurant businesses using the same names and identities. Similarly, it is difficult for them to appeal to health-conscious, healthy-eating and vegetarian market segments (although they are trying to). Despite such difficulties, however, changing tastes and market requirements demand that these 'giants' need to change their approaches over time to ensure they maintain their consumer appeal.

In practice, however, companies operate with limited and imperfect information and resources. It is not always possible to meet all of the criteria above. Under such circumstances, the challenge is to consistently improve so that better segmentation (and subsequently targeting, which will be introduced later) can be achieved.

Segmentation approaches

There are many ways to approach the segmentation of a market and a summary of these is given in Exhibit 4.1. Although the approaches can be used singly, it is common to use them in combination. Exhibit 4.2 gives an indication of how this works to produce a much more focused segment for targeting. Variables used singly would still represent a fairly indiscriminate market, while, used collectively, a more clearly defined segment emerges.

SEGMENTATION IN CONSUMER MARKETS

Geographic and demographic segmentation are probably the most popular forms of segmentation. Where customers are physically located (**geographic segmentation**) is of obvious concern to marketers, and determines the length and breadth of their marketing activities from the very local to global, international marketing. Markets can be segmented by areas, regions and by country. In many markets, the Internet and World Wide Web have opened up national and international opportunities to even the smallest of companies. Operating in many countries or areas, however, can have significant resource implications and should only be entered into after careful consideration. McDonald's, for example, operates around 22,000 restaurants in 109 different countries.

geographic segmentation
markets are segmented by countries, regions and areas

The world is getting smaller

global focus

The world is getting smaller, or so it seems, with improvements in transportation and telecommunications technologies. Writer and thinker Marshall McLuhan has coined the term 'global village'. International trade is increasing all around the world and trade barriers are being lifted. With an Internet website, email and text messaging, and greatly improved physical distribution operators, even the smallest company can attract and satisfy international customers. But you do not need to market overseas to face international competition. International competitors are on your own doorstep. Moving into international markets is not without its problems, though. Even greater attention to segmentation may be needed to avert failure. Around 230 nations each have their own unique cultures, subcultures, languages, customs, ethics, beliefs, religions and demographic patterns. All these differences complicate the segmentation process, especially as the quantity and quality of relevant information will vary significantly from country to country.

Demographic segmentation (demographics) has to do with the study of population characteristics and provides a range of useful variables. These variables have the particular advantages that they are relatively easy to measure and that a wealth of information on them is readily available from both government and commercial

demographic segmentation
markets segmented by population characteristics such as age, gender, occupation and income

Exhibit 4.1   The main variables used as bases to segment markets

Consumer (B2C) markets	Examples of variables
• Demographic segmentation	Age, gender, family size, life stage, e.g. family life cycle (FLC), religion, race, nationality, education, ethnic group
• Socio-economics	Income, occupation – social grade (A, B, C1, C2, D, E)
• Geographic segmentation	Country, region, city, urban–rural
• Geo-demographic segmentation	House type and house location (e.g. ACORN, MOSAIC)
• Psychographic segmentation	Lifestyles, values, motives, personalities, e.g. VALS
• Mediagraphic segmentation	Media habits (i.e. TV viewing, papers read, etc.)
• Behavioural segmentation	
purchase occasion	Day-to-day purchase, special occasion
benefits sought	Value for money, service, status, quality, brand image
usage rate	Heavy, medium, light user
user status	None, ex, potential, first time, regular user
readiness stage	Unaware, aware, informed, interested, desirous, intending to buy, bought, used
attitude to product	Enthusiastic, uninterested, positive, negative
involvement	Low involvement, high involvement (see Chapter 3 for more details)
adopter type	Innovator, early adopter, early majority, late majority, laggard
loyalty status	Total, strong, medium, light, none
Business-to-business (B2B) markets	**Examples of variables**
Macrosegmentation variables	
• Geographic location	country, region, city, urban–rural, industrial estate
• Type of organisation	manufacturer, service, government, local authority, private, local, international
• Industry grouping/business sector	standard industrial classification (SIC), e.g. textiles, computing, telecommunications, etc.
• Customer size	large, medium, small, key customer
Microsegmentation variables	
• User status	none, ex, potential, first time, regular user
• Trade category	agent, wholesaler, retailer, producer
• Benefits sought	economy, quality, service
• Loyalty status	total, strong, medium, light, none
• Readiness stage	unaware, aware, informed, interested, desirous, intending to buy, bought, used
• Adopter type	innovator, early adopter, early majority, late majority, laggard
• Purchasing practices	centralised, decentralised, tendering
• Buy class	straight rebuy, modified rebuy, new task

Exhibit 4.2 Using multiple segmentation variables

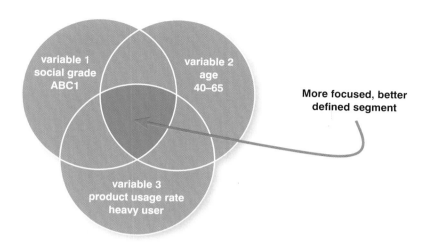

sources. As can be seen in Exhibit 4.1, demographic segmentation variables include age, gender, ethnic group and many more. If you are a manufacturer or retailer of shoes, even size of feet would be relevant; or size of chest/bust if you make clothing. By focusing on large sizes only, retailers Long Tall Sally and High and Mighty have made use of size to segment and target the women's and men's market, respectively, for clothes. Life stage is another useful variable and an example of this is the **family life cycle** (FLC), which is described in the Insight box on p.128. In this segmentation, the stages in the family life cycle create different needs. Young families have very different purchasing behaviour and leisure activities than solitary survivors.

family life cycle
a form of market segmentation based on the recognition that we pass through a series of quite distinct phases in our lives

ACTIVITY

For each of the stages in the family life cycle, identify a range of different goods and services you think are most likely to appeal.

Social grading is when *occupations* (of heads of households) are classified to provide groupings, which in the UK are best known as A, B, C1, C2, D and E (Exhibit 4.3). These are often inaccurately referred to as social classes, which is a related and overlapping concept but has wider connotations than just the occupational measure that is used in social grading. By implication, measures of occupation are closely linked to income and so social grading is classified as a socio-economic segmentation variable. Social grading has proved to be a particularly useful measure as it is used so widely in market research and the collection of government statistics. For this reason, there is a wealth of data available to the marketer that relates social grades to buying behaviour, disposable and discretionary income, media habits, hobbies and interests – all the sorts of things that marketers need to know. Unfortunately, social grading is not very good at determining discrete segments (homogeneous within, heterogeneous between), which is an important aspect of analysing market segments. The information may be fairly easy to collect and it may be widely available, but it is limited in its usefulness. Despite this, it remains popular. Of course, as pointed out above, segmentation variables do not have to be used singly; they can be combined to improve their usefulness.

social grading
segmentation by occupation of head of household; the typical classifications used are A, B, C1, C2, D and E groups

insight   Stages in the family life cycle

© iStockphoto.com/Rebecca Ellis

amily life cycle segmentation is based on the recognition that we pass through a series of quite distinct phases in our lives, each typified by a different set of circumstances, and within each we display some very different behaviour. Each stage gives rise to, or is associated with, different needs, social behaviour and purchasing patterns. The buying and consumption needs of a family with a young child or children (Full Nest I) are very different from those of an older couple with no children (Empty Nest II). Since its first inception, there has been far greater emphasis placed on the buying and influencing behaviour of children and, given the increasing longevity of life, the Empty Nest and Solitary Survivor stages.

People at different stages in the family life cycle
a) young couple
b) young family
c) older family
d) elderly single

© iStockphoto.com/Pascal Genest

© iStockphoto.com/Justin Horrocks

© iStockphoto.com/Catherine Yeulet

Stage	Characteristics
Bachelor	Young, single, not living at parental home, few financial burdens, recreation orientated – holiday, entertainment
Newlyweds	Young couples, no children, better off financially, two incomes – purchase home, home household consumer durables
Full Nest I	Youngest child under six, home purchase is significant emphasis, increasing financial pressures, may have only one income, purchase of household necessities
Full Nest II	Youngest child over six, financial position improving, some working spouses
Full Nest III	Older married couples with dependent children, financial position better still, replace household furnishings and products
Empty Nest I	Older married couples, no children at home, home ownership is peak, renewed interest in travel and leisure pursuits
Empty Nest II	Older couples, no children at home, retired, drastic cut in income, medical services emphasised
Solitary Survivor I	Still working, income good but likely to sell home
Solitary Survivor II	Retired, low income, special needs for medical care, affection and security

Exhibit 4.3   Social grading

Occupational Groups		% of population
A	Higher managerial, administrative and professional	4
B	Intermediate managerial, administrative and professional	23
C1	Supervisory, clerical and junior managerial, administrative and professional	29
C2	Skilled manual workers	21
D	Semi-skilled and unskilled manual workers	15
E	State pensioners, casual and lowest grade workers, unemployed with state benefits only	8

SOURCE: NRS data, 2008

To clarify, the implication behind demographic segmentation is that age or life stage or occupation, etc. will be factors that will tend to affect your buying and usage behaviour. Thus, for example, an older person is likely to want different things from a younger person. A 20-year-old male will exhibit different purchase and use behaviour from a 50-year-old female.

Geo-demographic segmentation has become an increasingly popular method for segmenting consumer markets. It combines aspects of both geographic and demographic data (hence its name). Developed first in the early 1980s by the CACI organisation, ACORN (A Classification Of Residential Neighbourhoods) makes use of household census data (data collected by the government on the total population) and specifically focuses on where people live and what types of house they live in. Using sophisticated statistical techniques, it has been possible to 'cluster' the population into defined groups according to two variables: house location and house type. The implication is that the area and the sort of house we live in say something about the sort of people we are and, importantly for the marketer, the sort of things we do, buy and use. We can contrast this with social grading, which attempts to relate the sort of people we are and the things we do with our occupations (and income). Geo-demographic systems that have already analysed and grouped the population for every area in the country (in all large economies) are commercially available to the marketer to analyse a huge range of markets. Examples include: ACORN, MOSAIC, EuroMOSAIC, GlobalMOSAIC, PIN and SuperProfile (details of MOSAIC are provided in Exhibit 4.4). Significantly, geo-demographic groupings have been extensively cross-referenced with other shopping and behaviour databases, such as Target Group Index (TGI) and BARB (see also Chapter 5) so that the actual buying habits of these groups are widely known and analysed. The geo-demographic systems that are offered for commercial purposes, such as ACORN and MOSAIC, are updated frequently so it should be noted that the categories and details are subject to change.

geo-demographic segmentation
markets are segmented by a combination of geographic and demographic approaches using house location and house type

Exhibit 4.4 MOSAIC geo-demographics

Group	Description	Approx % population	Examples of types within each group
A	Alpha Territory	4	A01 Global Power Brokers A02 Voices of Authority
B	Professional Rewards	10	B06 Yesterday's Captains B10 Parish Guardians
C	Rural Solitude	5	C11 Squires Among Locals C13 Modern Agribusiness
D	Small Town Diversity	9	D17 Jacks of All Trades D 18 Hardworking Families
E	Active Retirement	3	E20 Golden Retirement E23 Balcony Downsizers
F	Suburban Mindsets	13	F26 Mid-Market Families F27 Shop Floor Affluence
G	Careers and Kids	5	G30 Soccer Dads and Mums G32 Childcare Years
H	New Homemakers	4	H34 Buy-to-Let Territory H36 Foot on the Ladder
I	Ex-Council Community	11	I 38 Settled Ex-Tenants I41 Stressed Borrowers
J	Claimant Cultures	5	J42 Worn-Out Workers J43 Streetwise Kids
K	Upper Floor Living	4	K48 Multicultural Towers K49 Re-Housed Migrants
L	Elderly Needs	4	L50 Pensioners in Blocks L53 Low Spending Elders
M	Industrial Heritage	7	M54 Clocking Off M55 Backyard Regeneration
N	Terraced Melting Pot	7	N60 Back-to-Back Basics N61 Asian Identities
O	Liberal Opinions	9	O63 Urban Cool O67 Study Buddies

SOURCE: Based on the latest version of MOSAIC UK launched in July 2009 which classifies consumers in the United Kingdom into one of 67 types and 15 groups. MOSAIC is a registered trademark of Experian Ltd

ACTIVITY

Walk around an area of housing you are familiar with. Using the brief MOSAIC descriptions given in Exhibit 4.4, try to guess what categories the types of house fit into. How much do the houses vary? How many different categories can you identify? Alternatively, if you know the postcodes for the area, you can go on to www.upmystreet.com, click on Neighbours in the dropdown menu under 'LOCAL AREA' and put in the postcodes of your choice. The website will identify the ACORN category the postcode has been allocated and will give a brief description of it. Compare the description with your impressions of the area.

Psychographic segmentation attempts to measure and understand people's lifestyles, values and personalities. As an approach, it more directly addresses the issue of understanding buyer and usage behaviour through an understanding of the buyers and users themselves. It is a particularly useful approach for creating a more detailed understanding of particular segments within an overall market and can be used in conjunction with other approaches, such as demographic segmentation. For example, classifying shoppers into different types, as follows, is an interesting and useful lifestyle approach:

psychographic segmentation
using lifestyles, values and personalities to split up markets

- the convenience shopper
- the recreational shopper
- the 'shop-till-I-drop' shopper
- the price-bargain shopper
- the store-loyal shopper
- the traditionalist shopper
- the outgoing/individualistic shopper
- the quality service shopper
- the socially conscious shopper
- the other directed shopper (concerned about asking others for opinions).

A popular consumer psychographic classification model is VALS™ developed originally by SRI International and now owned and operated by Strategic Business Insights (SBI). The most recent version of VALS™ consists of eight categories based on a combination of demographic and psychological characteristics that correlate with consumer behaviour. The main dimensions of the framework are primary motivations on the horizontal axis and resources on the vertical axis. Exhibit 4.5 shows the eight types grouped into three broad categories of primary motivations associated with ideals, achievement and self-expression. The extent to which these primary motivations may be realised is affected by the resources available. SBI describe their primary motivations and resources as follows:

Primary motivation

Consumers buy products and services and seek experiences that fulfill [sic] their characteristic preferences and give shape, substance, and satisfaction to their lives. An individual's primary motivation determines what in particular about the self or the world is the meaningful core that governs his or her activities. Consumers are inspired by one of three primary motivations: ideals, achievement, and self-expression. Consumers who are primarily motivated by ideals are guided by knowledge and principles. Consumers who are primarily motivated by achievement look for products and services that demonstrate success to their peers. Consumers who are primarily motivated by self-expression desire social or physical activity, variety, and risk.

Resources

A person's tendency to consume goods and services extends beyond age, income, and education. Energy, self-confidence, intellectualism, novelty seeking, innovativeness, impulsiveness, leadership, and vanity play a critical role. These personality traits in conjunction with key demographics determine an individual's resources. Different levels of resources enhance or constrain a person's expression of his or her primary motivation.

More details of the VALS™ model can be found at www.strategicbusinessinsights.com/vals.

ACTIVITY

Visit the SBI website (www.strategicbusinessinsights.com) and make notes on each of the eight types identified in the VALS™ model. As an additional exercise, try out the survey questions for yourself and see which VALS™ type you fit into.

mediagraphic segmentation
markets segmented by reading and viewing habits

Mediagraphic segmentation is based on the reading and viewing habits of the population. This might at first appear a strange approach to segmentation as it measures media behaviour rather than attempting to measure buying or product usage behaviour. However, in developing this approach, Carat International, maintained that the approach is more discriminatory than demographics or geo-demographics. The company has cross-referenced data collected through readership and television viewing surveys (e.g. NRS and BARB, see Chapter 5) with purchase surveys (e.g. TGI, see Chapter 5) and has developed a range of mediagraphic categories, each relating media behaviour to purchase behaviour. The implication is that the sort of media consumed says something about the sort of products purchased and used. At an obvious level, this can clearly be related to the reading of specialist magazines and particular purchases. For example, somebody interested in reading hi-fi magazines is likely to be interested in hi-fi products too.

behavioural segmentation
dividing a market into subgroups (segments) of customers/users according to how they buy, use and feel about products

Behavioural segmentation is described by Dibb (2000) as grouping customers and consumers according to how they buy, use and feel about products, and, as such, can

Exhibit 4.5   VALS™ segmentation

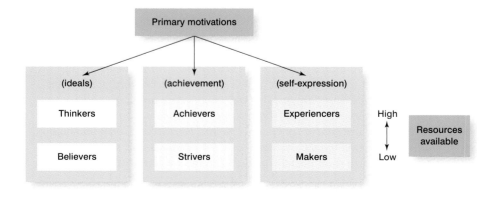

be very effective in identifying segments. She quotes the example of tea consumption to illustrate the point:

Research into tea consumption has revealed that most consumers no longer prepare the beverage in a teapot. Instead, they place a single teabag directly into their cup and add hot water. Unfortunately, these consumers often find that the teabags drip when taken out of the cup. Now manufacturer Tetley has devised a new teabag design to appeal directly to these consumers. The bag features two drawstrings that are meant to ensure that when it is removed the liquid all drains into the cup. (Dibb, 2000: 391)

Similarly, a change in behaviour has accompanied the growth of out-of-town and edge-of-town supermarkets and shopping malls. As most shoppers arrive in cars, it has been possible to increase the size of bulk packaging of such items as soap powders as they now only have to be transported to the car park. In contrast, social changes and growth in what the Henley Centre for Forecasting has described as the 'secular household', in which individuals 'do their own thing', has resulted in increased sales of pre-packaged meals for one that can be prepared quickly in the microwave.

Behavioural segmentation can involve many different variables, as indicated in Exhibit 4.1, and these can include product or brand loyalty, frequency of purchase or rate of consumption, attitudes towards the product, whether the product is perceived

insight   Lifestyle groups 1

There are many strange terms used to describe specific lifestyle groups. 'Yuppies' – young urban professionals – aspired to a good life. This grouping was popular in the 1980s and early 1990s. They were young, upwardly mobile and were high achievers. Their disposable income was the envy of many and their spending followed suit. They were 'conspicuous consumers'. They bought expensive, status-brand products and everyone could see this in the cars they drove, the clothing they wore and the leisure activities they pursued.

Although not so popularly referred to today, Yuppies (as status-conscious parents) have given birth to 'Yuppie Puppies', children whom they dress in kiddie designer clothing by Versace, Moschino, Hermes and Kenso.

'Baby boomers' is a term used to describe people born after the Second World War between 1946 and 1964. 'Generation X', a term coined by the writer Douglas Copeland, describes people born between 1965 and 1979. They grew up with television and computers. They are independent minded and cynical due to the economic and social problems present when they were young (economic recession, AIDS epidemic, etc.). 'Generation Y' (people born since 1980) have also been called the 'Digital Generation' ('Generation D') because they have grown up with the Internet, and computer and communication technologies. They are more opportunistic, better informed, more empowered and entrepreneurial. Older members of the population have been called the 'grey market' and 'Woopies' – well-off older persons.

Other intriguing titles include: 'Dinkies', double income (young couples) with no kids yet; 'Biddies', baby boomers in debt; 'Skippies', school kids with income and purchasing power; 'Guppies', grey, upwardly mobile professionals; 'Maffies', middle-aged, affluent folks; 'Mossies', middle-aged, over-stressed, semi-affluent suburbanites; and 'Dimps', dual-income couples with money problems.

SOURCE: Duncan, 2002

insight   Lifestyle groups 2: Teenage Tribes

It would be wrong (but is frequently done nevertheless) to segment 13–19 year old teenagers as a single group. The same sort of mistake is made with many other age groupings and other over-generalised segments as well! Here is a selection of teenage groupings and the music, brands and styles they like.

Group	Preferred music genre	Example bands	Common brands	Clothes styles	Shoe styles
Emo (Emotional Punk)	Emotional pop-punk/rock	My Chemical Romance, Taking Back Sunday, Fall Out Boy, Dashboard Confessional	Converse, Vans, Von Dutch, Heartcare, Atticus, Dickies	Very tight jeans, stripy long-sleeve tops/jumpers, zip-up hoodies, 'trucker' (mesh) baseball caps. Lots of black, red and stripes	Converse All Star baseball boots, old-school Vans slip-ons
Goth/metaller	Metal/Heavy metal	Marilyn Manson, Nightwish, Dragonforce	New Rock, Criminal Damage, Underground, Dr Martens	Long, black trench coats, baggy black trousers with straps. Metallers wear heavy metal band t-shirts	Big, chunky high-leg leather boots with metal buckles, mega-high platform shoes
Chav	R'n'B/Rap/ Hip-hop/D'n'B	Eminem, The Streets, D12, Nelly, 50 Cent	Nike, Adidas, Reebok, Puma, Umbro, Ecko, leCoqsportif, Patrick, fake Burberry	Sports clothes – tracksuit trousers, zip-up tracksuit tops, hoodies, fake Burberry items, baseball caps, thick fake gold chains	Expensive sports trainers
Grunger	Heavy rock, 'screamo'	System of a Down, Rage Against the Machine, Nirvana, Slipknot	Hoodies with brand logos, Criminal Damage, Vans, not much branded stuff	Ripped jeans, band t-shirts and hoodies, dad's old shirts over t-shirts, bandanas	Skate shoes, Dr Martens boots
Skater	Indie rock/punk rock	Rage Against the Machine, The Offspring, Green Day, Rancid, Bad Religion	Vans, DC, Globe, DVS, Element, Emerica, Adio, Etnies, Osiris, Dickies	Baggy jeans and combat trousers, t-shirts, hoodies, polo shirts, Beanie hats and trucker baseball caps	Big, fat, chunky, padded skateboard shoes

(Continued)

(Continued)

Group	Preferred music genre	Example bands	Common brands	Clothes styles	Shoe styles
Surfer	Surf rock, modern rock	The Beach Boys, Jack Johnson	Vans, Animal, BillabongReef, Mambo, Weird Fish, Oakley, Fat Face	Baggy combat trousers and shorts, baggy hoodies and t-shirts, sunglasses, 'boardshorts' in the summer	Skateboard shoes or sandals
Hippy	Reggae, old rock, trip-hop, jungle/D'n'B	Bob Marley, The Beatles, Jimi Hendrix, Massive Attack, Aphrodite	None – at a push, fair-trade brands such as Namaste	Baggy, cotton, hemp, very casual, earthy colours, 'flowy' materials. Fair-trade stuff from Nepal, woolly jumpers	Simple canvas/ cotton shoes, sandals or skate shoes
Fashionistas	Indie rock, charts	Kaiser Chiefs, Artic Monkeys	Top Shop, New Look, FCUK, Ted Baker	Whatever's fashionable – jeans, skirts, tops, cardigans, handbags, etc. all in the latest fashion	Shoes in the latest fashion, whether it be ballet pumps, wedges or chunky lace-ups
Normal	Charts, pop	Gnarls Barkley, Coldplay, Kooks, Kaiser Chiefs, Katie Melua, Red Hot Chilli Peppers	Top Shop, New Look, Next, Adidas	Jeans, zip-up tops, t-shirts	Normal shoes and trainers, skate shoes

SOURCE: Jellyellie, 2007

as a high-involvement product, in which great care will be taken over the purchase, or a low-involvement product that may be bought more out of habit (see Chapter 3), what the product is bought for – general use or a special occasion such as a party – and so on.

Some have described behavioural segmentation as the best segmentation approach. Others disagree with this contention, not least based on the argument that relevant information is not so readily available or can be expensive to collect. In fact, it would be difficult to state that any one segmentation approach or variable is the best – it would typically depend on the particular application. What *is* true is that behaviourally based variables can provide very powerful descriptors for distinguishing between segments.

insight

Camera manufacturers and insurance companies make use of behavioural differences

Some manufacturers in the camera industry make use of behavioural segmentation in designing their models.

Point-and-clickers look for ease of use, reliability and auto-settings so that the camera effectively takes all of the guess work out of taking photos

Budget buyers look for value for money and more 'bang for their bucks'

Gadget freaks just can't have enough of those twiddly bits, buttons and menus, they look for extra functionality

Settings junkies really want manual controls and overrides of the auto settings or lots of auto settings to choose from to suit each photo occasion

Professionals and serious enthusiasts are looking for high performance, which probably means auto and manual control, digital SLR, high-specification body and lenses, superior photo chip and data capture in compressed and non-compressed formats as standard.

You may have already noticed the advertising that insurance companies carry out when encouraging the purchase of car insurance. The next time you see this advertising you might want to test yourself in working out whom each company is trying to focus upon (target). For example, SAGA appear to aim at the over 50s whereas Admiral seem to woo younger drivers looking for cheaper quotes. Sheila's Wheels and Diamond focus not on age but emphasise gender in targeting females. Esure and Privilege have aimed towards careful drivers offering cheaper quotes for those with three or four years no claims bonuses. Elephant.com and Directline target those wanting quick and convenient arrangements. In each case, the insurance companies are offering the same basic product but with emphasis on different elements of the marketing mix designed to appeal to different market segments. The price quoted varies significantly and this has given rise to a whole new set of online companies that offer comparison websites to make the process of choosing easier.

EXPAND YOUR KNOWLEDGE

Haley, R.I. (1968) 'Benefit segmentation: a decision-oriented research tool', *Journal of Marketing*, 32 (Jul): 30–35.

Haley introduces the concept of segmenting on the basis of the benefits offered by the brand as a legitimate new approach.

Loyalty status is of increasing interest as a segmentation variable. As the value of maintaining loyal customers has become more widely recognised, degrees of loyalty have become more relevant to marketers. In today's market environment, it is difficult to believe in totally loyal customers. Even those that hold loyalty cards frequently hold such cards from a variety of competitors. One way of classifying customer loyalty is as follows.

> **Hard core loyals**: have absolute loyalty to a single brand or company (e.g. brands AAAAAA – each time they buy, these customers always buy the same brand).
> **Soft core loyals**: divide their loyalty between two, or sometimes more, brands or companies (e.g. brands AABABBA – these customers may first buy brand A

once or twice, then switch to another brand (brand B) before returning to their original brand, then perhaps back again to another brand).

Shifting loyals: brand-switch, spending some time on one brand, or favouring one company, and then moving to another (e.g. brands AAABBB).

Switchers: show no brand loyalty, often purchasing products that are the lowest price or have a special offer (e.g. brands BCBAACD).

User status (which may vary from non-user to regular user) and usage rate (light usage to heavy usage) may seem similar to loyalty status. Like loyalty, they are both important concepts to marketers. Even when potential customers/consumers are within a specified segment of interest to the marketer, their user status or usage rate may heighten their worth or reduce it to zero. User/usage behaviour is therefore something to which marketers should pay particular attention. Increasingly, the concept of **customer lifetime value** has become a focus of attention for marketers, as the importance of longer-term customer relationships has become more widely recognised. The use of customer databases allows organisations to maintain vast amounts of data on their customer's purchasing habits and segment different customer groups accordingly.

customer lifetime value
a calculation of the long-term worth of a customer using estimates of expected purchases

The actual benefits sought by customers/consumers is another interesting way of distinguishing between them. The key benefit for some might simply be a low price, for others ease of use. In the toothpaste market, we can see how different brands are aimed at different benefit groups. There are brands for sensitive teeth such as Sensodyne, brands for tooth whitening such as Pearl Drops, brands for fresh breath such as Aquafresh, brands for tartar and plaque control such as Crest, brands that tackle tough smokers' stains such as Topol, brands that fight against cavities such as Oracle, and those that claim 'total' care such as Colgate. Each relevant benefit can provide a substantial market segment and help to create opportunities for brand **positioning** which will be discussed later in this chapter.

insight   Nectar segments, targets and pinpoints for added loyalty

The Nectar customer loyalty scheme was launched in the UK in 2002 by Loyalty Management UK (LMUK) and it generates a vast amount of data that can be used by the companies that have signed up to it. Around half of all UK households have the card which can be used in about 6,000 retail outlets, but unlike most other loyalty schemes, Nectar is not linked to a single company but to a range of companies, all of which benefit from the data analytics that LMUK produce. This data provides insights into customer shopping trends based on till sales and other Nectar information. LMUK have developed a segmentation scheme that groups its active customer base into seven levels of commitment that range from 'engaged collectors' to 'passive swipers'. Personal information provided by members when registering for Nectar is regularly updated with Experian Mosaic data, giving insight into life stages and helping to highlight targeting opportunities. John Sheekey, Nectar's Marketing Director, states that Nectar is moving towards more 'trigger-based' communications, with consumer behaviour identified from data changes triggering action. For example, when Nectar cardholders change address, a 'home mover' pack is sent which includes a map with the cardholder's new home featured and indicates where Nectar points can be collected locally. Coupons with offers are included to help track impact.

SOURCE: Anon, 2007

ACTIVITY

Visit a supermarket and choose a category of heavily branded products such as soap, detergents or toiletries. Take a close look at the different brands and their packaging, and identify what benefits each is trying to emphasise. Think about the different ways the competing products are trying to be positioned in terms of the similarities and differences in the benefits they claim to offer. Can you identify the sort of different behavioural characteristics they appeal to?

product adopters model (product diffusion model) categorises product buyers/users according to their take-up rate of new products

personality a person's distinguishing psychological characteristics that lead them to respond in particular ways

The **product adopters model** is another way of conceptualising purchasing behaviour. This approach has already been identified in Chapter 3 in which each of the categories or adopter groups was introduced. Researchers have found that people tend to be more or less adventurous in their purchase and consumption behaviours, and these findings have been linked to particular **personality** and behavioural tendencies. Marketers have found this way of segmenting the market can be very insightful and helps to explain why product sales follow the typical product life cycle curve that is described in Chapter 6. As new products to the market are launched, they appeal to innovators who are quick to respond to novel ideas. Over time these products are adopted by each of the adopter categories in turn until those new products become dated and really only appeal to the laggards, who are the slowest to accept new ideas and change. Therefore, it is possible to modify the marketing activities to best appeal to each of the groups in turn as the product is first launched, becomes accepted in the marketplace and, eventually, declines in popularity. Exhibit 4.6 briefly summarises the different adopter groups.

Exhibit 4.6   Categories of adopter

Category	Characteristics	Percentage of the population
Innovators	Risk-takers, often affluent and well educated	2.5
Early adopters	Adopt early, are opinion leaders in their communities and a source of information about new things	13.5
Early majority	Follow the lead set by the early adopters, delay while making sure of new ideas and things	34
Late majority	Older than average and often less well educated, tend to be more sceptical, more traditional and more comfortable with older values	34
Laggards	Suspicious of innovation, often associated with lower education and low income, often social outsiders	16

SEGMENTATION IN BUSINESS MARKETS

Segmentation principles apply in just the same way to business markets: markets that we may refer to as B2B (business to business) or industrial markets or commercial

Helping customers or manipulating them?

What is your view? Does understanding customer and consumer behaviour better mean that companies can provide products better suited to their needs? Or does this give companies improved abilities to manipulate their customers?

markets, i.e. those situations where one business does business directly with another, rather than with an individual. Although marketing is most readily associated with consumer markets (or B2C markets as they are also known), and even more particularly with fast-moving consumer goods (**FMCG**) markets (e.g. the sorts of products we associate with supermarkets), a great deal of marketing takes place B2B. The importance of this is frequently underestimated. The marketing takes place in industrial and commercial contexts, which is also a fundamental part of consumer marketing. If we consider for a moment the very well-recognised large consumer goods companies, such as Unilever and Procter & Gamble, Coca-Cola and PepsiCo, Ford and General Motors, Sony and Philips, much of their marketing efforts are directed towards doing business with other businesses. They less commonly, if ever, sell directly to us, the final customers, even though they do advertise and promote themselves and their brands to us (through **pull** marketing activities, see Chapter 8). They put significant marketing effort into working through the trade – wholesalers, retailers, agents, franchisees, etc. (**push** marketing activities, see Chapter 8), however, in describing their markets, it is the final customers and end consumers who are significant.

For true B2B organisations, their customers are other organisations and so it is these that need to be segmented. Similar variables can be used in B2B markets to those used in consumer markets. For example, the location of their potential customers, what type of business or industry they are in, size of business, and so on. In B2B markets, the segmentation variables can be grouped into macrosegmentation variables and microsegmentation variables, as shown in Exhibit 4.1. As with segmentation in consumer markets, the advent of cheaper databases has drastically reduced the cost of collecting, and vastly increased the opportunity of maintaining, mountains of customer information on a continual basis, making the segmentation process much easier.

Shapiro and Bonoma (1984) have proposed a detailed, nested approach in which they identify five general segmentation bases arranged in a nested hierarchy. The process of segmentation should work from the more general outer area (macrosegmentation) towards the more specific inner area (microsegmentation), probing deeper as it goes (see Exhibit 4.7). The five general segmentation bases are as follows.

1 *Demographic variables* are used to give a broad description of the business segments based on such variables as location (which Shapiro and Bonoma included as a demographic, rather than geographic, variable), size of business, type of business and business sector (e.g. SIC code, for details see below).

2 *Operating variables* enable a more precise identification of existing and potential customers within demographic categories. User status and technologies applied might be considered here.

3 *Purchasing approach* looks at customers' purchasing practices (e.g. centralised or decentralised purchasing). It also includes purchasing policies and buying criteria, and the nature of the buyer/seller relationship.

4 *Situational factors* consider the tactical role of the purchasing situation requiring a more detailed knowledge of the individual buyer, others involved and the specific buying situation. This might include potential order size, urgency of order and any particular requirements.

5 *Personal characteristics* relate to the people who make the purchasing decisions. Different customers may display different attitudes to risk and different levels of loyalty to suppliers.

Exhibit 4.7   The nested approach to B2B segmentation

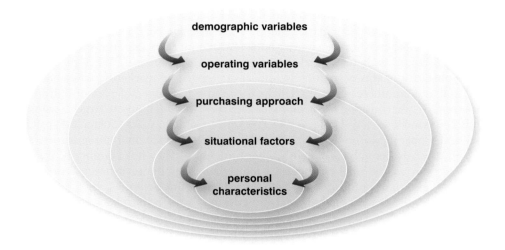

EXPAND YOUR KNOWLEDGE

Shapiro, B.P. and Bonoma, T.V. (1984) 'How to segment industrial markets', *Harvard Business Review*, May-Jun: 104–110.

The difficulty of segmenting industrial markets has dissuaded companies from trying despite the benefits derived from so doing. This article explores the ways of segmenting industrial markets and proposes a nested hierarchy approach.

SIC (Standard Industrial Classification)
system of classifying products by allocating numbers (codes) to every product category, industry or business sector

As with consumer markets, a great deal of information may already be available in published form. For example, type of business/industry will be defined by industrial classifications, such as the **SIC (Standard Industrial Classification)**, which governments use to categorise the companies within their countries. Government publications summarise this data and company details can readily be found in a wide range of business directories. The SIC system simply allocates numbers (codes) to every industry or business sector. The first digit, or couple of digits, indicate the broad industry area. The succeeding digits provide greater detail and are more specific about individual products or product groupings. Exhibit 4.8 shows example details of UK SICs by providing just the first digit of the code showing the major industry

B2B focus

Selling buses to America

Approximately 5,000 transit buses are sold per annum in North America to some 350 transport authorities. Segmentation in this B2B bus market has historically involved the macrosegmentation approach, namely focusing on customer size and geographical variables. Essentially, the most important consideration has been the size of the bus fleet. Transport authorities with over 750 buses are considered large, authorities with between 200 and 750 are medium, and authorities with fewer than 200 buses are small. In addition, the North American market is divided into 11 geographical regions. Research into microsegmentation characteristics in this market has revealed two new approaches to segmentation. The first highlights the importance of the purchase decision process and the second highlights the importance of the product evaluation process, which emphasises the significance placed by buyers on particular product features. Six distinctly different decision process segments and a further six product feature segments have been identified. These new ways of segmenting B2B markets are providing far greater insight into marketing issues, and overcoming the criticisms voiced and difficulties faced over not being able to adequately operationalise segmentation approaches into marketing strategy (Dibb and Wensley, 2002).

Crittenden et al. (2002) have termed these two different groups of segments as shown below:

Decision process segments	Product feature segments
• The rider-conscious and low-cost bid segment. Importance was given to standardisation of products with current fleet, low-cost bid and rider opinion.	• The drive train and not drivers segment. Importance was given to drive train and low maintenance cost, but not to efficiency of use for drivers.
• The government regulation-prone advanced design bus (ADB) lovers segment. Importance was given to issues of government intervention and compliance.	• The cool climate drive train and not drivers segment. Similar to segment above, but both air conditioning and driver efficiency were less important.
• The low-cost bid and manufacturer reputation segment. Importance was given to low-cost bid, perception of manufacturers and manufacturers' nationalities.	• The rider-sensitive and forget the fuel segment. Concern was given to attractiveness and air conditioning. Fuel efficiency and bus power were less important.
• The staff-poor ADB big spenders segment. Importance was given to comparisons with and the opinions of other transport authorities. Staff opinion was considered less important.	• The more rider-sensitive and less driver-sensitive segment. More concern was given to location-specific operating conditions, air conditioning and exterior styling, with less importance given to maintenance cost and driver efficiency.
• The large, new-look buyers segment. Importance was given to standardisation with current fleet, perception of manufacturers and local manufacture.	• The power-hungry segment. The unique characteristic of this segment was the importance given to bus power and location-specific operating conditions.
• The 'others' opinions and not dollars count' segment. Importance was given to board of directors' opinions and opinions of other transport authorities. Low-cost bid was of low importance.	• The style conscious and cool segment. This segment was primarily characterised by high ratings for exterior styling and low ratings for bus power and air conditioning.

and service areas. The North American SICs (North American Industry Classification System – NAICS) code examples show how the code number is built up from the general to the specific. European SICs and other countries' SIC approaches adopt similar principles.

Exhibit 4.8   Standard Industrial Classifications (SICs)

UK SIC code	Description
0	Agriculture, forestry, fishing
1	Energy and water-supply industries
2	Extraction of minerals and ores (excluding fuels), manufacture of metals, mineral products and chemicals
3	Manufacture of metal goods, engineering, vehicles
4	Other manufacturing industries
5	Construction
6	Distribution, hotels/catering, repairs
7	Transport and communication
8	Banking, finance, insurance, business services, leasing
9	Other services

NAICS code	Description
	The first two digits of the NAICS code show the Major Group Category, for example:
20–39	digits in this range are for the Manufacturing Industry Division, for example:
34	these first two digits give the industry group code for 'Fabricated Metals'
342	the addition of the third digit, 2, gives the industry group code for 'Cutlery and hand tools'
3423	the addition of the fourth digit, 3, gives the specific industry code for 'Hand and edge tools'
34231	the addition of the fifth digit, 1, gives the product class code for 'Mechanics hand service tools'
342311	the addition of the sixth digit, 1, gives the specific product code for 'Pliers' so allocating Code 342311 to a company (among any other codes it might also be allocated) would indicate that it was a manufacturer of pliers

target marketing (targeting)
the selection of one or more market segments towards which marketing efforts can be directed; sometimes called market targeting

Target marketing

Target marketing involves making decisions about which part of the market an organisation wishes to focus on. It follows from market segmentation, in which the total

B2B focus

The case for customer segmentation for improved marketing and cohesive customer experience at Dell Computers

In the late 1990s, Dell Computers in the USA segmented its customers into groups based on each group's unique needs. Its segments included Global enterprise accounts, Large organisations, Mid-size organisations, Federal agencies, State and local government agencies, Educational institutions, Small organisations and Individual consumers. In 1998, 90 per cent of Dell's sales were to business or government institutions, and of those, 70 per cent were to large corporate customers who spent at least $1 million on PCs annually. Dell had hundreds of sales representatives calling on large corporate and institutional accounts. The organisation regularly had prominent ads in such leading computer publications as *PC Magazine* and *PC World*, as well as in *USA Today*, the *Wall Street Journal* and other business publications.

Sales-account managers were coached on how to lead large customers through a discussion of their future needs for PCs, workstations, servers and peripheral equipment. Distinctions were made between purchases that were virtually certain and those that were contingent on some event. Salespeople made note of the contingent events so they could follow up at the appropriate time. Dell's value proposition to corporate customers included services highly valued by corporate accounts – services such as bundled service agreements, customer software loading and asset-tagging services, customised intranet support sites and vendor financing – all of which resulted in Dell becoming the preferred provider of computers and peripherals for this segment.

Dell's sales to individuals and small businesses were made nationally and internationally by telephone, fax and the Internet. It had a call centre in the USA with free phone lines so that customers could talk with a sales representative about specific models, get information faxed or mailed to them, place an order and pay by credit card. The call centres were equipped with technology that routed calls from a particular country to a particular call centre so that customers could speak to knowledgeable representatives in their own language. Customers could also build their own system (i.e. configure options and features from available alternatives) as well as check the status of orders, troubleshoot problems, order in-home service and arrange returns through a personalised website.

potential market is subdivided according to its characteristics. Targeting is then the choice of which single segment or group of segments the organisation wishes to select. A **target market,** therefore, would actually be better described as a target sub-market or target segment.

EVALUATING A SEGMENT FOR TARGETING

There are five principal characteristics that will make a market segment particularly attractive for targeting but, before selecting, the organisation must undertake a full PRESTCOM analysis (see Chapter 2), which will include consideration of its own company resources and capabilities, its strengths and weaknesses, the competition and the company's objectives. The characteristics of an attractive segment are that it includes one or, preferably, more of the following:

target market
a group of buyers and consumers who share common needs/wants or characteristics and upon whom the organisation focuses

- has sufficient current and potential sales and profits
- has the potential for sufficient future growth
- is not over-competitive
- does not have excessive barriers or costs to entry or exit
- has some relatively unsatisfied needs that the company can serve particularly well.

It should be noted that the distinction here is really about the way in which a company *focuses* its marketing efforts towards those customers (targets) that it really believes will give it greatest success. Customers from outside the target can, of course, be accepted, but these will not be the focus of attention. The result could be that companies may lose some potential customers but, within their limited resources, they will have directed their efforts in ways that they have decided are likely to be most effective and cost-efficient. Certainly, marketers recognise that trying to appeal to *everyone* may well have the effect of not appealing successfully to *anyone*.

REASONS FOR TARGETING AND POSITIONING

The underlying rationale behind the total process from market segmentation to targeting and positioning is well accepted in marketing and is a logical development of the marketing concept that was introduced in Chapter 1. As all marketing authors emphasise, segmentation, targeting and positioning are key decision areas in marketing and strategic planning, and are the foundation of successful marketing management.

Applying the principles outlined in this chapter allows organisations to handle market diversity by focusing resources on particular customer/consumer groups. Having a better understanding of the media habits, buying behaviour and product use of subgroups of the market creates the opportunity for organisations to fine-tune their offerings, allocate scarce resources more effectively, and provide the basis for strategic marketing decisions. Analysis of the market allows organisations to improve their competitiveness, exploit market gaps, avoid or reduce direct competition, and develop their competitive advantage. In short, they are fundamental parts of good marketing, facilitating marketing effectiveness, efficiency and economy. How well an organisation then puts these to use is an implementational issue that will be affected by managerial willingness and ability.

targeting strategies
used to select a single target market or a group of target markets

undifferentiated marketing
where the market is believed to be composed of customers/consumers whose needs and wants from the product are fundamentally the same

TARGETING STRATEGIES

Having analysed the chosen market and determined the attractiveness of the various segments in that market, a decision then has to be made concerning which segments to target. There are some basic options available. Exhibit 4.9 lists these and Exhibit 4.10 illustrates the different **targeting strategies** visually.

Undifferentiated marketing

Undifferentiated marketing is where the market is believed to be composed of customers/consumers whose needs and wants in the context of the product being

---

Targeting children

ethical focus

A number of companies are now quite directly targeting children. This is clearly evident during Saturday-morning TV and in marketing activities focused directly at schools. Companies are providing books, other teaching and learning materials, and free gifts.

While it can clearly be argued that children benefit from the donations and support given to their schools, what do you consider the motives behind this support to be? What ethical issues are raised by these companies' actions?

Exhibit 4.9   Targeting strategies

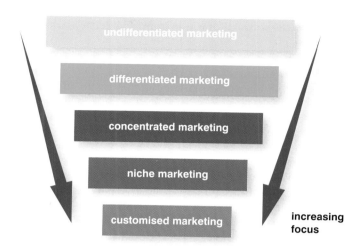

offered are fundamentally the same, i.e. there is no basic difference between them, they are undifferentiated. This is the area of mass marketing. In undifferentiated or **mass marketing**, a single marketing programme is used for all. Although this may result in lower costs and prices (and/or higher profit margins), it is very difficult to satisfy all customers/consumers with one marketing mix. An organisation using undifferentiated marketing may also be providing an excellent opportunity for its competition to capture a portion of its sales by appealing to the desires of specific segments. Few, if any, products are marketed totally in this way. Usually, some form of differentiation takes place, even if only on a small scale. Products such as Coca-Cola and Pepsi are reasonable examples of undifferentiated marketing, although it should be recognised that some modifications are made to the marketing effort in different countries even if this is only to recognise language differences. Both companies have also recognised particular benefit segments within the general market and so, in this way, really practise a differentiated marketing strategy to some extent. For example, Coca-Cola has Diet Coke and Pepsi has Pepsi Max as sugar-free alternatives.

Marketeers may use an undifferentiated marketing strategy even when some differences between customer/consumer groups are recognised. The segments are aggregated in the belief that the differences are not significant or can otherwise be ignored. However, too much aggregation of segments can be risky. Combining segments to enlarge the target, and adopting **mass-marketing** approaches, inevitably means that the target becomes less and less homogeneous – the differences between each segment begin to outweigh their similarities. Thus, the mass marketer (when adopting an undifferentiated targeting strategy) needs to be convinced that the nature of its product offering can, indeed, meet the requirements of a large market, e.g. cola drinkers. Other organisations, such as McDonald's, Burger King, Wendy's and KFC, take a similar stance, although each of these businesses does modify its product offering in different countries (geographical segmentation) to reflect different cultural preferences (demographic segmentation). It is each company's intention, though, to maintain its general image and promotional effort throughout.

Lindgren and Shimp (1996) point out that by pursuing an undifferentiated marketing strategy an organisation can build and maintain a specific image with customers/consumers, minimise its production costs, achieve greater efficiencies and be able to offer its products at competitive prices (or otherwise achieve higher profit margins).

They cite three instances, in general, when a mass, or undifferentiated, marketing strategy is most appropriate:

1 When the market is so small that it is unprofitable to market to just a portion of it.
2 When heavy users are the only relevant target because they make up a large proportion of the market.
3 When the brand dominates the market and appeals to all segments of the market, thus making segmentation unnecessary.

Differentiated marketing

differentiated marketing
differences between market segments are recognised and two or more target markets are selected, each receiving a different marketing programme

Differentiated marketing occurs when differences between market segments are recognised and two or more target markets are selected, each receiving a different marketing programme. The Ford Motor Company is a very good example of an organisation that uses a differentiated target marketing strategy effectively. By developing a range of models, it is able to meet the needs of a wide range of targeted segments. Most large organisations have adopted the principles of differentiated marketing, even if the specific approaches they have adopted vary (see Chapter 11, on branding strategies). Even the Coca-Cola Company, as an organisation, has adopted a differentiated approach to its total business. Although Coke may be relatively undifferentiated, as an organisation it owns and markets a range of drinks brands to cater for different segments.

Exhibit 4.10   Targeting strategies

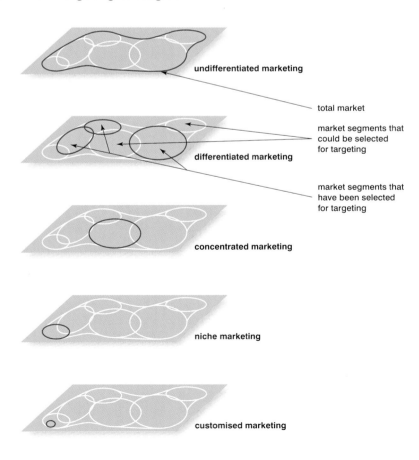

Concentrated marketing

Concentrated marketing uses the term 'concentrated' to describe this strategy because only one, single market segment is chosen for targeting – hence, there is a concentration of marketing effort. If the market is relatively small, well defined and very focused, the term **niche marketing** is used. In the car market, this might apply to Aston Martin and Morgan cars. At an even greater level of focusing, where individual customer preferences are important to the organisation, marketing effort may be defined entirely by the need to satisfy a single customer. Here, the term **customised marketing** may be used. In consumer markets, this may be for one-off products such as items hand-built to a customer's specification. Tailors will custom-make suits; architects will design and build new houses for clients. More frequently, this degree of targeting is found in B2B markets, especially for large-value orders. This might apply, say, to a custom-made factory, engineering project or the organising of a special event on behalf of a company.

Targeting strategies can therefore be seen as a continuum of strategies ranging from the very broad to the very narrow (see Exhibit 4.11).

concentrated marketing
where only one market segment is chosen for targeting

niche market
a market segment that can be treated as a target market; a small, well-defined market, often part of a larger market

customised marketing
producing one-off products/services to match a specific customer's requirements, e.g. a made-to-measure suit or the organisation of a product launch party

Exhibit 4.11   Continuum of targeting strategies

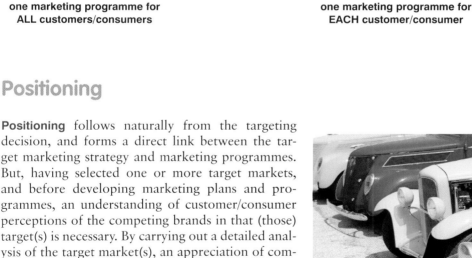

| undifferentiated marketing | differentiated marketing | concentrated marketing | niche marketing | customised marketing |

one marketing programme for ALL customers/consumers   **one marketing programme for EACH customer/consumer**

positioning
the place a brand holds in the minds of customers/users, usually in relation to competitors' brands, e.g. better value, more upmarket

Positioning

Positioning follows naturally from the targeting decision, and forms a direct link between the target marketing strategy and marketing programmes. But, having selected one or more target markets, and before developing marketing plans and programmes, an understanding of customer/consumer perceptions of the competing brands in that (those) target(s) is necessary. By carrying out a detailed analysis of the target market(s), an appreciation of competing offerings and where one's own brand might fit into the market can be developed, especially in the context of how customers/consumers think and feel about the brands. It is to do with their perceptions and preferences. This will typically be a consequence of their previous knowledge and experience of the brands themselves and the companies associated with those brands – thus a brand is frequently a function of perceptions held about both the company and its products. Apple, for example, creates close links between itself as a company and its **brands** (e.g. iPhone, iPod, iPad). Likewise, Cadbury's chocolate brands

Customisation in the car market

adopt a similar strategy. In contrast, some companies prefer to allow their brands to stand alone. Kiwi shoe polish is actually a brand of the Sara Lee company but very few people would realise this. Whiskas is a cat food, but few may recognise that it is made by Pedigree Petfoods, and fewer still may realise that this is a part of the Mars group, manufacturer of Mars bars (see Chapter 11 for more details about branding).

Positioning, then, is the place a brand is perceived to occupy in the minds of the target market relative to other competing brands. It has been referred to as a battle for the hearts and minds of customers/consumers. Any one company may have a range of brands that it markets. This is referred to as its **product (or brand) portfolio** (see Chapters 6 and 11). When referring to competing brands it is possible, therefore, to be referring not only to brands owned by other companies, but also brands owned by the same company. To avoid undesired cannibalisation of sales (i.e. where one brand steals sales from other brands owned by the same company), it is necessary to ensure that such competing brands are either offered to different markets or market segments (through differentiated targeting) or that they hold different positions within a given target market (through careful market positioning). Good examples to illustrate this point are the large soap powder manufacturers, Unilever/Lever Brothers and Procter & Gamble, and the major car companies which have a range of models to choose from and, moreover, through major efficiencies in manufacturing techniques, can offer customisation at the time of ordering a new vehicle.

Exhibit 4.12 shows how the VW/Audi Group (VAG), which makes the Skoda, Seat, Volkswagen and Audi brands, have differentiated these brand families through careful positioning so that they do not compete directly with each other. VAG refer to these as product platform developments. Although the brands in Exhibit 4.12 are compared with each other on the basis of price and cost-leadership/differentiation, the actual process of creating brand differentiation and distinctiveness (and, thereby,

product portfolio
all a company's or strategic business unit's products

Exhibit 4.12   VAG brand differentiation

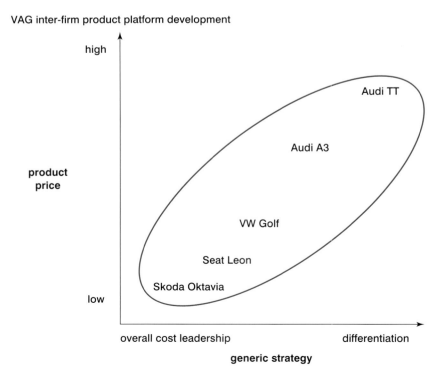

positioning the brand in the marketplace) involves many more marketing dimensions and heavy reliance on marketing communications to create specific brand identities and images. If you are familiar with the Skoda car, you may remember it as one of the cheapest cars available with a reputation for poor quality. This was before VAG acquired ownership of Skoda. Since then they have tried very hard to change the brand image of the Skoda models. They have worked hard to improve the car's design, quality and market acceptance. The result has been that Skoda is increasingly accepted as a significant brand that competes with many other mid-range vehicles. It will be interesting to see if this repositioning of the Skoda brand will result in it taking sales away from some of the other VAG brands in the future. It has certainly captured market share from competitors and has won industry awards in the process.

ACTIVITY

An activity earlier in this chapter suggested a visit to a supermarket to investigate different brands. Think about that activity now or carry out the activity again but this time specifically look for brands made by the same company. You might look at carbonated drinks such as Coke, Lilt and Fanta, for example. But there are many other product groups you could choose. Consider what each brand is trying to achieve, how it is positioned and whether the brands are likely to appeal to the same target customers. Consider what the manufacturing company is trying to do in marketing such similar brands and the extent to which the company could be competing against itself.

PERCEPTUAL MAPS

Rothschild (1987) highlights two particularly important techniques in ascertaining customer/consumer perceptions relative to competing bands. These are both represented visually as **perceptual maps**, which are also called brand maps, position maps or space maps. The first technique is **Multi-attribute Attitude Mapping (MAM)** and the second is **Multidimensional Scaling (MDS)**, both of which sound significantly more frightening than they really are. Both forms of analysis can be presented pictorially, which makes the comparison between brand perceptions very straightforward.

perceptual map
results from the perceptual mapping process and shows brands' relative positions (also called a brand map, position map or space map)

Multi-attribute Attitude Mapping (MAM)
a form of perceptual mapping comparing a product's key features (according to their importance to target customers) with features offered by competitive brands

Multidimensional Scaling (MDS)
a form of perceptual mapping that establishes similarities and differences between competing brands

EXPAND YOUR KNOWLEDGE

Smith, W.R. (1956) 'Product differentiation and market segmentation as alternative marketing strategies', *Journal of Marketing*, 21 (1): 3–8.

Wendell Smith recognises, in this paper, the limitations of economic theory to explain market behaviour due to the imperfections within the marketplace and economic theory's notions of perfect competition and pure monopoly. Product differentiation and market segmentation are offered as two, distinct, alternative marketing strategies which are appropriate in real-life economic/market conditions.

Multi-attribute Attitude Mapping (MAM)

MAM is achieved by, first, determining the key features or attributes of products in the group – for cars these might include fuel consumption, style, comfort, etc.

People are asked to assess competing **brands** against these attributes by indicating how important each attribute is (from high to low) and how each brand is rated for each attribute (from high to low). Scoring can be used in both cases. For example, a mark out of 10 might be given. In all cases, it is important to confine the analysis to the perceptions of the members of the **target market(s)**. Obtaining the views of the general market or general population would only serve to confuse the findings. The findings might then be presented as shown in Exhibit 4.13. The horizontal lines indicate how important each of the six identified attributes are perceived to be, and the relative position of brands A, B, C, D and E are shown against each of these attributes. Also shown is what is deemed to be the ideal position according to the respondents. This is identified as brand 'I'.

From this, comparisons can be made between competitor brands and also against the ideal position. Brand C, for example, is near the ideal position regarding price, while brand A is close to the ideal position regarding low running costs. None of the brands appears to be close to the ideal regarding style and comfort, although it may be argued that brand C greatly exceeds the expected ideal for performance.

Rothschild emphasises a further feature of the MAM approach. If it is recognised that, for any one purchase, a range of people may be involved (see Chapter 3 for more on the **decision-making unit** (DMU)), then different constituent members of the target market may hold different views about the importance of specific attributes because of their particular interests or perspectives. Under these circumstances, the views of the different DMU members can be isolated, rather than being aggregated into the total data, and a multi-attribute attitude map produced for each. He quotes an industrial market example to illustrate this:

> *The most important attributes for the engineer are related to the technical specifications of the product, while the purchasing agent is most concerned with price issues. In such a case the firm can develop a technical ad for engineers and deliver it in* Engineering Digest, *while developing a price/value ad for purchasing agents that can be delivered in* Purchasing Agents Weekly. *(Rothschild, 1987: 89)*

MAM is a useful tool in analysing and determining positioning in that it is easy to implement, it identifies which attributes are important to customers/consumers,

Exhibit 4.13   Possible Multi-attribute Attitude Map for a compact car

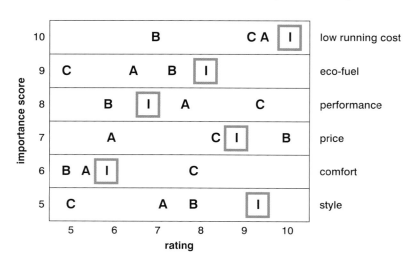

it identifies how competitors are perceived in relation to each other and to an ideal, and provides further insight into positioning strategies for different constituent customers/consumers within the target market. In the context of this latter point, understanding perceptions of product attributes can assist in highlighting benefit segments, which may then be specifically catered for by launching new products, changing marketing programmes and repositioning.

Multidimensional Scaling (MDS)

Multidimensional Scaling is a popular approach to visualising brand positions. It is easiest to illustrate this approach by considering an example. Eight competing brands of soap are compared by asking members of the target market to consider the brands in groups of three. This is known as **triadic comparisons** and is a technique that is used because it is easier for respondents to compare such groups rather than try to consider all the brands together in one go. The respondents simply have to say which two of the three are most similar or, in other words, which they feel is the odd one out. The respondents do not have to work out why they feel this, it is enough that they can choose. All combinations of three brands are assessed in this way and a picture is developed of how similar or dissimilar the brands are to each other. These relative positions are analysed by a computer multidimensional scaling programme, which takes into account all the responses and plots the aggregate positions on a chart. The resulting map, known as a **perceptual map**, **brand map** or **position map**, shows how close to or how far away the brands are from each other (hence the reason why these maps are sometimes referred to as **space maps**) (see Exhibit 4.13). A modified approach to this would be to use **dyadic comparisons**, in which the brands are compared in pairs and a judgement is made as to how similar each pair is by allocating a score. All combinations of pairs are considered and, again, a computer multidimensional scaling programme is used to plot the resulting map. The map at this stage would not have any axes. These are added by the researcher using judgement to guess what are the major underlying dimensions or attributes that account for the respondents' perceptions. In Exhibit 4.14, the differentiating attributes appear to be the deodorising and moisturising qualities of the soaps.

It is also possible to question respondents about their ideal product and plot the different responses to this as well. As might be anticipated, this does not result in a single ideal position but a range of positions according to the different preferences expressed. These preferences will tend to cluster into particular positions and are shown in Exhibit 4.14 by the circles. The larger the size of circle, the more people who have expressed that ideal preference.

For the purposes of this text, the actual mechanisms of how perceptual maps are constructed are not too important. What is important is to recognise that such maps are used and what they represent. By referring to the **positioning** of competing brands, the closeness of competition can be assessed, as can possible market opportunities, as represented both by ideal positions and by market gaps. The latter are represented by areas on a map left uncovered by any brand. Market opportunities can be filled by launching a new brand or by repositioning an existing brand. Repositioning can also be considered as an appropriate strategy where two brands appear to be too close together. (Repositioning is considered a little later in this chapter.)

A much simpler, if less accurate, way of developing a perceptual map is to pre-select the axes and ask respondents to place brands on the map where they think each competing brand should lie. This is often used as an approach when first trying to illustrate the development and use of such maps to marketing students, but it should be clearly understood that this is not a methodologically sound approach.

triadic comparisons technique used in perceptual mapping in which three products are compared to each other at a time

perceptual map results from the perceptual mapping process and shows brands' relative positions (also called a brand map, position map or space map)

dyadic comparisons technique used in perceptual mapping in which two products are compared to each other at a time

Exhibit 4.14   A possible perceptual map for soaps

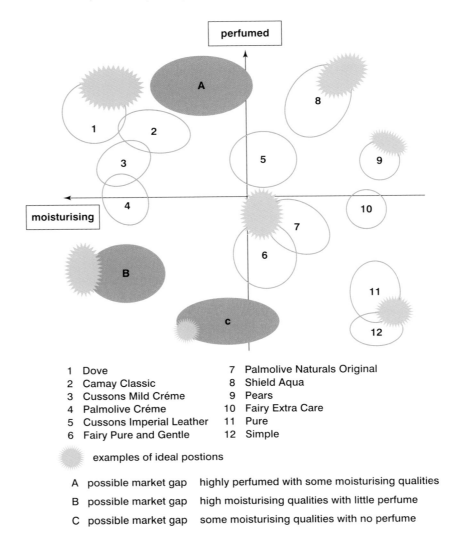

1 Dove	7 Palmolive Naturals Original
2 Camay Classic	8 Shield Aqua
3 Cussons Mild Créme	9 Pears
4 Palmolive Créme	10 Fairy Extra Care
5 Cussons Imperial Leather	11 Pure
6 Fairy Pure and Gentle	12 Simple

examples of ideal postions

A	possible market gap	highly perfumed with some moisturising qualities
B	possible market gap	high moisturising qualities with little perfume
C	possible market gap	some moisturising qualities with no perfume

It is only suitable for basic illustrative purposes to give an idea of what a perceptual map may look like.

EXPAND YOUR KNOWLEDGE

Johnson, R.M. (1971) 'Market segmentation: a strategic management tool', *Journal of Marketing Research*, Feb: 13–18.

This paper illustrates the use of market research in studying market segmentation and the construction of 'product spaces'.

POSITIONING STRATEGIES

A range of different strategies can be considered when positioning a brand against the competition. These strategies are largely to do with the way in which the brand is promoted through advertising and other marketing communications approaches (see Chapter 8), and are outlined below.

● *Positioning on attributes/product features.* A common way to position is to differentiate it from other brands by emphasising its distinctive product feature(s). Head & Shoulders shampoo eliminates dandruff.
● *Positioning by price/quality.* For some brands, high price or high quality is featured, others are promoted for their relatively low prices or adequate quality. Stella Artois beer has advertised itself as 'Reassuringly expensive'. Value for money is often emphasised, although this does not always clearly differentiate the brand well from other offerings. Wal-Mart's ASDA promotes 'ASDA price', Tesco promotes 'Every little helps'.
● *Positioning for specific usage occasions.* After Eight mints have consistently been promoted as an after-dinner chocolate.
● *Positioning on benefits or needs.* Bold washing powder is a powder and fabric conditioner in one. Some fabric conditioners reduce the need for ironing. Tesco also promotes itself as 'You shop, we drop' to highlight online ordering with home delivery.
● *Positioning by the product user.* Marlboro cigarettes, originally aimed at women, are now positioned towards men – and adverts specifically feature outdoor ruggedness.
● *Positioning against another brand or with respect to a competitor.* 'In tests, our washing powder washes whiter than . . .'.
● *Positioning with respect to another product class.* Rather than showing a direct comparison against another brand, the positioning can be against a product class. The 'I Can't Believe It's Not Butter' brand is a spread that clearly compares itself to butter.

REPOSITIONING

Repositioning is the marketing process of manoeuvring a brand from its current position to a new one in people's minds relative to competing brands. Repositioning arises out of a need to respond to competitor activity and/or changes in the marketplace. Such repositioning might involve relatively minor shifts in perception or moving into totally new segments.

insight   A truly great beer

There are risks associated with repositioning and, as a strategic approach, if the brand is already well established and strong, repositioning may be unwise and difficult to achieve. However, where it is triggered by falling sales or the anticipation of faltering performance, repositioning may be a necessity. Lowenbrau was a successful beer before attempts to reposition it caused it to falter. Originally positioned as 'a truly great German beer', it was exported out of Europe. When the brand was bought by the American company, Miller, from Philip Morris, the new owners decided that they would not be able to continue importing it quickly enough and started brewing it in the USA. The position was changed to 'a truly great American beer' but this was at odds with the beer's established perception. Production issues led to the change of position and Miller had to spend millions of dollars creating a new position after losing a truly great position.

ACTIVITY

Choose a number of different hotel chains (such as Holiday Inn, Travelodge, Best Western, Hilton, Sheraton, Holiday Inn Express, Hyatt) and consider how they each try to position themselves within the market. What are the marketing features that suggest their positions? Write a brief description of the market position of each and discuss your ideas with a colleague or friend.

McDonald's has been trying to reposition itself as a healthier fast food brand

Hellmann's mayonnaise found that sales were decreasing not just through competition with other mayonnaise brands but through competition with other dressings. The market for mayonnaise was being attacked and Hellmann's was losing out. Initially, changes to its promotional activities achieved a repositioning of its mayonnaise in relation to other dressings such as salad creams. Mayonnaise sales increased, but not only for Hellmann's – it had improved the market for its competitors, too. The company's next task was to position itself favourably compared with its mayonnaise brand rivals, and this it succeeded in doing.

Marlboro cigarettes were originally launched to appeal to women. They were repositioned, with their now familiar rugged brand image, to appeal to real men. The tobacco company introduced Virginia Slims as a more suitable brand for women smokers.

Johnson & Johnson's Baby Shampoo brand used to be specifically positioned for baby/infant use. To widen the market, the company successfully repositioned it as an adult, gentle, frequent-use shampoo. It achieved this without sacrificing its original position and now maintains two quite distinct positions within the market. This is not often achieved. So successful was this strategy that the company extended it to its other baby products and enjoys similar success for its Baby Oil and Baby Powder brands.

EXPAND YOUR KNOWLEDGE

Trout, J. and Ries, A. (1972) 'Positioning cuts through chaos in the marketplace', *Advertising Age*, May: 51–53.

Ries and Trout are early supporters of the need to ensure the correct positioning of brands in the marketplace to achieve competitive differentiation and advantage.

The five-stage process from market segmentation to positioning

By considering all the relevant points above, we can identify a step-by-step process by which companies can move from an early understanding of the total market through to finally determining their own brand positions. Dibb (2000) refers to this as the STP of market segmentation: segmentation, targeting and positioning. Exhibit 4.15 shows the full five-stage process.

From RAP to K3: repositioning on multiple levels – company, product and market

RAP was a successful Swedish-owned rubber and plastics supplier and manufacturer, selling its products to large DIY chains such as B&Q. Its repositioning transformation since 2000 has been miraculous. At corporate level, it has acquired new businesses and it is selling off others. It is completely moving out of its original business and into computing software. At this corporate level, the approach is best described as moving into different markets rather than repositioning. The company has bought out Kewill's enterprise software business, which itself started life in the form of computerised production and stock control systems, and is repositioning this as a total enterprise resource planning (ERP) business with the inclusion of customer relationship management (CRM) capabilities. It has fully updated the software from DOS to the more modern Windows operating environment. It has renamed the company K3.

This total repositioning has required both corporate and product changes, a move from one customer base to others, and from one competitive environment to another. The original RAP business has been sold off and the old Kewill business has been revamped with product and image updates under the newly named K3. Existing Kewill customers, who could have become disenfranchised with the company and product changes, have remained loyal (now to K3) and are responding well to new product developments. New customers are coming online. Kewill competitors are now experiencing stronger competition in their target markets under K3. Software products and services within the K3 range have been modified and repositioned as integrated systems solutions.

There is a logical progression from one stage to another. The total potential market is analysed and market segments are identified. Through an understanding of the market segments, the market attractiveness of each can be determined and one or more segments can be targeted. Further analysis can reveal an understanding of the perceptions of the potential customers and consumers in the target(s), and the relative positions of competing products (brands) can be assessed. The complete analysis can then be used as a foundation for selecting appropriate marketing strategies and tactics, leading to the implementation of specific marketing activities and actions.

insight   Coffee on the move

When starting out, branded coffee retail chains, such as Starbucks, Costa Coffee and Coffee Republic, focused their marketing efforts and resources on the gourmet coffee drinking segments of the coffee drinking market. As coffee drinking and the wish for better coffees have increased, the nature of the market has moved on, creating new opportunities and growth. These chains have become the new cafés. It is no longer the gourmet drinkers who frequent them. Tastes for quality coffee have spread throughout the market and the nature of the segments within the market have changed. Don't ever presume that segments and targets are fixed. Changes in consumer tastes and competitive activities can fundamentally affect otherwise stable market environments. It is interesting to see that these new coffee shops have moved into new retail positions, such as inside bookstores.

Exhibit 4.15 Stages in the market segmentation, targeting and positioning process

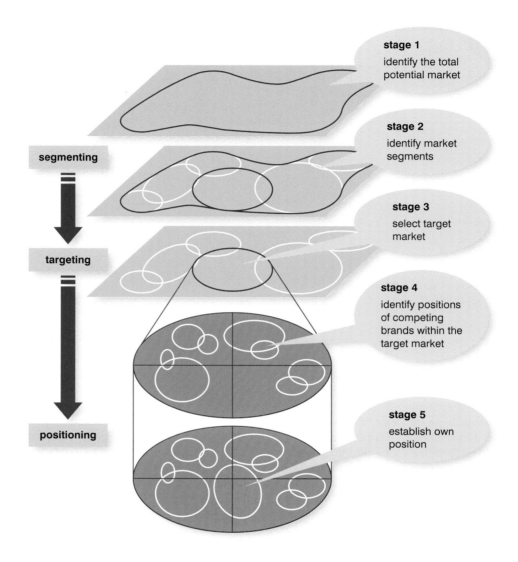

EXPAND YOUR KNOWLEDGE

Trout, J. and Ries, A. (1979) 'Positioning: ten years later', *Industrial Marketing*, July: 32–40.

This article is a retrospective on positioning, a concept the authors popularised 10 years earlier. Having looked backwards, they turn to face forwards to consider the changes they predict and what companies will need to do to succeed.

SUMMARY

Market selection is one of the most fundamental aspects of marketing. The choice will be affected by what market opportunities seem to be available matched against a company's objectives, its resources and an assessment of its general business environment, which can be undertaken through the use of PRESTCOM analysis.

Markets consist of customers and consumers, whether they are B2C or B2B markets, but no single company can fulfil the needs of all and so careful attention to defining customer and consumer requirements is vital. While individuals are different, people do share similarities in terms of some of their habits, lifestyles, preferences, where they are located or, in the case of B2B, what type of business they are in, etc. An understanding of these similarities can be used to divide a total market into subgroups that each consist of customers and consumers (buyers and users) who share similar characteristics that are different from those of the other subgroups. This process is called market segmentation.

There are many ways to segment markets and this chapter has briefly described the use of geographic, demographic, geo-demographic, psychographic, mediagraphic and behavioural segmentation in the case of consumer markets and macro- and microsegmentation approaches in the case of B2B markets. It is up to marketers to decide which of the segments are attractive enough to target. This is the process of targeting or target marketing.

In this chapter, a number of different targeting strategies have been described. These range from the general to the specific. They have been identified as undifferentiated marketing, differentiated marketing, concentrated marketing, niche marketing and customised marketing. A useful way to think of them is as a continuum from undifferentiated, where there is no targeting and the product is considered suitable for all, to totally customised, in which the product is provided on a totally individual basis.

Having identified one or more potential target markets, an understanding of customer/consumer perceptions of the competing brands in those target(s) is necessary so that the most appropriate marketing activities can be determined. This is the process of positioning and is achieved by, first, carrying out a detailed analysis of the target market(s) so that an appreciation of competing offerings and where one's own brand might fit into the market can be developed. Positioning is very much about understanding customer and consumer perceptions of the brands on offer. These can be plotted on a perceptual (brand) map. With an understanding of the brands competing in the target market(s), a range of positioning strategies is possible. Marketers should carry out a regular check on their brands' perceived positions as this provides an ongoing assessment of a brand's competitive position. If necessary, repositioning should be considered to reduce or eliminate head-on competition.

The chapter ends by summarising the total segmentation-to-positioning procedure as a five-stage process, which starts by identifying the total potential market and goes on to the identification of market segments, the selection of target market(s) and the identification of the positions of competing brands within the target market(s), and finishes by establishing one's own position within the target market(s).

CHALLENGES REVIEWED

Now that you have finished reading the chapter, look back at the challenges you were set at the beginning. Do you have a clearer idea of what's involved?

Hints:

- segmentation and targeting strategies
- differentiated or undifferentiated?
- perceptual mapping
- segmentation bases.

READING AROUND

Book chapter

David Pickton and Amanda Broderick (2004) *Integrated Marketing Communications*
(2nd edn). Harlow: FT/ Prentice Hall. Chapter 17, 'Identifying target audiences and
profiling target markets'.

Books

Sally Dibb and Lyndon Simkin (2007) *Market Segmentation Success: Making It Happen!*
New York: Haworth Press.
Siebel e-business White Paper (October 2003) *Customer Segmentation: A Core Tenet of
Customer Strategy*. Available at: www.siebel.com.

Journal articles

Benson P. Shapiro and Thomas V. Bonoma (1984) 'How to segment industrial markets',
Harvard Business Review (May–June): 104–10. (This is a dated article but is one of the
classics.)

Websites

www.caci.co.uk – for information on ACORN.
www.experian.co.uk – for information on MOSAIC.
www.strategicbusinessinsights.com/vals – for information on VALS lifestyle segmentation.
www.upmystreet.com – to check out neighbourhood types based on ACORN categories.

SELF-REVIEW QUESTIONS

1. Broadly speaking, it is suggested that marketers should address three areas of concern
   when assessing market attractiveness. What are they? (see page 120)
2. What is the difference between market segmentation and target marketing? (see page 123)
3. What are the main criteria for assessing how good a market segment might be? (see
   page 123–4)
4. What are the main bases that can be used for segmenting consumer markets? (see
   Exhibit 4.1, page 126)
5. What is social grading and how is it measured? Is it the same as social class? (see
   page 127)
6. What is geo-demographic segmentation? (see page 129)
7. Why are lifestyles useful for segmentation purposes? Identify an example of lifestyle
   segmentation. (see page 131)
8. Why is behavioural segmentation a useful approach for marketers? Identify some
   examples of behavioural segmentation variables. (see pages 132–3)
9. What are the main bases that can be used for segmenting business markets? (see
   Exhibit 4.1, page 126)
10. Why should macrovariables be used before analysing microvariables in business
    markets? (see page 139)
11. What is the difference between targeting and positioning? (see page 147)
12. What is the difference between mass marketing and niche marketing? (see pages
    144–6)
13. Under what conditions is mass marketing an appropriate marketing strategy? (see page
    145)
14. What is the five-stage process from market segmentation to positioning? (see page
    154–5)

mini case study

Auto-Tecnic GmbH

Read the questions, then the case material, and then answer the questions.

This is a short case but it is really quite sophisticated and deceptively insightful. It invites you to question the nature of products by taking the perspective of the benefits that products offer, not just their features. This opens up many market segmentation considerations and very many market opportunities for the company. It encourages you to develop a marketing manager mindset and use a number of basic foundations of marketing thought.

Questions

1. What really is this product? Hint: Marketing has to do with matching product offerings with customer/consumer demands. Review the benefits that Peter's product provides. Do not be happy with Peter's view that this is only a garage door opening device. Reappraise his definition of the product and identify as many possible uses for the product as you can (a garage door-opening device is just one possibility, and some uses may be in industrial and commercial situations).
2. For each use you have identified, what segmentation variables would you use to segment the market?
3. Consider Auto-Tecnic's situation and resources. What target market or target markets would you advise the company to focus on?

Auto-Tecnic is a small German company founded and run by a clever electronics engineer, Peter Schnider. He has built his successful, though small, business over the past five years by undertaking subcontract work for large electronics companies. The work has mainly involved producing small control devices (automatic switches, timers, etc.) in response to his business customers' requests. Peter's expertise is valued by the organisations with which he has dealt. Having returned from trips outside Germany, Peter noticed an increase in the number of homes making use of automatic garage doors. Drivers would either press a button on a device kept in the car, which activated a switch in a door-opening mechanism fitted to the garage door, or a device would be fixed in the car that automatically triggered a sensor as the car approached, which then operated the garage door-opening mechanism.

With his electronics expertise, Peter designed a better electronic system than the ones he had seen on his trips. His system contains extra security features that ensure constantly changing but synchronised coding between the transmitter (fixed in the car) and the receiver (fixed on the garage door). In other words, other people should not be able to activate the opening switch. In Peter's system, the garage door would automatically open as the car approached the receiving sensor. Peter has arranged for his system to be patented.

Peter recognises his limited understanding of marketing; his skills lie in technical electronic product development. He is convinced, however, that his new product idea will be profitable. As a first stage, he has asked you, as marketing consultant, to advise him how to define his market – just who would be interested in buying and using his product? He realises that, as with any product, his system is unlikely to have universal appeal.

REFERENCES

Anon (2007) 'Nectar case study', *Marketing*, 13 June: 35.

Crittenden, V.L., Crittenden, W.F. and Muzyka, D.F. (2002) 'Segmenting the business-to-business marketplace by product attributes and the decision process', *Journal of Strategic Marketing*, 10 (1): 3–20.

Dibb, S. (2000) 'Market segmentation', in K. Blois (ed.), *The Oxford Textbook of Marketing*. Oxford: Oxford University Press.

Dibb, S. and Simkin, L. (1996) *The Market Segmentation Workbook: Target Marketing for Managers*. London: Routledge.

Dibb, S. and Wensley, R. (2002) 'Segmentation analysis for industrial markets: problems of integrating customer requirements into operations strategy', *European Journal of Marketing*, 36 (1/2): 231–51.

Duncan, T. (2002) *IMC: Using Advertising and Promotion to Build Brands*. New York: McGraw-Hill Irwin.

Haley, R.I. (1968) 'Benefit segmentation: a decision-oriented research tool', *Journal of Marketing*, 32 (Jul): 30–35.

Jellyellie (2007) *How Teenagers Think*. White Ladder Press.

Johnson, R.M. (1971) 'Market segmentation: a strategic management tool', *Journal of Marketing Research*, Feb: 13–18.

Lindgren Jr, J.H. and Shimp, T.A. (1996) *Marketing: An Interactive Learning System*. Fort Worth, TX: The Dryden Press.

Louden, D.L. and Della Bitta, A.J. (1993) *Consumer Behavior* (4th edn). New York: McGraw-Hill.

Pickton, D.W. and Broderick, A. (2004) *Integrated Marketing Communications* (2nd edn). Harlow: FT/Prentice Hall.

Rothschild, M.L. (1987) *Marketing Communications*. New York: DC Heath.

Shapiro, B.P. and Bonoma, T.V. (1984) 'How to segment industrial markets', *Harvard Business Review*, May–June: 104–10.

Smith, W.R. (1956) 'Product differentiation and market segmentation as alternative marketing strategies', *Journal of Marketing*, 21 (1): 3–8.

Trout, J. and Ries, A. (1972) 'Positioning cuts through chaos in the marketplace', *Advertising Age*, May: 51–53.

Trout, J. and Ries, A. (1979) 'Positioning: ten years later', *Industrial Marketing*, July: 32–40.

5

Marketing research

CHAPTER CONTENTS

Introduction
The use and value of marketing
  research
The marketing research process
Ethics in marketing research
Areas of marketing research
Secondary (desk) research
Commercially available research
Primary (field) research
Primary research methods and
  techniques
Sampling
Questionnaire design
Quality of marketing information
Forecasting and trend spotting
Summary
Challenges reviewed
Reading around
Self-review questions
Mini case study
References

MARKETING RESEARCH CHALLENGES

The following are illustrations of the types of decision that marketers have to take or issues they face. *You aren't expected to know how to deal with the challenges now*; just bear them in mind as you read the chapter and see what you can find that helps.

- You run a travel agency. You have found a fabulous hotel in the Swiss Alps that you have never used before. However, the hotel wants to know how many rooms to reserve for you next season. What information do you need to work this out, and how will you collect it?

- Your company's skateboard sales have been falling steadily over the last two years. How would you make a case to a sceptical managing director that the expense of research into the causes of the fall would be worthwhile?

- The editor of a Lad's Mag, a monthly magazine read by men and women (e.g. the men's wives and girlfriends), has invited you to research the attitudes of readers to its contents. How would you do this?

- Your company is hoping to launch a new beer and wants to find out what would be popular across Europe. This is difficult because different European countries traditionally drink different types of beer. However, recently you have seen an Italian drinking British beer, a British man drinking French beer and a Swede drinking German beer. You need to get views from a huge number of beer drinkers to be sure you get the complete picture. It is not practical to interview every beer drinker in Europe. What could you do?

Introduction

If any plan is to be successful, it must be based on good intelligence. If you want to change something, first you must understand the true nature of the thing that you want to change. To understand a marketing situation, and its future possibilities, you must have good information about it, i.e. you have to conduct market research.

The environmental analysis discussed in Chapter 2 (the marketing environment) is only possible if there is sufficient data available. The segmentation processes described in Chapter 4 are totally dependent upon sound market intelligence. How can a company design products, develop advertising campaigns, set prices, choose outlets, encourage customer loyalty or build its brands without information about its customers, its competitors and the worlds they inhabit?

This chapter will outline the research process, list typical areas for marketing research and then examine the techniques used by researchers to gather data. Much of this data is personal, some of it is sensitive and so market researchers have to be careful of their research subjects' wishes, rights and potential reactions. Market researchers should be honest, open and, above all, ethical in their dealings with research subjects. Finally, the chapter briefly considers one of the main purposes of all this research and analysis: forecasting marketing trends.

ACTIVITY

Reflecting on previous chapters, write a list of all the things you might need to research in the following situations:

* starting up a small, top-quality ice cream business and hoping to sell to local businesses (shops, restaurants, etc.)
* a top brand of perfume is losing market share
* a firm of accountants is considering setting up a new office in a different town

If you can, compare lists with someone else. Why do you want to know these things?

DEFINITIONS

Marketing research covers a broad range of activities including *market* research, which is a term frequently used interchangeably with *marketing* research, although there are distinctions that can be made between them. (See the Insight box for details.) The breadth of marketing research is illustrated by the following definitions and descriptions. The AMA's (American Marketing Association) view of marketing research is that it is an objective and systematic process centred on the customer. The research process, by collecting, recording and analysing data, results in the identification and refinement of information about customers that is important for marketing decisions:

> *Marketing research is the function that links the consumer, customer, and public to the marketer through information – information used to identify and define marketing opportunities and problems; generate, refine, and evaluate marketing actions; monitor marketing performance; and improve understanding of marketing as a process. Marketing research specifies the information required to address these issues, designs the method for collecting information, manages and implements the data collection process, analyzes the results, and communicates the findings and their implications. (American Marketing Association, 2004)*

The Market Research Society (MRS), in a UK definition, embraces all types of data gathering and investigations for market and social research:

Market research or marketing research?

What is the difference between market research and marketing research?

The phrase 'market research' is a familiar one. It has connotations of people with clipboards stopping others on the street and asking questions. Market research is usually about solving marketing problems, e.g. finding out the existing and future product needs of customers. How do people use certain products and services? When they do, what are their attitudes and preferences? What are their backgrounds and lifestyle characteristics? For example, a footwear brand manufacturer might want to find out what are the most popular types of shoe and what colours people want. The company might also want to know if its type of trainers is still considered to be fashionable streetwear. They may want to know customer media habits, that is what papers and magazines they read, what films they watch, what their favourite TV programmes are and so on.

'Marketing research' has evolved to cover the activities of market research. It is a broad term that covers the whole body of theories and processes of research that are carried out by governments, public corporations, private-sector companies and individuals concerning what works, or does not work, with industries, organisations and customers in markets. It involves deeper understanding of buying and usage processes, competitive behaviour, demographic profiles, technological developments, social change. Marketers want information to help them refine the whole of the marketing mix. With reference to the example of a footwear brand manufacturer, marketing research into the marketing mix will cover: competitors' prices; locations of shoe shops; which types of shoe the shops specialise in; what their footfall (number of passing customers) is; how memorable the manufacturer's latest advertising campaign is; and how much a teenage customer is prepared to pay for a pair of high-fashion shoes.

Market research can be viewed as a subset of marketing research and this chapter, which is about the broader spectrum of activities, is therefore called 'Marketing research'.

Research is the collection and analysis of data from a sample of individuals or organisations relating to their characteristics, behaviour, attitudes, opinions or possessions ... such as consumer and industrial surveys, psychological investigations, observational and panel studies. (Market Research Society, n.d.)

The use and value of marketing research

Marketing research is a planned activity. It is carried out methodically so that the results can be supported by evidence that can be validated by others. This is crucial because of the need to maintain trust and confidence between the clients (buyers of research) and agencies (providers of research studies). Marketing research provides vital information for key marketing decisions, e.g. which products should be developed, how they should be packaged, what price should be charged, how they should be distributed, who they should be aimed at, what benefits and features those customers would want and how the products should be promoted. In order to make these decisions, marketing managers need to know (among other things): what competitors currently offer, what their reactions might be to these new products, what would make customers buy these products in preference to those of their competitors and how retailers will respond (e.g. will they be prepared to stock the new products?) Without marketing research it would be very difficult to make such decisions. Marketing research is so important to good marketing that organisations spend billions on it each year (see Exhibit 5.1).

Exhibit 5.1   Market research expenditure (in millions of US dollars, 2008)

Top six largest markets (2008)	Value (in millions US$)	Market share	Growth rate (adjusted for inflation)
Europe	16,066	49%	0.9%
North America	9,629	30%	−2.1 %
Asia Pacific	4,538	14%	2.1%
Latin America	1,700	5%	5.6%
Middle East and Africa	529	2%	1.1%
WORLD	32,000	100%	0.4%

SOURCE: ESOMAR, 2006

The marketing research process

Marketing research is a continuous process of information gathering and analysis into which ad hoc marketing research activities may also be fitted as and when management problems arise. Exhibit 5.2 shows the stages involved in the marketing research process.

Exhibit 5.2   The marketing research process

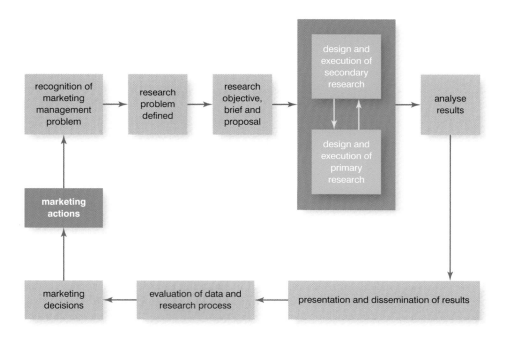

1. Recognise the marketing management problem

The starting point for the research process is the recognition of a marketing problem. Perhaps there has been a loss of sales or market share? It could be that there are problems with distribution or that customers are choosing to shop elsewhere.

2. Define the research problem

Once the marketing management problem has been recognised and understood, it needs to be restated as a research problem. This may require some background information. For example, a local authority may be concerned that few people shop locally, preferring large, out-of-town superstores and malls. Neighbourhoods are becoming rundown as shops close. The research problem, at its broadest, is to find out why customers shop outside their local community. More specifically, the research will investigate: who tends to shop outside, what local shopping is available, customer attitudes to the local facilities, what might make people change their shopping habits, and what are the costs and benefits involved from the points of views of the shoppers, the local shop owners, the supermarket owners and developers, etc. These are research questions to be answered.

3. Set research objectives, write research brief

The next step is to set research objectives. These provide a clearly defined direction for the research activity. From the objectives, basic decisions can be made as to the form the research will take, including the use of both secondary and primary research (see below). Management will need to think through the resources required and set a suitable budget. There is a trade-off to be made here between cost and certainty. The more information managers have, the better the decisions they can make, but costs rise as the research goes on and on, and so a reasonable budget must be set.

Organisations do not always undertake their own research. Frequently, they employ research agencies to carry out some or all of the research tasks. These agencies will need to be thoroughly briefed on what is required. The agency then expands the brief into a complete research proposal, i.e. a document that details exactly what they propose to do. An agreed proposal makes it much less likely that misunderstandings will arise in the future and also encourages the agency to take more responsibility for the research.

4. Carry out research (design and execution)

Secondary research (also known as **desk research**) should always be considered *before* **primary research** (also known as **field research**) is undertaken. If the right information already exists, then it may be possible to answer a number of the research questions and address the research problem through secondary research alone. This would make primary research unnecessary, saving time and money.

There are many sources of secondary information and the Internet has made them easier to find and to use. There are also many primary research methods, the most commonly used being surveys (see below for primary and secondary research).

5. Analyse data

As the data from the research is gathered, it is collated and analysed. The type of analysis will depend on the nature of the data and the information and answers required. Analysis, especially qualitative analysis, can be very subjective. However, it is important for analysts to be as objective as possible. Quantitative analysis claims greater objectivity thanks to the mathematical techniques it employs, but even this is dependent upon the skills of, and the decisions made by, researchers and analysts.

One way of looking at analysis is to think of it as a sense-making process. Analysis is the means by which raw data (e.g. the number of people who shop out of town on a Tuesday) is converted into valuable information (e.g. which are the most popular shopping days and why) that can be used for marketing decisions.

secondary research (desk research)
the search for good-quality data that has been validated and is now published for use by others

field research (primary research)
carried out specifically for the research task in question

6. Present and disseminate results

There is little value in researchers keeping their findings to themselves. After the sense-making process of analysis, the results need to be shared and made available to all staff who could benefit. Some of the results may be considered confidential and so restricted access is needed. However, the more usual problem is to ensure findings are distributed widely, are well understood and acted upon. Researchers are expected to comment on the quality of the findings (in terms of confirming their accuracy, validity and reliability (see below)) and make appropriate recommendations related to the findings to management.

7. Evaluate data and research process

Evaluation should not be limited to the results themselves but should extend to the whole research process. Has the research brief been fulfilled? Has this been done within budget? On time? Have the results shed light on the management problem? Could it have been done better?

8. Make marketing decisions and carry them out

The purpose of research is to make well-informed decisions and to improve marketing actions, e.g. raise prices or develop a new product. These changes will elicit a response from the market which may then form the basis of a new marketing research cycle.

EXPAND YOUR KNOWLEDGE

Brien, R.H. and James, E.S. (1968) 'Marketing information systems: a new dimension for marketing research', *Journal of Marketing*, 32 (Jul): 19–23.

An article that emphasises the need to view marketing research as an integrated system rather than ad hoc research projects.

Ethics in marketing research

Ethical practice is important in good marketing research. Professional body codes of conduct have, over the more recent years, been strengthened by changes in laws and regulations covering data protection and freedom of information. Codes of behaviour for researchers are about honesty and are mostly common sense. They should be observed by anybody involved in designing and conducting research. They cover disclosing whenever research is being undertaken and being truthful about its purpose. Marketing research has been practised by unscrupulous practitioners in the past and continues to carry the stigma created by unethical salespeople claiming to be carrying out research as a selling tactic. When approaching potential respondents, you should clearly identify who you are, that you are carrying out research, and the broad purpose for which the research is being conducted. Confidentiality should be assured or, if it is not, permission of the respondent should be confirmed. Similar ethical considerations should be borne in mind when recording, analysing and reporting research findings. The storage of data will be affected by legal controls.

A full version of the Market Research Society Code of Conduct can be found on their website (www.mrs.org.uk) and other professional bodies related to marketing research in other countries will also have their own versions of the codes.

Areas of marketing research

Marketing research can be grouped according to the focus of the research. This is not the only way in which research can be classified but it is one of the most straight-forward approaches.

- marketing environment research
- competitor research
- product research
- customer and consumer research
- pricing research
- advertising and promotions research
- sales and distribution research
- business-to-business (B2B) research.

MARKETING ENVIRONMENT RESEARCH

It is important for organisations to understand the wider environment in which they are operating. Research in this area is of a broader, more general nature. An understanding of the macro environment allows an organisation to complete the 'PREST' part of its **PRESTCOM** analysis. (See Chapter 2 for more on the marketing environment and PRESTCOM.)

COMPETITOR RESEARCH

It is clearly important for an organisation to know as much as it reasonably can about who its competitors are and what they are doing. This includes not only past and current activities, but also indications of their future plans.

unique selling proposition (USP)
a clear point of differentiation for a product/service

ACTIVITY

The cola blind taste test is perhaps one of the most famous pieces of commercial research ever, although it was used mainly as advertising for Pepsi Cola. Pepsi claimed that in blind taste tests the majority of people preferred the taste of Pepsi. Yet they still buy more Coca-Cola. Why do you think that is?

PRODUCT RESEARCH

Much of product research is about testing the design concept, performance, ease of use, reliability, special features, appearance and packaging of products. Research about brand superiority, in terms of qualities, higher prices and snobbery/image appeal to create distinctive brands and **unique selling propositions (USPs)** with customers and consumers, is also important. Customers and consumers develop strong brand loyalties to products and their manufacturers' trading names. There are many examples of products we use daily that have been tested with customers by marketing researchers. Customers are asked about their preferences concerning design features of products,

Try this at home.
Can you tell the difference? Are you surprised by which tastes best?

consumer durables
products for use by individuals that can be expected to last for some time, e.g. a washing machine

FMCG
(fast-moving consumer goods) low-value items that are bought regularly (the shelves empty quickly), e.g. toothpaste

pre-testing
evaluating the effectiveness of an aspect of marketing with its target audience *before* release

post-testing
evaluating the effectiveness of an aspect of marketing with its target audience *after* release

e.g. **consumer durables** such as cars and **FMCG** products such as toothpaste and soap. Products, or parts of products, can be evaluated through **pre-testing** and **post-testing**. New product development is an important part of marketing and marketing research has a key role to play in each of the stages of development (see Chapter 6), whether this be research into new technologies, competitor products, screening, concept testing, market potential analysis, market segments, consumer preferences, etc. Marketing research has helped new industries such as mobile phones, flat-screen monitors and games machines to expand. However, food and drinks products consistently top the list as the most researched categories.

Research is not confined to physical, manufactured goods but also extends into the service industries (see Chapter 7). These industries (e.g. financial services, travel, tourism and leisure, media, public services and utilities) have generated considerable work for marketing researchers. Marketing research has helped insurance companies and banks such as EGG (banking and insurance) and First Direct (banking) to provide new services and products online and offline (by telephone and mail). In the travel sector, low-cost flights have tempted many holidaymakers from traditional large carriers to the new, lower-cost operating airlines such as easyJet, Ryanair and BMI Baby. Customers are regularly asked for their opinions on a range of services from beauty care and therapy to second-hand book sales.

ACTIVITY

Log on to www.amazon.co.uk (or your local Amazon site) and pick a book to buy. Find one where Amazon offers you an alternative through Marketplace. Click through. Look at the seller ratings. What purpose do they serve? How are they arrived at? (Note: there is no need to buy anything to view these ratings. As long as you do not enter a credit card number you will not be charged.)

insight   Visit Scotland

Tourism agency, VisitScotland, used qualitative market research to optimise a pan-European marketing campaign. It needed to know what consumers would respond to and whether different approaches would be required for Germany, France and Spain. Research agency, Nunwood, set up two workshops in each country, for walkers, tourers and city breakers (based on previous research which identified these segments). Discussions centred on possible objections to Scotland as a holiday destination, such as lack of awareness of what it could offer. Responses to images of Scotland were used to elicit views. A key insight was that consumers' interests were similar in all three countries. This justified a single pan-European campaign.

A second round of research was carried out to evaluate different creative executions. Print ads and inserts were released across Europe. Return on investment increased compared to earlier campaigns. Brochure requests increased by 68 per cent in Germany and 126 per cent in France. There were an extra 180,000 hits on the French and German websites. Such was the success of the project that it won the award for Outstanding Research at the Marketing Research Society Annual Awards.

SOURCE: McLuhan, 2006

CUSTOMER AND CONSUMER RESEARCH

Customer and consumer research is central to understanding what determines customer buying behaviour, customers' decision-making processes and how consumers use products (goods and services). Why do some customers buy and others don't? Why do some choose certain suppliers and others remain loyal to one supplier? Analysing customer behaviour, purchase intentions and product use has led to a large and valuable body of knowledge that also includes greater understanding of customer attitudes, preferences and repurchasing patterns.

Over the past decade or so there has been an explosion of customer data collection activities fuelled through the growth and availability of facilitating technologies. Modern computing power, in terms of storage and analysis of data, has meant that companies can easily capture data on all customer transactions: what is bought, by whom, how frequently, by what means and where are questions that can be answered with little difficulty provided that the company has set up the appropriate database. Tesco, for example, has gained a reputation for using customer transaction data to segment their customers and provide highly targeted offers based on their buying and usage behaviour.

EXPAND YOUR KNOWLEDGE

Dichter, E. (1947) 'Psychology in marketing research', *Harvard Business Review*, 25 (Summer): 432–443.

An early extension to the scope of marketing research and its methodology includes lessons learned from the discipline of psychology to help understand customer and consumer motivations.

PRICING RESEARCH

Sales of some product types, such as most grocery products, are highly sensitive to price movements and so pricing research is important to many firms. Research tests customers' reactions to price changes, in-store discounts, price promotions, seasonal prices, and differences in expected price bands for different sizes, packaging and quantities. Even prestige, branded products, such as Gucci and Calvin Klein, are susceptible to price competition when there are reasonably priced quality **substitutes** available. Demand can be elastic when there is choice, as there is with many household cleaning products (see Chapter 10 for an explanation of **elasticity**). For many products, the manipulation of prices can be risky as a result of the competitive forces in play, so pricing research is done to establish just how much customers would be prepared to pay.

substitutes
other products that might be bought as alternatives; they satisfy the same or similar needs

elasticity
a significant response to changes in a marketing variable, most commonly price; quantity demanded changes by a greater percentage than the percentage change in price (i.e. if the price rises, the revenue falls)

ADVERTISING AND PROMOTION RESEARCH

Advertising and promoting big brands such as Nike and Reebok is very expensive. Marketing research helps to reduce the risks and costs involved. Marketing

Reaping the rewards

e-focus

The Nectar scheme, initially used by a consortium of large UK companies, including Sainsburys, Debenhams and Barclaycard, was launched in 2002 with a campaign budget in excess of £40 million (approximately €60 million) (Sainsbury's, 2002). About half the households in the UK have a Nectar card, using the points collected to claim money off purchases or special treats like a day at a theme park. However, Barclaycard and Debenhams have now dropped out of the scheme.

The information gained from Nectar application forms and computer records of individual purchases builds to a detailed profile of each Nectar card holder. The data is stored in a huge central database so that a variety of queries can be made and reports run off. For example, the information held will reveal whether you have pets and what kind they are – even whether your dog is large or small. From the amount of toilet roll bought, the computer can calculate how many people there are in a household. Purchases reveal whether there are any children and approximately how old they are. A suitably written database query can even work out when you are going on holiday.

Knowing their customers profiles enables the stores to stock the kinds of products that will appeal to those customers. For example, if a lot of large families shop there, it makes sense to stock family and economy sizes. If there are a lot of young professionals, then upmarket ready meals may sell well. This profile information also allows the companies involved to target their communications better, e.g. by not sending special offers on meat to someone who appears to be vegetarian. There are some consumer concerns though. Just how comfortable are you with a firm knowing so much? Just think how this data could be misused if it was in the hands of less reputable organisations.

---

market segments
distinct parts of a larger marker – customers and consumers in each segment share similar characteristics

research about customers and consumers not only uncovers their desires and needs, it also provides valuable databases of customers' details, which companies such as Kaleidoscope and Sears use to target their mail-order offerings. Crucial marketing decisions will concern which **market segments** (see Chapter 4) they wish to reach and how best to appeal to them. Research in this area includes **pre- and post-testing** of communications, **tracking** studies, media planning research, readership/viewership/listenership **surveys**, exhibition and **sponsorship** evaluation, direct marketing communications research, including the use of e-communications, among other considerations.

SALES AND DISTRIBUTION RESEARCH

supply chain
network of businesses and organisations through which goods pass to get to their final destination

There may be many intermediaries in a **supply chain** (e.g. in the food chain, from farm to fork). Sales and distribution research can discover where companies could improve their selling functions or increase the selling effectiveness of their distribution outlets, perhaps by helping distributors with promotions or providing training in the use of products. Sales and distribution research can be carried out by manufacturing companies and producers into their use of intermediaries (warehouse operators, **wholesalers**, insurance and financial brokers and agencies, retail store outlets) to find out how to get the best service for customers. Even small rural businesses, selling what they produce directly to customers, need to know how competitive their markets are and where they can make the most impact. In short, many firms require information to assist them with decisions such as: the kinds of outlets to sell through; which territories to sell in; what field supervision and training are required; and what sales information to provide. For retailers, research about sales and **distribution** is crucial to help with management decisions about siting new stores, in-store layouts, car parking, stock quantities, deliveries, etc. As with all these categories of research, it is common for companies to appoint research agencies to investigate their selling activities and the effectiveness of sales outlets and distribution networks. Some research companies undertake research like this under their own initiative and sell their findings to interested companies. Retail audits of the type produced by AC Nielsen would be examples of this.

distribution
the processes involved in moving goods from the supplier to the customer or user

BUSINESS-TO-BUSINESS RESEARCH

In business markets, goods and services are bought either for use and consumption or for resale in the commercial, industrial and/or **public sector**. This is a vast area because it involves all organisations that buy and sell from each other, from one-person companies to huge **multinationals** and government corporations. Business-to-business (B2B) research involves not only commercial and industrial research, but also government institutions such as local authorities and hospitals, which are large buyers and users of goods and services. Former public utilities that were privatised, e.g. the gas and electricity companies, frequently conduct B2B research with their industrial and commercial customers. Business-to-business research has continued to grow as these sectors have expanded.

public sector
government-owned organisations

multinationals
corporations with subsidiaries in multiple countries

Secondary (desk) research

Desk research is the search for good-quality **secondary data** that have been validated and are now published for use by others. Such information is freely accessible in libraries or can be purchased from the publishers. Researchers have to be careful in acknowledging the sources used and in gaining permission from the publishers of such sources if any data are to be reproduced in their marketing research reports. The terms 'desk research' and 'secondary research' have become interchangeable so, for the purposes of this chapter, the term 'secondary research' will be used to embrace 'desk research' as well.

secondary data
data previously collected for other purposes that can be used in the current research task

Information about past events, and the dates they occurred, can be helpful in establishing the background of significant product and market developments. Desk research is important in establishing what has already been achieved so that researchers can build on information already known. There is no need to reinvent the wheel. Researchers can also use this information to help forecast future patterns or trends (assuming past and current assumptions hold). Secondary data usage has expanded as there is more and more information added year after year and as the Internet makes access to data more easily and widely available.

Secondary or desk research is the search for published data that are available and pertinent to the research problem at hand. The starting point is usually the 'internal data' and records of market and customer information held by an organisation.

Drowning in data

There's a story popular with marketing folk, that when Tesco first introduced its now familiar Club-card, it produced so much more data than envis-aged, it just didn't know what to do with it. This may, of course, not really be true of Tesco, but it has surely happened somewhere to some unsuspecting but enthusiastic loyalty schemer.

Over 70 per cent of Tesco's customers now have a Clubcard. Every time they use it they provide Tesco with a breakdown of their shopping – and not just Tesco shopping – the card is taken at a number of outlets, including the optician, Dollond & Aitchinson. The more recently launched Nectar card is taken by an even wider range of retailers and so builds an even more complete picture. Combine this data with the demographic information supplied on the card appli-cation form, and you can build a detailed profile of shoppers.

The possibilities are enormous. A well-managed loy-alty scheme can help a company do so much more than just promote repeat sales (important though that is). Armed with that kind of information, firms can man-age the way they interact with their customers and so increase customer satisfaction and long-term profita-bility. For example, if Tesco has a regular customer who has the right profile for Internet shopping but who does not do it, it might want to find out why. If it can fix the issue, then it can encourage them into a better shop-ping pattern and, as it is unlikely that this issue is unique, it will probably pick up other new online shoppers too.

They know us so well.

---

marketing environment
the forces and organisations that impact on an organisation's marketing activities

When there is a lack of specific data for a new market, or new types of customer, or where we need to understand the reasons for changes in the **marketing environ-ment**, researchers will then look for alternative data sources that are external to the organisations they work for.

'External data' collection of secondary information involves examining books and printed materials in libraries, conducting searches by computer through data-bases created by other organisations (e.g. large publishers, companies, government institutions and international bodies) or buying information already collected about markets, products and customers from firms such as Mintel and the British Market Research Bureau. There is a wealth of information that can be accessed free or at least quite cheaply. For instance, anyone can carry out secondary or desk research for the names of firms in specific industries using directories such as those produced by Kompass or Dun & Bradstreet. They can access World Bank and UNESCO statistics concerning wealth distribution figures in terms of per capita income levels.

Secondary data collection has its attractions:

- it is non-reactive – i.e. it can be carried out without alerting any organisation or business
- it is unobtrusive because it only seeks out what is already available
- the issue of confidentiality in the use of materials is not usually a problem (so long as copyright permission has been obtained)

- accountability is rarely a problem because such published data have been vetted by previous research and reviewers, so the data collected can be used to back up one's own opinions and statements about what is known about the research problem at hand
- it is an economical method whose costs (e.g. travel and access) are usually known very quickly
- it is a speedy research method, finding existing information, so that only what is not available is uncovered by the more expensive form of field research.

Exhibit 5.3 gives an account of the types of data collection from internal and external sources for secondary and primary research. The provision of information from secondary (desk) research and primary (field) research underpins the activities of marketing research.

However, there are limitations to secondary data collection. Such data have been compiled both within and outside organisations for their own purposes. So the data collected are relevant to those organisations and might not be applicable to independent studies currently being conducted by others. The secondary data might also be out of date, depending on how many years ago they were collected. Therefore, the limitations of secondary research to find data that are relevant, up to date and easily available makes the choice of field research an appropriate one. The terms 'field research' and 'primary research' are now used interchangeably.

Commercially available research

There are a number of commercial organisations (such as Mintel, AC Nielsen, TNS and Keynote) which conduct research and publish substantial reports which other researchers and client companies can then purchase. For example, the Target Group Index (TGI) is produced by the British Market Research Bureau (BMRB). It is based on a long questionnaire with over 45 pages, sent out to representative consumers (**consumer panels**). The selected consumers, usually in their own homes, answer questions or perform small tasks and return their responses to the research agency. In this way information is obtained about respondents' general purchasing habits, lifestyles and needs. The surveys cover a comprehensive range of topics, such as brands consumed, levels of income and expenditure. Information collected in this way can be sold to businesses that are interested in any of these consumer topics. More information on TGI can be found on BMRB's website (www.bmrb-tgi.co.uk/gateway.asp).

consumer panels
a primary research technique that seeks the views, attitudes, behaviour or buying habits of a group of consumers

The Broadcasters' Audience Research Board (BARB) collects information on a regular basis on what television programmes are watched. These data are sold to television stations and media buyers, and used to compile the 'most popular programme' lists often published in magazines.

AC Nielsen Worldwide, and other research agencies, provide data about the total sales of retailers' and manufacturers' brands in many product categories. A product's barcode contains information such as contents, manufacturer, price and country of origin. Each product is scanned at the store's checkout and this information can then be used by marketing research agencies to compile **retail audits**.

retail audit
a research implement that provides information on retail product sales, e.g. value, volume, market/brand share

Exhibit 5.3   Examples of secondary and primary data collection

	Internal sources	External sources
Secondary data collection	Customer records Sales reports Retail outlet/dealer's feedback Financial figures about customers, suppliers and dealers Research and development studies Production and technical records Management reviews Marketing intelligence assessments	Trade and consumer press Periodicals and journals Commercial and industrial reports Government publications Trade association reports Other companies' reports Directories Market reports Retail audits
Primary data collection	Current customer feedback Current customer complaints Sales interviews and daily feedback Current delivery situation Current state of stock turnover Current feedback from marketing, discounts and promotional activity State of current production levels to keep pace with dealer and customer demand Current research and development activity to give competitive edge	Observing behaviour: • watching customers and situations • surveillance by electronic means Questioning respondents: • asking questions in personal interviews • asking questions by telephone • using mailed questionnaires • using computer-assisted interviewing • using video links to ask questions Carrying out experiments: • carrying out product trials in a laboratory setting • carrying out consumer tests, e.g. eye tracking • carrying out trials in the field, e.g. with a sample of respondents trying a product at home or in a public place within a specified period

EXPAND YOUR KNOWLEDGE

Montgomery, D.B. and Weinberg, C.B. (1979) 'Toward strategic intelligence systems', *Journal of Marketing,* 43: 41–52.

The paper argues that as strategic planning tools become more sophisticated, the quality of information inputted into the planning process becomes more important such that increased attention should be paid to the range of information used and to the systematic development of strategic intelligence systems to deal with this information. An intelligence cycle is introduced emphasising information, sources of intelligence and analysis and processing considerations.

Primary (field) research

When relevant **secondary data** are not available, information has to be gathered in the field, directly from individuals and the market. This is known as primary research. Researchers always begin with secondary research as this is cheaper and usually quicker. Primary research is then used to fill in the gaps or examine findings in greater detail.

External primary research may involve dealers, suppliers, customers, consumers, trade associations, industry groups and government institutions. The **primary data** gathered is useful in building up a picture of the level of satisfaction of such groups with the products and services, or of their general attitudes towards the particular organisation and its activities.

primary data
first-hand data gathered to solve a particular problem or to exploit a current opportunity

Advances in computing have made gathering, recording and analysing information much easier and quicker. Researchers can involve substantially greater numbers of respondents, or respondents who might be difficult to reach by other means. Computer-based research also has the advantage of automatically providing a record of what was said.

There are two broad approaches to **primary research, quantitative** and **qualitative,** which should be seen as mutually supportive. There are core strengths in both approaches that benefit research clients in terms of problem-solving and decision-making. As described by ESOMAR, **quantitative research** is numerically orientated, requires significant attention to the measurement of market phenomena and often involves statistical analysis. By contrast, **qualitative research** provides an understanding of how and why things are as they are.

quantitative research
seeks numerical answers, e.g. how many people have similar characteristics and views

qualitative research
investigates people's feelings, opinions and attitudes, often using unstructured, in-depth methods

QUALITATIVE RESEARCH

Qualitative research allows researchers to offer their clients new or different ways of looking at problems. Unlike quantitative research, it consists of a body of research techniques that 'do not attempt to make measurements, [but] seek insights through a less structured, more flexible approach' (Birn et al., 1990). It is used to 'increase understanding, expand knowledge, clarify the real issues, identify distinct behavioural groups' (Gordon and Langmaid, 1988). Qualitative research is about finding out what people think and feel and it can be used prior to undertaking a quantitative research programme. It can be **exploratory,** i.e. a small-scale attempt to find out the particular circumstances of a market and its customers. It can be unstructured, e.g. in an interview situation where the interviewees can discuss answers freely and so

exploratory (research)
initial research to see whether a more comprehensive study is needed

biographical research
an individual's story or experiences told to a researcher or found in other materials

phenomenological research
describes the experiences of individuals concerning some specific phenomena or occurrence

unearth a greater wealth of information for the researchers. It can be descriptive, as in the narratives offered in **biographical** or **phenomenological** research. It can be explanatory in nature, trying to discover why people do particular things, unearthing their attitudes and motivations.

In marketing research there are many good examples of qualitative work. The most common qualitative research methods are **in-depth interviews, focus groups** and **consumer panels**, all of which are covered in more detail later in this chapter. Qualitative work takes place in most markets, including B2B, consumer, youth, financial, industrial, fast-moving consumer goods (**FMCG**), pharmaceutical, retail, international, leisure, tourism and travel, and across a range of disciplines – e.g. **advertising**, branding, customer care, design, idea generation, media, new media, new product development, and social and organisational studies (Wright and Crimp, 2000).

Most qualitative research falls into five areas:

- biography
- phenomenology
- grounded theory
- ethnography
- case study.

Biography

Biography is the story of an individual and his or her experiences as told to a researcher or as found in documents and archived materials. The biographical tradition includes autobiographies, or life histories, and the turning points in particular individuals' lives, which are retold and assessed. Researchers will explore meanings from the recollections of individuals.

Phenomenology

Phenomenology describes the lived experiences of individuals concerning a specific phenomenon or occurrence. Researchers will explore the consciousness of the human experience, i.e. how individuals have lived these experiences, in order to construct social acts or outcomes, and to find meanings from such individual experiences.

grounded theory
starts from the intention to generate, or to discover, a theory by studying how people interact in response to a particular phenomenon; theoretical propositions are developed from interview data and field research

Grounded theory

Grounded theory starts from the intention to generate, or to discover, a theory by studying how people interact in response to a particular phenomenon. Theoretical propositions are developed from interview data and field research. Grounded theory is often about looking at how people react in a visual way and for signs or cues in their group behaviour. It is about defining and refining categories, and revisiting the questions arising from the research repeatedly until specific, tenable propositions arise. These propositions are then developed for further research.

ethnography
the description, or interpretation, of the patterns of behaviour in a social group or setting; the researcher will immerse himself or herself in a variety of ways into the culture of the group to be studied

Ethnography

Ethnography is the description, or interpretation, of the observable and learned patterns of behaviour in a social group or setting. The researcher will immerse him/herself in a variety of ways into the culture of the group to be studied. For example, he or she might live with the community, experiencing its day-to-day life and/or pursuing one-to-one interviews with members of the group. By doing this, researchers can experience at first hand how the subjects of the study are living, working and behaving.

insight   At home with your research subjects

Ethnography may be described as a research approach in which time is spent with consumers in their own environment. Bruce Davies, an ethnographic researcher, explained: 'Rather than bringing consumers into companies, it's about bringing a company to consumers . ... It's good at finding new perspectives from old topics and unmet needs in mature markets'. His ethnographic research has helped develop two new brands in established markets: Zopa, an online financial exchange based on the eBay approach, which connects a community of users who want to borrow and lend money to each other; and Monkey Shoulder, a whisky brand from William Grant and Sons, aimed at appealing to younger (but of legal age) whisky drinkers. For Zopa, ethnography identified a community of entrepreneurs who were willing to exchange funds with each other rather than using the traditional channels of banks or financial institutions. The ethnographic research led Davies to recognise that the brand needed to be about exchange relationships that were social rather than just economic.

According to Fiona Jack, Chair of the Association of Qualitative Research, ethnography can sometimes be more effective than focus groups because it allows consumers to show how they do things in context rather than talking about what they do: 'Often consumers can't remember what they do until they're stood in front of something. Don't tell me but show me. It could involve anything from observing a consumer cleaning their toilet to accompanying them on a shopping trip for mascara'.

Pampers realised the benefits of this approach over ten years ago when their marketing team spent a week with different consumers in their own homes. They realised that the nappy itself was not the only important part of the experience of being a new mum, but that mums really cared about information and knowledge. Based on their consumer insight, the brand launched Pampers.com, an online community for mothers, and the website now has 650,000 unique users across Europe.

Ewan Jones, partner at Lippincott Mercer, a brand strategy and design consultancy, emphasises that ethnographic techniques can be especially useful for brands in the service sector that need to understand consumers' unmet needs: 'It helps brand positioning in a fact-based way. Should an airline invest in cabin seating or in-flight entertainment or staff? It helps to define the "touchpoints" in an experience'.

SOURCE: Lewis, 2005: 19–21

© iStockPhoto.com/quavondo

Case study

A **case study** could be about an event, an activity or individuals. A case study contains detailed, in-depth information using multiple sources of information to build up a picture of individuals and their contributions to a particular situation.

case study
contains in-depth information, built from multiple sources, that forms a detailed picture of a particular situation

QUANTITATIVE RESEARCH

Quantitative research requires much larger numbers of respondents than qualitative research. Its aim is to find out how many people have similar or specific characteristics and views. If there are large numbers of respondents, a quantitative survey is used to collect the data. It would be too time-consuming and costly to cover a large number of respondents with a qualitative approach. Use of questionnaires is a

SPSS
(Statistical Package for the Social Sciences) a software program for statistical analysis

Minitab
a software program for statistical analysis

sample
a smaller number of people, or cases, drawn from a population that should be representative of it in every significant characteristic

population
a complete group of people, cases or objects that share similarities that can be studied in a survey

popular technique adopted, and these can be cost-effective in reaching many people when posted, faxed, emailed or completed online. The answers are then subjected to analyses using statistical computing software (e.g. **SPSS** or **Minitab**).

The largest type of quantitative study, and the most complete way of collecting data, is to conduct a full-scale census of the entire population within a country. Full-scale census surveys are used by governments all over the world as aids to planning and forecasting. Each census provides a large amount of information that gives reliable statistical data about population characteristics. The heads of households, or chief income earners, in each household have to fill in the census questionnaire. The process is expensive and time-consuming so population censuses are only conducted every ten years in the UK.

It is impossible for market research organisations to draw data from every member of the country's population in the way a census does. Respondents do not have to cooperate and, anyway, the costs involved would be huge. Therefore, they question a sample of the population. Each member of that sample group may represent hundreds, or even thousands, of people. It is therefore vital to choose your **sample** carefully to ensure you have the same balance of characteristics (sex, age, background, etc.) that are representative of the statistical **population** that is being studied. Sampling is considered later in this chapter as it is such an important part of the survey process. However, before leaving the issue of the use of census data, it is worth noting here that researchers use the term 'population' in a particular way and this does not necessarily mean the whole population of a country. Marketing researchers are concerned with the research population. If the research only needs to be focused on a particular group of people, such as attendees at a specific concert, then this would be the relevant research population. While it may still be inappropriate to survey all of them for cost and time reasons, a census would be a survey of all of these people, not of everybody in the population at large. From a research perspective, the important consideration is the definition of the research population which might be used for a census or from which a sample can be drawn.

The strength of quantitative research lies in the way the science of mathematical analysis and modelling is used to explain marketing phenomena. Marketers can base their decisions on statistically proven facts with known margins of error. The development of computer-aided simulations and database applications has greatly enhanced the ability of marketing researchers to build customer characteristics from geo-demographic data (see Chapter 4 for more information on market segmentation and geo-demographics) and purchasing records to build up more accurate customer profiles.

ACTIVITY

Go to the library and find examples of recent market research reports and company directories. Look for company directories such as Kompas and Dunn and Bradstreet, and market research reports such as Mintel and Keynote. What information do they provide? What other examples containing useful marketing information can you find and what do they cover?

Quantitative research can be criticised for its inflexibility and the impersonal nature of the collection of data through large-scale surveys – i.e. quantitative work may be limited as it fails to fully understand respondents' attitudes, motivations and behaviour. However, quantitative research has the reliability of numbers and statistically proven large-scale results. For example, quantitative research might be used to find out how much of a product is bought, when it is bought and where. This information shows marketing managers how and what customers have purchased, from which they can deduce what customers are likely to consume in the near future. However, should the marketing team want to know *why* people buy what they do, numbers alone will not suffice. A qualitative approach is better at discovering such customers' purchase intentions. The customers would need to be interviewed and probed for in-depth answers.

Qualitative and quantitative research should be seen as mutually supportive. For instance, as quantitative surveys taking in large numbers of people are expensive to conduct, a smaller-scale exploratory qualitative study is useful to find out whether its results would support undertaking a quantitative survey. If the exploratory study unearths only very limited demand for a new product, then the need for an expensive quantitative survey is questionable.

Primary research methods and techniques

Primary research is original research, i.e. it is not reliant on previously published information. There are three major forms of primary research:

- watching how people behave (**observation**)
- testing (**experimentation**)
- asking questions (**survey**).

OBSERVATION TECHNIQUES

Observation, as the name suggests, is about watching how people behave rather than asking them questions about their behaviour. Simple observation involves watching and recording people and their activities: perhaps using products or doing their shopping. A 'pantry audit' is an example of simple observation. Researchers list all the products or brands that are kept in someone's home. A useful observation for a toy manufacturer is watching children play with their toys to see exactly how they behave and enjoy themselves. For a restaurant owner, watching people use their services can be highly insightful. Participant observation, which is a variant, requires the researcher to become involved in the activity or task being observed, e.g. the researcher might accompany the respondent on a shopping trip.

observation
a primary research technique that involves watching how subjects behave in their normal environment

An advantage of using observation as the research approach is that there should be no researcher or response bias in the observation process, although the recording of the observed behaviour may cause problems. Technology helps to overcome this problem. Observees can be filmed or sound-recorded unobtrusively (though this should always be done with their permission, of course). For example, television viewing habits can be monitored electronically as the television is turned on and channels changed.

Other recording devices include:

- eye movement camera – used for such things as assessing advertisement designs by electronically tracking exactly what the eye is looking at (see Exhibit 5.4)
- tachistoscope – used to show images very quickly which can be used, for example, to measure brand image awareness
- pupilometer – used to measure pupil dilation (the size of the pupil in the eye); the larger the pupil, the more it indicates how much the image being viewed is liked
- psycho-galvanometer – used to measure changes on the surface of the skin when the respondent is viewing images or answering questions or performing a task
- neuro-research – this is a growing area of research which involves the measurement of brainwave patterns as respondents are presented with different messages or images and using different media.

The immense advantage all these techniques share is that they measure autonomic responses in respondents. These are biological changes that are automatic and well documented for their reliability.

Exhibit 5.4   Example of a stationary eye-tracking sytem; alternative systems are smaller and can be more conveniently head mounted

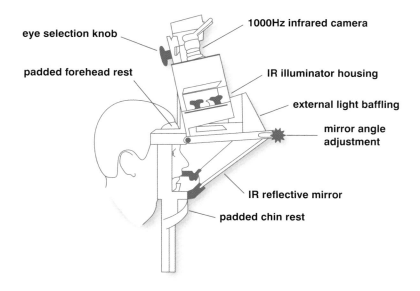

EXPAND YOUR KNOWLEDGE

Krugman, H.E. (1965) 'The impact of television advertising: learning without involvement', *Public Opinion Quarterly*, 29 (Fall): 349–356.

Herbert Krugman was a pioneer of what is now frequently referred to as neuro marketing. Krugman researched autonomic brainwave patterns in response to external stimuli.

EXPERIMENTATION TECHNIQUES

experimentation
a primary research technique that seeks to understand the behaviour of specified variables under controlled conditions, i.e. not real-world

Experimentation can take place in the field or in the laboratory. Field experiments endeavour to exert a level of control (although this is not always easily achieved in a market setting) so that a change in the experimental variable (e.g. advertising, price, distribution) can be related to any resulting changes, such as in sales, levels of recall, brand awareness, etc. Examples include coupon trials, split-run advertising and test marketing. Laboratory tests make use of the observational techniques listed above.

Pre-testing, tracking and post-testing

Consumer responses to a product launch are affected by how it is introduced as well as how it is priced, packaged and finally presented to the market in terms of distribution and promotions. Similarly, any proposed changes to any of the elements of the marketing mix can have critical effects on the achievement of marketing objectives. While a planned programme of pre-testing, tracking and post-testing can be expensive, the results can yield useful data for marketers.

insight   Simply Software Ltd

As an illustration of how primary research might work, let us consider the case of Simply Software Ltd. The firm is considering an option of a new offering of hardware maintenance services. It might start by sending an email to its entire salesforce asking how many customers have enquired about such services. Then it might ask a sales team to sound out its customers next time they visit. Additionally, it could write to all local members of the Computer Users' Association. The company may have already built up records of customer usage and of customer complaints.

Having established that there is some interest in the new service, it would want to make sure that it designed it in the most appealing way. To find out what would appeal to customers, it could invite groups to come in and talk about their current hardware service arrangements: what's good and what's not; what extra services they would like; and what they would be prepared to pay. The opinions of the salesforce and other key employee groups may be elicited. The company may design a questionnaire that it posts out to all of its current customers.

This scenario makes use of a variety of research techniques and approaches: internal data analysis, salesforce information, trade association information, electronic questionnaires, focus groups, face-to-face interviews and a postal survey. This may be described as a process of triangulation in which the information and insight that the company is seeking is gathered from a variety of sources and perspectives.

Pre-testing can be carried out on a range of products, packaging, marketing communications (promotions) and prices. For instance, respondents can be asked for their views on a range of products (product research) by attending product 'clinics' (research on models of cars make use of this approach); or they can be shown different pack sizes (for packaging research); or they can be asked about advertising treatments, brand names and brand images, and promotional offers (for marketing communications research); or they can be asked about what they would be prepared to pay for a product given high/moderate/low prices (for pricing research). Without divulging either the product name or producer identity for the product that is being researched along with the other known brands, marketing researchers can find out valuable information to help the producer to refine its product prior to market launch.

Post-testing with the same sample of respondents, or varied by the inclusion of new respondent samples, can provide further observations about the final price, pack, taste and marketing communications effects. For example, we can pre-test the effects of marketing communications by showing advertising material in advance of a new advertising campaign and post-test the effects after the campaign has been run.

Tracking is simply the testing process that measures what is going on over a period of time. Such testing is commonplace in the marketing communications industry where pre-testing may be used to evaluate and select advertising concepts, tracking is used to measure changes in recognition and recall of the advertising, branding and attitudes, and post-testing is used to assess the overall effect of a campaign. However, all these approaches to testing can be applied to many other areas of marketing and marketing research.

tracking
ongoing campaign information fed back into the marketing planning process

Statistical modelling

Computer-aided models based on data collected from the market are used to emulate market conditions and outcomes so that the effects of price changes or competitor actions or promotional expenditures, etc. can be assessed as simulations.

Test marketing

test market
a subset of a market in which a product offering can be sold for a short period of time in order to predict demand and to try out and refine the marketing mix

A **test market** is a mini-market – a smaller version of the whole market, in which changes to any or all elements of the marketing mix can be tried out, e.g. new products, promotions, distribution, retail display, pricing, etc. If the testing is successful in the test market, then it can be rolled out to the real market with more confidence; there is less risk of it proving an expensive failure. In the UK, television advertising campaigns are sometimes tested in one of the television regions before going national. However, not all countries have regionalised television (e.g. Germany, for instance, does not), so TV adverts are more difficult to test.

The use of test marketing is a recognition of the difficulties of researching matters, as a scientist might, by controlling conditions in order to test a particular variable. In the world of marketing and social research, variables cannot be controlled in the field. The test market therefore needs to be as close as is reasonable (or variations accounted for) to the whole of the market. While the variables cannot be controlled, they are at least presumed to have approximately the same effect in the test market as they would in the full market. Test marketing may be particularly useful when launching a new product or significantly changing or experimenting with changes to the marketing mix.

insight   Recruiting the right respondents

Recruiting the right people to interview is a crucial, but can be a difficult, part of the research process. One recruitment approach is to use an agency for the task. Another approach that has both its advocates and critics is to use a technique known as 'snowballing', in which the participants recruit each other.

Ipsos MORI's Participation Unit explored these approaches as part of a project designed as a methodological trial to assess the impact of different recruitment methods on a particularly hard-to-reach group – irregular drug users. The snowballing technique resulted in peer interviewers accessing a wider spectrum and diversity of drug-user interviewees in locations not usually reached. In contrast, interviewees recruited by agency staff were all participants in rehabilitation programmes. Of course, appropriate training needs to be given to ensure that peer interviewers do not create bias in the way the interviews are conducted when using a snowballing approach.

SURVEY TECHNIQUES

survey
direct questioning of market research subjects

Surveys involve *asking* respondents questions and recording their responses to those questions. A range of techniques are available to the researcher. Some are qualitative, some quantitative, and some techniques can be adapted for both approaches. The following are some of the more popular methods.

Qualitative techniques include:

- interviews
- focus groups
- projective techniques
- clinics.

Quantitative techniques include:

- postal surveys
- telephone surveys

- face-to-face surveys
- online surveys
- omnibus surveys
- syndicated surveys
- panels.

Interviews

In an **in-depth interview,** the interviewer will usually start off by asking a few general questions or putting up a problem situation or case scenario. Each interviewer will vary in his or her approach to a respondent, but the main idea is to create a situation where the respondent will feel at ease and can talk freely about the subject, thereby generating more information and insights for the interviewer. The aim is to encourage the respondent to freely express her or his opinions, attitudes, experiences, interpretations and motivations. Interviews are time-consuming and can take from one to several hours. Recording the responses can be challenging as can the analysis of those responses. A voice or video recorder can be helpful if its use is agreed with the respondent and analytical software such as NVivo is useful when analysing qualitative data.

in-depth interviews
one-to-one research interviews; commonly used in qualitative research

Elusive data

global focus

Marketing research in less developed countries (LDCs) can present particular problems. Often, there is very little secondary data available, and what there is may be out of date or unreliable. Population censuses are expensive and so poorer countries are unlikely to do these often, if at all. Few houses, especially in rural areas, may have phones and so the telephone directory will be a slim volume. (In many LDCs, people in remote areas are more likely to have mobile phones than land-line telephones.)

This lack of secondary data also affects primary research as it is hard to obtain an accurate sampling frame. As a consequence, convenience samples are often used.

The very collection of primary data can also be difficult in itself. In some countries, women still play a subservient role to their menfolk and would not be permitted to talk to a strange man – certainly not alone. So who do you send to do the interview? The obvious answer would be a woman. But how will you find a trained female market researcher in a country where women do not work outside the family? In such countries, people can also be reluctant to talk to strangers at all, especially about personal matters.

On the other hand, countries that have not always enjoyed the privilege of free speech may prove a researcher's dream. Response rates to surveys can be very high – though whether this is because people are accustomed to cooperating with official enquiries, or just because they find being asked their opinion on consumer products a novelty, is as yet unclear.

Focus groups

A **focus group** is where a number of respondents (6–12 people) meet and where leadership of the group is provided by a moderator. The researcher/moderator will start by asking questions or prompting individuals to respond to the words, sights, sounds and touch of visual images, or the actual products themselves, in order to get the group discussion flowing freely about the subjects or objects. By observing the interactions and recording the discussions, the moderator can gain useful insights about the groups' intentions and feelings towards the subjects or objects.

focus groups
a qualitative research technique using a group discussion overseen by a moderator, used to explore views, attitudes and behaviour with regard to a marketing issue; common in advertising research

Focus groups can give useful insights into people's views and feelings

Projective techniques

Projective techniques are based on approaches used in psychological testing to understand respondents' perspectives better. Examples of projective techniques include word associations – one word is said and the respondent supplies her/his own immediate associated word in response; picture associations – respondents are shown a range of pictures and asked to choose those that best represent the item being researched, e.g. the pictures that best represent a particular brand; sentence completion – respondents are asked to complete incomplete sentences; cartoon test or thought bubbles – a cartoon or picture is shown and the respondent has to fill in the captions or thought bubbles; third-person techniques – the respondent is asked what they imagine a specified other person might say in a given situation; personalisation of objects – e.g. respondents are asked to imagine if the brand was a celebrity who it would be; collages – respondents are asked to create a collage representing the research item from a pile of pictures.

EXPAND YOUR KNOWLEDGE

Haire, M. (1950) 'Projective techniques in marketing research', *Journal of Marketing*, Apr: 649–656.

Another foray into the world of psychology to seek research approaches that can be applied to marketing situations to improve marketing research techniques.

Clinics

Clinics are laboratory situations in which respondents, frequently in groups, are asked to view the items being tested. New car designs or modifications to designs are tested in this way. Clinics such as these can be used to show actual products that respondents can walk around, touch and discuss.

Quantitative survey techniques

Quantitative surveys are what most people think of when they think of market research. They can be administered in a number of ways. Respondents may complete the survey forms themselves (e.g. if it is sent by post or is online) or they may be asked questions by a researcher (e.g. on the phone or face to face), who then completes the questionnaire on their behalf.

Omnibus surveys

omnibus surveys
a large questionnaire that provides data for multiple clients

In an **omnibus survey** research agencies collect information on behalf of a number of their business clients at the same time. Typically, clients pay to have one or a series of questions put into a larger questionnaire. Such a questionnaire might contain different sections relating to lifestyles, consumption habits, financial circumstances, ownership of motor vehicles, etc. In the motor car and financial services industries, where manufacturers and institutions are very protective of their corporate reputations, omnibus surveys are useful in helping to hide from the respondents the purposes for which the answers to the questionnaire are sought. When reporting the findings, the research agency will just report back the responses to the specific questions asked by the client and not the full questionnaire results.

Syndicated surveys

Syndicated surveys are similar to omnibus studies in that they are undertaken on behalf of a range of clients who pay into the syndicate. The difference here, however, is that where omnibus research involves a questionnaire composed of questions from different clients and each client only sees the responses to its question(s), syndicated research is designed by the research agency as a complete piece of research which is sold to each of the clients with full results from the research made available at a cost. For example, an organisation with a small research budget may buy into a syndicated advertising tracking study along with other organisations as a cost-effective way of finding out how its and others advertising is being received by the target market.

Panels

Panels are most often associated with consumer panels but can equally be formed in industrial and B2B situations. Groups of people are recruited to respond to a specific survey over a period of time, and some are set up permanently by research agencies who only have to recruit new members if existing ones drop out or if they choose to increase the size of the panel. They can be expensive to set up but relatively cheap to run and maintain. A big advantage is that once recruited, high response rates can be assured and the same group of people are available throughout the research process. Consumer panels are frequently used for surveying buying habits and usage behaviour of grocery goods and for researching media habits such as watching TV, listening to the radio and reading the press.

Exhibit 5.5   Comparison of some of the primary research methods

	Advantages	Disadvantages
Postal survey	Low cost per interview Avoids cost of travel A large number can be surveyed	Limited to short questionnaire to avoid non-response Non-personal so there is inflexibility in probing respondents Low response rates
Telephone survey	Cost limited to time spent on the phone Allows probing Avoids cost of travel Computer-assisted telephone interviewing (CATI) can speed up automated data collection	Intrusive into privacy Development of call centres with resulting increase in calls to homes can make people less willing to answer questions Can be time-consuming – CATI is more expensive to set up than using phone

Exhibit 5.5   Comparison of some of the primary research methods

	Advantages	Disadvantages
Personal interview	Flexibility – visual materials and other aids can be used to test respondents' reactions Allows probing Trust can be built up to get more reliable data Computer-assisted personal interviewing (CAPI) is faster and more accurate in handling multivariate data analysis	More expensive (e.g. travel, time taken) Have to set up individual interviews on an appointment basis, which can be cancelled at short notice CAPI is more expensive to set up and more staff training is required
Focus groups	More flexibility – visual materials and other products can be used to test/probe respondents' reactions Flow of discussion encourages greater intensity of ideas and participation of individuals	More expensive and time-consuming Needs good control by the 'moderator' otherwise group dynamics can cause a loss of direction Can be problematic in getting a truly representative sample of individuals
Consumer panels	Flexibility and participation – consumer can do product testing or give responses from home Diaries are filled in and/or use of recording devices with computer link	Expensive and time-consuming to set up Can be problematic in getting a truly representative sample of individuals
Email	Very cheap compared to methods above No international boundaries Words, images and sounds can be sent Versatile and very quick	Incomplete directories of names Poor lists are unrepresentative of sample Brevity of responses can be a problem
Websites/ online	Intranets are free and accessible to a ready-made population within an organisation Internet websites can give easy access to freely available information and to potential respondents Have similar advantages to email Bulletin boards and social networking groups can facilitate extensive discussion	Respondents select themselves Little control over sample Limited to those with access to computers Reliance on people to find and visit a website Vested interests may distort the findings

Exhibit 5.5 (Continued)

	Advantages	Disadvantages
Use of observational equipment and recorders	Cameras and CCTV can be left for long periods to gather evidence in everyday or test/experimenting situations Audience ratings can be measured by leaving videos recording in respondents' homes	Much information is useless Time-consuming to sort out the required details Monitoring of respondents needed in test situations – more researcher time needed
Autonomic response measurement, e.g. eye tracking, galvanic response, pupilometer, tachistoscope, neuro-measurement	Measures natural and unconscious responses and thus overcomes respondent bias created through answering questions Can provide useful insights of materials to be tested before use in the market to allow for modification and improvement Alternative materials and treatments can be tested	Needs to be used in laboratory situations and needs specialised equipment Only limited number of respondents is feasible

Sampling

Qualitative research samples are small and are not used to draw general conclusions about the research population as a whole, whereas quantitative research samples should be large enough, and representative enough, to allow researchers to draw general conclusions about the population being studied.

The first step in sampling is to identify a suitable sampling frame from which the sample can be drawn. The frame might be a telephone directory, an electoral register, a list of members of a club, or any other list that represents the research population as a whole (or is as close to it as possible). The list should contain records of the entire, statistical population. The second step is to determine the appropriate sample size. How many people need to be surveyed? Finally, the researcher must choose a sampling method.

It is important that the characteristics of the sample should be as close to those of the population as possible, as the sample is meant to be representative of the population from which it is drawn.

There are several, popular sampling methods available to researchers, as shown in Exhibit 5.6. The first three are based on random sampling approaches and are therefore suitable for statistical manipulation. The second three can deliver quantified

Exhibit 5.6 Sampling methods

Random (probability) sampling	Non-random (non-probability) sampling
Simple random	Convenience
Stratified random	Purposive
Area or cluster sample	Quota

insight   Sampling

Let us imagine that you want to find out how female children spend their money. Clearly, you cannot question *all* the children in the country, so you will try to find a representative sample. Then you can ask this sub-set of children and scale up to get a close approximation of the picture across the whole country. You establish (perhaps through a smaller qualitative study) that the key factors that influence what children buy are:

- their gender (boy or girl), and
- their age.

The country's child population breaks down as follows:

52 per cent are girls
20 per cent are 0–3 years
20 per cent are 4–6 years
30 per cent are 7–12 years
30 per cent are 13–15 years.

The names you select for your survey (perhaps 1,000 names from the total million or so), should also be: 52 per cent girls, 20 per cent 0–3, etc. This will then be a suitably representative sample of the whole.

results but care has to be taken in making presumptions about how representative they are of the wider population.

SIMPLE RANDOM SAMPLING

simple random sample
the Rolls-Royce of sampling methods, every member of the population has an equal chance of being selected; this can be expensive and often difficult

In **simple random sampling**, every member of the population should have an equal chance of being selected. This complete randomness can be quite difficult to achieve in larger populations and so there is a useful variant on this pure simple random sampling: **systematic random sampling**.

For systematic random sampling, each individual in the sampling frame is identified by means of a number and then regularly spaced numbers are chosen until the sample has been filled. For example, a telephone directory can provide a convenient **sampling frame** and, say, every seventh name can be picked out of the directory.

systematic random sampling
uses the whole population as a sampling frame but draws subjects from it at regular intervals, e.g. every 10th name on the list

STRATIFIED RANDOM SAMPLING

In the use of stratified random sampling, the population is divided into mutually exclusive groups and random samples are drawn *from each group*. For example, we can stratify the population by social grade and then by age group. Be aware, though, that classifying people according to social grades has always been one of the most dubious areas of market research investigation, although it is still one of the most widely used classification systems.

sampling frame
a list of the actual members of a population from which a sample is then chosen

AREA OR CLUSTER SAMPLING

The population is divided into mutually exclusive groups (e.g. geographical region) so that a random sample *of the groups* can be selected.

Take, for example, electoral polling. The decision as to how many constituencies to use, and then how many polling districts, is based on informed judgement. If we were using a postcode file as a sampling frame, we would have to find out how many postcode areas there were. Then we select the sectors within these postcode areas to draw. So, in the UK, this cluster sampling could, for example, be concentrated in 200 out of over 630 voting constituencies.

CONVENIENCE SAMPLING

A **convenience sample** is picked on the basis of convenience to the researcher. Organisations sometimes use their own employees to evaluate new products or prototypes that their research and development departments have come up with. Universities and colleges carry out market research surveys based on convenience samples of students and visitors to their campuses.

Convenience sampling lends itself to qualitative research, where consumer information can be obtained fairly quickly, inexpensively and effectively from convenient respondents who are close to hand. The rationale is to select the most accessible members of the population from which to conveniently draw the sample. Unless the members of the population are reasonably uniform (e.g. in expectations, socio-demographic make-up, etc.), there can be problems as the sample may not be representative of the population. In such a case a purposive **sample** (see below) would be a better method.

convenience sample
a sample picked on the basis of convenience to the researcher, e.g. work colleagues

sample
see quota sample

PURPOSIVE (JUDGEMENTAL) SAMPLING

This is a non-probability sampling method, where every member of the population does *not* have an equal chance of being picked. For example, if it is known who the experts are within a particular industry, purposive sampling is used simply to pick these people to represent the expertise of the industry. Knowledge gleaned from these people would be more useful than knowledge from a larger sample of people who are less expert in the particular field. In another example, we know that there are a vast number of retail outlets selling food in Britain, but there are only a few national supermarket chains (Tesco, Wal-mart/ASDA, Sainsbury's, Morrison's and Gateway). So a purposive sample of large retail firms would include these stores.

QUOTA SAMPLING

In marketing research it is common practice to use **quota samples**. What this means is that we put a prescribed figure or a number of the members of the population in each of several categories or quotas. For instance, in industrial and trade research we may be interested in sampling output or sales turnover. Our base for sample design is, therefore, the output or turnover and not the number of establishments or shops in a particular industry. We would therefore include a quota or selected number of firms based upon output and turnover for our study.

As another example, a survey of the manufacturers of paints should include a selected number or quota of the large companies, such as ICI Paints. Judgement is involved in selecting the quota because the firms sampled should be representative of the paints industry. In consumer studies we can set quotas based upon socio-economic and demographic characteristics such as age, race, gender and education attained.

quota samples
picks respondents in proportion to the population's profile, e.g. if 25 per cent of the population are under 25 and female, then researchers set a quota of 25 per cent females under 25 for the sample

Questionnaire design

Questionnaires are frequently thought of first when thinking about research, their use is so extensive. The **questionnaire** is a very useful, flexible and far-reaching tool for the market researcher, who can use it to obtain important information about consumer behaviour, attitudes to products, shopping habits, media habits and many

questionnaire
a set of questions for use during a survey

other marketing-related issues. In quantitative research, standardised questionnaires are common **survey** instruments and are used with samples of several hundreds or even thousands of respondents. Such questionnaires normally contain structured questions for ease of coding and statistical analysis. Designing questionnaires looks easy but designing *good* questionnaires is a highly skilled task. Questionnaires should always be pilot tested with typical respondents for whom the questionnaire was constructed. Such testing invariably reveals errors and shows ways to make the questionnaire more effective.

There are three basic types of questionnaire:

- fully structured with **closed questions** and no comments invited
- a compromise form of semi-structured questionnaire with mixed question types and room for comments
- completely unstructured with **open-ended questions** seeking to discover or explore the respondents' minds.

closed questions
questions that expect a one-word (usually yes or no) answer

open-ended questions
questions that invite the respondent to comment rather than just give a one-word answer

STRUCTURED QUESTIONNAIRE

The order in which questions are asked, together with their exact wording, is laid down. The interviewer must not alter or explain questions. Many questions are *closed* and the possible answers to most questions are pre-coded so that all the interviewer has to do is to ring around a code number or tick a box.

SEMI-STRUCTURED QUESTIONNAIRE

This usually constitutes a mixture of closed or fixed-response questions (yes/no), quick response ranking (e.g. 1 = highest-ranked favourite, 10 = lowest-ranked favourite) or rating scales (e.g. 1 = most wanted, 7 = least wanted) for measuring attitudes to organisations and their products. There are also open-ended questions or spaces for respondents to fill in their comments. Semi-structured questionnaires are useful in enabling the interviewer to stage-manage the interview by making sure that all questions are covered, with room for the interviewee (respondent) to add comments to the specific questions already asked.

© iStockphoto.com/Winston Davidian

Face-to-face interviewing

UNSTRUCTURED QUESTIONNAIRE

Most of the questions are open-ended. The interviewer is free to change the order of asking questions and to explain them. The questionnaire may take the form of a checklist for discussion. The unstructured questionnaire is used in in-depth interviews, group discussions and in non-domestic surveys. The interview may be respondent-led, particularly if the interviewee is an expert in the field, so that the observations and expertise of the respondent can be taken fully into account.

Exhibit 5.7   Examples of ways of asking questions

(Please tick or circle as appropriate.)

Closed questions:
'What is your age?'   16–25   26–35
'Do you have a bank account?'   Yes/No
'Do you like cheese?'   Like/Dislike

Semi-structured questions:
These can use a mixture of attitude scales and rank order types, followed by room on
the questionnaire for 'comments'.
(a) Likert scale

Do you agree with speed limits?

☐   ☐   ☐   ☐   ☐
strongly   slightly   neither agree   slightly   strongly
agree   agree   nor disagree   disagree   disagree

Comments:

(b) Semantic differential scale
Was Rosannica Restaurant's service:
Good   _ _ _ _ _ _   Poor
Reliable   _ _ _ _ _ _   Unreliable
Fast   _ _ _ _ _ _   Slow
Expensive   _ _ _ _ _ _   Cheap?

Comments:

(C) Rank order scale
Please rank in order of importance: 1 = very important, 5 = least important, in the boxes.

In your opinion, how important is your university's provision of the following facilities?

Sports facilities   ☐
Medical centre facilities   ☐
Library facilities   ☐
Parking facilities   ☐
Restaurant facilities   ☐

Comments:

Open-ended questions:
'What did you enjoy about the play last night?'
'Describe your feelings concerning the news about ...'
'What do you think the level of competition will be like in the next five years?'

Comments:

e-questions

Researchers often use email to send out their questionnaires and there are a number of software programs that construct and administer online questionnaires. This means that information can be collected much faster and that physical distance is no obstacle. With email and the Internet it is no more expensive to contact people on the other side of the world than it is to talk to people in the next office.

Computerised questionnaires have significant advantages over their old-fashioned paper counterparts. The computer does away with that tedious (and confusing) business of 'if you ticked yes, now go to question 44b, otherwise go to question 16'. Each answer can determine what the next question will be.

The information collected from all the respondents is then downloaded, collated, statistically analysed, cross-related and systematically grouped into the types of categories that will allow researchers to make meaningful statements to their clients about the findings. This type of computer-assisted personal interviewing (CAPI) saves a lot of time. Computer-assisted telephone interviewing (CATI) works on the same principle, by allowing responses on the telephone to be recorded on to the computer and computer-generated analyses to be carried out speedily and impartially. Further examples of electronic assistance include small, digital, handheld cameras, traffic sensor devices and closed-circuit television (CCTV) equipment, often used in stores and shopping precincts to observe and record the behaviour of customers.

EXPAND YOUR KNOWLEDGE

Oppenheim, A.N. (1992) *Questionnaire Design, Interviewing and Attitude Measurement*. London: Pinter Publications.

This book has received widespread acclaim as an insightful introduction to various aspects of marketing research and, in particular, is a useful reference for questionnaire design issues. Use this book to overcome many of the pitfalls associated with questionnaires.

Quality of marketing information

If the information we have is wrong in some way or it is not available when needed, then it is little use. Sound marketing decisions can only be made on the basis of good quality information. The data must be:

Timely
Accurate
Reliable
Valid

TIMELINESS

It is important that research is finished on time. If it is late, then it may be too late to be of any use. For example, the management problem may have become acute or the marketing environment may have changed. Out-of-date data is worthless.

insight   **Analysing a database to segment the market**

Simple marketing research and analysis, coupled with a basic understanding of market segmentation and targeting principles, can result in more effective marketing.

Dudley College, Further Education Institution, recognised that information it regularly collected and stored in its database would reveal valuable information that could be used to improve the efficiency and effectiveness of its recruitment publicity for part-time adult students. The College dropped its blanket marketing communications approach and targeted likely students more precisely.

Consultancy, Rocket Science, purged and deduplicated the College's adult student database, reducing the 34,000 records by almost half. It then segmented students by demographic and lifestyle characteristics (see Chapter 4). The analysis showed that its students tended to be young, of average affluence, and married with 2.4 children. They also tended to work in craft or trade occupations and enjoyed practical activities such as DIY and home computing.

The next step was to identify local postcode clusters with the greatest proportion of people matching its profile. This can be done by subscribing to geo-demographic data such as Mosaic or ACORN. By focusing its efforts on these, the College reduced the number of brochures it needed to distribute, achieved an increase in enrolment of 19 per cent across all targeted areas, and a decrease in promotional costs of 23 per cent.

ACCURACY

Accuracy is about correctness or precision. Clearly it is desirable to have absolutely accurate data. However, this is not always possible (complete accuracy is rare) and comes at a high cost. Frequently, researchers have to make estimates and it is important that they make it clear when this is the case. Relying on inaccurate data can lead to poor decisions, but if we know how inaccurate a figure may be, then we can make allowances. For example, if a thermometer consistently shows boiling water to be 91°C, instead of 100°C, then we know it is inaccurate and by how much.

RELIABILITY

Reliability refers to the consistency of results. If a piece of research is repeated, would we obtain the same results? In the example above, does the thermometer read 91°C each time? Even though the measurement is inaccurate, if it returns the same result, it is reliable.

This issue of reliability is significant because most research is conducted with a sample of respondents rather than a **census**. For instance, **focus group** members should be representative of the targeted group of consumers as a whole. If one were to repeat the focus group with a new set of participants, would the findings be the same? It is hard to prove reliability in **qualitative research** because people are different. However, it is good practice to aim for consistency of research, e.g. by administering a questionnaire in the same way to each respondent.

census
a survey that includes all members of a population

It is easier to achieve consistency in **quantitative research** by asking the same structured questions, in the same format. However, the reliability of research is ultimately down to the integrity of the researchers concerned. Their work must be unbiased. When entrusting the researchers with their projects and their money, client organisations need to know that they can depend upon the findings when making crucial managerial decisions about their marketing strategies and their markets.

VALIDITY

Validity is a key concept in assessing the quality of research. Research should deliver evidence that can be used to answer the research problem. 'Internal validity' is an indicator of whether the research measures what it claims to measure. It is no use using a barometer (which measures pressure) if you want to measure temperature. That requires a thermometer. If research has 'external validity' it means that generalisations can be made from the research carried out on a sample to the wider population from which the sample is drawn.

Researchers have ways to deal with issues of validity which are beyond the scope of this book. Just remember the importance of taking care over research design to ensure that the research outcomes are valid.

Forecasting and trend spotting

Forecasting can be defined as the estimation of the future value of a variable (most commonly sales). A key assumption is that a relationship does exist between the variable being forecast (the dependent variable) and the other one or more variables that are being measured against, i.e. the independent variable(s). For example, it is assumed that growth in sales is in some way related to advertising.

Marketing activities are designed ultimately to deliver sales and so sales forecasting is a key input to marketing planning. Accurate forecasting is the basis for what managers predict will happen within their markets. Spreadsheets are used to plot trends and compounded growth rates before predictions are reached.

Developing a new product, entering a new market or making changes to any of the elements of the marketing mix is risky. Organisations need to predict how customers will react and also what competitors' retaliatory strategies might be. A costly failure can be disastrous for an organisation. Equally, standing still with no change brings its risks. Marketing management is about basing decisions for change on sound information obtained through professional marketing research.

SUMMARY

Marketing research is a crucial aspect of marketing. It provides the basis for all marketing decisions.

Good marketing research is essential to the objectives and successes of both profit and not-for-profit organisations. The procedures used are well-established forms of collecting, analysing and conveying information about people and markets. Markets can be described and analysed in detail so that opportunities can be taken, the performances of organisations assessed and competitors' activities tracked. Marketing research is, therefore, indispensable for the marketing intelligence purposes of organisations and in helping them to develop their marketing strategies.

Marketing research starts with secondary data which should be collected before any primary research is undertaken. The broad categories of qualitative and quantitative research have been described along with the many and varied primary research methods that fit into these categories. The decision of which method or methods to use is a direct function of the information needed which, in turn, is a function of the marketing management problem the researcher is trying to solve.

CHALLENGES REVIEWED

Now that you have finished reading the chapter, look back at the challenges you were set at the beginning. Do you have a clearer idea of what's involved?

Hints:

- sources of secondary information, internal records, primary research approaches
- objectives of research
- appropriate qualitative research methods
- sampling.

READING AROUND

Books

Yvonne McGivern (2006) *The Practice of Market and Social Research* (2nd edn). Harlow: FT/Prentice Hall.

Len Tiu Wright and Margaret Crimp (2000) *The Marketing Research Process* (5th edn). Harlow: FT/Pearson.

Journal articles

Mark Earls (2003) 'Advertising to the herd', *International Journal of Market Research*, 45 (3): 311–36.

Clive Nancarrow, Andy Barker and Len Tiu Wright (2001) 'Engaging the right mindset in qualitative marketing research', *Marketing Intelligence & Planning*, 19 (4): 236–44.

Brian Tarran (2003) 'The birth of an idea', *Research* (the magazine of the Market Research Society), August: 22–4.

Websites

www.barb.co.uk – Broadcasters Audience Research Board, e.g. market research applications.
www.cia.gov/library/publications/the-world-factbook – the CIA's world factbook, for country information.
www.mrs.org.uk – home of the Market Research Society.

Market research reports

Mintel, *Keynote* and *Euromonitor* are commonly found in univerisity libraries or can be accessed online by subscription.

SELF-REVIEW QUESTIONS

1. Why is marketing research sometimes referred to as market research? (see page 163)
2. If marketing managers know about their customers from past purchases why do they need to conduct marketing research? (see pages 163–4)
3. What are retail audits and consumer panels? (see page 185)
4. What is meant by defining a research problem? (see page 165)
5. What is random, quota and stratified or area sampling? (see page 189)
6. What are the advantages of secondary data over primary data? (see pages 172–3)
7. What is qualitative research? (see pages 175–7)
8. What is the difference between simple random sampling and stratified random sampling? (see page 188)
9. List four qualitative survey techniques (see page 182)
10. Name atleast three commercial market research organisations (see page 173)

Holidaying at home

mini case study

Your company is considering developing a small, UK-based chain of Bed and Breakfast accommodation (B&B) but first you need to do some market research to see if this is likely to be a good investment.

1. Start with some secondary research. Check the latest relevant market reports (e.g. Mintel and Keynote), specialist travel sites and the travel sections of newspapers. What trends might be relevant?
2. Check the competition. What are the key differences between a B&B and a hotel? What do they offer to guests? (Tip: you can use the Internet for this but do not just rely on a search engine such as Google – this will mainly be trying to sell you holidays, so think it through and check a variety of sites, e.g. Tourist Boards).
3. Develop three research objectives for a small primary research project to help you to assess the B&B's potential.
4. Which primary research method(s) would you use and why?

Millions of Britons go abroad each year – largely to escape the British weather. For many people, holiday sunshine has become an essential that only the gravest of crises would persuade them to forego. However in 2009, about 60% of Britons took their holidays in the UK. It wasn't global warming that changed their minds, but the recession and the weakness of the pound which together made trips abroad unaffordable.

Britain offers a wide variety of holiday options: from posh hotels to B&Bs and camping sites, from seaside resorts to stunning countryside to cosmopolitan cities, from ancient to modern. One of the newer accommodation trends was the emergence of boutique hotels such as those owned by Hotel du Vin: relatively small, luxurious and decidedly chic. Such treats were beyond the budget of many holidaymakers though and so there seemed to be an opportunity for something with the same kind of feel but cheaper rates: perhaps an ultra-comfortable, fashionably decorated budget hotel or B&B.

REFERENCES

American Marketing Association (2004) 'Definition of marketing'. Available at: **http://www. marketingpower.com/aboutma/pages/definitionofmarketing.aspx** (accessed 6/03/2010).

Birn, R., Hayne, P. and Vangelder, P. (1990) *A Handbook of Market Research Techniques*. London: Kogan Page.

Brien, R.H. and James, E.S. (1968) 'Marketing information systems: a new dimension for marketing research', *Journal of Marketing*, 32 (Jul): 19–23.

Dichter, E. (1947) 'Psychology in marketing research', *Harvard Business Review*, 25 (Summer): 432–443.

ESOMAR (2006) Global Market Research 2008 Report, September. Available at: **www. esomar.com** (accessed 9/03/2010).

Gordon, W. and Langmaid, R. (1988) *Qualitative Research: A Practitioner's and Buyer's Guide*. Aldershot: Gower.

Haire, M. (1950) 'Projective techniques in marketing research', *Journal of Marketing*, Apr: 649–656.

Lewis, E. (2005) 'Getting involved', *The Marketer*, September: 19–21.

Krugman, H.E. (1965) 'The impact of television advertising: learning without involvement', *Public Opinion Quarterly*, 29 (Fall): 349–356.

Market Research Society (n.d.) 'Standards and guidelines'. Available at: **http://www.mrs.org. uk/standards/revised_code_definitions.htm** (accessed 6/03/2010).

McLuhan, R. (2006) 'Informed decisions', *Marketing*, 13 December.

Montgomery, D.B. and Weinberg, C.B. (1979) 'Toward strategic intelligence systems', *Journal of Marketing,* 43: 41–52.

Oppenheim, A.N. (1992) *Questionnaire Design, Interviewing and Attitude Measurement.* London: Pinter Publications.

Sainsbury's (2002) 'Nectar launches today', J Sainsbury plc (10 September). Available at: **www.j-sainsbury.co.uk/cr/index.asp?PageID=115&subsection=&Year=2002&NewsID=291** (accessed 13/07/2007).

Wright, L.T. and Crimp, M. (2000) *The Marketing Research Process* (5th edn). Harlow: FT/ Pearson.

Part three

THE MARKETING MIX

THIS PART CONTAINS:

6 Product

7 Service products

8 Promotion (marketing communications)

9 Place

10 Price

WHAT THIS PART IS ABOUT:

When they have completed their research and analysis, and so have developed an in-depth understanding of their marketing environment and of their customers, marketers make plans to satisfy those customers' needs. At the heart of these plans is a set of tools known as the marketing mix. The marketing mix is commonly referred to as the 4Ps: product, promotion, place and price. All four elements must be blended together to produce an integrated plan of action to build brands and deliver long-term profits.

The 4Ps sounds deceptively simple, but a product is so much more than the item you buy. The product that is offered to customers includes its packaging, its brand and its supporting services and the decision to buy it may have more to do with those things than with the make-up of the item itself. Promotion or marketing communications is so much more than just advertising and is much more subtle than simply saying 'buy this'. Place is about getting the right products to the right people at the right time and about making it easier for customers to buy our products. Without a price, a product is a gift. Set the wrong price (either too high or too low) and products may not sell at all.

Decisions about the 4Ps should not be make in isolation. The Ps need to fit with each other. An exclusive product, such as a designer suit or a Bang and Olufsen stereo, commands a high price, is sold in upmarket shops, or delivered to your door in a smart van, and should be high quality. An everyday product, such as shampoo or cat litter, should do its job reliably, be inexpensive and be widely available. If just one of the Ps is out of sync, then the whole of the product offering will be devalued.

Product

6

CHAPTER CONTENTS

Introduction
What is a product?
The total product offering
Product types
Branding
Product development
The product life cycle
Product portfolio management
Summary
Challenges reviewed
Reading around
Self-review questions
Mini case study
References

PRODUCT CHALLENGES

The following are illustrations of the types of decision that marketers have to take or issues they face. *You aren't expected to know how to deal with the challenges now*; just bear them in mind as you read the chapter and see what you can find that helps.

● You are a manager in a large confectionery company which has just taken over another company. You now have too many chocolate products which are proving to be complex to manage. You have been asked to recommend which should be kept and which dropped. How will you decide?

● You are the marketing director of a large car company. The finance director wants to cut the product development budget. She cannot see why you need to keep launching new models so often. Can you convince her that this is necessary?

● You are given the task of managing a well-known and long-established brand of jeans. The brand is showing its age and sales are slowly falling year on year. What might you do to halt the decline and revitalise the brand?

● You are a salesperson at an electronics retailer. You stock the same PCs as everyone else and cannot change the basic products themselves. How can you make it more attractive for customers to come to your store rather than go to your rivals?

● You have recently been appointed Marketing Manager for a manufacturer of kitchen appliances (fridges, microwaves, dishwashers, etc.) and have just discovered that your products have built-in obsolescence, i.e. they are made to last five years only and then they have to be replaced. It would be easy to make them so that they lasted longer, but then you would not make the replacement sales. What is your position on this?

Introduction

Product is one of the 4Ps of the marketing mix: the central elements of a marketing plan. The other 3Ps are promotion, place and price, and these 4Ps together are the basic tools marketers use. They must be carefully planned out so that they all work together in order to meet companies' targets for sales and profit.

> Product
>
> Promotion
>
> Place
>
> Price

All commercial enterprises have products to sell and these products are both the result of, and the reason for, marketing activities. Products are developed to meet customer needs and so those needs must be researched and understood. The product can then be targeted at a specific market segment and a **marketing mix** developed to support its desired **positioning**. Product managers, or brand managers, have to design marketing programmes for their products and develop good customer relationships to ensure their brands' ongoing success.

The ways in which research into new products can be carried out was discussed in Chapter 5. Targeting and positioning were covered in Chapter 4 and customer needs in Chapter 3. Chapters 8–10 are on the other major marketing mix elements and how they can be blended to support each other in an integrated marketing programme.

Some products are tangible (i.e. they have physical substance, they can be touched) and some are intangible (without physical substance, they cannot be touched), such as insurance or a dental check-up. The tangible products are often referred to as **goods**, while the intangible products are referred to as services. However, no product is completely physical; all have service elements to them, e.g. after-sales service, warranties, guarantees, installation assistance. Equally, very few services are pure service; most have a physical element to them. When you have your car cleaned, the cleaner uses detergent, wax, etc. When you eat in a restaurant, you are served food. Goods providers often use the service aspects of their products to differentiate them from the competition, whereas service providers may try to use the products associated with their services to do this.

This chapter will concentrate on tangible products, or goods (i.e. the ones you can actually touch), leaving services to be dealt with in more depth in the next chapter. It will consider what makes a new product a success in the marketplace and why so many fail. Most companies sell more than one product and the entire range must be managed so that individual products contribute to the success of the brand. Product managers use a number of analysis tools and these will be considered here, along with the strategies they feed into.

Branding is one of modern marketing's most popular tools and much has been written about the power of the brand. Branding was perhaps the primary competitive weapon of the 1990s, and in the twenty-first century it has become almost ubiquitous – everyone wants a brand. In this chapter, we will look at branding as a part of the product offering. Chapter 11 will revisit branding and its place in the whole of the marketing mix and in marketing strategy.

What is a product?

A product can be described as a bundle of attributes or characteristics. A loaf of bread may be large, sliced and wholemeal, or it may be small, white and unsliced. These are

---

marketing mix
the basics of marketing plan implementation, usually product, promotion, place and price

positioning
the place a product is perceived to occupy in the minds of customers/consumers relative to other competing brands

goods
tangible products, i.e. those with physical substance

its physical attributes and they provide benefits to the person who buys and/or eats the loaf. For example, the loaf may be good value for money, good for your health or convenient for sandwich making. Products exist to satisfy people's needs. The primary purpose of bread is to satisfy hunger whereas a watch satisfies our need to know the time, a car satisfies the need to travel from one place to another and washing powder cleans clothes. The product's attributes (or characteristics) must satisfy the customers' needs.

Customers judge the value of a product by weighing up all its aspects – the **total product offering**. The total product may have to satisfy a range of needs, e.g. Diet Pepsi has to quench thirst, taste good, be low calorie, be convenient to drink and convey a suitable image. Needs range from the simple (e.g. quench thirst) to the elaborate (e.g. convey suitable image). Some of these are fulfilled by basic product characteristics, e.g. the water in Diet Pepsi satisfies thirst, but some needs require more than just product ingredients. For instance, Pepsi's image is largely created by its advertising and the convenience of drinking is down to the size and design of the can or bottle. Whether or not an exchange (see Chapter 1) will take place, i.e. a sale be made, depends upon the customer's judgement of the total product's value. The customer's perception of a product's value may differ greatly from the company's perception, and is dependent upon all the elements of the marketing mix, i.e. the 4Ps (product, promotion, place and price). Customers have expectations of products that go beyond product performance. They may expect helpful product support, clear instructions and a fair price. They may also want their purchases to be ethically sound: non-exploitative, safe to use and environmentally friendly, perhaps. The marketing mix must therefore be well planned and integrated to create a total product offering that matches, or exceeds, the customer's expectations and needs.

> **total product offering**
> the total package that makes up and surrounds the product, including all supporting features, such as branding, packaging, servicing and warranties

TYPICAL REASONS PRODUCTS FAIL TO MEET CUSTOMER EXPECTATIONS

Ways in which products may fail to live up to consumer expectations include the following:

- **Non-performance**: the product may not deliver the core benefit required. It may not meet the basic need for which it is being bought (i.e. it may not work). The car may not start, the CD may not play. There are degrees of non-performance. The product may meet the core benefit but not deliver all the additional benefits anticipated (e.g. the car works but there is a strange squeak coming from somewhere), or it may be too complicated (e.g. the car radio has more functions than required) or, at the extreme, it may turn out to be physically dangerous (e.g. the car's brakes do not work).
- **Not me**: the product may not suit the customer after all. They get it home and do not feel good about it. A skirt may be unflattering, paint can turn out to be the wrong colour after all, pizzas sometimes have too little or too much topping.
- **Social disapproval**: the customer's friends and family may not like the product.
- **Poor value**: there are several elements to this. A customer may wonder whether he or she could have got the product cheaper, or it may turn out to be of lower quality or a lower specification than anticipated. Alternatively, it may take up too much time, either in the purchasing or in the installation, in learning how to use it or in its ongoing use.
- **Non-delivery**: the product may never arrive. This is a common fear of Internet shoppers.

Playing with lives

Channel 4 transmitted a stunt featuring the illusionist Derren Brown. The stunt was Russian roulette – with a real bullet. The programme was billed as going out live but, in actual fact, there was a slight delay in the transmission just in case something went wrong and he actually did kill himself.

On the night there was indeed a hitch, but fortunately only in that Derren mistook a blank bullet for a live one, and fired it into the waiting sandbag rather than his head.

The show was not universally popular. Parents' groups and police criticised it on the grounds that it might inspire youngsters to copy it. There were also complaints that, in a week when there had been a number of shootings and gun crime was a hot topic in all the newspapers, the programme was in bad taste. Channel 4 defended the show by pointing out that it contained a number of warnings of the dangers, and explanations that the game was enacted within a controlled environment and under the supervision of firearms experts.

Was this programme an ethically sound product?

The total product offering

Thanks to modern manufacturing techniques, most products can be copied by competitors with relative ease – and often made more cheaply than the originals. Firms rarely compete on the basis of their products' physical features alone; they offer their customers much more than that. A product may enhance the customer's image, it may offer better value than others, or better after-sales service, or come in a handier packet, or it may be a preferred brand. Mass-produced products are usually differentiated from each other by their additional characteristics rather than by their fundamentals and so marketers must design a complete package, a **total product**.

total product
the complete product offering, including all marketing mix elements

Exhibit 6.1 The total product offering

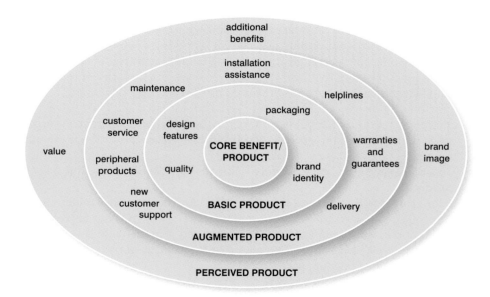

CORE BENEFITS (OR THE CORE PRODUCT)

A product's main reason for existence is called its **core benefit**. It is the simplest possible answer to an expressed need: no frills, no branding or packaging, no warranties or service promises, just the most basic reason why that product would be needed. The core benefit of a food product is to provide nutrition. A coat is needed to keep a person warm. Medicine is meant to cure an illness.

core benefit (core product)
the minimum benefits a product should confer, e.g. a pen must write, a car must go

Surprisingly, perhaps, there is no such thing as a new need; just new or different ways of solving a problem, i.e. satisfying that need. For example, riding horses was an improvement over walking from one place to another, trains replaced the horses, cars have largely supplanted trains and aeroplanes have, in many types of journey, replaced trains and boats. The transport problem is being solved in new and different ways. Electric light replaced gas for lighting, which in turn had replaced paraffin and candles, which in turn had replaced tallow wicks. The core benefit of all these things is to light the dark.

It is dangerous to lose sight of this important concept. Marketers must be sure that their products satisfy a need in its most basic sense. Products that do not offer a sound core benefit will usually fail. For example, it would be an uphill task for Rolex to attempt to sell watches that are not accurate timekeepers. No matter how precious the metals they are made of, or how many jewels are used to decorate them, watches must keep good time. Likewise, no matter how cheap it is, a washing powder that fails to get clothes clean has little chance of success since it does not deliver the core benefit it was bought for.

Marketing managers have to keep focused on the basic problems to be solved: understand them well, address them precisely and directly and place these solutions at the core of their products. This satisfaction of needs may be upfront or concealed within the complete product, but it must be there as it is central to the customer's perception of the product's value. The next stage is to consider how the product offering can be improved so that it will appeal to more customers. This requires a thorough understanding of what customers want from this type of product (see Chapter 5), as well as awareness of what is already being offered by the competition.

ACTIVITY

There are a number of coffee shops in most shopping areas (e.g. Starbucks, Costa Coffee, Caffè Nero) and they generally sell very similar products: lattes, cappuccinos, etc. Visit two, or more, of them and observe how they try to differentiate themselves from their competitors. It may be by service, quality, product range, surroundings and so on. How well do they do it?

In a monopoly situation, where there is only one provider of the means to satisfy needs, that provider can get away with offering just the bare minimum. If there is no choice, customers have to satisfy their requirements as best they can with whatever is available, however poor the product. When there are multiple providers of a product, they have to compete with each other for customers. There will therefore be a variety of products available, all designed to meet the same basic needs. Customers have choices as to what to eat or wear, which hamburger or trainers to buy. With choice comes the opportunity for customers to express their individuality in the way they make this choice. They will choose the products and services that have the most value to them. An understanding of how customers see value gives the organisation a chance to make a product offer that matches their preferences better than the competition's products do.

Most products on sale will meet customers' basic need for that product, i.e. they all offer the same core benefit, and so the choice is often made on the basis of what else the products offer; on their points of difference. It may be the flavour of the burger, the type of bun it comes in, the restaurant where it is served, the extras, the way it is packaged. These things all form part of the total product and are illustrated in Exhibit 6.1 above.

BASIC PRODUCT

basic product
a bundle of essential characteristics; a product described in terms of the features that deliver its core benefit (e.g. the ingredients of a soft drink – fizzy orange) without reference to branding, service or other more sophisticated elements

The **basic product** is just what it sounds like – the product stripped down to its essentials. These include its features (for a car, these would be the engine, the gear box, the braking system, the available colours, etc.), quality level, brand name and logo, and packaging. These things are the means by which the core benefit is delivered and, to the customer's thinking, they add up to the product itself. These product attributes attract the customer's attention, and are often the first things used to judge the product against the competitors' offerings.

AUGMENTED PRODUCT

The next level of the total product model contains supporting features. Among these are guarantees, service network, delivery, after-sales service and credit facilities. These can be an important source of differentiation from the competition. They enhance the product offering and can be used to counter objections or resolve doubts in a customer's mind. For example, a guarantee reassures a customer who is worried about quality and a credit agreement helps convince a customer who is concerned about the price.

As such extras are not physically part of the product, they can often be changed without modifying the basic product itself. For example, Fiat offered a 12-year anti-perforation warranty on the bodywork of its cars. The cars were the same as in previous years, so the basic product was the same, there was no change in production, only the augmented product changed – and could easily be changed again. Despite there being no change in the way the cars were produced, there may have been some actual costs incurred in this augmentation process (especially, for example, if someone claimed under the warranty) that must be borne by someone, either by the supplier or by the customer, or both. A balance always needs to be struck between increased cost and increased perceived value.

These products all share the same core benefit, though they differ in other ways.

PERCEIVED PRODUCT

The outer ring of the total product model (see Exhibit 6.1) is the perceived product. Customers' perceptions of a product vary, e.g. different customers have different views on what a

I'll have the usual please

global focus

Unfortunately, you may not be able to get your usual product abroad. There is an ever increasing number of global brands available but, although they may look the same as the ones at home, there are sometimes subtle differences.

Take Coca-Cola, for example. The US drink is not quite the same as the one you can buy in parts of Asia, where it has more sugar added. McDonald's? Well, you can hardly sell hamburgers in India where the cow is sacred, so those burgers are made of lamb instead. Then there's the strange story of the Mars bar.

Mars was founded in the USA – and Britain. The first company was the US one, and it was so successful that its founder could see no reason to change. However, as is the way of the world, his son wanted to make improvements. Frustrated by his father's blocking his ambitions, the son emigrated to England where he set up his own company.

Mr Mars Senior's bestselling line in the USA was Milky Way. The new British company started with the same product but called it the Mars bar instead. Eventually father and son, and the two companies, were reunited. However, the Mars bar and Milky Way are still confused – if you know someone who is going to the USA, ask them to bring you a Mars bar and see what you get.

product is worth or how fashionable it is. Perception involves the way in which we interpret our world and is built from our life experiences and our personalities. We have different likes and dislikes, different tastes – that is largely why suppliers offer us a choice of products.

One of the big challenges of marketing is to ensure that customers perceive a product in the way that is intended. If there is a mismatch of customer perception and supplier intention, then there is a problem. For example, when Sunny Delight was launched, it was positioned as a healthy drink for children – as one that children would like the taste of and parents would feel was doing them good. Children did like the taste but parents did not share Procter and Gamble's view of the product's healthy qualities. There was a rethink, a redesign and a relaunch.

ACTIVITY

Ask some friends to describe a well-known branded product – for example, the Big Mac, Marks and Spencer underwear, Nike shoes, Bounty chocolate bars. It is likely that they will have different views, i.e. they will each perceive that product differently.

Products deliver benefits other than the core ones. A car's core benefit may be flexible travel – there is no need to go to specific departure or arrival points, such as bus stations or airports, at specific times, and they also carry one or several people, with luggage if required. All cars provide this benefit and so a customer's choice of car will depend upon the other rings in the total product model (see Exhibit 6.1) and upon individual preference. Some people want fast cars, some want safe cars, some want cars that keep them cool, some want enough room for the whole family and others want cars that are easy to park. In a competitive market, the customer's perception of the total product (is it fast, safe, roomy, etc.?) is the main determinant of their choice.

Towards a learning organisation

By the close of the twentieth century, the UK manu-facturing industry was in a bad way. One of the worst-hit sectors was textiles, where high-cost Western firms were having trouble competing with manufacturers from the low-wage economies of the East. It became clear to one small Leicestershire textile components manufacturer (130 employees) that, if it was to survive, it needed to find new ways to improve long-term profits.

When it looked closely at its order history, it saw that it had a variety of customers, both large and small, and that many of them bought products made to their own specifications. The obvious course of action was to cut out the smaller customers and reduce the range of products offered – especially the bespoke ones. How-ever, that's a strategy that cannot be repeated endlessly and, anyway, the company was reluctant to let down loyal customers who had stuck with it. So it decided that it would prefer to understand its customers better, and serve their needs more precisely and profitably.

A postgraduate student, supervised by experienced university staff, worked with the company to introduce more modern management techniques. During the initial business analysis process, it was discovered that many people within the company had areas of specialist knowledge (e.g. ways to improve knitting quality), which they did not share with their colleagues – or customers. Such expertise was not usually delib-erately withheld, it was just the way things worked. Procedures had not changed very much in a long time. It was time they did.

The company installed a computer database sys-tem that would integrate all the information sources within the business (sales records, product details, contact reports, etc.) together with outside sources (databases, suppliers' information, journals, etc.). This improved access to better-quality information means that the firm can serve its existing customers more effectively. It has greatly improved existing relationships as well as helping forge relation-ships with new customers. By sharing knowledge throughout the company, and with customers, strik-ing results have been achieved. The total product offering has been improved immeasurably. Sales revenues are up and, most importantly, profits are increasing.

A NOTE ON BRANDING

branding
the process of building a brand

brand identity
all the outward trappings of the brand, e.g. logo, name, colours, strap line and packaging

brand image
people's perception of the brand

Branding spans two levels in the total product model. As **brand identity**, it is a part of the basic product, giving it a name and signalling its level of quality. **Brand image** is also an important part of the customer's perception of the product and so fits into the model's outer ring (see below and Chapter 11 for further explanation of branding).

Product types

Products differ in the way they do things, the way they are used, the way they are dis-tributed and who they are aimed at. The successful management of a product, brand or group of products and brands, depends to a great extent on an understanding of the types of products and brands to be managed. This is essential in order to select the most appropriate way in which to design and communicate a properly integrated and focused set of images, messages and customer relationship activities. Products can be grouped with others which satisfy broadly the same needs (Exhibit 6.2).

Exhibit 6.2   Product types

Consumer products	Examples
durable goods	fridges, bicycles
non-durable goods	fresh food, toiletries
services	theatre seats, haircuts
convenience goods:	
impulse buys	snacks, flowers
staples	bread, washing-up liquid
emergency	headache pills, tissues
shopping goods	stereos, cars
speciality goods	antiques, sports cars
B2B/industrial products	
capital goods	fork-lift trucks, computers
accessories	screwdrivers, hard hats
raw materials	flour, steel
sub-assemblies/components	engines, wheels
supplies	stationery, paper cups
services	cleaning, accountancy

CONSUMER PRODUCTS

The following are some common categorisations of products. There is overlap and some products may fit more than one category. For example, shampoo is both a non-durable good and a convenience good – and it is usually categorised as **FMCG**.

FMCG (fast-moving consumer goods) low-value items, frequently bought, e.g. toothpaste

Durable goods

These products are expected to last a considerable length of time. They are not used up all at once but can be used repeatedly. A washing machine, for example, is expected to perform a large number of washes, a car a large number of journeys.

Non-durable goods

These products are used up in the process of consumption. They do not last. Fruit is eaten. Soap dissolves.

Service products

Services cannot be stored at all. Normally they are used there and then. You watch a film and are left with only a memory (and possibly a ticket stub). You get off the bus and have no further claim on it. Services present marketers with particular challenges and will be discussed in more depth in the next chapter.

Convenience goods

These are products that customers buy frequently and think little about. They are of little value and have many close substitutes so they need strong **branding** and eye-catching colours and designs to make them stand out from the rest. There are a number of subcategories of convenience good:

- **Impulse goods**: spur-of-the-moment purchases that have no advance planning, e.g. an ice cream bought while queuing to get in somewhere or flowers bought at the station on the way home. Customers are not usually prepared to pay a high price for such purchases.
- **Staple goods** (essential goods): staple goods are purchased regularly, perhaps always kept in the cupboard or fridge (e.g. coffee, milk, shampoo). Customers usually look for good value.
- **Emergency goods**: emergency goods are infrequently purchased but needed at short notice (e.g. rain capes, sun hats, plasters). Such products may be location-specific (rain capes sell well at Disney World and Wimbledon) and have a high value to customers at that time, so their prices can be higher.

ACTIVITY

Classify the products in the photo. Are they:

- impulse goods?
- staples?
- emergency purchases?

Fast-moving consumer goods (**FMCG**) are a form of convenience good, but in this case looked at from the retailer's point of view. They are the products that move off the shelves quickly and so need frequent restocking, e.g. toothpaste, washing-up liquid, instant coffee.

Shopping goods

Shopping goods carry a higher associated risk for a customer than convenience products do. They may be set at a higher price or it may be that the cost of product failure is high.

Customers usually shop around to find the right car, stereo, furniture, necklace or lawn mower (hence the name shopping goods). For many, shopping for such things is an enjoyable leisure activity in its own right. Customers are likely to spend some time over the decision-making process, assessing the options, seeking information and opinions, trying things out. These products are therefore sometimes referred to as **high-involvement purchases**, i.e. the customer gets very involved in the decision-making. For more on decision-making processes, see Chapter 3.

Speciality goods

Speciality goods are unusual, and often quite expensive, products which are commonly sold in niche markets. They may be high-risk products and so customers may need extensive emotional support and encouragement from the supplier before they buy. This often means that they are sold through limited outlets (see 'exclusive distribution' in Chapter 9) by highly trained staff. Examples of speciality goods include model aeroplanes, health foods, wedding clothes, horses and classic cars.

EXPAND YOUR KNOWLEDGE

Bucklin, L.P. (1963) 'Retail strategy and the classification of consumer goods', *Journal of Marketing*, 27 (Jan): 51–56.

This article takes as its starting point Copeland's classification of consumer goods: convenience, shopping and speciality, and develops the concept and classification extending it to apply to retail strategy formulation.

B2B AND INDUSTRIAL PRODUCTS

Capital goods

Capital goods are durable products (i.e. they are designed to last for a number of years), such as machinery and buildings. They are usually high cost, bought infrequently and carry high potential risk. Consequently, great care is normally taken over these purchases.

Accessories

These are smaller capital items, e.g. chairs, shelving, hand tools such as screwdrivers. They support the production process. As they are lower cost, they represent a lower financial risk to a company. However, some accessories are essential and their failure may have far-reaching consequences so not all are low risk. For example, a hand tool that breaks may cause serious injury. The total product still plays a part in the differentiation of such products.

Raw materials

Raw materials are goods that will be processed, and added to, by the manufacturing process. Together they become the finished article. For example, cotton is knitted into socks, crude oil is refined and becomes petrol (and a number of other products), water, hops and yeast are brewed into beer. At this level it may be difficult to distinguish one supplier's products from another since, by their nature, raw materials may be similar. They are often **generic products**. However, service, delivery terms, technical assistance and many other aspects can be exploited to make the organisation different and thus the preferred supplier (see Exhibit 6.1).

generic products
physical products that have no discernible difference from each other; often used to mean unbranded products

Sub-assemblies, components and parts

These products have already been manufactured but are not finished goods. They are bought by businesses to incorporate into their own products. For example, Levi's buys denim fabric to make into jeans, Nokia buys microchips for its mobile phones, Siemens buys condensers to put into its fridges.

Supplies

Numerous minor items are used in the production process; and they are important in the smooth running of the whole process. Companies depend on such things as soap, stationery, pens, copier paper and cleaning materials. These are not capital goods as they are non-durable (i.e. they are used up relatively quickly rather than being reused over and over).

Services

Manufacturing businesses rely on efficient machinery so maintenance and repair services are important to them. All workplaces need regular cleaning. Buildings must be painted and repaired. In addition, there are a large number of business services, such as consultancy, accountancy, legal advice and IT support. The special nature of services is discussed in the next chapter.

There are many different ways to categorise products and different markets have their own preferred descriptors. Many products are bought both by businesses and by consumers (though the specifications may be different). For example, envelopes may be B2B supplies and bought in bulk, or a consumer staple good bought in smaller packs.

These product types refer to basic products. However, most of the products we buy today are not generic products – they are branded.

Branding

branding
the process of building a brand

Branding is a strategy used 'to differentiate products and companies, and to build economic value for both the consumer and the brand owner' (Pickton and Broderick, 2004). This section will discuss branding as part of the total product offering, whereas the strategic nature of branding, along with the building of strong brands, will be considered in Chapter 11.

WHAT IS A BRAND?

From the earliest times, people have marked their possessions in order to differentiate them from other people's. The term 'branding' seems to originate with American ranchers, who branded their cattle to advertise their ownership. Each branding iron was unique and formed an indelible, identifying mark. That mark was an assurance that the animal in question was from that particular ranch and also came to be used as a guide to the quality of the beef. However, modern brands are:

much more than just logos or names. They are the culmination of a user's total experience with the product ... over many years. That experience is made of a multitude of good, neutral and bad encounters such as the way a product performs, an advertising message, a press report, a telephone call, or a rapport with a sales assistant. (CIM, n.d.)

What's in a name?

global focus

Increasingly, manufacturers are trying to use the same name for their products worldwide. In Britain, Jif cleaning cream became Cif to match the rest of Europe. Marathon bars became Snickers and Oil of Ulay, rather oddly, became Oil of Olay. The UK won on Twix, though; that used to be called Raider elsewhere, but now it's Twix to everyone.

Those name changes were made as part of global branding exercises. Having the same name helps to standardise brand positioning, promotes global recognition and, of course, it's cheaper in terms of packaging, support literature and promotion. Sometimes, though, the name changes because it has to. The existing name just will not do in other languages. For example, Vauxhall used to make a car called the Nova. Ask someone who speaks Spanish what that means and you'll see why they changed it. In China, Coca-Cola translated as 'bite the wax tadpole'. The Jolly Green Giant turned into 'Intimidating Green Ogre' in its Arabic translation.

Here are some products that never made it in English-speaking countries:

- Pocari Sweat and Mucos (soft drinks, Japan)
- Pipi (orangeade, Yugoslavia)
- Pschitt (soft drink, France)
- Skinababe (baby cleanser, Japan)
- Polio (detergent, Czechoslovakia)
- Shitto (hot pepper sauce, Ghana)
- Krapp (toilet paper, Sweden)

SOURCES: Dennis, 2001; Paliwoda and Thomas, 1999

Business branding's origins lie with craftsmen who made especially good tools or leather, and later with manufacturers who could provide consistent quality. They realised that they could attract more customers and could charge a higher price than their rivals if they could label their products to make them easily recognisable. Through the latter part of the twentieth century, branding developed alongside marketing as a managerial process, although some of today's well-known brand names existed as company names long before they became part of a branding strategy, e.g. Sunlight Soap, Swan Vesta matches, Daimler motor cars, His Master's Voice records (HMV), Boots the Chemists. Today a strong brand brings with it a wealth of quality, value and high performance cues and can even be an intrinsic part of its customers' lifestyles.

With the growth of branding has come a change in emphasis within organisations. Companies used to be centred on the production of goods or services. The emphasis was very much on quality and efficiency (see Chapter 1 for production and product orientation). The importance of marketing has long been well accepted in most organisations, although unfortunately rivalries do still exist between the marketing, finance and production functions. Customer satisfaction is now seen as being at the heart of success rather than excellence in production or selling, largely as a result of increased competition making it harder to attract and keep customers.

Brands are differentiated by their unique names, logos and packaging. This makes up their **brand identity.** That identity is designed to represent the brand's values and to signal them to potential customers. The way they see values then helps the customers to form a brand image in their minds (see Chapter 11).

brand identity
all the outward trappings of the brand, e.g. logo, name, colours, strap line and packaging

THE ADVANTAGES OF BRANDING PRODUCTS

Companies invest millions in the development and protection of their brands. A strong brand is seen as key to commercial success, providing the following advantages (and more):

brand equity
the monetary value of a
brand

- high **brand equity**
- increased product awareness levels
- the ability to charge a premium price
- reduced susceptibility to price wars
- competitive edge
- a sound basis for building strong customer relationships
- higher likelihood of repeat purchases
- retail leverage
- the fact that new products have a better chance of success thanks to the brand name.

Brands must be built in order to become strong and benefit from the advantages listed above. It is not enough just to attach a name and a logo to a product. Nor do brands automatically maintain their strength. They must be nurtured and carefully managed (see Chapters 8 and 11 for more on building brands).

High brand equity

A well-known brand adds value to a product both from the customer perspective and from the company's. Brands may be the most valuable assets that a company has. For more on brand equity, see Chapter 11.

Increased product awareness

Clearly, it is crucial that potential customers should be aware of a product. It is the first stage on their journey to buying it (see sequential models in Chapter 8). One of the key roles of advertising is to build that awareness and an easily recognised brand makes that task much easier. Product and packaging design play key roles here as well, by making the product more visible and reinforcing the brand's values.

Premium pricing and reduced susceptibility to price wars

A good brand name helps a firm achieve a premium price for its products. Think of the differences in the prices of trainers. The well-known brands, e.g. Nike and Reebok, can charge much more for their products than lesser known brands. It is not just a question of having a well-known name. The strength of the brand depends upon the values associated with it in that particular market. Marks and Spencer is a well-known brand but they cannot get away with charging Nike prices for their trainers, even if the quality is comparable.

Without a brand, a firm will have to settle for a commodity position in the market where low prices alone drive sales. Some firms actively choose this position, e.g. the makers of generic pharmaceuticals, but it does not sit well with the concept of marketing as a series of complex management tasks leading to greater success for the organisation. In very price-conscious markets, e.g. children's shoes and clothing, or in economic downturns, marketers can come under great pressure to compete on price but this might devalue their brand (assuming it already has a reputation). Aaker (2002) argues that pressure to compete on prices can even undermine attempts to build up a brand as one of the main impetuses for branding, i.e. the differentiation from the competition that allows a firm to charge premium prices, is removed.

product adoption process
the stages a buyer goes
through before purchasing
a product

Competitive edge

A branded product simplifies shopping by assisting with a customer's **product adoption process** (see Chapter 4). If the marketing communications have worked well, then the potential customer will already have built up a set of associations with the brand, short-circuiting a lot of the information searching that they might otherwise have to do. This is good for customers as they save time and effort (this assumes that their image of the brand is correct) and is certainly an advantage to the branded product as it is likely to be preferred to other unknown or less well thought of products.

ACTIVITY

What do these car marques say to you? What values do you associate with each of the brands?
How does Porsche's logo compare to that of Jaguar or Mini? What do the differences say about each brand's personality?

The Porsche, Jaguar, Mini Cooper, and Mercedes logos are the registered trademarks of each respective corporation. Use of the logos here does not imply endorsement of the organisations.

Building relationships

The strength of the customer's relationship with a brand is central to that brand's growth. The relationship is normally between the customer and the brand, rather than between the customer and the brand's owner, which may even be a company that the customer has never heard of. There are many big companies which own many brands that do not bear their owner's name. For example, Diageo is the owner of a large number of drinks brands (Smirnoff, Bailey's, Guinness, Johnny Walker, Captain Morgan) and yet 'I'll have a Diageo please' is never heard in bars (see 'Brand types' in Chapter 11).

The importance of this brand relationship has prompted companies to develop various relationship-building activities which establish a two-way flow of communication with their customers and encourage them to integrate brands into their lives. Examples of these activities include club memberships, loyalty card schemes, registration of warranties, other products such as T-shirts and bags with the brand name and logo on and website activities.

The number of brand communities is increasing rapidly, thanks in part to the World Wide Web, and they form a significant part of a growing number of people's social lives. Muniz and O'Guinn (2001) first coined the term 'brand community' and they defined it as 'a specialised, non-geographically bound community, based on a structured set of social relations among admirers of a brand'. **Brand communities** are characterised by a set of shared attitudes towards, and beliefs about, the brand (shared consciousness), rituals and traditions connected with the brand and a sense of moral guardianship for the brand. A brand that is liked well enough to inspire a community to grow around it clearly has a number of loyal consumers and therefore this is generally held to be a positive thing for the brand – though members of brand communities can be the brand's greatest critics as well as its greatest fans. Brand communities can be very possessive towards brands and the importance of understanding their views is illustrated by the reaction of loyal customers to the introduction of a new recipe for Coca-Cola. They boycotted the product and sales slumped so badly that the original recipe had to be reinstated. New Coke lasted about three months (see Insight box)

brand communities a group of people, usually consumers, formed on the basis of their shared admiration for a particular branded product or range of products, e.g. the BMW owners group

insight   Brand new love

Coca-Cola is one of the most successful products ever but even the Coca-Cola company makes product mistakes sometimes. In 1985, they changed the tried-and-tested secret formula and introduced New Coke. They did this in response to Pepsi's repositioning as a youth brand and its much publicised triumph in blind taste tests – people generally preferred its sweeter taste. Sure enough, the taste of New Coke was popular in all the trials.

However, Coke had underestimated the power of its brand and its customers' loyalty to the original Coca-Cola. When the new replaced the old on the shelves, there was a storm of protest across the USA. A part of American history had been devalued, replaced. According to its advertising, Coca-Cola was *the real thing* and yet now it seemed there was a new real thing – a contradiction in terms. Within three months, New Coke was withdrawn and the old favourite was back on the shelves.

SOURCE: Haig, 2003

Repeat purchases

Most human beings instinctively avoid unnecessary risk. Buying things represents at least a financial risk in that money may be wasted if the product is not fit for purpose. There are other possible risks too. For example, there is ego risk if the product is unflattering (e.g. clothes) or ridiculed by others (e.g. an unpopular scent), or physical risk if the product turns out to be unsafe (e.g. faulty machinery). A brand that has been bought before and found to be satisfactory reduces these risks and so people are more likely to buy that trusted brand again.

A good experience of a brand results in a happy customer who continues to purchase. Conversely, a bad experience can lead to an unhappy customer who may very well reject future offerings bearing this brand, no matter how attractive the offering appears to be. Worse still, they may tell their friends, family and acquaintances of their bad experience, influencing them against the brand. Attraction and retention are the key words when thinking about the development of a brand.

Retail leverage

In many countries, notably in the UK, large retailers have enormous power when it comes to setting prices and dictating terms of purchase and sale. Tesco, for example, is one of the largest companies in the world, much larger than many of the manufacturers who supply it. Tesco therefore has a great deal of buying power (see Chapter 9). However, there are some branded products that are so popular that even a retailer as powerful as Tesco is unlikely to leave them off its shelves, e.g. Heinz Tomato Ketchup, Heinz Baked Beans, Kellogg's cereals, Coca-Cola, Kleenex tissues.

New product success

Even the most innovative and high-quality new products struggle to make headway in today's markets. Many entrepreneurs have launched seemingly superb products only to watch them fail. A strong brand gives that vulnerable new product a much better chance of success. The customers can call on their experience of previous products of the same brand, and transfer those brand values to the new product.

evoked set
the shortlist of products from which a purchaser will make a final choice

This reduces the risk associated with trying something new and so the new product is more likely to make it into their **evoked set** of products, and therefore they are more likely to try it. Take the BBC iPlayer, for example. It was launched into a market that was struggling to gain consumer acceptance. ITV and Channel 4's catch-up TV services were not attracting sufficient viewers but the BBC's new product changed the market profile completely by reassuring reluctant viewers and encouraging them to try the catch-up service. Now all three services are doing well and others, e.g. Sky, have joined them.

For more on branding, including brand components, types of brand, branding strategies and brand equity, see Chapter 11.

EXPAND YOUR KNOWLEDGE

Belen del Rio, A., Vazquez, R. and Iglesia, V. (2001) 'The effects of brand associations on consumer response', *Journal of Consumer Marketing*, 18 (5): 410–425.

This paper studies the dimensions of brand image by focusing on the value of the brand as perceived by consumers. Four categories of functions are identified: guarantee, personal identification, social identification and status. These functions are shown to have a positive influence on the consumer's willingness to recommend the brand, pay a price premium and accept brand extensions.

Product development

New products are the lifeblood of a company. Competitors improve their product offerings all the time and customers usually prefer to buy the latest products. They want this year's fashions, the technology with the latest features, the most convenient household products, the healthier version or the greener version or just the more economical one. This philosophy of constant innovation, especially in consumer goods markets, has been adhered to by leading companies for many years. However, it is important to plan and to manage the process carefully. Too much innovation too quickly can be disruptive and make product lines too complicated to manage effectively. As the complexity of the management task increases, so the organisation's costs rise and its profit margins shrink. To maximise its profit potential, the company needs to be sure that any additional products add more value than the costs they create.

It is a key marketing task to deliver products that meet needs. If those needs change, e.g. there is now a need for green fuels that will not harm the atmosphere,

insight   Boots march on

It used to be called Boots the Chemist but that may not be appropriate for much longer. The high street retailer long ago extended its range of products beyond medicines. In a Boots store today, you can have your eyes tested and get films developed as well as buy cosmetics, toiletries, baby clothes, gifts and sandwiches. However, the electrical goods and kitchen utensils have gone. The brand has already successfully stretched into health services. There are Boots dentists and laser eye clinics. Its most recent addition is fitness equipment – a complementary product for its West London gym.

Whatever brand type or strategy is adopted, it is important that the idea of the brand is not limited to the actual product. It should be part of the whole experience. A brand promise is made to the customer. Fulfilling that promise, hopefully even exceeding it, is a key part of brand management.

then marketers must find new ways to satisfy those needs – and this often means that they must develop new products. The better a product offering matches customer needs, the more likely it is to achieve customer satisfaction, and consequent success in the marketplace.

Innovation is expensive and requires the support of top management and an organisational culture that encourages new ideas. The new product development process can take a number of forms. It may be an informal exercise in encouraging ideas or a formal, structured approach with its own staff and facilities dedicated to the research of changing customer needs and the development of new ways to fulfil them.

New products do not have to be totally new inventions. In fact, truly new products are very rare. Even those that seem to be so innovative, e.g. MP3 players and mobile phones, are really advancements on previous products that played music (gramophones, CD players, tape machines) or made calls (landlines and telephones). Most new products are modifications of previous offerings rather than new-to-the-world products. So the PC manufacturers make their laptops lighter and with better screens, mobile phones have more features, skirt lengths go up (or down), food has less fat, etc.

THE IMPORTANCE OF INNOVATION

New products can be used to:

- increase or defend market share by offering more choice within the range or by updating older products (e.g. Ford has developed people-carrier versions of most of its models)
- appeal to a different market segment (e.g. Guinness bitter, Häagen-Dazs frozen yoghurt)
- maintain reputation as a leading-edge company (e.g. Apple iPhones and iPods)
- diversify into new markets and thereby spread risk (e.g. Dyson hand dryers)
- improve relationships within distribution channels (e.g. Allied Domecq offering its Baskin-Robbins franchisees further franchise opportunities in Dunkin' Donuts and Togo's)
- make better use of resources such as production capacity (e.g. some chocolate bars can be made on the same production machinery as others)
- even out peaks and troughs in demand (e.g. ice cream parlours selling baked potatoes; Father's Day was invented by greetings card companies).

TYPES OF NEW PRODUCT

Most new products' newness stems from innovation in the basic, augmented or perceived product rather than from true innovation in the product's core (see total product offering). Very few are designed for an entirely new purpose, i.e. to meet a new need or one that was not met by any product before. New products can be classified as follows:

- *Innovative product*: this is a really new product, one that meets a need that was not previously fulfilled. It is likely to be a technological or medical breakthrough, e.g. Biodiesel (a vegetable oil-based fuel), the Internet, text messaging, laser eye surgery. There are relatively few of these types of new-to-the-market products and services. Innovative new products may be protected by a patent, requiring imitators to obtain a licence to produce their version or risk being sued.

- *Replacement product*: these are more common than innovative ones. The customer need has been satisfied by a previous product but the replacement product does it better (or at least differently), e.g. MP3 players may replace CD players just as they (more or less) replaced record players and tape decks; the Ford Focus replaced the Ford Escort.
- *Variant product*: many companies frequently introduce new, related products to their ranges. These may be temporary or more permanent additions, e.g. Kit Kat Chunky (long term), Ford Fiesta Flame (special edition).
- *Me-too product*: these are imitations of products already on the market, e.g. Wrigley's Extramints, Trebor 24/7 chewing gum or the many portable music players that followed Sony's on to the market. It makes sense to let others do the costly market research and development first – to let them take the risks.
- *Relaunched product*: this is not really a new product at all. Rather, the physical characteristics of the basic product may not be altered (or only slightly) but the total product offering has changed. There will be a different marketing strategy, perhaps changing the emphasis on product benefits, e.g. the magazine *Inside Soap* was relaunched as a weekly, rather than a fortnightly, publication.

THE NEW PRODUCT DEVELOPMENT PROCESS

New products are evaluated at each stage in their development process. If an idea is not going to make it to launch, then it is better if it is eliminated as early in the process as possible. The product's development costs mount up as it moves further through the development process.

Producers should not always rely on customers to judge the merits of a new-to-the-world product idea. Sometimes new products fulfil a need that it had not occurred to customers *could* be met, and so it is not really possible to assess customer reaction accurately before they see the finished item. Take, for example, electric light. It is taken for granted now, but 100 years ago people were quite happy with gaslight and it didn't occur to them that a better, clearer artificial light source might be possible. They liked the greenish glow gaslighting gave and appreciated the extra warmth in winter. Thomas Edison knew that electric light would sweep civilisation but he was greeted with scepticism at first and had to give many demonstrations and use his own money to pay for generators to light the streets of New York before he got his point across. In the early days of domestic electricity, the electricity companies had to offer to wire up houses free of charge to encourage use – rather like modern-day digital television services.

The model in Exhibit 6.3 shows the stages of the product development process. Product development should not be seen as a one-off or ad hoc activity but as a continuous process. That way, there will be a fairly consistent stream of new product ideas available to be taken to the next stage and ready to replace older products when their time comes.

Constant monitoring and evaluation is essential in this product development process. The aim is that only the right products should progress while those with little chance of commercial success are disposed of as early as possible. The number of products in development reduces at each stage as some are rejected. However, the costs associated with the development of each product mount as it goes through the stages. So the costs associated with the product development process escalate, and the number of viable product ideas reduce, as time passes.

Exhibit 6.3   New product development process

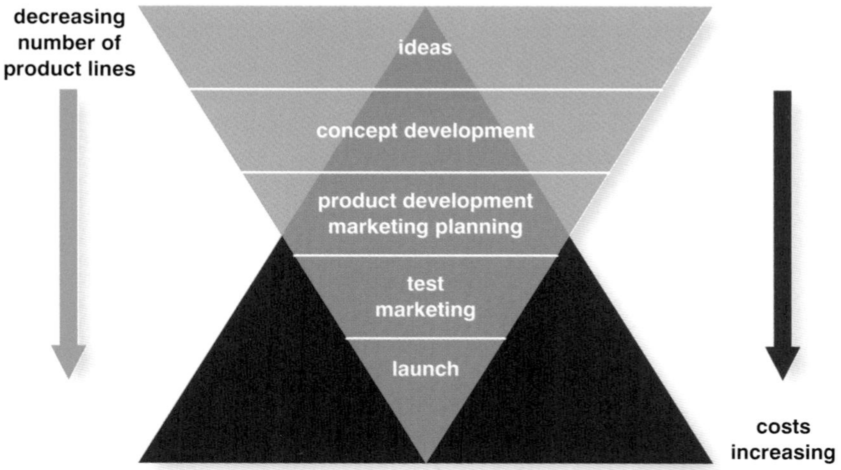

Idea stage (generation and initial screening of ideas)

Ideas for new products may be generated internally or externally. Some companies are technology led, e.g. Dyson and Apple, and get the inspiration for most of their new products from their own product research. They have substantial research and development departments whose job it is to design technologically advanced products. Other companies, particularly the more market-orientated ones, take their lead from their customers and look to develop products that match explicitly stated customer needs. Others may employ a marketing agency which specialises in new product ideas.

Market research seems a sound way to find ideas for new products and it will certainly help establish customers' views on the firm's existing product offering and, by establishing what is wrong with it, suggesting new ideas. It is better at uncovering customer needs than in finding specific product solutions, as customers are rarely able to imagine the design of a product that does not exist.

ACTIVITY

Be a market researcher briefly. Ask some of your friends, family or classmates what new communications products they would like. Do not lead or prompt them. Then ask them what is wrong with the products they already own (computers, mobile phones, telephones, etc.) and if they can think of any improvements to them.

How many new product possibilities have you discovered? Which technique generated more?

There are many ways to generate new product ideas: from brainstorming (a lively group session where ideas spark other ideas and all are captured, none discounted or disparaged), to analysing customer complaints and competitive products, to establishing original research facilities. 3M (the makers of Scotch Tape and Post-it Notes) deliberately encourages a culture of creativity and allows its employees to spend some of their time on personal projects that may, or may not, produce ideas the company can use. The company expects all of its employees to devote some of their time to thinking up new ideas, but also has sophisticated research facilities. Any source of new ideas is acceptable although many ideas will be discarded, sometimes very early in the process of monitoring and evaluation.

At the start of the process, the focus is on generating as many ideas as possible. The impractical ones are then quickly discarded while the possibles will progress to the next stage.

Concept stage (development and testing of the product concept)

A product concept is much more than just an idea. The product has to be thought through from both technical and **consumer**, or end user, points of view. This may involve the production of drawings, detailed descriptions and theoretical models – all of them aim to assess whether the idea works. As well as testing the product design and consumer reactions, at this stage the concept should be examined to see whether or not it fits in with the organisation's marketing strategy. Is it a product that will add to and complement the company's existing range of products?

In the motor industry many ideas are floated but get rejected quickly. Those that have potential are passed to the design studio where the proposed car is mocked up, perhaps even as a full-size model that can be seen in three dimensions. Individuals, both inside and outside the organisation, are then shown the model and asked for their opinions.

The product concept is tested both for its viability as a product and as a business proposition. Business analysis involves reviewing costs and sales projections in order to arrive at a profit forecast and to assess the likelihood of this product meeting the company's objectives for it. Products that meet the company's criteria, move on to the next stage: product development.

Product development stage (prototyping and pilot production)

Prototyping and/or pilot production of a product is very costly and so only products with good potential are allowed to get this far. Such products have passed concept tests and are now ready for production, but first the company may make a prototype (or prototypes) in order to conduct further tests. These tests check the safety of the product, its durability, usability, etc. Car manufacturers such as Volvo use crash test dummies to see what happens when the car crashes at various speeds. Toy manufacturers call children in to play with the new toy to see how well it stands up to their misuse. Many organisations use computer simulations for this stage, especially if the prototype would be expensive to make and/or would require an actual production facility. The results from these tests are used to refine the design before production starts.

Full-scale production is very expensive and so most companies start by making one, or a small number, of the products so that they can test their production plans and make any necessary changes before committing to large-scale manufacture. These initial pilot runs may involve making the product entirely by hand as setting up a working production line is expensive and time-consuming and may be a waste if the product does not make it to the next stage of the development process. Critical evaluation now takes place, assessing the product in its approximate final form.

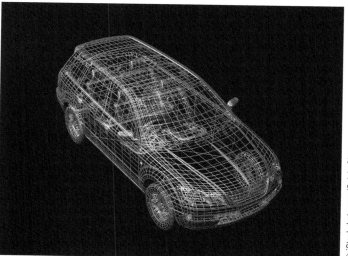

Computer-aided design is widely used in product development

© iStockphoto.com/Golgin Oleg

Marketing planning

The marketing planning process will have already begun – sometimes these stages overlap at least a little. The marketing department have to work out what price to charge, how much advertising and other communication will be required and where and how the product will be sold. They will develop a formal product marketing plan that sets out the product's proposed positioning, their sales targets and other formal marketing objectives. See Chapter 12 for more on the drawing up of marketing plans.

Test marketing stage

test market
a subset of a market in which a product offering can be sold for a short period of time in order to predict demand and to try out and refine the marketing mix

Concepts will only progress this far if the company believes that those products will sell. They may now be made in small quantities and sold to a small, selected market, usually a geographic region, in order to obtain information about customer reactions. A **test market** is the market in miniature. The area chosen should represent the whole market as closely as possible in all its key characteristics, e.g. demographics, lifestyles, media, outlets, competition. Not only the product itself, but also all the related marketing mix activities are tested. If the mix works well, then the product may be launched immediately afterwards. Alternatively, the test-marketing exercise may suggest modifications to the mix, or that the product should not be launched at all.

Test marketing is expensive and time-consuming and also has the disadvantage of allowing the competition to assess the new product. Competitors may even attempt to spoil a test market, perhaps by deliberately lowering the price of their own products in that area, or launching their own, local promotional campaign. Some have even been known to launch special, limited edition versions of their own products in order to spoil the sales and market research data from the test market.

Test marketing is not essential, only desirable, and in any one case the drawbacks may outweigh the benefits. If the new product is a simple modification of an existing one, the market is well known and understood, and the data is therefore likely to suggest only minimal changes, then the product may be launched without exposure to a test market.

Launch (commercialisation)

This is the final stage in the product development process. The company is now committed to full-scale manufacture and distribution, and has many decisions to make before the product is ready to be shipped out. All marketing mix elements must be finalised: prices set, promotion booked, packaging arranged, the distribution chain set up and all the operational issues involved in supplying the product to the market resolved. The company's personnel will need to be trained on the new product and enthused about it. Timing is crucial to a successful product launch and therefore there must be a detailed project plan. Companies trading internationally will have to decide where to launch as well as when. Very few will roll out a new product in all their markets at the same time as that would place too great a burden on even a multinational's resources.

The launch of a new-to-the-world product (or even a major innovation on an old one) is a time for the company to celebrate. They might host an event for customers, staff and journalists with the intention of gaining publicity for the new product. The launch of a new consumer product needs to be well publicised as its initial reception and the speed with which early sales build up are often crucial to its long-term success.

New products are launched regularly. The continued existence of many large high-tech corporations relies upon the successful launch of their next product. The producers of computer games frequently battle to be the first to launch the latest technology. Sega used to be a major player in this market, producing its own consoles and equipment, but now they have to be content to produce software for other

Clockwork power

As the pace of technological change gathers speed, there are, apparently, fewer and fewer areas where customers might be surprised by new-to-the-world ideas. New and wonderful electronic gizmos, both for entertainment and for more serious applications, are everywhere and have become the norm. Yet it is still possible to be surprised. Take, for example, the Bayliss wind-up radio, which exploited old clockwork technology, applied modern techniques and produced a fully portable power source that is now being exploited elsewhere – e.g. in powering laptop computers, satellite navigation systems and even for recharging mobile phones by use of a device included in a pair of hiking boots (every step generates power for the user's phone).

Initially, Trevor Bayliss found it next to impossible to find a manufacturer prepared to back him. They were unable to envisage the potential of his radical, old idea.

manufacturers' platforms. Fall behind on the technology and billions of pounds' worth of sales can slip into the hands of competitors. So much depends on the effectiveness with which target markets have been researched, and expectations matched, when the new product is launched.

New products are launched to replace old ones that no longer have significant markets. Most new products will, unfortunately, fail despite companies' best efforts in their development. The time in between their launch and their deletion can be viewed as the life of that product and one of the tools available to aid managers with their product planning is the product life cycle.

The product life cycle

The **product life cycle** concept is one that has many opponents and many supporters. On the one hand, it has limited usefulness as a management tool since it provides no absolute answers. On the other hand, it does help analyse the market for the product and so can be a helpful decision-making aid. The position of a product in its life cycle can indicate whether there are likely to be further significant increases in sales or not – and provide pointers on what to do in order to maximise those sales.

product life cycle
a product analysis tool based on the idea that a product has life stages: introduction, growth, maturity, decline, deletion

The model in Exhibit 6.4 illustrates how products move through a series of stages in their progress from introduction to a market to their final replacement with another product – i.e. another way to deliver the core benefit that the old product delivered or another solution to a particular customer need. The product's progress is mapped out in a similar way to a human being's progress through life: birth, growing up, reaching maturity, declining into old age and ultimately death – or, in the product's case, deletion.

THE STAGES OF THE PRODUCT LIFE CYCLE

Introduction

At the introduction stage, sales are low (initially zero) and the product is usually making a loss. The challenge is to get people to try the product. The people most

Exhibit 6.4   Product life cycle

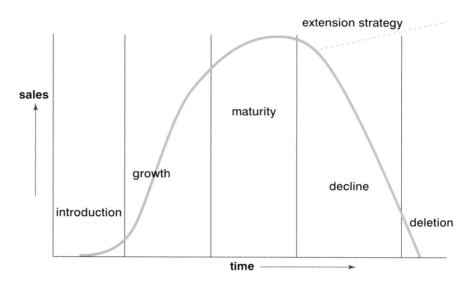

likely to try it are the innovators (see the section on the product adoption process in Chapter 3) and so marketing efforts are usually directed at them.

Growth

Sales increase during the growth stage, as does customer understanding and appreciation of the product. This stage is critical to the product's long-term survival as it is now that customers decide whether to make the product one of their regular purchases (in the case of **FMCG**) or not. For shopping goods such as DVD players, the decision is more whether to buy a second one or to replace worn-out products as clearly these goods are not regular, repeat purchases. Aggressive pricing and intensive promotional campaigns are often used during this stage as competitors fight to capture, and retain, customers.

The product should be settling down during the growth stage and any teething problems should have been dealt with. This is the time to introduce new members of the product range and add features. A more heavily featured product may attract more customers. The **early majority** (see Chapter 3) should be displaying an interest by now and they are likely to be tempted by a lower price.

early majority
a substantial group of customers who follow early adopters in buying a new product or service

Maturity

Sales peak during the maturity stage of the life cycle although their growth rate slows as this is now a relatively stable market. This is the stage at which the greatest profit may be made as development and launch costs should have been covered. Competition hots up in the maturity stage. The market is likely to have been split into numerous segments. For example, when chocolate was first introduced into the UK market, it was sold as cocoa to be made into drinks. In today's mature confectionery market, just think how many different types of product, aimed at different types of people, are chocolate-based.

Mature products are likely to be more standardised, although they may be more sophisticated than the original basic ones. This makes manufacturing easier and cheaper. However, there may still be a number of variations. For example, kitchen furniture may have a standard, modular design but come in a choice of colours, finishes, handles, etc. There may also be special editions available for limited time periods.

This is the time to look for an extension strategy in order to delay decline.

Extension strategies

It may be possible to extend the profitable life of a product which is starting to decline. The product might do better in another market, e.g. in another country or aimed at a different age group. Guinness is a classic example of how successful re-targeting can extend the life of a product. Many years ago, Guinness was regarded as an old person's drink, with its slogan 'Guinness is good for you'. There was a distinct problem: its market was dying – literally. Award-winning advertising helped to make the drink trendy and more appealing to a younger market segment, and so it lives on today.

The product may need to be repositioned in order to bring in new customers. Lucozade, for example, was known for many years as a drink for invalids to 'aid recovery'. The product's owners then repositioned the drink as an energy boost for sports people and it assumed a much more youthful, isotonic personality. The brand personality has been changed yet again to become a mixture of a health drink and an energy drink. Each change has been to target different market segments.

Product sales may be increased by persuading existing customers to use more of it, e.g. by finding new uses for it, perhaps in different combinations with other products, or by using the product in a different way (100 uses for WD40, or Rice Crispies made into a dessert for children's parties).

There are numerous strategies to try but they need to be planned and implemented before the product goes too far into decline. Despite marketing departments' best efforts, sadly most products do eventually decline and die.

Decline

The decline stage, which companies try to delay for as long as possible, is characterised by falling sales. This may not be as catastrophic as it at first appears, as there are numerous examples of products being well managed in their decline and producing very satisfactory profits. This time can also be used to prepare the market for the successful introduction of the old product's replacement.

In the decline stage, everything starts to wind down. Product ranges and features are cut to a minimum, with unprofitable products and less popular features being phased out and so the customer has a lot less choice. Unless an extension strategy can be found quickly, or the product gains cult or classic status (as some music or fashion products might), it is headed for deletion.

Deletion

The final stage in a product's life cycle is its end – the deletion stage, when the decision is taken to withdraw the product from sale. The product may be costing more to maintain and support than it brings in. The market is shrinking, as evidenced by falling sales, declining profits and the existence of new, alternative ways of satisfying customer needs and wants.

Pony traps, hula-hoops (the plastic toys, not the snack), yo-yos and typewriters have one thing in common: they are all products that were introduced, grew, matured and declined, and no longer hold any significant commercial value (apart from occasional reappearances as novelty items). They were all replaced by other products that better satisfied customers' needs.

Deleting a product is a big decision and there a number of things to consider before it is reached.

- Is the company prepared to risk losing other business because of this?
- What effect will the deletion have on the rest of the product range? Would it leave a gap that would drive customers to competitors? For example, if a restaurant stopped offering a salad bar, customers might go elsewhere for the sake of the one salad eater in their group.
- Will the products' disappearance upset loyal customers?
- What residual problems may the company be left with? Previously sold products may still have outstanding warranties and will require support.

Take, for example, an airline that has decided to delete a service. Frequent users of this service may have accumulated a substantial number of Air Miles, which they are now no longer able to use. These will continue to show as a debt on the airline's books until the customers use them and yet these customers can no longer use them as there are no flights. There is a serious customer relations issue here. Since the Air Miles have no expiry date, this debt can apparently exist forever. The airline can solve the problem by converting the value of the Air Miles into shopping vouchers, which the customers can spend at home. Microsoft and most other software companies give notice before discontinuing support for their obsolete products. Many users do not upgrade to the latest versions of the software and they must be supported for a reasonable time. Eventually products enter the 'limited support phase' and the company makes renewed attempts to get them to upgrade to the newer products.

EXPAND YOUR KNOWLEDGE

Enis, B.M., LaGarce, R. and Prell, A.E. (1977) 'Extending the product life cycle', *Business Horizons,* 20 (Jun): 46–56.

The paper questions the concept of the product life cycle, particularly in accepting inevitable decline and proposes that the product life cycle can be extended further. It proposes strategies for each stage of the life cycle and for its extension.

USING THE PRODUCT LIFE CYCLE AS AN INPUT TO PLANNING

It is difficult to determine exactly where a product is in its life cycle. Any management action the life stage suggests will be an opinion based on past experience. The product life cycle model is just one of many inputs into the decision-making process.

The product's life stage can be helpful when making marketing plans. Should new features or even new models be introduced? Should the price be changed? Is it time to step up promotional activity? Should the emphasis of that activity be changed from informational to persuasive? Would the product benefit from being offered more widely or perhaps distribution should be cut down?

A product's life is governed by the market forces it is subjected to and the decisions that its managers make. Its life can be terminated or extended. Aspects of the product can be changed to help it adjust to changing market conditions, e.g. new competition, changing customer tastes or reduced incomes. The product life cycle model is an aid to understanding products and their markets, and a useful tool for helping to manage **product portfolios.** A company with too many products in the decline stage would need to think of ways to extend some of those products' lives rapidly or to hurry the introduction of some new ones. If they had paid more attention to the mapping of their products' life cycles earlier, then they might have avoided the problem by ensuring that new products were in the pipeline ready to replace these older ones. Equally, a company with most of its products in the growth stage would be in a high risk category because of the high expenditure needed to support them in what is likely to be a competitive marketplace.

insight   New life for an old product

Some of today's popular products are surprisingly old. They have lived through huge changes and some have changed substantially during their lives, while others have hardly changed at all. Here is a brief history of a very old product that is enjoying a revival recently. Can you guess what it is?

This medicine is first mentioned in East European records from the ninth century but the first commercial version is more likely to have been produced in the eleventh or twelfth centuries. In addition to being a popular cure for a range of illnesses, it was a key ingredient in early formulations of gunpowder. In Russia, where it was believed to have a spirit of its own, it was an important element in religious ceremonies.

In the fourteenth century, people realised that it was also a highly intoxicating drink. Early batches were rough and needed fruits, spices or herbs added to make the drink more palatable. Popular early flavours included absinthe, acorn, birch, calamus root, cherry, ginger, hazelnut, horseradish, peppermint, raspberry and sage.

In the eighteenth century, a Russian professor discovered a more effective purification method and this product's quality improved enormously – although there were still local brews that would never meet today's health and safety standards. The disguising flavours were no longer required and the quest for purity began.

The product was virtually unknown in Western Europe until the Napoleonic wars when Russian soldiers introduced it to new enthusiasts. The first Western distillery was set up in Paris in 1934 by a Russian exile called Vladimir Smirnov. The product quickly gained favour with the French and they introduced it to the rest of Europe and to the USA.

Today this drink is the UK sector leader and the favoured spirit of younger drinkers, largely because of its lack of flavour and its purity (thank those eighteenth-century distillers). It mixes well and is the base for many popular cocktails, including Screwdrivers, Harvey Wallbangers and Bloody Marys. In a declining spirits market, it is the one bright note. Between 2003 and 2008, sales grew by 20 per cent and, despite the recession slowing the growth rate, they are predicted to increase further.

It has been a long and varied life but this old drink doesn't seem ready to slide into decline just yet. It has been helped by a number of innovations: improved quality; additional features (e.g. flavourings); launch into numerous markets; word of mouth; new uses (e.g. cocktail recipes); product line additions (e.g. single portion ready-mixed drinks and alcopops such as Smirnoff ice and WKD); clever advertising aimed at a younger audience and a very loyal following.

Na zdorove!

SOURCES: Anon, n.d.; Courtney, 2009; Mintel, 2009

The product life cycle model was originally devised for generic products, i.e. the product type, not the individual branded item (shoes, not Clarks shoes). It is often, however, applied to products, product classes or to specific brands. The idea behind the product life cycle is that products have an inbuilt life that can be mapped and so its application to a specific branded product can be difficult. One brand may be out of step with the rest of the products in its class, i.e. it is following a differently timed life cycle. The reason for that is likely to lie with its marketing mix, i.e. it is likely to be an internal cause rather than an external one which would affect other similar products as well. For this reason, as well as to ensure that you are comparing like with like, it is always important to be clear what you are analysing. Is it hatchbacks, cars or Volkswagens?

This model can also be related (though not precisely) to the stages of product adoption (see Chapter 3). In the early stages of a product's life, its buyers will largely be innovators, i.e. the risk takers who are happy to try a new product and who like to own the latest thing. In the growth stages of the product life cycle, customers may be early adopters or the early majority. These people may have a special interest in, or knowledge of, such products and are quite adventurous in their product choices. The majority of customers will buy the product during its maturity phase – this is when sales peak. In the early stages of decline, most customers will be from the late majority and the laggards categories. These are people who prefer to wait until a product is tried and tested (by other people) before they buy it and may even wait until it is a product that other people will be surprised that they do not have.

It is often claimed that product life cycles are getting shorter. Certainly, high technology products, such as computers, have noticeably short lives as newer, improved models seem to come out almost immediately after purchase. Some products have always had short lives, such as fashion items, but others seem to live on forever. There is no sign of a significant decline in the demand for bread, for example, and that has been around for thousands of years. The belief in shorter product life cycles can become a self-fulfilling prophecy if decisions on product development and management are based on it. This might lead companies to withdraw or sell off products before their time. Equally, this perception that products have shorter lives can encourage companies to step up research and development and so decrease the time between innovations, and to introduce more and more new products as quickly as possible (Rifkin, 1994) which, given the expense of development and the frequency with which new products fail, may be a costly exercise.

EXPAND YOUR KNOWLEDGE

Levitt, T. (1965) 'Exploit the product life cycle', *Harvard Business Review*, 43 (Nov/Dec): 81–94.
Smallwood, J.E. (1973) 'The product life cycle: a key to strategic marketing planning', *MSU Business Topics*, (21) Winter: 29–35.

The product life cycle is a well accepted concept in marketing although it needs to be applied wisely. In both these articles, the authors demonstrate how the product life cycle can be used in marketing planning.

Critique

The product life cycle model is not without its critics. Its simplicity leads many to say it cannot possibly represent the situation in a complex and dynamic marketplace accurately. Not all products follow this pattern, of course. Some just never seem to die. For example, gin, cutlery and bread have been with us for centuries, if not millennia. They have been adapted, e.g. the gin may be purer, the cutlery may now be dishwasher proof and the bread now has E numbers, but those product classes live on. Others, of course, never actually grow to maturity. It is estimated that at least 50 per cent of new products fail within a year of their launch: they die before they have lived. So the product life cycle is a model of a successful product, not a failure.

Product life cycles vary in the time they take to run their course. The lives of some highly successful products are so short that they cannot be mapped before they are over. High fashion products fall into this category.

Dhalla and Yuspeh (1976) claimed that the product life cycle was dangerously misleading and often caused companies to delete products that could have been profitable for many more years with the right adjustments to their marketing mix. They found that the concept was even less helpful in assessing the potential of brands where the brand's apparent decline could be reversed. A product can defy the rules of the product life cycle through clever repositioning, perhaps even taking up a position outside its current category, as the Fox network did in the USA when it aired a cartoon aimed at adults in a prime time television slot normally reserved for family sitcoms. When a breakaway position such as this works, the product redefines its competition. *The Simpsons* cartoon is the longest running sitcom ever in the USA (Moon, 2005).

Product portfolio management

Few companies sell just one product; some sell thousands. Their products are collectively referred to as their **product portfolio**, and this needs careful management.

The number of **product lines** a company sells is referred to as **product breadth**. Within each line, there will be several products (**product depth**). For example, the Ford Fiesta is one product line, while the Ford Focus is another. The Fiesta line has a number of models (Finesse, LX, Zetec, Ghia, etc.), which may have different engines and other features. That is its depth. The product manager lays down guidelines for the consistency required within each line, both in terms of product features and in terms of marketing activities. Products may be introduced, dropped, modified, replaced. Sufficient resources must be allocated (e.g. budgets for advertising, research, customer support). The manager must also agree what contribution to profits the product ought to make and this will become a target or sales objective. The company must have enough cash-generating products to support the cash eaters.

A number of management tools have been developed to help managers to manage their product portfolios. These help to judge how individual products and brands, or ranges of products and brands, or **strategic business units (SBUs)** are performing. Then decisions can be taken on the various products' futures.

Although these **product portfolio analysis** tools may appear simple, they require considerable research, calculation and analysis if they are to be a useful management tool. The Boston Consulting Group matrix (BCG matrix) considers the growth of the market and the size of the product's share of that market relative to the market leader's share (see Exhibit 6.5). The GE-McKinsey matrix uses market attractiveness and competitive position (see Exhibit 6.6).

BOSTON CONSULTING GROUP (BCG) PORTFOLIO MATRIX

The **Boston Consulting Group (BCG) portfolio matrix** shows the relationship between cash-generating products and cash-eaters. This model plots products, or SBUs, in a matrix formed by two axes: market growth rate and relative **market share**. It is important to note that this is the growth rate of the *whole* market and so it takes into account all sales within that category, including competitors' sales. So, if, for example, the matrix was being drawn up for Nestlé's chocolate products, then the market would be chocolate generally and Cadbury's, Mars and many other brands would be added in when working out its size and growth rate. The market needs to be carefully

---

product portfolio
all a company's products

product line
a product and all its variants (models, colours, styles, sizes, etc.)

product breadth
the number of product lines a company supports

product depth
the number of items within a product line

product portfolio analysis
the process of comparing products/services to see which are deserving of further investment and which should be discontinued

SBU (strategic business unit)
a distinct part of an organisation that has an external market for its products

Boston Consulting Group (BCG) portfolio matrix
a portfolio analysis tool involving classifying products, or SBUs, according to their market share and market growth rate, as stars, cash cows, problem children or dogs

market share
a firm's sales expressed as a percentage of the total sales of that type of product in the defined market

defined and this may not be easy. For example, are Green and Black's chocolate bars part of the chocolate bar (countline) market, or a general chocolate market, or confectionery, or snacks, or organic foods? Once the market has been defined, the market growth rate is calculated by working out the percentage increase (or decrease) in sales from the previous year.

For example:
current market sales   £2,200,000
minus last year's sales   £2,000,000
equals sales increase   £   200,000
as a percentage of last year's sales   £   200,000 × 100
                                                    £2,000,000

market growth rate = 10 per cent

High growth markets are attractive to companies as they offer a better chance to increase sales; the company's sales just have to move with the market's and they will go up. Exactly what constitutes high growth for a market, and what is low, is uncertain. The mid-point is often taken as 10 per cent and so it can be construed that anything over that may be high and anything below it may be low (Doyle, 2002). However, different markets are likely to vary and so a judgement must be made.

The other axis is labelled 'relative market share' and measures the product's success (in terms of sales) against the market leader in its field. The company's product(s) are placed in one of the four boxes of the model and thereby categorised as stars, problem children (sometimes referred to as question marks or wild cats), cash cows or dogs. The boxes are not absolutes. The products do not always have to be in the middle of a box. For example, a product in the medium growth market may be categorised as a dog but placed towards the top of the box, or as a problem child but near the bottom of the box.

It may be more profitable to have a small share of a large market than it is to have a large share of a small market (so a problem child in a large market can be more valuable than a star in a smaller one), and so the BCG portfolio Matrix can also be refined to reflect market size.

Exhibit 6.5   Boston Consulting Group portfolio matrix

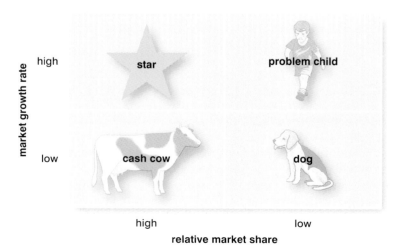

Star

Products in rapidly growing markets in which the company has a high relative market share are called **stars** (e.g. Sony's desktop video-cam, HSBC's First Direct Internet banking service). They generate a large amount of cash but are also expensive to support. They are good investments as they have high earning potential both at the present time and in the future. That investment is likely to be needed if the company wants to retain its market position, as competitors will be trying to emulate stars.

Stars therefore often require high promotional expenditure and perhaps additional product development in order to keep their competitive edge. If this is managed successfully, then when the market's growth rate slows down (as markets inevitably do), these stars will become cash cows.

stars
a category within the Boston Consulting Group matrix; products or SBUs (strategic business units) with high market share in a high-growth market

Cash cow

Products in slow growth, or even static, markets in which they have relatively high market share are called **cash cows**. They require little promotion although under-investment can turn them into **dogs** (see below) so they should not be taken for granted. The company's objective is likely to be to hold this position in order to obtain maximum return on investment (ROI). The profits from cash cows can be used to invest in stars, which are high maintenance, or problem children (who need help).

cash cows
a category within the Boston Consulting Group matrix, products or SBUs (strategic business units) with relatively high market share in low-growth markets

Problem child

Products in this quadrant are in a rapidly growing market but hold a relatively low market share. They are usually called **question marks** or **wild cats**. The market looks attractive (as long as it keeps growing) and just maintaining current market share will increase sales as the company would then have the same percentage of a bigger market. However, the company may be unsure how the market will develop or whether it can acquire enough customers to make further investment here worthwhile. Small companies often suffer by having too many problem children in their portfolios.

Problem children will require heavy investment in a successful marketing mix if they are to develop into stars. Left alone, they will almost certainly go to the dogs. If they prove to be too much of a drain on resources, it may be prudent to sell them off, if possible.

problem children
a category within the Boston Consulting Group portfolio matrix; products or SBUs (strategic business units) with relatively low market share in high-growth markets

Dog

Dogs are in stagnant or slow-growing markets and have relatively low market share. When a dog gets old it may be kindest to put it to sleep but, from a company's perspective, there may be sound reasons to keep it alive. It might be an effective loss leader or barrier to market entry by competitors. It can be quite difficult to judge just when a product has reached the end of its useful life and, ideally, rather than just phase it out, it is often worth trying to sell it on to another company. One company's dog can become another's cash cow or even a star if they are operating in different markets or market segments.

Attempts are sometimes made to relate the BCG portfolio matrix to the product life cycle. Problem children may be in the introduction phase, stars are in the growth stage, cash cows are generally mature products and dogs are in old age (decline). However, this is not necessarily the case and to characterise a problem child as being in the introductory phase may be unhelpful if the product has in fact been around for some time. Additionally, the match is of limited help in analysing the product portfolio.

dogs
a category within the Boston Consulting Group matrix, products or SBUs (strategic business units) with relatively low market share in low-growth markets

insight

The BCG Portfolio Matrix

Milk the cow to feed the problem child, in the hope that it will grow up to be a star. And shoot the old dog.

(Although you may, of course, find reasons not to do that last bit!)

Here is a saying that may help you to remember the BCG matrix:

GE-MCKINSEY MATRIX

This is another classic portfolio analysis tool which is also known as the market attractiveness, market share matrix. This nine-box matrix is a systematic approach to determining which products or SBUs (strategic business units) are the best ones for investment. Rather than rely on managers' forecasts, the company judges how well a product may do in the future on the basis of two, currently known factors: the attractiveness of the industry it is in and its competitive strength within that industry.

Attractiveness can be defined in a number of ways depending on the particular circumstances of the company, for example:

- market size
- market growth rate
- ease of market entry
- competition
- profitability
- social and environmental impact
- technological requirements
- legal implications
- energy and other resource requirements.

The business's competitive position may be calculated by assessing its:

- market share
- market share growth rate
- management team's skills and competences
- product quality
- brand strength
- distribution channels
- promotional effectiveness
- production capacity
- production efficiency
- unit costs
- research and development success.

These criteria are then weighted according to their relative importance to the company and the market.

Exhibit 6.6   GE-McKinsey 9-box matrix

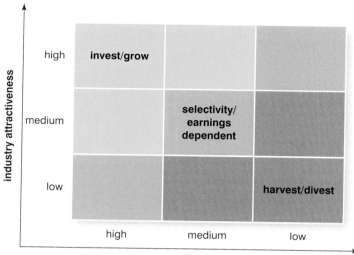

SOURCE   Mckinsey, used with permission

Products that fall into the three boxes in the top left corner of Exhibit 6.6, would appear to have the growth potential to be worth investing in. Those in the three boxes on the diagonal, are borderline. The company may invest in them if it has sufficient funds, or it may let them go (divest). Those below the diagonal, i.e. in the bottom right-hand corner are likely to be sold off (divested) or kept in the portfolio only if they can generate sufficient short-term cash (harvested). Their long-term potential is poor.

Placing products or SBUs in these three categories is a good starting point for strategic analysis, but sound managerial judgement is still needed to ensure the right decisions are made. For example, a strong brand that dominates an unattractive market, perhaps a slow-growing one, may still be a far better prospect than a weak brand in a highly attractive market and yet they both fall into the selective investment section of the matrix (Coyne, 2008).

There are many different portfolio analysis tools and organisations will have their favourites – even their own variants. The BCG Portfolio Matrix (see above) and the GE-McKinsey matrix are, however, the basis for many of these more modern techniques.

EXPAND YOUR KNOWLEDGE:

Gluck, F.W., Kaufman, S.P., Walleck, A.S. and Stuckey, J. (2000) 'Thinking strategically', *McKinsey Quarterly*, June. Available at: www.mckinseyquarterly.com (accessed 10 January 2010).

The Boston Consulting Group portfolio and the GE-McKinsey matrices were radical innovations of their time. They are included here as they formed the basis for many

(Cont'd)

(*Cont'd*)

other portfolio analysis tools, e.g. MACS (Market Activated Corporate Strategy) and the Portfolio of Initiatives.

For further information on Portfolio of Initiatives, see:

Bryan, L.L. (2002) 'Just-in-time strategy for a turbulent world', *McKinsey Quarterly*, June. Available at: www.mckinseyquarterly.com (accessed 10 January 2010).

Critique

It has been argued that portfolio analysis tools over-simplify what are actually complex situations. Ironically, some of these tools have now grown so complex that they cannot meaningfully be applied in real life. Some of the criticisms are briefly outlined below.

First, they merely provide a snapshot of the company's portfolio at a single point in time. The next day, things may have changed. Also, they ignore products in development that have yet to be launched into the market.

Second, consider how market share is calculated. At best, it is a guesstimate, often based on knowledge of one's own business and estimates of competitors' sales, sometimes informed by industry analysts (usually only when the stock market has a keen interest). How, then, is it possible to calculate market share accurately or to compare the relative growth of one market to another in order to map the company's portfolio? Furthermore, is market growth the best criterion for analysis? Perhaps profitability is more important?

Third, these tools fail to recognise any interdependencies between elements of the company's product portfolio. For example, a dog may be essential to the sales of a cash cow if they are complementary products such as an inkjet printer and print cartridges.

This is not to say these tools are not useful as a systematic approach to portfolio analysis. They are a sound base for further exploration of issues and subsequent management decisions. Also, these product portfolio tools can be useful when allocating resources, but it is important to recognise their general limitations and not follow them blindly.

EXPAND YOUR KNOWLEDGE

Day, G.S. (1975) 'A strategic perspective on product planning', *Journal of Contemporary Business*, 39 (Spring): 1–34.

George Day is a widely recognised academic, researcher and author on strategic matters. In this paper he uses the product life cycle and portfolio analysis to introduce strategic perspectives on product planning.

SUMMARY

In this chapter we have attempted to look at products from all angles. There are many different types of product and each has particular characteristics that influence its marketing, but all must be designed to deliver a core benefit. Competitive advantage often comes through differentiating aspects of the total product, rather than just the basic product, and the service elements of a product can be a key selling point (as can the product elements of a service). Branding is today a key differentiator and this is often at the heart of the customer's choice of product and may even inspire loyalty to a particular product.

Management of a product portfolio is a huge marketing challenge. Products are launched, build sales and eventually die. There are a number of portfolio analysis tools which can help managers to judge a product's contribution to the company and to decide what course of action to take next. In this chapter we have briefly considered two of them: the Boston Consulting Group portfolio matrix and the GE-McKinsey matrix. There are criticisms to be made of these tools, as there are of the product life cycle concept, but they all provide useful insights to help manage the product offering.

CHALLENGES REVIEWED

Now that you have finished reading the chapter, look back at the challenges you were set at the beginning. Do you have a clearer idea of what's involved?

Hints:

- product portfolio management
- importance of innovation
- product life cycle – extension strategies
- total product concept – augmented and perceived product, particularly service aspects
- is this right? Can preserving our environment be compatible with making products? Would customers pay more perhaps for products that lasted longer? Would they choose your company over others if it had a more responsible attitude? Bear in mind that there are likely to be laws about manufacturers' responsibilities for disposal of old products soon.

READING AROUND

Book chapters

Susan Hart (2008) 'New product development', in Michael J. Baker and and Susan Hart (eds), *The Marketing Book* (6th edn). Oxford: Butterworth Heinemann.
Robert F. Hartley (1995) 'A giant fails to cope', in Robert F. Hartley, *Marketing Mistakes* (6th edn). New York: John Wiley, pp. 57–73.

Books

Matt Haig (2003) *Brand Failures: The Truth about the 100 Biggest Branding Mistakes of All Time*. London: Kogan Page.

Articles

Mark Gottfredson and Keith Aspinall (2005) 'Innovation vs complexity', *Harvard Business Review*, 83 (12): 62–71.
Theodore Levitt (1965) 'Exploit the product life cycle', *Harvard Business Review*, Nov–Dec: 81–94.
Helena Rubinstein (1996) '"Brand first" management', *Journal of Marketing Management,* 12 (4): 269–80.

Websites

www.cim.co.uk/ – the Chartered Institute of Marketing.
www.designcouncil.org.uk – the Design Council, includes articles on product design.

SELF-REVIEW QUESTIONS

1. Define a product. (see pages 202–3)
2. What is meant by the term core product? (see page 205)
3. How can core products be differentiated? (see page 206)
4. Which usually attracts higher customer involvement – convenience goods or shopping goods? (see page 210)
5. What does FMCG mean? (see page 209)
6. Why are good brands so important to companies? (see pages 213–4)
7. Draw the product life cycle diagram. (see page 224)
8. What is an extension strategy? Give two examples. (see page 225)
9. Is the product life cycle universally applicable? If not, why not? (see pages 228–9)
10. Draw the BCG matrix. (see page 230)
11. What should you do with a dog? (see pages 231–2)
12. Why is innovation important? (see page 218)

Piège à Souris – 'SuperCat', the better mousetrap

Read the questions, then the case material, and then answer the questions.

Questions

1. What do you think the marketing professor meant when he said, 'the aim of marketing is to make selling superfluous'?

2. What stage in the product life cycle (PLC) are mousetraps in, in general? Why would a company think it a good idea to introduce a new mousetrap when they are generally in this stage of the PLC? Would the new product be in the same stage or could such a product innovation be said to be in a different PLC stage? If so, which?

3. Consider the description of the mousetrap and draw a total product offering (TPO) diagram to highlight its main elements. Can the TPO be helpful in understanding why the SuperCat has been successful in European markets? Do you think the launch of the product is likely to be successful in Britain, Ireland and Scandinavia? Are there specific elements in the TPO that you would highlight to which particular attention should be given to increase the chances of success in launching the product in new markets?

It has been said that if you build a better mousetrap, the world will beat a path to your door. But what does this mean? The mousetrap has been around for a long time and sales of mousetraps in general are in decline. The mousetrap, a device for catching and killing mice and other small rodents that may infest a home, is a pretty basic product. Yet it is one that many householders value for those times when they need to eradicate that nuisance mouse or family of mice that have made the householder's home their own. The traditional mousetrap is a small wooden device with a spring-loaded clip. Cheese, which mice are said to love, is used as bait and the mousetrap is set in a place that the mouse is expected to visit. One nibble of the cheese and the spring clip flips down across the neck of the mouse, catching it and killing it. Sometimes this works, sometimes it does not. If a

better, more effective mousetrap could be designed, then, as the saying goes, the world will beat a path to your door – or in other words, the product will be in high demand. Indeed, the idea is that the product will be so good that marketing will almost be unnecessary – it will practically sell itself. As one eminent marketing professor has said, 'the aim of marketing is to make selling superfluous'.

So entering into the marketplace is a new and more effective mousetrap. A Swiss-based company, which prides itself on developing and marketing innovative products, launched its better mousetrap originally in Germany, Switzerland and Austria in 1999. In 2000, it extended its international distribution to France, Italy, Holland and Spain. It is now looking to improve sales in those countries as well as launching in Britain, Ireland and Scandinavia. The mousetrap is called 'SuperCat'. It is new and it comes with its own permanent, non-toxic, more enticing bait. The company claims it has four innovations that make it better than other traps: it can be used immediately (it does not need to be baited); it is efficient and hygienic; it is easy to use; and it does not cause harm to children or domestic pets (presumably this assumes you do not have a pet mouse or hamster). It carries a 100 per cent guarantee. It is packed for sale in pairs. To operate the trap, the rear clip is pushed down. It is ready to use. When a mouse is caught, it can be disposed of without having to touch the mouse. You simply carry the trap to a bin and push the rear clip down again, and the mouse falls out. The trap is once again ready for use. The bait lasts a long time although refills can be bought. In fact the trap is so cheap, it could be thrown away and a new one purchased.

Since 2002, the company has extended its product range and entered into collaboration with other companies in international markets. Its own designed and own-produced devices now include other pest control products (rat traps, mole traps and fly traps) and household products (paint brushes and fire-lighter sticks). It distributes these itself and through its collaborative partners, and also distributes other garden and household goods. But the SuperCat remains its central focus.

REFERENCES

Aaker, D.A. (2002) *Building Strong Brands*. Sydney: Simon and Schuster.

Anon (n.d.) *Vodka: History Development and Origin*, Gin and Vodka Association. Available at: **www.ginvodka.org/history/vodkaHistory.asp** (accessed 17/07/2009).

Belen del Rio, A., Vazquez, R. and Iglesia, V. (2001) 'The effects of brand associations on consumer response', *Journal of Consumer Marketing*, 18 (5): 410–425.

Bryan, L.L. (2002) 'Just-in-time strategy for a turbulent world', *McKinsey Quarterly*, June.

Bucklin, L.P. (1963) 'Retail strategy and the classification of consumer goods', *Journal of Marketing*, 27 (Jan): 51–56.

CIM (n.d.) *Defining Brands*. Chartered Institute of Marketing, Maidenhead. Available at: **www.cim.co.uk/mediastore/Brand_eGuides/eGuide1.pdf** (accessed 1/03/2007).

Courtney, G.M. Jr (n.d.) *The History of the Vodka Drink from its Origins in Russia and Eastern Europe*. The Authentic Bartender. Available at: **www.the-authentic-bartender.com/Vodkahistory.html** (accessed 17/07/2009).

Coyne, K. (2008) 'Enduring ideas: the GE–McKinsey nine-box matrix', *McKinsey Quarterly Strategic Thinking*, September 2008. Available at: **www.mckinseyquarterly.com/Enduring_ideas_The_GE-McKinsey_nine-box_matrix_2198** (accessed on 5/12/2009).

Day, G.S. (1975) 'A strategic perspective on product planning', *Journal of Contemporary Business*, 39 (Spring): 1–34.

Dennis (2001) 'Life's bloopers, foreign brand names', True North Strong and Free, Canada. Available at: tnsf.ca/bloopers/files/foreign_brands.shtml (accessed 29/03/2007).

Dhalla, N.K. and Yuspeh, S. (1976) 'Forget the product life cycle concept!', *Harvard Business Review*, 54 (1): 102–12.

Doyle, P. (2002) *Marketing Management and Strategy*. Harlow: FT/Prentice Hall.

Enis, B.M., LaGarce, R. and Prell, A.E. (1977) 'Extending the product life cycle', *Business Horizons,* 20 (Jun): 46–56.

Gluck, F.W., Kaufman, S.P., Walleck, A.S. and Stuckey, J. (2000) 'Thinking strategically', *McKinsey Quarterly*, June. Available at: www.mckinseyquarterly.com (accessed 10 January 2010).

Haig, M. (2003) *Brand Failures: The Truth about the 100 Biggest Branding Mistakes of all Time*. London: Kogan Page.

Levitt, T. (1965) 'Exploit the product life cycle', *Harvard Business Review*, 43 (Nov/Dec): 81–94.

Mintel (2009) *Vodka UK Market Report March 2009*. London: Mintel.

Moon, Y. (2005) 'Break free from the product life cycle', *Harvard Business Review*, 83 (5): 86–94.

Muniz Jr, A.M. and O'Guinn, T.C. (2001) 'Brand community', *The Journal of Consumer Research*, 27 (4): 412–32.

Paliwoda, S.J. and Thomas, M.J. (1999) *International Marketing* (3rd edn). Oxford: Butterworth Heinemann.

Pickton, D. and Broderick, A. (2004) *Integrated Marketing Communications* (2nd edn). Harlow: FT/Prentice Hall.

Rifkin, G. (1994) 'The myth of short life cycles', *Harvard Business Review*, 72 (11): 11.

Smallwood, J.E. (1973) 'The product life cycle: a key to strategic marketing planning', *MSU Business Topics*, (21) Winter: 29–35.

7

Service products

CHAPTER CONTENTS

Introduction
The importance of services
The nature of services
Different types of service
The services marketing mix
Service quality
Branding services
Service recovery
Summary
Challenges reviewed
Reading around
Self-review questions
Mini case study
References

SERVICE PRODUCTS CHALLENGES

The following are illustrations of the types of decision that marketers have to take or issues they face. *You aren't expected to know how to deal with the challenges now*; just bear them in mind as you read the chapter and see what you can find that helps.

- You are at the bank asking for a loan to help your chauffeuring service through a slump. If you are refused the loan, then you will have to sell off some of your limousines at a fraction of their value to you. It is unlikely that you will ever be able to afford to buy such cars again. The bank manager is not impressed with your business. He says it can never be a source of real wealth as it does not make anything. What could you say to convince him that the business is worthwhile?

- You manage the check-in operation for a major airline. You are visiting your staff at Gatwick airport when ten of your planes have to be withdrawn from service for safety checks. The queues of angry passengers are building up and you can see staff at a competitor's check-in looking smug and preparing to lure some of your customers away. What are you going to do? How can you come out of this with an even better reputation for great service?

- You are the marketing manager for a company that makes office furniture. Despite being one of the best recognised brands in your home business-to-business market, you have recently lost a couple of big orders to a foreign rival whose prices are much lower. To make matters worse, their furniture is just as well designed and as good quality as yours. Their brand name is as well recognised too. The production manager has shown that there is no way your company can match their low prices. You need a way to make customers value your products more highly. What are the possibilities?

- You used to sell cars but now you are a travel agent and you have two, difficult, potential customers in front of you: a bride and groom who want to fly an entire wedding party to a Caribbean island and put them up in a smart hotel. This would be a major sale but they are nervous about signing the agreements and want to be reassured that everything will be just perfect. When you were a car salesperson, you would have shown them the car and taken them for a test drive in it, but your budget does not stretch to flying the couple to the Caribbean – and anyway it is currently the monsoon season. How will you reassure them and make the sale?

Introduction

Products come in many forms, from ice creams to consultancy, from photocopiers to physiotherapy. Many products have no substantial physical form: we cannot pick them up, put them away in a cupboard, sell them on to someone else. Hairdressing, cleaning, insurance, maintenance, teaching – these are all service products and they are just as real, and potentially just as profitable, as the products that you can touch.

The study of services marketing encroaches into other disciplines rather more than most marketing topics do, incorporating aspects of design, human resource management and operations. Europeans sometimes use the term *service management* instead as a more accurate, and less restricting, description (Grove et al., 2003). There is no clear defining line between the sale of a service, its production and its use. These aspects of a service product are often inseparable.

Take hand car washing as an example. A motorist pulls into a petrol station, or parks in a car park, and is approached by a young man who asks if she would like her car washed. She says 'yes' and the same young man produces bucket and sponge and gets to work. That young man has sold the service and delivered the service and his customer has used the service all within a very short space of time. In fact the production of the service (the young man wielding bucket and sponge), and the use of the service (the car becoming clean) happen simultaneously. It is possible to build in a delay between sale and consumption, if, for example, there had been a queue for car washes, but often the whole process happens all together.

So service products are indeed rather different from the goods we studied in the last chapter, although they still have to be priced, delivered and promoted. This chapter will explore those differences, the challenges they present and the recognised ways of overcoming them. It will also show why service products are so important to all businesses today – to goods manufacturers as well as to service companies.

DEFINITIONS

A defining feature of service products is that they are intangible (they cannot be touched) as opposed to goods, or physical products, that are tangible. Unfortunately life, and business, is rarely that straightforward. Few products are exclusively tangible or intangible. A car is a solid object but it comes with a warranty which is not. The car needs insurance and will need servicing in the future. It may be wise to have a roadside recovery package such as that offered by the AA in the UK or ANWB in Holland. The availability, price and quality of these additional services are often important factors in a customer's decision to buy a car.

services
intangible products

Similarly, many things that are classed as **services** have substantial physical products at their heart. Take the restaurant business, for example. A key determinant of the diner's satisfaction will be the food itself. The surroundings and the service are important, but if the food is no good then the restaurant is no good either. So although marketers, and governments and other interested parties, like to distinguish between goods and services, there are significant overlaps between the two.

There are a number of definitions of services, most of them have at their heart this idea of intangibility. According to Palmer, services are:

The production of an essentially intangible benefit, either in its own right or as a significant element of a tangible product, which through some form of exchange, satisfies an identified need. (Palmer, 2005: 2–3)

World services

Services create a high proportion of many countries' GDP (Gross Domestic Product) and the bulk of their working populations may be employed in service industries.

Exhibit 7.1 shows the approximate proportion of GDP that services contribute, and the approximate percentage of workers in service industries in a selection of countries/regions.

China, possibly the fastest developing, major economy today, is still focused on agriculture and manufacturing, but there are signs of a fast-developing service sector there too.

Exhibit 7.1   Contribution of service industries

Country	Services GDP (as % of total GDP)	Services jobs (as % of all jobs)
European Union	71	67
India	53 (2008 est.)	28 (2003)
China	40	32 (2006 est.)
Japan	72	66 (2004)
UK	75 (2008 est.)	80
USA	80 (2008 est.)	80 (est.)
(CIA, n.d.)		

Another defining feature of a service is that the customer does not actually own anything as a direct result of receiving the service:

Any activity or benefit that one party can offer to another which is essentially intangible and does not result in the ownership of anything. Its production may or may not be tied to a physical product. (Kotler et al., 2001: 535)

Here is an alternative definition:

A service is an activity which benefits recipients even though they own nothing extra as a result.

This simple definition encapsulates the key ideas of conferring a product benefit, no rights of ownership and of services being processes, or activities, rather than material things.

The importance of services

Services are becoming more and more important to both businesses and consumers. The majority of business start-ups are service businesses, although admittedly many of them are very small.

Some countries are said to have service economies, i.e. they rely on services businesses for the bulk of their wealth. Services businesses are sometimes criticised on the grounds that, unlike manufacturing businesses, they do not produce any increase in wealth. Restaurant or hotel customers spend their money and are poorer – they have nothing of ongoing value in exchange. Food has been eaten, sleep has been had, but customers own nothing new that they can sell on. This idea dates back to Adam Smith, an eighteenth-century economist who argued that intangible products did not create anything of real value unlike the products of manufacturing or agriculture (Palmer, 2005). As we can see from Exhibit 7.1 though, service customers contribute significantly to the income of a country. One of Britain's main foreign currency earners is the City of London, where banks, insurance companies and other financial institutions carry out their business. However, hotels and restaurants also bring huge amounts of money into most European capitals, largely thanks to visiting tourists. The more traditional services still have their part to play – even highly paid city bankers have to eat.

KNOWLEDGE-BASED ECONOMIES

The trend towards service industries is at its most advanced in the MDCs (most developed countries), but it is notable worldwide. The MDCs could be said now to have moved beyond services and into a new era of knowledge-based activities where expertise is prized above all else. These are nations of consultants, financiers and lawyers, who outsource more basic services such as call centres and computer programming to other countries which possess skilled workforces (particularly in IT).

So Europe has become a continent of knowledge-based workers who are paid for their expertise while other countries, with cheaper labour costs, do the manufacturing. Current thinking is that it is a company's intellectual capital that is its most valuable asset, rather than the more tangible things it owns. This, as Handy (2002) points out, can cause a problem because companies do not actually *own* their employees. They are not slaves. They are free to leave and take their expertise with them. Handy quotes a story about the world-renowned advertising agency Saatchi & Saatchi. The board fired Maurice Saatchi, one of the agency's founders, who duly left, taking major clients and some of the agency's best staff with him. These things did not belong to the company or its shareholders.

REASONS FOR THE GROWTH IN THE SERVICES SECTOR

There are a number of reasons behind this rise in the popularity of service businesses, including:

- more employment in knowledge-based industries
- increased consumer leisure time and consequent demand for leisure services
- the popularity of outsourcing services as a cost-cutting and efficiency measure
- displaced workers setting up their own small businesses, notably consultancy, training and coaching
- complex modern products requiring support services
- the fact that the service element is now often the key (if not only) way to differentiate a goods item (physical product).

First, the knowledge workers and other highly skilled service staff, who are the backbones of advanced economies, have to keep their knowledge and skills up to date. ('Knowledge worker' is a term first used by Peter Drucker to describe people who work with information rather than in more traditional industries. Knowledge workers may be thought of as the ultimate service industry employees.) Such personnel need ready access to detailed information banks as they are insatiable users of information services and they also need training, even coaching and mentoring. Corporate coaching is a service that has taken off in the last few years. Experienced business people, with specific coaching training, help hard-pressed executives to make the most of their talents and their time.

Second, people in the more developed nations have larger incomes and a lot more free time to spend it in. This means that the demand for leisure activities, largely services, has gone up. Hotels, restaurants, cafés, bars and health clubs have been the main beneficiaries of this new-found wealth, closely followed by retailing. So many people love to shop! This increase in disposable income also means that many people can afford to pay others to do things that most of their grandparents would have done themselves: mending pipes, fixing windows, cleaning, gardening, laying patios, decorating, etc. However, many services are considered luxuries, e.g. restaurants and travel, and these suffer badly during hard times such as recession.

The increased popularity of **outsourcing** has also encouraged new service businesses to start up. Company profits are under closer scrutiny as more businesses are publicly quoted or are registered as limited liability companies – meaning they have shareholders who demand higher profits. Consequently, today's businesses are always looking for ways to cut costs and one of the recommended routes to lower cost operations is to focus on the core business and outsource as much of the rest as possible. Many businesses employ other companies to perform key tasks such as delivery, installation, maintenance, call centres, even new product development, as well as more peripheral, but nonetheless important, activities such as cleaning, vehicle fleet management and staff training. All the above-mentioned examples are services and this outsourcing has created a lot of new businesses whose core business is to provide these services.

outsourcing
the subcontracting of a business process, e.g. delivery or maintenance, to another organisation

Outsourcing is not without its drawbacks, however. Although costs may be saved up front, there may be further expense incurred if the outsourcing goes wrong. Firms who outsource customer contact activities, such as call centres or Internet order taking, are handing over a significant part of their customer relationship to another company. They are trusting the outsource partner to care for their company's image and reputation, and not to set up a rival business and poach their customers.

The outsourcing of work to other countries where land and labour costs are cheaper boosts those countries' economies and helps to turn them into viable markets for the home country's products. However, outsourcing to other countries can sometimes create a level of dissatisfaction in the home country. In the UK, for example, some banks and insurance companies are endeavouring to create competitive advantage by making a virtue of returning all of their call centres to the UK.

This trend towards setting up operations in lower-cost countries has meant that the displaced workers of Western Europe, North America, Japan and other post-industrial nations have had to seek alternative employment. Many have turned to self-employment, either in a new industry or as consultants or trainers to their old one. Service businesses are often relatively cheap to set up as many require little in the way of heavy machinery, land or premises. A cleaning service needs mops, buckets, brushes, polish, etc., and maybe a small van to travel from place to place, but little else. A consultant may only need an office, a car and communications equipment. Many service businesses are small and so the investment needed to start one up is also small. It is actually an advantage to be small in some types of service, particularly where personal service is prized (e.g. decorators). Recent years have seen a huge increase in the number of self-employed workers and small business owners, many of which are offering services.

Another reason for the increase in service products can be found in the world of physical products. Modern technology has created ever more complex products, such as laptops, MP3 players, hard disk recorders, intelligent cars and all the technical paraphernalia (routers, Bluetooth devices, scanners, etc.) that surround computers. Such complex products can be prone to breakdowns and so they need maintenance and repair services. Some, such as heavy industrial plant or highly technical products, need training courses for users before they can even be started up.

As advanced production techniques have made products more standardised, it is often the service aspects (the support: helpdesks, training, service engineers, etc.) that are the means of differentiating one product from another. Customers frequently choose a more expensive supplier on the grounds that they believe the installation or the ongoing service will be better. They are wise enough to recognise that the cost of their new central heating boiler, car or PC does not end at the point of purchase. They take account of the ongoing service costs and the hassle factor when deciding what to buy and from whom (see Chapter 3 for more on how customers make purchase decisions).

Training and support is another major growth area. Services are people-intensive and rely on the skills of those who provide them. All these lawyers, accountants, nurses, IT technicians, plumbers, consultants and trainers need to be trained and supported themselves and so we have a self-perpetuating cycle of service (see Exhibit 7.2).

Exhibit 7.2   Circle of service creation

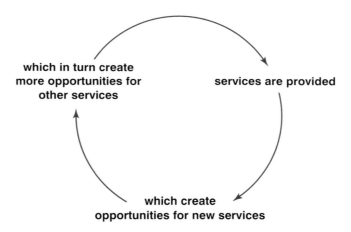

Most of today's products have a strong service element, which may be the source of their competitive advantage. Equally, many services have a physical product element and this may be the source of theirs, although skills are a more common determinant of the quality of a service. Service products can use physical elements within the offering, and physical products can use service elements, to add to the satisfaction provided by the product.

EXPAND YOUR KNOWLEDGE

Shostack, G.L. (1977) 'Breaking free from product marketing', *Journal of Marketing*, 41 (Apr): 73–80.

New concepts are necessary if service marketing is to succeed. Lynn Shostack argues that marketing is too overwhelmingly product-oriented. This is an early paper moving marketing into a new era.

The nature of services

A cut and blow dry needs shampoo. A car service needs filters. A consultancy project produces a report. A night's sleep in a hotel room means there must be a bed. There are very few pure services (i.e. with no physical element at all) in existence, just as there are increasingly few pure goods (i.e. with no service element). Whether a product is primarily a good or a service makes a great deal of difference to the way in which it will be marketed.

Exhibit 7.3 presents a continuum upon which example products are placed according to their degree of physicality.

Exhibit 7.3   A product continuum, tangible to intangible

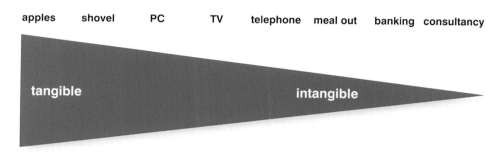

Apples bought in a shop have the benefit of all the retail and distribution services that got them there. However, apples picked on a pick-your-own farm or from your own garden have no service element. A shovel will probably be bought from a shop but requires no maintenance or other services, unlike a PC where the warranty and back-up service may be important. Televisions may well be chosen for their features: widescreen, digital, surround sound, portable, etc., but they are of no use without a signal from one of the television broadcasters – unless you just want to play DVDs of course. Telephones usually have fewer features than televisions but their whole point is to receive telephone calls. Restaurants are selected for their standards of service and their ambience as much as for their food. Traditional banking provides us with little of substance: bank notes, cheque books, cards. Online banking is even less tangible. The ultimate intangible product is perhaps consultancy. Although consultants usually provide a written report at the end of their work, it is not the writing down that clients are really paying for but the ideas contained within the report – the consultant's expertise.

The overlap between goods and services is so large and yet so difficult to pinpoint that some marketers have expressed doubts as to whether services marketing is a distinct marketing area at all.

EXPAND YOUR KNOWLEDGE

Shostack, G.L. (1984) 'Designing services that deliver', *Harvard Business Review*, 62 (Jan–Feb): 133–139.

The author notes that despite the importance of the services sector, little effort is exerted to apply the sort of rational management techniques so common in the goods-producing sector. The article reviews this position and presents a systematic management process that can be applied to services.

CHARACTERISTICS OF SERVICES

Throughout much of this book, goods and services are treated similarly. A service is a product and it needs pricing and promoting just as any product does. As Theodore Levitt said, 'There are no such things as service industries. There are only industries whose service components are greater or less than those of other industries. Everybody is in service' (cited in Kotler, 2003). However, the provision of and marketing of services presents some additional challenges. Many of these arise from the nature of services – the way they differ from goods.

Services have a number of defining characteristics which set them apart from goods. The following are typical service characteristics and will be discussed in the section that follows:

- services confer benefits
- services are intangible – they have no (or little) physical form and so cannot be touched
- services are time and place dependent – they cannot be stored or moved
- the service provider is part of the service
- the consumer is part of the service
- services are inconsistent
- services cannot be owned.

Some academics believe that the distinctions between goods and services have become so blurred that even these key characteristics are unreliable and should be revised (Grove et al., 2003). It is certainly true that technology has made a difference. Some Internet services can, in a way, be stored. Purchases can be left in a shopping basket and paid for later, downloads can be bought and then watched later. The Internet has also meant that the service provider and customer do not always have to be together. Think of Internet banking, for example. So it may be best to consider these as typical characteristics of traditional services, some of which can be mediated by technology.

Services confer benefits

Just like goods, services are designed to meet customer needs and so services also have core benefits. The core benefit from having your car serviced is the prevention of a breakdown. The core benefit from a haircut is to look better. The core benefit from most medical services is to feel better. There may be additional benefits, e.g. the car being worth more, but marketers must ensure that the service provides the core benefit well, or customers will not return. Once you have had a bad haircut, you do not usually go back to that hairdresser no matter how good the coffee was, unless the service recovery was really good, of course. (Service recovery will be examined later in the chapter.)

This does not mean, however, that service products can be analysed in the same way as physical products. Chapter 6 presented a total product model, with outer rings comprising largely service elements or other intangibles. While the idea of a core benefit from services is useful, much of the rest of the total product offering model needs modification when applied to services.

The concept of the total service product offering is illustrated in Exhibit 7.4 using the example of a concert.

Music fans go to concerts in the hope of being entertained, maybe leaving the venue feeling exhilarated or even inspired. Those are the benefits that they are looking to the concert to provide. The second ring shows the things that may contribute

Exhibit 7.4   Total service offering for a concert

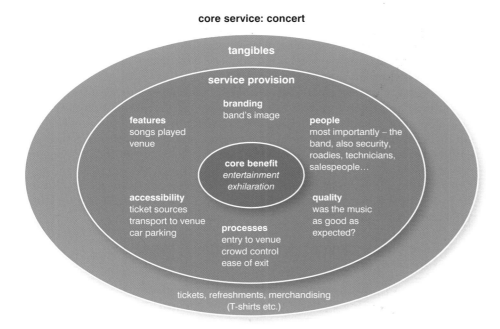

to that core benefit. Clearly, the band itself is a major factor, along with what they play (features) and how well they play it (quality). The sound system will also contribute to the quality of the event and technicians (people) will be important to ensure that sound and lighting work properly. The thrill of the concert may be spoilt if the audience has to queue for hours to get out of car parks or on to buses at the end (accessibility) or if crowd control is too aggressive (processes). The idea of branding a band is not novel. Bands can effectively be considered as brands – some even have logos and merchandising (the sale of branded goods such as T-shirts and posters) is typically a key part of concert activity. The experience will be enhanced if the desired refreshments are available (tangibles) and these tangibles are represented in the third ring of the model.

Services are intangible

Services are, at their core, intangible. You cannot smell them, touch them or throw them at anyone. However, some services are more intangible than others (see Exhibit 7.3). For example, a dental check-up is almost completely intangible. There may be no products involved beyond the dentist's instruments. The essence of the service lies in the dentist's skill and that has to be taken on trust. On the other hand, a meal in a restaurant has a lot of tangible things associated with it, especially the food. This intangibility

Promotional merchandise is one of the tangibles at a rock concert

peripheral products
a secondary product often provided as part of a service, e.g. the complimentary mints at the end of a meal, shampoo at the hairdressers

patent
a legal protection for inventions that prohibits unauthorised copying

makes services harder to market than goods. Potential customers feel more confident buying something that they can see and feel – and take back if necessary. So one of the key challenges for marketers is to reduce the perceived risk involved in buying a service by making it appear more tangible, often by emphasising the **peripheral products** used in carrying out the service. Restaurants usually try to convince potential diners that the food is really good. Beauticians stress the properties of the face masks and moisturisers they use.

This intangibility presents marketers with an additional competitive headache. It is more difficult to protect a service from imitation. The inventors of physical products can apply for **patents** to safeguard the product in its early years while they recoup their development investments. Patent laws, and the rigour with which they are enforced, vary from country to country but few, if any, allow for the patenting of service products. Other intellectual property laws, such as copyright and trade mark registration, afford some protection but are even harder to enforce, and recent efforts to extend UK patent laws to include business processes and software have failed (Patents Office, n.d).

Services are time and place dependent (they cannot be stored or moved)

Services are transient. They happen at a particular time and cannot be stored for later sale or use. You cannot buy a service to keep in the cupboard and use at your convenience like you might a tin of soup or a bottle of shampoo. Planes and trains leave at specific times and customers have to be on board if they want to take advantage of the service. The train or plane operator has to sell seat tickets before departure. If seats remain unsold, they have lost potential income. This perishability of services, as some writers refer to it, greatly complicates the planning of service operations.

The management of peaks and troughs of demand is more difficult for service providers. Whereas a retailer or a manufacturer has a stock room in which to keep surplus products until demand picks up again, service providers just lose business if they do not have enough products. The retailer or manufacturer can stockpile in anticipation of a future peak in demand, fans for the summer perhaps, and so keep their workforce employed, but a hairdresser cannot get ahead by doing extra haircuts and keeping them for later. Service providers may need to employ seasonal staff and lay them off again when demand is low – a reason why so many students find jobs in the holiday industry. Another way that service providers can manage these peaks and troughs is through changing the price (see price discrimination in Chapter 10) to attract extra customers when business is slack or to increase profits in times of high demand.

Additionally, for most services, the number of customers that can be accommodated at any one time is limited and so services often involve appointments, e.g. for the dentist, or queuing, and service customers are more often turned away than are customers for goods. There are a limited number of tickets for a concert. There are a limited number of seats on the plane.

Service products cannot be moved like physical products which can be bought in one place and then transported to another location. Few services can be delivered long distance (though modern electronic technologies do facilitate this for some services). A hotel room cannot be moved; you must sleep in the hotel. A play is not performed whenever and wherever you want; it must be at the theatre and at a scheduled performance time.

The time dependency of many services has major implications for the service supplier, who must be a master of demand forecasting if they are not to be left with time on their hands or unsold seats. Late customers cause significant problems. If a customer misses an appointment or is late for it, then this can cause serious scheduling problems. The person who was to perform the service (the hairdresser, the dentist, the bank manager) will be left with extra time that they could have used more profitably while any revised scheduling may impact on the quality of service for subsequent customers.

The service provider is part of the service

A service provider is an intrinsic part of the service. It is rarely possible to disassociate the person or organisation that performs the service from the service itself. This is often referred to as the inseparability of services and it is a key difference between services and physical products. Customers frequently buy products with no knowledge at all about how and where they were produced and by whom. Do you know which company made the bread for your sandwich? Have you visited their factory? Do you know the name of the baker?

In the case of personal services, such as dentistry, the service provider must actually be physically present at the point that the service is consumed, e.g. the tooth is filled. This is not true for all services. The less personal the service, the more likely it is that it can be performed remotely. For example, an Internet user may shop in the middle of the night, while all the online retailer's staff are asleep. Technology is often the facilitator of remote services. We no longer need telephonists to make connections for us; we can dial the numbers ourselves. We do not always need computer programmers to search databases for us, nor do we need a salesperson to place an order online.

Technology also allows service providers to cut costs. Traditionally, services have been very staff intensive, much more so than manufacturing, and this is expensive, especially in the more developed nations where wages are high. Thanks to advanced telecommunications, organisations can move their customer service operations to other countries where staff costs are lower and often employment law is less stringent. A number of British companies have call centres in India, for example.

Thanks to the Internet, organisations can get their customers to do some of the work for themselves, e.g. placing orders online or filing tax returns electronically. This offloading of work on to the customer is not a particularly new idea and it is not solely due to technological advance. Self-service in supermarkets and cafés has the same cost-cutting motivation.

The consumer is part of the service

The consumer of the service is part of the experience whether or not they perform a part of the service themselves, e.g. by serving themselves in a petrol station. Because the production and consumption of services cannot be separated, the consumer has to be considered as an element of the production process and their actions, reactions or inaction need to be taken into account in the service offering's design. This brings into sharp focus the emphasis that is now placed on customer relationship management (CRM). Not only has the importance of customer loyalty been recognised in successful marketing, but also the way in which building relationships is a fundamental part of the service offering. Early work in recognising the shift of marketing emphasis from goods to services and the roles of relationship marketing can be found in the publications of such authors as Grönroos and Gummesson in the late 1970s and 1980s.

For most service customers, ease of use of a service will be important. They do not want to be over-involved in the service delivery. If an investment service is too complicated or there are too many forms to fill in, then the potential customer may

service convenience
a measure of how much time and effort consumers need to expend to use the service offered

be put off. Most people shop at the supermarket that is the closest to them or has good parking. Consumers value **service convenience** which they measure in terms of the time and effort they have to expend on the service. Berry et al. (2002) have proposed five categories of service convenience:

- decision convenience
- access convenience
- transaction convenience
- benefit convenience
- post-benefit convenience.

First, there is the question of the ease of decision-making. People are more likely to consider performing a service themselves (e.g. DIY) than they are to consider making a physical product. Service providers must ensure that there is enough information available, and in the right form, to inform this decision as well as the choice of supplier.

Second, the customer may consider how easy it will be to ask for the service, e.g. do they have to go to the restaurant or can they order by phone and have their food delivered? Is the website easy to navigate or is it disjointed and slow?

e-tailers
online retailers

service encounter
the time during which a customer is the recipient of a service, e.g. the duration of a meal in a restaurant

The third category is transaction convenience: how long will it take to pay and how secure is the payment? Often you have to pay for services before you actually receive them, e.g. you have to buy a ticket for a play. If it takes too long to pay (perhaps there is a queue) people may give up. **E-tailers** suffer particularly from this as many shoppers abandon their baskets before the check-out.

Next is benefit convenience: the time and effort that the consumer has to expend in order to actually receive the core benefit of the service while the service is happening, i.e. during the **service encounter**. For example, the benefit of a taxi ride would be considerably reduced if the customer had to walk the last mile of their journey.

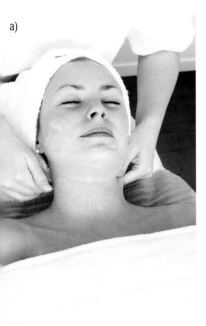

a)

© iStockphoto.com/Tyler olson

b)

c)

© Mark Richardson

a) Most personal services, such as beauty treatments, require both people to be present.

b) Some services have been delegated to customers so that the service provider does not need to be present.

c) Non-personal services are less likely to require the presence of both people, e.g. windows are often cleaned in the householder's absence.

Internet banking

New technologies have overcome some of the difficulties normally found in the marketing of services. In particular, technology has helped address the issues of inconsistency and inseparability (the service provider having to be there to deliver the service).

In the virtual world, consumption *can* take place without both provider and customer being in the same place at the same time. Automation also improves service consistency, although the differences in consumers and their skills may make them experience the service differently. This has a major advantage in terms of opening hours. Internet banking, for example, is available 24/7 without staff having to be there.

First Direct, now a division of HSBC, was a pioneer of telephone banking and was also among the first to move into Internet banking. Customers can manage most aspects of their accounts online: view balances and statements, transfer money, pay bills and set up direct debits. First Direct has no branches, which means it makes considerable cost savings.

The website helps First Direct in other ways too: the technology provides a more consistent service delivery than a person would; imagery and branding are more tightly controlled; and a record of transactions is created automatically. On the other hand, customers are at the mercy of the unpredictability of the Internet service itself and this may affect their perception of the service. Also, an Internet service is quite easy to mimic, making it harder for brands to differentiate themselves from the competition.

This is the one point of the service process where customers do not always mind spending extra time. If the service is a hedonistic one, e.g. a holiday, then customers may well be happy to prolong the experience.

Finally, there is post-benefit convenience. Customers want hassle-free ongoing benefits from the service provided and not to have to return to complain or to have the fillings replaced in their teeth too quickly (see **service recovery** later in this chapter).

EXPAND YOUR KNOWLEDGE

Farquar, J.D. and Rowley, J. (2009) 'Convenience: a service perspective', *Journal of Marketing Theory*, 9 (4): 425–438.

Farquar and Rowley argue: 'The concept and construct of convenience is at the forefront of customer and user evaluation of services experiences and should therefore play a much more pivotal role in marketing theory than it does at present'.

Other people may also be part of the service

Consumers' enjoyment of a service is also affected by other people, particularly other consumers, and especially if the service is one that is offered to a group rather than just to individuals. For example, a play can be spoilt by someone else's mobile phone. A train journey can be turned into a distressing rather than relaxing experience by the bad behaviour of fellow passengers. Equally, a holiday may be made so much more fun thanks to good company. It can be hard for service providers to control the behaviour of their customers and sometimes their very attempts at control cause a problem for others, e.g. the puzzled old ladies who are no longer allowed to take their nail scissors on to aeroplanes because of increased security measures.

ACTIVITY

Imagine you are a holiday rep at a Mediterranean beach resort. You are based in a large hotel that is popular with both young people, who want to go out clubbing, stay out late and then stay in bed until the afternoon, and with families. What problems might you anticipate and what can you do to resolve them?

Local people have complained about the behaviour of both groups of customers. Is that your concern? What can you do about it?

Services are inconsistent

Physical products aim for consistency in quality, packaging and features and many can rely on advanced manufacturing equipment to help them deliver it. Even physical products are not infallibly the same though. Flaws in ingredients or components may have an adverse effect on manufactured goods. Nature is not always as bothered about consistency as some fussy humans are either – fruit and vegetables come in various shapes and sizes, and often with blemishes despite farmers' best efforts with pesticides. The EU has rules about the shape of some produce, there was a media fuss about the requirement for straight cucumbers not long ago, and supermarkets demand standard sizes and shapes and have had a major influence on which varieties are grown and sold. Sometimes inconsistencies are viewed positively, as in home-baked goods, where the slightly irregular shapes are proof that they are genuinely hand prepared, but usually standardisation is preferred.

The issue of consistency is even more pronounced for service products. Variability is inherently part of services. They are difficult to standardise. The intangibility of services means that we cannot know exactly what we are getting until it is too late. We can try on clothes to see if they fit. However, if we ask a plumber to mend a leak for us, we will not know whether we are going to receive a good service until after it has been performed. Only then can we tell if the leak is fixed. This is so much more risky and one of the ways that customers reduce the risk is by relying on past performance as a guide to the future (something that the financial services adverts point out that you should never do). If the plumber did a good job last time, we assume that this job will also be good. If our expectations are not met, if the standard of work is inconsistent, then we will be unhappy with it, and possibly protracted and bitter arguments and negotiations will ensue. It is not a question of just putting the trousers back on the rail and trying another pair, the quality of the work is often a matter of judgement.

Service products are dependent upon humans, and humans are not always consistent. It is rare that two hair cuts would be exactly the same. In a restaurant, you might order the same food as before but it is unlikely that it will be prepared and served by the same staff – and, even if it was, it could still be a little different.

Consistency is something that many services strive for, but few deliver. It is more important for some services, e.g. financial ones, than it is for others. Lawyers and accountants rely upon documentation to try to provide consistent services. The Internet has been of great assistance here. Services provided online are made more consistent by the constraints of the technology. However, it could be argued that with this consistency comes an inflexibility that does not always provide the service that customers actually want.

Another way to provide consistent service is by following strict procedures. Service owners devise a plan for their employees to follow so that each service encounter will be as similar to the previous one as possible. Fast-food chains have tight controls over what their staff do. Kitchen staff walk along set paths from fryer to sink

Free-(down)loaders

ethical focus

If you cannot see it, touch it or smell it, can you steal it? Police in West London arrested a man for stealing a wireless broadband connection. He was sitting on a garden wall outside a house (not his own), using his laptop and the house owner's broadband. Many people would claim that this was a victimless crime. The broadband subscriber did not have to pay more because of the extra use that was made of his connection, and his service was not affected in any way.

The first person to be prosecuted was another West London man who was fined £500 and given a 12-month conditional discharge in 2005. The number of arrests in the UK, under the Communications Act 2003, for dishonestly obtaining free access to networks has risen steadily. However, it may prove difficult, if not totally impractical, to arrest all the perpetrators of this crime.

Critics argue that it is not difficult to password protect a connection and so, if people want to prevent others from using their broadband, then they should secure the connection. In a further blow to attempts to police these connections, some Internet Service Providers, e.g. British Telecom, are encouraging their users to make the connections available to others and so build up national wireless access. They advertise 'hot spots' where any of their broadband customers can access the Internet by piggybacking on someone else's connection.

The police, and consumer groups, maintain that it is unacceptable to use services without the subscriber's permission. They argue that the freeloaders, by getting services without paying, increase the costs for those who do pay – and someone has to pay or there will be no service provided.

What do you think? Is it acceptable to use another's service or not?

SOURCE: Topping, 2007

to serving hatch. Bells ring when it is time to turn the burger or take the chips out of the fat. Nothing is left to chance. This heavily proscribed way of working has the added advantage of meaning that trained chefs are not required. The work, however, is repetitive and can soon become boring. Staff turnover is often high in such restaurants.

Flow charts are often used to work out how best to provide a consistent, quality service (see Exhibit 7.6 on p. 259) or there may be a service **blueprint**. These tried-and-tested procedures are part of what a **franchisee** is paying for when they buy their business idea from the **franchiser**.

The best service providers go to great lengths to ensure that they provide a high-quality service, one that customers can rely on – and still they will receive some complaints. Customers are no more consistent than staff. Some will like their burgers overcooked, others will not. One customer will love their haircut, but it will not suit her friend. There are diners who like loud music in restaurants and there are those who complain that they cannot hear their companions talk – and those may actually be the same people but at different times, or with different companions. Services are often inconsistent in their reception as well as in their delivery and so all service businesses must be adept at handling complaints if they are to be successful (see service recovery later in this chapter).

Services cannot be owned

This is largely a function of the intangibility of the service. There is nothing to actually own. A client pays for the beautician's skill (and the lotions and potions applied) but at the end of the treatment has nothing more than a good feeling (and possibly

blueprint
an original plan or set of instructions for how something should operate

franchisee
the person or organisation granted permission (a licence) to market a business idea or product whose rights are owned by someone else

franchiser
owner of a business idea or product who grants a licence to someone else to market it

better skin) to take home. Services clients are paying for expertise, experience, advice, skills, knowledge and the benefits these bring. The benefits may last, but the service itself is of limited duration. Of course, it is possible to augment the service offering with additional items (peripheral products) some of which may be physical goods. For example, in the case of hairdressing or beauty treatments, the client may be able to purchase hair care and beauty goods for use at home.

EXPAND YOUR KNOWLEDGE

Voss, G.B., Parasuraman, A. and Grewal, D. (1998) 'The roles of price, performance and expectations in determining satisfaction in services exchanges', *Journal of Marketing*, 62 (Oct): 46–61.

This paper analyses the contributors to customer satisfaction with service products.

Different types of service

The services sector is a very large one and so it is easier to study if it is broken down into smaller groupings or subcategories. Traditionally, similar activities have been grouped together, e.g. the UK government groups together 'retail, hire and repair', 'media and creative services', 'health and social care services', 'personal services', 'IT and telecommunications services' (Business Link, n.d.). While this is easy to do, it is a business-based categorisation rather than a customer-based one and therefore not **market-orientated**. A marketer would prefer to see the groupings based on customer needs and the way the services are used rather than the type of skills and resources needed to provide them. However, classifying activities in this way can lead to some very broad categories which are not particularly useful for marketing. Palmer (2005: 52) suggests that it would be better to group them along the lines of 'processes by which customers make decisions, methods of pricing and promotional strategies'.

Additionally, there are problems when classifying some large and diverse organisations. For example, Tesco would be classed as a **retailer** even though it also offers banking services. That category of **retail** is so broad anyway, incorporating organisations as diverse as Tesco, Holland & Barrett (health food chain) and individually owned corner shops – all, incidentally, food retailers but with very little in common in terms of their business operations.

Academics tend to place services on a continuum according to their nature – most commonly their degree of intangibility. Dibb et al. (2006) also propose a five-category classification scheme:

1 Type of market.
2 Degree of labour intensiveness.
3 Degree of customer contact.
4 Skill of the service provider.
5 Goal of the service provider.

In this schema, type of market would typically be 'consumer' or 'business' and a description of the core activity, e.g. consumer legal advice. The degree of labour intensiveness would be classed as either high or low depending on how automated it was. The degree of customer contact would also be classed as high or low, with healthcare being an example of a service with a high degree of customer contact and the postal service being an example of a low level of customer contact. Dibb et al. (2006) consider the skill of the service provider in terms of professional or non-professional. Accountancy is a professional skill whereas dry cleaning is not. The rationale behind this is that professional services are more complex and their practitioners have to be sure to comply with more regulations than non-professionals do. Clearly, there is a cross-over area here as it is not only the traditional professions, such as lawyers, doctors, accountants, who are highly regulated, as anyone who works with children in the UK will vouch. The final classification category, the goal of the service provider, refers to whether they are a profit or non-profit organisation (e.g. charities, national health service).

There is no general agreement on a useful classification system for services and it may well be that service products are so diverse that any system will be flawed. It is important to remember that these categorisations are meant to assist the study and marketing of services and, if they do not do so, then there is little point to them. Choose a category or system that fits the service you are considering, and do not be afraid to choose a different one in a different situation.

Another consideration in categorising services as an aid to marketing them well is to think about the degree of involvement of both the service provider and the consumers. In considering the nature of services in the section above, it was identified that both the service provider and the consumer are integral parts of service provision but the extent of their involvement in the process will vary: some services require high levels of direct involvement by the provider (e.g. dentistry) and some low levels (e.g. online ordering). Similarly, this is the case with the **level of involvement** by the consumer. It is possible to consider the marketing implications of each in defining the service provision.

ACTIVITY

The following services vary in terms of how reliant they are on goods. Try placing them on a scale from pure service to high use of (peripheral) products. Then try and categorise them using any of the systems mentioned above.

- banks
- insurance companies
- hotels
- casinos
- bookmakers
- restaurants
- travel agencies
- airlines
- educational establishments
- crèches

- debt collectors
- beauticians
- doctors' surgeries
- plumbers
- management consultancies
- cleaners
- stockbrokers
- garages
- personal trainers
- life coaches

RETAILING AND E-TAILING

personal selling
an oral presentation, in a conversation with one or more prospective purchasers, for the purpose of making sales

distribution channel
a chain of organisations through which products pass on their way to a target market

In many of the more developed countries, shopping is a major pastime. This is a relatively new phenomenon. Shopping used to be considered a chore rather than a leisure activity. This change in shopping's status has significant implications for **retailers** and for retailing's place in marketing. Is it a service or is it a form of **personal selling** or is it the final stage in the **distribution channel**? (See Chapter 9.) So which P of the marketing mix (see below) should we put it in: product, promotion or place? The answer is, of course, that there are aspects of retailing which fit into all of these categories. Here in the service products chapter, we are mainly concerned with **retail** as a service to the consumer: a provider of goods and services and a leisure activity.

As the main source of goods, retailing has a special place in the services spectrum. Its *raison d'être* is to provide other products and it is difficult to separate it out from those products. So we have two issues of inseparability here: the service provider (in this case the efforts of the retailer, including shop staff) is an integral part of the service and so are the goods sold. Retailers will be judged on the quality of both.

ACTIVITY

Refer back to Exhibit 7.4 of the total service offering. Re-draw the diagram for a retailer of your choice.

Whereas traditional retailers are tied to a particular place, a high street or out-of-town shopping centre perhaps, there are other retailers who are not. Mail order (or catalogue) companies have sold their goods and services through the post for many years. Their business is based upon the convenience of bringing the shop to the shopper's own home. A modern variant of home shopping is provided by the Internet. A large proportion of books and CDs are now sold online and a greater variety of goods are being bought there, from groceries to concert tickets to financial services. High street retailing and Internet retailing are becoming blurred. Tesco's, for example, extol the virtue of 'You shop, we drop' as customers order online while Tesco's deliver to your door.

As the Internet becomes a mass marketplace, ease of use becomes more and more important: high quality and service convenience are demanded by e-shoppers too. The early Internet shoppers were computer-skilled bargain hunters, but this is no longer true. Today's online shoppers are motivated by the convenience of shopping from home at any time of the day or night, and having products delivered to their door. Ease of use is paramount and numerous customers give up and abandon their shopping baskets before they make it all the way through to the check-out pages (Jayawardhena et al., 2003). If the process takes too long, it may not only negate the service convenience advantage, but also anger the customer to the point that they never return.

The services marketing mix

physical evidence
the tangible aspects of a service

process
one of the 7Ps of the services marketing mix; the way in which a service is provided

THE OTHER 3PS

The traditional **marketing mix** of **4Ps** (product, promotion, place and price) needs some expanding in order to cope with the distinctive qualities of services. In 1981, Bernard Booms and Mary Jo Bitner proposed the addition of a further 3Ps: **physical evidence**, participants (**people**) and **process** (cited in Bitner, 1990).

Service companies have an even greater need to build customers' trust in the products they offer than do goods providers. They need to reassure customers that the service will be a quality experience, especially as most of the time the service is bought untried. One obvious strategy to overcome fears associated with the service product's intangibility is to turn it into something more tangible. It is generally recognised that the surroundings in which a service is delivered are a key part of customer satisfaction. The ambience of the restaurant, the plates, the music, the state of the toilets – all these things contribute as much to a meal out as does the quality of the food. These more tangible aspects of services are called **physical evidence** and they are important contributors to customer satisfaction. These things are largely within the control of the staff and so, if they are not pleasing to the customers, then it is often the fault of the staff. However, if the service environment is good, and seems well organised, customers are less likely to blame the staff for service failures, even when it is really their fault (Bitner, 1990).

The second P of this extended marketing mix is more commonly referred to as 'people' rather than as 'participants' (the original term). Delivery of a service is usually reliant on staff and so they are important, but the customers and consumers are also important factors affecting the delivery of the service and so they are included in the mix too.

Then there is the question of the actual provision of the service: the **process**. When a customer buys a product, such as a DVD, it is put in a bag, taken home and watched whenever the new owner feels like watching it. They do not actually see the product being made, they just buy the end result. However, a service only exists while it is being delivered. When a customer has a haircut, the only thing that gets taken home is a new look – and if it is a bad look, then little can be done about it. The actual process of hair cutting is the chargeable thing. Exhibit 7.5 illustrates the 7Ps of the service marketing mix.

Exhibit 7.5   The 7Ps of services marketing

P	Description	Example
Product	The core service offering	Haircut
Promotion	Advertising and other tools	Student discount
Place	Where the service is delivered Intermediaries involved in service delivery	The salon Franchises (e.g. Toni and Guy)
Price	The money part of the exchange	May be scaled according to stylist's experience
People	Who deliver the service and who receive it	Hair stylist, junior, receptionist, service consumer
Process	How the service is delivered	From booking the appointment to leaving the salon – and beyond
Physical evidence	The tangible aspects of the service	Shampoo

The first 4Ps of the marketing mix were introduced in Chapter 6 and have their own individual chapters in this book. The extra 3Ps of services marketing are discussed individually below.

PEOPLE

It is the organisation's people who deliver the service, and their attitudes, skills and efficiency often determine how satisfied customers are. It is therefore important that customer-facing staff should be well trained, appropriately turned out and courteous. It is often people that build relationships rather than companies. (In some industries, employees have to sign a contract preventing them from working in the same area for a specified time period in an attempt to prevent them from taking customers with them when they leave.)

If the service personnel are on the end of a telephone line, then it is good telephone manner that is essential. If they are communicating by email, it is their written communication and efficiency that is important.

Technology does not replace people completely in the delivery of most services, it just makes them more remote (and means that the company needs fewer of them). The loss of the personal touch means that it is even harder to build customer relationships. The Internet has the potential to remove all human interaction from transactions, reducing them to mere routines (Pincott and Branthwaite, 2000). Amazon and other online booksellers work really hard to build relationships with their customers. They personalise web pages and greet their returning visitors by name. However, there is growing evidence that too much personalisation is unpopular with some customers, who find it intrusive and who do not want so close a relationship with their bookseller (O'Connor and Galvin, 2001).

The quality of a service is largely dependent upon the skills of the people who provide it, and so the quality of the people who provide a service is even more important than the quality and skills of those who make products. Good, up-to-date training is important. Faulty products may be caught by quality control before they leave the factory, but there are no second chances with services. It is not possible to rewind and start again.

PROCESS

Process is the way in which the service is provided. Burger King is self-service whereas Pizza Express offers waiter service. The processes involved are different, although each scenario is capable of providing competitive advantage.

How bookings are made and how customer enquiries are handled is part of the service process. This is an aspect of service management that is becoming increasingly outsourced and automated through ticket agents, and Internet and telephone sales. This **outsourcing** is potentially damaging for the customer relationship. Customers may actually build relationships with the firm's subcontractor rather than the firm itself. This makes the customers harder to retain in the future. Even worse, it has been known for companies that started as subcontractors to expand and take on the whole business themselves (e.g. plumbers contracted to a home services company could decide to take on the customers themselves).

The **service encounter**, which determines the perceived quality of the service, should be carefully thought through. Flow charts may help us to understand the process better (see Exhibit 7.6 below for an example).

PHYSICAL EVIDENCE

Although fundamentally intangible, most services do have a tangible element (just as goods, physical products, frequently have intangible service elements). Even dentists give you appointment cards and occasionally free toothpaste, and they certainly have instruments and a chair, and reception and waiting areas designed to look pleasant and comfortable.

ACTIVITY

Next time you use a service provider, whether it is a dentist, a hairdresser, a bar, a library or any other, note down all the items of physical evidence you can spot. What is their role in the service's marketing? What changes and improvements would you suggest?

These tangible aspects are known as physical evidence and are key in shaping the customers' perception of the quality of the service. Physical evidence takes many forms. It may be a **peripheral product**, e.g. the oil used in a car service or the soap provided in a hotel. It may be the surroundings in which the service is delivered – the ambience. This comprises décor, music, colour scheme, etc., which is particularly important in places of entertainment such as bars and restaurants (see **services-capes** below for more on the environment in which a service is delivered). It may be a ticket or a contract, the physical proof that you have paid for the service. Tickets may sound trivial but they play a vital role in reassuring customers that their flight, theatre seat or concert is booked. There is no real need for an airline to issue a ticket, indeed some Internet-based airlines do not, but the ticket tells the customer where to go to catch the plane and is a chance to check that the flight is correctly booked. Even when booking on the Internet, airlines usually send a confirming email as, increasingly, do online retailers seeking to reassure customers that their order has been registered and will be dispatched.

Taking a visit to the hairdresser, for example (see Exhibit 7.6), the experience starts with the booking of the appointment. What impression is created by the

Exhibit 7.6   Simple flowchart for a hairdressing service encounter

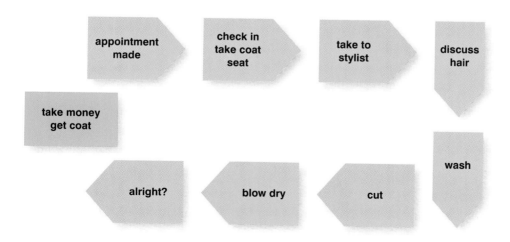

person who answers the phone? Their courtesy and helpfulness, along with the availability of appointments, will be the first point at which the experience could go bad. When the customer arrives at the salon, the welcome they receive is important. This is the start of the service encounter and sets the tone for the rest of the experience. Each stage in the process must be carefully managed so as to meet customer expectations.

EXPAND YOUR KNOWLEDGE

Gronroos, C. (1984) 'A service quality model and its marketing implications', *European Journal of Marketing*, 18 (4): 36–44.

This is one of the early articles highlighting the need to add issues of service quality to marketing thinking. A model of service quality is introduced which identifies perceived and expected service as important contributions to customers' overall perception of a services's quality.

Servicescapes

servicescape
the total environment in which a service is experienced

The environment in which the service is provided and experienced plays a significant part in the overall effect and assessment of the service. Consumers do not typically go to too much trouble in analysing individual components (unless prompted to do so), but rather experience a totality. Booms and Bitner (1981) proposed the concept of the **servicescape** to describe the total (and frequently complex) environment in which the service encounter takes place. They defined servicescape as:

The environment in which the service is assembled and in which the seller and customer interact, combined with tangible commodities that facilitate performance or communication of the service. (Booms and Bitner, 1981: 56)

The ambiance, décor, staffing, layout, accessories, and so on contribute to the total experience of the **service encounter** of a theatre or bar or other service offerings. The environment is one that helps to define the service, distinguish it from competitor offerings and ultimately generate customer satisfaction or dissatisfaction.

insight   A retail experience

Abercrombie and Fitch is not just any shop. Customers go there for the experience as much as for the clothes. The ultra trendy décor is inspired. Lighting is dim (apart from strategically placed spots so that shoppers can see the clothes on offer), music is loud (check their website for playlists), the assistants are all young and good looking (they are 'cast' rather than hired), and bare-chested male models adorn the entrance. There are queues both outside the shop (a wonderful advert) and inside for the tills where people queue for up to an hour just to pay.

In a virtual or online situation, the environment becomes the website and the situation surrounding the computer in which the Internet is being viewed. Servicescapes thus become composites of what the service provider offers and what the consumer brings to the service encounter. Again, this emphasises the potential for inconsistency in the service offering as different customers interact in different ways and at different times with the service being offered.

Upmarket servicescape: a luxury service such as a trip on the Orient Express demands luxury surroundings

Service quality

Services companies need to build the customer's trust in the services they offer. They need to reassure the customer that the service will be a quality experience. Given that services are intangible and inconsistent (see 'the characteristics of services' section above), it is all the more important to pay particular attention to the quality of service offered. Many papers and articles have been written on customer expectations and perceptions of service quality. Perhaps the most famous model used to measure service quality is SERVQUAL (Parasuraman et al., 1988), which employs five dimensions that contribute to service quality:

1 Tangibles (see physical evidence above)
2 Reliability (how dependable is the service, can its performance be relied upon?)
3 Responsiveness (speed of response and helpfulness of staff)
4 Assurance (confidence in the service offering, credibility and consistency)
5 Empathy (good customer understanding).

Customers are asked to complete a questionnaire that uses a series of questions related to the five dimensions listed above. Importantly, SERVQUAL has two parts: the first asks about the service in general and the second part asks the same questions about the specific service received. For example, if the service was a restaurant, Part A would be about restaurants of a similar type more generally and Part B would ask about the specific restaurant whose service quality was being measured. The reason why this is significant is that Part A gives an indication, a benchmark, against which the service being evaluated can be assessed. Gaps between expectations in general and the perception of the service offered in particular can be highlighted and improvements made where relevant. It is important to assess service quality against the right benchmarks. There would be little point in trying to assess the service quality of a small, local restaurant against what may be expected of a particularly high-class, expensive restaurant of the type run by celebrity chefs.

Customers and consumers do not expect perfection. Typically, they have a tolerance range and are willing to accept anything that falls with it. Things can and do go wrong. What is usually important is what the service provider is able to do about it and this is where service recovery comes in (see below).

Google.cn (censored)

ethical focus

The world's favourite search engine has never thought of itself as a mainstream company. More traditional businesses have watched and waited for the company to come crashing down. Analysts thought its stock market floatation would fail but it was a success. IT gurus thought that search engines had a limited life and that eventually people would go straight to their favourite sites without searching, but they don't. Google has been a phenomenal success and, through it all, maintained that quirky, alternative image that made it so popular in the first place. That was until they expanded into China. Initially, they offered a Chinese language version of the site but, in 2005, they launched a Chinese site – censored by Google itself. The idea was that the new address would make the search engine easier and quicker to use. The company argued that, while removing search results was inconsistent with Google's mission, cutting the Chinese people off from information was even worse. The number of Internet search users in China is predicted to increase to 187 million by the end of 2008 and competition was hotting up – notably from Beijing-based Baidu.com.

The Chinese government keeps a tight rein on the Internet and what users can access. The BBC news site is inaccessible and a search for the banned Falun Gong spiritual movement directs users to a string of negative articles. Google, whose motto is 'Do no evil', modified the version of its search engine in China to exclude these and other controversial topics such as the Tiananmen Square massacre, freedom for Tibet and the independence for Taiwan.

Email, chat room and blogging services were not made available on the Chinese site because of concerns the government might demand users' personal information. The US government had already tried something similar but Google refused to pass data on. Not long before, Yahoo had been accused of supplying data to the Chinese authorities that was used as evidence to jail a journalist for ten years.

The censorship of the Chinese site has provoked a backlash in Google's core Western markets. Google is now often compared to Microsoft because of its dominant position and power, and many people feel the company's values have been undermined. In its defence, Google says that much of this is based on misperceptions caused by inflammatory newspaper headlines. Asked whether he regretted the decision, Sergey Brin, one of Google's founders admitted: 'On a business level, that decision to censor ... was a net negative'.

What do you think? Given that Google could not have operated in China uncensored, should they have given up that market?

SOURCE: Martinson, 2007

EXPAND YOUR KNOWLEDGE

Parasuraman, A., Zeithaml, V.A.I. and Malhotra, A. (2005) 'E-S-QUAL a multiple-item scale for assessing electronic service quality', *Journal of Service Research*, 7 (3): 213–233.

These authors, experts and key researchers in the field of service quality, investigate service quality on the web. They use a multiple-item scale to measure the service quality delivered on e-tailing sites.

Branding services

The idea of branding a service is a relatively new one although there are a few notable exceptions that have been around for a while. Branding started in the world of the physical product, at the time when manufacturing processes had advanced to the stage at which consistency and quality could pretty much be assured. Services tend to be inconsistent, which makes them harder to **brand**. However, there are lots of famous service brands today: British Airways, Avis rent a car, Barclay's Bank, NHS (National Health Service), McDonald's, J. Walter Thomson, Computacab, etc. Brands are seen as a badge of quality. Consumers have been educated by the physical products companies to understand this and so, in our age of the brand, services companies are able to switch things around and create brands that confer quality – rather than products of quality that therefore deserve brands.

ACTIVITY

Identify ten major service brands. It may help if you look at advertising in the press to jog your memory. Try to identify examples from a range of different sectors, such as travel/tourism, financial services, high street and online retailing, telephony and communications, etc. Consider the ways in which the companies have created and promoted their brands and what you think those brands represent. What message do they convey to customers?

A good brand not only reduces the customer's perceived risk, but actually enables a company to charge a higher price for its services.

EXPAND YOUR KNOWLEDGE

Tax, S.S., Brown, S.W. and Chandrashekaran, M. (1998) 'Customer evaluations of service complaint experiences: implications for relationship marketing', *Journal of Marketing*, 62 (Apr): 60–76.

The authors research complaining customers and find that the majority are dissatisfied with their experiences. Their findings suggest that satisfaction, or otherwise, has a direct impact on trust and commitment but that positive prior experiences can mitigate this poor complaint handling to a limited extent. Implications abound for improving handling procedures which affect customer relationships and loyalty.

Service recovery

Nobody can guarantee that all **service encounters** will run smoothly or as intended. Things go wrong. Trains, boats and planes run late and are delayed. A financial transaction may contain errors. The food may not taste as it should in a restaurant. The plumber may not fix a leak or an electrician may charge more than expected. These things may occur despite the best efforts of the service provider and may be simple but unfortunate mistakes.

One bad service encounter is a serious thing that may lead to a significant loss of custom, not only from the person directly affected but also from others if that person tells family and friends of the bad experience. Bad news travels fast! Consequently, **service recovery** is very important. If the service does go wrong, then the customer's

service recovery
trying to retrieve a situation caused by a poor product or bad service encounter

complaint must be handled with great care. Good customer relationships are even more important to service businesses.

A complaint should be looked at as an opportunity to provide great service. It is often possible to turn the situation around and impress the customer after all. Bars and clubs may apologise profusely and take things off the bill or offer free drinks. Airlines may upgrade seats to first class or offer free tickets for another flight. The result can be a more satisfied customer than the one who received good service in the first place.

While poor service encounters need to be avoided, service recovery provides opportunities for greater customer satisfaction if dealt with well. Encouraging customers to state their complaints may seem counter-productive but analysis of complaints can be an important research activity that can avoid customer disappointment at the time of the service delivery and can be built into overall improvement plans to avoid future complaints by other customers.

EXPAND YOUR KNOWLEDGE

Hocutt, M.A., Bowers, M.R. and Donavan, D.T. (2006) 'The art of service recovery: fact or fiction', *Journal of Services Marketing*, 20 (3): 199–207.

As it is impossible to ensure all customer experiences are positive, it becomes all the more relevant to understand the importance of what companies do about poor customer experiences. Bad experiences may be spread to others through word-of-mouth creating even lower levels of customer satisfaction and loyalty. Service recovery is, therefore, a critical concept. If handled well, service recovery can lead to greater levels of customer satisfaction.

SUMMARY

Services are aspects of the total product offering. While it is convenient to think of physical products and service products as different, in reality they are part of the same product continuum (Exhibit 7.3), in which services have greater intangibility than physical goods. From a marketing perspective, it is always wise to consider what services may be added to enhance physical products and what physical products can be used to enhance the service offering.

In most developed countries (MDCs) there has been a significant economic shift from manufacturing output to service provision. For this reason, the economies of MDCs place great reliance on services and on those companies that provide them. In marketing, therefore, it is important to recognise the distinctiveness, and key characteristics, of services. This chapter has highlighted the nature of services and identified seven particular characteristics: the customer gains some benefit from them; they are mostly intangible; they are time and place dependent (they cannot be stored); the service provider is an intrinsic part of the service itself; the consumer is also an intrinsic part of the service itself; services are inconsistent; and there is no resulting ownership of anything significant.

The interest in services marketing has led to an expansion of the traditional marketing mix from 4Ps to 7Ps by the inclusion of physical evidence, people and process. While the 7Ps clearly relate to services, many physical products also contain elements of services and therefore the 7Ps can usefully be used for all types of products.

This chapter also highlighted a number of other key concepts, such as service convenience, service encounter, service quality, servicescape and service recovery as important considerations when marketing services. Branding is a strategy that evolved in the world of physical goods, but it has lately been successfully applied to services. Branding is covered in greater depth in Chapters 6 and 11.

CHALLENGES REVIEWED

Now that you have finished reading the chapter, look back at the challenges you were set at the beginning. Do you have a clearer idea of what's involved?

Hints:

- the UK and most other highly developed counties are service economies so talk about how much income service businesses generate, the jobs they create and how they facilitate other businesses
- service recovery – remember that people often think more highly of a company that treats them really well after a mistake has been made than they do of companies who have never made mistakes
- there are a number of answers to this problem, an obvious one relies on offering a better service; think about peripheral products, processes and how to exploit the skills of your people (who have the advantage of being more local)
- this is about the intangibility of services and how that makes them high-risk purchases. You need to reduce the perceived risk somehow, e.g. by emphasising the tangible aspects of the service being offered (such as the hotel's facilities) and the brand values of the airline, and/or by reference to previous satisfied customers. Do not forget about what guarantees and assurances you can offer.

READING AROUND

Book chapters

Dave Chaffey, and Paul Smith (2008) *Emarketing Excellence*: *Planning and Optimising Your Digital Marketing (Emarketing Essentials)*. Oxford: Butterworth Heinemann. Chapter 2, 'Remix'.

Books

Evert Gummesson (2001) *Total Relationship Marketing*. Oxford: Butterworth Heinemann.
Adrian Palmer (2005) *Principles of Services Marketing* (4th edn). Maidenhead: McGraw Hill.

Journal articles

Leonard Berry (1980) 'Services marketing is different', *Business*, 30 (3): 52–6.
Christian Grönroos (1978) 'A service-oriented approach to the marketing of services', *European Journal of Marketing*, 12 (8): 588–601.
Christian Grönroos (1997) 'From marketing mix to relationship marketing – towards a paradigm shift in marketing', *Management Decision*, 35 (4): 322–39.
G. Lynn Shostack (1977) 'Breaking free from product marketing', *Journal of Marketing*, 41 (2): 73–80.

A journal article that gives insights into the future of services marketing:
Stephen J. Grove, Raymond P. Fisk and John Joby (2003) 'The future of services marketing: forecasts from ten services experts', *Journal of Services Marketing*, 17(2): 107–21.

Websites

www.hospitalityassured.com – a website for an organisation (Hospitality Assured) dedicated to raising standards in the hospitality industry. Check out *The Standard* with its ten key steps to achieving service and business excellence.

SELF-REVIEW QUESTIONS

1. Define services. (see page 240)
2. Why should marketers be more concerned in today's economies with the marketing of services? (see pages 242–4)
3. What does the product continuum describe? (see page 245)
4. Identify the six characteristics that describe the nature of services. (see page 246)
5. What is meant when we say that services are inconstant? (see page 252)
6. Dibb et al. propose a way of classifying services based on five criteria. What are they? (see page 254)
7. What is meant by the consumer being part of the service? (see pages 249–51)
8. What is 'service convenience'? (see page 250)
9. What are the 7Ps? (see page 256)
10. Why is physical evidence important to the marketing of services? (see page 259)
11. Why is it important to assess service quality and what is SERVQUAL? (see page 261)
12. Why is service recovery an important concept? (see page 263)

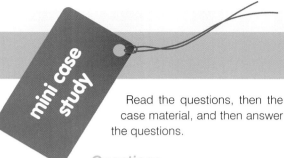

Read the questions, then the case material, and then answer the questions.

Questions

1. Identify and explain examples of the 7Ps at work in the case study.
2. What is Rock Planet doing well? Where does it fall down?
3. Using the 7Ps to guide you, recommend three improvements the restaurant can make. You should explain and justify your ideas.

The Rock Planet restaurant opened with a burst of publicity and a celebrity launch party just over a year ago. For the first few months it was the place to eat, although even then there were mutterings about slow service and rude waiters. Now it's a familiar London landmark, particularly popular with tourists who like the inexpensive set lunch menu. Its reasonable prices and rock star connections also attract the young for celebrations such as birthdays and leaving parties. The bouncers look formidable, but they've never been known to refuse anyone entrance unreasonably.

The restaurant is usually full, so diners wait in the bar, which is loud and crowded. A 1960s-style jukebox adds to the din. Customers get a Rock Planet buzzer, one of five designs (each a model of an artist), which lights up and sings when their table is ready. Flamboyant waiters shake cocktails in dramatic style against a backdrop of rock memorabilia. Electric guitars adorn the walls alongside pictures of their famous former owners. One of Jimi Hendrix's guitars has pride of place above the bar. To its right, under thick glass, is a scrap of paper on which John Lennon jotted some of the words to 'She Loves You'. On the left is Badly Drawn Boy's hat.

The rock décor is carried through to the restaurant, as is the music. All the waiters are young and dressed up. There are the teddy boy suits and the flared skirts and short socks of the 1950s, glam rock, grunge and some of the latest club styles. The restaurant serves fast food American style: hamburgers (and a veggie burger), fries, salads, chicken and ribs. It also does take-aways and delivers within a five-mile radius.

The biggest complaint is that food doesn't come to the table fast enough – something that is rubbed in by the lights that flash on a neon map of the USA to tell the waiters when an order is ready for collection. However, many diners find the friendly service makes up for their building hunger. And they tend to order more drinks. Home-delivery customers have to order at least two hours before they want the food.

Rock Planet is a place where people like to celebrate their birthdays and so the staff have a birthday routine. They dance through the restaurant carrying sparklers and then, when they reach the birthday table, they sing 'Happy Birthday' and encourage the rest of the diners to join in. The birthday boy or girl is presented with a cup cake with an everlasting candle on it and a small bag of inexpensive Rock Planet merchandise.

Further entertainment comes from the Rock Planet Moments. Each day, the manager chooses three dishes to be the special recommendations of the day. When the 20th order for that dish is delivered to a table, there is a fanfare and lights flash. The lucky diner gets the featured dish on the house and a complimentary cocktail (alcoholic or non-alcoholic) of their choice. For the 50th order, the diner gets their whole meal free.

Very lucky diners may get to sit at a table next to the stars. The restaurant is owned by a group of well-known musicians who make a point of eating there as often as possible. Sometimes, you might even get 'Happy Birthday' sung by a megastar.

One of the biggest challenges for the management is keeping the place clean. It's a large, busy restaurant and lots of children eat there. Inevitably this means that there are spills and it can be hard to get them cleaned up while people are eating. The toilets are checked every hour but they still sometimes run out of towels or soap. The floor seems always in need of a clean. The problem in the bar is even worse. Staff have trouble fighting their way to tables to collect glasses and wipe down tabletops. A dropped tray of glasses means dangerous glass on the floor, so staff are reluctant to collect too many at once. Frequently the bar staff run out of clean glasses altogether.

Rock Planet has had some bad reviews recently. Critics say the food is unimaginative and of low quality, the restaurant too loud and too dirty, the service too slow and the waiters often get the orders, or the bill, wrong. But apparently the diners disagree – it's still packed out every night.

(Rock Planet and this case study are entirely fictional.)

REFERENCES

Berry, L.L., Seiders, K. and Grewal, D. (2002) 'Understanding service convenience', *Journal of Marketing*, 66 (3): 1–17.

Bitner, M.J. (1990) 'Evaluating service encounters: the effects of physical surroundings and employee responses', *Journal of Marketing*, 54 (2): 69–82.

Booms, B.H. and Bitner, M.J. (1981) 'Marketing strategies and organization structures for service firms', in J.H. Donnelly and W.R. George (eds), *Marketing of Services*. Chicago: American Marketing Association. pp. 51–67.

Business Link (n.d.) *Your Type of Business*, UK government. Available at: **www.businesslink. gov.uk/bdotg/action/sectorsSIMLandingPage;jsessionid=GH8pKT1yJqhKys9yn55LMJh4qDC DcWBpWJ6PCVT2yKF20KrdSK7F!476980321!1153907934766?r.s=tl** (accessed 27/07/2006).

Central Intelligence Agency (CIA) (n.d.) *The World Factbook*. Available at: **https://www.cia. gov/library/publications/the-world-factbook/** (accessed 16/12/2009).

Dibb, S., Simkin, L., Pride, W.M. and Ferrell, O.C. (2006) *Marketing Concepts and Strategies* (5th edn). Boston: Houghton Mifflin.

Farquar, J.D. and Rowley, J. (2009) 'Convenience: a service perspective', *Journal of Marketing Theory*, 9 (4): 425–438.

Gronroos, C. (1984) 'A service quality model and its marketing implications', *European Journal of Marketing*, 18 (4): 36–44.

Grove, S.J., Fisk, R.P. and Joby, J. (2003) 'The future of services marketing: forecasts from ten services experts', *Journal of Services Marketing*, 17 (2): 107–21.

Handy, C. (2002) *The Elephant and the Flea*. London: Arrow.

Hocutt, M.A., Bowers, M.R. and Donavan, D.T. (2006) 'The art of service recovery: fact or fiction', *Journal of Services Marketing*, 20 (3): 199–207.

Jayawardhena, C., Wright, L.T. and Masterson, R. (2003) 'An investigation of online consumer purchasing', *Qualitative Market Research: An International Journal*, 6 (1): 58–65.

Kotler, P. (2003) *Marketing Insights from A to Z: 80 Concepts Every Manager Needs to Know*. New York: John Wiley & Sons Inc.

Kotler, P., Armstrong, G., Saunders, J. and Wong, V. (2001) *Principles of Marketing* (European edition). Harlow: Pearson Education.

Martinson, J. (2007) 'China censorship damaged us, Google founders admit', *Guardian*, 27 January.

O'Connor, J. and Galvin, E. (2001) *Marketing in the Digital Age*. Harlow: FT/Prentice Hall.

Palmer, A. (2005) *Principles of Services Marketing* (4th edn). Maidenhead: McGraw Hill.

Parasuraman, A. Zeitham, V.A. and Berry, L.B. (1988) 'SERVQUAL: A multiple-item scale for measuring consumer perceptions of service quality', *Journal of Retailing*, 64 (1): 12–40.

Parasuraman, A., Zeithaml, V.A.l. and Malhotra, A. (2005) 'E-S-QUAL a multiple-item scale for assessing electronic service quality', *Journal of Service Research*, 7 (3): 213–233.

Patents Office (n.d.) *Media Centre: Journalists' Guide to Intellectual Property*, UK government. Available at: **www.patent.gov.uk/media/journalistguide** (accessed 19/07/2006).

Pincott, G. and Branthwaite, A. (2000) 'Nothing new under the sun?', *International Journal of Market Research*, 42 (2): 137–55.

Shostack, G.L. (1977) 'Breaking free from product marketing', *Journal of Marketing*, 41 (Apr): 73–80.

Shostack, G.L. (1984) 'Designing services that deliver', *Harvard Business Review*, 62 (Jan-Feb): 133–139.

Tax, S.S., Brown, S.W. and Chandrashekaran, M. (1998) 'Customer evaluations of service complaint experiences: implications for relationship marketing', *Journal of Marketing*, 62 (Apr): 60–76.

Topping, A. (2007) 'Man using laptop on garden wall charged with wireless theft', *The Guardian,* 23 August, p. 3.

Voss, G.B., Parasuraman, A. and Grewal, D. (1998) 'The roles of price, performance and expectations in determining satisfaction in services exchanges', *Journal of Marketing*, 62 (Oct): 46–61.

Promotion (marketing communications)

CHAPTER CONTENTS

Introduction
Managing promotion
Marketing communications objectives
Promotional strategy
The marketing communications process
Influencing customers
The marketing communications mix
Advertising
Public relations (PR)
Sales promotion
Personal selling
Direct marketing
Regulations
Setting the marketing budget
Summary
Challenges reviewed
Reading around
Self-review questions
Mini case study
References

PROMOTION CHALLENGES

The following are illustrations of the types of decision that marketers have to take or issues they face. *You aren't expected to know how to deal with the challenges now*; just bear them in mind as you read the chapter and see what you can find that helps.

- You are a marketing manager responsible for a new range of chilled fruit drinks. What budget would be appropriate for the launch?

- You run a small, specialist soft drinks firm. Your marketing budget is a tiny fraction of that of your major competitor and you certainly cannot afford television advertising. How will you get your brand noticed by potential customers?

- You believe that your new manager has an unusual sense of humour. He wants to incorporate some of his jokes into a television advertising campaign for your long-established brand of mid-market, male footwear and he wants your views. His ideas don't make you laugh but you're not sure how your customers will react. What will you do?

- Disaster! You are the public relations manager for a major airline. The check-in staff and baggage handlers have gone on strike, leaving thousands of passengers stranded at an international airport. They are angry and frustrated. What will you do now? What will you do later when the crisis has passed?

- You are an advertising account manager and one of your clients is a multi-national snack food manufacturer whose account is worth £30 million per year to your agency. In the past, most of that money has been spent on advertising during children's television programmes but recently there has been a consumer backlash against adverts, and junk foods, which target young children. You need to advise your client on their future marketing communications strategy.

Introduction

Promotion, another term for **marketing communications**, is one of the 4Ps of the marketing mix and an essential part of the total product offering. No matter how good your product is, if people do not *know* it is good, then they will not buy it. Equally, no matter how good your promotion is, if your product is poor, then people will not continue to buy it. Some form of promotion, or marketing communication, is necessary to make customers aware of the existence of the product, help create its brand identity, and persuade them to try it and even to incorporate it into their life.

To be effective, promotional activity must be based on a sound understanding of how and why products are bought, consumed, used and of current market trends. Clearly, this involves in-depth research as well as an understanding of the principles of buyer behaviour (see Chapters 5 and 3 respectively). Marketers segment their potential audiences (using the techniques discussed in Chapter 4) in order to select the best group(s) at which to aim their communications.

DEFINITIONS

promotion
another name for marketing communications, communication designed and implemented to persuade others to accept ideas, concepts or things; to motivate consumers to action

In its broadest sense, **promotion** means to move forwards. Think about the term in relation to a promotion to a higher grade or more senior position at work. Over time, this meaning has evolved so that, in marketing, promotion refers to communication designed and implemented to persuade others to accept ideas, concepts or things; to motivate customers and consumers to take action, i.e. it moves them forward towards a purchase decision.

This chapter will examine the reasons why it is necessary for organisations to communicate, who they communicate with and how they can get their message across. It will also consider the regulatory environment within which marketers operate (with particular reference to UK regulatory bodies). The chapter concludes with a brief section on setting marketing budgets.

THE PROMOTION MIX

promotion mix
traditionally, advertising, PR, sales promotion and personal selling

There are many potential promotional tools or activities and the traditional way of categorising all of them is as the **promotion mix**, which (at its most basic) comprises:

● advertising
● public relations (PR)
● sales promotions
● personal selling.

4Ps
a mnemonic (memory aid) for the marketing mix: product, promotion, place, price

So there are **4Ps** in the marketing mix – product, promotion, place and price – and also four main elements to the promotional mix.

Although it is sometimes used as yet another alternative term for promotion or marketing communications, in its stricter sense the term 'advertising' describes any paid form of non-personal presentation of ideas, goods and services by an identified advertiser. It is paid-for promotional messages carried by the mass media (TV, radio, press, cinema, posters, the Internet).

public relations (PR)
planned activities designed to promote goodwill between an organisation and its publics

Public relations (PR) uses different activities designed to promote goodwill between an organisation and the outside world. These activities may include providing news and features stories for the media, running events, **sponsorship**, or building relationships with influential individuals and groups. PR may use the same media (e.g. television, radio, the Internet) as **advertising** but in a very different way. While advertisers buy space or airtime and control (within the regulations) what goes into it, PROs (Public Relations Officers) have to persuade journalists to include stories about their brands and cannot control what those journalists say.

Sales promotions are short term, special offers and other added-value activities intended to induce buyers to buy, or try, a product. Such offers include two for the price of one, money-off coupons and instant wins.

Personal selling, as the name suggests, is the most personal of the promotional tools. It involves persuading customers of the benefits of products and services, usually on a one-to-one basis. Such personal communication is costly – imagine sending a salesperson out to sell single bottles of shampoo to individuals. Consequently, it is an approach favoured in B2B sales where the order quantities are higher. Similarly, it would be a waste of television advertising if it was used to sell ball bearings as the vast majority of those who saw the ad would not be interested, so it would be more efficient to send sales representatives to the few companies that might be interested.

Different techniques are needed in different markets, in different situations and to achieve different ends. This chapter will examine those techniques and their effective use.

MARKETING COMMUNICATIONS OR PROMOTION?

These two terms mean the same thing: promotion is the older name and fits within the mnemonic the 4Ps. In this chapter (as in life), the two terms will be used interchangeably.

Each tool in the promotion mix has certain strengths that will be outlined below. Some organisations – e.g. Nike, Cadbury and Volkswagen – emphasise advertising and public relations efforts in their promotional mixes. Others, especially those engaged in business-to-business (B2B) marketing, choose personal selling as a significant promotion mix ingredient. Smith & Nephew, Johnson & Johnson and 3M sell healthcare products to hospitals and all tend to favour personal selling in these situations. This is, in part, because of the complex nature of the **decision-making** units involved (see Chapter 3) and the need to identify and nurture different **stakeholders.**

sales promotion
a short-term special offer, e.g. two for the price of one

personal selling
an oral presentation, in a conversation with one or more prospective purchasers, for the purpose of making sales

marketing communications
another name for promotion; communication designed and implemented to persuade others to accept ideas, concepts or things; to motivate audience members to action

---

ACTIVITY

Collect or identify as many examples of promotional material from one organisation as you can. How do they differ? Why do you think they differ? Who are the audiences?

Managing promotion

A key part of a marketing communications manager's job is to coordinate the promotional mix elements:

- setting objectives for what the elements are intended to accomplish
- setting budgets that are sufficient to support the objectives
- designing marketing programmes (e.g. advertising campaigns) that will achieve those objectives
- checking the results of the campaign regularly to ensure that it is on track to achieve the marketing communications objectives (evaluation and control).

CAMPAIGNS

A campaign is a series of coordinated marketing activities designed to achieve specific objectives, e.g. to reposition a product or to educate people about its correct use or to raise a brand's awareness levels. Each of these objectives would require a different set of promotional activities. Educating people about products' use is quite different from raising brand awareness: different messages, different techniques. Managers must decide what emphasis to put on interpersonal versus mass communication, whether to select a push strategy or a pull strategy, and how much importance to place on each of the different promotion mix elements.

As well as being internally coordinated, all a company's campaigns should fit with each other. Managers need to be able to think in a joined-up way. It is counterproductive to have one campaign's message or feel contradicting another one's. Consequently, the design of campaigns starts higher up. It starts with the development of overall marketing communications objectives and a promotional strategy.

Marketing communications objectives

An objective is something that an organisation wants to achieve: a target to aim for. Well-chosen marketing communications techniques are capable of achieving many positive things for a company, but clearly it makes sense to think through exactly what the organisation wants to achieve before designing, and then spending money on, a campaign. Heinz's Classic Soup campaign won a silver award in the Design Business Association's 2009 Design Effectiveness Awards. The campaign's objectives were to:

- reinvigorate the brand
- 'remind consumers that Heinz provides good, nourishing food made with wholesome ingredients'
- 'make the range feel relevant to a contemporary audience and get consumers to "fall in love" with Heinz again'
- get people to eat more soup

(DBA, 2009).

Without clear-cut objectives it is impossible to know whether a campaign was a success or not. It really is not enough to produce an attractive campaign that people like, or even one that wins awards. Companies expect their advertising to help their business. They expect it to achieve something worthwhile.

THE IMPORTANCE OF TARGETED OBJECTIVES

A strategy is the means by which a firm tries to achieve its objectives. Objectives are fundamental in providing direction for an organisation and can only do this if they are clearly stated, compatible with each other, known, understood and followed (Pickton and Broderick, 2004a). A marketing manager must set the promotion objectives before deciding on the optimal promotion mix.

In order to set realistic promotional objectives, the firm needs a clear statement of its target market. However, a promotional campaign may not be aimed at the entire market; it may even be aimed at people who are not part of the market at all. Promotional campaigns reach out to **target audiences.**

target audience
the people, or organisations, that are selected to receive communications

TARGET AUDIENCE OR TARGET MARKET?

Target markets are customers (i.e. the people who buy goods and services). The term is also used to refer to consumers or users (who may or may not have bought the product themselves). However, in marketing communications, everyone involved in the purchase decision, however indirectly, needs to be understood and addressed. The people that organisations want to *talk* to are target *audiences* and may include potential agents, distributors, retailers, opinion leaders and formers, journalists, employees, the government, present and potential shareholders – anybody who is important to the organisation. So the term 'audience' is potentially much broader and may, or may not, include the market. Markets are places where things are bought and sold, while audiences are the people that communicators want to listen to them.

For example, Domino Pizza's target market is broad and encompasses families, singles and students, but the target *audience* for a very successful campaign was:

- customers of competitor stores (specifically Pizza Hut)
- lapsed or occasional pizza eaters who have (through experience) low expectations of home delivered pizza

(Makin, 2002).

The target audience is often more specific and narrower than the target market and closely targeted communications tend to be more effective.

> **Products are sold to target markets.**
> **Marketing communications**
> **are addressed to target audiences.**

A good deal of marketing has international dimensions. Although not all organisations are global, many audiences are worldwide and major brands try to maintain consistency in their worldwide positioning. How disappointing to visit a foreign country and find that your favourite designer is considered downmarket, or that your beer is thought to be poor quality. Some beers that are 'reassuringly expensive' in the UK might not have quite the same image elsewhere. Many marketers have to take a varied international audience into account when designing their marketing communications strategies.

Promotional strategy

There is no one clear definition of the term 'strategy'. Over the years strategy has acquired a number of meanings, and academics and practitioners are not in total agreement. Broadly speaking, Engel et al. (1994) used the term 'promotional strategy' to refer to a controlled, integrated programme of communication methods designed to present an organisation and its products or services to prospective customers, to communicate need-satisfying attributes, to facilitate sales, and thus to contribute to long-term profit performance. Pickton and Broderick (2004a) emphasised the need to consider a range of target audiences when determining strategy and not just to focus on customers.

insight   A big job for a small car

Volkswagen was well established in New Zealand as a small-car specialist with understated Euro-styling and an affordable price. Car buyers with youthful memories of the Beetle had moved on to the cost-competitive Polo and the Golf.

Volkswagen had successfully positioned itself as a sub-prestige brand, nicely located in between prestige brands like BMW and Mercedes-Benz and mass-market brands like Toyota and Ford. Then the company announced plans to launch a new car in a totally different category. It was now up to their advertising agency (DDB) to launch the Touareg as a prestige SUV (sport utility vehicle).

For upmarket competitors like Mercedes and Range Rover, a brand extension into the prestige SUV category was a small one. For Volkswagen, starting from its Polo and Golf base, the distance to be closed was huge.

DDB's campaign's objectives were to:

- raise awareness of the Touareg among existing and potential prestige SUV buyers
- close the perception gap and so position Volkswagen as a credible and attractive competitor in the prestige SUV category
- encourage potential buyers to see and test-drive the Touareg.

The campaign's target audience was 'the new generation of entrepreneurs and self-employed' – a subset of the ABC1 market for the product.

The campaign theme that the agency developed was: 'Surprise!' The idea behind this was that a prestige-level Volkswagen vehicle would come as rather a surprise to the prospects who did not expect a Volkswagen to be so luxurious and powerful, nor to be based on such world-beating technology. The audience would also be surprised by the humorous, convention-challenging brand attitude of Volkswagen overall and the new Touareg particularly.

The creative executions showed a Touareg owner who had driven to a place never previously visited by humans and where animals were behaving in unusual ways, e.g. possums were playing cards, rabbits playing rugby. The Touareg owner had surprised them doing things that they usually hide from human eyes.

The adverts were placed in the kind of magazines and newspapers which the target audience read, during their favourite television programmes and on urban billboards that they would be likely to drive by. The total media expenditure was just under $500,000.

The other major campaign element was designed to help dealers to persuade prospects to test drive the car. This 'Yeti kit' stuck with the 'Surprise Nature' theme by providing a camera for the first ever Yeti photo, a fabricated public relations release on how the driver had discovered the Yeti and an invitation to a Yeti-finding adventure (and picnic) with the dealer in a hard-to-reach place where Yetis might be found.

Within its first six months, the Touareg exceeded its ambitious sales targets and became the number two brand in the category, second only to BMW and well ahead of those other, prestige rivals.

SOURCE: DDB, 2004

PUSH AND PULL STRATEGIES

One way of understanding the different promotional emphases of various organisations is to think of them as push or pull. Who are the target audiences? If the campaign is directed towards consumers or end users, then it is hoped that by demanding the product, they will pull it through the supply chain. If, on the other hand, the campaign is directed at intermediaries, e.g. retailers, then its purpose is to persuade them to push the products.

In some companies, marketing efforts and tactics are aimed primarily at the trade, such as wholesalers, distributors and retailers. In this case, advertising and sales promotion, selling effort, as well as pricing strategies, are aimed at generating trade interest and demand for the company's products. This promotional focus is designed to push a product into, and through, the distribution channel. **Push strategies** are common in the industrial sector and also the field of medicine. Medical sales representatives from companies such as Astra-Zenica promote (push) products very strongly to general practitioners and support this push with promotional material from the marketing department. This promotional material may include brochures and branded merchandise. Next time you visit your doctor, observe the different promotional materials in the surgery, such as posters, post-its, pens and mouse mats.

push strategy
a promotional strategy aimed at distribution channels

B2B focus — Getting the drinks in

Consumers of premium spirit brands, such as Bacardi light rum and Gordon's Gin, can be fierce champions of their favourite brand, claiming it has superior taste and that they can always pick it out. Such spirits are rarely drunk neat though – they are mixed with something else and that something else is usually a larger measure than the alcohol. Take gin and tonic or rum and coke, for example – in both cases there is more mixer than spirit in the drink. How can the superiority of the chosen spirit be best preserved? The answer clearly lies in a premium quality mixer.

The Fever-Tree range of mixer drinks was developed to fill this gap in the market. However, it is one thing to come up with the idea, but quite another to make it into a success. There was a clear need for the product: consumers wanted more natural drinks and most existing mixers were highly artificial and stuffed with additives. Fever-Tree used only the best, exotic natural ingredients, even producing the world's first naturally low-calorie tonic water (no artificial sweeteners; just a blend of fruit sugars, citrus, aromatic botanicals, natural quinine and spring water).

It was a great product but the challenge was to get it to the consumers. To do that, Fever-Tree needed to convince retailers to stock it. They began with sales calls to upmarket hotels and restaurants, including The Ritz and Claridges, but they needed a supermarket stockist if they were to make significant inroads into this market.

A major advertising campaign was out of the question as their marketing budget was tiny, so the Fever-Tree communications team concentrated on food and drinks journalists. Media coverage in papers such as the *Sunday Times* helped them to convince Waitrose to stock the brand and the brand's market share soon increased by a percentage point (a significant amount in a market as large as this one).

Fever-Tree is now available from Tesco, Sainsbury's, Harrods's, Fortnum and Mason's and many smaller retailers, cafes and bars. It is served in six out of the top 10 restaurants in the world (as voted for by *Restaurant* magazine in 2008). World-renowned chef Ferran Adria of Spain's El Bulli restaurant has turned Fever-Tree Premium Indian Tonic Water into a course in itself: 'Sopa de Fever-Tree tonica'. In the USA, the world's largest mixers market, Fever-Tree was awarded 'Best New Product' at the 2008 Tales of the Cocktail awards. Fever-Tree also won the new brand (SME) award at the Marketing Society's Golden Jubilee Awards 2009.

Conversely, a **pull strategy** focuses a company's marketing efforts on the final customer or consumer. The objective of this strategy is to generate sufficient consumer interest and demand for the company's products to be pulled through the distribution channels. The goal is to generate demand at the retail level in the belief that such demand will encourage retailers and wholesalers to stock the product.

pull strategy
a promotional strategy aimed at end customers or consumers

Although we see push and pull as distinctive strategies, it is usually not a case of deciding between one or the other, but more of determining where the balance should be. An effective marketing communications strategy often uses a combination of push and pull.

The strategy is implemented through the marketing communications mix, which is considered in more detail later.

The marketing communications process

An understanding of the communications theory that underpins the marketing communications process is helpful in ensuring that messages arrive safely. Schramm (1955) is attributed with first modelling the communications process and the model presented in Exhibit 8.1 is based on his initial, simple model.

Exhibit 8.1   Simple communications model – after Schramm (1955)

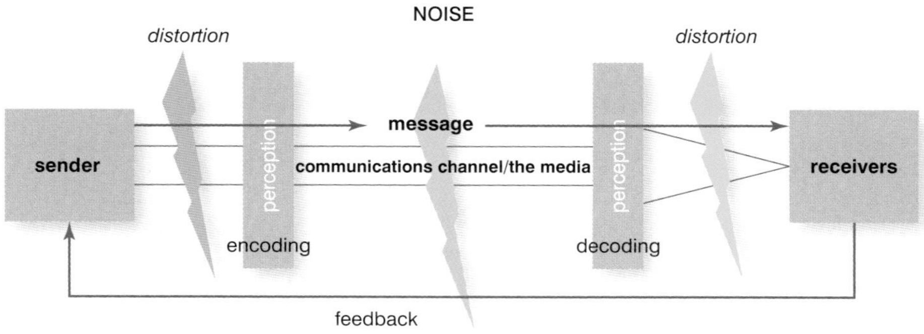

There are two principal participants (or sets of participants) in the communications process:

1 The sender is the originator or source of the message. This is the company which is doing the advertising, such as BT or Coca-Cola. Although in practice, agents or consultants may actually do a lot of the work on behalf of the sender.
2 Receivers are the people to whom the message is sent, the target audience(s).

message
the impression a promotion leaves on its audience

Advertising will be used for the purposes of this explanation; however, the model is applicable to all forms of marketing communications. The advertiser wishes to communicate with a chosen target audience. The **message** is the actual information and impressions it wishes to send. This message is coded into an advert by the agency's creative team (they make the ad). It can then be sent. The 'media/channels' are the means used to carry the message, e.g. in the case of advertising this may be by television, radio, cinema, etc.

The challenge of marketing communications is to ensure that this process communicates the right message, in the right way, to the right people, in the right place, at the right time. Communication only actually takes place when the receiver understands the message and, ideally, acts upon it. This may not be a physical action – it may be a change of attitude (a frequent objective of advertising) – but something happens to the receiver as a result of receiving the message – even if it is only an increase in knowledge.

Senders are not usually telepathic. They cannot transmit pure thought so they have to put the message across through a commonly understood code, such as words, pictures, symbols and/or actions. Senders *encode* messages, using their skills and resources (e.g. film studios or printers). Encoding is the first step in the communications process. Ideally, the sender's intended message is transmitted, although in reality this does not always occur. Have you ever tried, unsuccessfully, to express an idea? You know what you intended to say, but the words that came out of your mouth failed to reflect your thoughts? Media advertising is an expensive business. An advert that does not come across well to its target audience is a major waste of time and money. That is why agencies, and their clients, put so much into getting them right.

Messages that are encoded badly get distorted and are not received correctly: **distortion** is a coding problem, a lack of skill, or care, either on the part of the sender (who encodes) or the receiver (who decodes).

distortion
a barrier to communication; poor coding skills, e.g. a badly devised ad or a badly worded sales promotion, that prevent the message from being received correctly

The message may get distorted at either end of the channel. For example, the press release may be badly written, the prize for the sales promotion poorly selected, the salesperson might be disagreeable that day or the problem may lie with the poor language skills of the receiver or their lack of attention. In marketing communications, it is up to the sender to try to ensure that the way the message is coded is suitable for the intended target audience.

Distortion is not the only barrier to communication. There are a number of other things that may get in the message's way: poor television reception, graffiti on a poster, a computer going down, crackle on a telephone line, the receiver having a headache – this is all **noise**.

noise
a barrier to communication, usually from an external source

There is no excuse for poor coding by professional communicators such as advertising agencies. However, decoding happens at the other end of the channel as well and the receivers' decoding skills are less certain. Whether or not the message is correctly received depends upon the receivers' receipt and interpretation of the message transmitted. The sender hopes that the message received is identical to the one transmitted, but this is not always the case.

Levels of coding skill and external noise are easier to deal with than the distortion that comes from perceptual problems. **Perception** is how we see the world. Our perception is built up over the years through all of our experiences. Without it, we would be unable to interpret the world around us. Think of a newborn baby. It knows nothing and may well misinterpret its world. How puzzling those new shiny toys must be – especially the ones that make its mother shout when it reaches for them. There is no understanding, no ability to interpret external stimuli, without learning and experience. As no two people's lives are exactly the same, then their perceptions will not be the same either, and this can cause communication problems. The person whose experience includes severe seasickness may view a boat sailing out to sea with dread, while others might see that as an invitation to relaxation or adventure. So be careful what images you use in your advertisements.

perception
the process by which people select, organise and interpret sensory stimulation (sounds, visions, smell, touch) into a meaningful picture of the world

Individual perceptions are influenced by selective attention and selective distortion (see Chapter 3).

After the decoding process, the receiver responds to the message. The receiver may show interest in the message and may accept everything that is communicated without question. However, the receiver may also react unfavourably to the communication or may totally ignore it. From the marketer's perspective, the message will not be effective unless it elicits the desired response. This may be covert, such as a favourable attitude change towards a product or increased awareness or knowledge of a product. Sometimes the response is overt, such as redeeming a coupon, or returning a form to order a product or to receive more information. The sender needs to know that the message has been understood: **feedback** is the response from a receiver back to the sender.

feedback
a part of the two-way communications process whereby the receiver sends a message back to the original sender

Feedback can sometimes, especially with advertising, be hard to pick up. The change in the receiver may be slight, e.g. an increased awareness of the shampoo on offer. The original Schramm model portrayed one-way communications, where there was no feedback. This is no longer accepted as correct. Communication must be two-way. It should be a dialogue, not a monologue.

This two-way communication may be asymmetric or symmetric. In two-way asymmetric communication, there is communication from a sender to a receiver with little or delayed feedback, producing a non-direct dialogue, such as in most advertising. In two-way symmetric communication, which according to Pickton and Broderick (2004a) is the richest form, there is a direct dialogue between the sender and the audience. Traditionally, personal selling activities have provided this major benefit. However, new technologies are creating new opportunities for interactivity and near immediate response. Interactive digital television, the Internet and telephone call centres are aiding this process.

The more comprehensive models of the communications process regard communication as an exchange process in which thoughts or ideas are the things exchanged.

EXPAND YOUR KNOWLEDGE

Pickton, D. and Broderick, A. (2004b) 'Creating shared meaning in marketing communications – from sender to receiver', in D. Pickton and A. Broderick *Integrated Marketing Communications*. Harlow: Financial Times/Prentice Hall, Chapter 3.

In this chapter the authors describe the marketing communications process from sender to receiver and introduce the communications loop.

Influencing customers

Influencing and encouraging buyers to accept or adopt goods, services and ideas are among the key objectives of marketing communications. In fact, some argue that the ultimate effectiveness of promotion is determined by its impact upon product adoption among new buyers or the increases in the frequency of current buyers' purchases. A single promotional activity rarely causes an individual to buy a previously unfamiliar product and so, to have realistic expectations about what promotion can do, product adoption should be viewed not as a one-stop process, but as a multi-stage process.

In Chapter 3, the five stages of the consumer buying process were identified as:

1 Need or problem recognition
2 Information search
3 Evaluation of alternatives
4 Purchase decision
5 Post-purchase evaluation.

Throughout this process the consumer deliberately, or unconsciously, adopts various attitudes, or has various mind-states, in relation to the product/service offer. The nature and objectives of marketing communications need to alter to take account of these in order to encourage the correct purchase, or re-purchase, decision.

hierarchy of effects models
describe the stages individuals go through when making a purchase or consumption decision

Several models, known as **hierarchy of effects models**, have been developed to illustrate the activities required to take a consumer from the state of unawareness about the product to one of willingness to purchase the product or service.

AIDA is a simple model commonly used by marketing professionals. According to this model, potential buyers go through a psychological or behavioural process before purchasing a product. AIDA is an acronym for:

Attention
Interest
Desire
Action.

It incorporates various psychological processes. Attention (or awareness) is a cognitive process. It relates to how and what we think and believe. Interest and desire are affective processes; they relate to our emotions, how we feel about something. Finally, action takes the form of manifest behaviour (i.e. actually doing something) – we buy the product or tell others about it.

AIDA AND SETTING PROMOTIONAL OBJECTIVES

Although a simple model, AIDA is very helpful when setting promotional objectives.

Attention

In the initial stage, say for a new product, the promotion objective is to get the product seen and, ideally, talked about by the target audience. For example, an effective advertisement must grab attention from the very first viewing or hearing. If the target audience's attention has not been caught, then whatever follows will be of little use.

Interest

After the audience's attention has been gained, their interest in the product must be aroused. This may be achieved by creating an understanding of the benefits of the product in relation to the personal need(s) of customers, and focusing the message on how the product or service being advertised actually meets these needs. Much modern advertising tries hard to be entertaining and to generate interest in the product behind the advert in that way. The main objective of the interest stage is to motivate individuals to want information about the product: its features, uses, advantages, disadvantages, price and location, etc.

Desire

At this stage, a company tries to appeal to the target audience's wish to fulfil some need. While it is usually best to aim advertisements (or other promotional material) at moving the audience from one stage to the next, interest in, and desire for, the product can often be established simultaneously.

Action

As the name suggests, the action stage aims to get individuals to do something such as purchase the product or service. This is often helped by making it easier for the potential customer to take action. This can be done by giving a phone number, an Internet address or closing with a note saying that credit cards are accepted. Personal selling and sales promotion are particularly effective at closing sales, the latter by offering an additional incentive to buy, e.g. money off or a free gift with purchase.

AIDA AND THE PROMOTION MIX

Think for a moment about the sequential nature of AIDA. It comprises a number of stages that follow on, one from the other. However, it is not always necessary for organisations to start promotional campaigns at the top of the hierarchy, at the attention or awareness stage. The product may have been around for a while and everyone has already heard of it.

The choice of promotion mix will depend on where in the response hierarchy the organisation wishes to direct its promotional effort. For example, if the firm's primary objective is to catch the audience's attention, then advertising is often the most effective promotional tool. Advertising can also be very effective at creating and holding interest, and at reinforcing positive aspects of the product to develop post-purchase satisfaction. PR is also extensively used to raise interest levels in a product. Personal selling tends to be effective at creating desire and motivating purchasing behaviour. Sales promotion is good at getting a customer to try something new. For example, a half-price offer reduces the risk associated with trying a new hair gel.

Exhibit 8.2 illustrates the uses of the various promotional tools. Hierarchical models such as AIDA describe the step-by-step process through which individuals move

Exhibit 8.2   AIDA and the promotion mix

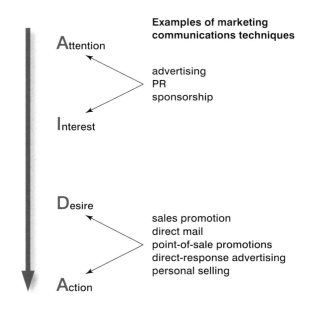

Exhibit 8.3   DAGMAR, a hierarchical model

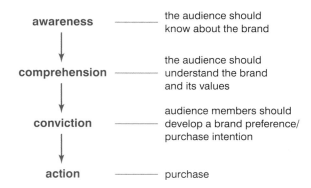

when exposed to marketing communications; these encompass the cognitive (thinking), affective (feeling) and conative (doing) steps.

Russell Colley (1961) developed a hierarchy of effects model known as **DAGMAR** (Define Advertising Goals for Measured Advertising Results). In this he stressed the importance of setting objectives against each element within the hierarchy (or at least those that were relevant to the promotional campaign being devised). Although his focus was on advertising objectives, his ideas are equally appropriate for consideration across all marketing communication tools (see Exhibit 8.3).

DAGMAR
acronym for Defining Advertising Goals for Measured Advertising Results, a hierarchy of effects model describing the stages individuals go through when making a purchase, or consumption, decision

EXTEND YOUR KNOWLEDGE

Colley, R. (1961) *Defining Advertising Goals for Measured Advertising Results*. New York: Association of National Advertisers.

Colley introduced DAGMAR to the world in this article. He argued that advertising outcomes can be improved by firstly recognising that a hierarchical process of communications is involved then setting appropriate advertising goals related to this process. (Others have criticised Colley's specific hierarchy and, even, whether any specific hierarchy exists that covers all eventualities.)

The marketing communications mix

Marketers have a large number of promotional tools which they can use to achieve their communications objectives. Historically these tools, or techniques, have been organised into four broad categories: advertising, public relations, sales promotion and personal selling. This is known as the promotion mix (or marketing communications mix). However, increasingly, other categories are being added that either do not fit neatly into these four or that some people feel deserve their own category heading. Examples include **direct marketing, sponsorship** and packaging. Whichever classification is used, what is most important is to recognise the vast array of promotional activities that is available to marketers.

These promotional tools involve either direct (i.e. personal) communication, usually on a face-to-face basis or on the telephone (and, perhaps, through videoconferencing), or indirect (i.e. non-personal) communication via some medium such as television, magazines or radio, or through packaging, leaflets, etc. It is the responsibility of the marketer to determine which approach is best for each situation.

Whichever element, or elements, of the promotion mix organisations choose, the purpose is to communicate a message to an appropriate target audience in order to elicit a favourable response, such as purchasing a product or changing an attitude. The term 'integrated marketing communication' is used to emphasise that all elements of the promotion mix should be coordinated and systematically planned to complement each other.

The separate elements of the promotion mix will now be discussed in more depth.

direct marketing
'all activities that make it possible to offer goods or services or to transmit other messages to a segment of the population by post, telephone, email or other direct means' (Chartered Institute of Marketing)

sponsorship
giving financial aid, or other resources, to an individual, organisation (usually non-profit making) or event in return for a positive association with them, e.g. the Coca-Cola Cup

Advertising

Advertising includes any paid form of non-personal presentation of ideas, goods and services by an identified advertiser. Communication by advertising is transmitted to a

advertising
paid-for promotional messages

B2B focus

Talking shop

Although much of marketing and marketing communications theory focuses on consumer goods, particularly fast-moving consumer goods (FMCG), a significant amount of marketing communications is conducted between businesses. Interestingly, the big FMCG manufacturers' primary contact is with the trade, not end customers. Managing trade contacts (e.g. wholesalers and retailers) is quite different from dealing with end customers and consumers. For example, whereas a consumer might want one bottle of wine, a retailer may want many cases of different types.

Such major sales warrant a different approach. The supplier may well send a sales representative cold-calling or use techniques such as telesales, direct mail (post, fax or email) or trade exhibitions, either to make sales or to set up appointments for the rep to call.

target audience through what is known as the mass media, which include television, radio, cinema, press, posters and the Internet.

The major benefit of mass media advertising is its ability to communicate to a large number of people all at once, e.g. all the existing and potential consumers for McDonald's fast food.

As traditional mass media advertising is indirect and non-personal, it allows marketers to send a uniform message with great frequency. However, it does have several disadvantages. Even though, for example, the cost per person reached by the advertising may be relatively low, the total financial outlay can be extremely high – especially for commercials shown during popular television programmes such as *Coronation Street* or *The X Factor*. These high costs can limit, and sometimes prevent, the use of this type of advertising in an organisation's promotional mix. It should be remembered that not all companies have huge marketing communications budgets like Nike or Coca-Cola (and that even these aim for effectiveness and efficiency in using their companies' budgets). Television advertising is now within the reach of those with a smaller budget thanks to the many digital channels available. Costs can also be kept down by focusing on specific ITV regions. Another disadvantage is that advertising rarely provides rapid feedback, although technology is helping to overcome this limitation. Interactive television, mobile and Internet advertising all make two-way communication so much easier.

HOW DOES ADVERTISING WORK?

Over the years, researchers have designed a number of models to investigate how advertising and other marketing communications tools work. Two of the more popular ones, AIDA and DAGMAR, are outlined above. The truth is that we still do not know exactly how advertising works – but we do know that good advertising *can* have positive effects on customers and on sales. Many of these explanatory models are sequential, showing the customer moving through stages beginning by becoming aware of a product and ending with a sale or some form of post-purchase re-evaluation. Such models are essentially about persuasion, about moving people on to the next stage. Although these sequential models have been much criticised in recent years, they are still helpful to marketing communicators seeking to understand their customers and to help them to make the right decisions.

A rather simpler approach is to look at the sorts of things that advertising might achieve without attempting to put these things into a sequence or hierarchy. There are four basic purposes that advertising can be used for and DRIP is an acronym designed to help remember these:

- **Differentiate** – it is widely accepted that marketing communications can act as a differentiator of products, especially in markets where there are many similar products. Today this is largely achieved by making vivid and positive brand associations.
- **Remind** – promotional messages may be aimed at reminding people who already buy a product of reasons why they should continue to do so. As well as product quality, reasons could include some form of reward for loyalty, such as a price discount, or even a free prize draw.
- **Inform** – promotion provides a great deal of factual information about products and places of business, such as where a shop is located. In the UK, for example, multiples such as Tesco and Waitrose, as well as franchises, such as Londis, often advertise and produce flyer inserts in local newspapers giving information about special price promotions and special buys – plus directions on finding the shop.
- **Persuade** – persuasion is a primary goal of promotion and encourages purchases or changes in attitude. In fact, many people regard promotion as persuasive communication. Think again about the contents of the supermarket flyers – what might they contain that would induce or urge you to visit and buy from them?

EXPAND YOUR KNOWLEDGE

Ehrenberg, A.S.C., Barnard, N.R. and Scriven, J.A. (1997) 'Justifying our advertising budgets', *Journal of Marketing*.

Ehrenberg and colleagues have argued that advertising works as a weak (but nevertheless significant) force. This article is supported by other articles in a series that covers an extensive research programme.

Jones, J.P. (1990) 'Advertising: strong or weak force? Two views oceans apart', *International Journal of Advertising*, 9 (3): 233–246.

This article reviews the conventional view of advertising – the strong theory – which is all but universally believed in the USA and which sees advertising as a dynamic force operating as an engine for brand innovation and other types of change in the marketplace. Andrew Ehrenberg's theory sees advertising as a weak force. This paper argues that a good deal of confusion has been caused by an uncritical belief that the strong theory operates in all circumstances. As a result, advertising has been associated too much with over-promise and under-delivery.

ADVERTISING OBJECTIVES

Marketers use advertising in a number of ways. Most consumer advertising is product (or brand) advertising, however, there are other forms, for example corporate, that communicates the values and ideas of organisations.

Advertising is rarely the best tool for closing a deal, so advertising objectives tend to relate to the early stages of sequential models like AIDA. Advertising can create awareness of a brand, ensure improved knowledge of that brand and its attributes, create a more favourable image, stimulate positive attitudes and achieve many other things, but product advertising's underlying objective is usually sales and its ultimate function is to sustain a brand and make it profitable.

Exhibit 8.4   Typical categories of advertising objectives

Awareness or attention	Usually of a new product
Recognition (or prompted recall)	A form of awareness – particularly important for a new product, where the purchase decision is made at the point of purchase, e.g. anything sold in a supermarket
Recall	Another form of awareness – the ability to remember the product rather than just to recognise it; useful where decisions are made in advance of purchase, e.g. seeing a film at the cinema
Reminder	For established products that may be being overlooked
Repositioning	Altering the way the brand is viewed by the target audience, e.g. Baileys is an anytime drink, not just an after-dinner liqueur
Differentiation	Making the brand stand out from the competition
Information	Telling the audience something about the brand, e.g. that it has new features
Image change	A form of repositioning, altering the market's perception of the brand, e.g. a Skoda is a top-quality car
Education	Tell the audience what the product is for, or how to use it – especially new products
Information gathering	For example, direct-response advertising gives audience information back to the advertiser
Attitude change	Change a negative to a positive, e.g. 'Volvos are not for me' to 'That's a cool car'
Attitude reinforcement	Encourage positive attitudes, e.g. 'I like brand x'
Correction of a misconception	Give the audience a new angle, e.g. 'I can't afford a new car' to 'That's cheaper than I thought'
Trial stimulation	If a person never tries your product, then they can never become a regular purchaser
Sales	Purchase of the new product

The problem with trying to measure advertising's effectiveness on sales alone is that it is hard to prove that the advert really did cause the increase in sales. Of course, there is a lot of anecdotal evidence to suggest that advertising has a positive effect on sales. Sales do tend to rise during an advertising campaign – and then to fall off soon after. However, that is not conclusive proof. There could be any number of other reasons why the sales rose, e.g. a competitor was short of stock, there was a price reduction at major retailers, a journalist wrote a good review. Conversely, it might be unfair to judge the advertising as bad just because sales do not rise. It may not be the advertising's fault. Many companies today advertise just to keep up. It is not so much a question of trying to increase sales, but of protecting their market share. If they stop advertising, they hand an advantage to the competition.

THE ESSENTIALS OF ADVERTISING

A way of simplifying our study of advertising (and of marketing communications as a whole) is to consider its four essential elements as identified in Exhibit 8.5 and discussed in turn in the section that follows.

Exhibit 8.5   Advertising essentials

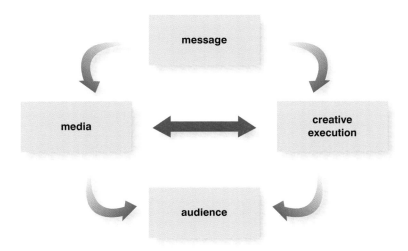

AUDIENCE

Get the right message to the right audience and you have a good ad. It sounds simple, but unfortunately it is not. Advertising agencies put a lot of time and effort into understanding audiences and into developing **audience profiles.** If you want to communicate effectively with someone, it helps to know them well. (See Exhibit 8.6 for an example of an audience profile.)

   Remember that a target audience is not the same as a target market. The audience for an advert is the people at whom the message of the ad is aimed. They may be part, or all, of the target market, or they may not. Sometimes adverts are deliberately aimed at influencers rather than actual purchasers, e.g. many toy ads are (rather controversially) aimed at toy consumers (children) rather than customers (parents). In the past, anti-smoking campaigners have also aimed at children, urging them to nag their parents into giving up. Trade audiences are often wider. Take, for example, an advert in a trade magazine for cars. It could be aimed at the fleet manager (who manages the company's car fleet), professional buyers (who negotiate terms of purchase), the company owner or the finance director (who may make the ultimate decision), the people who have cars (who may push for new ones) or the PR department (which guards the company's image) – in fact at any member of the decision-making unit (see Chapter 3).

audience profile
a detailed description of audience characteristics used by communicators to tailor their promotional efforts

Sun readers

This is an example of an audience pro-file. 'Cover (%)' refers to the percentage of people in that category who read the newspa-per, e.g. 19.2 per cent of 25–34-year-olds read *The Sun*. 'Profile (%)' refers to the percentage of the overall *Sun* readership that falls into that category, e.g. 19 per cent of *Sun* readers are DE men. Adver-tisers and PR agents use these newspaper profiles when planning their media strategies.

Exhibit 8.6   Audience profile of the *Sun*

Circulation
Circulation refers to the number of sold, reduced price and free copies of a title distrib-uted on an average day (excluding Sundays) over the stated period of time.

05 Oct–01 Nov 09: **3,026,556**

Estimated Readership
Estimated Readership refers to the number of people reading a title on an average day (excluding Sundays) over the stated time period.

Jan–Jun 09: **7,986,000**

Demographic profile

Source: NRS Jan–Jun 09	Estimated Readership (000s)	Cover (%)	Profile (%)
All adults	7,986	16.1	100
Men	4,469	18.5	56
Women	3,517	13.8	44
Age			
15–24	1,475	18.4	18
25–34	1,541	19.8	19
35–44	1,446	16.5	18
45–54	1,302	16.1	16
55–64	1,065	15.0	13
65+	1,158	11.8	14
Social class			
AB Adults	953	7.2	12
ABC1 Adults	3,066	11.0	38
ABC1C2 Adults	5,493	14.4	69

Reproduced with kind permission of the National Readership Survey

(Continued)

(Continued)

Source: NRS Jan–Jun 09	Estimated Readership (000s)	Cover (%)	Profile (%)
C1 Adults	2,113	14.5	26
C2 Adults	2,427	23.4	30
DE Adults	2,493	21.8	31
AB Men	605	9.0	8
ABC1 Men	1,771	13.1	22
ABC1C2 Men	3,282	17.2	41
C1 Men	1,166	17.2	15
C2 Men	1,510	27.2	19
DE Men	1,187	23.3	15
AB Women	348	5.4	4
ABC1 Women	1,295	9.1	16
ABC1C2 Women	2,211	11.6	28
C1 Women	947	12.2	12
C2 Women	917	18.9	11
DE Women	1,306	20.5	16
ITV region			
Anglia	802	17.1	10
Border	145	22.8	2
London	2,393	19.9	30
Central	1,616	17.2	20
Wales & West	551	12.0	7
Grampian	216	17.8	3
Yorkshire	781	13.3	10
West Country	225	12.0	3
Meridian	908	16.3	11
Granada	541	8.6	7
Tyne Tees	517	18.4	6
Central Scotland	791	24.8	10

SOURCE: NRS Jan–Jun 2000

Reproduced with kind permission of the National Readership Survey

MESSAGE

Once the advertisers have established exactly who it is they want to talk to, they can develop the correct message to achieve their advertising objectives. They develop an **advertising proposition**: what the advertising should say and the impression it should create, but not necessarily phrased in the way that the ad will say it. For example, the message that this is a fun beer that enhances sociability while also providing refreshment might result in the slogan 'refreshes the parts other beers cannot reach'. The slogan is the clever, catchy form of words that goes into the actual ad. It is part of the creative work and is written by a copywriter (copy just means text, i.e. the words in an ad).

advertising proposition
what the overall advert should say to the target audience, the impression that should be left in their minds (this is not the slogan; the whole of the advert should communicate the proposition)

CREATIVE EXECUTION

The message is not normally put across through words alone. There are visual elements to most advertising that assist its transmission: a picture, a scene, colours, designs. There may also be music, other sound effects, acting – all of these form part of the **creative execution**. This is the heart of the advert. Advertisers appeal to our emotions (e.g. through humour or sex) and/or to our rational side (e.g. through value for money or product features), in order to interest us in their products.

creative execution
the way an advert is designed in order to put the message across

There are a number of common execution approaches including those below. Look out for these and others as you see and listen to advertisements. Think of them as movie genres, as types of advertising.

Slice of life: a real, everyday situation shows the product in normal use, e.g. a little boy plays his separated parents off against each other and persuades them both to take him to McDonald's.

Animation: cartoon characters can liven up a dull product or deal with an embarrassing subject, e.g. the Tetley tea folk, Volvic's talking volcano and npower's use of Wallace and Gromit to push an energy-saving message.

Testimonial: uses supposed experts, or past users, to verify the merits of the product, e.g. 'my washing has never been so white'. Testimonials are commonly used in Internet advertising. There is more space to print endorsing statements, making them more credible. Testimonials are reassuring in a medium where lack of trust is a problem. References in blogs are even more reassuring as they have the impartiality of word-of-mouth advertising, which is perhaps why less scrupulous advertisers sometimes write these themselves.

News style: common in press adverts, makes the advert look more like part of the publication.

Fantasy: catches the imagination, particularly useful when the product cannot be shown in use, e.g. Smirnoff vodka ads. Advanced CGI has made many fantasy executions even more fantastical, e.g. a Coca-Cola advert had someone disappear into a vending machine and emerge in a completely different world.

Spoof or parody: catches attention through humour, e.g. a woman sends her lover to the fridge for more Häagen-Dazs but he spots the Fosters lager and takes it with him to watch TV rather than return to the bedroom. The original Gary Lineker Walker's crisps ads played on his good guy reputation.

Guarantee: reassures prospective purchasers, e.g. 'a closer shave or I'll give you your money back'.

Demonstration: shows how the product works, e.g. how Flash can clean up a floor so quickly. These can be more imaginative than a straight demonstration and may be combined with a fantastical element, e.g. in a mini convertible ad, a man was surrounded by threatening hoodies every time he tried to close the roof, but they disappeared when he desisted. Eventually we got the message: 'leave it open'.

Celebrity: attracts attention, gives the product credibility, e.g. David Beckham and Gillette, Uma Thurman and Virgin media, Richard Hammond and Morrisons.

Problem solution: lends a helping hand, e.g. the *Yellow Pages* ads, or the www.gotomypc.com ad where a man in a meeting needs his PC (left back in his office) and sends pigeons to get it for him but they forget the keyboard. He would have been better off using the Internet-based GoToMyPC application to access the PC remotely.

Music: often a key part of the creative execution, it creates mood, attracts attention, reinforces a message, inspires word of mouth and makes the ad more memorable. Music is not a stand-alone execution, of course – it is most commonly in the background – but it can be a major element as in the Cadbury's gorilla ad ('In the Air Tonight'), John Lewis's 2009 Christmas ad ('Sweet Child of Mine') or X box 360 lips ('The Fear') which made more of the music by featuring singer Lily Allen singing along with hundreds of X boxers (so there was a celebrity element too).

Sirens calling

Lever Fabergé used the interactivity of e-media along with the impact of ambient media to launch Siren, a fragrance in the Impulse body spray range.

The campaign was targeted at 16–24-year-old females. Posters displayed photos of nine, supposedly missing, male models alongside the strap line, 'Where have all the men gone?' The ambient media campaign was supported by a website, SMS voting, a text message advice line and viral marketing.

Visitors to the website were encouraged to vote by text or email for their favourite man. Voting entered them into a prize draw where they could win an invitation to an exclusive Siren party.

MEDIA

The final essential of advertising is the media: the carriers of the message. Without media, no one will hear or see it. The right choice of media is essential to the effectiveness of a campaign. It has to be appropriate to the target audience and to the message.

There is little point in advertising in *Cosmopolitan* if you are trying to reach elderly men (though there may be some point if you are trying to reach younger men as, apparently, a large number of them read it; they do not buy it, they just read their girlfriends' copies). It is important to establish the readership/viewership profile of **media vehicles** and match this to your audience profile. Newspapers, TV channels, etc., provide guides to assist with this and to help sell their advertising space.

The choice of media also affects how the message comes across. If your message is a complex, informative one, perhaps explaining the technical advantages of a new computer system, then a 30-second TV ad just will not do. You need the space and copy possibilities of press. However, if you want your new jeans to catch the eye of the younger generation, then the creative scope offered by a cinema ad may be the best thing (and then you can cut it down to show on TV as well).

Advertisers must choose a **media class** (the inter-media decision, e.g. television or Internet or press) and then a media vehicle (the intra-media decision, i.e. the actual TV programmes or websites or magazine titles). This decision is based on the creative scope a medium offers and its audience profile. For example, a TV advert aired during *Big Brother* would allow the advertisers to use colour, sound and movement (actors, props and/or animation) to create an impact on a young audience. An ad or a page on *Facebook* could use interactivity to engage a sociable, IT-literate audience.

Exhibit 8.7 lists examples of the media available although, as new ones appear all the time, you can probably add to the list. Of the traditional mass media, press advertising takes in the most money despite being a less expensive medium than TV – there is just so much more of it. The picture is constantly changing, though. New digital channels keep coming online. These are cheaper vehicles than terrestrial television and can be targeted more closely as many channels are very specialist and so appeal to clearly defined audiences, e.g. a home improvement channel is clearly a good place to advertise DIY equipment.

The traditional mass media is still commonly used, although other media types are becoming increasingly popular, e.g. e-media and ambient media.

The Internet, along with other digital technologies such as iTV and mobile phones, is still often referred to as the new media – although e-media is becoming a more accepted term as the newness wears off. The technology behind e-media has a number of advantages:

- interactivity
- faster response times
- more direct communications
- greater possibilities for interaction between audience members and user-generated content
- the ability to put the message across in a more sophisticated way.

Ambient media is a term that was originally applied to unusual outdoor media. It is becoming more widely used now to describe any outdoor media, although some ambient media may be indoors. Used in this broader way, the original, and still the biggest, ambient media are poster sites. Advertising is getting everywhere and the discovery of new media possibilities is a great source of differentiation and a way to cut through the noise created by communications overload. More unusual ambient media include cars, laser light shows, people, tickets, stairs, postcards, balloons and skywriting.

---

media vehicle
the newspaper, magazine, poster site, etc. where adverts appear

media class or **media category**
type of media, e.g. television, press, posters, cinema

Posters can have great impact

ambient media
outdoor (usually) media, classically posters but now including more imaginative forms, e.g. laser-light shows, tickets, students wearing promotional clothing or tattoos

EXHIBIT 8.7   Examples of promotional media

TV	Posters	Underground stations
Newspapers	Magazines	Tickets
Cinema	Buses	Trains
Video	Taxis	Telephones
CD/DVD	Search engines	Mobile phones
Radio	Websites	Cars
Email	Directories	Teletext
Shop fronts	Escalator steps	Beer mats
Pavements	Post-it notes	Promotional gifts
Sides of buildings	Packaging	Clothing, e.g. T-shirts
Skywriting	Blimps	Road signs
Electronic games	Noticeboards	Blogs and wikis
Outdoor screens	Windows	Bar optics
Social networking sites	Rubbish bins	Bus shelters
The sky (through laser projection)	Students' heads (transfers or shaved into hair)	Anything else that could carry a promotional message!
What else can you think of?		

insight   Zipping and zapping

Television advertising just isn't as effective as it used to be. There are so many adverts that audiences just tune out – sometimes literally. If viewing a programme as it is aired, they use the remote control to zap and channel hop to a station where there are no ads. When watching recorded programmes, they zip through the adverts and watch only the programme.

There is a silver lining here for advertisers and it comes in the form of TV sponsorship. Think about it. When you're zipping through the ads, what are you looking out for so that you know when to stop? Is it the sponsor's message (ident) perhaps?

Another way the TV companies are fighting back is by placing ads at the beginning of the playback on their online catch-up services. These can't be fast forwarded, and viewers have to watch them before the programme will start.

ACTIVITY

Take a walk around your local high street. Note down the different types of ambient media you find.

The final medium to mention is **word of mouth**. This is probably the most pervasive of all. When friends and relatives talk positively about a product or service, it sounds so much more convincing than when the words come from an actor on television who has been paid. Some adverts are deliberately designed to stimulate word of mouth, to get people talking, e.g. Budweiser's 'Wassup?' – remember that? Did you ever say it yourself? Budweiser's budget reached many more members of its audience thanks to the creative excellence of that campaign.

Is that a real gorilla?

Cadbury's gorilla was the star of a TV advert that got everyone talking. The ad won numerous awards and generated massive media coverage. It showed a gorilla playing the drums on Phil Collins's song, *In the Air Tonight*. It was a long ad (90 seconds) with a slow build-up and the gorilla was perfect. Chocolate sales rose and so did sales of the song. Within a week of the ad being aired, *In the Air Tonight* went to number 14 in the UK singles chart and 9 in the downloads chart. Many of the younger purchasers had never heard of Phil Collins before.

The gorilla rapidly became an Internet sensation. Over 4 million people have viewed the advert on *You Tube* and the gorilla has several *Facebook* pages, the most popular of which has over 2,600 members. Fans made their own versions, dubbing in different songs. Some of those became *You Tube* sensations too.

The buzz surrounding this ad centred on what the ad was about. The majority found it puzzling and couldn't see what it had to do with chocolate – but they didn't care, they loved it anyway. The sharper-eyed viewer spotted the purple background and linked that to Cadbury's. The cynical declared that it wasn't actually made as a Cadbury's ad, but was meant to promote the new Phil Collins greatest hits album. Gradually a *You Tube* consensus formed. The advert was about joy: the joy of playing the drums, the joy of eating the chocolate. Despite that glorious opening drum roll, the song itself isn't joyful though. After its release in 1981, the talk was of its dark side.

The other major topic of speculation was who was in the gorilla suit? Was it actually Phil Collins? Was it a real gorilla? People expressing this view were quickly laughed down – but wouldn't that have been great!

viral marketing
modern form of word-of-mouth advertising, often uses new media (e.g. email and texting)

Electronic media, such as email and text messaging, lend themselves well to word-of-mouth advertising as they make it easy to pass a message on. The use of electronic media in this is referred to as **viral marketing** and it is becoming increasingly well used. Advertisers look for ways to engage their audience and encourage them to pass the message on. They hope to create a buzz. This encouragement may involve some financial reward (e.g. Virgin Wines offered their customers money-off vouchers for passing messages on to their friends), or may just be based on entertainment value. Levi's Flat Eric campaign included a website with images of the orange puppet character deliberately made easy to copy and edit (web widgets). People made their own mini ads and sent them on.

ACTIVITY

Check *You Tube* for tribute adverts and other user-generated advertising content. Try Cadbury's, Lynx and McDonald's as starting points and then see what's new.

Public relations (PR)

Traditionally, **PR** was perceived to be a corporate function. Nowadays, there are a number of types of PR, and **marketing communications** has embraced and adapted the various elements of the discipline. Creating and maintaining goodwill is just as relevant to product **brands** as it is to corporations as a whole.

Raising the visibility of organisations and encouraging interest in them and goodwill towards them is an important function of marketing communications. In recent times, public relations has assumed a greater significance at both the corporate level and within the promotion mix.

WHAT IS PUBLIC RELATIONS?

According to the Institute of Public Relations:

> *Public relations is the planned and sustained effort to establish and maintain goodwill and mutual understanding between an organisation and its publics.*

Reflecting on this definition, the words *planning*, *sustained effort* and *mutual understanding* need emphasising. Good public relations involves conducting planned programmes with clear objectives, so that results can be assessed and understood. Good public relations involves sustained activity over time. The objectives of creating and maintaining goodwill are not achieved by short-term activities alone. Finally, good public relations requires mutual understanding between the organisation and its various publics. In public relations, the organisation receives as well as transmits information, listens as well as speaks (Jefkins, 1989).

THE SCOPE OF PUBLIC RELATIONS

Public relations can raise awareness, inform, interest, excite, educate, generate understanding, build trust, encourage loyalty and even help generate sales (Pickton and Broderick, 2004a). PR can raise visibility and also help develop corporate and product credibility in ways that other promotional tools cannot. It can also be used to enhance the effectiveness of advertising.

Any solid management planning relies on research and analysis and PR is no exception. The planning and management of PR is a systematic process of identifying PR tasks, setting objectives, defining PR **publics**, integrating PR within the promotion or marketing communications mix, scheduling, managing the implementation of PR techniques and assessing their effectiveness.

publics
the groups of people with whom the organisation communicates

PR TECHNIQUES

Media relations/publicity

Publicity can be described as stimulation of demand for goods or services by generating news about them in the mass media. This is done by means of press releases, press conferences and events or publicity stunts (e.g. Richard Branson flying across the Atlantic in a hot-air balloon to get the Virgin name in the news).

Good media relations encourage media coverage and favourable, positive publicity. Equally valuably, they also discourage negative coverage. This is an important function of professional public relations specialists and involves developing strong personal relationships with editors and journalists. Media releases contain information about the organisation and its products or brands in the hope of obtaining positive editorial coverage and are sent to journalists who may, or may not, use all (or more usually part) of the content. Publicity may use the same mass media as advertising. However, unlike advertising, the media costs are not paid for directly by the company, nor does it identify itself as coming directly from the company, and it therefore can have greater impact as it has the appearance of coming from an impartial source.

ACTIVITY

Press releases are often written as articles suitable for publication. Time-strapped editors sometimes print them with little or no amendment. Browse through a newspaper or magazine and try to find stories that may have been placed by a commercial company (the weekend glossies or special interest magazines are often the best source). What's the objective behind the story?

Publicity can be an impressive and effective promotional tool. However, as it involves a third party, such as a newspaper reporter or editor, who has the power to determine the nature of the message, a firm has little control over its timing and content. An extreme example of this is the publicity, good, bad or indifferent, a company's products get in *Which?* consumer magazine. *Which?* regularly evaluates products, and publishes the results of the tests. Companies have no control over the tests or the resultant publicity. Visit www.which.co.uk for examples.

insight   Families at war are good for ratings

A Channel 4 programme, *Masters and Servants*, was just one of a long line of reality TV shows. It featured two families, one playing the role of masters while the members of the other family became servants. The Rose and Mills families fell out so spectacularly that it led to press speculation that the whole thing might have been staged. The extensive media coverage attracted an additional 300,000 viewers to the next programme in the series.

Such accusations have been levelled more recently at a number of other reality shows, notably *Big Brother*, although publicity-seeking contestants are as often accused as the programme producers.

Publications

The PR department or agency is usually responsible for this important task, although advertising agencies and others also offer the service. Organisations produce a variety of publications, e.g. employee newsletters, financial reports, consumer magazines, brochures and media packs. Such publications are a major tool of much organisational PR.

Corporate communications

Aspects of corporate communications that fall into the category of PR include corporate identity programmes, corporate image management, corporate advertising, some internal communications and some communications with other publics or stakeholder groups.

Public affairs and community relations

This involves contact with the government and government agencies, special interest and professional groups, as well as the local community, with a view to building and maintaining local, national and international relations.

Lobbying

An approach associated with public affairs and media relations. It aims to build and maintain positive relations with, for example, group leaders, legislators and officials, through negotiation and persuasion.

Sponsorship

A business relationship in which one organisation provides funds or other resources/ services to another organisation (or an individual) and gains commercial advantage through being linked to them. It may be on a relatively small scale directed at a local activity, or involve millions of pounds. Typical **sponsorship** vehicles include sports (events, teams, individuals), television programmes and the arts.

sponsorship
giving financial aid, or other resources, to an individual, organisation or event in return for a positive association with them

Product placement

This is another promotional tool that is growing in importance. How many times have you rented a video or DVD and zapped through the adverts to the start of the film itself? The marketing communications industry is aware that adverts, whether on television or in other media, can irritate some of the audience. This, as well as clutter in the marketplace, was the impetus behind **product placement**. Today, a wide variety of brands is directly placed in television programmes and films. The brands become props and are seen being used (and thus, by implication, endorsed), although the audience is not always fully aware that this is effectively advertising. The communications process is quite subtle.

Branded content

A natural progression from media **sponsorship** and **product placement**, branded content is more common in the USA than in Europe, where it has been slow to take off. It is still in the early enough stages of development to have a number of different names. In the USA, it is more likely to be called 'branded entertainment' and it is also sometimes called 'advertiser-funded programming'. Branded content is a logical progression from sponsorship. Instead of selecting a suitable event to sponsor, the advertiser creates one. For example, Heinz, having discovered that their products were most often consumed by families eating together, created a family cooking television programme.

Events management

This is the staging of events such as conferences or festivals. They may be one-offs or something that occurs regularly. If a new product is to be launched, there may be internal announcement meetings. External events may be staged to attract, hopefully, favourable publicity and extensive media coverage.

insight   Sponsorship: a rising star

Should the Notting Hill Carnival or school lessons or sport be sponsored? These, and many similar questions, are being hotly debated by various publics worried about the sponsor's influence on the event or person sponsored. So if sponsorship can be controversial, why does it have such an important role in marketing communications?

Sponsorship is an effective and valuable marketing communications tool. The sponsorship of events, activities and organisations will continue to grow because it provides access to specific target audiences and enhances the sponsor's image.

The key reasons for sponsorship's increase in popularity are: national and European policies on tobacco and alcohol, which prevent them being advertised, a greater focus on promotional cost-effectiveness, the proven ability of sponsorship to deliver good results in terms of brand awareness and image change, new opportunities for sponsorship as people have more leisure time, greater media coverage of events resulting in a wider reach for the sponsorship, and the recognition of the inefficiencies associated with more traditional media. At the same time, sponsorship has become recognised as a good way to raise money for any vaguely worthy or socially popular activity. Most football clubs have sponsors, as do most athletes. Exhibitions look for sponsorship funds from the outset. Concerts and plays rely on sponsors to subsidise the revenues from ticket sales.

Certain activities have attracted sponsorship more than others: sports, programmes and broadcasts, the arts and other areas that encompass socially responsible activities such as wildlife conservation and education. Without sponsorship, many of our favourite pastimes and pet projects just wouldn't happen.

© Pascal Guyot/AFP/Getty Images

Formula 1 has always provided attractive sponsorship vehicles

Crisis management

Dealing with unforeseen events is an important facet of PR and is often referred to as damage limitation. It may involve product recall, such as in the now famous Perrier case, or dealing with major ecological disasters, such as the *Exxon Valdez* oil spillage, or a scandal such as a football manager being overheard insulting his club's fans.

ACTIVITY

Visit an exhibition. Observe and evaluate all the activities that are going on. Consider the organisation of the exhibition as a whole – the number of stands, layout, visitor attendance, exhibitor attendance, promotional/informational materials, atmosphere and all the supporting services.

- Evaluate the whole event from a visitor's perspective.
- Evaluate the event from an exhibitor's perspective.
- What recommendations would you make for future exhibitions?

McLibel

McDonald's is one of the largest and best-known brands in the world. The company's revenues exceed those of a number of smaller, less well-off countries. There are over 25,000 McDonald's restaurants in the world and about 40 million people eat there every day. But not everyone loves McDonald's. Towards the end of the twentieth century, protests against their products, and the means of producing them, were growing steadily. Still, McDonald's fans outweighed the critics massively and so the company seemed secure.

Then, one day in a flat in North London, a postman and a gardener wrote a little pamphlet lambasting McDonald's for its unethical products, employment practices and means of production. They handed it out to passers-by on the local streets and got vegetarian restaurants to display it. The pamphlet was fairly innocuous, a little out of date and, according to Naomi Klein, clearly the product of a 'meat is murder' vegetarian attitude. It was therefore unlikely to worry the core McDonald's customer. McDonald's really should have let it go, but they didn't, they sued.

The two activists, Helen Steel and Dave Morris, had little money and were denied legal aid. In court, these two quite ordinary looking people had to face a battery of top lawyers on the other side. The trial was the longest in the history of English law – and the newspapers gleefully reported on it every day. Helen and Dave's views, previously only communicated to the few Londoners who had bothered to read the pamphlet, were now written up with commentary by leading journalists and posted on the web for the world to see and blog about. As for the original pamphlet, that had become a collector's item. More recently, in 2005, a documentary film was made about the McLibel two. Who won and who lost the case is largely irrelevant. This was one of the biggest corporate PR disasters of all time and its effects are still being felt – and seen – in McDonald's current marketing strategies.

For the full story of the McLibel trial, visit www.mcspotlight.org/case.

SOURCES: BBC News, 1999; Haig, 2003

Sales promotion

Organisations spend more of their marketing budgets on sales promotion than they do on advertising. Clearly, then, this is a very important promotional weapon, so what exactly is it? The Institute of Sales Promotion (ISP), the professional body that represents all the major sales promotion practitioners in the UK, gives this definition of sales promotion:

> *Sales promotion comprises that range of techniques used to attain sales/marketing objectives in a cost-effective manner by* adding value *to a product or service, either to intermediaries or end-users, normally, but not exclusively, within a defined time period.*

'Adding value' has been emphasised in the definition above because this is the single most important thing about **sales promotion**. It works by making a product into a better deal. It offers something extra for free or money off or the chance to win something else and most people, it seems, like to think that they have got something for nothing. It could perhaps be free conditioner with your shampoo, or money off a badly wanted DVD or an instant-win competition. Sales promotions are intended to induce buyers to purchase, or try, a product, or to improve the effectiveness of marketing channel members (e.g. retailers or wholesalers).

sales promotion
a short-term special offer and other added value activites, e.g. two for the price of one

Advantages of sales promotion as a marketing communications technique include:

- They have been shown to work. Sales promotion campaigns usually produce notable increases in sales, or trial of a product.

- This effectiveness can be measured, and therefore proved, quite easily. A sales promotion's impact on sales is more directly attributable to the promotion (rather than other activities) because it is a short-term offer and because there is usually some easy means to collect data, e.g. counting money-off coupons handed in, or counting competition entries.
- They can be closely targeted. Thanks to computer databases, a special offer can be directed at specific groups of people within particular market segments, e.g. online retailers might send out incentives to people who have registered but never bought.
- They are managageable within a smaller budget. By managing the length of time the promotion is available, and the number of winning entries or coupons or free products available, sales promotion can maximise the effectiveness of a limited budget. This is a very important aspect of sales promotion, although it must be managed carefully or the costs can get out of hand.
- They have an almost immediate effect. The fortunes of brands and companies are increasingly volatile. Sales promotions can be devised, implemented and take effect far more quickly than other forms of promotion.
- They create interest. Sales promotion brings in an element of novelty, excitement and humour, which customers enjoy and to which, more importantly, they respond.

SALES PROMOTION OBJECTIVES

Sales promotion is usually used to achieve short-term objectives such as to:

- introduce a new product
- encourage greater usage
- combat or offset competitors' marketing efforts
- stimulate product trial.

It should be fully integrated with other promotional tools to form a cohesive plan that supports the organisation's long-term objectives. Many sales promotions are seen as downmarket and therefore unsuited to campaigns that are promoting an upmarket image. Also, some types of promotion would be too expensive to fund if extended to high-priced goods, and so BOGOF promotions, for example, tend to be found on low-priced products such as toiletries, food and drinks. Sales promotion is at its most effective in the latter stages of the buying process. Promotions are good at prompting action.

There are three categories of sales promotion: consumer, trade and salesforce.

CONSUMER PROMOTIONS

Trial is regarded as the most important action objective for almost every brand. In FMCG, getting a customer to buy for the first time is harder than getting repeat purchases. Customers making high-involvement purchases may also want to try them out, e.g. test driving a car. Sales promotions are a good way to stimulate trial, to add value and to reassure.

Consumer promotions are generally one of three types: save, win or free. For example:

Supermarkets use a lot of sales promotion

- samples – standard or trial size giveaways
- coupons, e.g. 25p off your next purchase
- premiums – an extra, free item, e.g. BOGOF
- special offers, e.g. half price this week
- bonus packs – extra quantity or larger product, e.g. 25 per cent bigger bar
- multipacks – cheaper than buying separately
- competitions, e.g. answer the following questions . . .
- prize draws, e.g. check the number by ringing/writing in
- instant wins, e.g. Kit Kat's 'Win a Million' promotion
- points to collect, e.g. Air Miles or Nectar card points
- tie-ins – giving a different product away, e.g. cereal gifts
- cause-related promotions – the seller gives a donation to a worthy cause for every product sold, e.g. Pizza Express donates to the Venice in Peril Fund every time one of its Veneziana pizzas is sold
- **self-liquidating special offers**, e.g. a cereal company offering a set of breakfast bowls in return for £10 and four tokens.

Consumer sales promotion programmes may be paid for by the retailer but are commonly financed by the manufacturer. They are often supported by advertising, **point-of-sale (POS) promotions** and **merchandising** activities within retail outlets.

self-liquidating special offer
a sales promotion that pays for itself (usually because the company making the offer has bought the promotional items in vast quantities and so obtained a substantial discount)

point-of-sale (POS) promotion
the general term for any type of promotion found where the sale takes place. Most usually associated with retail outlets

merchandising
selection and display of products within a retail environment

TRADE PROMOTIONS

Consumer goods suppliers spend a great deal on trade promotions to distributors, including retailers, as part of their push strategy.

Promotions by manufacturers to their distributors, generally called trade promotions, are often some form of price promotion because the main factor motivating distributors is their reseller profit margin.

Price promotion is often used to stimulate trial, i.e. persuading the distributor to stock a product for the first time. There are three main types of trade trial promotion:

1 New line fees (slotting allowances): these are cash payments or a proportion of the shipment (consignment of goods) donated free, which amounts to a price inducement, in return for stocking a new product or offering a new service for a specified period of time.
2 Price-offs: these are straight reductions in the selling price to the distributor and are sometimes called off-invoice promotions.
3 Returns: the manufacturer agrees to buy back unsold quantities of the product. Distributing on consignment is an extreme form of this. The distributor pays nothing to the manufacturer until the product is sold (also known as sale or return).

Price promotions are also important in encouraging repeat purchase by distributors. There are four types:

1 Price-offs: as described above, but on the understanding that part of the discount will be passed to the end

Eye-catching point-of-sale displays can boost sales

customer or consumer, or that the distributor will provide extra display, advertising or both.

2 Joint promotions: these are agreements by which the manufacturer and distributor both contribute funds towards promotional expenditure. The proportion of contribution may vary.

3 Sales contests: competitions in which retailers or other trade partners can win attractive prizes.

4 Sales education: this is applicable mainly to industrial products and services, or to the more technical types of consumer durable. Manufacturers train the retailer's or wholesaler's staff and all parties benefit from the increased sales.

SALESFORCE PROMOTIONS

Manufacturers have a salesforce to motivate. Salesforce promotions include monetary rewards, such as bonuses, and non-monetary rewards, such as prizes, training programmes, motivational meetings and selling aids.

WHAT CAN GO WRONG?

Sales promotions must be very carefully planned. There is a code of practice to abide by, and laws on gambling and competitions to be obeyed. For example, if someone has to pay to enter, then that is gambling and, in the UK, a licence is required to run gambling games. Hence that familiar phrase 'no purchase necessary'. There is a thriving sales promotion industry in the UK and, as the details of promotions can get quite complex, it is usually advisable to enlist expert help for anything but the simplest of offers. Some of the scenarios that might arise are outlined below.

- Over-redemption
  - bad promotion design, e.g. the classic case of the Hoover flights promotion. Hoover offered a free flight to New York with every vacuum cleaner purchase. Unfortunately, the vacuum cleaner was cheaper than the flight and people flocked to electrical appliance stores instead of to travel agents. That promotion is reported to have cost £48 million.
  - error in administration, e.g. Pepsi's Philippine subsidiary promised one million pesos (about £25,000) for bottle caps bearing the winning number 349. When Pepsi had paid out £8 million, it realised something was amiss – there were far too many winners. The withdrawal of the offer provoked riots.

- Misredemption: one of the advantages of sales promotion is the accuracy of its targeting. You can send a coupon to precisely the person you want to redeem it, but can you prevent it from being passed on to someone else?
- Malredemption: the likely number of winners for any promotion is carefully worked out and budgets are set. Lottery syndicates are encouraged but, if a promotion requires the collecting of a set of something, beware: joint efforts (and swaps arranged through newspaper columns or on the Internet) could blow the budget.
- Faulty pack design: some sales promotions require a special pack design to disguise which one is the winning pack. This packaging must be designed with

great care. If someone swallows a prize notification ticket when upending a packet of crisps into their mouth (as has happened), then trouble will ensue.

- Pilfering: if the pack design is not good enough to disguise a winner, the chances are it will never make it out of the shop. Bored sales assistants enjoy trying to spot a winning pack.
- Lost in the post: many samples fail to reach the right target. They may arrive but be picked up by another member of the household. Recently, there have been complaints that some of the promotional items that land on doormats are dangerous to young children who may think that they are toys or sweets, when they are not.

Sales promotions need careful, worst-case scenario planning – and professional indemnity insurance.

EXPAND YOUR KNOWLEDGE

Buttle, F. (1984) 'Merchandising', *European Journal of Marketing*, 18 (6/7): 104–123.

Buttle emphasises the significance of merchandising and its effectiveness while recognising that this is a little researched area that is often underestimated and under-valued. The article provides practical insights into merchandising activities and techniques.

Personal selling

There is talk of outlawing door-to-door selling in the UK. This will be good news for many people, who feel threatened and coerced by such salespeople, and bad news for the unprofessional sales organisations whose behaviour has prompted the ban. Putting to one side the ethical problems associated with extreme forms of personal selling, it has a major role to play in the promotion mix of many companies. Personal selling is an oral presentation, in a conversation with one or more prospective purchasers, for the purpose of making sales.

Personal selling involves informing customers of the benefits of products, and persuading them to buy through personal communication in a potential exchange situation. It includes such things as a salesperson explaining a product's features, a technician demonstrating a new MRI scanner to relevant hospital personnel, and even the person at the supermarket who gives you a free sample of a new luxury ice-cream while telling you something about it.

Personal selling differs from other forms of communication in that messages flow from a sender to a receiver directly (often face to face). This direct and interpersonal communication lets the sender receive and evaluate feedback from the receiver immediately. This communications process, known as dyadic communication (between two people or groups), allows the message to be tailored more specifically to the needs of the sender and receiver than do many of the other media.

Reaching a limited number of people through personal selling efforts costs, proportionately, a considerable amount more than it does through advertising. However, in many situations it is thought to be worth it because of the immediate feedback and its greater persuasive impact on customers.

Doing business abroad

Company representatives and salespeople have to learn the business conventions of other countries in order to do business there. Failure to do so can leave an impatient North American hanging around for hours in a South American office wondering what has happened to the meeting or a disappointed European waiting for a contract that they believe has been promised by a Japanese firm but which never materialises.

Many Latin Americans have a different attitude to time than do their North American counterparts. In the USA, meetings should start on time. Further south, they can see no point in starting before everyone is ready. The Japanese dislike saying an outright no, as it seems rude, and are also concerned not to lose face by admitting that they do not have the authority to say yes. Either or both of these situations can leave a European with the false impression that they have made a sale.

In many countries business is a much more personal thing than it is in the West. Arabs prefer to do business with people they know. The Japanese too spend time getting to know people and building trust before they commit to any business dealings. Much time may be spent on the golf course before business is even mentioned.

Conducting business in some countries is particularly awkward for women. There are many countries, notably Arab and African ones, where women are still not accepted as equals in the workplace. On a positive note here, Western women tend to be treated as representatives of their companies first, their countries second – and their sex third. So they do get on rather better than local women do and it is by no means impossible for women to strike deals in such countries. Some Western companies refuse to bow to local custom and send their female employees as trailblazers.

SALESPEOPLE

To develop a salesforce, a marketing manager needs to decide what kind of salesperson will sell the firm's products most effectively. Various authors classify sales roles in different ways. Some classify sales jobs into two broad categories: service selling, which concentrates on getting sales from the existing customer base, and developmental selling, which aims to convert prospects into customers. Others refer to three basic roles: order taking, order supporting and order getting. From reading the above, you will understand that there are many sales roles and, in reality, these roles may not be discrete. Salespeople now have to perform many tasks and activities daily (not just selling), which involve numerous skills, such as:

- buyer/seller team coordinator
- customer service provider
- buyer behaviour expert
- information gatherer
- market analyst and planner
- sales forecaster
- market cost analyst
- technologist.

EXPAND YOUR KNOWLEDGE

Storbacka, K., Ryals, L., Davies, I.A. and Nenonen, S. (2009) 'The changing role of sales: viewing sales as a strategic, cross-functional process', *The European Journal of Marketing*, 43 (7–8): 890–906.

The role of sales within the promotional mix is constantly changing. A study by Storbacka, Ryals, Davies and Nenonen revealed that the twenty-first-century sales function is changing in three interrelated aspects: from a function to a process; from an isolated activity to an integrated one; and from operational to strategic.

STAGES OF SELLING

A number of sequential steps go into making a sale. These are illustrated in Exhibit 8.8.

Exhibit 8.8   Personal selling

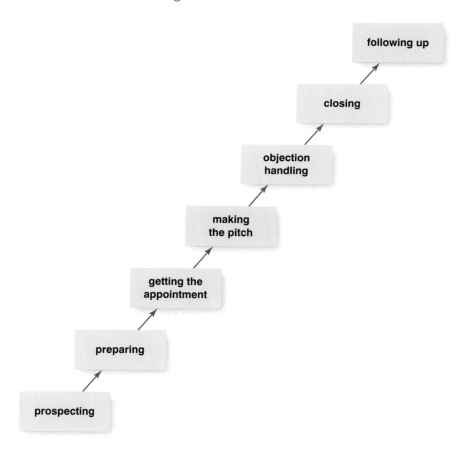

Prospecting is about finding potential customers. Exhibitions are good sources of prospects, as are direct-response promotions. Websites are often used to identify

prospecting
looking for prospective customers

people who are interested in a brand or product category. It is important that a salesperson should prepare before approaching a prospect. They need to know what kind of person they are dealing with, why they might want the product and what their likely hot buttons are. The next step is to get the appointment. This may be arranged in advance (e.g. over the phone) or the salesperson may **cold call**. The next step is a big one. Although, in Exhibit 8.8, it is labelled 'making the pitch', there is more to it than that. First, the salesperson should find out what the customer wants, then he or she can draw attention to the most appropriate products and their benefits. The best salespeople are good listeners. It is unlikely that the product will fit the customer's needs perfectly – there will be some objections raised (e.g. it is too expensive, it is the wrong colour, it has no cover). The salesperson must address these concerns honestly, and perhaps convince the customer that the things the product lacks are unimportant. Now comes the close. This is the part that many salespeople find the hardest: they just have to ask for the order. Finally, there is the follow-up: making sure the product is delivered, that it works properly and, of course, checking if the customer needs anything else. This could be the start of a long and profitable relationship.

Not all steps are used in all sales situations. The **retail** sales assistant, for example, will be in a very different situation from a key accounts salesperson who works for a manufacturer of heavy industrial equipment.

cold call
when a salesperson calls on a prospect without an appointment

insight   Closing techniques

Salespeople employ a number of closing techniques to persuade customers to place orders. Some are more effective than others and some are less ethical than others. Good salespeople are honest and straightforward. If customers like and trust them, they are far more likely to buy from them.

Some examples of closing techniques are:

- the straight close, e.g. 'So would you like one?' followed by silence

- the deadline close, e.g. 'There is only the one left in stock and I don't know when we'll be able to get more'
- the assumptive close, e.g. 'So I'll get it delivered next week then'
- the alternative close, e.g. 'Would you like the blue or the green?'
- the no problem close, e.g. 'Order it now and you can cancel it later if you change your mind'
- the sympathy close, e.g. 'I just need one more order to make my sales quota this month.'

Look out for these next time you're out shopping. You may even be able to add to the list.

Direct marketing

It is not always easy to fit all the elements of the marketing communications mix into four broad categories. Where to put **direct marketing** (or more accurately in the context of promotion, **direct marketing communication**) is one such problem, as it can make use of advertising as well as sales promotions and personal selling.

Most promotional tools are aimed at mass audiences but there are weaknesses with the mass approach and so many companies have adopted a more direct approach to their markets. They are motivated not just by cost advantages but also by opportunities to improve quality and service provision.

Direct marketing establishes personal contact with prospects and customers to encourage a direct response. Early direct marketing focused on providing a telephone number or a response card in advertisements (i.e. direct-response advertising). Today, **direct mail**, telemarketing, door-to-door, email and interactive website forms are among the main response media used.

Direct marketing has outgrown its early roots and has become a sophisticated marketing tool used for building relationships with customers. **Direct-response advertising** is now only a part of the huge direct marketing industry. The Institute of Direct Marketing's (IDM) definition emphasises the importance of building customer relationships through direct marketing efforts. 'Planned recording, analysis and tracking of individual customers' responses and transactions for the purpose of developing and prolonging mutually profitable customer relationships' (IDM, 2010). The primary objectives of direct marketing are to build and sustain a mutually rewarding relationship with individual customers, to reduce media cost and to improve the effectiveness of marketing communications and the measurement of results.

Undoubtedly, direct marketing has grown and developed because of rapid advances in computing and communications technology, transportation and changing market conditions. Technology has facilitated the collection, storage, analysis and retrieval of customer data. It has increased opportunities for direct communication even on an individual basis to millions of people. It offers a solution to the fragmentation of the marketplace. It can also create problems of unwanted communications.

direct marketing
all activities that make it possible to offer goods or services or to transmit other messages to a segment of the population by post, telephone, email or other direct means (according to the Chartered Institute of Marketing)

direct mail
advertising material delivered by post

direct-response advertising
'advertising, or selling, through any medium inviting the consumer to respond to the advertiser' (IDM Direct Marketing Guide)

DATABASE MARKETING

Database marketing is a sophisticated, modern direct marketing tool that owes everything to technology. Customer (and potential customer) data is held in a database, which is really an electronic filing system with extensive cross-referencing and processing capabilities (see Exhibit 8.9 for examples of the kind of data that would be held). This data is used to identify prospects for a company's products. These prospects are then targeted for marketing and sales activities, usually by being placed on specific mailing lists. Take the example of a department store. It may have lists for men, women, parents, customers of specific cosmetics companies, people who buy designer clothes, people who have its store card, people who do not have its store card, people who purchased electrical goods such as televisions or household appliances. This information is gathered from purchases made in store, data provided by customers when they fill in forms (such as applications for store cards, credit agreements, competition entries) and bought in from other sources (there are companies that specialise in buying in data and selling it on).

The targeted customers may be sent mailings, telephoned, emailed or just added to a list to receive regular newsletters, updates, etc.

Databases have been used for years to analyse customer buying patterns and identify prospects for other products and services. The technology has, of course, got more sophisticated and powerful, and so have the uses to which it can be put. Today, many companies have data warehouses and use **data mining** software to sift through the enormous amounts of data stored in them and make the connections between the data. For example, a company can match up customer profiles in different parts of the country with past sales at specific times of year and use this link to identify new ranges that might sell well. There is almost no limit to the connections data mining might make – as long as the data exists in the database, of course.

database marketing
the use of computerised customer data to communicate with customers and promote further sales

data mining
using specialist software to analyse large amounts of data (held in a database) to predict trends and likely customer behaviour

ACTIVITY

When you get home after your next shopping trip, take a look at what you've bought. What could a company work out about you from your purchases?

Exhibit 8.9   Examples of customer database information

Type of information	Possible source(s) include
Customer contact details	Order forms, sales team
Customer sales history	Past orders, loyalty cards
Customer demographics	Order forms, credit applications, market research reports
Customer psychographics	Customer surveys, sales team
Customer preferences	Customer correspondence, enquiries, sales team
Customer business details	Annual report and other publicly available documents, company website, sales team

These sophisticated computer systems are at the heart of customer relationship management (CRM). Organisations have more information on customers than they ever had before, as well as the technology and techniques to use it to understand and serve their customers better. There really is very little excuse for poor customer service today and yet it does still exist in some places. Have you ever received a standard response to a query that really just did not answer it? It can be a mistake for an organisation to become over-reliant on automation.

ACTIVITY

Gather together all the promotional items that you receive in a week (through the post and by email). Then sort them according to their relevance to you.

How many did you receive? Whose mailing lists are you on? How did you get there?

DIRECT-RESPONSE ADVERTISING

direct-response advertising
'advertising, or selling, through any medium inviting the consumer to respond to the advertiser' (IDM Direct Marketing Guide)

Direct-response advertising is, according to the IDM (2010), 'advertising or selling through any medium inviting the consumer to respond to the advertiser'. As with all advertising, it requires good audience profiling, creativity and wise media choice. Direct marketers make good use of database technology to build up information on customers and prospects. Using this, they can compile mailing lists, or lists suitable for other media, and so reach their target audiences.

MEDIA CHOICE

While most media can be used for direct communications, Exhibit 8.10 outlines the main media choices open to direct marketers.

Exhibit 8.10   Direct-response media

Display advertising (press)	Door to door
Classified advertising (press)	Websites and Internet advertising (e.g. banners)
Mail	Search engines
Telephone	Internet pop-ups and instant messages
SMS and other messaging systems	Email
TV	Inserts in magazines/newspapers
iTV	Flyers
Radio	Posters

Factors affecting media choice in direct marketing communications

No one medium always achieves the highest response at the lowest cost, and it is generally true that those media that elicit a higher response also tend to be the most expensive. For example, telephone responses are potentially the highest of any media, but the costs are also the highest.

To assess the media for a direct marketing campaign, the framework AIMRITE can be used as a decision-making aid (Pickton and Broderick, 2004a).

- **Audience**: does the media reach the desired target audience?
- **Impact**: does the media have sufficient impact to ensure the message has a chance of getting through the clutter?
- **Message**: does it help ensure the message is clearly communicated?
- **Response**: does it make responding easy?
- **Internal management**: does it enhance the efficient management of the campaign?
- **The end result**: what are the costs and projected likely revenues? Taking the above into account, and looking at the average response rates for the chosen media, how likely are you to hit target for the campaign?

ACTIVITY

Obtain a direct-response press or magazine advertisement or a piece of direct mail. Critically appraise the media choice made, using the AIMRITE framework (although you are not likely to be able to assess the end result).

Regulations

Throughout Europe and elsewhere, marketing communications are subject to constraints and regulations. Some controls are set by law and others are self-imposed voluntarily by the marketing communications industry itself. The balance of legal and self-regulations varies from country to country. Collectively, the UK regulations seek to uphold four guiding principles. Promotions should be:

● legal
● decent
● honest
● truthful.

These principles are used to produce a series of codes of practice covering different media and types of promotion. These codes can be seen on the web at www.asa. org.uk.

Despite attempts to ensure that these principles are maintained, there are examples of some dubious practices. Regulatory bodies police the industry and, where necessary, require that promotions are withdrawn if they contravene the principles above. Legal action can be taken in extreme cases. Where infringements do occur, it is more likely to be because of issues of decency, or moral, ethical or misrepresentation concerns, rather than outright lack of honesty or a deliberate attempt to mislead (although these do occur in a minority of cases through false claims and downright illegal practices). Notable examples that have been widely publicised are the poster promotions for Benetton in which the use of imagery has often been deemed to be too shocking to be seen in public places where it might create a degree of offence. In coming to a view on such matters, it is not a question of offending everybody that is the issue but, rather, one of creating what may be considered widespread offence.

In general, it is up to the media owners (TV, radio, cinema, newspaper and magazine owners, etc.) to come to a view as to whether or not an item is likely to contravene the codes of practice, and not accept the promotion where this may happen. In the case of TV and radio, any advertising should be pre-vetted – that is, checked before transmission, but in the case of most other promotions, such pre-vetting is impossible because of the volume of advertisements involved and so checks are made after the promotions have been circulated. Members of the public are encouraged to make complaints, which are subsequently investigated. In the case of the UK, a great deal of voluntary self-regulation is relied on to enhance the legal controls. The Advertising Standards Authority (ASA) is responsible for regulating advertising, sales promotions and direct marketing (including the Internet). There are also numerous other professional bodies representing the different elements of marketing communications, which also have their own codes of professional practice. Most other countries have similar arrangements although the extent, and nature, of the control exerted varies significantly.

Setting the marketing budget

Marketing communications should be seen as an investment. It can, however, be quite expensive and so attention should be paid to getting the budget right. Setting the promotional budget is not an exact science. Various techniques are used by organisations, the five most popular ones being:

● Arbitrary method
● Affordable method
● Competitive parity method
● Objective and task method
● Percentage of sales method.

Breaking the code

ethical focus

It's in the nature of human beings to push boundaries to see how far they'll stretch, and advertisers are no different. The ASA and OFCOM are there to maintain standards.

The most complained about ad of 2006 was placed in *The Independent* by the Gay Police Association and sought to draw attention to the rising incidence of violence towards gay people. The ad was headlined 'In the name of the father' and showed a Bible in a pool of blood. Although three of the five complaints about the ad were upheld by the ASA, it was a one-off ad timed to coincide with the Gay Pride March, so the advertisers were warned not to take the same approach again, but little else could be done. *The Independent* published an apology to its readers.

A Carphone Warehouse ad attracted complaints from 145 people including some of its competitors. Ads in a range of media, including TV, press and on a CD, promoted a new TalkTalk telephone package with 'free broadband forever'. The complaint was that it was misleading to suggest that the broadband was free when it involved an 18-month contractual commitment to the calls package, a connection charge of £29.99, ongoing costs of £9.99 per month plus line rental (£20.99 in total) and a disconnection fee of £70. The complaints were upheld.

Ninety-six viewers complained about a Kellogg's Crunchy Nut Cornflakes ad which showed a man riding a large dog in order to get home quicker to eat his cornflakes. Despite an on-screen warning of 'Don't try this with your dog at home', viewers felt that it might encourage cruelty to animals. The ASA considered the ad obvious fantasy and so did not agree.

Dolce & Gabanna were clearly controversial in 2006. Three of their ads appear in the ASA's list of the ten most complained about ads. Two ads were claimed to glamorise knife crime while the other showed two men kissing and was thought offensive. None of these complaints was upheld.

To find out more about the advertising codes, and for examples of complaints, visit www.asa.org.uk.

Budgeting methods between organisations vary in popularity. Although the percentage of sales method is reputed to be a favoured approach in larger organisations. Small businesses are more likely to use arbitrary or affordable approaches.

ARBITRARY METHOD

Rather than a method, this is an approach to arriving at a budget figure. It is more a judgement that seems right at the time. It is unlikely to be based on any significant criteria and is more likely to be based on gut feel or intuition. It is an educated guess – but, remember, it may have been made by a very experienced marketing director.

AFFORDABLE METHOD

In essence, this means that the company will spend on promotion what it thinks is reasonable and can afford. Organisations using this approach, like the arbitrary approach, are more likely to reflect a view that marketing communications are an expense rather than an investment.

The affordable method causes problems with long-range planning. The company cannot guess the funds that will be available in the future to spend on promotion. Also, in times of recession or hardship, very little will be spent on promotion, and yet this is most likely to be the time when extra spending would be of benefit.

COMPETITIVE PARITY METHOD

A budget is set that matches, exceeds or is in proportion to competitors' budgets. Care has to be taken in applying this method. For example, not all companies have the same objectives. Some may want to become the market leader (market share objective), while others may wish to become more profitable (profitability objective). A company's nearest competitor may be much bigger or much smaller than it is. Simply matching expenditure in this situation would not be sensible. Setting the budget as an appropriate proportion would be a better approach.

OBJECTIVE AND TASK METHOD

The objective and task method determines a budget based on what the various communications activities need to achieve. In essence, objectives are set and then the marketing communications tasks to achieve the objectives are decided upon. By calculating the costs of those tasks, a budget is set.

Although this method may appear to be the best, it is a method that is rarely applied in its entirety. Difficulties in implementing this approach include:

- the company may not be able to afford the budget arrived at
- it is time-consuming (and therefore expensive to prepare)
- the task may not actually achieve the objective anyway, e.g. the planned PR campaign may not raise the company's credibility as intended.

PERCENTAGE OF SALES METHOD

The percentage of sales method is probably the most popular method. It is the classical approach partly because it is easy to calculate. It links marketing communications expenditure directly to levels of sales by allocating a fixed percentage of turnover to marketing communications.

However, there are difficulties. What percentage should be used and how should the turnover be determined? The percentage may be based on previous practice, on competitor allocations or on industry averages. Turnover could be based on historic sales, last year's sales or sales averaged over a number of years. It could be based on current sales levels, or it could be based on forecast sales (which may, of course, be wrong).

Perhaps unsurprisingly, in practice, most organisations use a combination of all these approaches to set their budgets.

SUMMARY

This chapter has introduced some basic concepts and models that will help you to understand how marketing communications decisions are made. The key model to understand is the communications process, since marketing communications, or promotion, is a communication process. This involves an understanding of the sender, the message, the media and the receivers.

Organisations can use a variety of promotional tools to communicate with potential customers, whether consumer or organisational. The major promotional tools are advertising, PR, sales promotion and personal selling. To these can be added direct marketing and sponsorship, together with many other activities such as packaging and exhibitions. Collectively, these are known as the promotion or marketing communications mix. Advertising, PR and sponsorship are primarily mass communications, whereas personal selling is interpersonal communication. Sales promotion and direct marketing may be either.

The organisation can use its promotion mix to develop both push and pull strategies. With a push strategy, the organisation directs its promotional efforts at marketing channel members. These then push the product forwards to the final buyer. With a pull strategy, the organisation directs its promotional efforts at the final buyer to develop a strong demand for the product that is used to pull a product through the marketing channel. Most organisations use a combination of push and pull.

The purpose of all marketing communications is to create a response from potential buyers. One response model, also known as a hierarchy of effects model, is AIDA (Awareness, Interest, Desire and Action). Each promotional tool has different degrees of effectiveness in eliciting these different responses.

One approach does not fit all. There is no single optimal promotion mix and no one accepted scientific approach to determining the promotion mix. Many factors need to be considered, such as: the objectives of the marketing plan; the size and characteristics of the target market/audience and their buying decision process; the type of products being promoted; the objectives of the promotional efforts; and competitors' promotional efforts.

CHALLENGES REVIEWED

Now that you have finished reading the chapter, look back at the challenges you were set at the beginning. Do you have a clearer idea of what's involved?

Hints:

- see 'setting the promotional budget'
- think beyond mass media advertising to other promotional tools and more targeted media
- audience profiling and research – but be wary of jokes in advertising (how funny are they the fourth time you hear them?)
- time for crisis management – see 'publics' and 'media relations'
- think about repositioning and take great care not to be misleading in your approach – check the advertising code carefully.

READING AROUND

Websites

www.asa.org.uk – the website for the Advertising Standards Authority, check out the complaints and adjudications.
www.brandrepublic.com – access to news stories and feature articles.
www.creativeclub.co.uk – subscription-only site; excellent source for current advertising.
www.nmauk.co.uk – the Newspaper Marketing Agency, check out its 'breaking ads' page.
www.theidm.co.uk – the Institute of Direct Marketing, go to the knowledge centre and browse.
www.warc.com – the World Advertising Research Centre: journals, case studies, papers on best practice and much more.

Journals

International Journal of Advertising
Journal of Advertising
Journal of Marketing Communications

Magazines

Campaign
Marketing
Marketing Week
PR Week
Admap

Books

Amanda Barry (with a foreword by Sir Richard Branson) (2005) *PR Power: Inside Secrets from the World of Spin.* London: Virgin Books.
Chris Hackley (2010) *Advertising and Promotion* (2nd edn). London: Sage.
Joseph Jaffe (2005) *Life after the 30 Second Spot*. Wiley/Adweek.
Jay Conrad Levinson, Mitch Meyerson and Mary Eule Scarborough (2008) *Guerilla Marketing on the Internet: The Definitive Guide from the Father of Guerilla Marketing.* Entrpreneur Press.
Carol J. Pardun (ed.) (2009) *Advertising and Society: Controversies and Consequences*. Wiley-Blackwell
Gerard J. Tellis (ed.) (2007) *The Sage Handbook of Advertising.* London: Sage.

Book chapters

Mehta Abilasha (1999) 'Celebrities in advertising', in J.P Jones (ed.), *The Advertising Business.* London: Sage. Chapter 17.
Jackie L'Etang (2007) *Public Relations Concepts: Practice and Critique*. See Chapter 10, 'Public relations in promotional culture and in everyday life'. London: Sage.
Paul Springer (2007) *Ads to Icons.* London: Kogan Page. See Chapter 1 'Rethinking mass media'.

Video

BBC4 (2008) *Hard Sell programmes 1–6* – Phil Jupitus narrates a series exploring 50 years of British TV advertising.
Minority Report (2002) starring Tom Cruise – look for the possible future of marketing communications.

SELF-REVIEW QUESTIONS

1. List and explain the key elements in the communications process model. (see pages 276–8)
2. Identify sources of noise in the communications process. (see page 277)
3. What are the main elements, or tools, of the promotion mix? (see pages 270–1)
4. What are the advantages and disadvantages of mass communication and interpersonal communication? (see page 282)
5. Define push and pull strategies. (see pages 274–5)
6. What are the problems with using 'increase sales' as a promotional objective? (see page 284)
7. How is advertising controlled or regulated in the UK? (see page 308)
8. What is the AIDA model and how can it be used to set promotional objectives? (see page 280 and 283–5)
9. Explain how personal selling is a two-way communications process. (see page 301)
10. Explain and give examples of the major types of consumer sales promotion. (see page 299)
11. What is direct-response advertising? (see pages 298–300)
12. Discuss the strengths and limitations of each budgeting method. (see pages 308–10)

mini case study

British Airways strike wrecks £6,000 honeymoon

Read the questions, then the case material, and then answer the questions.

Questions

1. As marketing consultant to British Airways (BA), you have been asked to develop a post-strike marketing communications campaign. Consider the nature of the problem from a marketing communications perspective. Reflect on the public perception of BA, as indicated in the case study, to assist you with your decision-making. Your campaign suggestions should:

   - identify key target audiences and their issues with BA
   - list the objectives your campaign should achieve
   - identify the marketing communications techniques you would use to achieve these objectives.

Thousands of holidaymakers faced misery when check-in staff, working for British Airways at Heathrow, went on a series of strikes. The troubled company lost an estimated £40 million through the industrial action, and ruined the travel plans of more than 90,000 people. Thousands of passengers switched to other airlines.

The unofficial walkout by 250 check-in staff was triggered by the imposition of a swipe-card entry system, which workers felt could lead to new working practices, such as being sent home during quiet periods and called in at busy times.

Union leaders said that workers would strike for 'as long as necessary to force BA into a climb-down on its introduction of the controversial swipe-card system for staff' as it was unacceptable. One union leader also said, 'We are not backing down on this. BA must withdraw the swipe-card system or face a series of very damaging strikes. If we wipe out the company's profits as a result, it will have to face that.'

For many BA travellers, the misery was not over when they did eventually get a flight. BA admitted that 18,000 cases had not made it on to the flights and many passengers were not reunited with their possessions until a full week later.

Tabloid press in the UK took advantage of the situation and published many stories focusing on how the strike had caused personal misery for stranded customers. One story was about newlyweds who spent their first day of marriage on the airport floor, rather than at their honeymoon destination. They swore that they would never fly with BA again. No apologising was ever going to give them their honeymoon back.

Brand image and corporate reputation is crucial for an airline such as BA. Its position is that, unlike the low-cost flight operators, it offers more than just a cheap seat. It believes its reputation for reliability, comfort and customer service is particularly important and worth paying a little more for.

The first decade of the twenty-first century has been tough for the travel industry and particularly for airlines. The economic downturn and increased fears about flying following 9/11, other terrorist attacks such as the shoe bomber and the wars in Iraq and Afghanistan have severely reduced passenger numbers. At the same time, competition from low-cost airlines such as easyJet and Ryanair has increased. All this has meant that BA needed to make major changes. However, some commentators have expressed doubt that BA's internal culture was well suited to the task of winning back the respect of its customers and restoring good industrial relations.

In the last quarter of 2008, BA made a loss of £122m. In July 2009, in an attempt to stem the losses, they proposed radical changes to working practices including reducing the number of cabin crew on long haul flights from 15 to 14 and a two-year pay freeze from 2010. The unions rejected these proposals but BA introduced them in November prompting another strike call from the unions. The courts declared the strike ballot illegal and thus saved numerous travellers' Christmas holidays but the dispute rumbled on into the following year. The union balloted again for strike action and BA threatened to take away strikers' generous travel perks. BA's management wanted to protect the company from collapse and safeguard shareholders' interests. The unions were concerned for the future of their members. The dispute rumbled on.

SOURCES: BBC News, 2010a, 2010b

REFERENCES

Bartle, J. (2000) 'The advertising contribution', in L. Butterfield (ed.), *Excellence in Advertising: The IPA Guide to Best Practice* (2nd edn). Oxford: Butterworth Heinemann. pp. 27–42.

BBC News (1999) *McLibel Duo Gain Part Victory*. Available at: **news.bbc.co.uk/1/hi/uk/308453.stm** (accessed 21/05/2007).

BBC News (2010a) 'British Airways cabin crew strike talks to resume' 10 March. Available at: **news.bbc.co.uk/1/hi/business/8558399.stm** (accessed 10/03/2010).

BBC News (2010b) 'Union loses legal battle with British Airways' 19 February. Available at: **news.bbc.co.uk/1/hi/business/8523758.stm** (accessed 10/03/2010).

Buttle, F. (1984) 'Merchandising', *European Journal of Marketing*, 18 (6/7): 104–123.

Colley, R. (1961) *Defining Advertising Goals for Measured Advertising Results*. New York: Association of National Advertisers.

Cummins, J. (1989) *Sales Promotion: How to Create and Implement Campaigns that Really Work*. London: Kogan Page.

DBA (2009) *Heinz Classic Soups*, Design Business Association Effectiveness Awards 2009. Available at **www.warc.com** (accessed 13/12/2009).

DDB (2004) *Touareg launch*, IPA Effectiveness Awards. Available at: **www.warc.com** (accessed 22/05/2007).

Ehrenberg, A.S.C., Barnard, N.R. and Scriven, J.A. (1997) 'Justifying our advertising budgets', *Journal of Marketing*.

Engel, J.F., Warshaw, M.R. and Kinnear, T.C. (1994) *Promotional Strategy* (8th edn). New York: Irwin.

Haig, M. (2003) *Brand Failures: The Truth about the 100 Biggest Branding Mistakes of All Time*. London: Kogan Page.

IDM (2010) Institute of Direct Marketing website. Available at: www.theidm.com/resources/jargon-ouster (accessed 15/05/2010)

Jefkins, F. (1989) *Public Relations Techniques*. London: Heinemann.

Jones, J.P. (1990) 'Advertising: strong or weak force? Two views oceans apart', *International Journal of Advertising*, 9 (3): 233–246.

Makin, C. (2002) *Domino's Pizza: building a high street brand through a change in media strategy*, IPA Effectiveness Awards, Best Interactive. Available at: **www.warc.com** (accessed 01/09/2003).

Meenaghan, T. (1991) 'Sponsorship – legitimising the medium', *European Journal of Marketing*, 25 (11).

National Readership Survey (2007) London: NRS.

Pickton, D.W. and Broderick, A. (2004a) *Integrated Marketing Communications* (2nd edn). Harlow: FT/Prentice Hall.

Pickton, D. and Broderick, A. (2004b) 'Creating shared meaning in marketing communications – from sender to receiver', in D. Pickton and A. Broderick *Integrated Marketing Communications*. Harlow: Financial Times/Prentice Hall, Chapter 3.

Schramm, W. (1955) 'How communication works', in W. Schramm (ed.), *The Process and Effects of Mass Communications*. University of Illinois Press. pp. 3–26.

Storbacka, K., Ryals, L., Davies, I.A. and Nenonen, S. (2009) 'The changing role of sales: viewing sales as a strategic, cross-functional process', *The European Journal of Marketing*, 43 (7–8): 890–906.

Place

CHAPTER CONTENTS

Introduction
The importance of distribution
Channel members
The right space and time
Differing views of place
Place management
Designing the supply chain
Overseas operations and market entry
    options
Sources of power and conflict in the
    supply chain
Marketing functions in the supply chain
e-channels
Summary
Challenges reviewed
Reading around
Self-review questions
Mini case study
References

PLACE CHALLENGES

The following are illustrations of the types of decision that marketers have to take or issues they face. *You aren't expected to know how to deal with the challenges now*; just bear them in mind as you read the chapter and see what you can find that helps.

● Imagine that you work for Reebok. Your objectives are to increase the number of sales made in your home market and to maintain the relative exclusivity of the brand. How can you use the stores to achieve your objectives?

● A journalist you know is writing a story about the increase in direct marketing and has come to you, as a marketing consultant, for some advice. You have told her that getting the right product to the customer on time is critically important. In reply, she has asked you to explain why, if it is so important, all manufacturers do not take responsibility for every aspect of deliveries themselves.

● You are working for a French wine company. You know that Australian and American wine producers are seen as more technologically advanced and better value. How can you compete?

● Your small furniture company is located in a small industrial estate in Cornwall. You know that your products have great potential if only consumers could see them. Unfortunately the major retailers tell you that you cannot make enough furniture to be worth their while working with you. How can you develop to get around this?

● You are the headteacher of a large secondary school which is always in need of cash. A snack food manufacturer wants to install vending machines in the school to sell crisps, chocolates and biscuits. They will stock and maintain the machines and give the school 15 per cent of the takings. What do you need to consider before accepting or rejecting the deal?

Introduction

Where did you buy your last T-shirt? Do you know where it was made and how it got from there to you? Billions are spent on products every year but few people look beyond the places where they buy things. They do not think about the plantation that their bananas came from or the factory in which their television was made. For a marketer, place includes *all* the activities and all the organisations involved in getting goods from their point of origin to their point of sale.

Place is one of the elements of the **marketing mix** and is really more accurately referred to as distribution, but then the marketing mix would not be **the 4Ps**; it would be 3Ps and a D which would be far less memorable.

Many of the activities involved in managing product distribution are crucial to effective targeting and positioning (see Chapter 4). For example, placement in an upmarket store sends an upmarket message that helps build a brand image in customers' minds. The timely arrival of goods is seen as good customer service. Contrarily, late arrival of goods, or the arrival of the wrong goods, or of goods in poor condition can undermine all the good work of the product managers and marketing communications managers and cause customers to reject a brand completely. There is a significant management challenge here: a challenge requiring the management of both time and space.

This chapter looks at some key elements of the exchange relationship (see Exhibit 9.1), in particular how this idea of place brings together sellers and buyers, products and the needs they are designed to fulfil. We will discuss the importance of time, space, information, bargaining power and what sellers have to do to match buyers' expectations. By the end of the chapter, you will begin to realise just how much work has been done to put those trainers in your local sports shop or to make your next dream holiday a reality.

Exhibit 9.1   The exchange relationship system

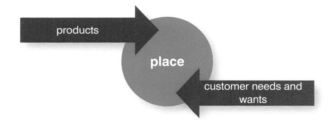

The importance of distribution

All businesses depend on marketing opportunities to meet potential customers' needs. Opportunities, whether taken or missed, are what shape the future of the enterprise.

marketing opportunity
a chance to reach a particular group of customers with a product offer

Changes that affect place frequently bring new **marketing opportunities**. These may be technological changes. For example, the Internet has changed the way in which many products are delivered to customers. Newspapers are able to meet their customers' demand for continuously updated and instantly accessible news and information, for instance. They may be changes in the competitive environment, such as a company withdrawing from a market and so freeing up its channels of distribution. Changes in the political and regulatory environments can affect how and when companies get products to customers, e.g. the relaxation of Sunday trading laws or the granting of new casino licences. All of these things provide marketing opportunities.

In a competitive environment, the customer can shop around. It is not generally desirable to be second choice. The tension between consumer needs and business capabilities creates a constant dynamic for change. One of the key roles for marketing management is the creation of attractive opportunities for exchange and that means monitoring the changes carefully and getting the place right.

---

insight   An opportunity to become one of the most successful companies in the world

Most of today's PCs are based on IBM's architecture, as originally developed for the IBM PC launched in 1981 (the only sizeable alternative is Apple), but IBM was not the first into the field. Towards the end of the 1970s, the market leader for large business computers realised that it had to get into the growing market for small home and personal computers quickly or it would miss out on a huge opportunity. That meant, unusually for IBM, contracting out some of the development. IBM was one of the largest companies in the world and many smaller companies did not want to get involved in a project where the power was so one-sided. However, IBM's decision to work with others presented major, and unusual, marketing opportunities for smaller firms who were prepared to develop components and software for the new PC.

Two of the main beneficiaries of these opportunities were newcomers Intel and Microsoft (at that time, just another small software company). Microsoft produced the original IBM PC operating system: DOS. DOS has long since been replaced by Windows. Microsoft was handed a new product opportunity but its real value lay in the chance to have its operating system sold with every IBM PC. So this was really a distribution (or place) opportunity.

IBM no longer make PCs, having sold that part of its business to Lenovo, but a large number of other companies (e.g. Dell, Toshiba, Compaq, Sony, Acer, Fujitsu, Siemens, Hewlett Packard) do make computers which use Microsoft's operating system and they hugely outsell the IBM-branded ones – just as Microsoft's profits far exceed IBM's.

SOURCES: Bellis, 2007; IBM, n.d.

Channel members

A **supply chain** is a network of businesses and organisations through which goods pass to get to their final destination (see Exhibit 9.2). In most developed markets, these networks will be extensive and have many participant businesses. A global business, such as the Ford Motor Company, has a supply chain that runs through a number of countries. Each of the businesses within that chain is likely to have further international suppliers so that the whole network spans the world. So, Ford buys raw materials and parts from a number of other businesses and sends cars on to a number of resellers.

A **distribution channel** (sometimes called a marketing channel) is a product's route through the supply chain. The distribution channel is a specific product's path through the supply chain. Its shape is determined by the product's manufacturer in order to meet their marketing objectives. For example, Rolex watches target quite a

supply chain
the network of businesses involved in distributing goods and services

distribution channel
a chain of organisations through which products pass on their way to a target market

Exhibit 9.2   Example of a supply chain: suppliers, intermediaries, customers

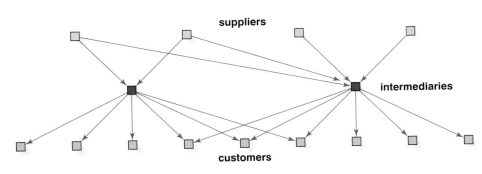

small customer group (the relatively affluent), offer high-quality service and want to project a quality image. Consequently, Rolex generally uses upmarket retail partners with comparatively few stores. This is called selective distribution (see 'Designing the supply chain' below).

To summarise, a supply chain includes all of the channel members but a distribution channel is limited to just one group of channel members chosen to deliver a particular product to a particular market.

BUYERS – CONSUMERS, BUSINESSES AND OTHER ORGANISATIONS

This group is at the end of a supply chain. Its members do not sell the product on but buy it to be used by themselves or their organisations. (For more on customer types see Chapters 1 and 3.)

SELLERS – MANUFACTURERS, RETAILERS, WHOLESALERS, RESELLERS

Manufacturers and producers are the major group of sellers. Many of the largest manufacturers achieve global recognition for their products. For example, Hewlett Packard is considered to be one of the world's leading computer printer manufacturers. Its products are sold to customers in different markets through a global network of outlets, some of which are **retailers** selling to end-user customers, and some of which are **resellers** selling the products on. Coca-Cola is known globally as a producer of soft drinks, although in many countries the drinks are produced by another company under licence rather than by Coca-Cola itself.

Products are transformed as they move through the **supply chain**, i.e. each company that receives products uses its expertise and resources to change them in some way before passing them on. For example, FAG buys steel and then transforms it into ball bearings, which it then sells to motor manufacturers across the world. The motor manufacturers sell their motors to quarry plant manufacturers, who make equipment to extract material from the earth. At each stage, value is added to the bought-in product, i.e. it is transformed into something more desirable or useful and can command a higher price (e.g. steel into ball bearings or fresh peas into frozen ones). The length of a product's supply chain is determined by the complexity of the final product and its user's needs.

Intermediaries within the part of the supply chain that makes up the distribution channel (or marketing channel) also add value to the product. They deal in finished products, in bars of soap and televisions rather than ingredients or sub-assemblies such as vegetable fat and electrical components. Marketing channel members may, for example, re-package goods, take them to more convenient places for sale or offer extra services such as delivery, installation or advice on the product's use.

The seller that most consumers buy from is the retailer. The retailer is usually the last member of the supply chain before the end customer. Retailers may operate from a shop, a catalogue, a phone line, a **direct-response advert** in the press or on television, or a website (sometimes a combination, as is the case with Argos, for example). The retailer uses their market knowledge to select goods and services that their customers will want to buy. When this is done well, the retailer thrives; when it is done poorly, the retailer does poorly too.

Magna Park in Leicestershire is Europe's largest distribution park. Companies based there include ASDA, Argos, Britvic, DHL, The Disney Store, Exel, Honda, Lidl, Merck, Nissan, Panasonic, P&O, Sara Lee, TNT, Toyota and many others.

Retail organisations come in all sizes. The biggest retailers, such as Wal-Mart and IKEA, are global household names and can offer consumers products from around the world. The smallest are corner shops or even businesses run from home.

Retailers buy goods in and sell them on, transforming them and adding value to them (partly through providing a more convenient way to buy them) in the process. It is this transformation that turns the buying business into a selling business. An illustration of this is Sainsbury's transformation of Heinz beans. Sainsbury's buy millions of cans of beans which arrive at its distribution depots packed in cartons and on pallets. These pallet loads are then broken down into individual cans that can be stacked on the supermarket's shelves. Sainsbury's sell the individual cans of beans to the final customer. In an IKEA store it may be the customer who has to take the product from the stack of products in the warehouse, which directly passes the cost of the work to the customer.

Wholesalers are one step further away from the final customer than retailers are. They usually buy products to sell on to other members of the supply chain and they support smaller retailers by holding stock in a more convenient location, thus reducing the delivery time from the manufacturers. Most retail wholesalers (e.g. cash and carries) also transform the products by **breaking down** the quantities supplied by the manufacturer. In this respect they are quite similar to the retailer.

This type of business is often found in clothing and food markets because the volume of transactions is high and that helps reduce the risk in holding quantities of stock available for other channel members to buy.

Wholesalers are currently in decline and the main reason for this is the growth of large retail businesses, such as the big supermarkets and high street multiples, which generate significant **economies of scale** by buying in bulk direct from the manufacturers. This makes it more difficult for the wholesaler to sell their products at prices that earn sufficient profit.

In business-to-business (B2B) markets, many businesses carry out the breakdown of bulk function. They are called resellers, i.e. businesses that buy the product from the manufacturer with the purpose of selling it on to another business further down the chain.

wholesalers
buy products in bulk to sell on to other businesses in smaller quantities

breaking down
the process of reducing the quantity of product to be moved

economies of scale
unit costs fall as larger quantities are produced; a cost advantage associated with large organisations

Exhibit 9.3   Types of retailer

Type of retailer	Description	Examples
Market traders	Stall in open or covered market, low rent, few facilities, may move location regularly, specialist or variety; markets are traditional across the world but have fallen out of favour in the UK; some have been repositioned upmarket and there is also an upsurge in farmers' markets	Leicester market (traditional), Borough market (more upmarket), Columbia Road market (flowers and plants)
Independents	The majority of shops are independent but, in the UK and many other industrialised nations, they account for only a small proportion of sales; they have fewer resources and usually less expertise than the large high street multiples	One-off newsagents, restaurants, hairdressers
Multiples and chains	Have a standardised image; they may specialise in a specific range of goods (e.g. women's fashion) or may stock a wider range or be service providers	Topshop, Marks and Spencer, Toni and Guy, Starbucks, Slug and Lettuce, Shell
Supermarkets, superstores and hypermarkets	Usually multiples, common in food but also found in specialist categories such as golf or hardware; hypermarkets are usually out of town	Tesco, Aldi, PC World
Convenience stores	Smaller than supermarkets and with more limited stock but easier for shoppers to pop in to; local shops and garage forecourt shops	Spar, Londis, Tesco Metro, BP Connect
Department stores	A collection of shops or departments under one roof; the store is centrally owned although parts may be rented out	House of Fraser, Debenhams, El Corte Inglés, Printemps, Vendex
Discount stores	Traditionally large, warehouse-like shops with cheap prices; their cost savings come from: lower rents (they are often out of town), minimum service levels, rudimentary display and bulk purchase; increasingly moving online for further cost savings and wider reach	Lidl, Mountain Warehouse
Warehouse clubs	Large stores offering wholesale prices to members only; members may be individual and/or trade; a cross between a cash and carry and a discount store (see above)	Costco, Sam's Club (USA)
Voluntary chains	A network of individually owned shops which club together to benefit from economies of scale and to gain marketing advantages	Mace, Spar

(Continued)

Exhibit 9.3   *(Continued)*

Type of retailer	Description	Examples
Franchises	A type of multiple, the outlets are individually owned but licensed by a larger company to sell their products	Body Shop, Domino's Pizza, Merry Maids (cleaning service)
Factory outlets	May be large and out of town (and grouped into a factory outlet or shopping village) or smaller and more central; originally sold seconds but are now also used to get rid of excess stock; paradise for bargain hunters	Bicester Outlet Village, Cheshire Oaks, The Galleria Outlet Centre
E-tailers	Primarily sell online; many offline retailers also sell online (bricks and clicks), few are pure Internet businesses (pure plays)	Amazon, Ocado

FACILITATORS – AGENTS AND LOGISTICS SERVICES

This group of businesses smoothes the flow of products through the **supply chain**. Members of this group usually have specific expertise in a market, or other specialist resources that enable them to undertake distribution tasks more efficiently.

Agents are businesses that represent other businesses in a particular market. Smaller businesses often use locally based agents as a means of entering new or distant markets because the agent has knowledge of the market and access to local facilities. The agent can thus reduce the costs and risks associated with entering the new market. These businesses do not usually buy the products from the manufacturer so they cannot be classed as **resellers**. They take orders and are paid a commission.

The UK housing market provides a good example of how agents work. In this market, the buyers and sellers tend to be individuals or families with just one house to sell. The estate agency does not take ownership of the house at any point, it brings buyers and sellers together by communicating the property's details to potential buyers and showing them around the house. The agency then charges the seller a commission for any subsequent sale of the property.

Eddie Stobart are well-known logistics contractors

The final category of participants is that of the businesses that transport and store products for the various members of the supply chain. They are known as **logistics** services, and include warehouses, distribution depots and transport services.

The simplest form of transportation is the postal service. For bigger items, courier services or small transport companies may be used. If there are vast quantities of products to be moved around, then the logistics business will also need to be a big company. These businesses have specialist facilities and knowledge. Some, e.g.

logistics
the flow of goods and services through the supply chain

UPS, have grown to a global scale and can take products to market anywhere in the world. The vast majority of logistics businesses, however, are much smaller.

Companies who use specialist logistics companies do so primarily to reduce costs. By concentrating on just this one specialist function, logistics businesses benefit from **economies of scale** (e.g. they can use larger lorries and so make fewer trips) and so are able to deliver goods more cheaply than most manufacturers can. They also transport a large enough volume of products frequently enough to make it worthwhile investing in specialist storage and transport. For example, Christian Salvesen operates a number of cold-storage depots across the country. Manufacturers and retailers that need special conditions to store chilled food products use these depots rather than buying and maintaining these facilities for themselves.

There are drawbacks to contracting out deliveries. For a mail-order company, the only face-to-face contact with the customer may come at the point of delivery and then that is not with one of its own employees. The customer service provided by the logistics company is therefore a major determinant of customer satisfaction, but it is not in the seller's control. Apart from the impact this has on customer relationships, there are a number of marketing opportunities lost here. For example, the lorries and packaging may not bear the seller's name. To get around this, many major retailers who contract out their distribution insist that the transportation company paints its vehicles in the retailer's corporate colours. Those Marks and Spencer lorries you see on the motorway actually belong to Exel Logistics and are driven by that company's staff.

EXPAND YOUR KNOWLEDGE

Hollander, S.C. (1960) 'The Wheel of Retailing', *Journal of Marketing*, 25 (Jul): 37–42.

The 'Wheel of Retailing' was a termed coined by McNair. It describes the process by which new retailers enter the market and over time change and grow and by so doing create opportunities for new entrants. Hollander explains the Wheel and examines examples that conform and some that do not conform to the Wheel.

The right space and time

Customers choose where and when to buy something. For example, if they want farm-fresh fruit and vegetables, they may go to the farm on the day they want these things. If they want designer clothes, they go to an appropriate upmarket store at a time that is convenient to them. These are fixed, geographic spaces – geography is the simplest idea of place. Whether you can buy the food that you want also depends on the growing season of the product (or it used to, now food is flown in from around the world all year round). Whether you can buy the jacket you want depends on the season and what is fashionable at that time. It also depends on the opening times of the outlets and whether you have time to get there. So another fixed point, a point in time, can be added to the concept of place.

In our increasingly technology-driven world, these concepts of space and time have become more flexible. Thanks to the Internet, customers can shop at any time of day or night. They can stay at home and have everything delivered to them. Most purchases, however, are still made from conventional, offline retailers.

Place, or distribution, is often summed up as *getting the right product to the right place at the right time*. No matter how good the product, if it is not available when and where the customer wants it, then there will be no sale. So if the shop is closed, or too far or away, or if the salesperson calls at a bad time, customers are likely to make their purchases elsewhere. The time and place and manner of the sale are important parts of the product offer.

RIGHT SPACE

There is an old saying, which has been attributed to a number of famous **retailers**, that there are three secrets to business success: 'location, location, location'. So how do businesses, not just shops but all the other members of the supply chain too, choose their locations?

According to McGoldrick (2003), the most important consideration is the firm's target market. Who are they, where are they, and where do they want to buy things? Other considerations include the competition and costs.

There are several questions businesses need to ask when choosing the right location for retail premises:

- Are there enough of the right type of customers there?
- Where do they go now? What would make them become your customers instead?
- Is it easy to get to? Is there good public transport? Car parking?
- Will staff be able to travel there at a price they can afford (this can be a problem with some of the more exclusive areas)?
- What are the costs involved?
- How many competitive outlets are there? Is there enough business to support a newcomer?
- Are there complementary businesses nearby? For example, customers of a real meat butcher may be good prospects for an organic vegetable shop or a good bakery.
- Is there a suitable building available in the right timescale?
- Do you need planning permission? Is it likely to be granted? If the premises were used for another purpose before, then you are likely to need permission for 'change of use'.
- Has there been a similar business in the area? How did it do? Many people take over a failing business, e.g. a restaurant, and then fail too. It is important to analyse why the previous business failed *before* starting up.
- What other legal restrictions are there? For example, some areas are conservation areas, making it difficult to alter premises, others are residential only areas, still others may prohibit certain types of business, e.g. pubs.
- For chains, what impact will the new outlet have on existing ones? Is it too close? Will it take away trade?
- What does the location say about your business? Does it project the right image?

Sometimes a **retailer** spots a marketing opportunity – a high street with no food store, a vacant shop near a school, a residential area with no bars or restaurants, an out-of-town site large enough to take a superstore with parking. These are places where there is little or no competition and where the retailer could reasonably expect to make good profits.

If a clothing retailer wants to attract the rich and fashionable, then its stores will need to be in exclusive locations, such as Bond Street in London or the Quadrilatero della Moda in Milan. The image of an area, its surroundings (e.g. residential or business), is a good indicator of the type of customer likely to be found there. If, however, the retailer depends on high sales volumes, then they will need to be somewhere busy, such as London's Oxford Street or in a popular shopping mall. Here they are also more likely to get passing trade (i.e. people who are just passing on their way somewhere else but who might pop in).

A busy location with lots of passing trade is a popular place for many retailers of low-value goods – they need a high volume of sales in order to make profits. There is usually a newsagent and a café near a railway station. People want things to read and eat on train journeys. When they miss their train (or it is delayed), then they want a drink and a snack to while away the time. In the early days, McDonald's used to snap up sites near highway intersections – often in the middle of nowhere. It had realised that the bulk of its customers came by car, usually on their way somewhere else, and could be tempted to take a break by the sight of those famous golden arches. Other fast-food retailers sometimes set up shop anywhere McDonald's did – just because McDonald's was so good at picking locations.

The death of the high street

ethical focus

In the UK, the trend recently has been towards bigger and bigger stores. These superstores are too big to fit into the centre of town and so out-of-town shopping centres have become commonplace. These are clearly popular with many consumers, as hordes of people drive out to them every day. However, there are those who object to the building of these retail parks.

The only way to get to many of these out-of-town stores is by car, so people who do not have cars cannot shop there. This does not seem to be too much of a problem. After all, they can just carry on shopping on the high street, can't they? Well no, not for everything. So much business has gone out of town that many high street shops have had to pack up.

Not all of them, of course. Walk through any UK city or town centre and you will see a lot of familiar names: WH Smith, Boots, Marks and Spencer, Topshop, Starbucks, Caffe Nero, Pizza Express. In fact, there are so many familiar names on every big shopping street that it has given rise to another complaint – that everywhere looks the same. Not so long ago, every shopping street was different – each had its own character largely thanks to the shops, restaurants and cafés there. There used to be many one-off coffee and tea shops in Britain. They were owner-run places and they were all different. There were butchers and bakers and fishmongers and hardware stores. Does your high street still have those?

Nowadays almost all regular purchases are made in the big supermarkets and they have put a lot of effort into brand building. Those brands are a guarantee of quality – and of uniformity. You can buy the same products in ASDA anywhere in the country. By being different, the old one-off shops offered choices. In their quest for standardisation and economies of scale, the big chains have actually reduced choice. This affects the whole supply chain. Farmers will only grow what they can sell and if the supermarkets want Braeburn and Red Delicious apples, then that is what is grown – and orchards of more unusual apples, such as the Bloody Ploughman or the Knobby Russet, are destroyed to make way for them.

Some smaller shops have survived, notably the corner shop whose demise was widely predicted. Corner shops cannot compete with the big supermarkets on price, but they offer convenience – they are local to the customers. Some are now part of chains, notably Spar, and their success has attracted the big supermarkets back into town. Sales are growing faster in London's neighbourhood shops than they are in the big stores and both Tesco and Sainsbury's now have a number of smaller stores. It remains to be seen whether local shops have built sufficiently strong relationships with their customers to survive this strong competition.

Where do you prefer to shop? And why?

Clusters of similar businesses are quite common. Some areas become known for certain types of shop. For example, London's Tottenham Court Road is full of PC dealers, the Lanes in Brighton is known for antiques, Hatton Garden is the place for jewellery. Clearly, these retailers are not trying to avoid the competition, rather they seem to revel in it. So why do they do it? Again, it is about volume of customers. If an area is known for a product type (e.g. PCs), then customers will flock there and not bother to go anywhere else. They know that they have a wide choice in that one place.

ACTIVITY

Find a map of your local area. Where would you want to open the following types of retail outlet:

* an upmarket restaurant
* a bar
* a clothing store
* a DIY store
* a sweet shop?

What problems might you face, i.e. what are the constraints?

Any retail business has to decide whether its strategy will be to take its stores to the customers or to try to attract customers to its stores. Desirable as it may be to set up shop in a busy area with lots of the right type of customer, it is not always possible to find suitable premises there and so it may be necessary to attract customers away from their usual haunts. This was the idea behind the first of the out-of-town superstores in the UK. There just were not sites big enough to house the vast stores that the retailers had in mind in the town centres, and so they went out of town – making sure there were good roads and ample parking, of course.

Intermediaries further up the **supply chain** (e.g. **wholesalers, agents,** distributors) may deliver goods to their customers and that makes a big difference to how they choose their location. In fact they may choose to be nearer their suppliers. It is unlikely that they will be reliant on passing trade and so they can afford to be in a more out of the way place. Good transport links are important, as is cost-effectiveness of course.

intermediaries businesses that form part of the distribution channel, passing goods on towards the end customer

Many businesses now choose to locate themselves on the Internet. This is a wonderful way to be close to the customers – right in their homes. It is important not to forget that any goods ordered will need to be delivered, though, so the location of warehouses, or suppliers if goods are coming direct, still needs to be thought through carefully.

RIGHT TIME

To deliver what the customers want exactly when they want it requires flexibility in the **supply chain** and that usually results in higher operating costs. Think about how food is sold. For millions of people, the superstore has become part of everyday life. These huge buildings frequently offer over 20,000 different products. Millions are spent weekly on food and drink. Some of these stores are open 24 hours a day, six days out of seven. This creates the impression that you can get anything you want at any time. Stores have to live up to this expectation by trying to ensure that their whole range is always in stock. Clearly, stock costs money and so accountants will always try to minimise stock levels and the capital that is tied up in that stock. Overstocks (stock that cannot be sold) are expensive as they have to be sold off cheaply or binned. This is especially a problem with perishable goods such as food.

There is therefore a tricky balancing act with stock: stores need enough to meet demand without running out, but not so much that there is a lot of waste. Stock, or inventory, management is a very difficult thing.

The only thing that stops some shops being permanently open is government legislation, i.e. the UK laws limiting the hours of trading on Sundays, and even this last hurdle can be overcome thanks to modern technology. The large grocery businesses, such as Tesco and Sainsbury's, provide Internet ordering services so that shoppers can order their food and drink at any time to suit their own needs. For a small fee, these products are then brought to the location specified by the shopper at the time specified by the shopper. However, this still will not get you a pint of milk in the middle of the night. Available delivery slots are limited to more sociable hours.

stock out
when a supplier runs out of a particular product

Making sure that goods are always available requires good logistics planning. This is a complex process with lots of scope for mistakes which may lead to **stock outs** or overstocks. An empty space on a shelf inevitably means lost sales – missed opportunities for both **retailer** and manufacturer. If customer demand was constant, then logistics would be much easier, but unfortunately demand fluctuates with people's changing tastes, the weather, changes in competitive offerings, items on the news, new campaigns – the list is endless. Imagine buying food for a small seaside café early in an English summer. How would you know how much ice cream to get in? How much soup and other warming dishes? Will the demand be for iced lattés or for hot chocolate? Alternatively, take pity on department store buyers at Christmas. If they buy too many Christmas goods, they are left with stock nobody wants in January. If they buy too few, they have missed valuable sales and gained frustrated customers.

Fernie and Sparks (2004) identified five key aspects of logistics management:

- suitable storage facilities for stock
- keeping the right amount of stock – not too much nor too little
- good communications throughout the **distribution channel** so that suppliers can respond quickly to requests for products
- transport that is capable of carrying the required quantities of products safely to their destinations
- packaging that will protect the product in transit and storage while being easily handled – so boxes should not be too big or heavy, nor too small as small packages take longer to pack.

Some products need specialist storage facilities, e.g. refrigeration or a dust-free atmosphere. All need to be located conveniently, to be secure and to be accessible for onward transportation. Retailers used to keep their stock on the premises so that they could refill shelves quickly, but only the smallest do this today. Retail space is expensive and so is better used for displaying goods rather than storing them. Large retailers have their own **distribution centres** situated close to clusters of stores so that they can restock easily. Some manage these themselves but others contract out to logistics specialists. For example, Exel manages seven of Marks and Spencer's 11 UK distribution centres as part of a range of activities that Exel is responsible for across Marks and Spencer's entire **supply chain**. These functions include imports, in-store logistics, home delivery, systems design and transportation (*Logistics Today*, 2003).

EPOS (electronic point of sale)
a computerised system that collects sales data at a retail checkout

Keeping the right amount of stock requires good sales forecasting. Most retailers and wholesalers use computerised stock control programs fed with data from **electronic point of sale systems (EPOS)**. Bar-coded products are scanned at checkouts, or by hand-held scanners in **warehouses**, and stock figures are adjusted automatically. This information can then be communicated, either by the Internet or the company's own system (Intranet) to other members of the supply chain. Replacement stock may be ordered with no further human intervention at all.

Transporting goods may sound straightforward but it is not. Some town centre shops are difficult to access and deliveries may only be permitted at certain times (usually out of hours) so as to prevent traffic hold-ups. There are restrictions on lorry size and how long drivers can drive. The thoughtless driving of lorries with the company's logo emblazoned on the side is a **PR** problem. There are environmental considerations. Trains and boats are considered less polluting than road or air, but boats are slow and so are unsuitable for the shipment of perishable goods from a distance. In the UK, there is a growing **consumer** preference for local products. Not only are they perceived as fresher, but their purchase is seen as supporting the local economy and as less polluting because they have travelled a shorter distance. Marks and Spencer tries to fill any spare space in its lorries by making it available to other companies with goods to ship. With the help of the Strategic Rail Authority, the company has also set up a rail system to deliver wine from France directly to its Midlands distribution centre (Marks and Spencer, n.d.).

Packaging has a number of functions within the supply chain. It may have a promotional role (see Chapter 8) and even be an intrinsic part of the product, e.g. an individual ice cream tub, a toothpaste tube or a bottle for shower gel. Its logistics role is protecting the goods during transit, storage and handling, and making them easier to handle, stack and secure.

Differing views of place

THE CONSUMERS' VIEW

Generally speaking, shoppers do not think very much about place or the management of the supply chain. Shoppers are usually more concerned with the availability of the goods and services that they want. The shoppers' perceptions are thus largely focused on the last link in the supply chain, usually the **retailer** (Piercy, 2002). Just

Delivering the goods

UK shoppers spent nearly £18 billion online in 2009. While there were some 'pure play' (online only) retail success stories, such as Amazon, most of the big e-tailers were well known offline brands who added the Internet to their more traditional marketing channels.

It wasn't easy to attract regular, online customers. Early e-shoppers had many concerns. Would they get the right goods? Was payment secure? Would the goods arrive on time? For e-tailers trying to build trust, getting the right product to the right place at the right time was vital. Supermarkets were unused to making customer deliveries and they struggled with the logistics. Early e-shoppers had to wait in for hours for their groceries and were frequently given substitute products for out of stock items – some of them laughably unsuitable, e.g. rat position instead of ant powder.

For most supermarkets, e-tailing was an extension on their in-store service. The ordered goods were just picked from the shop's shelves. Waitrose however, outsourced their online shopping service to e-tailing specialists Ocado. Ocado had a high-tech customer fulfilment center rather than expensive, customer-friendly stores. They could offer shorter delivery slots and their advanced stock control meant fewer substitutions. They were also the first to provide an iPhone app. Perhaps it's no surprise that they were voted online retailer of the year four times in the last five years. Although even Ocado had still not made a profit by 2009.

SOURCES: Mintel, 2010; Ocado, n.d.

take a moment to think about your daily newspaper. Millions of people take it for granted that their preferred title will be available in a local shop each morning. They don't think about how it gets there or how its components have been brought together. They want the information or entertainment it contains and they will be frustrated if it is not there when they want it. Similarly, when was the last time that you thought about where your trousers came from and the activities that made it possible for you to buy them from the outlet you did? The key management task is to ensure that the right goods are there when and where the customer wants them.

Sometimes shoppers will be very concerned about the source of the goods. These usually reflect some concern about health or ethical issues.

First, shoppers who want organic food will seek reassurance from the retailer that the original source is reliable and truly organic. This is fairly easy for a major grocer to do as the reassurance comes from their own brand and the trust that the shopper has in that reputation. You can see from this example that the provision of relevant information to help the decision-makers is critical to completing the buying process. (For more on branding, see Chapters 6, 8 and 11.)

Second, there are sometimes ethical issues that concern the shopper. For example, there have been numerous instances of child labour being used to produce goods and many shoppers in developed countries do not approve of this, considering it to be the exploitation of vulnerable children. Sellers can respond by collectively organising to reassure shoppers that their products are ethically produced. The Rugmark label is an example of one such scheme. Retailers subscribe to a neutral third-party organisation that checks the product's source to ensure that it does not use child labour. Only products that meet the specification can bear the label.

FAIRTRADE

ethical focus

The FAIRTRADE Foundation, which awards the FAIR-TRADE Mark in the UK, is made up of different organisations, such as Oxfam, the World Development Movement and Christian Aid. The Fairtrade Foundation is a member of the standard-setting umbrella organisation Fairtrade Labelling Organization International, FLO. The FAIRTRADE Mark shows consumers that the farmers and workers who produced the products received a fair and stable price. They also have safe working conditions, stronger rights and treat their environment with care.

FAIRTRADE products include cocoa, coffee, tea, sugar, bananas, orange juice, honey and cotton. Any end product that is awarded the FAIRTRADE Mark must meet strict conditions of production and the Foundation has independent assessors to check that these conditions are being met.

Through such third-party schemes, the concerns of the consumers are passed up through the supply chain to the original source of the products. The customer can be satisfied that the farmers and workers who grew the products are getting a better deal. In this way, the FAIRTRADE Mark meets consumers' need to avoid exploiting poorer workers in the developing world.

Clearly, the design, and ongoing management, of the distribution channel is extremely important. The specific design will vary from product to product and will be discussed later in this chapter. Shoppers need more than just quality goods and services; they also need a reassuring purchase experience so that they feel they can trust their suppliers and are comfortable with their purchases.

Organisations buy more things than consumers do and, just like consumers, they want to know where their goods and services come from and to buy them from suppliers they can trust.

THE ORGANISATION'S VIEW

Does a business see the **supply chain** in the same way as the shopper? The answer is that it depends on the business, what it is buying (or selling) and what it intends to do with that purchase. A local newsagent selling pick 'n' mix sweets needs small paper bags which will have to be bought in. How much effort should the newsagent put in to finding the cheapest source? After all, these are low-value items with limited impact upon the business. This is a tactical, not a strategic, decision. It is likely that the newsagent will simply add the bags to its shopping list for the next visit to the **cash and carry** (a form of **wholesaler**). In this respect, the business is acting like a typical **consumer** and will be just as frustrated if the bags are not in stock.

On the other hand, a **multinational** buying electrical components to build into its products is likely to see the supply chain in a very different way from an individual shopper. The buyer for such a company will have to answer to others for their purchase decision and so will seek a different level of reassurance about the goods and the buying situation – quite likely in writing. They will also be treated differently. Organisational buyers rarely go to the shops. Instead, salespeople call on them at their convenience.

Organisations have a view both up and down the supply chain. They may be at its end for some purchases, in its middle (as intermediaries) for others, and, if they are manufacturers, at the start of it for some. At times they are buyers, at others they are sellers.

To ensure that potential suppliers are able to meet the organisation's needs, many large organisations engage in a process of **vendor rating**, which involves evaluating sellers' performances against a set of predetermined measures. These measures usually include reviews of product range (both the current offerings and potential new ones), product quality, production capability and capacity. For example, Daimler Chrysler, the car manufacturer, uses a vendor rating system that has four broad headings, each with its own importance weighting:

- quality (40 per cent)
- delivery (25 per cent)
- price (25 per cent)
- technology (10 per cent).

Each of these broad headings has four further measures within it so the overall vendor rating system considers 16 elements of the supply relationship. Such systems can be used to assess not just potential sellers, but also existing sellers to ensure that they are still the best choice. The organisation's purpose in using a vendor rating system is to ensure that they identify and select the best suppliers for each item that they buy. In this way the company tries to make its supply chain as effective and efficient as possible (Lysons and Gillingham, 2003). Its supply chain can make or break a business and so its design is a strategic decision which requires the best information available to ensure that it is right. Vendor rating data is a key input to the decision.

When things go wrong in the supply chain, the impact is often felt throughout it; all the companies involved in the production and delivery of the goods suffer. This is one reason why it is considered good practice to view other channel members as partners rather than merely suppliers or customers. Sometimes the damage can be permanent. The BSE crisis in the early 1990s is still affecting sales of British beef across the world.

cash and carry
a wholesaler whose main customers are small retailers who visit the premises, pay for their goods, and carry them away. Cash and carry outlets do not deliver

vendor rating
a vetting process to help buyers identify where there may be potential benefits or difficulties associated with a particular supplier

insight   Faulty tyres

The Firestone Tyre Company's contract to supply the tyres for Ford's Explorer had serious consequences for a large number of people. Ford fitted the tyres to its Explorers, and sold the cars on to their own customers, i.e. dealers and distributors, who in turn sold them on to their customers, some of whom were individuals, while others were trade customers who used the Explorers in the course of their businesses.

Unfortunately, the tyres performed very badly on the road. US regulators linked accidents involving Ford Explorers and Firestone tyres to more than 250 deaths and over 800 injuries. The result has been damage claims running into millions of dollars from the relatives of the dead, and personal injury claims against both companies. The claims from the injured represent only part of the total picture. In addition, there are economic loss claims from people seeking compensation for the reduced resale value of their cars, and further lost sales as negative publicity impacts on consumers' perceptions of the two manufacturers' products.

THE PARTNERSHIP VIEW

It has become normal practice for businesses to organise partnerships both upwards and downwards in the **supply chain**. This is most evident in the **retail** field. It is now common for the tills in a store to be linked to a head-office computer. This machine checks stock quantities against predetermined levels and produces an order that is transmitted electronically to the seller's computer. The seller then takes responsibility for delivering the order to the store. There is a considerable degree of trust built into such relationships. The **retailer** benefits from reduced stock risks but pays a higher price for the flexibility that this gives. The seller has to be more flexible in production but receives a higher unit price to cover the increased costs. Thus, with the improved flow of information between the buyer and seller, both can benefit.

A seller that always delivers quality goods on time, with no subsequent problems, at a price that is acceptable to the market develops a reputation as a good company to do business with and is therefore more likely to be a successful operation. This can help it to develop its business beyond its existing set of customers or to strengthen its defences against possible newcomers to the market, providing they disseminate this information widely enough and well, perhaps through the media or, even better, **word of mouth**. Good suppliers help make the buyer's business better too. Additionally, if a business treats its sellers well, then they may be offered support in the development of new products or in helping to establish new ways of trading.

word of mouth
where members of the target audience pass on information or promotional messages to each other; *see also* viral marketing

Place management

In its simplest form, place management is only concerned with the moment at which an **exchange** of value happens. In reality, although the moment may be simple, there is usually some preparation needed to make the exchange possible. For example, you might go into a corner shop and buy a bar of chocolate. If the owner of the shop had not previously been out and bought it (usually from a **wholesaler**), then your visit would have been a waste of time. This also holds true for the wholesaler, who would have had to purchase the bars from the manufacturer. From this simple example you

Petrol crisis

Motorists were dismayed by a spate of reports about car engines unexpectedly seizing up. Many of the broken down cars were taken to garages who suspected a problem with the fuel. It took a while to track down the source of the problem as the motorists had filled their cars at a number of different places – but all the pumps used were at either Tesco's or Morrison's stores. One immediate effect of this discovery was a surge in demand for petrol from competitive outlets – some of which ran out.

The two supermarket chains accused of supplying faulty fuel then had the task of tracing the suspect petrol back up through their distribution channels. The common source of the contaminated petrol proved to be the Royal Vopak oil terminal in Essex. This storage facility was used by a number of companies, including Greenergy, a blender and wholesaler of fuels and both Tesco's and Morrison's supplier. The source of the contamination appeared to have been a component product bought for the production of unleaded fuel by yet another company which shared the Royal Vopak storage tanks, Harvest Energy.

All the supply chain members involved had to work together to solve this problem. The supermarket managers at the retail end of the supply chain had little chance of preventing this crisis, but they had to bear the brunt of the consumers' anger and their companies had to make the apologies and offer the compensation.

Then petrol prices went up a little.

SOURCES: Anon, 2009; Greenergy, 2007; Harvest Energy, 2007

Professional purchasers

Most large retail chains have teams of buyers and merchandisers who choose and source the goods that we see in store. The entry point for these careers is usually trainee assistant buyer or merchandiser, from where you can work your way up to buyer or merchandiser for your own designated ranges. The department store, Debenhams, describe these roles as follows.

Buyers take control for the overall style and direction of their department and work closely with Merchandisers and Designers so that all elements of the product make them irresistible to the customer. They must be numerate – as it's all about making money for Debenhams – as well as having outstanding people management and negotiating skills, along with an instinctive fashion sense.

Merchandisers run their own departments as independent profit centres and, by working with the Buyer, make all the key decisions relating to the product positioning, price and quantity. With the potential to manage large teams and a worldwide supply base, their strong people management and negotiation skills are tested daily.

SOURCE: Debenhams, n.d.

A shopfloor showcases the work of buyers and merchandisers throughout the supply chain

Photo courtesy of Debenhams and www.prshots.com

can see that the **supply chain** extends away from the final exchange by a series of prior exchanges. If this chain is broken at any stage, then the final exchange is at risk. Ensuring that the chain is in place and delivering the expectations of all businesses involved is an important part of the management function.

In a small business, the buying and selling tasks are likely to be only part of a manager's job. In a larger organisation, these functions are likely to be carried out by specialists in dedicated departments. In such departments there are likely to be individuals with significant amounts of product expertise. There will often be a group of people focused on selling the organisation's products: the sales team or sales department. This group has a crucial role in the relationship with customers and potential customers. Having taken the orders and made the delivery promises, it is also usual for sales departments to organise the physical delivery of the product to the customer. There may also be a buying department, or a **merchandising** department, with specialist personnel who buy particular types of product, e.g. homewares, children's fashion, men's grooming products.

ACTIVITY

Think about something important that you bought recently. How did you choose the place that you bought it from? Did you just go somewhere you'd been before, or did something else affect your choice?

Finding, and keeping, the right place for the exchange usually requires the development of successful long-term business partnerships within the **distribution channel**. Only rarely will it benefit a business to change sellers regularly. There is usually much more to be gained from working together.

THE SUPPLY CHAIN AS A NETWORK OF PARTNERS

Substantial networks, both horizontal and vertical, may be developed in pursuit of the right place design. Consider the linkages necessary for a pick-your-own (PYO) fruit farm to reach its market. Initially it might seem that there could not be a simpler form of exchange. After all, customers just take the food from the ground and pay for it. However, if we look backwards up the **supply chain**, there are a considerable number of other participants in the process. For a crop such as strawberries, most PYO farms will buy in the plants from a dedicated nursery that has grown the plants from seeds. The growth of the plants can be further encouraged by the use of fertilisers bought from agricultural merchants. Next the potential customer has to be told about the opportunity to pick fruit, and so another relationship is needed to develop the promotional aspects of the business. This may be with a local printer or the local newspaper. The place where the exchange happens affects all other aspects of marketing function (Michel et al., 2003).

Designing the supply chain

The design of the **supply chain** is a strategic management function. Its consequences are long term and far reaching. A well designed supply chain can reduce costs by minimising overlaps between channel members and cutting out redundant parts of

Delivery terms

global focus

Different countries have different trading practices. In some it may be customary for the buyer to arrange delivery of the goods, while in others it is the seller who does this. In some countries it is common practice to pay for the goods up front, whereas in others this might be considered sharp practice. It is therefore hardly surprising that this is an area where misunderstandings frequently arise.

In order to try to minimise such misunderstandings, in 1936 the International Chamber of Commerce devised a set of rules for the interpretation of international terms and conditions. These became known as **incoterms** (international commercial terms) and although they have been revised many times since, incoterms are still helping to simplify international trade today. The last revision was in 2000 and so the set of rules in force today are known as incoterms 2000. Incoterms set out how activities, costs and risks are to be split between the buyer and seller. There are 13 different terms, which fall into four main categories (see Exhibit 9.4) and they range from everything being fundamentally the responsibility of the buyer to the other extreme, where everything is fundamentally the responsibility of the seller.

Within each group there are a number of variations in the exact terms. For example, group F includes FOB (free on board), i.e. delivery is deemed to have taken place when the goods pass the ship's rail at the named port of shipment and they then become the buyer's responsibility, and FAS (free alongside ship), i.e. the seller must place the goods, cleared for export, alongside the vessel at the named port of shipment.

Exhibit 9.4 Extract from incoterms 2000

Incoterms	Description
Group C	The seller must contract for the carriage of the goods but without assuming risk of loss of, or damage to, the goods or any additional costs caused by events occurring after shipment
Group D	The seller has to bear all costs and risks required to deliver the goods to the customer
Group E	The goods are made available to the buyer at the seller's premises
Group F	The seller must deliver the goods to a carrier appointed by the buyer – the carrier then delivers the goods

SOURCE: Sitpro, n.d.

incoterms
a set of rules governing the delivery terms for international sales

the network. It can also increase companies' responsiveness to market conditions, enabling them to restock or deliver more quickly, for example.

No one channel member can control the entire supply chain. Until relatively recently, marketers focused exclusively on the chain downwards (towards the final customer) from them, i.e. their **distribution channel**. However, all the sellers in the supply chain have an impact upon each other and so the network does need to be considered as a whole – despite its sometimes awesome complexity. Chain is perhaps a misnomer as it suggests linearity, a set of links with a beginning and an end. A supply chain is really more of a network (see Exhibit 9.2). There are many different branches and routes through. Each of the network's members has something to offer and something to gain. In addition, the businesses in a network all have customers to whom they address their efforts and for whom they design a product offering. These customers may become sellers in their turn. The supply chain is built upon a succession of negotiated agreements between buyers and sellers.

There are two key words in supply chain design: effectiveness and efficiency. These two words shape the objectives for the operation of any supply chain. If the goods are not in the right place at the right time, then the **exchange** is not likely to take place and the supply chain is not effective. If there are too many costs being added to the basic product by the various players, then the final product will be too expensive and the customer may choose to buy from another source. Lack of efficiency at any stage will add to these costs and thus put the whole exchange process at risk. It takes a coordinated effort from all channel members to create an effective and efficient supply chain.

The choice of supply chain members depends on the product, the market and the tasks to be undertaken. If there are many stages in the process of manufacturing a product, the supply chain is likely to have many members. It does not stop there. Many other companies may become involved before the final customer takes delivery of their product.

Take aeroplane manufacture as an example. There can be hundreds of companies involved in the production of these large and complex products which the manufacturer, e.g. Airbus, sells to airlines or governments. To make the planes into passenger carriers, these organisational customers need other products, e.g. catering, cleaning, refuelling, airport, services, films. The providers of all these purchases form part of the airline's supply chain. The tasks of partner selection and the maintenance of the relationships are now critical issues for management (Gattorna and Walters, 1996). To further complicate the issue, companies may need to find different partners, and design different channels, in different countries as distribution infrastructures are not the same the world over.

Some products might have specific requirements for their handling from manufacturer to final customer, and this can have an influence on the choice of partner. Take ice cream, for example. Many customers have this product at home, but how did it get there? Just as customers need freezers to store the product, so does every business involved in moving the product from the manufacturer to the retailer's store. There has to be a transport system capable of moving the product in its frozen condition. Not every transport business has such resources and this limits the potential number of partners. The same idea applies to other types of product. For example, specialist transport companies transport industrial gasses in specially designed bulk tankers. The specific needs of the supply chain can thus create niche business opportunities.

ACTIVITY

You are planning a twenty-first birthday party for 400 guests. Identify the different businesses that you will need to work with to make the event a success. How will you choose each of the businesses?

MASS MARKETING OR SELECTIVE MARKETING?

The next thing to think about is the nature of the market that the company is trying to reach (Hutt and Speh, 2001). The wider the range of potential customers, the wider the **supply chain**. If there is only one customer, then the relationship between manufacturer and customer is likely to be very direct. The **distribution channel** will be exclusive, i.e. there will only be one outlet. Exhibit 9.5 illustrates this connection.

Exhibit 9.5 Exclusive distribution

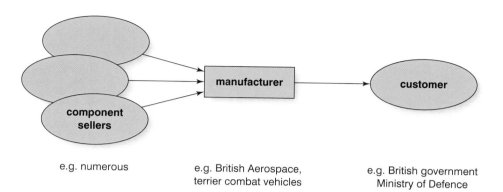

e.g. numerous   e.g. British Aerospace,   e.g. British government
                       terrier combat vehicles   Ministry of Defence

exclusive distribution
the distribution channel
has only one or two
outlets

intensive distribution
products are available at
numerous outlets

selective distribution
the distribution channel is
restricted to a few outlets

multichannel distribution
the use of different types
of channel to reach the
same target market

Exclusive, luxury goods, such as designer clothing, would normally have most restricted distribution channels, i.e. **exclusive distribution**. In extreme cases, the designers may only support one or two outlets for their products, often those directly owned by the designer. This allows them to keep very close control over their distribution.

Where there are many different types of customer, perhaps in different locations, then the pattern of connections becomes more complicated. Such situations call for **intensive distribution**, in which numerous outlets are used. In between these two extremes, there are products that are available in a number of places, but not all. This is termed **selective distribution**.

A company like Nike could not have become as large as it has by using selective or exclusive channels – it had to be intensive. Nike operates its own stores and has a large number of major retail partners, both specialist sportswear outlets (such as JJB Sports) and clothing stores. The range offered in the general clothing stores is limited so as not to challenge the specialist sports sector. This use of different types of channel to reach the same potential target group is also known as **multichannel distribution** (see Exhibit 9.6).

Exhibit 9.6 Multichannel distribution

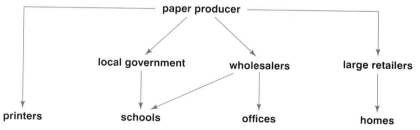

NOTE: Each member of the supply network will have numerous contacts with other businesses.

SHORT, SIMPLE CHAINS OR LONG, COMPLICATED CHAINS?

Exclusive, selective and intensive distribution are to do with the breadth of the distribution channel, i.e. how many members it has at each level in the channel. When designing a channel, it is also important to think carefully about its depth, i.e. how many levels (or intermediaries) there will be *between* the producer and the final customer (see Exhibit 9.7).

A zero-level supply chain, straight
from farmer to customer

Exhibit 9.7   Distribution channels: simple

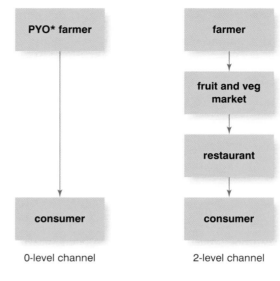

0-level channel   2-level channel

*PYO: Pick your own

The simplest distribution channel is the one that connects the producer directly to the consumer. Contrast this with the multiple channels design between a paper manufacturer and its customers in Exhibit 9.8.

Exhibit 9.8   Distribution channels: multiple

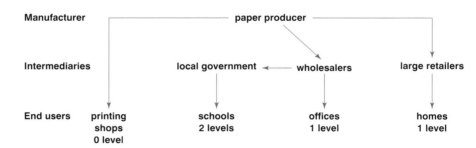

NOTE: To achieve the broadest market coverage some suppliers use many intermediaries while smaller, or more specialist, suppliers will use only some of the intermediaries available. Each member of the supply network will have numerous contacts with other businesses.

The shortest channel has no intermediaries at all. The producer sells direct to the end customer. This is called a 0-level channel or direct selling (direct sales). If there is one intermediary between the producer and the end customer, we call that a 1-level channel, while two intermediaries make a 2-level channel, etc. The longer the channel, the less control the producer has over how its products are presented to consumers (or to the final customer organisations in the case of B2B markets). You will have in your home products made by companies that you have never heard of. Do you know who made the components in your television? What about the zips in your jeans? Or who grew, or cooked, the food with a supermarket label on it in your fridge? Many producers **advertise** to consumers even though they do not deal directly with them. This is part of building a **brand** name and thereby making their goods more attractive to the intermediaries so that they stock them. A company such as Heinz is entirely dependent upon **retailers** to make sales. It redresses the power imbalance through **marketing communications** campaigns designed to persuade end customers to ask for its products when they go to the shop. In the UK, even the largest of supermarkets would not want to be without Heinz baked beans and ketchup.

ACTIVITY

Visit the Heinz website at www.heinz.com. What is its business purpose? How does it try to achieve this?

There are a number of different ways to create the potential for **exchange** between customer and business. All channels depend on a number of participants of different types who are called **channel members**. Some of the channel members are manufacturing businesses, others may be retailers and some businesses exist to provide supporting services, e.g. transport companies (see 'Channel members' above).

EXPAND YOUR KNOWLEDGE

Chandra, C. and Kumar, S. (2000) 'Supply chain management in theory and practice: a passing fad or a fundamental change?', *Industrial Management and Data Systems*, 100 (3): 100–113.

Supply chain management is seen as an integrative activity creating relationships with suppliers and customers which offer improved competitiveness and enhanced customer service. The paper provides a broader awareness of supply chain principles and concepts.

Overseas operations and market entry options

Most marketing textbooks include a substantial section on market entry options, but it is important to remember that marketing efforts do not finish once a market has been successfully entered. Very few organisations enter international markets with a short-term involvement in mind. Breaking into a new market is a complicated and costly business and most who take on the challenge will be hoping that they are setting up a long-term, profitable part of their business.

The first choice facing any seller who wishes to trade internationally is whether to:

- make the products at home and export them, or
- make the products abroad.

Most firms start by exporting. This is an easier route, with lower financial risks. Manufacturers can continue to use their existing facilities (perhaps expanded) and

indirect export
using a third party (e.g. an export management company), based in the firm's home country, to sell products abroad

direct export
when a company makes products in its home country for sale abroad and then manages the overseas sales and marketing of them itself

suppliers, just as they have always done for their domestic markets. They find an **agent** or distributor with knowledge of the target market and use them to sell, arrange delivery of, and service products overseas. This is known as **indirect export**. Larger, or more experienced, firms may handle the export themselves (**direct export**), sending personnel overseas as required. As business builds and becomes more profitable, and as the firm's knowledge of the market grows, it may set up facilities overseas – perhaps a sales or servicing office, an assembly plant, even a fully-fledged factory. (See Exhibit 9.9.)

Exhibit 9.9   Market entry and operational options

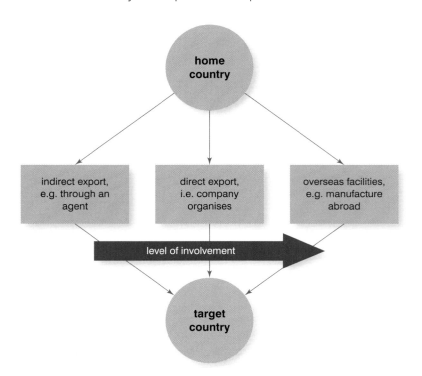

How to enter an overseas market becomes a more complex choice for services marketers who, because of the nature of services (which are intangible and cannot be stored – see Chapter 7), can rarely make the product at home and export it. Electronic services, such as banking and credit card transactions, can indeed be hosted in one country while sold and used elsewhere, but services which require the personal touch, e.g. medical care or maintenance, generally cannot. So the choices for services marketers depend upon the nature of the service. Most service companies will have to set up operations overseas if they wish to sell their product there (see 'Services' below).

In global markets expansion is often crucial to long-term business success. A larger organisation can reduce its overall costs thanks to economies of scale. These cost reductions can then be used to increase the business's competitiveness (usually by lowering prices, although there are other ways, e.g. increasing advertising) and/or its profit margins. The world's biggest retailer, Wal-Mart, has cost reduction as a key objective and although it has not always been successful in its overseas developments, it is globally feared by all of its competitors.

To become a global business a company needs to consider carefully the extension of its supply chain and the development of the new distribution channels needed.

Exhibit 9.10   Comparison of direct and indirect export

Indirect export	Direct export
The least effort for the exporter, as long as the trading partner performs well	Requires more effort, finance and resources from exporter, e.g. logistics management
Lowest risk option	Higher risk than indirect export as more investment is required, but still low risk compared to setting up more substantial overseas operations
Usually the easiest exit strategy (can cancel agreements, depending upon terms of contracts, and withdraw form market)	Ease of market exit depends on the degree of involvement, i.e. how much the firm has invested in the operation
Little or no customer contact	Owns the customer relationship, but has to manage customer-facing staff from a distance
Gains no market experience and is reliant upon agents to feed back data	Builds up market experience within the exporting organisation

In order to grow, it will need suitable partners to help provide the benefits that new customers seek.

SERVICES

Many developed countries have huge service exports, e.g. one of the UK's biggest earners of foreign currency is the City of London with its financial services products. Service providers can export their services either by sending personnel abroad, as consultants or lawyers might, or through **direct marketing** via the Internet or other communications technologies, as insurance providers or bankers might. Another alternative is to bring foreign customers to the service provider, as hospitals sometimes do. The marketing of this service happens abroad, though the service encounter would be in the hospital's home country.

Clearly, service providers do not need factories, but they may well need bases of operations. Franchising is particularly popular with **retailers** and restaurant chains. Both Marks and Spencer and McDonald's **franchise** many of their overseas outlets. At the same time, both companies also own and manage some of the stores or restaurants themselves.

Just as it is for manufacturing firms, ownership of overseas facilities represents the riskiest option for service providers because of the financial investment involved and because there is no local partner to provide the needed skills and market knowledge. This risky strategy has claimed many high-profile victims, such as British Airways which failed in their attempt to break into the US market by purchasing US Air. The American staff objected to the imposition of British working practices and BA were unable to maintain standards or to turn a profit. Sainsbury's failed in Egypt, but Tesco have done well in Ireland, the Far East and Eastern Europe. Also, the Carphone Warehouse have been hugely successful in pursuing their overseas expansion plans and can now be found in France, Spain, Germany, Sweden and the Netherlands where they use the less-limiting name 'The Phone House' (Palmer, 2005).

Topshop storms Manhattan

global focus

Glitzy, celebrity-crammed opening nights have long been a favourite with the film industry but in April 2009, it was a British fashion store that was attracting the queues: Topshop had arrived in New York.

It wasn't just the clothes that people were dying to see, Topshop's website had been hyping this opening for at least a year and promised celebrity appearances along with the coveted British street fashion. Their most famous designer, Kate Moss, was expected to open the store. Her range of floaty florals and clever layers looked like it was going to be as popular in the USA as it had already proved in the UK. Kate, wearing a long emerald green chiffon dress split to the thigh and a black leather biker jacket, arrived to rapturous applause. The crowd chanted her name along with 'we love Topshop'. On the first floor, the 'five purchases only per customer' rule was being completely ignored as her designs flew off the racks.

The USA is a notoriously difficult market to break into but, thanks to the pre-publicity and celebrity buzz, this was a highly promising beginning for the British retailer.

© Andrew H. Walker/Getty Images

Sources of power and conflict in the supply chain

The different routes through the **supply chain** to the final customer are known as **distribution channels**. Each business involved is known as a **channel member**. Any supply chain is dependent for its success on the individual contributions of its members, which are selected for their resources and skills. Each member has some power in the particular distribution channel of which it is a part (see Exhibit 9.11). Businesses with greater power have significant advantages. An extreme example is provided by Marks and Spencer. By 1996 Marks and Spencer had grown to be the world's fifth largest retailer and was making profits of £1 billion (€1.4 billion) per year. Under the chairmanship of Sir Richard Greenbury, the company was proud to announce that the vast majority of its products came from British sources. Unfortunately, the company's financial performance stalled and then collapsed. As profits slumped, Sir Richard was replaced and the management of Marks and Spencer's operations was severely overhauled. One result of these changes was a new approach to buying products. The old 'Buy British' strategy went and, as a result, several of Marks and Spencer's old suppliers collapsed. In this channel, Marks and Spencer was the dominant player and even had the power to close down other members' businesses.

This example is related here because it illustrates the importance of the relationships between channel members. In most cases businesses recognise that being too dependent on another business is potentially dangerous (in fact, Marks and Spencer did, at one time, have a policy of never allowing a supplier to become dependent upon its orders so as to avoid this situation). Most businesses aim to have a variety of different customers, which spreads the risks and reduces the chance of collapse if one partner fails.

Exhibit 9.11   Factors influencing the relationship between buyers and sellers

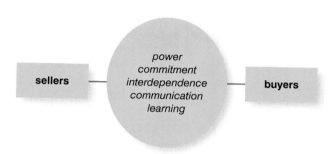

In the example above, Marks and Spencer had power because of its size and consequent financial strength. Most businesses do not have sufficient resources to control the whole supply chain. There are, however, other sources of power that channel members can use to gain advantage in their relationships. The main source of power, outside that of financial influence, is knowledge or expertise. This is known as **referent power**.

Businesses that are expanding into new areas look for partners that have knowledge of that particular market. This knowledge will help to reduce mistakes and to build relationships that may lead to further profitable developments. Specialist retailers such as UK multiple Jessops (cameras and other optical instruments) survive because customers come to their stores expecting the staff to be well informed. This is the basis of specialist retailing across the globe: from fashion shops, where the merchandisers are expected to be aware of trends and details, to delicatessens, where staff should know a serrano from a parma.

referent power
influence over others gained through superior knowledge or expertise

A third source of power in the supply chain comes from specific regulations or laws that are used to regulate markets. This is also known as **legitimate power**. This form of power can be used to increase control over the other channel members. This is definitely the case when one partner owns a patent on the required item. This type of power is commonly found in pharmaceutical markets where drug companies can legally protect their investment in new products for a number of years. No competitor can make Viagra until its legal protection runs out, unless its inventor, Pfizer, decides to allow other businesses to buy production licences. The Insight box below, 'Pause', contains another illustration of how control of a specific technology can bring about market power.

legitimate power
influence over others conferred by law or regulations

Creating a **brand** is another way of gaining legal support for your products. Millions are spent on creating images that position the brands in the market. A brand needs to be able to protect its image if it is to be able to charge a premium price for the products it offers. The law can be used to protect a brand in a number of ways. There have been cases of **retailers** virtually copying a manufacturer's branded product and selling it as if it were the retailer's own product. ASDA was found guilty of this when it copied the McVitie's Penguin biscuit bar. The court took the view that

JVC is a Japanese electronics company that invented VHS, a system for recording TV pictures. A few years before JVC patented its invention, Sony had launched its own TV recording system, which was known as Betamax. Although the two companies had an agreement to share each other's technologies, both of them wanted to create the dominant system. The stage was set for a global battle between these two Japanese companies and other recording systems, such as those invented by Philips and Grundig (two European companies), and RCA in America. The non-Japanese companies did not provide the business support needed for their systems to engage in global marketing and their products gradually disappeared.

Sony had the technically superior system but wanted to maintain control over its distribution and restricted production to a small number of manufacturing sites. JVC, recognising the technical inferiority of the VHS system, decided to allow many other companies to make VHS-based video recorders. The company now had partners across the world and could thus reduce the costs of manufacture, allowing lower prices for consumers. These two advantages, of price and availability, sped up consumer acceptance of the JVC system. To reach this wider audience Hollywood made more videos in VHS format than in Betamax format, and this gave JVC even more advantage in the market. Allowing its technology to be used widely did not weaken JVC. Instead, it gave it a winning advantage over its rival.

Some years later a similar format war arose between Sony's Blu-ray and Toshiba's and NEC's HDD DVD technologies.

such activities were intended to mislead the customer as to the origin of the product, and were therefore unacceptable. This case illustrates the problems that can arise between channel members when one challenges the power of another's brand. (For more on branding, see Chapters 6 and 11.)

A well-designed supply chain should limit the potential for conflict between the channel members. Any conflict reduces effectiveness in the supply chain and may ultimately lead to channels being closed off. Failure to resolve conflict between members, without the use of the law courts, should be seen as a failure of the management of the buyer–seller relationship.

EXPAND YOUR KNOWLEDGE

Cox, A (1999) 'Power, value and supply chain management', *Supply Chain Management: An International Journal*, 4 (4): 167–175.

Andrew Cox provides a review of the dominant ideas that inform supply chain management thinking. A more analytically robust way of understanding supply chains is laid out.

Marketing functions in the supply chain

As a product passes along the **supply chain,** its costs rise, partly because the activities carried out at each stage (e.g. transport, storage, re-packaging) have to be paid for, but also because each intermediary needs to make a profit. This is why the shorter the channel, generally speaking, the lower the final price. There would be no point to this if each stage in the chain did not also add value to the product. Both parties to an exchange want good value and so customers must value the product more highly than the **retailer** did and so be prepared to pay more for it (see Chapters 1 and 10 for exchanges and customer value). The members of the supply chain make their contributions to the eventual product experience in a number of ways.

STOCK HOLDING

For a retailer, having stock available is critical to success because usually no stock means no sales. Stock that does not sell is a waste of the retailer's money, so every effort is made to minimise this. This often means putting pressure on sellers to hold stocks away from the retailer's stores but ready to be called in at short notice if required. This **just-in-time** (JIT) or quick response (QR) approach reduces the retailer's waste but increases the seller's financial risk if the products do not sell.

TRANSPORTATION

Clearly, there must be a means to get the product to the customer. Consumers often visit stores themselves and so they take care of the transport of their purchases themselves. Businesses are likely to require delivery. Transportation is often contracted out to **logistics** services who are outside the buyer–seller relationship (see 'Channel members' above) or companies may use couriers, or even the post office. Online bookseller Amazon may now have its own warehouse (it did not originally, but relied on others to fulfil orders), but they outsource their deliveries.

For some products the task of transportation is complicated by the nature of the product itself (e.g. moving natural gas from the North Sea to homes). The transportation system for this example includes production platforms, pumping stations and thousands of miles of pipeline. Without that specialist transportation system this market could not exist.

INFORMATION GATHERING

This is a function that is undertaken by all participants. Information gathering does not necessarily require a formal market research project as all businesses obtain information on the markets that they serve as the result of their day-to-day operations. Many small businesses fail to recognise the value of this by-product of their work and therefore lose out on numerous marketing opportunities. Successful businesses, however, will analyse the information to shape the ways in which they approach their customers, both current and potential.

In some cases, the information is shared with other members of the supply chain. This sharing activity helps to improve the efficiency and effectiveness of the chain as a whole, and is evidence of healthy relationships between the participants.

COMMUNICATING

This function helps to develop efficiency in the supply chain. If information can be shared quickly, then the costs of operation can be reduced. Most major retail businesses use **EPOS (electronic point of sale)** systems to capture information from their stores. Such systems use the barcodes on products to identify the items and quantities that have been sold. This data is then sent to a head-office computer that adds up all of the individual stores' information. If more stock is needed, the central

EPOS (electronic point of sale)
a computerised system that collects sales data at a retail checkout

computer can place an order with the seller's computer using an EDI (electronic data interchange) system. Replacement products can thus be ordered without any human effort. These systems can work 24 hours a day, seven days a week and are a major force in the globalisation of retailing.

Constantly swapping business partners is inefficient. It leads to additional costs in selecting and evaluating prospective candidates. The development of long-term relationships helps to create trust and facilitates the exchange of information between the partners. In the longer term, this reduces the costs in the supply chain and brings financial benefits to all members.

PROMOTING

All buyers and sellers in the supply chain will promote their goods and services to each other. The final consumer does not see the majority of such promotional efforts, but they are vital to the development of the various relationships in the supply chain.

Promotional activities can be very sophisticated and behind the scenes, such as a manufacturer giving the retailer a retrospective discount dependent on the volume of product sold in a particular period of time. Alternatively, the effort can be blatant, such as Debenhams' Blue Cross Sale advertisements that announce 20 per cent discounts on specific days (often on Tuesdays to boost sales in the quieter part of the week). Some retailers combine the two forms, such as KwikSave's '£1 off Beefeater Gin' promotion. In this case, the product is a brand of Allied Domecq, a wine and spirit distribution company. This company sees it as in its own interests to support the retailer in promoting its product in preference to those of its competitors.

The possible objectives and the various methods for these promotional activities are discussed more fully in Chapter 8.

e-channels

ELECTRONIC DISTRIBUTION

One of the biggest changes the Internet has brought to our lives is through electronic distribution. Anyone who has played a game through their mobile telephone or listened to music on an MP3 player has probably downloaded some software from a website. Computers' anti-virus protection can be automatically updated online at a time that is convenient to the customer – even in the middle of the night.

The possibilities are growing almost daily. You can download a complete movie through the Internet or watch missed television programmes on a PC. With the spread of new technologies, download speeds are constantly increasing and the quality of transmission is improving. The Internet offers 24/7 access to services delivered directly to the receiver's PC. This level of convenience is something that store-based retailers cannot match and gives **e-tailers** (using e-distribution) a distinct market advantage.

e-tailers
online retailers

BUSINESS TO BUSINESS (B2B)

Over the last decade, the revolution in communications technology has affected almost all businesses. As defined in this chapter, the concept of place has two major components: time and space. The Internet has affected both of these.

In the B2B sector, some small businesses still use paper-based ordering systems. Salespeople may collect orders personally and forward them to a central sales office. However, hand-held computers and other electronic devices are rapidly replacing the old systems. The Internet creates opportunities for customers to send in their orders without any such visits from salespeople. Online customers can choose the time when the ordering will take place and can be shown a much wider variety of products than any sales representative is able to carry.

It is this capacity for carrying information, and for transmitting it so speedily, that makes the Internet so effective as a channel for communication. Buyers can surf the net looking for potential suppliers from anywhere in the world. Similarly, suppliers can also use the Internet to find potential customers anywhere in the world. Some facilitating businesses exist simply as portals, allowing sellers to post their products on the host site (for a fee, of course). This saves the buyers search time and the sellers gain access to a worldwide marketplace. One such business is click2procure, which has over 1, 000 supplier businesses listed, each paying around €3,000 for the privilege. This may seem expensive but the payback comes from the €1 billion worth of contracts that have been arranged via the online trading system. One estimate is that this system has reduced buying costs by up to 25 per cent for some contracts.

For example, the German electronics giant Siemens has set up an EDI system that allows it to communicate directly with its suppliers for a quarter of all its procurement. Although this represents a significant advance, there are still some major drawbacks associated with EDI systems. Most importantly, the initial development costs are high. Then there is a requirement for the suppliers to buy in to the system. Also not all members of the **distribution channel** will have the same systems which can cause compatibility problems. The Internet helps here as it provides a common communications platform. Siemens recognised the benefits of this type of structure for its operations and set a target of 50 per cent of all products to be sourced via the Internet. For Siemens, this means that products worth around €20 billion will be traded annually over the Internet. As the software available

CRM focus — Web support

The British Red Cross ran an online campaign to encourage repeat contributions. The interactive campaign was also designed to provide greater understanding of its supporters.

It employed an e-CRM specialist company to analyse the paths that visitors to the website followed. From this, it was able to work out what prompts people to donate online and what aspects of the site visitors found most attractive. Later development was planned to include the ability to monitor individuals' donation records. Knowing how much, and how often, people donate will mean that they will know when a request for cash is more likely to be successful and how much to ask for. Charities routinely ask donors for a little more than they gave the last time.

Charities are always looking for ways to reduce the costs of obtaining donors and the new system should help there too. Thanks to digital technology, it will be cheaper for the Red Cross to communicate with donors and so a greater proportion of each pound will go directly towards its work.

In the longer term, the organisation hopes to provide supporters with personalised information about the campaigns they have contributed to via the website. This, it is hoped, will build on this positive relationship, and encourage people to give more, more often.

develops into mass-market applications, so the number of smaller companies able to take advantage of electronic trading will also grow dramatically, and the shape of the exchange relationship will alter accordingly.

BUSINESS TO CUSTOMER (B2C)

The bulk of commercial electronic transactions are B2B, but **consumers** are catching up as e-shopping becomes more popular. Many retailers who never used **direct marketing** techniques, such as catalogues or telesales, are now online – albeit reluctantly in some cases. In the UK, it is now unheard of for any major retailer not to have a web presence.

Initially, customers were reluctant to shop online as they did not trust the technology. They were worried about credit card fraud, whether the goods would ever turn up, whether they would be in good condition, what they could do if they wanted to return something. Advances in security, the experience of others, and the appearance of known and trusted companies and **brands** online have reassured them, and now books, music and flowers are commonplace online purchases while the more adventurous customers also buy such products as groceries, electronics, household goods and clothing. Convenience has won shoppers over and, far from being the bargain hunters that the early e-shoppers were, today's time-starved consumers are prepared to pay extra for their groceries, in the form of delivery charges, so that they can shop from home (Huang and Oppewal, 2006).

The willingness of consumers to shop online has had a knock-on effect in B2B markets. Previously, it was necessary to have shops, often large ones and often chains of them, if you wanted to sell to consumers. Now products can be sold from a website without the need for such expensive investment. This has changed the competitive nature of many markets (e.g. booksellers). It is easier for new competitors to enter markets and it is easier for producers to sell direct. Internet retailers are judged by the impression their website makes. It is much cheaper to build an impressive website than an impressive shop, and so smaller companies can compete much more easily with larger ones.

There are snags, of course. Manufacturers have little or no experience of dealing with consumers. They still need to break down bulk as consumers will not want to buy a case of mayonnaise, just a jar. Then there is delivery. This is where many of the direct sellers fall down and where they lose the trust of their customers. In the early days, Internet-ordered goods were frequently late, wrong, damaged or were 'no-shows'. It is still vital to get the right goods to the right customer at the right time – and that is not such an easy task.

CUSTOMER TO CUSTOMER (C2C)

One of the most radical changes that the Internet has made to supply chains is the introduction of another channel member – the consumers themselves. Some consumers have always passed on goods in a small way, usually second-hand goods, maybe some unwanted gifts (or more dubiously acquired items), but this activity was so small-scale that it barely registered in the commercial world. The World Wide Web has provided the means for individuals to access thousands, even millions, of other individuals and so has opened the way for a host of small-scale exchanges and facilitated the birth of numerous businesses.

Some businesses tap into this potential by offering services for individual sellers. For example, Amazon marketplace is a forum where individuals can offer books and other items for sale, either through a listing or by auction, but without the risks inherent in running an Internet business as Amazon manage the site and collect the payments for them (for a commission of course). Another, even bigger, example is eBay, which claimed 181 million users worldwide in 2007 (eBay, n.d.). Their phenomenal reach is often cited as the reason for the collapse of a number of small antiques and collectibles shops – they are just no longer competitive.

So **supply chains** become ever more complex, ever harder to manage. New members join, although sometimes they are uninvited. Others leave. The concept of place is a dynamic one and it is one of management's major challenges to keep up with it.

For the marketer, new technology allows new services to be created and these will need to be distributed to customers. These new opportunities also bring potential dangers. In a digital world, it is very difficult to control the distribution of a digital product. If you have an MP3 player, then you may be using pirated recordings. Services such as Napster grew from individuals illegally copying CD-based music and making it available through the Internet. With physical products a counterfeiter has to create a manufacturing facility, and that takes resources. With digital products the copying and distribution can be done at the press of a button. In the future, marketers will have to pay more attention to protecting the distribution of their digital products if they are to secure the maximum return on their investments.

EXPAND YOUR KNOWLEDGE

Pearson, M.M. (1981) 'Ten distribution myths', *Business Horizons*, 24 (3): 17–23.

Michael Pearson goes through 10 myths in turn, explaining that these myths exist due to our lack of understanding of the true nature of distribution.

SUMMARY

Throughout this chapter we have seen that effective place management is vitally important to the marketing function. The elements of space and time are combined to create opportunities in which buyers and sellers can come together. A clear understanding of the buyer's needs, not just from the product but from the exchange itself, helps the seller to shape an offer that maximises the chances of an exchange.

Most **exchanges** will use existing supply chain networks. These are formed from different types of business that are connected by their own exchange relationships. These networks have many forms, from the simple (farmer direct to consumer) to the complex (Boeing building a 747). As the networks become more sophisticated, so there is more likelihood that the members will begin to operate as business partners. These partnerships may be for a particular project or on a long-term basis.

Each business in the supply chain has its own skills and capabilities. These are a source of business power in its relationship with the other members of the network. In most cases there is little open conflict, but there is usually some tension because of the opposing profit objectives.

physical distribution
the process of moving goods and services between businesses and consumers

In the twenty-first century, business exchange relationships are increasingly global. We have seen how changes in communications and **physical distribution** have made this growth possible. As the distances between buyers and sellers have increased, the management of the physical movement of goods has become progressively more important and more complex. In recent times there has been massive technological changes, and these changes in communication and transportation technologies have had a massive impact on our ideas of place. As technology continues its rapid development, marketers will need to be open to change if they are to maintain their business's effectiveness.

Successful management of place also requires an understanding of its role in the marketing function. Place offers opportunities for information gathering, for testing new products, for trying out promotional techniques and for getting feedback on pricing strategies.

A manager's ability to create, sustain and develop relationships is a fundamental skill in generating business success. To manage place well requires that you manage relationships well. These relationships will be both internal (with other departments that affect the flow of products through the business) and external (with customers and suppliers) (Gadde and Håkansson, 2001).

Getting all the activities that come under the heading 'Place' right will set the scene for a successful exchange. For that to happen, marketers must ensure that the right goods get to the right customer in the right time and space.

CHALLENGES REVIEWED

Now that you have finished reading the chapter, look back at the challenges you were set at the beginning. Do you have a clearer idea of what's involved?

Hints:

- breadth of distribution coverage and merchandising support – see also 'Marketing functions in the supply chain'
- marketing functions in the supply chain
- how do the members of the supply chain add value? (Also branding)
- the importance of building relationships through the supply chain
- junk food and child obesity problems – what responsibilities do schools have to the children in their care?

READING AROUND

Classic article

Peter Drucker (1962) 'The economy's dark continent', *Fortune*, April: 265–70.

Website

www.upmystreet.com – where you can find out 'everything you want to know about an area'; also try ACORN's neighbourhood profiling system.

Directory

Yellow Pages – to see the variety of businesses, and the range of different suppliers that they can use.

Books

John Fernie and Leigh Sparks (2004) *Logistics and Retail Management: Insights into Current Practice and Trends from Leading Experts*. London: Kogan Page.
Harvard Business School (2006) *Harvard Business School on Supply Chain Management*. Boston: HBR Press.

Video

BBC *Mary Queen of Shops* – retailing insights.

Magazine

Retail Week, UK

SELF-REVIEW QUESTIONS

1. What is a supply chain and what is its purpose? (see page 319)
2. How can a manufacturing business be both a buyer and a seller? (see page 319)
3. What is the main function of an agent? (see page 323)

4. Why do major supermarkets, such as Tesco and Sainsbury's, have Internet stores when they have invested so much in physical supermarkets? (see pages 327–8)

5. How can a firm use the concept of place to help it position its business against its competitors? (see pages 325–6)

6. Heinz engages in direct marketing communications to the final consumers of its products. Why it is unlikely to engage in direct delivery of its products to those customers? (see pages 320–1)

7. Why would businesses want to create long-term relationships with their suppliers? (see page 332)

8. Why is it important that the supply chain should be responsive to customers' needs? (see page 330)

9. What is vendor rating and in what kind of business would you be most likely to find it? (see page 331)

10. Why is product expertise important to businesses? (see pages 342–3)

11. What is the difference between direct export and indirect export? (see page 340)

12. Why does the physical nature of the product sometimes affect the choice of supply chain participants? (see page 236)

Honest, tasty and real

Read the questions, then the case material, and then answer the questions.

Questions

1. How would you categorise Dorset Cereal's distribution strategy before and after the re-positioning exercise? Why?
2. Discuss the advantages and drawbacks of a brand like Dorset Cereals being stocked by large supermarkets such as Tesco and Sainsbury's.
3. Revisit the section headed 'marketing functions in the supply chain' above. How can Dorset Cereals and its retail partners manage these marketing activities to the best, mutual advantage? What would you expect them to do?

Muesli has gone through a rejuvenation of late and Dorset Cereals is largely responsible. Back in the early 2000s, muesli was worthy but rather dull. Everyone knew it was good for them but not everyone wanted to eat it. Supermarkets stocked the big brand names, such as Alpen, and their own label products. Health food stores stocked the real deal but it was often compared to sawdust or cat litter.

Dorset Cereals had been around since 1985 and was sold in most of the specialist health food shops such as Holland and Barrett. However, their sales figures were flat even though healthy cereals were the only category in the cereal market showing a healthy growth. The breakfast cereal market generally was saturated. Cereals had been so well marketed that it was hard to find new customers or ways to grow the business. Also, it was dominated by large multinationals like Kellogg's and Nestlé who filled whatever space remained on supermarket shelves once their own label products had been displayed.

According to Mintel (2008), grocery multiples like the well-known supermarkets account for 94 per cent of all breakfast cereal sales. There are a number of niche players who sell through health food shops or even, like Mymuesli, online but If they wanted to make any serious inroads into the market at all, Dorset Cereals needed to be on the supermarket shelves. To achieve that they needed a radical brand makeover.

They researched the market and interrogated their own brand, establishing its values clearly. They realised that the supermarket's shelves were already full of cereals that claimed to have natural qualities and healthy ingredients but none of them claimed to taste good! Dorset Cereals re-positioned itself as 'honest, tasty and real'. This new positioning was encapsulated in a radical new brand identity. A simple, eyecatching leaf icon

adorned the improved packaging. The leaf symbolised the natural ingredients of the muesli and was easily recognisable even when re-coloured for different recipes, or turned into a cellophane window on the pack through which the product could be seen. It soon came to represent Dorset Cereals in the minds of both consumers and trade.

Previously, the muesli had been packaged in basic plastic bags that:

- faded into the background on shelves and so were rarely noticed
- would not stay upright on display stands and so looked a mess in store and irritated shopkeepers
- failed to protect the product well enough in transit causing wastage
- regularly spilt cereal across kitchen tables to the intense annoyance of consumers.

The new packs were bigger and made from recyclable card. They stood out, stood up and kept the cereal in good condition whilst being transported, stored and displayed in store. They also featured the kind of quirky copy that makes a good breakfast time read.

Armed with this new look, the company approached the major supermarket chains, some of whom (notably Waitrose) took the brand on trial. With its more appealing brand identity, it flew off the shelves and further orders were placed. Soon it stopped being the preserve of upmarket stores like Waitrose, and became a staple on the shelves of Tesco, Sainsbury's, Morrisons and the rest. At the same time, the Dorset Cereals sales team persuaded a number of high end, independent retailers to stock the brand and so they kept up the muesli's luxury image. In a later development, the company launched individual portion catering packs for hotels and restaurants and so broke into yet another new market thanks to imaginative packaging.

As a result of the improved distribution, Dorset Cereal's market share more than doubled, outstripping competitor's mueslis and even growing the breakfast cereal category overall.

By making their cereal look more exciting, Dorset had got people more excited about breakfast.

SOURCES: Mintel, 2008; WARC, 2007

REFERENCES

Anon (2007) 'Tesco petrol "back to normal"', *The Independent* (online), 6 March. Available at: **news.independent.co.uk/uk/transport/article2332263.ece** (accessed 21/04/2007).

Bellis, M. (2007) *The unusual history of MS DOS the Microsoft operating system*, about.com, part of the New York Times Company. Available at: **inventors.about.com/library/weekly/aa033099.htm** (accessed 18/04/2007).

Chandra, C. and Kumar, S. (2000) 'Supply chain management in theory and practice: a passing fad or a fundamental change?', *Industrial Management and Data Systems*, 100 (3): 100–113.

Cox, A (1999) 'Power, value and supply chain management', *Supply Chain Management: An International Journal*, 4 (4): 167–175.

Debenhams (n.d.) *Buying and merchandising*, Debenhams. Available at: **www.debenhamsweddings.com/site_services/article_summary.jsp?FOLDER%3C%3Efolder_id=4112323&bmUID=1177242009406** (accessed 22/04/2007).

eBay (n.d.) *Business Centre*, eBay. Available at: **pages.ebay.co.uk/businesscentre/index.html** (accessed 24/04/2007).

Fernie, J. and Sparks, L. (2004) 'Retail logistics: changes and challenges', in J. Fernie and L. Sparks (eds), *Logistics and Retail Management*: *Insights into Current Practice and Trends from Leading Experts* (2nd edn). London: Kogan Page. pp. 1–25.

Gadde, L.E. and Håkansson, H. (2001) *Supply Network Strategies*. London: Wiley.

Gattorna, J. and Walters, D. (1996) *Managing the Supply Chain: A Strategic Perspective*. Basingstoke: Macmillan.

Greenergy (2007) *Fuel quality statement,* Greenergy, 2 March. Available at: **www.greenergy.com/company/news_media/current_releases.html#Feb_statement** (accessed 21/04/2007).

Harvest Energy (2007) *Statement by Harvest Energy on South East of England Fuel Supply Issues*, Harvest Energy, 4 March. Available at: **www.harvestenergy.co.uk/news_story.php?articleID=20** (accessed 21/04/2007).

Hollander, S.C. (1960) 'The Wheel of Retailing', *Journal of Marketing*, 25 (Jul): 37–42.

Huang,Y. and Oppewal, H. (2006) 'Why consumers hesitate to shop online: an experimental choice analysis of grocery shopping and the role of delivery fees', *International Journal of Retail and Distribution Management*, 34 (4/5): 334–53.

Hutt, M. and Speh, T. (2001) *Business Marketing Management*. New York: Harcourt.

IBM (n.d.) *IBM archives 1981*. Available at: **www-03.ibm.com/ibm/history/history/year_1981.html** (accessed 18/04/2007).

Logistics Today (staff reporter) (2003) 'Exel and Marks and Spencer announce supply chain partnership', *Logistics Today*, 31 March. Available at: **http://logistics today.com/mag/outlog-story-5000/**.

Lysons, K. and Gillingham, M. (2003) *Purchasing and Supply Chain Management*. Harlow: FT/Prentice Hall.

Marks and Spencer (n.d.) *The Company, Our Responsibilities, Environment, Transport*, Marks and Spencer. Available at: **www.marksandspencer.com/gp/node/n/45941031?ie=UTF8&mnSBrand=core** (accessed 21/04/2007).

McGoldrick, P. (2003) *Retail Marketing*. Maidenhead: McGraw-Hill.

Michel, D., Naudé, P., Salle, R. and Valla, J.P. (2003) *Business-to-Business Marketing*. Basingstoke: Palgrave Macmillan.

Mintel (2008) *UK Breakfast Cereals Market Report*. London: Mintel.

Mintel (2010) *e-commerce - UK February 2010*. London: Mintel.

Ocado (n.d.) 'Our awards', Available from *http://www.ocado.com/theocadoway/awardwinning%20service/our-awards.html*, (accessed 29/07/2010)

Ocado (n.d.) 'About as', Available from *http://www.ocadogroup.com/about-us/*, accessed 29/7/2010

Palmer, A. (2005) *Principles of Services Marketing* (4th edn). Maidenhead: McGraw Hill.

Pearson, M.M. (1981) 'Ten distribution myths', *Business Horizons*, 24 (3): 17–23.

Piercy, N. (2002) *Market-led Strategic Change*. Oxford: Butterworth Heinemann.

SITPRO (n.d.) *Incoterms – a general guide*, SITPRO. Available at: **www.sitpro.org.uk/trade/incoterms1.html** (accessed 27/10/2006).

WARC (2007) 'Design Effectiveness Awards', Design Business Association. Available at: **http://www.warc.com/ArticleCenter/Default.asp?CType=A&AID=Home EC90615 & Tab=A** (accessed 30/12/09).

Price

CHAPTER CONTENTS

Introduction
Why it is so important to get the price
  right
Pricing viewpoints
Pricing in the mix
Pricing objectives
Pricing techniques
Pricing methods
Pricing strategies
International pricing
Pricing tactics
Changing the price
Price elasticity of demand
Pricing on the Internet
Summary
Challenges reviewed
Reading around
Self-review questions
Mini case study
References
Appendix: additional cost-based pricing
  activity

PRICE CHALLENGES

The following are illustrations of the types of decision that marketers have to take or issues they face. *You aren't expected to know how to deal with the challenges now*; just bear them in mind as you read the chapter and see what you can find that helps.

- You run a medium-sized business, a second-hand car dealership. A competitor, the showroom on the other side of town, reduces its prices. Should you do the same? What will happen if you don't and if you do?

- You have decided that it is a good time for your business to grow. The business is fashion design and is just getting known. You need to make more money to fund that growth: to make sample garments for the shows and to give away to celebrities. Could changing prices help at all? Should you put them down, or up?

- You have developed a new product. It is brand new, a technological breakthrough: a teleporter. It will make most other forms of transport redundant. How do you know how much to charge for it?

- You work for a large chain of furniture stores. Business is slack and competition for the few customers buying furniture is fierce. Your boss suggests offering credit deals to low-income households who would find it hard to borrow money from a bank as they are too great a risk. What are the potential drawbacks to this idea?

- Yours is a multinational company with branches in most countries. Incomes and currencies vary. How can you set prices for your televisions that will maximise profits in the richer countries without losing business in the poorer markets?

Introduction

Price is often a seriously undervalued part of the marketing mix. On the one hand, this is a great shame as many companies miss out on the competitive edge that the creative use of pricing brings. On the other hand, it is a good thing for the marketers who do appreciate the finer points of pricing. Pricing can be a devastating competitive weapon.

Only about 8 per cent of companies base their pricing decisions on serious pricing research. Few companies revise their prices often enough, most thinking that it is good enough to set them once a year, along with the budgets (Cox, 2001). Other common mistakes include not taking into account the rest of the marketing mix and focusing too much on costs.

Price is the odd one out in the **marketing mix**. The other three elements can be perceived as costs but the price of the goods and services a firm sells is a major determinant of its profit – and most businesses' primary aim is to make high profits. Pricing strategy, therefore, is a key part of a firm's overall marketing strategy.

As an alternative to, or in combination with, other marketing mix elements, a company can use pricing to improve the customer's perception of the product's value. Lowering the price is not the only way to do this; in fact, it might be counterproductive, making the product seem cheap. This is where creativity and judgement come in. This chapter will attempt to show how that works.

Through most of this chapter, price will be used in the simpler sense of the money charged for a product (unless otherwise stated). However, there is more to price than the price tag. The price to the customer is everything they have to give up to obtain the product. This includes time, effort and alternative purchases. The chapter will begin by considering the implications of the price of a product and how it affects a business. It will move on to look at the different influences on price setting and how prices can be used to help achieve marketing objectives. Pricing strategies and tactics for both new and existing products will be covered alongside some of the additional complexities of pricing in multiple countries. Prices are not fixed once and for ever more, so it is important to understand the implications of changing prices. The chapter then makes a brief excursion into economics for price elasticity of demand – an important concept for marketers as it helps them to forecast sales at different price levels. It finishes with a brief look at the special case of pricing on the Internet.

Why it is so important to get the price right

(selling) price
how *much* each product is sold for

profit
the difference between what something costs to make and the price for which it is sold

objective
a goal or target

The **price** of the goods and services a firm sells is a major determinant of its **profit** – and most businesses' primary aim is to make high profits. Pricing strategy, therefore, is a key part of a firm's overall marketing strategy. Even not-for-profit organisations usually need to cover their costs if they want to continue their existence, and so their costs must be covered too. In hard times, companies may be focused on survival rather than on profits, but then too, they need to pay careful attention to their pricing strategies. As the one part of the marketing mix that delivers money to the firm, rather than takes it out, price is always important.

The prices an organisation charges have a direct bearing on key corporate and marketing **objectives**, as described below.

PROFIT AND REVENUE

It is easy enough to sell a lot of something – just sell it really cheaply. Firms that use this technique will lose out on profit, of course. So why not set the price really high?

insight   What is profit?

Profit is what's left over when all the bills have been paid.

sales revenue – costs = profit

So to make the most profit, you need to get in as much money as possible (revenue):

sales revenue = sales volume × selling price

and pay out as little as possible (costs).

Here's an example of how to work out profit. Kidzone clothing sells 100 T-shirts at £5.00 each. Each T-shirt costs £1.00 to make and sell. Sales revenue from the T-shirts is:

100 (volume) × £5 (price) = £500

The company's profit is:

£500 (sales revenue) – £100 (total costs) = £400.

Now the firm will not sell anything at all. This much is obvious, but what is not so easy is finding the spot in the middle: the highest price at which the most people will buy. This is the price that will earn the most profit.

Generally speaking, marketing focuses on maximising **sales revenue**, rather than on keeping **costs** down. However, if the costs are too high for the price, no amount of clever marketing can make up for it.

Finance people have been known to dismiss marketing as an unnecessary cost. The marketers' response is that marketing expenditure is an investment in the firm's future. It is true, however, that pricing is the only part of the marketing mix that does not involve financial outlay.

sales revenue (turnover)
the income a firm receives from the sale of goods and services

costs
a firm's payments to suppliers, etc.

IMAGE

'Pile it high, sell it cheap' is a motto that has been attributed to various supermarkets. Is this a strategy designed to promote an upmarket or downmarket image? The strategy of reducing price, and so selling large volumes, appears a downmarket ploy. Price affects image.

SURVIVAL

A sure way to go out of business is to set prices lower than costs. Firms may get away with this in the short term (see 'Contribution pricing' and 'Loss leaders' below), but keeping prices too low for too long is a recipe for disaster.

MARKET SHARE

If a company wants to increase sales, this is likely to mean taking customers away from a competitor. Any increase in one firm's **market share** means a decrease in another's. One of the most common ways to do this is by undercutting competitors' prices (see 'Market penetration' and 'Predatory pricing' below).

Pile it high, sell it cheap

© iStockphoto.com/Juanmonino

EXPAND YOUR KNOWLEDGE

Oxenfeldt, A.R. (1973) 'A decision-making structure for price decisions', *Journal of Marketing*, Jan: 48–53.

Alfred Oxenfeldt notes that many pricing decisions are intuitive. In this article he introduces a framework for pricing decisions, pricing objectives and data that can be used to help determine prices.

Pricing viewpoints

WHAT IS A PRICE?

A basic definition of **price** is:

The money charged for a product or service.

That does sound obvious and there is more to it than that. Think about what you *really* pay for a product, say a computer. There is the price of the PC itself, but then there are other things too: peripherals, software, maybe service agreements. The customer and the salesperson may see the price differently. The customer may have gone into the store to buy a PC and have a price in mind for that. The salesperson may see the PC as the starting point of a deal that will include numerous extras, and over a much longer period. They will try and sell extended warranties and service agreements as well as additional software and a higher specification PC.

A more comprehensive definition of price is:

Everything that a customer has to give up in order to acquire a product or service.

This second definition takes account of the added costs associated with the purchase. For example, buying a new pair of shoes takes time: going to the shop, trying them on, maybe taking them back. It costs additional money for transport, maybe for lunch too. Then there may be accessories to buy, such as cleaner, protector, a handbag. It takes effort. It involves giving up alternatives that the money could have bought (**opportunity cost**). It takes an investment of brain power and judgement to ensure you get the right pair. There is also the actual money paid for the shoes.

opportunity cost alternatives that could have been had/done instead, e.g. the opportunity cost of a lunchtime sandwich may be a pre-packed salad, and an evening at the cinema costs a night's study

Exhibit 10.1   Price in the balance

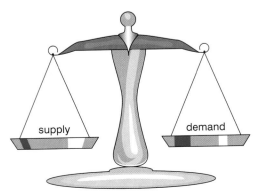

supply   demand

To illustrate the complexities of pricing decisions, Lancaster et al. (2000) consider three differing perspectives on pricing: the economist's, the accountant's and the marketer's. There is also the customer's view, of course.

THE ECONOMIST'S VIEW OF PRICING

In a free market, a product's price would be set by the forces of demand and supply (see Chapter 1). The idea is that the price goes up, and down, until it settles at the point where buyers are prepared to buy just exactly the same amount as sellers are prepared to sell (see Exhibit 10.1).

If there are more buyers than products, the price goes up until enough buyers fall out of the market and demand equals supply again. If there are more products than customers, the price falls until more customers are attracted into the market.

Take the example of a fruit and vegetable stall in a market towards the end of the day. The trader shouts out his or her prices, gradually reducing them until he or she attracts customers. At an auction, the potential buyers bid against each other, pushing the price up: the more buyers there are, the higher the price goes. If there is only one potential buyer, then the price stays low.

However, that is not the way business is done in shopping malls. The economist's view is more theoretical than the real world. In practice, shops and suppliers cannot change prices so dynamically; their prices are largely fixed in advance. The concept of supply and demand remains useful, though. Clearly, the higher the price of a product, the fewer people will be prepared to buy it, and so if a firm wants to clear out old stock, then it will usually reduce the price. The consequent increase in sales is evidence of the law of supply and demand.

Drawbacks in the economist's view of pricing include the following:

- It assumes that the firm's main objective is to maximise short-term profit. This is not always true, as they may want to break into a new market, or they may be a not-for-profit organisation, or in an industry where excess profits are unacceptable (e.g. electricity supply). There are many reasons why a firm may choose to make less profit than it could.
- Price is not the only thing that influences demand, and it is complicated to work out a demand function using all of the possible variables, e.g. **marketing communications**, competitors' prices. Therefore, demand forecasts are never 100 per cent accurate.

THE ACCOUNTANT'S VIEW OF PRICING

Accountants want to make sure that the price of a product or service covers all its costs, so that a profit can be shown (see 'Cost-based pricing' below). Drawbacks in the accountant's view of pricing include:

- it can be hard to work out all the costs involved
- focusing solely on the firm's own costs means ignoring the market and the power of the rest of the **marketing mix**. People may be prepared to pay more, especially if the brand is strong, or there has been a good advertising campaign, or a firm has shops in better locations, or all the competitive products are twice that price. This could be a missed opportunity for profit.

insight   Cheap cheers!

Christmas 2009 had even more sparkle than usual thanks to the availability of bargain bottles of champagne. Supermarkets cut prices of top brands such as Bollinger and Veuve Clicquot by as much as £15 per bottle. However, drinkers were warned not to get used to the high life as prices were unlikely to remain so low for long.

So why the unusually low prices? It was mainly because of the worldwide recession which meant fewer people could afford champagne, or at least not so often. Regular champagne drinkers traded down to Italian Prosecco and Spanish Cava and only went for the real French champagne for special occasions or when there was a need to impress.

Champagne growers had come to rely on the steadily increasing demand from countries such as Britain (the Brits are second only to France in champagne consumption), India, Russia and China. Sales had been so good that they had even extended the prestigious Champagne region so that nearly 40 new growing areas were able to call their products champagne: a privilege reserved for a strictly controlled area of France.

It takes two years to turn a grape harvest into market-ready champagne and so it is hard for the Champagne Houses to respond quickly to changes in demand. In 2009 there was too much champagne but it was predicted that there would be a shortage a couple of years later. Concerned that the drop in prices would harm their product's reputation and make it harder to command premium prices in the future, the champagne producers tried to reduce supply. Capping the volume of grapes that growers could legitimately produce would mean fewer bottles of champagne in the future. The consequent shortage would then push prices back up. Although, if consumers have developed a taste for sparkling wines from other regions, the Champagne Houses may find that they have overstocks once again.

Is it ethical to create a shortage deliberately in order to keep prices high? Is it good business?

THE CUSTOMER'S VIEW OF PRICING

Customers usually want the best quality at the lowest price. For a customer, the price has to represent good value:

$$\text{perceived value} = \text{perceived benefits} - \text{price}$$

Drawbacks in the customer's view of pricing include:

- quality costs money – there has to be a trade-off between the two; the highest-quality products cannot be sold at the lowest prices
- people's perception of the value of a product differs – e.g. some people will pay a lot more for branded goods such as Nike, while others will not.

THE MARKETER'S VIEW OF PRICING

Marketers see pricing as an opportunity to gain competitive advantage. It is vital to take account of what the market can bear: how much people are prepared to pay, and how much competitors are charging. Drawbacks in the marketer's view of pricing include:

- marketers may set a price that does not actually cover the costs of making a product. Clearly, this can only be sustained in the short term or the firm will make a loss (see 'Loss leaders' and 'Contribution pricing' below).

Pricing in the mix

Clearly, it is important to have a good product, but a product without a price is a gift. So, marketers must set a price. The key question is how much and the answer must take account of the rest of the mix. The price sends a message, just as the promotion, distribution channels, product and its packaging do. People do not expect Harrods to be cheap, but what about PriceRite? Which is likely to sell the highest-quality goods? The price sends a message about quality. Customers associate a high price, sometimes mistakenly, with high quality.

ACTIVITY

Visit a local department store (such as John Lewis, Fenwick or House of Fraser), go into the fashion, sport or perfumery department and find examples of expensive, and cheaper, products in the same category (e.g. tennis racquets, football boots, perfume, trainers, shirts). What are the differences in terms of packaging, materials used, presentation? Could you tell which was cheaper before you looked at the price tag?

Now go to a discount store or a chain store (such as Littlewoods, Matalan or BHS) and see if you can find the same brands. If you cannot find them, find the most similar thing you can and compare that with your impression of the more expensive department store brands.

Certain styles of promotion are associated with cheaper or more expensive products. When prices are rock bottom, the advertisers often shout – literally or through their choice of bold colours. There is more sales promotion (money-off coupons, two for the price of one, etc.) at the lower end of the market. Marks and Spencer used to think that all advertising and sales promotion was too downmarket and unnecessary for such a well-known brand. Top fashion brands only advertise in glossy high-fashion magazines such as *Vogue* (if they advertise at all – public relations is more their forte).

Pricing objectives

Pricing objectives can be grouped under two main headings:

- financial return, e.g. maximising revenue, recovering an investment made (usually in developing the product)
- market orientated, e.g. positioning, maintaining brand image, building market share, enticing customers to the store, rewarding customers for loyalty.

The financial objectives are largely inward-looking, while the market-orientated ones look to the external environment. Some of these objectives are really short term, e.g. 'enticing the customer into the store', and some should normally be long term, e.g. 'maximising revenue'. There may also be an ethical element to the setting of prices, e.g. governments may make services affordable to target social groups, such as the low paid, even pricing on a sliding scale to encourage those on low incomes to take advantage of services such as school dinners or education. Some companies also deliberately keep prices low for specific groups, e.g. IKEA's flatpack houses were only made available to people with combined incomes of under £35,000 (see ethical focus box).

There are numerous pricing techniques that are used to meet these objectives.

Flatpack homes

ethical focus

Gateshead on Tyneside has become a popular place to live. The once affordable, 1930s, council-built estates have long since been sold into private ownership and are now priced well beyond the means of first-time buyers or the low paid. There was a desperate shortage of good, cheap housing. Then Ikea moved in.

The Swedish furniture company had previously revolutionised Britain's furniture market with its range of well-produced, cheap, attractive flatpack furniture and fashionable home accessories. Then they went to the next stage and started to build the houses to put the furniture in. 'The principle of our stores is goods for the many. Now we are hoping to provide houses for the many', said an IKEA spokesperson.

The development won the support of the local council from whom planning permission was required for the 99 flatpack homes (ready assembled by experts). The houses' prices ranged from £99,000 for a one-bedroomed flat to £149,000 for a three-bedroomed house, and a range of shared ownership options put the homes within reach of someone earning as little as £15,000 per year.

High earners and property developers need not apply. Potential homeowners have to prove that their incomes total less than £35,000 a year and re-sale rules, such as that the houses must be sold through a designated agent (a specialist in low-cost housing), are designed to prevent re-sale prices from rising too rapidly.

SOURCE: Wainwright, 2007

Pricing techniques

STRATEGIES, TACTICS AND METHODS

Textbooks and commentators cannot seem to agree on which of the various ways of setting prices are strategies, tactics or methods. Some have apparently given up on categorisation altogether.

In this book, a pricing strategy is defined as being medium to long term and having a significant impact on the company's overall marketing strategy, or even corporate strategy. A pricing tactic is defined as a short-term action, or one with limited impact beyond the product being priced. Pricing methods are mechanical ways to set prices. They are a good starting point, or a good way to check that the price arrived at is sane, but, marketers would argue, not a way to set prices in isolation. It is also important to check out the ways price can be used to greater effect via a specific strategy or tactic. Some pricing techniques, e.g. market skimming (see below), could be used as strategies (longer term) or tactics (shorter term).

Pricing methods

There are three key elements to price setting: competitors' prices, customers' perceptions of the product's value, and costs.

A business's costs must be covered, but too great an emphasis on costs in a pricing strategy leads to missed opportunities. It is vital to take account of what is going on in the market. What are competitors charging? How much do customers want to pay? Exhibit 10.2 shows the key influencers on the pricing decisions.

In the case of a car manufacturer, there would be substantial costs in buying the materials required to make the cars. In the long run, these must be covered by the pricing of the car or the company will be out of business. Costs of supplies are an important consideration. The company buys in engine parts, sheets of metal, mirrors,

Exhibit 10.2   Price setting

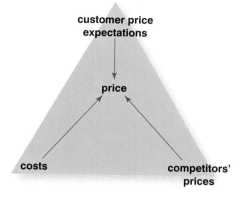

etc., and then adds value to them by turning them into a functional car. They have to pay wages, rents and other bills in order to do this. So additional cost is incurred here. But then there is the question of value. Is the car only worth the sum of its parts? Of course not, otherwise why bother to put it together at all? It is worth more as a car than as a pile of materials and sub-assemblies, but how much more?

Competitors and customers have a key role to play in determining how much value has been added by turning the parts into a car. Is it a better or worse car than the competition's? How much are customers prepared to give up for it?

Most methods of pricing can be classified as either:

- market-based pricing (taking account of competitors and/or customers), or
- cost-based pricing.

MARKET-BASED PRICING

There are a large number of different market-based pricing methods, including:

- **customer value pricing**
- **psychological price barriers**
- **going-rate pricing**
- **tenders**
- **cartels.**

Customer value pricing

A product is only worth what someone will pay for it. The price is the company's estimate of the product's value. The customer may place a different value on the product. The trick is to make these two concepts of value balance, so that the firm is paid a fair price and the customer gets a good deal. This is a difficult balancing act. The seller will have invested a great deal of time, money, effort and creativity into its offerings. They have great value. The customer has many choices as to what to buy, and will consider their relative values. The seller can increase the value of its offering in a number of ways, e.g. through added features, better quality, a superior brand image, better service, home delivery. Increases in value are usually created through the other elements of the marketing mix – one of the reasons why it is so important to coordinate all marketing mix elements.

In customer value pricing, the price is based on what customers value a product at, i.e. what it is worth to them, rather than on what it cost the firm to make. If the balance between value and price is right, then customers will see that the price they are being asked to pay is justified even if that price is higher than the competition's.

Psychological price barriers

Many people have a budget in mind before they go out to buy something. They may exceed the budget by a little, but there will be a price beyond which they will not go. That is their psychological price barrier. Some marketers set prices by conducting research to establish just where that barrier is. Then they set prices just below it.

ACTIVITY

How much are you prepared to pay for:

- lunch
- a CD
- a jacket
- a pair of shoes
- a concert ticket?

Work out your own psychological price barriers. Then, the next time you buy such things, see how well the products available match up to your budget.

You are likely to find a range of prices, e.g. lunch can cost anything from a sandwich at less than £2 to a fancy restaurant meal at £50 plus. Where do you fit in this range? (See also 'Product line pricing' below.)

Psychological pricing is a related concept (see 'Pricing tactics' below).

Auctions

Auctions used to be the preserve of art galleries and antique dealers, but the advent of the Internet has changed all that. Now auctions are a way to get products cheaper – online. Bandyopadhyay et al. (2001) attribute the success of auctions on the Internet to simplicity, real-time price negotiation and the large number of participants. There are a number of variants on the traditional auction, in which buyers kept bidding until only one was left in, e.g. some goods are sold by 'reverse auction'. At a reverse auction, suppliers make the bids, undercutting each other, and the customer takes the final offer and so gets the best price. (For a full explanation of Internet auctions see www.ebay.co.uk.)

Going-rate pricing

price leaders
set prices for a markets; other firms follow their lead

price makers
another term for price leaders

price followers
firms that set their prices in accordance with others in the market, notably a price leader

price takers
another name for price followers

Competitors' prices have to be taken into account when setting prices. Charge twice as much as the competition and the firm will make no sales; charge half as much and it is missing an opportunity for profit (as well as possibly sending the wrong message about quality).

Some established firms are considered to be **price leaders** or **price makers**. They set the prices that the others, the **price followers** or **price takers**, follow. Price leaders are often the largest competitors in the market but sometimes a smaller company is recognised as having particular expertise, and even larger firms will follow its lead. This happens quite often in the financial services industry.

Going-rate pricing is one of the most common ways of choosing a price. It is especially favoured by new entrants to a market who need to make sure that they set their prices at a realistic level in comparison to the competition, and who have no track record to guide them.

Advantages of going-rate pricing are that it:

- avoids **price wars** (see below)
- makes use of the expertise of more established firms.

Disadvantages are that it:

● assumes that competitors got their sums right and set the best price – they may not have
● firms have different cost bases; it is quite possible that Coca-Cola can charge 23p (€0.32) per can and still make a profit whereas it may cost a new competitor 25p (€0.35) just to make the drink and can it.

Tenders

There are numerous types of **tender**, but the basic premise of all of them is that a number of firms bid for a contract. The contract is awarded to the lowest bidder. This type of pricing is common in government, particularly for public works contracts such as road or bridge building, where the tender system is seen as being open and above reproach.

Tenders may be by sealed bid (when a firm does not know what the others are bidding) or open.

tender (tendering)
where firms bid for a contract and, usually, the lowest-priced bid wins

Cartels

A **cartel** is a group of companies that get together and fix prices between them. Cartels are most common in oligopolistic markets where they justify their joint price setting by saying that it avoids price wars. When companies get together and choose a mutually acceptable price, it tends to be higher than it would have been had they had to compete with one another. So it is cosy and safe for business, but bad news for consumers.

cartel
group of companies that get together and fix prices between them

Probably the most famous cartel is OPEC (the Organisation of the Petroleum Exporting Countries). In the 1970s and 1980s, OPEC set the prices for the world's crude oil. Now there are other countries involved, but the 12 OPEC members (Saudi Arabia, Iraq, Kuwait, Venezuela, Nigeria, Algeria, Libya, Iran, Indonesia, the United Arab Emirates, Angola and Qatar) still 'voluntarily restrain their crude oil production in order to stabilise the oil market and avoid harmful and unnecessary price fluctuations' (OPEC, n.d.).

Cartels are considered an anti-competitive practice and are illegal in the EU. However, that did not stop eight European drugs companies colluding to fix the price of vitamins. In 2001, they were fined €855.2 million (£529.5 million) for what the EU anti-trust chief, Mario Monti, described as the 'most damaging series of cartels the Commission has ever investigated' (Anon, 2001).

COST-BASED PRICING

Many marketers warn against placing too great an emphasis on costs when setting prices. However, they are important. If a firm does not cover its costs, then, sooner or later, it will go out of business. The downside of focusing on covering costs is that the firm may miss out on profit.

Cost plus pricing

Cost and price are different. Costs are monies that a firm has to pay to its suppliers. Prices are what they charge customers for the products/services they sell. The 50p a customer pays for a chocolate bar is a cost to him or her, but a price to the shop that sells it. Clearly, prices should be higher than costs – at least most of the time.

There are a number of pricing methods that take the costs of making the goods, or of delivering the service, and then add an amount on to arrive at a price. It is

insight   Types of costs

The different types of costs are:

- total costs – the sum of all costs
- direct costs – costs that are clearly due to the making of a particular product, e.g. cocoa and sugar are direct costs of Cadbury's Dairy Milk
- indirect costs – costs that cannot be attributed to a particular product as they are not directly associated with its production or sale, e.g. the running costs of the chief executive's car
- variable costs – costs that go up as production increases, e.g. electricity bills
- fixed costs – costs that do not vary with production, e.g. insurance premiums.

Costs will be either fixed or variable *and* either direct or indirect. Examples include:

- electricity is usually a variable, indirect cost – it costs more as production increases, but it is hard to work out just how much electricity went into the making of a particular product
- raw materials are variable, direct costs – you need more flour to make more cakes, and you still know just how much flour it takes to make a cake
- rent is usually a fixed, indirect cost – it does not vary month on month, and contributes to a number of different products
- highly specialised machinery may be a fixed, direct cost – the nozzle that pipes the perfect star on top of the coffee creams in the chocolate factory, perhaps.

therefore now necessary to take a slight detour into accounting, and briefly look at various types of costs (see insight box).

Cost plus pricing methods include:

- mark-up pricing
- full-cost pricing
- contribution pricing.

MARK-UP PRICING

This pricing method is common in **retail** as it is a relatively straightforward way for a shop to set prices: calculate the **direct cost** of the product, then add on an amount to cover **indirect costs** and provide a profit. For example, a boutique buys in dresses for £50 each. The £50 is the direct cost, but there are other costs involved in running the shop (heating, lighting, rent, wages, etc.). To price the dresses, it uses a simple formula, perhaps adding on 300 per cent of the direct cost. This should mean that each dress sold covers *all* costs, and makes a profit.

direct costs
costs that are clearly due to the making of a particular product, e.g. cocoa and sugar are direct costs of Cadbury's Dairy Milk

indirect costs
costs that cannot be attributed to a particular product as they are not directly associated with its production or sale, e.g. the running costs of the chief executive's car

direct cost	£50.00
mark-up	£150.00
selling price	£200.00

Advantages of mark-up pricing are that:

- it is a relatively simple way for **retailers** (and some other businesses) to set their prices
- unlike full-cost pricing (see below), mark-up takes account of demand. Retailers do not apply the same mark-up to all products – they are usually adept at varying prices to take account of the popularity of products.

Exhibit 10.3 The vicious circle of price setting

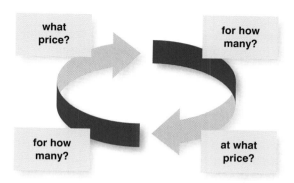

Disadvantages are that:

- the mark-up may not be high enough to cover all the indirect costs, especially if some products remain unsold
- a retailer knows the (direct) cost of products but it is not always so simple; direct cost per unit varies depending upon the level produced, e.g. there may be a discount available for buying a larger quantity, so costs come down (**economies of scale**).

So we need to know the demand for the product before we can set the price, and demand is largely determined by price. What output level shall we pick to get our cost base? It is a vicious circle (see Exhibit 10.3).

economies of scale
unit costs fall as larger quantities are produced; a cost advantage associated with large organisations

FULL-COST PRICING

This is also known as absorption costing.

Full-cost pricing is as it sounds: work out the total unit cost (i.e. the total cost per product) of making the product, then add a further amount, and that's the price. For example, the local pizzeria adds up the costs of all the ingredients on its four seasons pizza, adds in an amount for wages and the running costs of the restaurant, then adds 100 per cent – for profit.

full-cost pricing
prices are set by adding an amount (usually a percentage) to the full (i.e. total) costs of making and selling the product

per pizza	direct costs	= £0.75
	indirect costs	= £1.25
	total cost	= £2.00
	+100%	= £4.00, so that's the price

ACTIVITY

Using the full-cost pricing method, work out the price for a box of chocolates when:

fixed costs (rent, etc.)	= £40,000 per month
variable costs (ingredients, etc.)	= £1 per box
sales volume	= 100,000 per month

The accounts department has set 25 per cent as the profit margin.
(The answer is at the end of the chapter, on page 392)

Advantages of full-cost pricing are that:

- all production costs are covered by the price
- cost increases get passed on to the customer in the form of a price increase, so **profit margins** (in percentage terms) remain the same
- it may be the only way to price a job for which the amount of work cannot be predicted, i.e. the price is set retroactively, when all the costs are known, e.g. for a research and development project.

Disadvantages are as follows:

- direct costs, such as ingredients, are easy enough to allocate to a product (a baker knows how much flour was used in each loaf), but if a salesperson sells a range of products, of differing values, how much of his or her salary, company car costs, etc. should be added to the cost of each item? And just imagine how complicated that would be to work out for each of a thousand products sold by a hundred salespeople, all on different salaries. Then there's the other staff, buildings costs, etc. This allocation of costs to a product is often quite arbitrary – what percentage of the chief executive's car costs should be allocated to each Dream bar?
- it ignores market forces (demand and supply) and the price sensitivity of customers – they may be prepared to pay more, or they may not be prepared to pay that price at all, in which case a way would have to be found to reduce the costs.
- if a firm gets more efficient (i.e. fixed costs per unit go down – perhaps because you have installed more modern equipment), then their price goes down too, but if the product was selling well at a higher price, why lower it? In practice, a firm might not lower prices in this circumstance, but that would mean that it was no longer adhering to the firm's cost plus pricing policy and had allowed some market awareness to creep into its price setting.

CONTRIBUTION PRICING

Mark-up pricing uses direct costs as a basis on which to set the price. Full-cost pricing uses the **total cost** as a basis. **Contribution pricing** is based on **variable costs**.

It is being included here with the other cost-based pricing methods, but this one is rather different. Really, within the classifications given earlier in the chapter, contribution pricing is usually used as a pricing tactic. It is something that can only be used in the short term – usually just for one order. Try to use it all the time, on all products, and the company will rack up the losses and go under. However, it is also a way to price **loss leaders** (see below).

The idea behind contribution pricing is that, as long as the product is sold for more than its variable cost, it is making a **contribution** towards the **fixed costs** and profits.

Contribution pricing is often used for one-off orders. For example, the Alpha Company's monthly fixed costs (FC) are £3,000 and variable costs (VC) are £3 per product. It regularly sells 2,000 alarm clocks each month.

So:

fixed cost per product, i.e. average fixed cost (AFC) = the fixed costs divided by the sales volume, i.e.

$$= \frac{£3,000}{2,000} = £1.50$$

total cost per unit   = AFC + VC

                     = £1.50 + £3.00 = £4.50

---

profit margin
the difference between cost and price, expressed as a percentage

contribution
the amount of money remaining from the sale, when the variable costs have been paid

total cost
all product costs, i.e. direct + indirect, or fixed + variable

contribution pricing
pricing method based on variable costs

variable costs
costs that go up as production increases and down when it decreases, e.g. electricity bills

loss leader
a product that is sold at a loss, usually to tempt shoppers to make other purchases

fixed costs
costs that do not vary with production levels, e.g. insurance premiums

A new customer, Beta Holdings Ltd, wants to buy 500 clocks, but is only prepared to pay £4.00 per clock. This will not cover the total cost of making the clock, but it will cover the variable costs – anything over £3.00 makes a contribution. Should Alpha accept the order? It depends on:

- whether the fixed costs are actually already covered by other orders
- whether they have enough capacity to make the new order
- how much goodwill the acceptance of this order will generate – will Beta Holdings turn into a regular customer, maybe at a better price?
- how much bad feeling may be created if other, regular, customers find out and feel over-charged.

This is similar to the technique that economists call **marginal cost pricing**. Marginal cost is the cost of making additional units. So, in the example above, Alpha would work out what *additional* cost was involved in making the extra 500 clocks – it would need components, use more electricity, and perhaps would have to pay some overtime. Often, these additional costs will be the same as the variable costs of the order.

However, it is possible that Alpha would have to buy more machinery and, in that case, the additional cost (marginal cost) would be more than just the variable cost as additional fixed costs would be incurred too.

In a highly competitive business, a company may have the opportunity to achieve significant extra business by putting in a low bid.

Advantages of contribution pricing are that:

- it may mean keeping workers on, when otherwise they would have been laid off causing hardship for them and their families
- it keeps workers' skills honed – if they spend time idle, or doing other work, they are likely to get out of practice and will not be so efficient in the future
- if you let workers go, your competitors may snap up the best of them
- idle machinery sometimes seizes up and may require more maintenance in the future
- idle machinery is a wasted investment and still costs money in service agreements, etc.

A related concept is that of loss leaders (see below).

marginal cost pricing
similar to contribution pricing, a margin is added to the marginal cost (the cost of making an additional product) to arrive at a price

Target profit pricing

It would be useful for the firm to know how much, i.e. what **sales volume**, it has to sell in order to cover its costs. Then it can see if it is likely that the product will sell that many, and so if it is worthwhile. Clearly, price is one of the main determinants of how many products people will buy. The law of supply and demand (as well as common sense) tells us that higher prices result in lower sales, and vice versa.

The firm can work out the required sales volume, *at a given price*, that will cover costs. This is called the **breakeven point**.

sales volume
how *many* products are sold

Breakeven analysis

Breakeven analysis can be done graphically (see Exhibit 10.4) or as a calculation.

A breakeven chart is a clear, visual way of analysing a firm's profit at various levels of output, and a set price. By drawing a new chart, managers can see the impact of a change in price on the firm's profits, breakeven point and margin of safety. If

breakeven point
the amount of goods a firm needs to sell in order to cover its costs

costs change, a new chart will also show the impact of that. Increases in costs will push the breakeven point higher; increases in price will result in a lower breakeven point.

At any given price, the firm will break even at the point where total cost (TC) = total sales revenue (SR). Further graphs can be drawn to work out the breakeven points at different prices.

If it sells a larger quantity than the breakeven point, it makes a profit. If sales fall below breakeven, it makes a loss.

If you would like to try drawing a breakeven chart, have a go at the additional activity at the end of this chapter (Appendix: Additional cost-based pricing activity).

MARGIN OF SAFETY

If a firm sells more than is required to break even, then that extra quantity is referred to as its 'margin of safety'. In Exhibit 10.5, a firm sells 100,000 products, but breaks

Exhibit 10.4   Breakeven

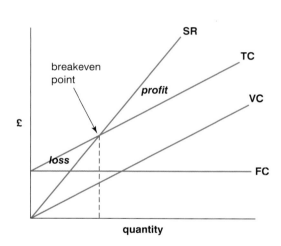

Key

SR = sales revenue
TC = total cost
VC = variable cost
FC = fixed cost

Exhibit 10.5   Margin of safety

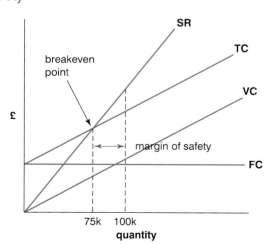

Key

SR = sales revenue
TC = total cost
VC = variable cost
FC = fixed cost

even when it sells 75,000. The margin of safety is 25,000. The significance of this is that the firm knows how many sales it can afford to lose before it hits crisis point.

SETTING A TARGET PROFIT

When firms use target profit pricing, they want to set a price that will result in a defined overall profit. This method of price setting is popular with the privatised utilities, which have a duty to provide fair prices and not to make excess profits. Firms set a target profit by, on a normal breakeven chart, finding the point at which the difference between sales revenue and total cost equals the target profit. Then they simply draw a line down to the quantity axis and read off the sales volume required to achieve that target profit (see Exhibit 10.6).

Exhibit 10.6   Roadrunner Co. target profit chart

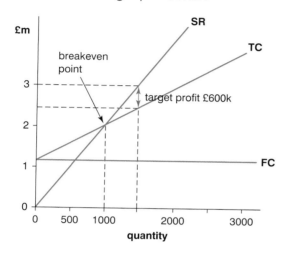

Target profit pricing can also be calculated. The formula for this is:

$$\frac{\text{fixed cost} + \text{profit target}}{\text{contribution per item}}$$
= required level of output

For example, the Roadrunner Co. wants to make £600,000 profit on its bicycles. Fixed costs total £1.2 million, while variable costs are £800 per bike. The bike is priced at £2,000.

contribution   = selling price – variable cost
                = £2,000 – £800 = £1,200

$$\frac{1,200,000 + £600,000}{£1,200}$$ = 1500 bicycles

So it knows that if it sells 1500 bicycles at a price of £2,000 each, then it will make £600,000 profit (see Exhibit 10.7). Alternatively, it could read this figure off a breakeven chart by finding the point at which the SR and the TC lines are £600,000 apart.

Remember that a breakeven chart works for one price only – you need to draw a new chart to try out the profit target at a new price.

Drawbacks to breakeven analysis include:

● it assumes that all the products made will be sold
● it is a static model – if costs change, then a new chart has to be drawn
● as with all analysis tools, its effectiveness depends upon the quality of the figures it uses: rubbish in = rubbish out
● it is actually more complicated than the example in Exhibit 10.6 shows because fixed costs are not always linear. They can increase (e.g. when the capacity of a machine is reached and a new one has to be bought) (see Exhibit 10.7).

Exhibit 10.7   Stepped breakeven chart

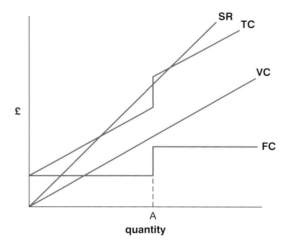

Pricing strategies

NEW PRODUCT PRICING STRATEGIES

The price is one of the most difficult things to get right for a new product. Many products fail because they are either too expensive, and therefore do not sell, or too cheap and so the company is unable to meet its costs. Small businesses often charge too little for their products and it is one of the reasons that so many of them fail. It is much harder to explain a price increase to customers than it is to explain a decrease. It is often difficult to raise a price once a product has been launched on to the market as customers by then have a view of the right price and are reluctant to pay more. This is why so many new products declare that they have an introductory price. This leads customers to expect a price rise in the near future.

The two major new pricing strategies are:

1 market penetration
2 market skimming.

Market penetration

When a company first enters a market, it needs to build **market share**. A low price should tempt people to try the new product. If they like it, they will buy it again. So product trial may lead to product adoption. The main objective of a penetration pricing strategy is to establish the product in the market: to build a customer base.

Advantages of **market penetration pricing** are that:

- it encourages people to try a product
- it encourages retailers to build up stocks – then they will not have room for competitors' products.

Disadvantages are that:

- it may provoke retaliation from existing companies
- it is not suitable for products with a short product life cycle as there may not be enough time to recover from the initial, low revenue.

The big disadvantage to the consumer is, of course, that the price does not stay low forever. New credit cards offer low, or no, interest. Then, when they are established, the 'introductory offer' disappears and they hope that their cardholders will not bother to change cards again.

Market skimming

This is really the opposite of penetration pricing. Firms following a skimming strategy set their prices higher than they need to, in order to maximise profits. The key to the success of a **market skimming** strategy is that there should be no significant competition – otherwise people will just buy the cheaper alternative. The company may be launching an entirely new product, or entering a new market.

This strategy works well where:

- there is insufficient market capacity and competitors cannot make more of the product
- there are no competitors
- the demand for the goods in question is relatively **price inelastic**
- a high price is seen as an indicator of high quality.

Advantages of market skimming are:

- early cash recovery – this is particularly important if this is a new product and the firm has made a significant investment in its development; it needs to get its money back before other firms copy the invention and the market becomes more crowded.

Disadvantages are that:

- there is a high danger of encouraging other firms to enter the market – they see high profits being made and they want to make them too
- depending upon the type of product and the market in question, there may be an ethical issue over charging high prices, e.g. for prescription drugs, or in less-developed countries.

market share
a firm's sales expressed as a percentage of the told sales of that type of product, in the defined market

market penetration pricing
pricing a product lower than competitors in order to gain market share

market skimming
setting a relatively high price to take advantage of limited competition

price inelastic demand
product sales are not very sensitive to price changes (see also inelasticity)

EXPAND YOUR KNOWLEDGE

Dean, J. (1970) 'Techniques for pricing new products and services', in V.P. Buell and C. Heyel (eds) *Handbook of Modern Marketing*. New York: McGraw-Hill, pp. 5–51 – 5–61. Also appeared in *Harvard Business Review* with retrospective commentary (Nov–Dec, 1978).

Determining the price level of a new product or service is one of the most important and most difficult marketing problems faced by a manager. Although such pricing decisions are more of an art than a science and require experienced judgement, making them can be facilitated by the concepts and procedures suggested in this article.

GENERAL PRICING STRATEGIES

General pricing strategies are:

prestige pricing
pricing a product high in order to enhance its status

● prestige pricing
● pre-emptive pricing
● product line pricing
● price discrimination.

Rolls-Royce: a prestige product sold at a prestige price and here being used to provide a special service

Prestige pricing

Prestige pricing sets a high price for a product. Unlike price skimming, this is an ongoing strategy – the product stays expensive throughout its life. The high price is designed to associate an image of quality and high status with the product. This high price is itself an important motivator for consumers. Customers with higher incomes are less price-sensitive and more interested in buying high-quality, prestigious products that enhance their image. Promotional strategies revolve around these aspects of the product, helping to justify the high price in the customer's mind. Typical prestige brands include Chanel, IBM, Bang & Olufsen, Cartier and BMW.

Pre-emptive pricing

pre-emptive pricing
setting prices relatively low in order to deter others from entering a market

predatory pricing
also known as destroyer pricing or extinction pricing, it is when a dominant company sells products at a loss with the intention of driving a rival firm out of the market

A company following a **pre-emptive pricing** strategy sets low prices to deter new entrants to the market. This is especially suitable in markets where there are few other barriers to entry, e.g. the company does not hold a patent and/or entry costs are low. (For more on barriers to entry, see Chapter 12.)

Pre-emptive pricing should not be confused with **predatory pricing** (see below). Pre-emptive pricing is a perfectly legitimate strategy, whereas predatory pricing, which sets prices below costs in order to drive another firm out of business, is illegal in many countries including Britain.

Product line pricing

Many companies develop **product lines**, rather than just single products, and these lines may be named and branded distinctly. A company's product range may contain a number of product lines, e.g. Ford produces the Ka, Fiesta, Focus, Fusion, Mondeo, Galaxy, Maverick . . . and all of these lines have a number of models with different engine sizes, different finishes and different features.

The product manager has to set price steps within the product lines. How much more will a customer pay for a Focus with 1.6-litre engine rather than 1.4? How much extra should be charged for a Zetec? There will be some overlap between the top of one line and the bottom of the next one up, but how much can they overlap without the top of the line losing business?

Some sellers use well-established price points for the products in their line: so a restaurant's main courses may be premier price (for a particularly special dish, such as lobster), top price (for more expensive ingredients such as steak), mid-price (for most dishes) and low price (perhaps for the vegetarian options).

product line
a product and all its variants (models, colours, styles, sizes, etc.)

Price discrimination

Price discrimination can be dangerous, but can also be very profitable. It relies heavily upon market segmentation (see Chapter 4). Price discriminators charge different prices *for the same products* to different market segments. The most common segments used are time, geography and age. Some examples are outlined below.

Time-based discrimination:

- many train services are more expensive if you want to travel before 9.30 am
- British Airways' return economy air fare from London to Sydney is approximately £1,460 over Christmas, but only £740 in June (BA, n.d.)
- many entertainment venues give a discount if you book in advance.

price discrimination
charging different prices for the same products/ services to different market segments, e.g. off-peak fares

Geographic discrimination:

- CDs are cheaper in the USA than they are in many European countries
- cars are cheaper on mainland Europe than they are in Britain (see e-focus box below)
- African countries are (at last) being allowed to buy AIDS drugs for a fraction of their normal price.

Age discrimination:

- children travel on public transport at reduced prices
- OAPs get discounts on cinema and theatre tickets
- if you are under 26, you can get a one-month Inter-rail ticket, valid for trains in 28 European countries, for about two-thirds of the price that over-26s pay (InterRail, n.d.).

The key to successful price discrimination is that customers should not be able to move between segments. It is surprising how many teenagers will happily take a couple of years off their age in order to get a cheaper bus fare. If people can move themselves into a cheaper segment, they will.

ACTIVITY

Search the World Wide Web. What's the best price you can find for a current top-10 CD?

In the European Union, borders are easy to cross, and there is no duty on goods brought in for personal use. Europeans frequently visit neighbouring countries to get a better deal – on a car, on alcohol and cigarettes, on Christmas presents. It gets harder to maintain different prices in different countries when people are able to travel freely.

The great British rip-off

For years, British consumers paid far more than their European counterparts for cars. The car companies gave a number of reasons for this, including the additional manufacturing costs incurred by putting the steering wheel on the other side and the additional distribution costs caused by having to cross the Channel.

They got away with it for so long largely because not enough people knew about it, but once customers found out there was a stream of car buyers catching ferries or the Eurostar across to France and Belgium and bringing their new cars home. They saved several thousands on the deal. So what changed?

One of the main reasons for the change was the advent of the Internet. It is so easy now to do price comparisons across the world. The Internet gives customers almost perfect pricing information, making it far harder for sellers to get away with high prices. Internet comparison shopping agents (programs such as Price Grabber and Kelkoo that automatically search a number of websites for the best price for a particular product) make it even easier for customers to get a better deal.

The Internet has been a major blow to the price discriminators. Now, consumers can surf the World Wide Web looking for bargains. They can check out prices all over the world and either buy online or use their superior pricing knowledge to drive down high-street prices.

International pricing

All the pricing methods, tactics and strategies covered in this chapter are valid in international marketing too, but here they are overlaid with all the difficulties of competing in a foreign environment. Goods and services sold in another country normally have to be priced in that country's currency. However, in business-to-business (B2B) deals, there may be arguments for pricing a contract in either the buyer's or the seller's currency – or even in a third-party currency such as the US dollar. Rates of exchange fluctuate and so it can be difficult for a company to maintain consistency in its pricing across countries. €120 may equate to £80 one day and £75 the next. Clearly, if the price has been set at the level that represents a fair exchange, then such fluctuations are not desirable.

PARALLEL IMPORTING (THE GREY MARKET)

Adapting prices to suit local income levels may sound like good business practice but it does have a downside. If a product is cheaper in one country than in others, then there is a danger that people will buy it in the cheaper country and then export it themselves to the more expensive one. Companies sometimes find themselves competing against their own products. In order to prevent this, either the product must be varied or the price must be pitched at a level that makes **parallel importing** (also called grey importing) unattractive. Different prices can still be charged so long as the difference is small enough that the additional cost of exporting means that it is not worthwhile. Many companies go to the courts to try and stop parallel importers but this is often unsuccessful and always time-consuming and expensive. It is better to avoid the problem entirely through judicious use of the marketing mix.

parallel importing
when someone outside of the official supply chain sells goods that were bought abroad (usually more cheaply)

Sometimes companies set different prices in different countries deliberately in order to maximise profits (see 'Price discrimination' above) and sometimes prices differ as a result of exchange rate changes or the actions of third parties, such as retailers. Varying prices across the world, and particularly across regions, such as the EU, can cause significant problems for a company. For example, they may have a negative effect on the product's image or they may provide the opportunity for parallel importing, i.e. when trade customers buy in a cheaper country and then import the goods themselves, thus undercutting the manufacturer and undermining their positioning strategies.

global focus

Cheap imports

Where do they come from, those piles of branded goods in the local supermarket? How can Superdrug afford to sell perfume so cheaply? Sometimes the goods are legitimate supplies – perhaps excess stock or the end of lines that the manufacturers are selling off. Sometimes their route to market is murkier – grey in fact. Grey importing is when someone outside the official supply chain buys goods, often in another country, for sale back home. Some of these products come from less-developed countries where prices have to be lower (otherwise people could not afford to buy them). This price discrimination tempts buyers from the more expensive markets who know they can then substantially undercut the manufacturer's recommended price and still make a profit.

There are further complexities to setting prices in foreign currencies:

- it may be harder to get reliable market information as the company is less familiar with this foreign market or because the information does not exist in the form that the company is used to (many third-world countries do not collect the market data that more developed countries do)

- prices in different currencies, and in multiple markets, require a lot of management time to monitor and to compare to competitive prices
- pricing laws vary from country to country (e.g. many Muslim countries do not allow credit, some governments will not allow foreign companies to undercut local ones).

Pricing tactics

Shorter-term, limited impact or special situation pricing options include:

- predatory pricing
- psychological pricing
- loss leaders
- promotional pricing and discounts.

PREDATORY PRICING (DESTROYER PRICING, EXTINCTION PRICING)

This pricing tactic is considered an anti-competitive practice in a number of countries, including the UK (i.e. it is against the law, but it is notoriously hard to prove).

Predatory pricing occurs when a dominant undertaking incurs losses with the intention of removing a rival and/or deterring other potential competitors. (Office of Fair Trading, 2002)

predatory pricing
also known as destroyer pricing or extinction pricing, it is when a dominant company sells products at a loss with the intention of driving a rival firm out of the market

The larger firm can carry this because it benefits from economies of scale. There have been some notorious examples of **predatory pricing** in the airline business and also in publishing.

The Times newspaper was accused of this back in 1998, when it reduced its cover price from 35p to 20p (€0.49 to €0.28) seriously undercutting its broadsheet rivals. However, the allegation was never proven. In 2002, Aberdeen Journals Ltd was fined £1.328 million (€1.86 million) for abusing a dominant market position. The Office of Fair Trading (OFT) decision followed a Competition Act investigation into allegations of predatory pricing by Aberdeen Journals, a sister paper of the *Daily Mail* (Office of Fair Trading, 2002).

PSYCHOLOGICAL PRICING

A surprisingly large number of products are priced at x number of pounds and 99p: £4.99 and £9.99 are particularly popular prices. The idea, of course, is to fool the customer into thinking that the item is cheaper than it really is. £1,000 sounds so much more than £999 – or so the theory goes.

This links to psychological price barriers (see above). If a customer's top price for a bunch of supermarket flowers is £3.00, then it makes sense to price some at £2.99. The customer feels he or she got a good deal and the supermarket has only lost out on a penny.

LOSS LEADERS

This tactic is often employed by retailers as a means of getting customers into a shop. Getting customers into the shop is a major retail objective as, once inside, they are

Microsoft vs Netscape

ethical focus

In 1996 Microsoft started giving away Internet Explorer, its web browser. In fact, it was argued that in some cases Microsoft effectively paid people to use Internet Explorer in preference to their existing browser, by giving them free software and marketing assistance. The strategy was crucial to the company's success in taking the market leadership away from arch-rival Netscape, which was, up until then, the most popular web browser. 'Even though Netscape constantly revised its pricing structure, it was impossible to stay competitive with "better than free"', testified Netscape CEO James L. Barksdale in the Justice Department's anti-trust suit against Microsoft (France and Hamm, 1998).

more susceptible to the in-store promotional displays and impulse buys. A loss leader is a product, prominently displayed and advertised, that is priced well below its normal price, even below its cost to the seller. It is a lure.

Advantages are that:

- the lower price provides a competitive advantage
- this can build the brand if people associate the company with value for money
- there may be opportunities to sell complementary products, upgrades or follow-on goods/services, e.g. a maintenance agreement
- it stimulates word-of-mouth promotion.

How can businesses afford to do this? Well, as with contribution pricing this is not a tactic that can be employed for everything, or all the time. Profits from the other items on sale have to cover the losses of the loss leader. Some retailers even put their other prices up in order to compensate, so watch out.

PROMOTIONAL PRICING AND DISCOUNTS

Short-term special offers are really sales promotions rather than price reductions, so see Chapter 8, which covers marketing communications, for discussion of those. Discounts are often part of the pricing policy, especially if offered as a matter of course, for a reason. For example, many firms give a discount for bulk purchase.

Sainsbury's gives a 5 per cent reduction to customers who buy six bottles of wine. Clearly, this is to encourage people to buy more, and, if they do buy more, then Sainsbury's can afford to charge a little less and still make a good profit.

Many restaurants have a table d'hôte menu: two, three or even four courses for a fixed price. The restaurant can afford to offer diners a good deal because this helps with its ordering and planning.

Seasonal sales and special offers are types of sales promotion

Not so happy hour

'The binge drinking girl who suffered liver failure at just 14' (*Daily Mail*, 14 April 2008).

'Italian children's binge drinking blamed on Britain' (*Daily Telegraph*, 17 August 2009).

It's not something the UK really wants to be known for, but some British youngsters are notorious for their binge drinking. Doctors worry that youthful drinkers are heading for long-term health problems. Local communities and police see them as troublemakers or potential victims of unscrupulous attackers. Pubs and clubs see a lucrative business opportunity. So what can, or should, be done?

A number of government-funded promotional campaigns have tried to reach youngsters with messages about health risks, about personal danger when drink makes them vulnerable, and even about making them see how ridiculous drunks look. One ad showed a night out in reverse. A young woman with messed up hair and smudged make-up, wearing ripped clothes covered in drink and vomit stains, staggers out of her front door on broken heels. A young man pours curry down his chest, rips his clothes and beats himself up. The strap line reads: 'You wouldn't start a night like this so why end it that way?'

Taxes on alcohol are high, making prices higher. This is partly to make it less affordable and partly because the taxes on alcohol sales raise valuable revenue for the government. If people drank less, the Treasury would actually suffer. Even so, there is talk of raising prices further to discourage excess drinking.

There are rules governing the sale of alcohol. In the UK you have to have a licence to sell it. Only over-18s can buy it. It can only be drunk in designated places such as bars and restaurants. Some councils have now banned drinking in the street, for example. In Sweden, the rules are even stricter.

The UK has regulations governing alcohol advertising, e.g. advertising cannot suggest that having a drink makes you more attractive or more capable. It must not target young people and so all the actors or models must look over 25. The ads mustn't plug into youth culture – as some alcopops advertising used to do. In France, mass media alcohol advertising is banned all together.

Drinks manufacturers have pledged to encourage more moderate drinking. Some cans and bottles carry advice to 'enjoy this drink sensibly'. Diageo, who make brands such as Guinness and Smirnoff, have run sensible drinking campaigns (though with a rather smaller budget than their brand advertising campaigns) At the same time, pubs are running sales promotions designed to get young people to drink more: happy hours where drinks are half price, buy one get one free promotions, reduced prices, loyalty cards – you can probably think of others. In December 2008, the government released a new code of practice for the drinks industry which outlawed a number of promotions including 'all you can drink for a set price' offers.

So what is the answer? Who is responsible? Should we rely on the drinks trade to police itself and on young people to take care of themselves? Should these promotions be banned? Should alcohol advertising be banned? Should the sale of alcohol be further restricted?

Would higher prices make young people drink less?

If it knows that a lot of people will order the same dish, then there is less waste, and so less cost.

Changing the price

For many businesses, changing prices is expensive and time-consuming, so it is not something they want to do frequently. They have to rework the figures, recalculate

VAT, redraw breakeven charts and work out new profit forecasts. Mail-order companies have to reprint their catalogues (the larger, glossier ones can cost as much as £5 (€7) each). Restaurants have to reprint their menus. Shops have to change price labels and tills have to be reprogrammed.

So, given the trouble and expense involved, why would a firm change its prices? There are a number of possible, pressing reasons:

- there is a substantial change in business costs, perhaps because raw materials have become cheaper or new production techniques have become more efficient (lower price can be charged), or materials or wages have become more expensive (an increase in prices is needed to compensate)
- there is an imbalance between supply and demand, i.e. customers want to buy more than the company has to sell; if there's a shortage, then prices may rise – possible causes include production hold-ups, such as strikes, shortages in materials, machine breakdowns, and the product suddenly becomes fashionable (the latest craze)
- there is an imbalance between supply and demand, i.e. customers do not want to buy as much as the company has to sell; if there's a surplus, then prices may fall – possible causes include a bumper harvest, a better product hitting the market, a health or safety scare (e.g. news stories about red meat being bad for you caused a massive drop in the sales of beef, pork and lamb)
- a change in competitors' marketing, e.g. a price decrease, a major advertising campaign, new stores opening up
- a changed economic situation, e.g. inflation
- new laws, new taxes or other government pressure, e.g. government-appointed regulators review the prices charged by privatised utilities (BT, water companies, gas and electricity providers)
- as a result of a change in the firm's marketing strategy, e.g. as part of a repositioning exercise.

EXPAND YOUR KNOWLEDGE

Guiltinan, J.P. (1976) 'Risk-aversive pricing policies: problems and alternatives', *Journal of Marketing*, 40 (1): 10–15.

Joseph Guiltinan reports on the increasingly important role of pricing for marketing. Current pricing responses to economic uncertainties are reviewed and key problems are identified. Alternative responses are developed.

PRICE WARS

A **price war** is a destructive spiral of reducing prices. It starts with one seller trying to undercut competitors by reducing prices. Others follow suit, meaning that the first firm has to reduce prices again in order to maintain its competitive advantage. So it goes on, sometimes until the weaker competitors (those with fewer financial resources) go out of business (see Exhibit 10.8).

In the short term, a price war is popular with consumers, but it is bad for business and, in the longer term, it is bad for consumers too.

price war
two or more firms keep undercutting each other in an attempt to build market share until one or other backs off or goes out of business

Exhibit 10.8   Price wars

market share
a firm's sales expressed as a percentage of the total sales of that type of product in the defined market

Businesses lose profits – they are cutting prices and, because others are matching their price cuts, they are not gaining **market share**. So they are just selling the same amount but at a reduced price. Eventually, either firms will go out of business, thus reducing consumer choice, or the firms involved will call a truce. Then they may have to put prices back even higher to recoup the profits they lost during the price war.

Price elasticity of demand

price elasticity of demand
a measure of the degree to which demand for a good changes when its price is changed

Price elasticity of demand is a measure of price sensitivity, i.e. it measures how many more, or fewer, products are sold when the price changes (see Exhibit 10.9).

Exhibit 10.9   Price elasticity of demand

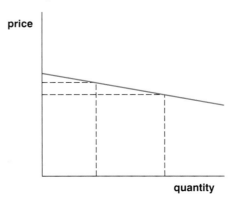

insight   Egg wars

The Easter weekend holiday is traditionally a happy time for many reasons. For food retailers it is second only to Christmas as a time of high sales, but lately those sales volumes have come at a price – a low price.

Easter is a time for eggs – chocolate eggs. The variety available has spiralled ever upwards but now the prices are spiralling downwards. This seems good news for the egg eaters, but it is not necessarily so good for the retailers. While the luxury end of the market is expanding, as discerning consumers trade up to organic and high cocoa content chocolate, the cheaper end of the market has contracted and a price war is being waged.

In 2002, a basic chocolate egg, such as those mass-produced by Cadbury, Mars and Nestlé, cost about £3. In 2006, they were priced at three for £5. In 2007, Woolworths were selling them at three for £3 – so you could get three for the price that just one would have cost four years back. Tesco went further. They were selling the eggs at two for £1.49, i.e. 75p each. Why did the price of Easter eggs drop so far so rapidly? It happened because some supermarkets slashed the prices to attract customers in to do their Easter shopping, and then the others felt they had to follow suit or miss out on sales. Then the smaller retailers, even newsagents, also had to slash the price of the chocolate eggs or they would not sell any at all.

According to Tony Page, Woolworth's commercial and marketing director, the Easter eggs were being used as loss leaders by the big chains, i.e. the prices were designed purely to attract customers into the stores and bore little or no relation to the costs of the eggs and produced little or no profit for the stores involved. 'The price deflation is driven by competition in the market. It does not reflect cost deflation. And it does not reflect the value of the product'. He also expressed concern that this downward pressure on prices was devaluing Easter eggs in the eyes of consumers. They were no longer seen as a special treat and children were buying them instead of a normal chocolate bar. In some cases, it was cheaper to buy an egg with a chocolate bar included than it was to buy the chocolate bar on its own.

SOURCE: Finch, 2007

We know from basic demand theory (and from common sense) that if the price of a product goes up, then fewer people will want to buy it, and vice versa. If a product's demand is very sensitive to a change in price, i.e. when the price goes up just a little, then far fewer products are sold and it is said to be **price elastic**. If the

price elastic
when the demand for a good changes significantly after a price change, e.g. price goes up by 10 per cent, demand falls by 20 per cent

Exhibit 10.10   Price inelasticity of demand

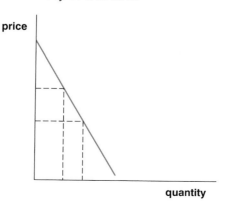

In order to calculate elasticity, the price *change* needs to be expressed as a *percentage* of the *original price*.

Price elasticity   = % change in quantity demanded / % change in price

The bigger the answer, the greater the elasticity. For example, Le Café is considering increasing the price of its café latte. It wants to know whether this price increase will achieve the aim of increasing revenue. This depends on how many customers stop buying the lattes because they are too expensive. Last time it increased the price, it went from £1.50 to £1.65, and Le Café sold 480 cups a week instead of 600. Price elasticity can help.

Step 1: work out price change

£1.65 – £1.50
  = 15p

Step 2: to express the price change as a percentage, divide the *change* in price by the *original price*

15p/150p × 100
  = 10%

Step 3: to express the quantity drop as a percentage, divide the *change* in quantity by the *original quantity*

480 – 600
= –120
  –120/600 × 100
= –20% (don't worry about the minus – it will be explained later)

Step 4: now substitute the figures into the elasticity equation

% change in quantity demanded / % change in price

20/10
  = 2

If the answer is higher than 1, the product's demand is elastic. The product is significantly sensitive to price changes and raising the price will lead to a large fall in sales. This is the case with the café lattes.

So, if you are the marketing manager of Le Café, you need to be wary of increasing the price. A better way to increase revenue would be to *decrease* the price, then a lot more people will buy the product, and the increase in the volume of lattes sold will outweigh the price decrease per latte.

If the answer is below 1, then the product in question has an inelastic demand curve. Raising the price will not put many people off and revenue should increase.

The minus sign just means that when price rises, demand falls, i.e. they have a negative relationship. If demand rose with price (as in the case of some antiques, works of art, shares), then there would be no minus sign.

product's sales do not vary by much when price changes, then its demand is said to be price inelastic (see Exhibit 10.10).

The steep curve is a price inelastic demand curve for a product such as cigarettes. As they are addictive, few people give up, even after a significant price increase.

FACTORS AFFECTING THE PRICE ELASTICITY OF DEMAND

prestige goods
high-status goods, e.g. Rolls-Royce, Rolex

● Necessity or luxury? To an economist, a luxury is anything inessential: chocolate, bubble bath, ready-made meals, DVDs, etc. Really luxurious products, such as diamonds, sports cars, top designer clothes, etc., are termed **prestige goods**. Generally, necessities and prestige goods have inelastic demand, while luxuries have elastic demand.

- Close substitutes: if there are many alternative products available, then the demand will tend to be elastic. A substitute is something that a customer could buy instead, e.g. there are lots of different makes of ballpoint pen or pencils.
- Habit forming? If it is, then the demand will tend to be inelastic, e.g. cigarettes.
- Time period: many products are more responsive to changes in price (i.e. more elastic) in the long term. It takes a while for people to find an alternative, although they eventually will. Also, higher prices will encourage new competitors into the market, and so more choice will be available.
- Frequency of purchase: the more often customers buy the product, the more impact a price increase has on their budget, and therefore the more price elastic the demand is, e.g. a student may have a favourite brand of beer, but if the price goes up, he or she may have to switch to a cheaper one.
- Customer loyalty: if a brand is well established, then it may have loyal customers who are reluctant to change. The demand will be inelastic.
- Price level: elasticity varies along the demand curve. When something is already very cheap (e.g. matches), making it cheaper may have little effect. Similarly, if something is too expensive for most people (e.g. a Rolls-Royce), making it even more expensive may have little effect on demand. So very expensive goods may have price inelastic demand above a certain level, but elastic below a certain level. Imagine £20 off trips to Australia – it is not enough to make a difference, but £200 off might be. Necessities are usually price inelastic at lower price levels, but may become elastic at higher levels as more alternative products become economically viable, e.g. cakes instead of bread, or would people take a bus to work if it cost the same as a taxi?
- Stage of the **product life cycle**: a new product may have price inelastic demand on introduction (little competition), be more price elastic during the growth phase, less elastic during maturity (assuming brand loyalty has been built up) and have a high level of price elasticity in its decline.

product life cycle
a product analysis tool based on the idea that a product has life stages: introduction, growth, maturity, decline, deletion

It is important for a company to know how demand for its product will react to a change in circumstances. This chapter has only considered elasticity in terms of price, but the concept can be applied to all marketing variables.

OTHER ELASTICITIES OF DEMAND

There are numerous different kinds of elasticity that can be calculated: advertising elasticity of demand measures how responsive sales are to a change in the advertising budget; income elasticity measures the response to a change in people's earnings. Of particular significance is cross-elasticity of demand. This measures the change in one company's sales in response to the change in price of a competitive product. For example, Coca-Cola would expect to sell more if Pepsi raised its price. Calculating the cross-elasticity would help Coca-Cola to know how many more cans to produce.

Pricing on the Internet

One of the things that makes pricing on the Internet unusual is the degree to which customers can participate in price setting – and turn into sellers themselves. eBay has been a phenomenal success, attracting many more customers than offline auctions do and even becoming a way of life for some devotees (and destroying the businesses

insight　　Price rise or price cut?

Although few marketing managers work out the exact elasticity of their products' demand curves, this is a concept that everyone involved in setting prices needs to be aware of. It is a vital consideration when changing prices as it determines whether lowering, or raising, prices is most likely to result in a revenue increase.

If a product has a price inelastic demand, then putting prices up will result in increased total sales revenue. Very few customers will stop buying the product, and their loss will be amply covered by the higher price that remaining customers pay.

If a product has a price elastic demand, then to increase revenue, the price should be lowered. Many more people will buy the product. So many that they will compensate for the lower price.

Most essential goods (bread, petrol, power, etc.) are not particularly price sensitive (inelastic). Whereas inessentials (cream cakes, bubble bath, meals in restaurants, etc.) are usually more sensitive to price changes (elastic).

This can be seen from the demand curves in Exhibits 10.11 and 10.12. The shallow curve is for a product with a price elastic demand, i.e. very sensitive to a change in price. A small price change results in a large change in the quantity of the product demanded.

of some others, e.g. sellers of collectibles). The Internet empowers bargain hunters who can more easily search out the best offers available (Wright and Jayawardhena, 2001) and at the same time provides a more convenient shopping experience for the time-starved.

There are a number of factors that combine to make Internet prices lower than their offline equivalents. Strauss et al.'s (2006) suggestions include:

- shopping agents (see below)
- reverse auctions, where sellers bid for the buyer's business
- venture capitalists, who are prepared to take a long-term view of their investment, meaning that the Internet company can charge less and sustain a loss for some time
- competition, which is fierce and worldwide
- lower costs, due to cutting out intermediaries (e.g. retailers), getting customers to do some of the administration (e.g. filling in order forms), cutting staff (automation), reduced printing requirements
- high price elasticity, i.e. price sensitivity (see above for a more detailed explanation) – online markets appear more price-sensitive than their offline equivalents
- frequent price changes – e-tailers can respond more quickly and easily to changes in competitive prices or in other market conditions.

To these can be added tax avoidance, as very few people pay the import duties on products bought over the Internet and shipped in from abroad.

In the early days of the Internet, economists gleefully anticipated the realisation of something that had, until then, been only a theory: an **efficient market**. In an efficient market, buyers have ready access to pricing information for all their choices of products to buy. The Internet provides this thanks to the ease of searching numerous possible suppliers, its interactivity (which enables real-time auctions), the ease with which prices can be changed and the availability of shopping agents. Shopping agents are software programs which search the Internet and then display a table of

efficient market
a market in which prices adjust quickly, and frequently, in response to new information (in economic theory)

comparative prices for a specified item, e.g. PriceSCAN or Kelkoo. Interestingly, despite the opportunities to shop around, not all Internet shoppers choose the lowest possible price. One of the reasons for this is the trust issue. Although e-shopping is now widely accepted, many consumers prefer to buy from known and trusted sites rather than risk their credit card details to less well-known ones – and they are prepared to pay a price premium for that privilege.

There is much debate as to whether the Internet is really a different marketplace or just a different marketing channel. Does it reach a new set of customers or just reach the same ones in a different way? Whether it is a new market or not, most of the old rules still apply to it – and that includes the pricing strategies, tactics and methods discussed elsewhere in this chapter. Sometimes, however, it does provide a new way to implement the old ideas. Take price discrimination, for example.

The Internet has provided companies with additional segmentation tools and price discrimination possibilities. Information about customers gained through cookies and registration forms can be used to segment the customers and charge them different prices. Companies need to exercise care here, though, as consumers are likely to perceive the charging of different prices on this basis as unfair and therefore to trust the suppliers less in the future (Grewal et al., 2004). The music industry has come in for a lot of criticism because of its pricing policies, both on- and offline. For example, Apple itunes customers are charged differently for downloads according to the country revealed by their email address – a practice which has resulted in an EU investigation of the record companies responsible for the differing charges (Jacoby, 2007).

SUMMARY

Pricing is a much neglected marketing tool. Too many firms take a mechanical approach to the setting of prices, often purely on the basis of costs. Far too few organisations review their prices regularly enough and so they miss marketing opportunities.

Pricing is a competitive weapon that should be deployed alongside the rest of the marketing mix. A product's price sends a message – of quality, of desirability, of status, of a good buy. It has to vary according to place of purchase – wholesale, retail, Internet. It is a key part of the brand.

Common pricing objectives include maximising revenue, maintaining brand image, building market share, recovering an investment made (usually in developing the product), enticing customers to the store, and rewarding customers for loyalty.

Pricing methods are largely either cost-based or market-based. Too great an emphasis on cost can lead to missed profit. Market-based methods take account of what the market can bear, but the price must always be high enough to cover costs in the long run.

Pricing strategies and tactics overlap. There are specific strategies for new product pricing. Firms following a market penetration strategy set their prices low. A market skimming strategy employs high prices. General pricing strategies include: prestige pricing, where a high price is set to confer status; pre-emptive pricing, where a lower price is set to discourage competition; product line pricing, where related products are sold at a variety of prices; and price discrimination, which charges different prices for the same product to different market segments.

Pricing tactics include psychological pricing, which sets a price that sounds cheaper (e.g. £999) and loss leaders, which are products sold very cheaply but made up for by the profits of others.

Elasticity is a key concept when changing prices. Products with price inelastic demand will earn more revenue if the price is increased. Prices for products with price elastic demand should be lowered if the firm wants to increase its sales revenue.

CHALLENGES REVIEWED

Now that you have finished reading the chapter, look back at the challenges you were set at the beginning. Do you have a clearer idea of what's involved?

Hints:

- profit margins and price wars
- price elasticity of demand and the impact of price on image
- new product pricing strategies – skimming
- think about why the banks will not make the loans – can these people afford to pay them back? What will happen if they cannot make the payments?
- remember parallel importing. The product may need simplifying in order to reduce costs.

READING AROUND

Journal articles

Jeffrey Paul Bray and Christine Harris (2006) 'The effect of 9-ending prices on retail sales: a quantitative UK-based field study', *Journal of Marketing Management*, 22 (5/6): 601–17.

Nirmalya Kumar (2006) 'Strategies to fight low cost rivals', *Harvard Business Review*, 84 (12): 104–12.

Vincent-Wayne Mitchell and Joseph Ka Lun Chan (2002) 'Investigating UK consumers' unethical attitudes and behaviours', *Journal of Marketing Management*, 18 (1/2): 5–26.

Magazine articles

Jane Bainbridge (2007) 'Sector insight: low-cost airlines – cheap flights expand reach: the appeal of low-cost carriers has extended from younger travellers to the business market', *Marketing*, 4 April.

Nicola Clark (2007) 'News analysis: over here and over priced: everyone's excited about Abercrombie & Fitch in London, but are the prices and positioning right?' *Marketing*, 11 April.

Websites

www.kelkoo.co.uk – a price-comparison site, to find cheaper prices.

SELF-REVIEW QUESTIONS

1. How does price affect a product's brand image? (see page 357)
2. How do the forces of supply and demand affect prices? (see pages 358–9)
3. Complete this formula: perceived value = perceived benefits –. (see page 360)
4. List three possible objectives of a pricing strategy. (see page 361)
5. List the three key influencers on pricing decisions. (see page 362)
6. What is a psychological price barrier? (see page 364)
7. Whose prices are taken into account in 'going-rate pricing'? (see page 364)
8. Which type of cost is mark-up pricing based on? (see page 366)
9. If a new customer wanted to place a large order but would only accept a low price, what would you take into account when deciding whether or not to take the order? (see pages 368–9)
10. What are the drawbacks to breakeven analysis? (see page 372)
11. Briefly describe two major new product pricing strategies. (see page 372)
12. Define price elasticity of demand. (see page 382)

Levi's vs Tesco

Read the questions, then the case material, then answer the questions.

Questions

1. Why was Levi's so reluctant to sell its jeans to Tesco?
2. How was Tesco able to sell the jeans so cheaply?
3. If large food retailers are able to sell designer brands at cheap prices, what are the long-term implications for branding?

The world's biggest brands have spent a fortune building their names and they protect their image jealously. Large retail chains have enormous amounts of marketing power and are used to being able to dictate terms to their suppliers. A clash seemed inevitable. The court case involving Levi Strauss and British supermarket chain Tesco was part of a power struggle between these two camps.

Britons spend an estimated £20 billion a year on branded fashion goods, and Tesco wants the right to sell those designer brands cheaply, but if it wins, then the brands' exclusivity is lost. Sourcing the goods was not easy. Tesco had to buy them through the grey market. Levi's would not sell to the supermarket directly

and bona fide Levi's distributors were worried about selling the jeans on to supermarkets.

Christine Cross, head of Tesco's non-food sales, felt that consumers should not have to pay such high prices: 'Consumers today are very well travelled, they see prices all over the world . . . why should Levi's be one price in America, another in France and a third price in the UK?' However, Levi's was concerned for the future of its business: 'Our brand is our most important asset. It is more valuable than all the other assets on our balance sheet. It's more valuable than our factories, our buildings, our warehouses and our inventory,' explained Joe Middleton, Levi's European president. 'The true cost of making this jean is not just the factory element. It is much more than that.'

Many were unconvinced by the brand's arguments. If the superstores gained the right to stock anything they wanted to, then Brits could buy cheaper jeans – either with their groceries or through traditional channels forced to reduce prices or lose sales. Of course, the longer-term casualty would be brand value, which would be unlikely to survive the shame of jeans being sold alongside baked beans.

The court decided that a manufacturer had a right to oversee the distribution of its products. Levi's won and its brand image was saved – until next time.

SOURCE: Datar, n.d.

REFERENCES

Anon (2001) 'Vitamin cartel fined for price fixing', *The Guardian*, 21 November.

Bandyopadhyay, S., Lin, G.B. and Zhong, Y. (2001) 'Under the gavel', *Marketing Management*, 10 (4): 24–8.

BA (n.d.) *Buy travel*, British Airways. Available at: **www.britishairways.com/travel/fx/public/** (accessed 14/04/2007).

Cox, J. (2001) 'Pricing practices that endanger profits', *Marketing Management*, 10 (3): 42–6.

Datar, R. (n.d.) 'Battle of the brands', *The Money Programme*, BBC TV. Available at: **news. bbc.co.uk/1/hi/programmes/the_money_programme/archive/1604636.stm** (accessed 20/10/2002).

Dean, J. (1970) 'Techniques for pricing new products and services', in V.P. Buell and C. Heyel (eds) *Handbook of Modern Marketing*. New York: McGraw-Hill, pp. 5–51 – 5–61. Also appeared in *Harvard Business Review* with retrospective commentary (Nov–Dec, 1978).

InterRail (n.d.) Untitled. Available at: **www.interrail.net** (accessed 14/04/2007).

Finch, J. (2007) 'Supermarkets wage Easter egg price war', *The Guardian*, 7 April, p. 35.

France, M. and Hamm, S. (1998) 'Does predatory pricing make Microsoft a predator?', *Business Week*, 23 November. Available at: **www.businessweek.com** (accessed 15/10/2002).

Grewal, D., Hardesty, D.M. and Gopalkrishnan, R.I. (2004) 'The effects of buyer identification and purchase timing on consumers' perceptions of trust, price fairness, and repurchase intentions', *Journal of Interactive Marketing*, 18 (4): 87–101.

Guiltinan, J.P. (1976) 'Risk-aversive pricing policies: problems and alternatives', *Journal of Marketing*, 40 (1): 10–15.

Jacoby, M. (2007) 'EU music complaint focuses on record firms: Apple's iTunes store Isn't getting scrutiny in price investigation', *Wall Street Journal* (Eastern Edition) Technology, 4 April, p. B5.

Lancaster, G., Withey, F. and Ashford, R. (2000) *Marketing Fundamentals*. CIM Workbook. Oxford: Butterworth-Heinemann.

Office of Fair Trading (2002) 'Aberdeen Journals Ltd has been fined £1.328 million for abusing a dominant market position'. Available at: **www.oft.gov.uk/news/press + releases/2002/ pn+58-02+oft+fines+scottish+newspaper+publisher+for+predatory+pricing.htm** (accessed 20/10/2002).

OPEC (n.d.) no title, Organisation of the Petroleum Exporting Countries. Available at: **www. opec.org** (accessed 14/04/2007).

Oxenfeldt, A.R. (1973) 'A decision-making structure for price decisions', *Journal of Marketing*, Jan: 48–53.

Strauss, J., El-Ansary, A. and Frost, R. (2006) *e-marketing* (4th international edn). Harlow: Pearson Prentice Hall.

Wainwright, M. (2007) 'Ikealand: where an Englishman's home is his Bo Klok', *The Guardian*, 31 January.

Wright, L. and Jayawardhena, C. (2001) 'Netting the consumer: the e-direct marketing imperative', *Proceedings of the Marketing Science Conference*. Cardiff: University of Cardiff.

APPENDIX: additional cost-based pricing activity

ACTIVITY: Drawing a breakeven chart

You will need proper graph paper, a ruler, pencil, rubber and calculator for this.

The Roadrunner Co. produces racing bicycles.

> fixed costs (FC) total £1.2 million
> variable costs (VC) are £800 per bike
> the bike sells for £2,000

1. The first challenge is to decide on the scale for the graph. In real life, you would know current output levels and could use that as a guide. Otherwise, it is really trial and error. Draw the y (vertical) axis along the short side of your paper. For our Roadrunner example, let's label the (vertical) y axis £m, and take it up to £4m, and the (horizontal) x axis (quantity of bicycles) to 3,500.
2. Now, plot the fixed costs. This is the easy one – fixed costs do not change so we draw a straight, horizontal line across from the y axis at £1.2 million. Label this line 'FC'.
3. Next, draw the variable costs (VC) line. VC are £800 per bike, so pick a number (any number between 1 and 3,500) and work out the VC at that level of output.

   For example, 500 × £800 = £400,000

   Now make a small mark at the point where 500 on the x axis meets £400,000 on the y axis. Repeat for another random point, say 2,000:

   2,000 × £800 = £1,600,000

   Next, taking 0 (bottom left corner of the graph) as your starting point, just join the dots to make a variable cost line (it should be a straight, diagonal line; if it is not, then check the two calculations). Label this line 'VC'.
       Why use 0 as a starting point? It is because if you don't make any products, then there will be no variable costs – they are ingredients and raw materials, remember.
4. The next line to draw is the total cost (TC) line and there's a cheat's way to do this.
       Take a ruler and lay it along the VC line, then carefully move it up, keeping the angle the same, until it crosses the y axis at the start of the FC line. Then draw a straight diagonal line, starting at the y axis. This line should be parallel to the VC line. Label this line 'TC'.

Exhibit 10.11   Roadrunner Co. breakeven chart

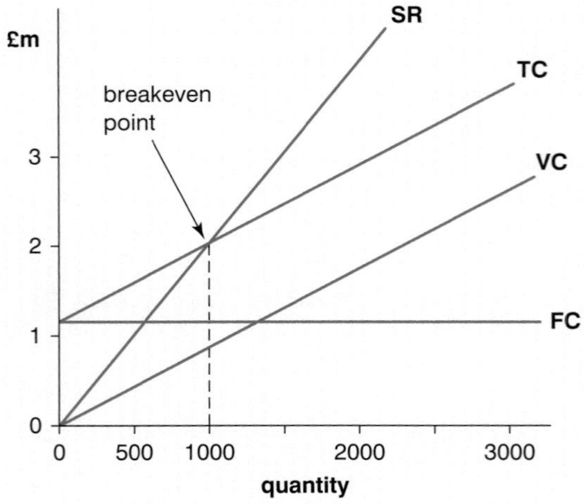

Why does the total cost line start at the FC line? Because total cost = fixed cost + variable cost, so it can never be *less* than fixed cost.

5. The sales revenue (SR) line is drawn in a similar way to the VC line. Pick two numbers (any two numbers within the scale of the graph). Work out the revenue at those sales volumes (quantity × price), then, using 0 as a starting point, plot a straight diagonal line that joins all three points. Label this line 'SR'.

6. Now you're ready to read off the breakeven point. X marks the spot, i.e. it is where the sales revenue and total cost lines cross. Draw a line down to the quantity axis – the answer should be 1,000.

Of course, if the company wants to know what happens if the price is increased to £2,100, it will have to draw a new line for sales revenue.

As an alternative to the graphical method, the firm might calculate breakeven points using this formula:

$$\frac{\text{Fixed costs}}{\text{Contribution }\textbf{per item}}$$

Let's revisit the Roadrunner Co. figures:

    fixed costs total £1.2 million
    variable costs are £800 per bike
    price is £2,000
    contribution = selling price – variable cost
                  = £2,000 – £800 = £1,200
    1,200,000   = 1,000
    1,200

So, it needs to sell 1,000 bicycles at £2,000 in order to cover all its costs, i.e. to break even.

ACTIVITY: Answer to full-cost pricing activity (see page 367).

total cost	= fixed costs + variable costs
fixed cost per unit (box)	= £ 40,000 = 40p
	100,000
total cost per unit (box)	= 40p + £1 = £1.40
price, i.e. total cost + 25%	
	= £1.40 + £1.40 × 25%
	= £1.75

Part four

MANAGING MARKETING

THIS PART CONTAINS:

11 Building brands using the marketing mix

12 Marketing planning

WHAT THIS PART IS ABOUT:

The final section of this book draws together all the previous areas and shows what marketers actually do with the resources at their disposal. Branding is a major weapon in a marketer's armoury and so Chapter 11 looks back at previous chapters on the marketing mix and shows how the 4Ps combine to build brands. Chapter 12 then explains the marketing planning process and how it is used to manage marketing activities and to achieve marketing goals.

Modern organisations are highly reliant upon marketing and successful marketing is dependent upon the skills of marketers. There is a wide range of different roles within marketing: research and analysis, logistics planning and management, account handling, brand management, new product development, price setting – it would take too much space to list them all here. However, we do want you to share our enthusiasm for marketing and to find your ideal marketing role. So we have put an extra, bonus, section on this book's companion website that explains what marketers do in more detail and how your career might develop.

Go to www.sagepub.co.uk/masterson

We wish you good luck in your future marketing career!

11

Building brands
using the marketing mix

CHAPTER CONTENTS

Introduction
Marketing mix objectives
The marketing mix: a reprise
Packaging – the fifth P?
The extended marketing mix: 7Ps
Mixing it (integrating the marketing mix)
Varying the mix through a product's life
Criticisms of the marketing mix
Branding
Brand equity
Brand types
Brand names
Branding strategies
Global branding
Brand loyalty
Summary
Challenges reviewed
Reading around
Self-review questions
Mini case study
References

BRAND-BUILDING CHALLENGES

The following are illustrations of the types of decision that marketers have to take or issues they face. *You aren't expected to know how to deal with the challenges now*; just bear them in mind as you read the chapter and see what you can find that helps.

● Aphrodite is a small, well-known confectionery brand that wants to change its image to that of a supplier of high-quality, special-occasion sweets. The marketing director has asked you to review current marketing activities to ensure that they support this new market position. What do you need to check?

● You are the marketing manager for a well-known designer fashion brand. A chain store has approached your company with a view to placing a large order. The finance manager is delighted and is prepared to discount the price. However, the managing director has some concerns. Do you think this order should be accepted? Do you want to impose any special terms and conditions?

● A friend owns two coffee bars, one in Leicester and one in Edinburgh. She now works in Edinburgh as that coffee bar is new and has no manager yet. Since she left, takings at the Leicester restaurant have dropped right down and she doesn't know why. She has asked you to help her find the problem. Do you know what to do?

● You are the brand manager for a range of jams that are one of the oldest brands in the world. The range has distinctive and well-recognised packaging. However, the packaging is plastic and not recyclable and you are under pressure to change it. You are worried about losing your brand's competitive advantage. What do you need to consider? What can you do?

Introduction

4Ps
a mnemonic (memory aid) for the marketing mix: product, promotion, place, price

7Ps
a mnemonic (memory aid) for the services marketing mix: product, promotion, place, price, physical evidence, people and process

The marketing mix is at the core of any marketing plan. The most commonly used schematic for the marketing mix is the **4Ps** and this has the advantage of being both widely recognised and easy to remember. This 4Ps mnemonic was first proposed by Jerome E. McCarthy in 1960 and, despite some criticism over the years, it is still taught in universities and used in practice today (McCarthy, 1960). However, with the increasing emphasis on services, and the service elements of physical products, the preferred framework today is the **7Ps.**

The marketing mix is a set of tools and should be treated as such. No one element can stand alone; they must all support each other. If they conflict, target markets will be confused, objectives will not be met and the brand's image will be diluted. Marketing managers blend their marketing mixes to make an integrated plan that will achieve their marketing objectives.

This chapter is a round up of the marketing mix, summarising the techniques, demonstrating how they fit together and showing how they can be integrated to build brands. The idea of branding as an integral part of a modern product was introduced in Chapter 6. It will be considered here as a strategy that employs all elements of the marketing mix.

If preferred, this chapter can be read first as an introduction to the more detailed chapters on each element of the mix (Chapters 6–10).

Marketing mix objectives

Before any decisions are taken on what to do with the marketing mix, it is important to know what you are trying to achieve. If you just get into your car and drive,

Exhibit 11.1   Planning to meet objectives

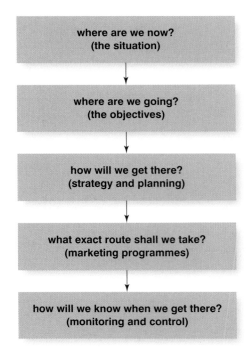

without first deciding where you want to go, then you will just drive around aimlessly. To reach a destination, you have to know where you want to be and plan a route to get there. The marketing mix is the organisation's route to its marketing objectives (see Exhibit 11.1).

An organisation's objectives work in a hierarchy. At the top level are the corporate objectives. All other objectives, including marketing, should be designed to contribute to those overall, corporate objectives.

Exhibit 11.2   Hierarchy of objectives

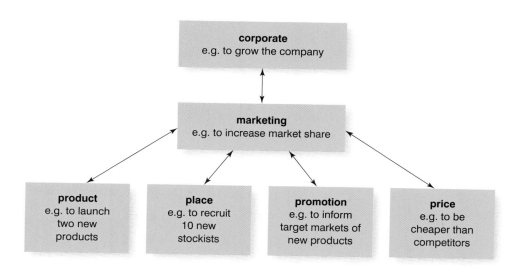

The objectives illustrated in Exhibit 11.2 are insufficiently detailed for the real world – more precision and explanation is required. For example, objectives should always try to be SMART:

Specific	clearly worded and directed at specific markets and/or audiences
Measurable	it will be clear that the objective really has been achieved; this normally means that it will be quantifiable, e.g. a percentage or absolute amount to be gained
Achievable	possible to do
Relevant	of value to the organisation and in keeping with other objectives; also objectives should always be challenging enough to act as motivators
Timed	with a deadline.

Objectives are not general across markets or even the whole of one market but directed at specific market segments (see Chapter 4).

So an example of a SMART objective might be to increase sales revenue from the pet food division (specific) by 10 per cent (measurable) by 31 December 2012 (timed). This objective could be relevant if the company was seeking to grow, and achievable if it has the resources (money, people, facilities) to put behind the sales drive. (For more on marketing objectives, see Chapter 12.)

A well-designed marketing mix will:

- achieve marketing objectives
- meet customers' needs
- create competitive advantage

- be well integrated (each element supporting the others)
- fit within the available marketing resources.

The meeting of customer needs is at the heart of good marketing. Marketers have to get inside their customers' heads and see the offering through their eyes. If the offering is noticeably better than that of the competition, then competitive advantage will be created. For example, it may be better quality, or cheaper, have a better image or be more readily available. The marketing mix will be more effective if it is well integrated, i.e. each element fits with the others so that there are no contradictory signals (see 'Mixing it' below). Resources are always a constraint on marketing activities. There is no point in designing a mix that the company does not have the resources (finance, expertise, time or a suitable infrastructure) to implement.

The marketing mix: a reprise

FIRST THERE WERE 4PS: THE TRADITIONAL MARKETING MIX

Each of the 4Ps is covered in more depth in its own chapter (Chapters 6–10). This chapter focuses on integrating the elements of the marketing mix to build brands and also introduces some of the additional complexities associated with international marketing. Exhibit 11.3 summarises the 4Ps and shows how they can fit together.

Exhibit 11.3   The 4Ps: key variables

Product	Price	Place	Promotion
Features (characteristics, attributes)	Price range	Intermediaries (retailers, wholesalers, etc.)	Advertising
Range	Discounts	Coverage	Personal selling
Support services	Allowances	Order processing	Public relations
Brand	Negotiation policy	Stock control	Sales promotion
Design	Credit policy	Delivery	Direct marketing
Packaging	Price changes	Transport	Sponsorship

PRODUCT

It may seem obvious just what a product is (a pen, a car, a ring, a bar of chocolate, etc.), but there is rather more to it than that.

Products of the same type, e.g. cars, and even produced by the same manufacturer, e.g. Ford, are differentiated by features, quality, size, speed, shape and colour. They have different features (engine size, braking system, colour, interior trim, etc.) and come in different sizes for different drivers (small car, small family car, family car, executive, limousine, van, minibus, people carrier, etc.). All these things are characteristics (or attributes) of a particular car and so a product could be said to be a bundle of characteristics. It is the quality of these features, coupled with the workmanship that goes into the product, that determines its quality. Quality is something that most customers look for in a product, even though they cannot always afford to buy the best. This is an example of how the marketing mix integrates. The best components, such as those that go into a Rolls-Royce (e.g. walnut veneer dashboards), cost more than others (e.g. plastic dashboards). This means that a higher price will have to be set for the products that have the higher-quality components. Some customers will be willing and able to pay that price (so long as the quality really is better), some will not. Those who do buy a Rolls-Royce will be buying not just a car but an exclusive image. They will therefore expect impeccable service, both before and after the sale.

Companies provide a range of products, of differing quality, with different features, different images and different levels of support, to match the prices that different customers are prepared to pay for that product type.

So a product is a bundle of characteristics but, of course, that is not what customers really want to buy. What the customer really wants is the benefit that the product brings. People do not just buy cars, they buy means of transport or status symbols. They do not really buy rings because they want small bands of metal, they want tokens of affection, gifts, decorated fingers, symbols of their engagement. Marketers must concentrate on the benefits their products bring to their purchasers – the product features and quality are really just the means by which those benefits are delivered.

ACTIVITY

Choose a pair of products from the list below. What are their features? What are the benefits that those features are designed to deliver?

- iPod and Sony Discman
- a tub of Häagen-Dazs ice cream and a Unilever Cornetto
- a pair of trainers and a pair of walking boots
- sleeping bags and duvets (think of all the possible variances)
- music downloads and CDs

Products have a number of levels, which together make up the total product offering. Customers may decide between two products on the basis of any of the attributes listed in Exhibit 11.4, e.g. new customer support, but they will not buy a product that does not deliver the core benefit required. A pen must write, chocolate must taste good, a car must go.

The basic product is the product itself and includes features, components and quality level. Remember that this may be a physical product or a service product. Service products also have features, components, quality levels, etc. Take a dry cleaning service, for example. It may be local (a feature), include ironing (a component), be standard or gold service (quality), and be given back to the customer in a plastic bag or a strong clothes carrier (packaging). The perceived product is the product as the customer actually sees it, which may not be in quite the way the supplier intended. For example, a restaurant may wish to be thought of as upmarket, but its target market may just think it is over-priced. The augmented product is the surrounding support for the product, including all support services, delivery and installation.

Exhibit 11.4   The total product offering

Take a shirt, as an example. Its core benefits are that it covers nakedness and provides some warmth. As a basic product, the shirt is blue, fashionably styled, available in most sizes and made of 100 per cent cotton of the highest quality. The supplier offers a no-quibble, money-back guarantee if the shirt fails to live up to expectations. This augments (adds to) the product. If the shirt in question also happens to be made by Armani, how does that affect your perception of it?

Previously, firms tried to differentiate themselves from their competition through tangible product advantages: their products might be better quality, come in more colours, have additional features, etc. Competitive strategies centred upon developing a

Augmented products

B2B focus

There is likely to be a greater emphasis on service in B2B markets, both pre- and post-sale. It is important to business customers that products are delivered on time and that they are repaired promptly, if necessary. If equipment is down, then this is likely to mean lost sales. Take PCs as an example. It is frustrating enough for a consumer when a computer won't work, but for a firm it might mean that orders don't get through, or customers cannot reach them, or sales cannot be processed because customer details are unavailable. It has much more serious implications.

Businesses usually order larger quantities and so are more valuable customers than individual consumers.

They are likely to be more particular about specifications too. Many companies have policies that state which computers must be bought for which purpose and exactly how large, fast, etc., they should be. They may insist on bespoke systems designed specifically to meet their needs and, if the order is big enough, the supplier is likely to provide these.

Customer relationships are more important in B2B markets. It is a lot of effort to win new business and so the emphasis is on retaining the good customers you have and benefiting from their repeat purchases. This often requires high-quality, responsive customer service.

insight   The age of the brand

Since it was first devised, the marketing mix has been a major source of competitive advantage for many firms: Aldi and ASDA charge cheaper prices, Mercedes makes superior cars, the founder of Woolworth claimed the three secrets of retail success were 'location, location, location', and most FMCG companies spend millions on promotion. However, towards the end of the twentieth century, branding was seen to be the main contributor to a company's competitive edge. The emphasis was on brand value. Leading brands battled for the loyalty of consumers, and few more fiercely than the big sportswear companies, Nike, Reebok and Adidas, who spent millions promoting their brands. They competed as fiercely to sponsor the best, or in some cases the most photogenic, sports stars as those athletes competed themselves.

Some highly successful organisations are just brands – they don't actually make anything and may franchise the selling operation too. For example, Virgin has lent its name to a number of products (vodka, cola, cosmetics) that it has very little to do with. At the beginning of the twenty-first century, the brand's power looks less sure. Customers seem to want more value than a brand alone can give Customer service looks set to be the key source of competitive edge over the next few years. What will the sportswear giants come up with next?

Famous faces can help make brands famous too

product that was demonstrably superior to competitors' products and then updating it regularly in order to maintain that superior position. However, as markets have become more competitive, tangible product differences are harder to maintain and so the augmented product has become the main source of competitive edge for many companies – their unique selling propositions (USPs).

The term USP originally stood for 'unique selling point' and was first used by Rosser Reeves, whose idea was that advertising worked best when it made one clear point. Unfortunately, the phrase was picked up and reinterpreted as meaning that a product must have a unique feature, something that it is increasingly hard to maintain (Pickton and Broderick, 2004). The word 'point' caused confusion and consequently 'unique selling proposition' is the definition now generally preferred.

The USPs of today are most likely to be derived from additional services or from brand values. (For more on services, see Chapter 7.)

International product decisions

Most consumer products are adapted in some way to suit the needs of different countries although we are now seeing a convergence of tastes and preferences, largely due to improved global communications and the efforts of multinational and global companies. This allows manufacturers to standardise products in certain categories. For example, Gillette's Mach 3 was developed as a world product. It is a standard shaving system designed to meet the needs of men who want a quicker, closer shave – whatever their nationality.

ACTIVITY

This exercise is perhaps best done in class, or at least with a group. List as many products as you can that are absolutely standard in all their features and characteristics, the world over. Then compare lists and see if you agree with the products that others have listed.

product life cycle
a product analysis tool based on the idea that a product has life stages: introduction, growth, maturity, decline, deletion

There are some products that look the same and are assumed to be the same, but even Coca-Cola is not the same in all countries, e.g. it has more sugar in India than it does in Europe. There are many more standardised products in B2B and industrial markets. Raw ingredients such as vegetables, commodities such as salt, metals, minerals and gemstones are all standard, as are many office and computer supplies. Analysis tools such as the **product life cycle** and the **Boston Consulting Group Portfolio Matrix** (BCG matrix) are used in international marketing as well as in domestic marketing. Products may be at different stages in their life cycles in different countries, although these differences are reducing as the forces of globalisation gather force. Exporting has long been seen as a means of extending a product's life cycle but, with the convergence of life cycles internationally, the general shortening of product lives and the trend for global brands to launch new products simultaneously in multiple countries, this is becoming less common. In terms of the BCG matrix, at the simplest level the 'market' referred to on the axes can be taken as the country in question, although it should be remembered that few countries are really just one big uniform market segment.

PROMOTION (MARKETING COMMUNICATIONS)

Today, consumers have a wide choice of products on which to spend their money. Sellers try to influence that choice through the use of promotion. This is the part of the marketing mix that is primarily concerned with communication, which is why it is now more commonly known as marketing communications. Unfortunately, that does not start with P, though, and so the old term of promotion is still used as well. Marketing communications is thought to be a better term as it is more accurate a description and because there was always the possibility of confusion between promotion and sales promotion. Marketing communications and promotion are interchangeable terms and this text uses both.

The promotional mix traditionally comprises:

hospitality
hosting clients (e.g. providing refreshments in a private room) at events

product placement
arranging for products to be seen, or referred to, in entertainment media, e.g. during TV or radio programmes, films, plays, video games

sponsorship
giving financial aid, or other resources, to an individual, organisation (usually non-profit making) or event in return for a positive association with them, e.g. the Coca-Cola cup

- advertising
- public relations (PR)
- sales promotion
- personal selling.

Direct marketing communication and **sponsorship** can be added to these.

Advertising uses paid-for mass media (advertisers buy space or air time in which to show their adverts), e.g. television, radio, cinema, Internet, leaflets. Media relations is a large part of **public relations (PR)** and this uses *unpaid*-for media, mainly through media releases, the placing of stories, press conferences and briefings, and publicity stunts. Although PR does not use paid-for space or air time, it would be a mistake to describe PR as free. PR agencies do not work for free and there are printing and other costs to account for as well. Organisations use a range of PR activities, including exhibitions, **hospitality, sponsorship** and **product placement**. All of these are designed to build relationships with audiences and promote understanding of the organisation and its activities. Short-term special offers (money-off coupons, multibuys, competitions, free trials, etc.) are called sales promotions and are a popular choice, especially among FMCG retailers. Personal selling ranges from sales assistants in shops, through door-to-door salespeople and telesales, to the high-level account managers who sell large capital items (such as bridges and mainframe computers) to governments and the boards of multinational clients.

All these activities must be integrated so that they support, rather than contradict, each other. The same message and tone should come through from each activity. This is an important part of building brand image. As well as being integrated with each other, marketing communications activities must also fit with the rest of the marketing mix as the message comes through from all of the mix, not just from explicit communications. Harrods sells quality products at premium prices, and we expect its communications to be similarly upmarket. A gaudy advert in a downmarket magazine offering a BOGOF would detract from its carefully cultivated image. (For more on marketing communications, see Chapter 8.)

B2B focus — Marketing communications

The biggest promotional tool in B2B is personal selling. Firms who operate in B2B markets, rather than consumer markets, usually have fewer customers who buy more. This makes the expense of salespeople worthwhile. Salespeople can explain complex products and build relationships with their customers. They are an important source of competitive edge and repeat business.

Trade shows and exhibitions are important in business markets. Most industries have these (e.g. Internet World, the Motor Show, the Boat Show). They are good for networking, product demonstrations, identifying prospects, building contact databases, entertaining customers and checking out the competition.

Businesses do use advertising to market to other businesses, but they use different media. Television would be overkill. Most adverts appear in the specialist trade press, such as *The Grocer*, *Computing*, *Accountancy Age*, *Environmental Engineering* and *The Hat* magazine. Sometimes businesses will do some consumer marketing to help their trade customers sell products on. So diamond miners might promote jewellery to increase the derived demand for diamonds.

International promotion (marketing communications) decisions

While promotional strategies may be global, differences of language and environment mean that they can rarely be absolutely standard in their detail. Adverts, packaging and promotions will all have to be translated. Different images, and actors, may need to be used if locals are to relate to them. Some countries insist on local actors appearing in all adverts and there are numerous other regulations that affect what promoters can and cannot do, country by country. There are a number of ways around these problems. Television and cinema adverts may be dubbed (although this does not help overcome the foreign looks of the actors). Some companies develop pattern adverts. These have a consistent look and tone, although some images and the slogan may be written for a specific audience.

Advertising media varies in its availability and quality. Some countries have no national press, some have no local press. In remote parts, television reception may be poor. The Internet is still banned in parts of the world (although this is hard to enforce in practice). In recent years, many companies have made their

Walls ice cream displays from around the world

first foray abroad via the Internet, which is an excellent direct sales medium provided that the product in question does not require too much personal support.

Trade fairs and exhibitions are often important to firms who are trying to get established in an overseas market. These provide the perfect place to demonstrate products, meet potential buyers and agents, and check out the competition.

PLACE (DISTRIBUTION AND LOGISTICS)

Place is perhaps the least descriptive of the marketing mix titles and therefore the most likely to cause confusion. Today, place refers to the whole distribution process – from customer enquiry to after-sales service. In consumer marketing, the place where the actual sale happens is part of that, but it is not the whole story. In B2B, the sale often takes place on the customer's premises, where a salesperson has called.

The **marketing channel**, or **distribution channel** illustrated in Exhibit 11.5, is a three-level channel (i.e. there are three links in the chain between the manufacturer of the product and the eventual customer).

Exhibit 11.5   Example marketing channel for clothing

fabric and trims suppliers ➡ manufacturer ➡ import agent ➡ wholesaler ➡ fashion stores ➡ customer

An important task of marketing management is to design the marketing channel. The longer the channel, the more removed the producer of the product is from its customers and the more opportunity there is for things to go wrong. Most manufacturers have little or no customer contact; it is the retailer who builds a relationship with the customer. This lack of contact makes it harder for manufacturers to get to know what their customers think of the products, what they would like to see changed, what new products they might like. It also means they have to work harder to build **brand loyalty**.

The shortest channel is a zero-level (0-level) channel. This means **direct sales** – there are no intermediaries. The product's producers deal with the customer themselves.

ACTIVITY

Given the availability of the Internet, the fact that most households now have access to it and its low-cost nature, why don't all manufacturers sell directly to customers? Why do they let their products be sold through traditional marketing channels at all? What is it that they may not be able to do, or not do as well as wholesalers and/or retailers?

Think this problem through from the point of view of:

- a PC manufacturer such as Hewlett Packard
- an FMCG manufacturer such as Kellogg's
- a car manufacturer such as Renault
- a shoe manufacturer such as Clarks

Marketing managers not only have to work out the length of a channel, but its breadth. How many **retailers**, distributors, etc. will handle the product? The answer will partly depend on whether this is an exclusive or a **mass-market** product. Is it cheap or expensive? Again, the mix intermingles. The nature of the product helps to determine the nature of the channel.

Channel conflict

The Internet has opened up new markets for all members of the supply chain, from raw materials suppliers through to retailers. This freer market access has brought new competition with it, both from companies at the same level in the supply chain and from those at different levels who were not previously seen as competitors at all. Organisations can now reach previously inaccessible markets, e.g. overseas markets, and at the same time the distinction between levels is blurring as wholesalers and manufacturers sell directly to consumers.

For example, a number of sportswear retailers have set up Internet sites to offer their customers an alternative way to buy sporting goods. In the world of e-commerce, these retailers may have to deal with competition from retailers in other countries (although in practice, many retailers cannot cope with supplying overseas orders and so only deliver to specific locations). Most of these retailers get their stocks from wholesalers, who can also now sell sports goods directly to consumers.

Wholesalers do not operate from smart high-street stores and so, in the past, were not equipped to deal with end customers. Now they can. With an Internet site, the wholesalers can cut out the retailers and sell direct. It doesn't stop there. If the wholesalers can do this, why not the manufacturers themselves?

This merging of customer bases is a cause of channel conflict. Supply chain members are able to compete with other members higher up, or lower down, the chain. Some manufacturers choose not to compete. They may offer products direct to customers but make sure that the deal is not as good as can be obtained at online retail sites. There is sound reasoning behind this strategy, and it is often to do with order administration and the problems of dealing with thousands of customers when you are only used to dealing with tens of customers.

Channel design is only the beginning. The **supply chain** for a product may be complex and will require careful ongoing management. Good relationships throughout the chain are essential for long-term success. Distributors need support and encouragement if they are to choose to **push** the right product forward.

Place is about getting the right product to the right customer at the right time. A lot goes on behind the scenes to ensure that this happens.

push strategy
a promotional strategy aimed at distribution channels

International Place decisions

Indirect exporters leave the job of getting goods to customers to someone else, but companies with a more direct involvement have to organise distribution themselves. This can be a difficult task as **distribution channels**, and the nature of the intermediaries available, can vary enormously. The Japanese distribution infrastructure used to be so fiendishly complicated that some would-be exporters claimed it was an unofficial barrier to trade. (For more on place, see Chapter 9.)

PRICE

Price is the one element of the marketing mix that does not need a budget. The other three tools all cost significant amounts. Price brings the money in.

At one level, the price is what a business charges its customer for the goods and services it provides. However, the product that the customer is buying may actually cost more than the price suggests. This may be because of hidden costs, such as a computer upgrade required before the software will run, or it may be more subtle, like the time it will take the customer to install the new software (time is money), or the loss of the benefits they would have got if they had bought a different package. So the organisation needs to bear these other things in mind when setting the actual price.

The price of a product is usually the most significant part of the value that a customer hands over in exchange for a product. Therefore, the perceived value of the product must be at least equal to the price. Other elements of the mix can be used to increase the perceived value and therefore allow the charging of a higher price, e.g. attractive or useful packaging, a free gift or an additional feature such as the bonus disks that come with some DVDs.

The price of a product sends a message to potential customers: high quality, cheap and cheerful, bargain, or somewhere in between. It is important that this message accords with the actual product. If Rolls-Royce halved its prices, people would be likely to think that the quality had dropped significantly. If Toshiba drops the price of its computers because a new model will be out soon, people may see this as a bargain and snap them up. The price and the product must match up if marketing is to work successfully.

Prices must also be in accord with place. If a restaurant wants to charge high prices, it usually needs not just good food, but also to be in a prime location. Perhaps then the restaurant critics will give it good write-ups (which is good PR). (For more on price, see Chapter 10.)

insight   Now with added extra!

Some organisations add new features to their products in an attempt to make them seem better value. However, if customers see no benefit to the additions, this ploy will only add to the firm's costs, eventually necessitating a higher price that customers may be unhappy to pay. For example, an online retailer offered a reduced-price DVD player in its clearance sale. As an added incentive, the player came with 50 free films. They were not well-known films and spanned a variety of genres – they looked like the titles that usually appear in the bargain tub.

Does this seem like a good deal?

International Pricing decisions

Organisations with trading partners or customers overseas, have to choose a currency in which to price contracts for sale. Given that marketing is about meeting customer needs, it would seem to be good marketing practice to price in the customer's currency. However, this has some disadvantages for the seller in terms of costs and practicalities of converting the customer's currency into their own. In practice, many contracts are priced in a well-accepted, stable, easily convertible currency, such as the US dollar – whether or not one of the parties is American.

Goods and services that are sold directly to end users or consumers, rather than through marketing channels, will normally have to be priced in the local currency.

Packaging – the fifth P?

Whether or not we grant packaging the status of a fifth P, it certainly warrants close attention. Packaging really transcends the traditional 4Ps, playing a part in each and every one. It is part of the product. Many products have to be packed or they cannot be sold. For example, the product may be liquid (e.g. cough syrup), dangerous (e.g. acid), potentially damaging (e.g. hair dye), delicate (e.g. contact lenses) or perishable (e.g. foodstuffs). As well as protecting the product, the packaging may be there to protect consumers. Childproof tops protect the young from accidental ingestion of harmful medicines. Tamper-proof packs prevent the malicious from poisoning, or otherwise spoiling, products.

Sometimes the packaging is more than a means to contain the product; it is an integral part. Products such as toothpaste turn packaging into a feature: pump or tube? Food can be packaged in different ways and this turns it into different products. For example, peas may be sold in tins, jars, packets, vacuum packs or their original pods. Individual drinks cartons have straws attached to make them easier to drink on the go.

Some packs are deliberately made attractive so that people will use them rather than put the product into something else (e.g., some of Marks and Spencer's desserts come in glass bowls). This can be good promotion too if the pack has the product's name on it. How many people, even in cafés, bother to decant ketchup out of the bottle rather than have it sitting on the table advertising Heinz?

ACTIVITY

Next time you go grocery shopping, look carefully at the different types of packaging used. Who are they designed to appeal to? Are you influenced in your choice of product by the packaging?

Packaging can be a key consumer decision criterion, especially for commodity products. Take milk as an example. Milk can be packaged in a number of ways: glass bottle, plastic bottle, paper carton, tin or packet (for dried milk). Some customers may choose the milk with the carton that is easiest to open, or the one that pours best, or keeps the milk freshest longest, or survives freezing.

Innovative packaging can confer competitive advantage. A supplier who invents a new and better way of packaging has an advantage over its competitors – at least until they catch up. Imagine having been the first to put fruit juice into a small carton with a straw, milk in an easy-pour carton, shampoo in a sachet or tissues in a pocket-sized pack.

The packaging is a key part of the **brand identity** and so is jealously guarded by brand owners. Coca-Cola watches competitors carefully and is quick to object if any rival product looks too similar to its own (e.g. the first can design for Sainsbury's

The lookalikes

Over the last few years, a number of manufacturers have taken retailers to court over own-label brands that just look too much like the real thing. The complaint may be about the make-up of the product itself or it may be about the packaging – an infringement of the brand is potentially even more damaging than a rip-off of the product itself.

- United Biscuits, makers of the much-loved Penguin, sued ASDA over its Puffin bars.

- Coca-Cola's objection to Sainsbury's Classic Cola can resulted in a redesign.
- Kellogg's has complained about the package design of Tesco's breakfast cereals.
- ASDA was in trouble again, this time over the appearance of its own-label versions of popular spirits such as Archers and Malibu.

The original manufacturers have put millions into brand development and don't see why these retailers should cash in. It is difficult to decide where to draw the line – when is it a product inspired by the original and when is it a cheap imitation?

Tesco, Marmite and Asda's own brand yeast spread – packaged inspiration

Cola bore too close a resemblance). Distinctive packaging becomes associated with the product and is the means by which the product is recognised: Jif's lemon juice is packed in a yellow plastic lemon. Perrier has a distinctive green bottle.

Packaging is sometimes referred to as the silent salesman because of its **marketing communications** role. Packaging sends a message about the product inside. This may be explicit (i.e. it may be a slogan or on-pack pro-

pack shot
a picture of the product, in its packaging, used in an advert to aid recognition

motion) or it may be implied through the packaging's style. Advertisements often contain a **pack shot**, usually at the end of the ad. It is hoped that this image of the pack will stay with the consumer and then, when they see it in the shop, they will remember the message of the advert. This is particularly useful for products that rely on recognition, i.e. when the customers may browse shelves looking for a suitable product to buy (this applies to most **FMCG**).

Packaging is also informative. It states country of origin, lists ingredients, gives instructions for use and carries warnings (e.g. not suitable for children under three).

The packaging can also be used to persuade people to use more of the product. Allegedly, Domestos increased its sales substantially by changing the instruction 'use sparingly' to 'use liberally'. Foodstuffs regularly carry recipes designed to encourage cooks to see how else the product can be used. Imaginative packaging can help to sell the firm's other products, e.g. by including other products in the recipes, attaching a trial-size packet of biscuits to the coffee (or vice versa). There are many possibilities.

Packaging can be varied to give a company more pricing options. Refill packs are cheaper than original products. Larger sizes are often better value.

Good packaging is essential to protect products during distribution. Secondary packaging (large cartons and palettes) may be needed here to make sure goods are

insight   Sweet and innocent

The Innocent brand is one of the big success stories of the 2000s. It has grown from a virtually unknown fruit drink found in just a few stores to a must-have for every food shop and sandwich store of note. The makers of Innocent smoothies take great care to ensure that the product is as high quality as it can be – pure fruit, no additives and no concentrates – but that is only part of their appeal.

Today, they use an intensive distribution strategy but this was not always the case. When the drinks were first launched, they were available only from a few, top-end outlets (e.g. Harrods). This helped build an upmarket brand image and meant that a correspondingly high price could be charged. Their promotion budgets were initially low but word of mouth worked well for them. Lately they have been advertising on television, demonstrating the quality of the product by showing the simplicity and purity of its ingredients but at the same time making fruit drinks fun.

Their strong brand identity has played a key role in building the Innocent brand. Their distinctive, apparently hand-sketched, fruits or shapes with halos logo has a childlike quality and is reassuringly simple looking. The brand personality seems to be good quality, good for you, pure and fun. The fun aspects come out through their advertising and most strongly through the packaging. Take the time to read an Innocent pack and you will not only find out exactly what's in your drink, but also what isn't, e.g.

No concentrates
No stabilisers
No flavourings
No GM stuff
No preservatives
No added sugar
No e numbers
No funny business

You may also find such things as a picture of a fireman's hat (drawn by Kat, aged 26½) alongside a little story about energy entitled *smoky bacon*.

A brand personality such as Innocent's demands environmental friendliness. The individual-size smoothie bottles are made of 100 per cent recycled plastic: 'greener than your seasick Auntie Sue on a cross-channel ferry after a big night out at Wetherspoons' (www.innocentdrinks.co.uk). Their green credentials are further strengthened by sourcing all their bananas from plantations certified by the Rainforest Alliance ('We love them') and by donating 10 per cent of their profits to charities working in the countries where their fruits come from.

Almost anyone can make smoothies. To make them without concentrated juices or other shortcuts is expensive, though. You need to be sure people will pay the price. Is there room in the market for another Innocent?

© innocent. Picture courtesy of innocent

easy to handle, can be stacked safely, and arrive at their destination in good condition. Sometimes this secondary packaging can be turned to good promotional advantage. Packets of crisps, which are notoriously hard to keep on the shelves (they sell fast and so run out, and they also slip about), are normally supplied to retailers in large brown boxes. One innovative crisp company decided to use these boxes to give their crisps an edge. They perforated a hole in one side of the box so that, when the hole was punched in, customers could reach into the box and pull out the crisps. The boxes had become display stands (all bearing the crisp manufacturer's name and logo, of course). Shops no longer had to unpack the crisps and restock shelves. When a box was empty they just brought in the next box.

INTERNATIONAL PACKAGING

Packaging is an important part of the mix and must be carefully designed for overseas markets. The following should be taken into account:

- any laws and regulations governing its composition, recycling, the languages used
- cultural issues that may affect the size of the packet, the colours used – and the languages used
- education and literacy levels in the country – how should the instructions be written? Perhaps they should be diagrammatic? Dangerous products (e.g. pharmaceuticals) must be especially carefully explained
- transport – one of packaging's main functions is to protect the goods during transit. How rough is the handling likely to be?

Internationally consistent packaging has the advantage of being recognisable to travellers and so is especially important for products that might be bought by visitors to a country: camera film, headache pills, toiletries, sun tan lotion, etc. They may not speak the language well enough to ask and so the sight of a familiar package will reassure them and give that product a competitive edge over others.

The extended marketing mix: 7Ps

The 4Ps do not provide enough scope for the support of modern products, many of which have a strong service element. The 7Ps were developed as a marketing mix for services, but are really more appropriate than four for all but the simplest products today. Exhibit 11.6 shows examples of the use of the additional 3Ps.

The first three products in Exhibit 11.6 are services, while the last one is a physical product, a PC, but it still has a number of service elements that are important to the customer. Retailing is itself a service and so the shopper is a service user. With a product like a PC, there may be more service elements involved: helplines, installation assistance, maintenance, etc. Contrast this with an FMCG purchase, such as soap powder. There is no installation help or maintenance required for this product, but there is still a retail service to be provided. Also, check the side of the box. Many FMCG products do offer advice lines or similar services – all are designed to try to establish a relationship with the customer and offer a better service.

These additional 3Ps must also be integrated into marketing plans. They too should support the rest of the mix, not clash with it.

PHYSICAL EVIDENCE

peripheral product
a secondary product often provided as part of a service, e.g. the complimentary mints at the end of a meal, shampoo at the hairdressers

Physical evidence includes **peripheral products**, such as free peanuts on a bar, products that are part of the service, such as ice in a drink, the décor of the place where the service is provided – and anything else that is tangible, but not the actual physical product itself.

Exhibit 11.6   Examples of the use of the 7Ps

Example products	Examples of physical evidence: the tangible aspects of the service	Examples of people: who deliver the service	Examples of process: how the service is delivered
Car cleaning	Car shampoo, sponges	The cleaners	While you shop
Restaurant meal	Food, tables, cutlery	Cooks, toilet cleaners	Self-service
Car hire	The car, maps	Receptionist, mechanics	Car delivered to home address
Personal computer	Retail environment	Shop assistants, helpline operators	Assistants approach to customers in store, call-queuing systems

The physical evidence may be the key thing in setting customer expectations. A smart, trendy bar with genuine art on the walls, expensive-looking furniture and waiters in tuxedos sets the expectation of superior service, a good wine list, high prices and a classy clientele. Contrast that with a typical local pub or bar, with posters and a wide-screen TV on the walls, a footrest around the base of the bar, hard-back chairs, a juke box and the bar staff in T-shirts. Quite a different customer expectation is set. Customer expectations are extremely important in marketing, and particularly in services marketing. A customer who has been let down, i.e. has received a service that does not meet their expectations, is an unhappy customer. They are liable to complain and to say unflattering things about the product to their friends. Often, if they had received the same service but had known what to expect beforehand and chosen it anyway, then they will be quite content with that situation.

Carrier bags: carrying the message home

So physical evidence is an important aspect of customer service and must match the rest of the mix if expectations are to be met.

PEOPLE

Most services require people to deliver them and to receive them. Although there are an increasing number of services delivered electronically, e.g. Internet messaging, where people's involvement is limited to the original set up and maintenance of the service and dealing with queries and complaints, people remain an important asset for most service providers. The quality of the service is liable to be largely dependent upon the quality of the people involved in its delivery and so, once again, the people must match the rest of the mix. A high-class restaurant needs silver service waiters; a burger joint does not.

The people who deliver the service are an integral part of its marketing mix, as are the people who receive that service. Customers are part of the interaction and influence the way a service operates. For example, it is quite possible for two people to eat the same meal in the same restaurant and experience the same service but one will love it and one hate it. This is equally true of concerts, haircuts and service from shop assistants.

PROCESS

Process starts long before a service is actually experienced. It starts with the prospect's very first contact with the service-providing organisation. This may be reading a brochure, visiting a website, making a phone call or calling into an office or shop. The process of service delivery is key to customer satisfaction and therefore to the stimulation of positive **word of mouth** and repeat business. The restaurant can be the smartest in the world, the staff the best trained and friendliest, but if customers find their booking has been lost, or if the food takes hours to arrive, they will not be happy. In a pizza restaurant, however, there may be no advance bookings and customers may be expected to queue. Customers may be happy to do this, especially if they are able to sit in the bar and have a drink, listen to music, read the menu. That is all part of the process.

Once again, the process has to be right, and fit with the rest of the marketing mix, if the product is to be a success. (For more on the 7Ps, see Chapter 7.)

word of mouth
where members of the target audience pass on information or promotional messages to each other; *see also* viral marketing

Mixing it (integrating the marketing mix)

Each element of the marketing mix should support the others. They should build to a consistent whole that accords with the organisation's brand values and so builds the brand's image. For example, an upmarket, exclusive fashion brand would:

- require high-quality products, made with top-class fabrics, that are well styled and well made, perhaps finished by hand (product)
- command premium prices (price)
- be sold in more exclusive, fabulously done-up stores (place, physical evidence)
- be sold by smart, fashionably dressed staff (people)
- provide an alteration service to achieve a perfect fit (process)
- be promoted in a tasteful, creative way, perhaps with adverts placed in fashion and lifestyle magazines, and with suitably upmarket celebrities wearing the clothes (promotion).

However, a mass-market clothing brand might:

- use cheaper fabrics and mass-production techniques while keeping fancy trims to a minimum
- undercut competitors' prices
- be sold everywhere
- be carried home in cheap plastic bags
- be promoted extensively, in the newspapers and magazines that the customers read, on billboards, even on flyers.

These mixes send clear, but very different, messages about the company's offering. If the messages are contradictory, then customers will become confused. You cannot charge a high price but use cheap materials (at least not for long). If your products are on sale everywhere, they lose their exclusive image (this is why Levi's was so keen to stop Tesco selling its jeans, and why perfumers such as Calvin Klein do not want their products sold in high-street stores such as Superdrug and Littlewoods).

The marketing mix is used to implement marketing strategies and plans. It is the marketer's tool kit, and deciding how to use each tool is a key part of the marketer's job. Those decisions are made in the light of the organisation's objectives and its overall strategy to meet those objectives. Look back at the above example: if a brand wants to maintain its upmarket position, then clearly it must be in the best shops and be made of high-quality materials. The desired market position informs the choice of how to use marketing tools. With the marketing purpose firmly in mind, marketing managers are able to design effective marketing programmes, which must be based on a well-coordinated marketing mix.

Varying the mix through a product's life

Marketers do not decide on the best marketing mix for a new product and leave it at that for ever. The mix has to be varied over time in response to, or in anticipation of, the changing marketing environment (see Chapter 2) and the brand's circumstances. The product life cycle (which was introduced in Chapter 6) provides an illustration of how the optimal marketing mix may change over time (see Exhibit 11.7).

The product life cycle model was originally devised for generic products, i.e. the product type not the individual branded item (e.g. shoes, not Clark's shoes). It can, however, be applied to individual, branded products as well.

Exhibit 11.7   Mixing it through the product life cycle

introduction	growth	maturity	decline	deletion
product: fairly standard **promotion:** high advertising spend; trade promotions; publicity; point of sale **place:** sign up distributors; build up stocks **price:** market skimming or market penetration	**product:** improve quality; add features; update style; add new products to range **promotion:** still a high spend; build brand loyalty **place:** look for new outlets; build relationships **price:** skimming stops now – price falls	**product:** further updating; few additions to range **promotion:** sales promotion; reminder advertising; database marketing **place:** keep costs down; stress customer service; maintain relationships **price:** needs to be competitive; depends on loyalty levels	**product:** scale back to basic; limited range; consider deletion **promotion:** lower spend; sales promotion **place:** cut back distribution; look for other markets **price:** keep low	

sales

time ⟶

INTRODUCTION

Products are often very expensive to launch. The research and development that goes into a new product can cost hundreds of thousands or even millions, and will have to be recouped in the early life of the product. Initially, the promotion budget will be at its highest. People do not know about this new product and so they must be told. There may be no distribution channels and so those need to be built up. If the product is a new-to-the-world invention (e.g. MP3 players), then the company may be able to use a price-skimming strategy to help recover some of its costs more quickly (see Chapter 10). However, the prospect of large profits will encourage competitors into the market (unless the new product is protected by patents – though often even these are not enough).

GROWTH

During the product's growth stage, organisations should be focusing on building brand loyalty and encouraging repeat purchases. They might introduce new products or lines and add more advanced features to existing products. A lower price may attract new customers or encourage existing ones to buy more. However, if the initial strategy was penetration pricing, perhaps for a me-too product, then prices may now be put up. Distribution coverage is vital to build up sales. A good push strategy (i.e. promoting the product to members of the distribution channel), may encourage retailers and other intermediaries to stock the product.

MATURITY

By this stage there are likely to be a larger number of competitors in the market and so competition for customers is fierce. Promotion strategies will be geared towards maintaining market share and extending this profitable maturity stage for as long as possible. Good customer service and the rewarding of loyal customers will help to retain them. Generally, the price of a mature product needs to be competitive, but if the firm has done a good job of building brand loyalty, then demand may now be more price inelastic. If its customers are truly loyal, truly committed to the brand, then the firm may actually be able to charge a slightly higher price than its competitors.

DECLINE

When a product is in decline, ranges and features are cut to a minimum. Unprofitable products, and less popular features, are phased out. Expensive promotion is unlikely to be worthwhile and so the marketing communications budget is cut. If there is no immediate replacement on the way, then some distributors may be dropped. Demand for the product is likely to be very price elastic and so prices need to stay low in order to make sales. The exception to this is when a product has built a highly loyal following (perhaps it has gained the status of a cult product), when a few people may be prepared to pay high prices to obtain their beloved product before it disappears forever.

EXPAND YOUR KNOWLEDGE

Enis, B.M., LaGarce, R. and Prell, A.E. (1977) 'Extending the product life cycle', *Business Horizons*, 20 (Jun): 46–56.

Levitt, T. (1965) 'Exploit the product life cycle', *Harvard Business Review*, 43 (Nov/Dec): 81–94.

Smallwood, J.E. (1973) 'The product life cycle: a key to strategic marketing planning', *MSU Business Topics*, 21 (Winter): 29–35.

The product life cycle is a well accepted concept in marketing although needs to be applied wisely. In these articles, the authors demonstrate the significance of product life cycle to marketing planning in each of the stages of the cycle and even beyond by adopting strategies to extend product life.

Criticisms of the marketing mix

The mix has been at the heart of marketing since the 1960s, but it is not universally acclaimed. There are those who find the 4Ps too limiting and so add further elements to the list. Some authors feel the fifth P should be packaging, others that it should be people. The element of people is formally included in the 7Ps of services marketing but packaging still moves around.

Jones and Vignali (1994) added an S, for service. It is today recognised that all products have a service element and that this is key to their acceptance and success. Customer service must be at the heart of a **market-orientated** organisation and the responsibility of everyone in the company, not just the marketing team. Grönroos (1997) considered that to view service as a separate element of the marketing mix would be disastrous for an organisation as it would isolate customer service as a distinct function apart from the rest of the organisation rather than being fully integrated at its core. This would downgrade its importance.

Modern marketing stresses the importance of building good relationships with customers and intermediaries, and so one problem with the marketing mix is that it emphasises techniques rather than customers and their needs. We could see relationship building as part of **promotion**, but this brings a danger of inducing customer cynicism. Card-based loyalty schemes are viewed by many as mere **sales promotion** – and customers are likely to have cards, and collect points, from all competitors.

The marketing mix has occasionally evolved into other letters. For example, Lauterborn (1990) proposed the 4Cs:

- customer needs and wants
- cost to the customer
- convenience
- communication.

The 4Cs have the advantage of being more customer focused. However, the 4Ps are indelibly lodged in the minds of several generations of marketers and are likely to be the preferred model for some time to come.

The development of faster and better methods of manufacture has led to the vastly increased level of choice being offered to the customer. This change from a supply-dominated marketplace to one where customers demand certain things, and are prepared to look for what they want, comes from the certain knowledge that those things will be available from one of the many possible sources now competing for their business. Increased distribution of goods and services nationally, internationally and globally, presents vast choice to customers. The challenge in such a world is to find customers in the first place, and to hang on to them in the future. This is one of the objectives of branding.

Brand strength is important and so maintaining and building this strength is an essential part of managing a brand. Strong brands sell more easily, both initially and to loyal customers and are therefore valuable organisational assets.

Branding

Brands are important assets for many companies, and building and maintaining their strength is a key marketing task that involves all of the marketing mix. A brand is more than a design or a concept. It is a combination of values which together promise customers the solution to their problems or the answer to their needs. The brand is greater than the products it encompasses and adds value to it. Modern branding has seemed to be the saviour of mass-produced products which often have little or no other means of differentiation. However, it has now become a victim of its own success. The credit for the success of many modern products has been attributed to their branding, but now it is often thought to be the brand that can cause a product to fail (Haig, 2003). If a brand's image deteriorates, then its sales will suffer as Levi's found to their cost when their jeans were no longer perceived as fashionable, nor even as a youth brand, in the late 1990s.

---

insight   The world's top brands

According to Interbrand, a leading global brand consultancy, the top ten brands (with values ranging from Coca-Cola's US$68,734 million to Disney's US$28,447 million) of 2009 were:

1	Coca-Cola	(USA)
2	IBM	(USA)
3	Microsoft	(USA)
4	GE	(USA)
5	Nokia	(Finland)
6	McDonald's	(USA)
7	Google	(USA)
8	Toyota	(Japan)
9	Intel	(USA)
10	Disney	(USA)

IT and electronics companies continued to dominate the listings, with another four computer companies in the next ten (Hewlett Packard, Cisco, Samsung and Apple). Top-ranked Coca-Cola's biggest rival, Pepsi, is in twenty-third place with a brand value of US$13.706 million. Only two of the top ten are from outside of the USA.

See www.interbrand.com for the full report.

SOURCE: Interbrand, 2009

Exhibit 11.8   Brand view

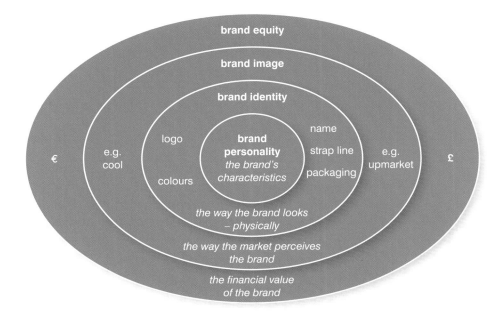

brand personality
the heart of the brand, the sum of its values, its character traits, e.g. bubbly, elegant, friendly

brand identity
all the outward trappings of the brand, e.g. logo, name, colours, strap line and packaging

BEHIND THE BRAND

Branding has given rise to a host of terms that are often used slightly differently in different texts and by different people. At the heart of a brand is its **brand personality** (see Exhibit 11.8). A brand can be described in a similar way to a person. Brands may be young (e.g. FCUK), mature (e.g. Epicure), rebellious (e.g. Virgin), understated (e.g. Liberty), classy (e.g. Aston Martin), forceful (e.g. Nike), caring (e.g. Body Shop) – any personality descriptor that can be applied to a person, can be (and probably has been) applied to a brand. Marketers develop their brands' personalities, which may be articulated in a brand personality statement, e.g. 'This is a chocolate bar that bites back. It's edgy and assertive whilst being absolutely dependable – a bar you want on your side.' This is not meant as a slogan for an advertising campaign, although it might help inspire one. This is the way the brand team see their product, and it is what they want their customers to see too. Their next challenge, therefore, is to find a way to express their chocolate bar's personality clearly to others.

Brand personality is encapsulated in **brand identity**. A brand's identity is a set of cues which help people to form their impressions of the brand, e.g. logo, name, colours, strap line and packaging. However, messages are not always received as intended (see Chapter 8). The target audience's perception of the brand may be different from its intended personality.

Cadbury has a strong brand identity

ACTIVITY

Pick two or three products within the same category, e.g. three cars or three clothing brands. Examine their brand identities and try to deduce the brand personalities that lie behind them. What else affects the way you see these brands?

Those identity cues represent values that the brand owner wants to be associated with the brand. For example, Pepsi is blue because it is a different cola and also refreshing and modern. Hovis packaging has an old-fashioned look because it is a traditional brand. Unleaded petrol comes out of a green-handled pump because it is more environmentally friendly. The internal processing of these brand values adds up to an overall **brand image**.

brand image
people's perception of the brand

Exhibit 11.9   Creating brand image

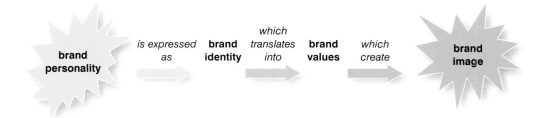

The target market's perception of the brand is called the brand image and it is this that really matters. Brand personalities and identities only exist in order to create an image. This is what people really think of the brand and, in an ideal world, it would match the brand personality as this is the image the brand team wanted people to have. A brand's power stems from the collective nature of these perceptions. One person's perception cannot create a powerful brand; it takes numerous people accepting the brand truth and reinforcing it in their everyday lives (Holt, 2004). Whether or not personality and image match will depend upon how well the brand team have constructed their brand's identity, and upon what else people hear about the brand. Brands exist independently of their owners. Brand owners cannot control everything that is said about them or how they are used. A person forms a brand image on the basis of all their experience with the brand – not just the official brand communications.

To sum up, the brand personality is put across through symbols known as the brand identity and these create, alongside other cues such as the advertising, a brand image in the minds of the target market.

Brand equity

A good brand image has a value. Branded goods usually carry higher prices than unbranded ones. Compare the prices of lesser-known brands of sportswear with those of Nike and Adidas. This value is known as **brand equity** and it is a difficult thing to calculate even though it is often one of the company's most valuable assets.

brand equity
the (monetary) value of a brand

High brand equity is clearly a desirable thing and the brand's marketing mix should be designed with this in mind. For example, frequent price promotions, such as discounts or sales, indicate low brand equity and will do nothing to build it up, whereas brands that have a high price, high distribution intensity, pleasant shopping environment and large advertising budget are likely also to enjoy significant brand equity (Yoo et al., 2000).

One way to value brands is to examine takeover bids. Companies usually have to pay more than the value of a firm's physical assets in order to buy it. They pay for goodwill (ongoing business prospects) and they pay for brands. In the early 1990s, Nestlé paid £2.5 billion (3.6 billion) for Rowntree's, which was much more than the company was apparently worth (Smith, 2006), in a deal that gave it rights to one of the biggest-selling chocolate snacks of all time: Kit Kat. Unfortunately, this technique does not help put a value on the balance sheet of a company that is not subject of a takeover bid.

An alternative way to value a brand is to ascertain how much extra customers are prepared to pay for the branded good rather than an unbranded one. So, how much more would you pay for a Kit Kat than for an unheard-of chocolate wafer biscuit? That price premium can then be multiplied by the number of bars sold (say in a year) to arrive at the brand equity. Neither these, nor the many other valuation methods tried, are entirely satisfactory. However, it is generally agreed that strong brands do have value – we are just not sure how much.

EXPAND YOUR KNOWLEDGE

Hennig-Thurau, T., Houston, M. and Heitjans, T. (2009) 'Conceptualizing and measuring the monetary value of brand extensions: the case of motion pictures', *Journal of Marketing*, 73 (6): 167–183.

Valuing brands is complicated; valuing brand extension potential is even more so but Thorsten et al. have developed a means to measure the monetary value of brand extension rights in the context of motion pictures (i.e. movie sequel rights) and to calculate the effect of variations of key product attributes, such as the continued participation of stars, on this value.

Brand types

There are a number of different types of brand in the marketplace today (see Exhibit 11.10) each of which has advantages and disadvantages. Most of Cadbury's products have an individual brand name as well as the corporate name. Cadbury's name is the badge of quality, while the individual name is an identifier for a particular recipe of confectionery. A purely descriptive name for a Cadbury's Flake would be too long and would not differentiate the product from the competition. Heinz, however, traditionally sticks to straightforward descriptions of its products alongside its corporate brand name, e.g. Heinz baked beans, Heinz tomato ketchup. The company relies on its own name to help establish the desired brand image. Even Heinz have now caught the brand name fever, though, by introducing, or acquiring, some range brands (e.g. Weight Watchers and Linda McCartney).

Exhibit 11.10   Brand types

Corporate umbrella brands	All products use corporate name	e.g. Heinz, Next
Range brands	Groups of products share a brand name	e.g. Taste the Difference (Sainsbury's), Lean Cuisine (Nestlé)
Individual brands	Each product has its own brand name	e.g. Twix (Mars), Bold (Procter & Gamble)
Own-label (private) brands	Products bear the retailer's (or wholesaler's) name	e.g. Tesco, Marks and Spencer

Own-label brands are a recent success story. Once the poor relation of branding, seen as inferior to manufacturer brands, they now take up the bulk of supermarket shoppers' trolleys. They are popular with retailers (and some wholesalers) because they enable them to earn better profits. These products are not manufactured by the retailers, just badged by them. The advantage to the manufacturer is that it can use up spare capacity this way. However, these brands can be the cause of friction in the supply chain if the manufacturer believes that the own-label product is too similar to its own (see ethical focus box on lookalikes on p. 408).

Brand names

brand name
the product's, or product line's, given name

There are historical reasons behind most corporate **brand names**. Companies often start out with the owner's name (e.g. Mars, Cadbury's, Guinness, Ford, Mercedes, Marks and Spencer, Dior). This remains the corporate brand name as it is well known and people make associations with it. In the 1990s, however, there was a management craze for renaming organisations, i.e. changing their brand names. There were a number of reasons behind this, including:

- a more attractive name that either described the organisation better or enhanced the brand identity
- a name that was more acceptable (or just easier to pronounce) in international markets (e.g. Jif household cleaner became Cif)
- distancing the organisation from its past (e.g. Andersen Consulting is now known as Accenture).

Not all of these renamings were successful. Take Consignia, for example. This was the new name chosen, after extensive consultation and market research, for the Royal Mail service. There were good reasons for wanting to change the name. The business had changed and was no longer merely a mail service. They operated call centres, courier services and logistics services and so the name no longer described the business that well. It was limiting their ability to add new services. Also, the organisation wanted to grow their business in overseas markets, beyond the rule of Queen Elizabeth II, where there might even be other 'Royals' and 'Royal Mails' to cause confusion. Finally, they wanted to revamp their image and be seen as a modern business rather than one stuck in the nineteenth century. Consignia was chosen because it does not actually mean anything in any language, but it sounds attractive and relevant.

It was a disaster. The organisation and its branding consultants severely underestimated the British public's attachment to the old name, and the media's will to sink the new one. Within about three years, the old name was back.

People do not like change. They get used to a brand and its look, and can react surprisingly strongly to management improvements. Such updates therefore need to be handled very carefully.

A good cup of coffee?

ethical focus

In October 2006, Oxfam accused Starbucks of sabotaging an attempt by the Ethiopian government to obtain trademark protection in the USA for the names of Ethiopia's highly sought-after, speciality coffee beans: Sidamo, Harar and Yirgacheffe. If the right to exclusive use of the names had been granted, then it would have proved a valuable source of income for Ethiopia, one of the world's poorest nations. The farmers would have been able to control the use of the names in lucrative Western markets and so obtain a greater share of the retail price (currently they get only a fraction of what Western consumers pay for coffee). Ethiopia's annual export earnings from coffee stood to increase by approximately 25 per cent.

Starbucks, whose annual turnover is about three times Ethiopia's gross domestic product (GDP), strongly denied meddling in the trademark application. The company countered that it was committed to paying premium prices to producers and had paid an average of 65p per pound last year, 23 per cent above the average market price. Tadesse Meskela, head of the Oromia coffee farmers cooperative union in Ethiopia, was unimpressed, however: 'We sell organic coffee for less than £1 a pound but that pound can make 52 specials in coffee shops selling for £2 each, meaning the retailer is selling it for £104. The people who are producing this in Ethiopia don't have enough food, clean water or health centres' (Seager, 2006).

The Ethiopians want Starbucks and other companies to sign voluntary licensing agreements that acknowledge the country's ownership of the coffee names, even without an official US trademark.

If you were the MD of a chain of coffee shops, would you agree?

Sources: Kelly, 2005; Oxfam, 2006; Seager, 2006

Branding strategies

The choice of brand type can almost be said to be a strategy in itself. It certainly has far-reaching consequences for the company's marketing. However, there are some specific strategies that relate to **branding**.

Branding strategies are used 'to differentiate products and companies, and to build economic value for both the consumer and the brand owner' (Pickton and Broderick, 2004). The following are some of the more commonly used strategies.

Co-branding is when two companies' brand names appear together, as on PCs when the brand name of the chip manufacturer appears alongside the PC maker (e.g. 'Intel inside'). Either or both brands should benefit from this as the good reputation of one rubs off on the other.

Multibranding is a strategy employed by companies that have multiple products within the same category. This gives the customer the illusion of choice. They can switch brand but still be buying from the same supplier. For example, Procter & Gamble has many different brands of washing powder: Ace, Dreft, Bold (Bolt), Ariel, Dash, Fairy, Daz, Bonus, Vizir and Tide. These are not all available in all countries, and each lays claim to slightly different properties, but they all clean clothes.

The above are ongoing strategies. However, one of the great advantages of a strong brand is that it can be used to launch new products with a far greater chance of success. According to Kotler (2003), there are three ways to introduce more products under the auspices of an existing brand:

- **line extension** – introducing product variants under the same brand name, e.g. a new flavour or colour
- **brand extension** – using the brand name on products in a new category but within the same, broadly defined market, e.g. a biscuit company starting to produce cakes
- **brand stretching** – using the name on products in a different market, e.g. a cigarette company making clothes.

For example, when Robinsons launched a new summer fruits drink flavour, that was a line extension. When Mars started making ice cream bars, that was a brand extension. The king of brand stretching is Richard Branson of Virgin, taking a brand name originally chosen for the music industry and launching it into airlines, drinks, trains, radio, cosmetics, mobile phones, etc. – that is really stretching a brand!

These new product strategies carry different levels of risk. The lowest risk would appear to be the line extension. It can be anticipated that existing, loyal customers will try a new variant of a product they already buy. However, all that is happening here is that they are substituting the new version for the old. There is no overall increase in sales. Line extension does have a role to play, though. It is essential to many brands that new versions be introduced or the line will become boring. Chocolate manufacturers launch new bars. Perfumiers introduce new scents or packaging. Drinks companies try out new flavours. New versions of products replace those that have reached the end of their lives and no longer sell well. A good **brand manager** anticipates that decline, and has the new variant ready in advance of it (refer to the section on the product life cycle in Chapter 6 and above).

Brand extension carries a higher risk of failure. People loved Mars ice cream. It was such a success that other chocolate manufacturers followed suit. So would you buy any kind of food from Mars? How about frozen ready meals? Baked beans? Breakfast cereal?

---

branding
the process of building a brand

co-branding
when two companies' brand names appear together, e.g. Intel on IBM computers

multibranding
a strategy employed by companies that have multiple products within the same category

line extension
using the brand name on products within the same category

brand extension
offering further products under an existing brand name but in a new category within the same, broadly defined market, e.g. Mars ice cream built on the Mars bar brand

brand stretching
using an existing brand name on products in a different market

brand manager
similar to a product manager, responsible for marketing a particular brand

Some brands are so strong that they have their own mythologies. It is a brand manager's dream to work on such a brand or, even better, to raise their brand to that status. Harley Davidson is one such brand. Its customers are more than loyal – they are in love with those bikes. Many Harley owners are tattooed with the brand name and imagery. Other motorcycles may be technologically superior or a better ride, but Harleys are more macho and they just belong on the road to freedom.

The temptation to capitalise on such a strong brand proved irresistible. The company opened a chain of shops with a wide range of Harley branded merchandise: T-shirts, socks, lighters, ornaments, even aftershave and perfume. It didn't go down well with their core market of bikers.

Harley had failed to remain true to their heritage and they had ignored the nature of those loyal bikers. In the past, they had been fussier about what they badged 'Harley Davidson', understanding the importance of focusing on motorbikes and so preserving the Harley mystique. Toiletries were too great a stretch for the bikers and therefore for the company. Fortunately, the error was recognised in time and the unsuitable merchandise has been withdrawn. So it's back to leather jackets and motor oil – and the open road.

SOURCE: Haig, 2003

Harley riders

Unilever successfully extended its Lynx brand. The original Lynx was just a deodorant, but now a wide range of grooming products are available under that brand name. Sometimes a brand carries with it associations that would be unhelpful to the new product. Companies may then actively try to disassociate the two. So Levi's did not call its cotton trouser 'Levi's' but Dockers instead. Sometimes, a company opts for a new family brand name, perhaps coupled with the corporate brand (e.g. Tesco Finest).

The riskiest of these three strategies is brand stretching. Often, the stretched brand breaks. Xerox computers were never as popular as the company's copiers and printers. *Cosmopolitan*'s move into the health food sector (with a range of low-fat dairy products) did not work, nor did its Cosmo Spirit Cafés (Anon, 2003). The strategy does work for some, however, even without a new family brand name. Yamaha successfully added musical instruments, home audio/video equipment, computer peripherals and sports equipment to its motorcycle range. Many retailers have successfully moved into financial services, offering credit cards, loans and insurance. Usually they do not run these services themselves, of course, but license others to do so, lending their name to the enterprise.

EXPAND YOUR KNOWLEDGE

Moorthi, Y.L.R. (2002) 'An approach to branding services', *Journal of Services Marketing*, 16 (3): 259–274.

As the title suggests, this papers focuses on branding from the perspective of services. It brings together Aaker's brand identity framework, the 7Ps and the economic classification of goods into search, experience and credence goods. 'Goods' is a term used in the wider sense, embracing service provision.

Global branding

Although it is rare to find globally standardised products, there are a number of global brands. A global brand may not have (in fact, almost certainly will not have) a completely standardised marketing mix, but it will have the same brand personality the world over and that personality will be expressed through a brand identity that is standard in its essential design, even though there may be some variance in packaging, languages used, etc.

McDonald's Beijing

Take McDonald's, for example. The golden arches are a well-recognised symbol throughout the world. Ronald McDonald has clowned his way through restaurant openings from New York to Shanghai. The writing beneath the arches may be in another language, or even another alphabet, but the brand identity is nonetheless the same. The products are not exactly the same though, and nor is the marketing mix. In India, Hindus do not eat beef products and so the burgers have to be made of something else, originally mutton but now the Maharaja burgers are chicken. Veggie burgers are also available in India, where the staff who make them wear a different uniform and prepare them separately from the meat (this is an example of a different process). The veggie burgers are also sold in other countries where there is a significant demand for vegetarian foods (e.g. some European countries), but are not generally available in the USA. In predominantly Muslim countries, the burgers are called beefburgers rather than hamburgers because Muslims do not eat pig products and the word 'ham' is therefore off-putting (even though there is no ham in the burger – the name comes from Hamburg where the recipe originated). In Australia, you can get a McOz: a quarter pounder with beetroot, tomato, lettuce and onions.

Prices vary according to local costs, ingredients and income levels. Promotions have to be in the right language and suited to local audiences. In some countries, McDonald's own their own restaurants; elsewhere they are franchised. Some outlets, e.g. in Japan, sell ranges of branded toys and other products; others do not. Yet McDonald's is held, quite rightly, to be the epitome of a global brand. Its image is consistent, as is its positioning.

EXPAND YOUR KNOWLEDGE

Levitt, T. (1983) 'The globalisation of markets', *Harvard Business Review*, 61 (May–Jun): 92–102.

Ohmae, K. (1989) 'Managing in a borderless world', *Harvard Business Review*, 67 (May–Jun): 152–61.

Wind, Y., Douglas, S.P. and Perlmutter, H.V. (1973) 'Guidelines for developing international marketing strategies', *Journal of Marketing*, 37 (Apr): 14–23.

These papers address the international dimensions and challenges of marketing. The challenges have changed as the marketing environment has changed to create worldwide and interlinked economies. The papers have at their hearts the inescapable view that marketing should no longer be thought of at a local level alone and suggestions are made in how to handle marketing across borders.

Brand loyalty

A company's loyal customers consistently choose that **brand** over any other. This **brand loyalty** has to be earned by the company and can be destroyed much more quickly and easily than it can be established. Loyalty is important because loyal customers make the best brand ambassadors, spreading positive **word of mouth** and so encouraging others to buy the product, and because repeat purchases mean a steadier, more reliable volume of sales for the company in question. Quality is crucial, both in the product itself, and in any supporting service. Poor service will lead to disappointment in the purchase and a reluctance, if not downright refusal, to ever buy that brand again.

A customer who repeatedly purchases the same brand may, or may not, be loyal to it. True loyalty comes from an ongoing relationship, not from convenience. So a customer who shops in their local supermarket every week may do so out of convenience rather than loyalty. It may sound like this does not matter, the sales are made anyway, but what happens when another store opens nearby? Does that supposedly loyal customer stay with the shop they have always used or do they switch? Also, where do they shop when they are away from home? Truly loyal customers will stick with their store and that makes them valuable.

Brand loyalty is based on an emotional bond between the customer and the brand. It can be very personal and powerful, and is usually formed on the basis of past experience, past brand encounters. When Coca-Cola launched New Coke in the USA in the 1980s, the reaction from their customers was phenomenal. The product had been extensively blind taste-tested in the marketplace and had been almost universally described as having a superior taste to original Coke. However, when the new version replaced the old, public reaction was violent. Street protests took place to demand that the old recipe be reinstated. Customers were so emotionally involved with the brand, it meant so much to them, that the change was felt as a personal blow. They felt betrayed and so their loyalty was tested to the limit. Wisely, just 79 days after the launch, Coca-Cola changed back – and apologised.

It is far more expensive to win a new customer than to keep an existing one and so it is cost-effective (as well as nice) to build these emotional linkages, and hence brand loyalty. Wise companies calculate the customer lifetime values (the net present

brand loyalty
the attachment that a customer or consumer feels to a favourite product

word of mouth
where members of the target audience pass on information or promotional messages to each other; *see also* viral marketing

value of all their purchases of the brand, past and future), rather than just looking at short-term sales. This approach is not without its drawbacks, however. The very act of calculation tends to reduce exchanges to transactions rather than relationships (Peelen, 2005), and without a good relationship with customers it is unlikely that the company will retain customers for a lifetime anyway.

EXPAND YOUR KNOWLEDGE

Kimiloglu, H. and Zarali, H. (2009) 'What signifies success in e-CRM?', *Marketing Intelligence and Planning*, 27 (2): 246–267.

The focus of this paper is on customer relationship management on of the Internet. The balanced scorecard approach is adopted to create a performance measurement tool for e-CRM implementation.

A strong brand is a good starting point for building brand loyalty, but the loyalty does not happen automatically. Loyalty comes out of a good, mutually beneficial relationship and its foundation is trust. This trust must go both ways. Clearly, customers must trust the brand. They must feel comfortable with it, secure that products will do what they are supposed to, that the quality will be maintained, that their brand experience will be the same as it was the last time they made a purchase, and the time before, and the time before that. Equally, the company must display some trust in its customers. A company that treats customers as if they are trying to con it will never build a relationship with those customers, will never gain their loyalty. This demonstration of trust can be an explicit part of the offer, or it may be demonstrated on an individual basis as part of the brand's customer service. For example, Virgin Wines will leave a delivery of 12 bottles of wine on a customer's doorstep if they are out when the delivery driver calls. If the wine is stolen, they replace it with no questions asked. Similarly, they encourage their customers to try wines by offering to refund any bottles that the customer does not like. Clearly, it would be easy to take advantage of this but, as the company has been making those offers for a large number of years now, it would seem that Virgin customers are generally honest and so the company's trust is not misplaced.

ACTIVITY

Pick a favourite product – one that you are loyal to (a chocolate bar, drink, restaurant, brand of sports equipment, TV programme). Make a list of what might cause you to buy, watch or consume something else instead.

Customer satisfaction is a key contributor to loyalty, but not all satisfied customers will be loyal. For example, you may have really enjoyed the last holiday you took – the flight, hotel, resort and value were all great – but you will probably want to go somewhere else next time. Satisfied customers will have a positive attitude towards the company and will probably intend to buy from it again. This, however, may not be enough to clinch the actual sale. A positive attitude is only a predisposition to behaviour; other things often get in the way and cause a person to do something else. They may even go out with the intention of buying one thing but come home with another. (For more on attitudes and their relationship to behaviour, see Chapter 3.)

Customers remain loyal because they value what they get from a firm (Reichfeld, 1994). This value mainly comes from product quality, functionality and style, service and support. These things are not all within the control of the marketing department, so if a company wants to build loyalty, it needs all departments to work together to achieve this. There needs to be an integration of customer-related activities across the whole organisation. This is easier for companies with a customer focus (see Chapter 1).

LOYALTY SCHEMES

The term **loyalty scheme** is really a misnomer. You cannot buy true loyalty; it has to be earned through excellence in products and customer care. The loyalty cards available from so many large retailers today are, more accurately, reward cards, and they are a sophisticated form of **sales promotion** and a source of customer data. Customers earn points on their bill, which they can exchange for money off the next bill or other treats, such as days out or tickets for the cinema or other entertainment venues. The Boots Advantage Card is one of the largest, and most generous, reward schemes in the UK, with nearly 15 million cards in circulation (Boots, n.d.). Advantage Card holders earn four points for every pound spent. Each point is worth a penny off future purchases. In-store machines give out points balances, vouchers and details of special offers.

> **loyalty schemes**
> ways in which companies try to retain customers and encourage repeat purchases, often accomplished by awarding points (e.g. Tesco Clubcard, Air Miles)

CRM focus — Punishing loyalty

There has been a finance battle going on in the UK. Credit cards have been employing some highly destructive weapons in their fight for new customers. The bait they offer is 0 per cent interest on balances transferred from other cards. This free offer has a time limit, of course, often six months. After that, the customer has to pay a standard interest rate. The offer is not usually available to existing customers, only to new ones when they first take out a card.

Many customers play a lucrative game with this, taking out a new card with a new company at the end of the honeymoon six-month period, transferring their outstanding balance on again and so still getting their 0 per cent finance. Some forget and so have to pay some interest at least some of the time. Are the credit card companies actively encouraging disloyalty? It seems hard to believe that this is their intention.

How would you feel as a long-standing customer who isn't getting such a good deal?

Most of the people who have a supermarket reward card have at least two. One of the biggest supermarket chains, ASDA, ditched its reward card scheme for a while, claiming that research shows that its customers prefer lower prices. ASDA's sales figures suggested that this strategy works well. Traditional retail thinking is that shoppers are largely motivated by convenience, i.e. they go to the nearest store or the one where they can park. Nowadays they may even choose the one with the best website.

These reward card schemes cost millions. Tesco issued vouchers worth £320 million (approximately €470 million) in 2005 (Tesco, 2006). On top of that, there is the cost of mailshots, the administration of the scheme, the customer support. Why are these companies prepared to spend all this money? Mainly, they do it for market research and improved **target marketing**. Every time a customer uses their card at the checkout, a computer records all their purchases. This information, combined with the personal information the cardholder gave when they filled out the application form, helps the companies build up a detailed customer profile of shoppers. They then use this information to improve their marketing by stocking the products such customers are most likely to buy and by tailoring offers to suit them.

Customer data can highlight a marketing opportunity that sales data would not. For example, according to sales data, the market for birdseed and feeders was very small. However, by analysing its customer data, Tesco found that people who bought bird feeders were also likely to buy organic foods. So it stocked a wider range of bird feeders, told its organic food customers about them – and watched the sales rocket (Shabi, 2003).

The information that stores gain from their reward card schemes is worth a lot to them. Market research can be expensive, yet here the stores have customers volunteering their information, electronically, every time they present their card at the till. The set-up costs are high but the research information pours in.

EXPAND YOUR KNOWLEDGE

Tybout, A.M. and Calkins, T. (eds) (2005) *Kellogg on Branding*. Hoboken, NJ: John Wiley. See Section 1, 'Key branding concepts' and Chapters 1, 2 and 3.

This book comes from the world renowned Kellogg School of Management at Northwestern University, USA home to the equally renowned Professor Philip Kotler who also provides a forward to this book. The chapters cover brand positioning, designing brands and brand meaning, all topics that offer a fitting finale to the end of this chapter.

SUMMARY

Most marketing plans rely heavily on the marketing mix for their implementation. The 4Ps has been the most commonly used framework for many years but this is always extended to 7Ps when considering services marketing. As so many products now have service elements to them (warranties, guarantees, after-sales service, retailing etc.), the 7Ps framework has become generally preferred for all products – tangible and intangible ones. Packaging is another important marketing tool and is often proposed as the fifth P.

Although they remain the most popular frameworks, the 4Ps and 7Ps models are not without their critics, mainly on the grounds that they are insufficiently customer-focused.

A brand's marketing mix should be integrated, each element working with the others to present a united front and support the organisation's marketing objectives. An uncoordinated mix sends conflicting messages to target customers and is much less effective in terms of building brand values and achieving marketing goals.

CHALLENGES REVIEWED

Now that you have finished reading the chapter, look back at the challenges you were set at the beginning. Do you have a clearer idea of what's involved?

Hints:

- the marketing mix must be integrated so all elements should support the organisation's desired position in its market
- see 'contribution pricing' in Chapter 10 but also remember that price is seen as a determinant of quality
- the 7Ps of services marketing are key determinants of the attractiveness of services to customers
- this is an ethical question – how important is the environment to your firm? Are there ways to maintain the brand identity even when changing packaging (Nestlé managed it with Kit Kat, for example)?

READING AROUND

Book chapters

Michael Baker (2008) 'The marketing mix', in M.J. Baker and S.J. Hart (eds), *The Marketing Book*. Oxford: Butterworth Heinemann. Chapter 12.

Dave Chaffey, Fiona Ellis-Chadwick, Kevin Johnston and Richard Mayer (2008) 'The Internet and the marketing mix', in *Internet Marketing: Strategy, Implementation and Practice*. Harlow: FT/Prentice Hall. Chapter 5.

Jan S. Slater (1999) 'Product packaging: the silent salesman', in John Philip Jones (ed.), *The Advertising Business*. London: Sage. Chapter 42.

Books

Matt Haig (2006) *Brand Royalty: How the World's Top 100 Brands Thrive and Survive*. London: Kogan Page.

Douglas Holt (2004) *How Brands Become Icons: The Principles of Cultural Branding*. Boston: Harvard Business Review Press.

Naomi Klein (2000) *No Logo*. London: Flamingo.

Journal articles

Neil Borden (1964) 'The concept of the marketing mix', *Journal of Advertising Research,* June: 7–12.

Christian Grönroos (1997) 'From marketing mix to relationship marketing – towards a paradigm shift in marketing', *Management Decision*, 32(2): 4–20.

Erich Joachimsthaler and David Aaker (1999) 'Building brands without mass media', *Harvard Business Review on Brand Management*. Boston: Harvard Business School Press. pp. 1–22. (Originally published in the *Harvard Business Review,* Jan.–Feb. 1997.)

Websites

www.cim.co.uk – the Chartered Institute of Marketing.
www.interbrand.com – Interbrand.

SELF-REVIEW QUESTIONS

1. What are the 7Ps? (see page 411)
2. Where does packaging fit in the marketing mix model? (see page 407)
3. What are the five characteristics of a well-designed marketing mix? (see 397)
4. Name and describe the levels of the total product offering. (see page 400)
5. What are the main tools of the promotional mix? (see page 402)
6. What is another name for 'promotion'? (see page 402)
7. How can packaging give a product a competitive advantage? (see page 407)
8. What is the relationship between brand personality and brand image? (see pages 417–8)
9. Why is it important that all elements of the marketing mix match and support each other? (see pages 412–3)
10. What faults can you find with the marketing mix as a framework for marketing activity? (see page 415)

Small objects of desire

Read the questions, then the case material, and then answer the questions.

Questions

1. Identify the elements of Apple's brand identity.
2. Was the launch of the iPhone a line extension, a brand extension or a brand stretch? Explain your answer and then discuss the advantages of this strategy.
3. What evidence is there that Apple enjoys a high level of brand loyalty? What advantages does this bring the company?
4. Is Apple a lifestyle brand? Give reasons for your answer. (You may want to refer back to the section on lifestyle branding in Chapter 1.)
5. Should electronics manufacturers take responsibility for the impact of their products on the environment? What could they do to make their businesses more environmentally friendly?

Why would anyone queue for over 24 hours to buy an (arguably) over-priced phone? Especially when they could buy it from a shop around the corner for the same price and without queuing at all? Questions like these were puzzling passers-by on the day that the Apple iPhone went on sale in London for the first time.

The queues outside Apple's flagship store in Regent Street started two days before the iPhone's much publicised arrival. It was November. It was cold and wet. Even the people queuing seemed bemused as to why they were doing it. 'I'm a Commercial Director. This is ridiculous behaviour for someone like me', said one member of the queue, while a civil servant near the front offered at least a partial explanation for why he wanted to be the one of the first to own the iPhone: 'Several of my colleagues have tried to arrange meetings with me on Monday just to have a look at it.'

The Apple iPhone combines a phone with fully featured web browser, advanced camera and music player. Even at the time of its launch, it was by no means the only device on the market to do all of these things. There were a number of cheaper rivals but none of them inspired the adulation given to Apple's new product. Fans of the iPhone raved over the deceptive simplicity of the design and were especially enthusiastic about the minimalist touch screen. The iPhone is beyond such restraints as a conventional keypad. Lucky iPhone owners just brush their fingertips over the sleek, full-colour display. *Time Magazine* called it 'the invention of the year'.

Over half a million iPhones were sold over the weekend of its launch in the USA. This extraordinary level of sales made the company's first-year sales target of 10 million look easily achievable. With that sales volume, Apple would achieve 1 per cent global mobile market share which, while impressive for a new entrant in such a short space of time, would still be a long way short of market domination – in volume terms at least.

Apple has a reputation for leading-edge technology and attention to detail, particularly style detail. Very few other brands generate such interest and inspire the number of brand ambassadors that Apple does. Apple customers believe that the company really cares about the way they use the technology – and about the way people look while using the technology. As a web designer in the iPhone queue on that wet November morning in London said: '...the point is the attention to detail. I'm actually going to enjoy using my phone, and Apple are the only company that I know in most of consumer electronics who care about this stuff.'

The Apple Mac pioneered an icon-based operating system (source of a long-running dispute with Microsoft over the Windows design) which was the starting point for Apple devotion. Mac users would not dream of trading in their computers for mere PCs and, years after the Mac revolution, Apple's entry into the MP3 market inspired a similar response. The iPod dominates that market, not least in terms of brand awareness and desired purchase. Apple products are recognised as style icons by a wide demographic: their appeal crosses divides of age, income, gender and taste – although approximately 93 per cent of the queue for the new phone were male.

The phone's launch price was a hefty £269 (€399) but there was speculation that the price might come down. In the USA, Apple cut the original price of the iPhone by $200 (£100, €135) and then had to offer refunds to early customers who complained vociferously.

Price was not the only off-putting feature of the iPhone. In the UK, broadband Internet access was

(Continued)

(Continued)

available through Edge but, at the time of the launch, Edge only covered 30 per cent of Britain, so in most places iPhoners would not be able to use that feature. Additionally, in an attempt to maximise revenues, Apple had negotiated exclusive contracts with specific network providers. All iPhones bought in the UK were tied into the O_2 network for 18 months. These network deals had already broken down in France and Germany, where local anti-competition laws had forced Apple to unbundle the iPhones and offer them with a free choice of network. This freedom of choice came at an even higher price, of course. In Germany, the unbundled iPhones were on sale at €999 (about £720), while it cost €399 (the same as in the UK) to buy an iPhone with a contract with Apple's German partner, T-Mobile.

Among all the Apple-inspired hype came a burst of bad publicity too. Green lobbyists took advantage of the interest in the iPhone's launch to make their own attack on the mobile phone market. Greenpeace claimed that mobile phones were significant polluters and that mobile companies needed to do far more to minimise their impact on the environment. Zeina Alhajj, Campaign Coordinator for Greenpeace, said:

'Over the life cycle of a phone there is massive pollution. The phone companies are making big changes – transparency and reporting is far ahead of what it was four years ago, for example – but it is still far away from being a really green industry.'

A recent Greenpeace report claimed to have found evidence of widespread, hazardous chemical contamination of rivers and underground wells in countries where electronics goods are manufactured. Greenpeace also complain that consumers are wasteful, replacing phones more often than is necessary and so artificially inflating the demand for new phones. Western consumers in particular frequently replace working phones with the latest models, keeping phones on average for only 18 months when they are designed to last for ten years.

Only a small proportion of these thousands of discarded phones are recycled. Nokia, the world's biggest mobile handset manufacturer, believes that about 48 per cent of old handsets are abandoned or forgotten by their owners – many of them are just lying at the bottom of drawers.

SOURCES: Burkeman, 2007; Judge, 2007a, 2007b

REFERENCES

Anon (2003) 'Cosmo forced to scrap branded cafe project', *Marketing Week*, 7 August.
Blackett, T. (2003) 'What is a brand?' (Ch. 1) and Brymer, C. 'What makes brands great?', (Ch. 4) in R. Clifton and J. Simmons (eds) *Brands and Branding: The Economist Series*. London: Profile Books.
Boots (n.d.) *About Boots*, Boots the Chemist, Nottingham. Available at: **www.boots-the-chemists.co.uk/main.asp?pid=1673** (accessed 13/07/2007).
Burkeman, O. (2007) 'At 6.02pm the worshippers got their reward', *The Guardian*, 10 November, p. 3.
Enis, B.M., LaGarce, R. and Prell, A.E. (1977) 'Extending the product life cycle', *Business Horizons*, 20 (Jun): 46–56.
Grönroos, C. (1997) 'From marketing mix to relationship marketing – towards a paradigm shift in marketing', *Management Decision*, 35 (4): 322–39.
Haig, M. (2003) *Brand Failures: The Truth about the 100 Biggest Branding Mistakes of All Time*. London: Kogan Page.
Hennig-Thurau, T., Houston, M. and Heitjans, T. (2009) 'Conceptualizing and measuring the monetary value of brand extensions: the case of motion pictures', *Journal of Marketing*, 73 (6): 167–183.
Holt, D.B. (2004) *How Brands Become Icons: The Principles of Cultural Branding*. Boston: Harvard Business Review Press.

Interbrand (2009) 'Best global brands 2009 rankings'. Available at: **www.interbrand.com/ best_global_brands_asp** (accessed 10 March 2010).

Jones, P. and Vignali, C. (1994) 'Commercial education', *Journal of Retail Education,* cited in Vignali, C. and Davies, B.J. (1994) 'The marketing mix redefined and mapped', *Management Decision*, 32 (8): 11–17.

Judge, E. (2007a) 'Green group shines light on safety of the Apple iPhone', *Times online*, 5 November. Available at: **business.timesonline.co.uk/tol/business/industry_sectors/technology/article2806228.ece** (accessed 27/11/2007).

Judge, E. (2007b) 'Fresh blow for exclusive Apple iPhone strategy', *Times online*, 21 November. Available at: **business.timesonline.co.uk/tol/business/industry_sectors/telecoms/article2914903.ece** (accessed 27/11/2007).

Kelly, A. (2005) 'Oxfam drops links with Starbucks', *The Guardian*, 4 March, Society section.

Kimiloglu, H. and Zarali, H. (2009) 'What signifies success in e-CRM?', *Marketing Intelligence and Planning*, 27 (2): 246–267.

Kotler, P. (2003) *Marketing Insights from A to Z: 80 Concepts Every Manager Needs to Know*. New York: John Wiley & Sons.

Lauterborn, R. (1990) 'New marketing litany: four Ps passé; C-words take over', *Advertising Age,* 61 (41): 26.

Levitt, T. (1965) 'Exploit the product life cycle', *Harvard Business Review*, 43 (Nov/Dec): 81–94.

Levitt, T. (1983) 'The globalisation of markets', *Harvard Business Review*, 61 (May–Jun): 92–102.

McCarthy, J.C. (1960) *Basic Marketing: A Managerial Approach*. Toronto: Irwin.

Moorthi, Y.L.R. (2002) 'An approach to branding services', *Journal of Services Marketing*, 16 (3): 259–274.

Ohmae, K. (1989) 'Managing in a borderless world', *Harvard Business Review*, 67 (May–Jun): 152–61.

Oxfam (2006) 'Starbucks opposes Ethiopia's plan to trademark specialty coffee names that could bring farmers an estimated £47 million annually', 26 October. Available at: **www.oxfam.org.uk/press/releases/starbucks261006.htm** (accessed 26/10/2006).

Peelen, E. (2005) *Customer Relationship Management*. Harlow: FT/Prentice Hall.

Pickton, D. and Broderick, A. (2004) *Integrated Marketing Communications* (2nd edn). Harlow: FT/Prentice Hall.

Reichfeld, F.F. (1994) 'Loyalty and the renaissance of marketing', *Journal of Marketing Management,* 2 (4): 10–21.

Seager, A. (2006) 'Starbucks, the coffee beans and the copyright row that cost Ethiopia £47m', *The Guardian,* 26 October, pp. 1–2.

Shabi, R. (2003) 'The card up their sleeve', *The Guardian Weekend,* 19 July, pp. 15–23.

Smallwood, J.E. (1973) 'The product life cycle: a key to strategic marketing planning', *MSU Business Topics*, 21 (Winter): 29–35.

Smith, S. (2006) 'The evil that men do lives after them...', *Marketing Week*, 9 March.

Tesco (2006) *Annual Review and Summary Financial Statements*. Tesco plc. Available at: **www.tescocorporate.com/annualreview06/index.html** (accessed 13/07/2007).

Tybout, A.M. and Calkins, T. (eds) (2005) *Kellogg on Branding*. Hoboken, NJ: John Wiley. See Section 1, 'Key branding concepts' and Chapters 1, 2 and 3.

Wind, Y., Douglas, S.P. and Perlmutter, H.V. (1973) 'Guidelines for developing international marketing strategies', *Journal of Marketing*, 37 (Apr): 14–23.

Yoo, B., Donthu, N. and Lee, S. (2000) 'An examination of selected marketing mix elements and brand equity', *Academy of Marketing Science*, 28 (2): 195–211.

12

Marketing planning

CHAPTER CONTENTS

Introduction
Organising for marketing
Top-down or bottom-up planning?
The marketing planning process
Situation analysis
Business mission and marketing
    objectives
Marketing strategy
Marketing operations and implementa-
    tion: tactics, resources and action
Contingency plans
Marketing evaluation and control
Summary
Challenges reviewed
Reading around
Self-review questions
Mini case study
References

MARKETING PLANNING CHALLENGES

The following are illustrations of the types of decision that marketers have to take or issues they face. *You aren't expected to know how to deal with the challenges now*; just bear them in mind as you read the chapter and see what you can find that helps.

- Your uncle runs a shoe factory that is struggling to compete with cheaper manufacturers from the developing world. He knows you've done a business course so he invites you to a management meeting to discuss the way forward. Do you have anything to contribute?

- A friend wants to start up her own company and needs a bank loan. The bank won't give her the loan without a marketing plan. She doesn't know how to write one. Can you help her?

- You run a medium-sized import/export agency. The international environment is turbulent and you are concerned that some of your markets and sources of supply will dry up. What should you be doing?

- You are the marketing director of a successful UK chain of restaurants. The company has money to put into expansion and you have been asked to present the options to the board.

- You work for a major British bank that is thinking of moving into the insurance market. You have to assess how well your bank is likely to be able to compete with the other insurance companies. How will you do this?

Introduction

Marketing decisions are key drivers to success in the modern marketplace. Marketing has the power to influence every part of the business and affect how organisations meet the needs of their customers, how they respond to competitors, deal with suppliers and financiers, as well as how they treat their employees. In turn, marketing outcomes and performance are influenced by a wide variety of individuals within the organisation and even many people outside the organisation who have associations with it. Even if an organisation has a marketing department, it is wrong to presume that they are the only ones who are involved in marketing activities. Other departments exert a strong influence and have significant effects on how well marketing is carried out.

How organisations manage their marketing activities is affected by many factors, not least the extent to which they are market-orientated or adopt an alternative orientation stance (see Chapter 1), what management style they choose to adopt, what preferences they have for organisational structure and the extent to which they carry out their planning as a **top-down approach** or a **bottom-up approach** (see below).

This chapter will consider marketing's place in the company's overall plan and how marketing can help the organisation achieve its goals. It will cover the basic planning process and marketing analysis tools. It will introduce you to a wide variety of key strategic and management aspects of marketing. The chapter will first consider organisational structures before moving on to some of the challenges faced in planning and implementing marketing (as well as other management functions): the approach to planning, barriers to planning, reasons for planning failure and organisational approaches to marketing. Having completed this overview, the rest of the chapter is structured in a way that mirrors the marketing planning process, taking each of the elements or stages in turn and introducing the more important concepts at each stage.

top-down approach
senior managers specify objectives, budgets, strategies and plans that are passed down to functions and departments to put into action

bottom-up approach
functions and departments recommend objectives, budgets, strategies and plans to senior management

Organising for marketing

An organisation's structure will give clues as to how customer-focused it is and, therefore, its likely attitude towards marketing. Although many companies have a marketing department, roles within this department will vary depending on the type of business conducted or types of customer it serves. For example, the marketing department in a B2B company, i.e. one that does not have direct contact with end users or consumers, may primarily be a sales team, while a company managing a number of brands is likely to have product, brand and category managers.

The following are examples of different types of typical organisational structure:

- functional, based on the different management functions that run the business, e.g. marketing, human resources, finance, manufacturing
- geographic, based on the regions where the company operates, e.g. Europe
- product, based on the products, groups of products or brands the company manages
- market/customer groups, based on the markets or customer groupings in which the company operates, e.g. Dell operates in both customer and B2B markets, which includes education, and small and medium-sized businesses. Particularly important customers, i.e. those that are strategically important to the company, may be dealt with as key accounts
- matrix, a hybrid-type structure where the company incorporates all functions into teams supporting different products or brands

insight

Some of the characteristics of a market-orientated company

Although there are different ways of organising companies, there are said to be certain features or characteristics that will be evident in a marketing-orientated company that may not be present at all or to only a limited extent in companies that may not be doing marketing quite so well. These characteristics follow, as would be expected, from the basic tenets and concepts of marketing. If marketing is to be done well, then certain aspects should be evident in the way that the organisation is structured and managed. Here are a few of the more obvious features:

- customer and consumer focused
- market led
- identifies and balances stakeholder needs
- marketing approach understood and practised throughout organisation
- knows and understands the marketing system
- has effective marketing intelligence system and established marketing database
- sensitive to market trends
- plans for the short term and long term
- adaptive and flexible
- proactive
- creative
- has strong internal communication.

- network, a highly versatile and relatively new approach that is, in essence, a coalition between a number of independent specialist firms, coordinated by a 'control centre' organisation. Specialist firms may be product designers, component manufacturers or distributors.

A company may choose a mix of the structure types in order to best serve their own purposes and structures may change over time. There is no single best solution. Exhibit 12.1 gives some examples of the different types of structure than can be adopted.

The structure adopted by a company will depend on the core values and strategies of the management team in line with the organisational aims and objectives. It is important to recognise that structure is evolutionary since companies operate in a dynamic environment and, in order to retain position, will evolve to ensure they remain at the forefront of their customers' minds. Such changes must be managed particularly well in order to ensure that the company's **stakeholders** are not alienated. It is why, yet again, we need to appreciate that internal marketing is an important part of the process in aligning the business to meet the needs of customers.

EXPAND YOUR KNOWLEDGE

Hanan, M. (1974) 'Reorganize your company around its markets', *Harvard Business Review*, Nov–Dec: 62–74.

While we frequently highlight the benefits of organising around market requirements, at the time of this article, this is a relatively new phenomenon. Marketcentering is a theme of this early paper. The virtues of organising companies around an understanding of market demands are extolled.

Weitz, B. and Anderson, E. (1981) 'Organizing the marketing function', in B.M. Enis and K.J. Roering (eds), *Review of Marketing*. New York: American Marketing Association.

Marketing effectiveness is, in part, a function of organisational structure. This paper reviews the relationships and interactions between organisation structure, environmental characteristics and organisational characteristics.

Exhibit 12.1   Illustration of organisational structures

(a) Marketing organisation – functional management structure

(b) Marketing organisation – hybrid of product, geographical and functional

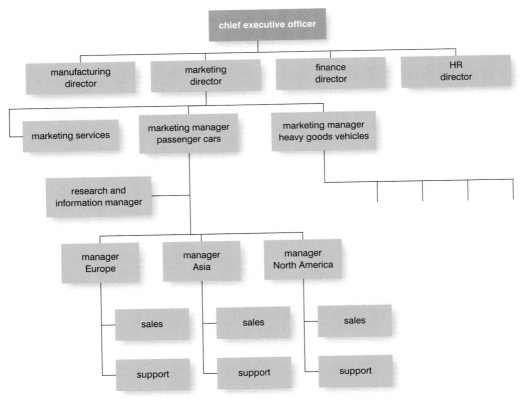

(c) Marketing organisation – product/brand management structure (FMCG)

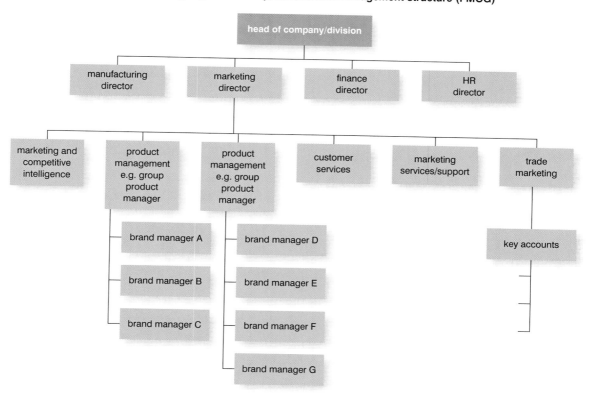

(d) Marketing organisation – market/customer management structure

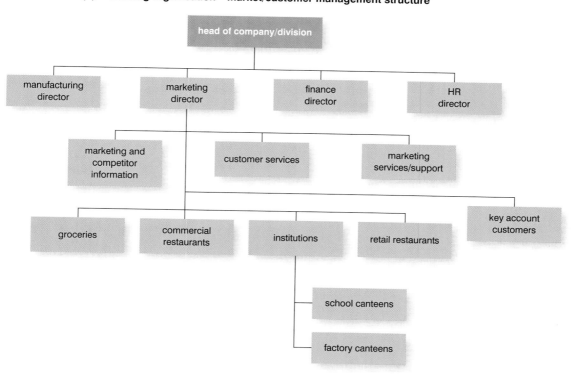

(e) Marketing organisation – matrix structure (product/market matrix)

		MARKET MANAGERS			
		Menswear	Womenswear	Furnishings	Industrial
PRODUCT MANAGERS	Rayon				
	Nylon				
	Orlon				
	Dacron				

Top-down or bottom-up planning?

The top-down process refers to the senior managers specifying objectives, budgets, strategies and plans that are then passed down to operating functions to put into action. The bottom-up approach works in reverse. Objectives, budgets and plans are set at operational level and are passed up to senior management for approval and consolidation into the company's overall plans (see Exhibit 12.2). Both processes have their advantages and disadvantages but they do not need to be mutually exclusive. It is often advisable to use both approaches together. Involving more people in the planning process makes it more likely that they will agree with and adhere to the plans developed.

outside-in approach the organisation looks outwards to focus on the needs of the marketplace to determine appropriate courses of marketing action

inside-out approach focuses on the needs of the organisation first, and customers and the marketplace second

Another consideration is the extent to which companies adopt an **outside-in approach** (Schultz, 1993a) to their management and planning, in contrast to an **inside-out approach**. An organisation with an outside-in approach, looks outwards, focusing on the needs of the marketplace to determine appropriate courses of

Exhibit 12.2   Focus of planning and management

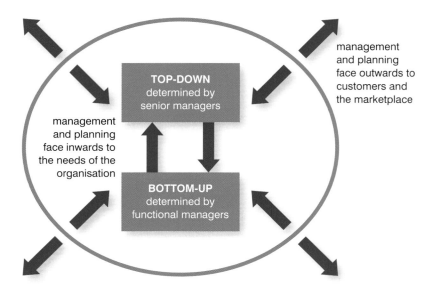

management and planning face outwards to customers and the marketplace

management and planning face inwards to the needs of the organisation

TOP-DOWN
determined by senior managers

BOTTOM-UP
determined by functional managers

insight   Outside-in not inside-out

Marketing principles have long extolled the virtues of starting with the customer and working back to the organisation. Some have criticised marketing communications for failing to do this. Emphasis has been on the organisation first and the customer second. Don Shultz, a leading exponent of integrated marketing, calls for an 'outside-in' approach rather than an 'inside-out' approach.

Start with the customer or prospect and work back to the brand or organisation. That's the outside-in approach. Most organisations are structured to deliver inside-out communications. That is, they're set up to send out messages when they want to send them, to people they want to send them to, in the form they want to use, at the time they want to send them, and so on. Much of this approach is dictated by the budget cycle or when money is available. Unfortunately, customers and prospects don't necessarily need or want communications when the organisation wants to communicate. They need and want communication when it is right for them. (Shultz, 1993a: 8)

marketing action. Customer perspectives are adopted and so this approach corresponds with a strong marketing orientation (see Chapter 1). The inside-out approach is inner-directed and focuses on the needs of the organisation first, and customers and the marketplace second. Clearly, a balance of the two is required if the basic outcomes of marketing are to be achieved, as identified in the Chartered Institute of Marketing's definition:

Marketing is a management process which identifies, anticipates and satisfies customer requirements efficiently and profitably.

Carrying out marketing well is not an easy task. The structure of organisations may make it difficult to coordinate and manage the different departments and specialisms as one entity. Management's response when faced with large, many-faceted tasks has been to divide them into sub-units (departments) in order to cope with the magnitude of operations and to outsource activities by commissioning specialists to undertake certain tasks (e.g. advertising and promotion agencies, market research agencies, call centres, etc.). While project teams and cross-functional assignments can help to improve working arrangements, organisational barriers remain that may impede the smooth implementation of marketing plans. Schultz (1993b) has identified these barriers as:

- **hierarchical management structures**
- **vertical communications**
- **horizontal communications**
- **turf battles**
- power struggles
- **functional silos.**

When faced with these barriers, individuals and groups may conflict as they protect their own specialisation and interests. These stakeholders may be within the organisation or outside it, and their vested interests can vary significantly.

Shareholders will be looking for profits and returns on investment. Suppliers will be looking for continuity of custom. Employees will want security, a good working

hierarchical management structure
each manager has a set place within a vertical chain of command

vertical communications
communications happen up and down the hierarchical organisation structure, e.g. sales manager to salesperson and vice versa

horizontal communications
communications happen sideways within an organisation, e.g. between workgroups or departments

turf battle
when individual managers or departments fight for their own interests at the expense of those of other managers or departments

functional silo
when departments or work groups act as independent entities rather than as components of a much larger system despite having many overlapping activities and information needs

insight   VW/Audi

The VW/Audi Group organises itself in relation to its brands and principal activities. It is a very complex organisation. There are separate marketing groups for each of its major brands: Audi, VW, SEAT and Skoda (among others). There is a separate marketing department for VW Commercial Vehicles and another that handles VW Finance. Within the departments, there are internal marketing staff based at headquarters and regional marketing staff throughout the country. Each brand has its own dedicated dealership. If that is not complicated enough, each of the marketing departments deals with its own external agencies. For example, one of the smaller departments, VW Commercial Vehicles, has 12 agencies with which it works. These range from advertising, PR, sales promotions and media buying to research, a call centre and a fulfilment agency.

environment and good wages. They will be concerned with fulfilling their own departmental objectives, which will differ between departments even though they may share the same organisational objectives, and so on.

Somehow, the organisation as a whole needs to balance these interests to achieve a level of satisfaction for all. An added complexity is that marketing departments frequently make use of a wide variety of external agencies which may, in turn, experience barriers and conflict not only with the organisation itself but also between themselves. Where distribution channels are used, such as wholesalers, retailers and physical distributors companies, these channel members also add to the complexity of interrelationships. Thus, from a marketing point of view, the complete and extended marketing organisation is a family of interrelated departments and organisations, many of which lie outside the direct control of marketing managers but which nevertheless have to be managed.

Exhibit 12.3   McKinsey's 7S framework

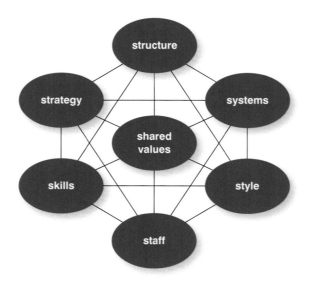

SOURCE: Peters and Waterman, 2004

McKinsey's 7S framework helps with understanding the interaction between these different elements (both inside and outside the company) in implementing marketing strategies and programmes (see Exhibit 12.3).

A company uses the particular *skills* of many different *staff* who require organising (*structuring*) in a way that maximises their benefit to the company. The company uses different *systems* in order to operate, e.g. computer systems, decision-making systems, work processing systems. It adopts a distinct *style* based on its leaders and organisational culture, and all individuals must *share values* that are similar in order to meet the *strategic* goals.

Making strategy happen, however, presents a distinct set of problems to many managers as, by its nature, it involves change, which is invariably resisted to some extent or another. Change within the marketplace is to be expected and welcomed and the organisation has to respond appropriately. Change is also initiated within the organisation, not only as a response to market changes but also in a proactive way as managers seek to improve their performance, their effectiveness and efficiency, and plan for anticipated future events.

Addressing issues such as this requires **internal marketing**. The purpose of internal marketing is to address the concerns, and therefore needs, of different groups or segments of employees. For some, concerns may come from a lack of information on the changes, while others may not possess the know-how or skills to act upon the changes proposed. Others may have both the knowledge and the know-how but lack the willpower or may hold different vested interests.

internal marketing
also called internal PR, it addresses the needs (particularly information needs) of employees

For each of these internal segments, management must inform, develop through appropriate training and incentivise appropriately. Needless to say, failure to implement successfully the changes proposed may ultimately result in the failure of the company or, at least, a swift change of position for those responsible for the failure. Failure may, however, be due to reasons other than a lack of support from employees. Quite simply, it may be the wrong strategic choice (see Exhibit 12.4 for possible reasons for failure).

Internal marketing is an important activity that will enable a company to remain focused on the needs of its customers.

Firms that do not or will not embrace the issues of internal marketing and incorporate those ingredients into their strategic marketing plan will see their market share and profit base erode. Internal promotion can create a positive and/or superior image of the firm and its products in the mind of the customer. (Greene et al., 1994: 10)

Exhibit 12.4   Reasons for failure in strategic planning

Lack of chief executive officer (CEO or MD) support

Too narrow an outlook

Irreversible decline of the company or market

Emphasis on *where* to complete, rather than *how* to compete

'Me-too' instinct

Not enough emphasis on *when* to complete

Failure to take account of individuals within the company

Using the wrong measures of success

Managerial conflict

Lack of information or wrong information or information withheld from key decision-makers

Results of planning ignored

EXPAND YOUR KNOWLEDGE

Ind, N. and Bjerke R. (2007) 'The concept of participatory market orientation: an organisation-wide approach to enhancing brand equity', *Journal of Brand Management*, 15 (Oct): 135–145.

The authors highlight that delivering the customer experience is an organisation-wide responsibility and thereby that a market-orientation can only be achieved through the participation of all organisation members. It is the role of marketing to connect the various elements of the organisation to achieve brand equity optimisation. Marketers need to be both outward and inward facing.

The marketing planning process

Marketing management and planning are parts of a wider activity that involve the whole organisation. The output of the total planning process is the production of a series of plans covering the various functional areas of the business. Such plans, while having a longer-term focus, usually cover a 12-month duration to coincide with the financial planning period. Although a great deal has been written about how plans should be developed, organisations and their managers tend to adopt processes with which they feel most comfortable. Sometimes this results in plans not always being fully documented and objectives and strategies left vague.

At its highest level, the organisation has to set its corporate (business) mission and goals that act as an overall direction for the business. To achieve these goals, each of the functional areas within each of the **strategic business units (SBUs)** (if an organisation has them) needs to set their own plans, involving objectives, strategies and tactics. In the VW/Audi Insight box presented earlier, each of the VW/Audi Group brands makes up a different SBU for the Group: one for VW, one for Audi, one for Seat and one for Skoda. The approach can be top-down or bottom-up, or a combination of the two. For this reason, the arrows shown in Exhibit 12.5 point in both directions. Collectively, the plans for production, finance, marketing, human resource management, and so on, form the composite that becomes the plan for

strategic business unit (SBU)
a distinct part of an organisation which has an external market for its products and services

Exhibit 12.5   How functional plans combine into the corporate plan

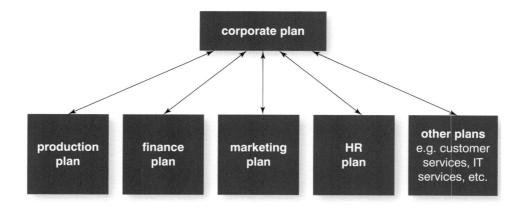

the SBU. The plans for the SBUs come together to create the corporate plan for the organisation as a whole. For companies that do not have SBUs, the functional plans simply form the basis of the corporate plan, as illustrated in Exhibit 12.5. It is important to recognise that marketing planning does not take place in isolation from the rest of the organisation, but is an integral part of it.

The process for setting each plan within the overall corporate plan is similar but we will concentrate solely on the marketing management and planning process.

Chapter 2 (Marketing environment) introduced the four basic questions that need to be answered in marketing planning (see page 72). Here the model is extended by adding three extra questions (questions 2, 3 and 6 in the list below) to make seven in total. These three extra questions are important additions because they emphasise the need to explore not only 'where are we now?' but highlight the danger of not considering trends in performance. By only asking 'where are we now?', we are only invited to consider the situation at a single moment in time. We need to know what we have done previously that has given rise to our current situation and also to consider if we continue to follow the same path of activities, where this will lead. Companies, unless just starting out, are continuing businesses that have a track record of performance in the marketplace that has to be recognised and understood in order to plan best for the future. Its past, present and future form integral parts of the planning process. The first three questions then become part of what is generally referred to as a situation analysis, and this provides an insight into the organisation's past and present, as shown in Exhibit 12.6.

The seven key planning questions, then, are:

1 Where are we now?
2 How did we get here?
3 Where will we be? (by the end of the planning period if we continue to do the same things)
4 Where do we want to be? (by the end of the planning period)
5 How are we going to get there?
6 Are we getting there?
7 Have we arrived?

By answering the first three questions and then posing the fourth, we can complete a strategic gap analysis. This is an important contribution to the marketing planning process. By knowing what we have done in the past and evaluating those activities (question 2), we can then forecast what would happen if we continued on our current path (question 3). Armed with this understanding and specifying where we would wish to be by the end of the planning period (question 4), we can determine what course of action would be necessary for us to make the shift from where we would be based on the current course to where we want to be based on our new objectives. It is rather like a boat changing tack and correcting its course so that it might reach its final destination. The answer to question six allows this change of tack to occur within a single planning period and the strategic gap analysis allows a change of tack as we move from one planning period to the next. Exhibit 12.6 shows this process and the strategic gap that needs to be filled as the organisation moves into its new planning period.

While there are a variety of marketing planning process models, there is general agreement on the sequence and stages involved. They relate directly to the seven basic questions above. Marketing planning and implementation thus require marketers to:

Exhibit 12.6   The strategic gap

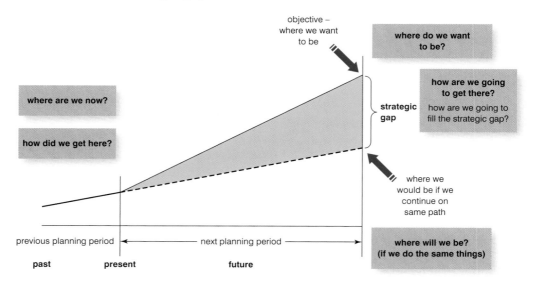

1 **Analyse the current situation.** This has implications for the use of databases, management/marketing information systems, and market research activities that have to be organised to deliver information in a timely fashion for the analysis to be undertaken. Data from previous planning periods can provide a basis for the analysis. It is important to consider trends in this process and not just what is happening at one point in time.

2 **Understand markets, customers and competitors.**

3 **Establish segmentation, targeting and positioning.**

4 **Determine objectives and direction in line with corporate objectives and strategies.**

5 **Develop marketing strategies and programmes** (and contingencies), including resource/budget implications. This has implications for collaboration with other departments within the organisation, outsourced agencies and with members of the distribution channel(s).

6 **Identify control approaches to evaluate progress and activities.**

7 **Implement plan.**

8 **Track progress.**

9 **Adjust activities as necessary.**

10 **Evaluate outcomes at end of planning period.**

11 **Use findings from tracking and final evaluation as part of the analysis of the current situation for the next planning period.**

Exhibit 12.7 shows the planning process in a diagrammatic form, linking the seven questions to the analysis and decision-making process. The stages enable marketers to produce plans that form the basis of how the company will approach and operate in the marketplace.

Exhibit 12.7 illustrates how the situation analysis forms the first stage of the planning process. Based on an understanding of the situation (past, present and future forecasts), new marketing objectives are set and strategies are determined to achieve the position the company wishes to be in by the end of the planning period. The

Exhibit 12.7   A model of the marketing planning process

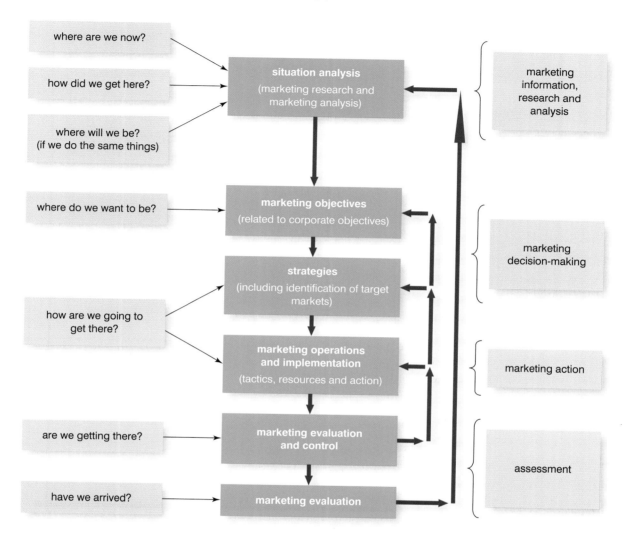

strategies which are of a general nature, indicating the direction that the marketing activities will take, are then made more detailed in terms of the tactics (operational activities) that will be implemented. Exhibit 12.7 also illustrates how the evaluation and control of marketing activities feeds back into the rest of the planning process to check that current plans are being achieved on an ongoing basis and whether or not they have been achieved at the end of the planning period. These final evaluations provide a basis for the development of future plans. The feedback process (frequently known as tracking) allows plans to be modified as necessary throughout the planning period. It is important to understand what works and why. If there have been changes in the marketing environment, perhaps competitor activity has increased, then the plans need to take account of these changes and the marketing activities need to be modified accordingly. This is the process of changing tack that was referred to earlier, as the marketing activities are modified in the light of the tracking evaluations so that the final outcome is reached as intended. Changes to plans may be at the strategic level or at the operational, tactical level. The tactical level of marketing is often

Exhibit 12.8 The marketing planning process and useful tools for analysis and decision-making

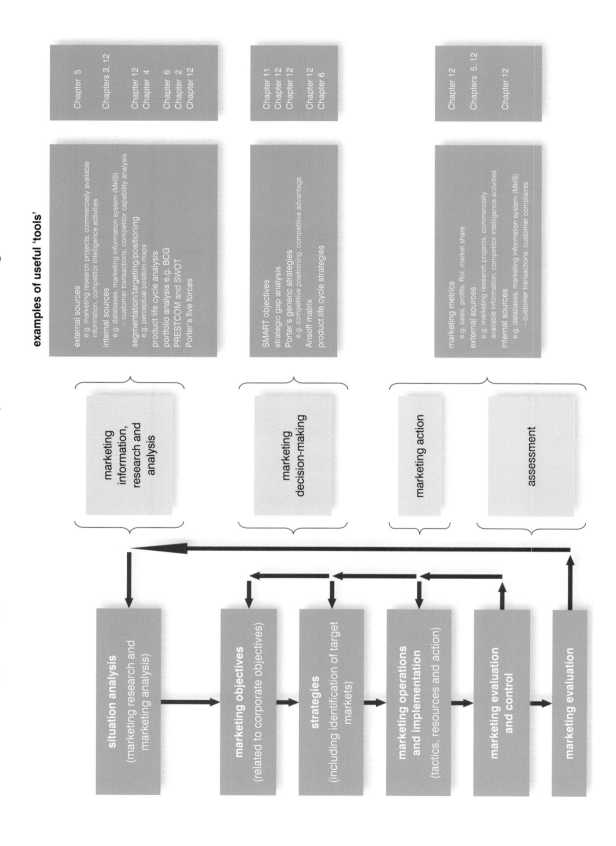

examples of useful 'tools'

marketing information, research and analysis

external sources
  e.g. marketing research projects, commercially available information; competitor intelligence activities | Chapter 5

internal sources
  e.g. databases, marketing information system (MkIS)
    – customer transactions, competitor capability analysis | Chapters 3, 12

segmentation/targeting/positioning
  e.g. perceptual/position maps | Chapter 12

product life cycle analysis | Chapter 4

portfolio analysis e.g. BCG | Chapter 6

PRESTCOM and SWOT | Chapter 2

Porter's five forces | Chapter 12

marketing decision-making

SMART objectives | Chapter 11

strategic gap analysis | Chapter 12

Porter's generic strategies
  e.g. competitive positioning; competitive advantage | Chapter 12

Ansoff matrix | Chapter 12

product life cycle strategies | Chapter 6

marketing action

marketing metrics
  e.g. sales, profits, RoI, market share

external sources
  e.g. marketing research projects, commercially available information; competitor intelligence activities

internal sources
  e.g. databases, marketing information system (MkIS)
    – customer transactions, customer complaints

assessment

marketing metrics | Chapter 12

external sources | Chapters 5, 12

internal sources | Chapter 12

situation analysis
(marketing research and marketing analysis)

marketing objectives
(related to corporate objectives)

strategies
(including identification of target markets)

marketing operations and implementation
(tactics, resources and action)

marketing evaluation and control

marketing evaluation

thought of as the use of the marketing mix elements. Aspects of marketing strategy that are broad-level decisions are considered later in this chapter.

Within the overall framework of the planning process model, there are a number of marketing management tools that can be used at the different stages in order to aid analysis and managerial decision-making. They help us achieve what is, basically, a systematic approach to identifying and analysing competitive advantage in the marketplace for our products, i.e. goods and services, thus helping to achieve long-term benefits for companies. A summary of examples of these tools is shown in Exhibit 12.8.

EXPAND YOUR KNOWLEDGE

Greenley, G.E. (1984) 'An understanding of marketing strategy', *European Journal of Marketing*, 18 (6/7): 90–103.

This article provides an overview of the marketing strategy process. It is concerned with developing 'an understanding of marketing strategy and with the differentiation and clarification of concepts used in conjunction with marketing strategy'.

What has been described above is a systematic, deliberate and prescriptive approach to planning and management. This is consistent with most texts and descriptions of the planning process (e.g. see McDonald, 2007). However, planning and management in practice tends to be a much less tidy business, in which ambiguity, inaccuracy, conflict and confusion can and do arise.

The main output from these planning activities is the marketing plan. The marketing plan is a document that summarises the key points of planning and highlights the marketing activities that will take place throughout the period of the plan. In reality, there may actually be a collection of marketing plans that together cover all products, markets and marketing functions rather than a single plan that covers everything. There may be separate plans for each brand or each main marketing function (e.g. advertising plan, sales plan, distribution plan, etc., covering all the elements of the marketing mix) or each target market or each market by area, region or country.

Marketing plans can appear in a range of different formats and structures but they should contain a basic minimum range of information. The planning period needs to be specified as part of the plan. This may be over a total of 3–5 years in outline, but the detail is likely to be over a single year to coincide with the organisation's financial planning periods – it may be broken down into quarter-year periods. The main sections of a plan are shown in Exhibit 12.9.

EXPAND YOUR KNOWLEDGE

Kotler, P., Gregor, W. and Rogers, W. (1977) 'The marketing audit comes of age', *Sloan Management Review*, 18 (2): 25–43.

Key areas of marketing analysis are identified and put together in a comprehensive 'audit'. The audit forms an early and essential part of the marketing planning process.

Exhibit 12.9 Outline marketing plan

Section	Description
1 Executive summary	A brief overview of the main points of the plan highlighting the main objectives/intended outcomes, activities and resource requirements.
2 Current marketing situation	Summarises the environmental situation *and* trends. This is the presentation of analysis of both internal and external factors and will include PRESTCOM and SWOT. Subheadings might include (but these are entirely at the discretion of the writer of the plan): 2.1 Key macro environmental influences (PREST factors) 2.2 Competitor analysis, e.g. direct and indirect competitors and their activities, competing brands and distinctions between them (position map), expectations of competitive activity, assessment of competitors and their brands' strengths, weaknesses and positions 2.3 Organisation analysis, e.g. sales and profits, mission and objectives, strengths and weaknesses 2.4 Product analysis, e.g. product portfolio, branding issues, product market analysis (Ansoff matrix), assessment brand performances 2.5 Market analysis, e.g. market structure and trends, channel issues 2.6 Customer/consumer analysis, e.g. identification of segments and targets, motivations, brand perceptions, buying habits, etc. 2.7 Identification of opportunities and threats.
3 Objectives	This is a statement about what should be achieved. Objectives should be as unambiguous as possible (SMART). It may contain a reiteration of the corporate objectives as well as the marketing objectives. Marketing objectives can be overall objectives as well as objectives set for each of the elements of the marketing mix (4Ps, 7Ps or similar) or, alternatively, the individual mix objectives may be presented in section 6 below.
4 Target markets	Explains the segmentation, targeting and positioning approaches and decisions. This section is really part of the section below as it is part of the marketing strategies adopted. It is given a separate section because of its importance to the plan.
5 Marketing strategies	Shows the strategy or strategies to be used to achieve the marketing objectives. This section will relate closely to the previous section on targeting, which itself is an aspect of the marketing strategy. This section includes the more general marketing approaches to be adopted (strategies) rather than presenting the detail of tactics/operations, which are given in the section below and which will form the bulk of the plan in terms of the amount of detail presented.

(Continued)

Exhibit 12.9   (*Continued*)

Section	Description
6 Marketing programmes	Provides the details of marketing activities to be undertaken. These are specific activities, schedules, costings and responsibilities. Subheadings for each key element of activity (each marketing mix element, e.g. 4Ps or 7Ps or similar, and any related elements) are likely to be used: 6.1 Product (may include details of product portfolio, branding issues, product development, new product launch, etc.) 6.2 Promotion/marketing communications, including such elements as creative approaches, objectives, executions, media selection, etc., covering advertising, sales promotions, public relations, direct marketing, salesforce, other (such as events, merchandising (further details may be given in one or more appendices). Increasingly, the use of the Internet is likely to be shown as a specific aspect, either under this subheading or under one of its own. Specific reference may be made to the use of push and pull promotional strategies related to promotions targeted at the trade (push) and promotions targeted at end customers and users (pull) 6.3 Place (channel and possibly physical distribution aspects) 6.4 Price (a range of price aspects may be included here such as trade pricing, recommended retail pricing, discount arrangements, etc.) 6.5 Service (this might include other aspects of the three remaining Ps of the 7Ps) 6.6 Other elements might include issues of brand and corporate identity and image and other branding considerations.
7 Resources and financial aspects (budgets)	This section should include statements of required financial budgets and human resources needed. There may be implications for recruitment, possibly downsizing the marketing department or other related department (e.g. customer services department) and salesforce. Outsourcing would be identified here, e.g. the use of promotional agencies, call centres, fulfilment companies, research agencies, etc.
8 Implementation controls	This is to do with evaluation and assessment of the plan *on an ongoing basis* and *not just* at the end of the plan. Contingencies may be identified at key points if the expected plan outcomes are not being achieved. It is important to consider possible changes to the plan over the period of the plan, rather than waiting to the end before seeing if things have worked. This section would highlight the research and assessment that would be carried out and the metrics (measurements) that would be used. By undertaking evaluation by tracking performance against the plan's objectives, it is possible to adjust the plan and corresponding activities to keep the programmes on track.

Situation analysis

Exhibit 12.10

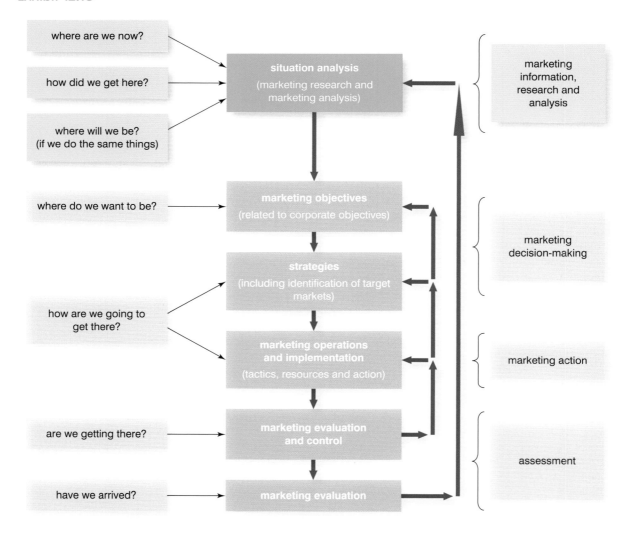

Marketing analysis involves an understanding of how the company is operating in its marketing environment. The marketing environment comprises a complex set of factors that affects marketing decisions and plans, and ultimately affect business performance. It is important that the company monitors itself and its environment in order to prepare for future activities and, particularly, to build and maintain competitive advantage. This type of analysis is not just a one-off, never to be repeated activity, but something that successful businesses do on an ongoing basis. Environmental analysis was covered in detail in Chapter 2 where situation analysis was also introduced. Some overview points are restated here to show how and why marketing analysis fits into the marketing management and planning process.

With the advent of sophisticated databases and the growth in readily available marketing research data, there is a wealth of information available to marketers, who are increasingly being required to assess their performance and measure the effectiveness and efficiency of marketing activities. This has been called **marketing metrics**.

marketing metrics
measurements that help with the quantification of marketing performance, such as market share, advertising spend and response rates elicited by advertising and direct marketing

Marketing is an expense to any organisation – a necessary one, but an expense none-theless. It is important that measurement systems are in place to analyse the value of marketing and to use those systems to improve marketing performance in the future. This information is fed into the analysis process from the marketing evaluation and control mechanisms that form part of the total marketing planning process. Where extra information is needed, such as other secondary or primary research, this needs to be budgeted for and carried out.

There are a variety of tools and approaches that can be used in marketing analy-sis. Some of the more important ones are outlined below. You should also reread Chapter 6, Product Portfolio Mangement, for further information.

PRESTCOM AND SWOT ANALYSIS

PRESTCOM was first introduced in Chapter 2 as a tool that can be systematically applied to analyse an organisation's internal and external environment. External factors are usually outside the control of an organisation or they may have only limited control over them. Internal factors are completely under the control of the organisation. PRESTCOM is a mnemonic to remind us of the main areas that should be analysed by organisations. It stands for Political, Regulatory, Economic, Social, Technological, Competitor, Organisational and Market factors.

Having identified the key factors impinging on an organisation, a SWOT analy-sis can then be undertaken to identify which of the factors represent the organisa-tion's strengths and weaknesses as part of the internal environment, and which of the factors represent external opportunities and threats to the organisation. Opportunity and threat analysis can be made more meaningful by using opportunity and threat matrices in which the likelihood of the factor occurring and the potential impact it might have can be assessed. For example, if a threat is not likely to occur, or if it does, its impact is assessed as minimal, then this can probably be ignored or relegated as being of low concern. If an opportunity has low-cost implications, is within the capa-bilities of the organisation and is likely to be very profitable with limited competitive interference, then it might be a good opportunity to pursue. Please reread Chapter 2 for more details on PRESTCOM and SWOT.

COMPETITOR ANALYSIS

Capability analysis and marketing information systems

It is particularly important to understand how the company's products and brands compare with those of the competition. **Competitor analysis** is important in deter-mining whether or not the products marketed by a company have a sustainable advantage in the marketplace. This is not something that should be done just once at the launch of a new product or service, but should be undertaken on a continuous basis throughout the life of the brand.

The process of competitor analysis must involve an analysis of the strengths and weaknesses of competitive products/brands and the basic capabilities of the com-petition. It may involve some form of **benchmarking**. This is where companies compare themselves to the best-in-class companies in their industry, typically the market leader. The purpose is to identify areas for potential improvement. A useful tool for this has been developed by Hooley et al. (1998) (see Exhibit 12.11).

Companies compete in the market using the elements of the marketing mix (the 4Ps or 7Ps). It is important to understand not only how competitors succeed in the market but also how they fail. You can learn from their mistakes just as well as your

competitor analysis
the process of obtaining an in-depth understanding of rival firms and their offerings

benchmarking
a process of systematic analysis and comparison of one company's performance, measured against another's (the industry leader's), in order to improve business performance

Exhibit 12.11

Key Success Factors	Our company	Competitor company
Strong R&D	1 2 3 **X**4 5 6 7 8 9 10	1 2 3 4 5 **X**6 7 8 9 10
Speed of response	1 2 3 4 5 6 7 **X**8 9 10	1 **X**2 3 4 5 6 7 8 9 10
International marketing experience	1 2 **X**3 4 5 6 7 8 9 10	1 2 3 4 5 6 **X**7 8 9 10
Technological capability	1 2 3 4 5 **X**6 7 8 9 10	1 2 3 4 5 **X**6 7 8 9 10
Financial strength	1 2 3 4 5 6 7 8 **X**9 10	1 2 **X**3 4 5 6 7 8 9 10
Strength of management	1 2 3 4 5 6 7 8 **X**9 10	1 2 3 **X**4 5 6 7 8 9 10

own and it is a lot cheaper! This sort of information can be gathered by talking to customers and other industry or market informants. Sources may include commissioned market research; commercially available market information such as Mintel, Target Group Index and retail audits; the press; suppliers; or other competitors with whom you have contact. Very often, companies will attend high-profile conferences and trade exhibitions with a view to gathering **competitive intelligence** quite openly, although some may engage in underhand corporate espionage (the latter is obviously not ethical or, indeed, recommended). Clearly, the closer you are to market intelligence, the better you will be able to make decisions – third- or fourth-hand data can be twisted out of all recognition, not unlike a game of Chinese whispers, and result in ineffective decision-making.

Souhami (2003) has argued that companies must stop 'staring at the same information and get the most out of competitor intelligence' and that 'competitive myopia' sets in when companies do not monitor their competitors systematically, which involves continuously gathering up-to-date information.

The Society of Competitive Intelligence Professionals (SCIP) is a worldwide professional body whose mission it is to raise the profile and recognition of the importance of competitive intelligence (CI), to get more companies involved in it and maintain and encourage ethical practices in CI. From a marketing point of view, it is not easy to distinguish where, or even if, CI differs from marketing information and intelligence. For our purposes here, it is helpful to consider CI as an important part of the total process of marketing intelligence. An approach to systematic gathering and disseminating competitive intelligence, together with other relevant marketing information, is referred to as a marketing information system (MkIS).

A fundamental function of the MkIS is to provide information when it is needed for decision-making. The information needs to be timely, accurate and trustworthy. The MkIS comprises a number of components:

- data collection and storage
- analysis
- reporting.

Data collection and storage

'Internal continuous data', as the name suggests, is data that is gathered continuously, e.g. financial accounts and salesforce records. The phenomenal growth in cheap computing power has revolutionised the process of information gathering, storage and analysis. Customer transaction data is an important part of any marketing intelligence system and there are many commercially available analytic systems to make greatest use of such data and companies willing to provide consultancy and data services to enhance this. 'Internal ad hoc data' is gathered from activities undertaken for specific events within the business, e.g. to see how well a particular promotion has performed. 'Environmental scanning' monitors the business environment (PRESTCOM factors) and 'marketing research', undertaken either continuously or as needed for particular purposes on an ad hoc basis, determines such things as customer attitudes to and opinions on product offerings.

Analysis

Companies gather huge amounts of data and managers need to make sense of it and turn it into useful information from which decisions may be made. Data needs to be distilled and disseminated to the right people at the right time in order for them to make optimum strategic, tactical or operational decisions.

Reporting

Based on the analysis conducted, reports should be produced from the MkIS on a regular basis, meeting the needs of the different marketing managers. Salesforce requirements differ from those of brand managers which differ from those of the marketing director, etc.

The sheer amount of data now available to managers, however, highlights particular management issues. Data was originally managed manually and sometimes with the assistance of press cuttings agencies, which helped companies to gather data. Now, growth in the range of media, facilitated by the development and growth of technologies, has resulted in the development of specialist computer software, e.g. SAS Textminer (www.sas.co.uk). This software helps manage the extraction of key information using techniques that industry frequently refers to as 'data integration management'. The use of such a wide array of data has given rise to the general term **database marketing**. Such databases are frequently thought of as holding customer data only, but they often hold much more.

Schultz (1997: 10) comments:

> *To integrate marketing you must integrate sales and selling, and to integrate those functions, you must integrate the entire organisation. ... The goal is to align the organisation to serve consumers and customers. Databases are rapidly becoming the primary management tool that drives the organisation's business strategy.*

database marketing
the use of computerised customer data to communicate with customers and promote further sales

Today's databases are very much more than simple customer listings. Computing power has created the ability to store and cross-analyse vast amounts of data, such as service and sales data, purchasing records, and attitudinal and behavioural data. There are many fields of data, covering millions of transactions and relationships. Without this information, it is unlikely that truly integrated marketing can exist. The database is the heart of a marketing intelligence system.

The aim of an efficient and successful MkIS is to turn data into information that, in turn, can be turned into management knowledge from which decisions can be made and action taken. Exhibit 12.12 illustrates an overview of a marketing intelligence system.

Exhibit 12.12   Marketing information/intelligence system

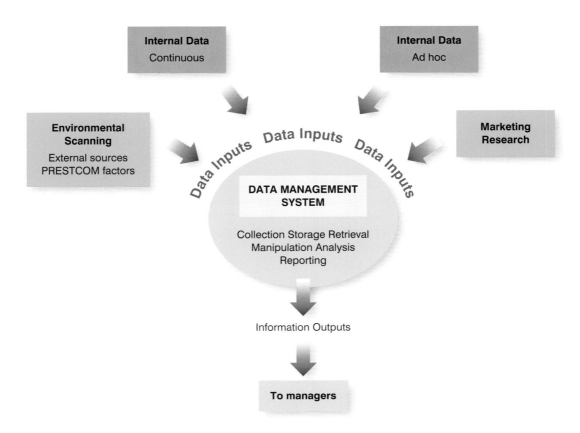

PORTER'S FIVE FORCES MODEL

Porter's five forces model
a competitive environment analysis tool

Porter's five forces model (Porter, 1985) is a useful tool for analysing competitive activity by helping firms determine the strength of competitive threats. This model enables businesses to analyse their competitive environment by focusing

insight   The man from Del Monte says 'Yes' to new database

Del Monte created a central database that sought to hold information, for example, about all of its thousands of retail customers. The database analysed buying patterns at each store and produced profiles of the stores' customer purchases. These were matched against local geo-demographic data.

Based on those profiles, Del Monte was able to identify if each store was reaching its expected target. Del Monte management were then able to direct their marketing effort with accuracy, from product launch, distribution and stocking decisions to marketing communications plans involving targeted salesforce effort, in-store promotions, direct mail and advertising.

The process created value-added information that Del Monte shared with all its trading partners to assist their efforts. Sales rose through closer partnership with distribution chain members and through better targeted marketing communications.

particularly on the competition and who has the bargaining power in the supply chain. Assessment can be made of the intensity of competition and the threat of new competitive entrants, the threat of substitute products, and the bargaining power of suppliers and customers (see Exhibit 12.13).

Threat of new entrants

An organisation needs to monitor the activities of potential competitors as well as existing competitors. The lower the market's **barriers to entry**, the more likely it is that these potential rivals will become actual rivals.

Barriers to entry include:

barriers to entry
things that make it difficult, or impossible, for new competitors to enter a market, e.g. patents, high set-up costs

- the costs of producing/providing for the marketplace. There may be the requirement for high capital outlay – perhaps to buy expensive production machinery, e.g. the nuclear power industry
- existing powerful brand names within the market, e.g. new entrants into the chocolate market would have to compete with Nestlé, Cadbury's, Mars, Suchard, etc.
- the size of the market – it may be too small to support any more competitors, e.g. a local high street may already have two good bakeries
- legal/regulatory barriers, e.g. a licence may be required to trade (selling alcohol, running a casino). Foreign firms are often banned from owning businesses in key sectors such as defence or the media. Patents are another means by which firms keep out potential rivals
- existing companies that control key resources, e.g. ownership or access to distribution chains or raw materials supplies
- existing companies that are large enough to benefit from economies of scale and therefore have lower cost bases than any new entrant would. This would mean that a new rival would be unable to match their prices without making a loss
- competitor reactions, e.g. fear or concern that competitors may react in ways either singularly or collectively that would make it difficult to enter a market successfully.

Exhibit 12.13   Porter's five forces model

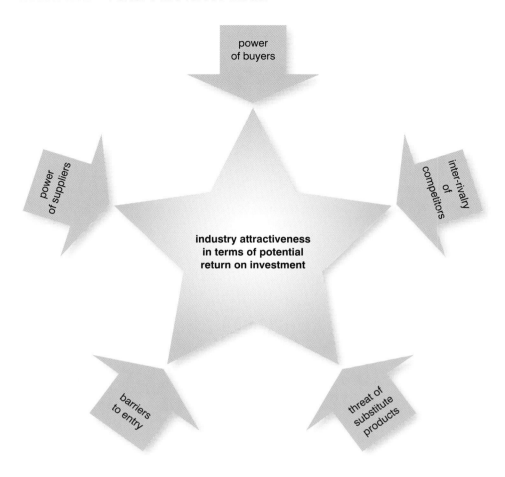

SOURCE: Based on
Porter, 1985

Threat of substitutes

The more alternative products and services there are, the harder it will be to maintain a competitive advantage and to make a good profit. For example, when crossing the channel, ferries and planes are substitutes for the Eurostar and Le Shuttle. The threat of substitutes may be determined by:

- the pricing of substitute products and, therefore, the sensitivity of customers to pricing
- the costs of the customer switching to a competitive product – if these are low, the risk of substitution is higher
- whether customers have a high propensity to substitute or, in other words, customers have low loyalty levels.

Bargaining power of buyers (customers)

Customers will be powerful if they, as individuals or buying groups, are more important to the suppliers than the suppliers are to them. Major grocery retailers such as Tesco and Aldi are able to dictate terms to most of their suppliers because of the bulk of groceries that are sold through their stores. Manufacturers such as Kellogg's and

Nestlé have to be seen on these supermarket giants' shelves. Smaller manufacturers actively compete for the supermarkets' shelf space. This has led to pressure on prices and, in some cases, insistence upon manufacturer-funded special offers such as BOGOFs (buy one get one free). Customers (buyers) are powerful when:

- there are few major buyers in the marketplace
- products are commoditised or standardised, i.e. there is little or no differentiation from the customer's perspective
- the company is not a key supplier to the customer and the customer holds the balance of power.

Bargaining power of suppliers

If raw materials or ingredients are scarce, then their suppliers can dictate terms. For example, after a bad coffee bean harvest, the price of coffee rose sharply in the shops (though little of this money went to the smaller coffee growers). Suppliers can redress the balance of power with retailers by developing strong **brands**. It would be a brave supermarket that refused to put Heinz baked beans on its UK shelves. **Market leaders** have a distinct advantage. Suppliers are powerful when:

- there are few other sources of supply for the company
- the suppliers threaten to integrate along the **supply chain,** in effect becoming a direct competitor to the company
- the costs of switching to other suppliers is great. Suppliers have been known to tie in their customers through financial pressure by extending credit terms so that companies they supply become dependent on such extended terms to help manage cash flow
- the company's business is not key to the supplier.

Intensity of rivalry of competitors

Just as some people are more competitive than others, so are some companies. Markets such as grocery retailing and fashion are highly competitive. In the first case, this is shown in **price wars** and intense **below-the-line activity.** In the second case, it is apparent in high **advertising** spend. Just how intensely firms compete with each other depends on a number of factors, one of which is the market growth rate. In a growing market, there is more business available for everyone and so firms do not need to steal each other's **market share** in order to make more sales. The intensity of rivalry between competitors may depend on:

- the number of competitors in the market – the more there are, the more intense the competitive activity
- the cost structure – high capital investment may actually result in lower unit costs because management will want to ensure that its machinery operates at optimum capacity rather than laying idle, waiting for orders
- the differential advantages between products and brands, i.e. those brands perceived by customers to be differentiated are less likely to attract competitive activity
- the costs involved in customers switching to competing products – if these are high, then customers are less likely to switch, negating the need for such intense rivalry
- the strategic objectives being pursued by the competitors – if a competitor is holding or harvesting its products, then it is not as concerned with highly competitive behaviour

competitive advantage or **competitive edge**
something about an organisation or its products that is perceived as being better than rival offerings

● the exit barriers, i.e. if these are high, then more competition will be encouraged to stay in the market, resulting in highly active competitive behaviour as they try to gain market share.

If a company is to develop a **competitive edge**, then it must understand its competitors' strengths and weaknesses. An in-depth, up-to-date analysis of the competitive environment is the basis of any sound competitive strategy.

ACTIVITY

Imagine you are the manager of your favourite football team. Apply Porter's five forces model to identify who has the greatest power in your market. Consider:

● who potential entrants into your market could be
● who the competition is and how competitive the game is
● who could be a substitute for your team
● who your suppliers are, what they supply to you and how important they are
● who your customers are, what they buy from you and how important they are to you and your team.

EXPAND YOUR KNOWLEDGE

Porter, M. (1980) 'Industry structure and competitive strategy: keys to profitability', *Financial Analysis*, 36 (4): 30–41.

Michael Porter's name is synonymous with competitive analysis and strategy. Here is an early paper in which he highlights the need to understand the competitive environment and outlines the key forces that drive industry competition.

Business mission and marketing objectives

Just as you set out on your studies to obtain a higher qualification, such as a degree or diploma, in order to become, perhaps, a marketing management expert, successful advertising executive or an entrepreneur, so a business will set out to achieve some broad aims. A **business mission**, or vision as it is sometimes called, is an explicit statement that captures the broad aims of the company. This is used to communicate those broad aims to all its stakeholders, both internal and external. Its purpose, ideally, is to provide an inspirational focus or strategic and operational direction for the whole company. Preferably, it should not be 'a long awkward sentence that demonstrates management's inability to think clearly', a criticism laid by Dilbert, one of the greatest cartoon characters who ever poked fun at business and management.

business mission
the broad aims a business hopes to achieve

There are a number of general components to a good business mission statement. It should:

● identify the company's philosophy, i.e. its approach to business
● specify its product–market domain, i.e. where the company will operate in the marketplace
● communicate key values for those involved, i.e. how it will operate
● be closely linked to critical success factors, i.e. the things the company has to be good at to survive.

insight   Mission possible . . . ?

Nike's mission statement is:

To bring inspiration and innovation to every athlete* in the world.

This appears quite narrow since it implies customers are purely competitive athletes. Its market, however, extends much wider than that. Do you own Nike clothing? Why? Perhaps you consider yourself to be a competitive sportsperson? No? Its purpose is, of course, not to limit its market to competitive sportspeople only. So, in order to qualify what it means by 'athlete'

(notice the asterisk in the mission statement), it goes on to use a quote from one of its legendary role models and co-founder of the company, Bill Bowerman:

'If you have a body, you are an athlete.'

This very cleverly puts Nike into the domain of every person in the world. It implies some of the mission statement components outlined in this section and it clearly incorporates the core values of the senior management.

To explore the many global Nike brands and products, go to www.nike.com. For more about Nike's business and to read more about its mission statement, go to www.nike.com/nikebiz.

SOURCE: www.nike.com

Exhibit 12.14

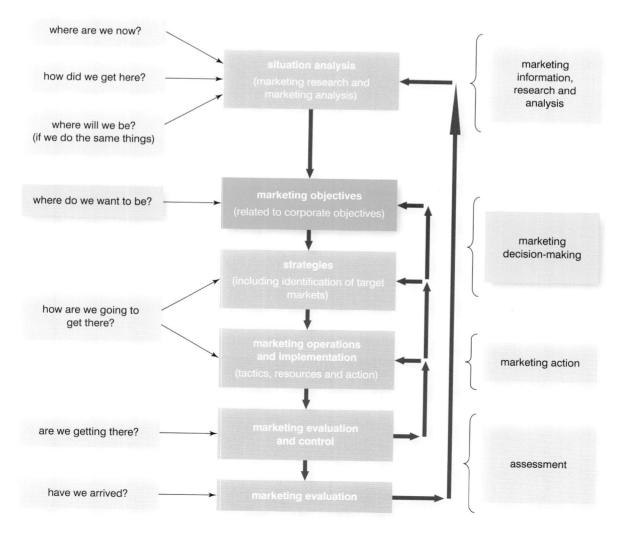

Nike's mission statement (in the Insight box) can be compared with that of the global activist organisation, Greenpeace (www.greenpeace.org):

Greenpeace is an independent non-profit global campaigning organisation that uses non-violent, creative confrontation to expose global environmental problems and their causes. We research the solutions and alternatives to help provide a path for a green and peaceful future.

This is less succinct than Nike's statement, but still incorporates the main components of a mission. It states what the organisation is trying to achieve and incorporates the strong beliefs that we know and see in some of its highly creative, attention-seeking behaviour reported in the news. It also qualifies its statement by going on to say:

Greenpeace's goal is to ensure the ability of the earth to nurture life in all its diversity.

ACTIVITY

Compare and contrast the Nike and Greenpeace mission statements. What similarities do they share? What are their distinctive differences? What do you think about the quality and value of these statements? How well do you think they will serve their purposes? Write a mission statement for yourself, incorporating the components outlined above. Remember, you do not need to have a sentence for each of these components – consider Nike's and Greenpeace's missions.

According to Levitt (1960), who is responsible for having created the concept of the business mission, in order to develop an appropriate mission a company's managers should ask some basic questions: 'What business are we in?', 'What business should we be in?' and 'What business can we be in?' The answers should be given in terms of customer needs, rather than the products the company makes (and are, therefore, another good indicator of market-orientation). See the example in Exhibit 12.15.

Exhibit 12.15   Defining the business

Traditional definition of business	Customer need-based definition of business
Electricity	Power/Energy/Heat/Light
Train travel	Transportation
Cinema	Entertainment
Computers	Information processing
Telephones	Communications

This type of extrapolation enables a company to identify much broader-based competition and think about how it could be more competitive and avoid 'marketing myopia' (Levitt, 1960). Marketing myopia is where a company forgets that a customer wants a product to solve a problem. The classic example highlighted by Levitt is a drill – he states that the customer actually wants the holes it makes. This can be taken further, however, because in fact customers do not usually want holes in walls, they want hooks for pictures or brackets for shelves.

Thinking about products in this way gives the company greater scope in its development of new products as well as highlighting the full range of products that may be competing for its customers. The process of identifying what business it is in, and could be in, will enable a company to develop an appropriate business mission. Having decided on a business mission, a company will use this to inform and develop its business objectives from which it will decide on specific strategies. The next paragraphs look at how business and marketing objectives are formulated, based on a systematic analysis of the marketplace.

Objectives should conform to three basic conventions (Walker et al., 1992/2003).

- What performance dimensions should the company and employees focus on?
- What is the target level of performance for each of these dimensions?
- What is the time frame in which the targets should be achieved?

Different organisations are trying to achieve different things. However, there are some things that most hope to achieve, for example:

- survival
- profits (however, not-for-profit organisations, such as charities or hospitals, usually just aim to break even)
- a good reputation
- competitive edge.

Everyone within the organisation is expected to pull together to meet these objectives and each business function will set its own objectives which are designed to help meet the overall corporate ones.

Typical marketing objectives include:

- a move into a new market (perhaps another country)
- the launch of a new product
- increased sales volume (i.e. quantity of goods sold)
- increased market share
- the acquisition of another brand.

Objectives are goals, targets, things that the organisation wants. Businesses then organise their resources (money, people, machinery, etc.) so as to achieve or acquire those things that they want, i.e. to meet their objectives. Clearly, objectives need to be within reach, so they need to be SMART: Specific, Measurable, Achievable, Relevant and Timed (see Chapter 11).

The next section will look at setting strategies to achieve the organisation's objectives.

Marketing strategy

With a clear picture of the business environment and of the objectives it wishes to achieve, the company can now decide how it is going to take its business forward into

Exhibit 12.16

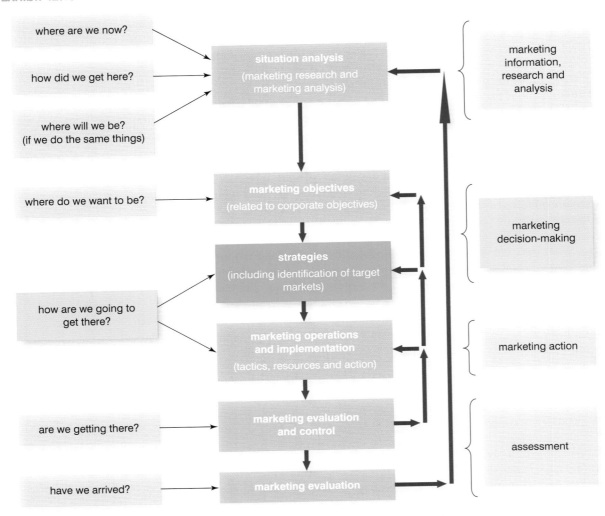

the next trading period. It can think about this in terms of shorter or longer time periods. It is often much easier for managers to make decisions for the short term because they will have more detailed and accurate information about the marketplace.

Long-term decisions require managers to see into the future. Longer-term success is about being visionary, reading the market, knowing the business well and, sometimes, getting lucky. Even Marks and Spencer's experienced managers have not been able to do this with complete accuracy or total success in the last ten years and have faced some very difficult times. On the other hand, Stelios Haji-Ioannou of easy-Group fame has been an artful player.

The next paragraphs look at how some marketing management tools can be utilised to develop strategic direction for the business (Johnson et al., 2007). It is the choice of strategic direction that provides focus for the company's longer-term continuation.

Porter's generic strategies
three main competitive strategies: cost leadership, differentiation or focus

PORTER'S GENERIC STRATEGIES

Porter's generic strategies is one model that provides an overview of strategic direction for the company (see Exhibit 12.17).

Exhibit 12.17 Generic competitive strategies

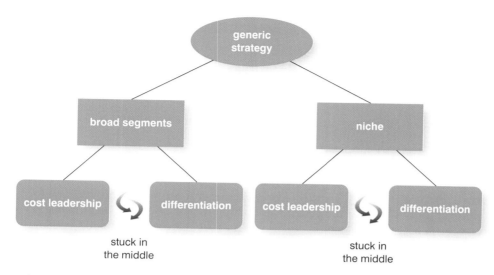

(based on Porter 1985)

SOURCE: Adapted from Porter, 1985

It highlights that the company can pursue one of three main competitive strategic directions based on its identification of competitive forces and view of the market:

- mass (broad segments) or **niche**. Does the company concentrate on one segment or try to serve many?
- differentiation, where the company chooses to differentiate itself based on some competitive advantage it has identified, e.g. **brand** or service offering
- cost leadership, where the company is able to offer low prices thanks to its low production costs

If the company ignores these choices, or attempts to pursue two simultaneously, Porter argues that it could be in danger of being stuck in the middle, i.e. where it has no clear direction and merely reacts to market conditions, therefore making it vulnerable to competitors.

EXPAND YOUR KNOWLEDGE

Abell, D.F. (1978) 'Strategic windows', *Journal of Marketing*, 42 (Jul): 21–26.

Strategic marketing planning involves management in anticipating and responding to changes in the marketplace. The term 'strategic window' is used to focus attention on marketing opportunities in which there is a fit between a firm's competencies and key market requirements. Emphasis is placed on a matching process between a firm and its market for successful outcomes.

ANSOFF'S MATRIX

The **Ansoff matrix** (Ansoff, 1957) is another tool managers can use to help determine their strategic direction (see Exhibit 12.18). It is also known as the Ansoff growth

Ansoff's matrix comprises four possible growth strategies: market development, product development, market penetration/ expansion and diversification

matrix because it focuses on the ways companies can grow through increased sales opportunities. It looks at the product in relation to its market and helps managers to identify their potential business opportunities. The matrix is one of the best-known strategic tools as, despite its simplicity, it is a very powerful way of looking at strategic options. The two-by-two matrix first defined by Ansoff can be made more sophisticated, and other authors have expanded the matrix into a three-by-three matrix that includes categories for modified products and modified markets. The quadrants defined by Ansoff are identified as having different levels of business risk associated them. In so far as the top-left quadrant is best understood and experienced by the company, it is said to carry the least risk for growth. However, if this proves to be a highly competitive market that is stagnant or declining, and if the company has limited power in the market, this level of risk might become significantly higher and the company might be wise to move into other areas. The top-right and bottom-left quadrants are said to carry greater risk and the bottom-right quadrant carries the greatest risk to the company in that diversification with new products in new markets represents new and uncharted territory in which the company has least or even no experience.

Quadrant 1: existing products in existing markets – market penetration strategy. This is about focusing effort in existing markets and encouraging existing customers

Exhibit 12.18   Ansoff's matrix

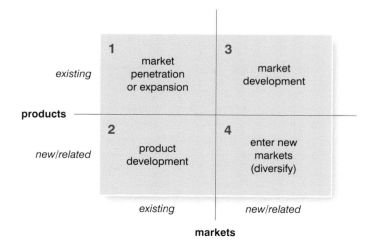

to use the product more (more at each use, or more frequently, or use competing products less). This quadrant emphasises strategies to develop sales from existing customers.

Quadrant 2: new or related products for existing markets – product development strategy. Involves some element of product development or improvement for existing customers. Car manufacturers are continually striving to improve their products, e.g. the Ford Escort has been replaced by the Ford Focus. This quadrant emphasises strategies to gain sales through product development or new products that are marketed to existing target customers (whether they are actual current customers or other potential customers in the target market(s) in which the company currently operates).

Quadrant 3: existing products in new or related markets – market development strategy. This is about finding new uses for products or launching into new markets e.g. different geographic areas of the world or different market segments. Lucozade was originally a drink for recuperating children, but when the company found that mothers were using it as a 'pick-me-up' during the day, it decided to relaunch the product. It is now firmly established as a 'sports' drink. This quadrant emphasises strategies related to marketing to newly defined target markets.

Quadrant 4: new or related products in new markets – diversification strategy. Taking new products into new markets is the hardest of the four directions from a company's perspective. This is because it involves moving into an area of business with which it is unfamiliar and, as a result, the risks of potential failure are high. The strategy works best when there is a close match with existing experiences. This quadrant emphasises strategies in which both product development and market development are combined and the consequential diversification can take many forms.

EXPAND YOUR KNOWLEDGE

Ansoff, I. (1957) 'Strategies for diversification', *Harvard Business Review*, 35 (5): 113–24.

Igor Ansoff has had a profound effect on our understanding of business strategies and was one of the early writers on the subject. In this article, he explores the strategies that relate to different diversification approaches.

The means by which a company chooses to adopt any of Ansoff's alternative strategic directions depend on how much the company wishes to control the activities related to the marketing of its products. Such expansion can be achieved through internal development or in unison with other companies through vertical or horizontal integration, which form different types of strategic alliance. Options include the following:

- **A network** – this is a loose association between a company and, for example, a series of distributors, such as pursued by many car manufacturers who sell through a range of different types of outlet. It can also be a network of agents, which is a strategy pursued by some companies when they enter an unfamiliar market or a new country. With a network, the company may have relatively little control over how the third party markets the products to end users, or how end users (consumers) are treated.

- **A contract or licence agreement** – here the company imposes conditions on the third party it uses to service its end-user needs. A contract or licence agreement may restrict the marketing operations to specifically those developed by the originating company. This is a strategy pursued by McDonald's, which specifies everything from outlet layout to the disposable packaging used by franchisees, and even the training received by counter and waiting staff.
- **A consortium or joint venture** – where two or more companies agree to develop joint operations on a contractual basis. This may be used by companies entering new markets or countries, and enables them to maximise their potential by taking on local working practices. This may also be a situation whereby companies remain focused on their core business but, through utilisation of each partner's specialisms, they develop a new or better product offering for the end user.
- **An acquisition or merger** – ultimately, complete control of the supply chain is achieved through this route. It does, however, necessitate the company to be cash rich or, at least, able to raise sufficient capital to invest and continue generating a profit. A number of companies have pursued this strategy in order to gain market share only to sell off their purchase at a later date, when they have been unable to realise the expected returns (e.g. EMAP Publications' procurement and then sale of a series of local FM radio stations during the 1980s and 1990s). Of course, the reason for a procurement or merger may be because a firm wants only a part of another company to add to existing operations, such as a brand name, or to achieve economies of scale by focusing on what each are good at, e.g. 3i's Go airline and easyJet merger in August 2002, whereby they have agreed both will use the easyJet flight booking system, among other things.

MOVING INTO OVERSEAS MARKETS

Why do firms trade internationally rather than stick with their familiar home markets? Most commonly, it is as part of a growth strategy. They want to increase sales.

The firm may want to market a wider range of products but has discovered that there is insufficient demand to support this in its home market, or it may be that the converse is true and the firm wishes to specialise in a narrower range of products. Either way, they will need a larger market for those products if they are to maintain sales revenue.

Apart from growth, there are a number of other good reasons for selling products internationally, including:

- as part of a competitive strategy
- risk spreading
- globalisation of markets
- excess capacity
- to extend the product life cycle.

Competitive strategy

Firms may trade abroad because competition has got too hot in their home market and they are looking for an easier market in which to trade. Alternatively, they may be trying to frighten off a new foreign competitor by keeping them busy back home. Internationalisation may be part of either a cost leadership or a focus strategy (see Porter's generic strategies above). Increasing sales is one way to increase profits, but the alternative (or complementary) way is through reducing costs. This can be achieved through the **economies of scale** that come from dealing in larger volumes of goods – volumes that the international marketplace can deliver. These cost savings can then be passed on to all customers as lower prices.

economies of scale
unit costs fall as larger quantities are produced; a cost advantage associated with large organisations

Risk spreading

Some firms trade in multiple markets in order to reduce risk through geographical diversification. The hope is that although some markets may suffer downturns, the others will make up for it. Unfortunately, as world trade becomes more and more globalised, and trading blocs such as the European Union emerge, the economies of countries are more closely linked and they have a greater tendency to move together.

Globalisation

One of the upsides of globalisation is that as markets become more similar, and more open to foreign products, it becomes easier to compete globally. It may even be necessary to trade internationally in order to maintain a reputation as a serious competitor.

Excess capacity

If demand is falling, or new technology has made a product easier to produce, or there have been significant productivity gains, then a company may have more products than it can sell. It will either have to downsize (produce less) or find new markets for its products – quite possibly overseas markets.

Extending the product life cycle

Moving to a new, foreign market, is a traditional method of extending a **product's life cycle**. Car manufacturers used to employ this strategy, selling their old models to third world countries when their home markets no longer wanted them. With the increase in international communications, this has become harder to do. Consumers the world over see the latest products and styles on television and the Internet. It is harder to fob them off with old products.

product life cycle
a product analysis tool based on the idea that a product has life stages: introduction, growth, maturity, decline, deletion

Market selection criteria

International marketing managers are constantly screening the international environment looking for threats and opportunities. These often present themselves in the form of new geographic markets for their products. They must select the most promising markets to trade in and reject the rest. They need to consider both the market generally and their own firm's potential within it. Management should set minimum acceptable levels for sales, profit, market share, and then analyse the potential of the new market to assess the likelihood of achieving those levels. This is called market screening. It requires managers asking the following questions:

- How does the market's potential for profit, sales, market share compare to the company's expectations from an overseas market?
- Does the country have an acceptable legal system (e.g. patent laws)?
- Is the market accessible?
- Is there a suitable marketing infrastructure (e.g. distributors, retailers, agencies)?

- Do existing competitors have too strong a hold on the market?
- Is the level of risk acceptable?

The assessment of political risk is especially important when considering whether to start trading in another country. Some countries have unstable governments that may be able to exercise powers that Western governments would not.

If the country passes the screening, then the company will then want to assess its own chances of success in that market.

- How much experience does the company have in similar markets and how well has it done there?
- Are there matches in terms of language and other cultural factors?
- Are there opportunities for standardisation?

The answers to these questions, and others like them, will determine whether the new market is likely to be a success.

INTERNATIONAL STRATEGY: STANDARDISATION VS ADAPTATION

A critical question in international marketing is whether to standardise your offerings worldwide or to adapt them to local needs. Remembering that the marketing philosophy is about satisfying customer needs and wants, it would seem that the best strategy would be to adapt to meet local needs. So if the Spanish want batter mix in smaller pack sizes, with less sugar and all the instructions in Spanish only – so be it. The snag with this approach is that it is expensive.

This is not just about products themselves. It is almost always cheaper to do things the same way everywhere. Promotion is cheaper if you can make one advert for the world; use the same prize draw, the same media. Distribution can be handled more effectively if a company can use the same retailers, the same logistics.

Standardisation is not just about costs. It also fits with a strategy of marketing integration – the philosophy behind which is that if we standardise, then our offering sends the same message the world over, reinforcing the desired positioning and avoiding conflict and confusion. However, most product offerings are difficult to standardise across multiple countries and consequently very few truly global (i.e. standardised) products exist. There are, however, an increasing number of global brands.

Reasons to standardise internationally

- economies of scale
- the Internet and other technologies have bridged culture and language gaps
- globalised communications media mean that people across the world get the same information and are exposed to the same influences
- some products have no cultural sensitivity – the main barrier to standardisation is national culture but some products really have no cultural values associated with them, e.g. paper clips, raw materials, computer mice
- there are market segments that exist across international boundaries, e.g. the youth market
- members of trading blocs, such as ASEAN, are growing more similar. It would be a big mistake to assume that the citizens of such blocs are all the same though as EU countries are enormously culturally varied

Reasons to adapt

- different cultures
- different income levels – this affects product design (number of features, quality of materials) as well as pricing
- different market infrastructure – e.g. different competitors, different types of distribution systems
- different climate – think about clothing, for instance, or duvets
- different legal requirements and regulations
- availability and level of local skills – can a complex product be supported properly?
- differing uses – will a product be used every day or occasionally? By one person or by many? For example, bicycles may be everyday transport (in China) or recreational (USA) or either (UK)
- brand history – sometimes a product is held dear by its customers and is hard to change, e.g. Coca-Cola still markets Thums Up in India though nowhere else. In Europe, Mars sell Mars bars while in the USA this product is called a Milky Way. Milky Ways can also be bought in Europe, but they, of course, have a different recipe to the US ones.

The above lists are not exhaustive but present the most common arguments on both sides of the standardisation vs adaptation debate. Particular markets or products may have special reasons for choosing one strategy or the other.

EXPAND YOUR KNOWLEDGE

Kotler, P. (1986) 'Global standardization – courting danger', *The Journal of Consumer Marketing*, 3 (Spring): 13–15.

Kotler takes a profoundly marketing orientated view to warn against presumption that international marketing can be a simple extension to marketing at a national level. Principles and practices of segmentation apply. Consumer behaviour varies significantly country by country.

Melewar, T.C., Pickton, D., Gupta, S. and Chigovanyika, T. (2009) 'MNE executive insights into international advertising programme standardisation', *Journal of Marketing Communications,* 15 (5): 345–365.

While the standardisation versus adaptation debate has long raged with expressions of the pros and cons of both approaches, this article sought to identify through in-depth interviews the factors that influence actual executive' decisions as determined by experienced and practising international marketing executives themselves and what factors they rated as important in their own businesses. These areas of standardisation or adaptation were considered: advertising theme, creative expression and media mix.

PUSH AND PULL STRATEGIES

If a company sells its goods or provides its services through third parties (intermediaries), then it needs to consider the roles of **push strategies** and **pull strategies.** One of the most significant yet basic strategic marketing decisions centres around the determination

push strategy
a promotional strategy aimed at distribution channels

pull strategy
a promotional strategy aimed at end customers or consumers

Trade customers for consumer goods

It is interesting to note that distinctions are made between B2C and B2B companies, as though they operate under significantly different circumstances. While the circumstances may vary, it is inappropriate for us to think in quite this way in strategic marketing terms. While the balance of the mix may vary, there is a lot in common between B2C companies and B2B companies. Among the biggest players in business to business marketing are, in fact, the B2C FMCG companies. Although their products are targeted towards consumers, their marketing activities have to cover trade customers as well. Push strategies feature strongly in their marketing, even if these are not so widely recognised or appreciated.

Likewise, B2B companies whose products may never be seen by the majority of consumers, can embark on elaborate pull strategies. In computing, Intel, with its Pentium processor, and in textiles, Dupont, with its Lycra fabric, are good examples. Both these companies have heavily branded their products and these are recognised in households throughout the world, yet they have never themselves sold a single product to consumers.

of push and pull strategies. These strategies are concerned with the marketing efforts focused towards trade/channel intermediaries (push strategies) and the final customers and consumers, and the decision influencers that affect them (pull strategies). These strategies are also known as 'selling into the pipeline' and 'selling out of the pipeline', referring to push and pull strategies respectively. The 'pipeline' is the channels that facilitate the movement of goods and services through intermediaries (**retailers, wholesalers, agents**, brokers, etc.). Wherever intermediaries are involved, *both* push and pull strategies should be used in an integrated fashion. To develop one strategy without consideration of the other can result in higher risks of failure.

Push strategies encourage the trade to carry and promote products. They help to achieve distribution coverage, create trade goodwill and partnership. Pull strategies encourage products to be demanded. A combination of push and pull provides a greater synergistic effect than can be achieved in the use of either strategy alone. Often joint promotions between channel members and manufacturers are undertaken to enhance trade partnership and improve pull promotions.

COMPETITIVE STANCE

The company needs to determine the position it wants in the marketplace, based on its assessment of the attractiveness of different market segments relative to business strengths. The company may aim to be:

- a leader
- a challenger
- a follower
- a nicher.

Clearly, these positions will necessitate particular approaches to the market. For example, it would be anticipated that market leader or challenger positions will

Too few cooks

Normally, B2B is about marketing to business customers, often with the aim of forming an alliance between them that benefits both parties. AWOL, a small recruitment company specialising in the placement of chefs and catering staff in the north-west of England, however, has a unique business problem: good-quality chefs are few and far between and notoriously prone to leaving jobs. Indeed, many are self-styled one-man businesses in their own right. So, as well as building relationships with restaurant and pub owners in its catchment area, who are the 'bread and butter' of AWOL's business, AWOL is also active in building strong relationships with its chefs. This means that as the chef rolls from one job he takes his recruitment company with him too, thus building a pyramid with a genuinely strong footing for the company.

This is a strategy of focused differentiation, which enables AWOL to retain its identity as distinct from other recruitment agencies with both restauranteurs and chefs.

SOURCE: Kim Brown, AWOL Recruitment, www.awolrecruitment.com

require aggressive defence or attacking behaviour, actively choosing to engage in pricing or promotional wars. As Ries and Trout (1986) contend, it is far easier to stay on top than to get there. Indeed, analogies between war and marketing have been extremely popular and strategic approaches to marketing based on military analogies for attacking and defending against opponents have been developed, although it is felt that this is something that goes beyond an initial introduction to marketing. On the other hand, a market follower is a company that is quite happy to take a background position, while a market nicher is one that focuses only on a small part of the overall market, thus avoiding direct attention or confrontation with the larger market leaders and challengers.

The application of marketing management tools enables the company to develop its strategic focus, by providing the detail behind the business objectives and strategies. In turn, these must be operationalised. The next section looks at marketing operations and implementation in more detail.

EXPAND YOUR KNOWLEDGE

Kotler, P. and Singh, R. (1981) 'Marketing warfare', *Journal of Business Strategy*, 1 (Winter): 30–41.

The analogy of war and military is used here to identify a range of strategic options available to firms from various forms of attack to various forms of defence.

Marketing operations and implementation: tactics, resources and action

Operational and implementation decisions necessitate the blending of different elements of the company in order to achieve its goals. In other words, they make the goals happen. (This is still part of the 'How are we going to get there?' question.) The

Exhibit 12.19

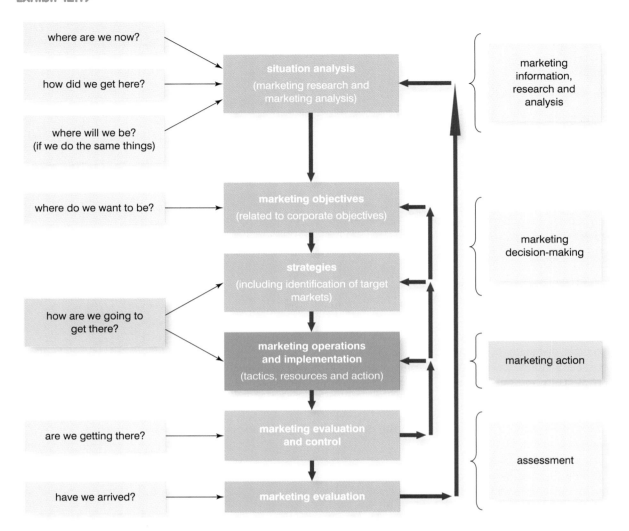

broad strategic decisions need to be turned into actual tactics and operational plans. The elements of the marketing mix form the basis of marketing tactics. Decisions have to be made about the specifics of the pricing, **marketing communications**, distribution and the product, together with issues of service delivery (see also Chapter 6, Product Life Cycle). Resources and timing need to be carefully considered. One way of considering the resource requirements is the 3Ms approach that was first suggested by Smith et al. (1997). The 3Ms stand for:

- money
- men
- minutes.

MONEY

Money refers to budgeting for the plan – the financial requirements needed to put the marketing plan into action. Various methods may be used to set the budget (see Chapter 8) and this may be done as part of the top-down or bottom-up approach referred to at the beginning of this chapter.

The budget is critical in determining what marketing activities can be afforded and also in assessing the overall contribution that marketing has made to the firm. Unless there are some particular and exceptional circumstances, companies expect the returns from marketing to exceed the expenditure so that marketing has made a positive financial contribution to the business. In practice, many related marketing costs may be hidden or placed in other budgets. For example, customer services may be part of a separate department and budgeted separately. Corporate branding, signage, livery and stationery may be a separate budget, PR and publicity may be separated from marketing, and so on. As a consequence, it is not necessarily easy to assess marketing contribution.

MEN

This element of the resources relates to the human resources (men and women) required by the plan, not only in terms of numbers of staff, but also their skills and experience and how they are to be organised. The marketing department may need extra staff, more sales staff may be needed, the staffing may need to be restructured, a new call centre may need to be set up, new agencies appointed, and so on. Consideration needs to be given to the extent to which in-house staffing will undertake the marketing activities versus outsourcing.

MINUTES

Minutes are to do with the timescale of the plan, the scheduling of activities and the time for tasks to be completed.

Contingency plans

Analysing the market is not just a means to facilitate strategic choice; it also helps to plan for an uncertain future. The theory, of course, is that by analysing the past, one can extrapolate forward. Consider what happens if there is a recession, a war, a new unknown competitor, a new alliance between two firms that wish to steal your market share, a takeover bid for your main customer, further **market fragmentation**, a new form of telepathic media developed, obviating the need for advertising, Internet meltdown, an increase in average life expectancy to 145 years. Clearly, some of these are more likely to happen than others, so events can be ranked by probability of their occurrence and their potential impact on the business. This can be part of the opportunities and threats analysis.

market fragmentation
a market characterised by a large number of relatively small players, none of which have significant competitive advantage

Although marketing research (see Chapter 5) provides good clues as to the nature of the problems that may arise in a market, there is always room for the unexpected. Piercy (2002) coined the term **market sensing**, which is the need for an understanding of the market rather than merely knowledge of it. Understanding is about synthesised knowledge – you may know a lot, but how well do you understand it? Piercy produced a framework to help managers categorise the potential series of events that may impact on their business (see Exhibit 12.20).

market sensing
the need for an understanding of the market, rather than merely a knowledge of it

The purpose, of course, in identifying potential problems is for the company to prepare itself to take some action, referred to as contingency planning (which may be called crisis management in another guise), i.e. plan B through to plan F, etc. should the possible change in outcome apply. In this way, the company is not left wondering what to do and can take the new course of action quickly. It is, however, not possible to develop a great number of options as they will take as much time and effort to develop as 'plan A', but it is prudent to have some rudimentary ideas that can be picked up in a timely manner should things go wrong. The implementation of contingency plans can only be made possible provided there is continuing **environmental scanning,** attention paid to competitor activity and the monitoring of your own plan as it is put into action. This involves tracking of performance and evaluation of the final outcomes at the end of the planned period and this is all part of the next stage of the marketing management and planning process – marketing evaluation and control.

Exhibit 12.20   Piercy's framework for market sensing

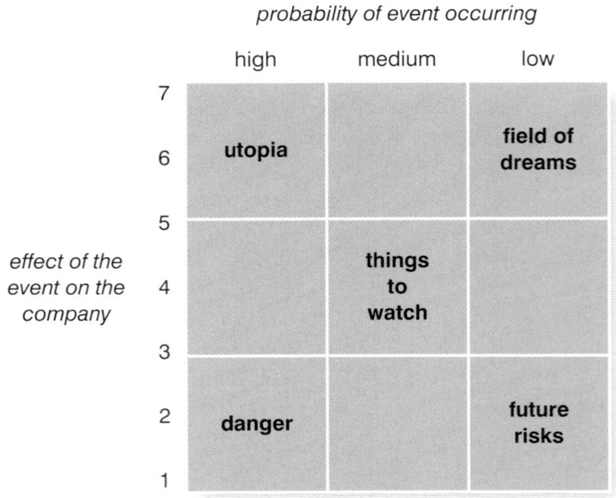

probability of event occurring

	high	medium	low
7			
6	utopia		field of dreams
5			
4		things to watch	
3			
2	danger		future risks
1			

effect of the event on the company

1 = disaster; 2 = very bad; 3 = bad; 4 = neutral; 5 = good; 6 = very good; 7 = ideal

SOURCE: Piercy, 2009: 256

EXPAND YOUR KNOWLEDGE

Buzzell, R.D., Gale, B.T. and Sultan, R.G.M. (1975) 'Market share: a key to profitability', *Harvard Business Review*, 53 (Jan–Feb): 97–106.

This article builds on the findings of the extensive PIMS project (Profit Impact of Market Strategies) and highlights the significance and impact of market share on profitability and return on investment. The paper explores the reasons for these links.

Marketing evaluation and control

Evaluation and control of marketing activities amounts to an understanding of how well the business is performing given the decisions made by its marketing managers. It addresses two of our strategic questions: 'Are we getting there?' and 'Have we arrived?'. This involves ongoing **tracking** over the period of the implementation of the plan and a final evaluation at the end of the period. Tracking facilitates modifications to the planned activities and, perhaps, the implementation

Exhibit 12.21

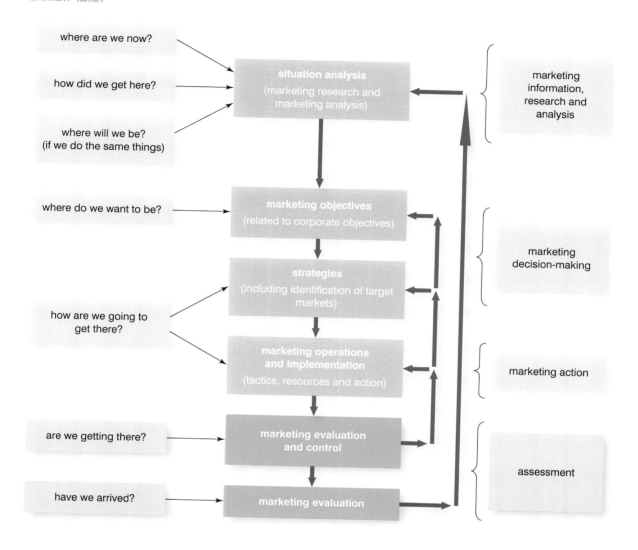

of contingency plans, as described above. If necessary, objectives and strategies can be amended (in more extreme circumstances), as can tactics and operations. The final evaluation is fed back into the next planning cycle. The process requires analysis of the variance between planned (target or budgeted) and actual performance across the range of activities that are affected by the decisions made. It may also, and indeed often does, take into account how well the company has performed in comparison to its competitors, especially the industry leaders. Effective evaluation and control therefore results in successful adjustments to activities in order to achieve the intended objectives. Exhibit 12.22 provides a summary of the evaluation and control process.

While it is clearly important to measure the extent to which the desired outcomes are being achieved, or have been achieved, it is also necessary to assess the efficiency and effectiveness of the marketing effort. It should not be the aim to achieve outcomes no matter what the cost. Marketing activities should always be carried out without wasting effort or resources. It is said that efficiency is about doing things right whereas effectiveness is about doing the right things, and both are important.

Exhibit 12.22   Marketing evaluation and control process

SOURCE: Chartered
Institute of Marketing, 2002

The sort of questions that should be asked include:

- What was expected to happen?
- What did happen?
- What was the effect of each of the marketing elements as well as their collective effect? Can these effects be separated from other factors? That is, are we sure that the results were due to our specific marketing efforts?
- What were the reasons for success or failure?
- What was learned from the plan?
- What does this tell us that we can apply to the next planning period?

The range of evaluation and control mechanisms is vast. The following are just a few examples:

- profitability analysis
- production analysis
- sales analysis
- customer service analysis
- benchmarking and competitor analysis.

All elements of the product offering and the marketing plan can, and should, be examined. Marketing metrics highlight the need to measure and assess all possible aspects of marketing that can be measured. The level and quantity of detail can be extensive. Measurements will include the following and a great deal more.

Exhibit 12.23   Elements of evaluation and control applied to the marketing mix

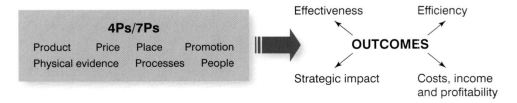

Product

- **market share**
- sales by segment and customer group
- performance of new products
- level of complaints.

Price

- **profit margin**
- discounts offered and level
- price analysis by customer segment
- comparisons to competing products
- level of **contribution.**

---

insight **evaluating promotions**

Exhibit 12.24   Common research and measures used in marketing communications

Type of effect	Relevant research
Retail sales	Retail audit
Direct sales	Consumer audit
	Percentage response to direct communications
	Percentage conversion to sales
Consumer buying behaviour	Panel data Own transactional data
Claimed consumer behaviour	Survey research
Attitude to brand	Survey/qualitative research
Perceptions/image of brand	Survey/qualitative research
Awareness of brand	Survey research
Attitudes to/communication of advertising	Survey/qualitative research
Recall of advertising	Survey research
Exposure to advertising	Media research

SOURCE: based on Coooper (1997)

Place

- channel costs
- channel volume
- delivery time
- stock levels
- performance of individual channel members.

Promotion

- cost per contact made
- media coverage
- customer awareness levels
- customer enquiries generated.

Physical evidence:

- customer awareness of, and attitudes towards, the physical aspects of service provision
- efficiency of store or outlet layout.

Processes:

- length of time from beginning to end
- efficiency and effectiveness of the process
- how well the planning and management was carried out
- the systems and procedures to ensure customer satisfaction.

People:

- number of people involved, agencies involved
- performance of the people, agencies involved
- skills and competencies
- training delivery
- qualifications
- rewards and incentives.

Having identified any areas of business that are underperforming, managers must decide how to address the shortfalls – either strategically or tactically – which is where contingency planning comes into force. The decisions, of course, will depend on the nature of the problem identified. For example, if there is a shortfall in sales, the company may decide to:

- target a new segment of the market (strategic)
- temporarily put prices down or up (tactical)
- redirect the sales effort or send salespeople on a training programme (operational).

The speed and efficiency with which shortfalls are addressed is often crucial to the ongoing success of the business.

ACTIVITY

The idea of evaluation and control can also be applied to your own studies. Consider how you measure your performance. You will think about the following:

- the results you have from previous assessments
- your intended results
- the amount of effort you have made to study
- what has given rise to the results achieved and what might have been done to improve them?
- do you monitor your performance regularly and make continual adjustments or do you just carry on regardless? Have you made contingency plans?
- what changes to your inputs should be considered?
- what are the results of your friends' and colleagues' assessments?
- how should you plan for improved performance if you did not get the result you expected?
- what are the resource requirements (time, effort and money)?

What other aspects of planning should you consider?

SUMMARY

This chapter has reviewed the marketing management and planning process. Consideration has been given to the types of question that managers need to ask. Before addressing the marketing planning process, aspects of organisation and management were highlighted to provide a necessary appreciation that marketing is, above all, a management activity with its corresponding challenges of organising, resourcing and working with people. The McKinsey 7S Framework was used as an overview.

A simple model of the planning process, which can be undertaken through a combination of top-down, bottom-up, outside-in and inside-out approaches, comprising five key stages that should be aligned to corporate mission, objectives and resources, was introduced. This was illustrated in Exhibit 12.7 and was used to provide the outline structure of this chapter.

CHALLENGES REVIEWED

Now that you have finished reading the chapter, look back at the challenges you were set at the beginning. Do you have a clearer idea of what's involved?

Hints:

- Porter's generic strategies, competitive positioning and portfolio analysis
- marketing planning process model and marketing plan
- contingency planning and situational analysis and environmental scanning (see also Chapter 2)
- Ansoff's matrix
- marketing analysis, Porter's 'five forces' model, competitor capability analysis.

READING AROUND

Articles

David Pickton and Sheila Wright (1998) 'What's swot in strategic analysis?', *Strategic Change*, 7 (2): 101–9.

Wyner, A.G. (2002) 'Top down or bottom up?', *Marketing Management*, 11 (5): 6.

James Richardson (2008) 'The business model: an integrative framework for strategy execution', *Strategic Change,* 17 (5 and 6): 133–44.

Robert Waggoner (1999) 'Have you made the wrong turn in your approach to market?', *Journal of Business Strategy*, 20 (6): 16–21.

Books

Malcolm McDonald (2007) *Malcolm McDonald on Marketing Planning*. London: Kogan Page.

Henry Mintzberg, Joseph Lampel, James Quinn and Sumantra Ghoshal (2002) *The Strategy Process* (European edn). Englewood Cliffs, NJ: Prentice Hall.

Richard Wilson and Colin Gilligan (2004) *Strategic Marketing Management* (3rd edn). Oxford: Elsevier Butterworth Heinemann.

Book chapters

Tim Ambler (2008) 'Marketing metrics', in Michael Baker and Susan Hart (eds), *The Marketing Book*. Oxford: Butterworth Heinemann. Chapter 21.

SELF-REVIEW QUESTIONS

1. What are the main stages of the marketing planning process? (see page 447)
2. List three marketing planning analysis tools. (see page 448)
3. How can the product life cycle be used by an organisation? (see pages 413–5)
4. What is portfolio analysis? (see pages 229–34)
5. What axes are used with the GE matrix? (see page 233)
6. What are Porter's three generic strategies? (see pages 464–5)
7. Define the four generic strategies from Ansoff's matrix. (see pages 465–8)
8. Name four competitive positioning strategies. (see page 472)
9. What is 'market sensing'? (see page 475)
10. Why is marketing control important? (see pages 476–7)

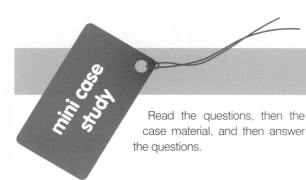

All Change!

Read the questions, then the case material, and then answer the questions.

Questions

1. Why would Procter & Gamble and Unilever want to take such apparently drastic actions by cutting the number of brands to a core few?

2. Recognised among the world's most influential marketing companies, Procter & Gamble and Unilever would have made extensive use of marketing tools of analysis and strategy development to arrive at their decisions. Which marketing tools discussed in this chapter would you have used? For each tool you have identified, explain why you would have used it by noting the benefits it gave.

3. What information and research would you have needed to use these tools and complete your analysis and decision-making?

4. Referring to the concepts covered in this chapter, how would you describe the strategic choice that these companies made? What other strategic choices could they have made?

Procter & Gamble (P&G) and Unilever have been cutting down their product portfolios recently in order to enable them to refocus their businesses. P&G has been making cuts for over ten years now, including global restructuring of its business operations, which in 1996 appeared to be 'bloated and fragmented' (Thomas, 2003). Its aims were to double sales within

a ten-year time frame. Since December 2002, the restructuring complete, its net income had risen from £1.76 billion (2001) to £2.62 billion (2002).

Meanwhile, in August 2003, Unilever announced a lower sales target for the year, down from an anticipated 5–6 per cent to 4 per cent. It has been selling off a considerable number of its long-established brands, such as Brut ('splash it all over') and Mentadent (the toothpaste with baking soda and peroxide) – some 850 in all since its restructuring began – but was still 350 brands over its target of just 400 core brands.

So, what is the slimline P&G going to do now? Apparently, the focus is going to be on household 'soaps' – Ariel, Bold and Daz! It planned a £20 million relaunch of Ariel in September 2003 with a new product formulation that is claimed to be even more effective at getting rid of those stuck-on stains. Its aim was to attract a bigger customer base, which, with its Bold and Daz brands, currently accounts for 49 per cent of the market.

Nonetheless, Unilever's Persil brand remains the strongest contender in the marketplace, growing at a rate of around 6 per cent per year, mainly as a result of constant innovation and advertising. It claims the title of the most trusted soap brand (in spite of its blip in 1995 when its reformulation quite literally shredded clothes), which leaves the market in a bit of a stink. Indeed, it seems poised for a good old-fashioned dust-up as both P&G and Unilever try to out-market each other for the top spot.

SOURCE: Thomas, 2003

REFERENCES

Abell, D.F. (1978) 'Strategic windows', *Journal of Marketing*, 42 (Jul): 21–26.

Ansoff, I. (1957) 'Strategies for diversification', *Harvard Business Review*, 35 (5): 113–24.

Buzzell, R.D., Gale, B.T. and Sultan, R.G.M. (1975) 'Market share: a key to profitability', *Harvard Business Review*, 53 (Jan–Feb): 97–106.

CIM (2008) **www.cim.co.uk**

Cooper, A. (1997) *How to Plan Advertising: The Account Planning Group*. London: Cassell.

Greene, W., Walls, G. and Schrest, L. (1994) 'Internal marketing: the key to external marketing success', *Journal of Services Marketing*, 8 (4): 5–13.

Greenley, G.E. (1984) 'An understanding of marketing strategy', *European Journal of Marketing*, 18 (6/7): 90–103.

Hanan, M. (1974) 'Reorganize your company around its markets', *Harvard Business Review*, Nov–Dec: 62–74.

Hooley, G., Saunders, J. and Piercy, N. (1998) *Marketing Strategy and Competitive Positioning*. Harlow: Prentice Hall.

Ind, N. and Bjerke R. (2007) 'The concept of participatory market orientation: an organisation-wide approach to enhancing brand equity', *Journal of Brand Management*, 15 (Oct): 135–145.

Johnson, G., Scholes, K. and Whittington, R. (2007) *Exploring Corporate Strategy*. Harlow: FT/Prentice Hall.

Kotler, P., Gregor, W. and Rogers, W. (1977) 'The marketing audit comes of age', *Sloan Management Review*, 18 (2): 25–43.

Kotler, P. and Singh, R. (1981) 'Marketing warfare', *Journal of Business Strategy*, 1 (Winter): 30–41.

Kotler, P. (1986) 'Global standardization – courting danger', *The Journal of Consumer Marketing*, 3 (Spring): 13–15.

Levitt, T. (1960) 'Marketing myopia', *Harvard Business Review*, July/August: 45–56.

McDonald, M. (2007) *Malcolm McDonald on Marketing Planning*. London: Kogan Page.

Melewar, T.C., Pickton, D., Gupta, S. and Chigovanyika, T. (2009) 'MNE executive insights into international advertising programme standardisation', *Journal of Marketing Communications,* 15 (5): 345–365.

Peters, T.J. and Waterman, R.H. (2004) *In Search of Excellence* (2nd edn). London: Profile Books.

Pickton, D. and Broderick, A. (2004) *Integrated Marketing Communications*. Harlow: FT/Prentice Hall.

Piercy, N. (2009) *Market-led Strategic Change* (4th edn). Oxford: Butterworth-Heinemann.

Porter, M. (1980) 'Industry structure and competitive strategy: keys to profitability', *Financial Analysis*, 36 (4): 30–41.

Porter, M.E. (1985) *Competitive Advantage: Creating and Sustaining Superior Performance*. Glencoe, IL: Free Press.

Ries, A. and Trout, J. (1986) *Marketing Warfare*. New York: McGraw-Hill.

Schultz, D.E. (1993a) 'Maybe we should start all over with an IMC organisation', *Marketing News*, 27 (22): 8.

Schultz, D.E. (1993b) 'How to overcome the barriers to integration', *Marketing News,* 27 (15): 16.

Schultz, D.E. (1997) 'Integrating information resources to develop strategies', *Marketing News*, 31 (2): 10.

Smith, P., Berry, C. and Pulford, A. (1997) *Strategic Marketing Communications*. London: Kogan Page.

Souhami, S. (2003) 'Competitive myopia', *Marketing Business*, April: 32–4.

Thomas, D. (2003) 'A good clean fight', *Marketing Week*, 3 July: 20–3.

Walker, O. Jr., Boyd, H. Jr. and Larreche, J.-C. (1992/2003) 'Marketing strategy', in D. Cravens and N. Piercy (eds), *Strategic Marketing* (7th edn). New York: McGraw-Hill.

Weitz, B. and Anderson, E. (1981) 'Organizing the marketing function', in B.M. Enis and K.J. Roering (eds), *Review of Marketing*. New York: American Marketing Association.

Glossary

4Ps a mnemonic (memory aid) for the marketing mix: product, promotion, place, price

7Ps a mnemonic (memory aid) for the services marketing mix: product, promotion, place, price, process, people, physical evidence

above the line advertising in commission-paying media, e.g. TV, posters, press, radio, cinema

adoption *see* product adoption process

advertising paid-for promotional messages

advertising proposition what the overall advert should say to the target audience, the impression that should be left in their minds (this is not the slogan; the whole of the advert should communicate the proposition)

agent represents other businesses and sells products on their behalf, does not usually hold stock or take ownership of the goods, just takes orders and is paid a commission

AIDA a sequential model showing the steps that marketing communications should lead potential buyers through: attention, interest, desire, action

ambient media outdoor (usually) media, classically posters but now including more imaginative forms, e.g. laser-light shows, tickets, students wearing promotional clothing or tattoos

Ansoff's matrix comprises four possible growth strategies: market development, product development, market penetration/expansion and diversification

aspirant (aspirational) groups groups to which an individual would like to belong, e.g. a professional football team or a particular club

asset-led *see* asset-led marketing

asset-led marketing basing the marketing strategy on the organisation's strengths rather than on customer needs and wants, e.g. by developing products that can be made with existing equipment or through brand extension

attitude describes a person's consistently favourable or unfavourable evaluation, feelings and tendencies towards an object or idea

audience profile a detailed description of audience characteristics used by marketing communicators to tailor their promotional efforts

awareness set a number of products or brands that may satisfy a customer/consumer need or solve a problem

B2B (business to business) business dealings with another business as opposed to a consumer

B2C (business to consumer) business dealings with consumers

barrier to communication anything that gets in the way of a message and prevents it from being received correctly

barriers to entry things that make it difficult, or impossible, for new competitors to enter a market, e.g. patents, high set-up costs

basic product a bundle of essential characteristics; a product described in terms of the features that deliver its core benefit (e.g. the ingredients of a soft drink – fizzy orange) without reference to branding, service or other more sophisticated elements

behavioural segmentation dividing a market into subgroups (segments) of customers/users according to how they buy, use and feel about products

belief how or what a person thinks about something, usually based on knowledge, opinion or faith

below the line non-commission-paying promotion, typically all forms except advertising

benchmarking a process of systematic analysis and comparison of one company's performance, measured against another's (the industry leader's), in order to improve business performance

biographical research an individual's story or experiences told to a researcher or found in other materials

blueprint the original, or master, plan for how to make or do something

bogof buy one get one free

boom when an economy experiences a rapid rise in spending, often accompanied by higher prices and raised investment levels

Boston Consultancy Group (BCG) portfolio matrix a product portfolio analysis tool involving classifying products or SBUs (strategic business units) according to their relative market share and market growth rate – as stars, cash cows, problem children or dogs

bottom-up approach functions and departments recommend objectives, budgets, strategies and plans to senior management

brand 'the intangible sum of a product's attributes: its name, packaging, and price, its history, its reputation, and the way it's advertised' (David Ogilvy)

brand communities a group of people, usually consumers, formed on the basis of their shared admiration for a particular branded product or range of products, e.g. the BMW owners group

brand equity the monetary value of a brand

brand extension offering further products under an existing brand name but in a new category within the same, broadly defined market, e.g. Mars ice cream built on the Mars bar brand

brand identity all the outward trappings of the brand, e.g. logo, name, colours, strap line and packaging

brand image people's perception of the brand

brand leader the brand with the highest sales within its particular market

brand loyalty the attachment that a customer or consumer feels to a favourite product

brand manager similar to a product manager, responsible for marketing a particular brand

brand map diagram of competing brand positions resulting from the perceptual mapping process, also called perceptual maps, position maps and space maps

brand name the product's, or product line's, given name

brand personality the heart of the brand, the sum of its values, its character traits, e.g. bubbly, elegant, friendly

brand portfolio *see* product portfolio

brand promise the way the brand sets out to fulfil a customer need, e.g. Pepsi Cola might promise to be thirst quenching

brand stretching   using an existing brand name on products in a different market

brand values   how a brand is perceived by the market

branded entertainment   leisure activities, most commonly television or radio programmes, paid for by an advertiser in order to draw attention to its products

branding   the process of building a brand

brand-switching   buying an alternative brand

break even   *see* breakeven point

breakeven point   the amount of goods a firm needs to sell in order to cover its costs

breaking down   the process of reducing the quantity of product to be moved

bricks and clicks   organisations that sell both online and offline, i.e. they have both actual and virtual stores

business mission   the broad aims a business hopes to achieve

buying centre   comprises all the individuals that participate in the business buying decision process

buying economies   i.e. economies of scale; companies may buy goods in large quantities and so obtain favourable terms

C2C (consumer to consumer)   business dealings between consumers, e.g. on eBay

capital goods (fixed assets)   substantial purchases that are not used up in one go but are expected to be used multiple times

cartel   a group of companies that get together and fix prices between them

case study   contains in-depth information, built from multiple sources, that forms a detailed picture of a particular situation

cash and carry   a wholesaler whose main customers are small retailers who visit the premises, pay for their goods and carry them away. Cash and carries do not deliver

cash cows   a category within the Boston Consulting Group matrix, products or SBUs (strategic business units) with relatively high market share in low-growth markets

cause-related marketing   a form of sponsorship whereby funds are raised for a worthy cause, often a charity (e.g. Tesco's Computers for Schools, Pizza Express's support of the National Trust through sales of its Neptune pizza)

census   a survey that includes all members of a population

channel members   the businesses that make up a distribution channel; intermediaries

classical conditioning   the process of using an established relationship between a stimulus and a response, which can then be used to evoke the same response

classified advertising   the small ads, usually placed into specific classifications, e.g. cars for sale, help wanted

closed questions   questions that expect a one-word (usually yes or no) answer

co-branding   when two companies' brand names appear together, e.g. Intel on IBM computers

cognitive learning   active learning using complex mental processing of information

cold call   when a salesperson calls on a prospect without an appointment

competitive advantage or **competitive edge**   something about an organisation or its products that is perceived as being better than rival offerings

competitive advertising   highlights and illustrates the uses, features and benefits that the advertised brand has and its rivals do not

competitive edge   *see* competitive advantage

competitive intelligence   information on rivals, their products and environments compared with one's own

competitor analysis   the process of obtaining an in-depth understanding of rival firms and their offerings

complementary product   one that is required by another product, e.g. a printer needs paper, a DVD player needs DVDs

concentrated marketing   where only one market segment is chosen for targeting

consideration set   a range of preferred products or brands that may satisfy the need or provide a solution to the problem

conspicuous purchase   a product or service that is likely to stand out, perhaps because it has unusual or high status or will be consumed in public

consumer   the individual end user of a product or service

consumer durables   products for use by individuals that can be expected to last for some time, e.g. a washing machine

consumer goods   goods that are bought/used by individuals rather than by companies

consumer models   representations of consumer buying behaviour, usually as diagrams

consumer panels   a primary research technique that seeks the views, attitudes, behaviour or buying habits of a group of consumers

consumerism   the belief that increasing consumption is economically desirable

consumerist   someone who believes in consumerism

contract manufacture   when a company employs another company to manufacture its goods, the employing company retains ownership of the goods and rights of sale

contribution   the amount of money remaining from the sale, when the variable costs have been paid

contribution pricing   a pricing method based on variable costs

controllables   events, issues, trends, etc. within the internal environment

convenience goods   products that customers buy frequently and think little about

convenience sample   a sample picked on the basis of convenience to the researcher, e.g. work colleagues

copy   text

copywriter   someone who writes the words for promotional materials, e.g. adverts

core benefit (core product)   the minimum benefits a product should confer, e.g. a pen must write, a car must go

corporate brand   a company brand name

corporate image   audiences' perception of an organisation

corporate social responsibility (CSR)   'the continuing commitment by business to behave ethically and contribute to economic development while improving the quality of life of the workforce and their families as well as of the local community and society at large' (World Business Council for Sustainable Development, 1999)

costs   a firm's payments to suppliers, etc.

countertrade   exchanging goods for other goods rather than for money. There are various forms of countertrade, the best known of which is barter

creative execution the way an advert is designed in order to put a message across

creative team an art director and a copywriter; they work together to create ads

CRM *see* customer relationship management

cross-selling persuading a customer to buy other products

CSR *see* corporate social responsibility

culture the set of basic values, perceptions, wants and behaviour learnt by a member of society from family and other institutions

customer a buyer of a product or service

customer lifetime value a calculation of the long-term worth of a customer using estimates of expected purchases

customer loyalty a mutually supportive, long-term relationship between customer and supplier, which results in customers making multiple repeat purchases

customer orientation the whole organisation is focused on the satisfaction of its customers' needs

customer profile a description of the firm's customer base, used to target customers more accurately

customer relationship management (CRM) attracting and keeping the right customers

customer value pricing pricing a product or service according to the value placed on it by the customer

customised marketing producing one-off products/services to match a specific customer's requirements, e.g. a made-to-measure suit or the organisation of a product launch party

DAGMAR acronym for Defining Advertising Goals for Measured Advertising Results, a hierarchy of effects model describing the stages individuals go through when making a purchase, or consumption, decision

data mining using specialist software to analyse large amounts of data (held in a database or a data warehouse) to predict trends and likely customer behaviour

data warehouse a large database holding copies of customer and environmental data taken from the organisation's other systems and designed specifically to make it easier to raise queries and produce reports

database marketing the use of computerised customer data to communicate with customers and promote further sales

decision-making unit (DMU) all the individuals who participate in and influence the customer's purchase decision

demand the quantity of goods that customers buy at a certain price

demand-driven when a surplus, or potential surplus, of goods to be sold gives the buyers more power than the sellers

demographic segmentation markets segmented by population characteristics such as age, gender, occupation and income

depression when an economy experiences a severe fall-off in sales, usually accompanied by unemployment, lower prices and low levels of investment; sometimes called a slump

desk research (secondary research) the search for good-quality data that has been validated and is now published for use by others

destroyer pricing *see* predatory pricing

differentiated marketing differences between market segments are recognised and two or more target markets are selected, each receiving a different marketing programme

direct costs costs that are clearly due to the making of a particular product, e.g. cocoa and sugar are direct costs of chocolate bars

direct export when a company makes products in its home country for sale abroad and then manages the overseas sales and marketing of them itself

direct mail promotional material delivered by post

direct marketing 'all activities that make it possible to offer goods or services or to transmit other messages to a segment of the population by post, telephone, email or other direct means' (Chartered Institute of Marketing)

direct marketing communications promotional materials designed to prompt a direct response from the recipient to the sender.

direct sales when a manufacturer deals directly with customers rather than through intermediaries in the supply chain

direct-response advertising 'advertising, or selling, through any medium inviting the consumer to respond to the advertiser' (IDM Direct Marketing Guide)

disassociative groups groups to which the individual does not want to belong or be seen to belong, e.g. an upmarket shopper may not wish to be seen in a discount store

discount a deduction from the price

disintermediation the removal of levels of intermediaries in distribution channels, often associated with the trend towards direct sales facilitated by the Internet

display advertising mainstream press advertising, usually with illustrations or other attention-drawing features

distortion a barrier to communication; poor coding skills, e.g. a badly devised ad or a badly worded sales promotion, that prevent the message from being received correctly

distribution the processes involved in moving goods from the supplier to the customer or user

distribution centres large warehouses that repackage goods into smaller units and ship them to trade customers; they may be exclusive to one large retailer

distribution channel a chain of organisations through which products pass on their way to a target market

diversification strategy developing new products to sell to new markets (customers) (part of Ansoff's growth matrix)

DMU *see* decision-making unit

dogs a category within the Boston Consulting Group portfolio matrix, products or SBUs (strategic business units) with relatively low market share in low-growth markets

domestic market a company's home market, i.e. markets in the same country as the company itself

dumping an anti-competitive practice whereby a company exports its products at a very low price and so undercuts competitors in the target country

duty an import tax charged by the government

dyadic comparisons a technique used in perceptual mapping in which two products are compared to each other at a time

early majority a substantial group of customers who follow early adopters in buying a new product or service

economies of scale unit costs fall as larger quantities are produced; a cost advantage associated with large organisations

efficient market a market in which prices adjust quickly, and frequently, in response to new information (economic theory)

elasticity a significant response to changes in a marketing variable, most commonly price; if the demand for a product is price elastic, sales volumes will change by a greater percentage than the percentage change in price, e.g. if the price goes up by 5%, sales fall by 7%; therefore if the price rises the sales revenue actually falls

embargo(es)   a ban on the trade of a particular category of goods (e.g. arms) or between certain areas (e.g. USA and Iraq)

emergency goods   goods infrequently purchased but needed at short notice, e.g. rain capes, sun hats, plasters

end user   the person who actually uses the product or service; this is not always the customer, e.g. a computer may be bought by a company's purchasing officer for use by the marketing manager (the end user)

environmental scanning   monitoring the forces that influence the organisation in order to identify changes that may affect performance

environmental variables   factors within an organisation's environment that may change, i.e. PRESTCOM elements

EPOS (electronic point of sale)   a computerised system that collects sales data at a retail checkout

e-tailers   online retailers

ethnocentrism   ethnocentric firms have a home country focus. There is an assumption that home country ways are best and that others should adapt to them

ethnography   the description, or interpretation, of the patterns of behaviour in a social group or setting; the researcher will immerse himself or herself in a variety of ways into the culture of the group to be studied

evoked set   the shortlist of products from which a purchaser will make a final choice

exchange   when two parties swap items perceived to be of approximately equal value

exclusive distribution   the distribution channel has only one or two specially selected outlets within a specified area

experimentation   a primary research technique that seeks to understand the behaviour of specified variables under controlled conditions, i.e. not real-world

exploratory (research)   initial research to see whether a more comprehensive study is needed

extension strategies   means of prolonging the product life cycle

external environment   organisations and influences that are not under the organisation's control, e.g. government, competitors, legislation

extinction pricing   *see* predatory pricing

extrapolate   use already established data (or experience) to predict the unknown, e.g. using last year's sales figures, adjusted for current conditions, to forecast this year's figures

family brand   a brand name that covers a group of related products

family life cycle   a form of market segmentation based on the recognition that we pass through a series of quite distinct phases in our lives

feedback   a part of the two-way communications process whereby the receiver sends a message back to the original sender

fees   payments made for services or for permission to use something, e.g. for a licence or a franchise

field research (primary research)   carried out specifically for the research task in question

first mover advantage   the first significant company to move into a market often becomes the market leader and can be hard to dislodge from that position

fixed costs   costs that do not vary with production levels, e.g. insurance premiums

FLC   *see* family life cycle

flyer   a short brochure

FMCG (fast-moving consumer goods)   low-value items that are bought regularly (the shelves empty quickly), e.g. toothpaste

focus groups   a qualitative research technique using a group discussion overseen by a moderator, used to explore views, attitudes and behaviour with regard to a marketing issue; common in advertising research

fragmented industry   one in which there are a lot of players, few of whom have any significant power

franchise   a form of licence; the franchisee pays for the rights to run a business that has already been successful elsewhere, in a new territory and benefits from the expertise of the original owners (franchisors)

franchisee   a person or company who has bought a franchise

franchisor or **franchiser**   a person or company who has sold a franchise

free trade   trade across international boundaries without government restrictions such as import duties and quotas

frequency   the number of times that an average member of the target audience is exposed to an advert during a campaign

full-cost pricing   prices are set by adding an amount (usually a percentage) to the full (i.e. total) costs of making and selling the product

functional silo   when departments or workgroups act as independent entities rather than as components of a much larger system despite having many overlapping activities and information needs

GE-Mckinsey   a portfolio analysis tool developed by McKinsey & Co and GE involving classifying product lines or SBUs (strategic business units) according to their competitive position and market attractiveness

generic products   goods that have no discernible difference from each other; often used to mean unbranded products

geocentrism   the middle ground between ethnocentrism and polycentrism. Geocentric firms have a worldwide outlook, picking and choosing the best practices from the various countries in which they do business

geo-demographic segmentation   markets are segmented by a combination of geographic and demographic approaches using house location and house type

geographic segmentation   markets are segmented by countries, regions and areas

globalisation   the process of growing to a worldwide scale; it often involves the standardisation of offerings and cultural convergence

goods   tangible products, i.e. those with physical substance

grey importing   when someone outside the official supply chain buys goods (usually very cheaply) in another country for sale in their home country

grey market   *see* grey importing

grounded theory   starts from the intention to generate, or to discover, a theory by studying how people interact in response to a particular phenomenon; theoretical propositions are developed from interview data and field research

hard currency   freely exchangeable currency, usually from one of the more developed countries, e.g. the euro, pound, US dollar

hedging   making a deal to buy or sell foreign currency in advance so that the exchange rate is fixed

hierarchical management structure   each manager has a set place within a vertical chain of command

hierarchy of effects models   describes the stages individuals go through when making a purchase or consumption decision

high-context culture   one where communication must be interpreted according to the situation; much of the message is in the context rather than being explicitly expressed in the words (*see also* low-context culture)

high-involvement purchases   purchases that customers expend time and effort on, usually high cost or high risk, e.g. cars, holidays, wedding dresses

high street multiples   chains of shops, such as WH Smith and Boots

horizontal communications   sideways communications within an organisation, e.g. between workgroups or departments

horizontal integration   where a company owns a number of different businesses at the same level in the supply chain, e.g. Curry's and Dixons electrical retailers are part of the same company

hospitality   hosting clients (e.g. providing refreshments in a private room) at events

hypothesis   a proposition put forward for testing

import duties   taxes paid when goods are brought into a country from outside

import licence   permission, usually granted by a government, to bring specified goods into a country

impulse purchase   buying behaviour, made on the spur of the moment

incoterms   a set of rules governing the delivery terms for international sales

in-depth interviews   one-to-one research interviews; commonly used in qualitative research

indirect costs   costs that cannot be attributed to a particular product as they are not directly associated with its production or sale, e.g. the running costs of the chief executive's car

indirect export   using a third party (e.g. an export management company), based in the firm's home country, to sell products abroad

inelasticity   little response to changes in the marketing variable being measured (commonly price, advertising, competitive products, income); the percentage change in demand is less than the percentage change in price (or other variable), so if price rises, sales rise

infinite elasticity   the product can only be sold at one price; there is no demand at any other. This is really just a theoretical term

inflation   when the prices of goods rise without a matching (or greater) increase in their actual value

information framing   the ways in which information is presented to people to ensure selective distortion does, or does not, happen

information search   identifying the various ways a need or problem can be satisfied

innovative products   a really new product, possibly a technological or medical breakthrough

inside-out approach   focuses on the needs of the organisation first, and customers and the marketplace second

integrated marketing communications   the process of ensuring that all elements of the promotional mix are complementary in order to avoid mixed messages and strengthen the brand

intensive distribution   products are available at numerous outlets

inter-media decision   the choice of media class

intermediaries   businesses that form part of the distribution channel, passing goods on towards the end customer

internal environment   the organisation itself, its functions, departments and resources

internal marketing   also called internal PR, it addresses the needs (particularly information needs) of employees

international organisations   there is a head office in the home country which controls overseas sales

Internet   worldwide computer network linking smaller networks via satellite and telephone links, and providing access to email services and the World Wide Web

intra-media decision   the choice of media vehicle

iTV   interactive television

judgemental sample   *see* quota sample

junk mail   unwanted promotional material sent by post

just in time (JIT)   a lean manufacturing technique where little or no stock is held

knowledge-based economy   one in which knowledge is the primary wealth creator

lead time   the time it takes for an order to reach the customer

learning   changes in an individual's behaviour arising from their experiences

legitimate power   influence over others conferred by law or regulations

level of confidence   the degree to which the researchers are sure that data are accurate

level of involvement   the extent to which the purchase is important to the purchaser

Likert scale   subjects are asked to indicate their agreement, or disagreement, with a statement by use of a five-point scale

line extension   using the brand name on products within the same category

lobbying   a means of influencing those with power, particularly politicians and legislators

logistics   the flow of goods and services through the supply chain

logo   a graphical device associated with an organisation

loss leader   a product that is sold at a loss, usually to tempt shoppers to make other purchases

low-context culture   the information to be communicated is put into words explicitly; there is little need to take account of the surrounding circumstances (*see also* high-context culture)

loyalty schemes   ways in which companies try to retain customers and encourage repeat purchases, often accomplished by awarding points (e.g. Tesco Clubcard, Air Miles)

macroenvironment   the broad, external influences that affect all organisations in a market, e.g. the political situation in a country

mailing lists   any list of names and addresses to which mail is sent, often potential customers

marginal cost pricing   similar to contribution pricing, a margin is added to the marginal cost (the cost of making an additional product) to arrive at a price

market   a composite of individuals or organisations that have a willingness and ability to purchase products; a market can consist of single or multiple segments

market attractiveness   an assessment of how desirable a particular market or market segment is to an organisation

market challenger a company that is trying to take over the market leader position

market development strategy selling existing products to new markets (customers) (part of Ansoff's growth matrix)

market followers take their lead from competitors and copy their successful ideas and strategies (*see also* market-led)

market fragmentation a market characterised by a large number of relatively small players, none of whom have significant competitive advantage

market growth rate the percentage increase in total sales within a category or market

market leader the company with the highest sales within a market (also sometimes used to refer to a groundbreaking firm that others follow)

market-led companies take their lead from competitors and copy their successful ideas and strategies (they are also called market followers), i.e. they are more cautious and wait for more radical ideas to be tested by others first

market-orientation provision of customer value determines an organisation's direction

market penetration pricing pricing a product lower than competitors in order to gain market share

market penetration strategy encouraging existing customers to buy more of a product in order to increase sales of existing products in existing markets (part of Ansoff's growth matrix)

market screening assessing the potential of a new market to achieve desired levels of sales, profit, market share and/or other objectives

market segment a group of buyers and users/consumers who share similar characteristics and who are distinct from the rest of the market for a product

market segmentation the process of dividing a total market into subgroups (segments) such that each segment consists of buyers and users who share similar characteristics but are different from those in other segments

market sensing the need for an understanding of the market, rather than merely a knowledge of it

market share a firm's sales expressed as a percentage of the total sales of that type of product in the defined market

market skimming setting a relatively high price to take advantage of limited competition

marketing channel another term for distribution channel

marketing communications another name for promotion; communication designed and implemented to persuade others to accept ideas, concepts or things; to motivate audience members to action

marketing environment the forces and organisations that impact on an organisation's marketing activities

marketing information system (MkIS) also know as a marketing intelligence system, the systematic gathering and dissemination of competitive and marketing information; this usually involves a computerised system

marketing metrics 'measurements that help with the quantification of marketing performance, such as market share, advertising spend, and response rates elicited by advertising and direct marketing' (Chartered Institute of Marketing)

marketing mix (*see* 4Ps, 7Ps) the basics of marketing plan implementation, usually product, promotion, place, price, sometimes with the addition of packaging; the services marketing mix also includes people, physical evidence and process

marketing opportunity a chance to reach a particular group of customers with a product offer

mark-up pricing the price is set by adding a percentage (a mark-up) to the direct cost

mass customisation tailoring product offerings almost to meet individual needs

mass market a homogeneous market, i.e. no distinction between segments

mass marketing delivering the same marketing programme to everybody without making any significant distinction between them

mass media communications channels that reach a large, relatively undifferentiated audience, e.g. posters, the Internet, press; plural of mass medium

McKinsey/General Electric matrix a portfolio analysis tool developed by McKinsey & Co and GE, involving classifying product lines or SBUs according to their competitive position and market attractiveness

media class or **media category** type of media, e.g. television, press, posters, cinema

media vehicle the actual TV programme, newspaper, magazine, film, etc., in which adverts appear

mediagraphic segmentation markets segmented by reading and viewing habits

membership groups groups an individual already belongs to and which therefore have a direct influence on his or her behaviour, e.g. students belong to a class

merchandise *see* merchandising

merchandising (1) selection and display of products within a retail environment; (2) a form of licensing spin-off products often inspired by entertainments (e.g. T-shirts at a concert)

message the impression a promotion leaves on its audience

me-too product a new product that is an imitation of an existing, competitive one

microenvironment comprises an organisation's competitors, distributors, suppliers and its own internal resources

Minitab a software program for statistical analysis

modified rebuy the buyer wants to modify an element of the rebuy, e.g. change colour, size, price or delivery time

monopoly a market in which there is only one supplier

Multi-attribute Attitude Mapping (MAM) a form of perceptual mapping comparing a product's key features (according to their importance to target customers) with features offered by competitive brands

multibranding a strategy employed by companies that have multiple products within the same category

multichannel distribution the use of different types of channel to reach the same target market

Multidimensional Scaling (MDS) a form of perceptual mapping that establishes similarities and differences between competing brands

multinational organisations has subsidiary companies in other countries which have significant power although they answer to the parent company

multinationals *see* multinational organisation

multivariate analysis two or more variables are analysed at the same time

new media makes use of modern technologies, e.g. the Internet, iTV, mobile phones, CD/DVD

new task when someone buys a product for the first time

niche market a market segment that can be treated as a target market; a small, well-defined market, often part of a larger market

niche marketing a form of concentrated marketing in which the target market is relatively small, well defined and very focused

noise a barrier to communication, usually from an external source, e.g. technological breakdown

not for profit organisations whose primary goal is something other than profit, e.g. government, charities, clubs, pressure groups

observation a primary research technique that involves watching how subjects behave in their normal environment

oligopoly a situation where the market is dominated by a small number of very large companies

omnibus surveys a large questionnaire that provides data for multiple clients

one-to-one marketing personalised marketing, typically on the Internet

on-pack promotion a promotional offer printed on the product's packaging

open-ended questions questions that invite the respondent to comment rather than just give a one-word answer

operant conditioning (instrumental conditioning) the learner's response produces a reinforcing stimulus

opportunities to see (OTS) a measure of media effectiveness

opportunity cost alternatives that could have been had/done instead, e.g. the opportunity cost of a lunchtime sandwich may be a pre-packed salad, and an evening at the cinema costs a night's study

outside-in approach the organisation looks outwards to focus on the needs of the marketplace to determine appropriate courses of marketing action

outsourcing the subcontracting of a business process, e.g. delivery or maintenance, to another organisation

own-label products that bear a retailer's brand name, e.g. Tesco; sometimes called 'private brands'

pack shot a picture of the product, in its packaging, used in an advert to aid recognition

participant observation a primary research technique in which the observer becomes involved with their subjects rather than remaining apart

patent a legal protection for inventions that prohibits unauthorised copying

pattern adverts partial standardisation of advertising, useful in international marketing; the adverts have the same look and feel although some images and the slogan may be written for a particular place or purpose

penetration pricing *see* market penetration pricing

perception the process by which people select, organise and interpret sensory stimulation (sounds, visions, smell, touch) into a meaningful picture of the world

perceptual map results from the perceptual mapping process and shows brands' relative positions (also called a brand map, position map or space map)

perceptual mapping the process of visually representing target-market perceptions of competing brands in relation to each other

perfect competition a theoretical market situation in which all product offerings are identical, and there are many small buyers and sellers, none of which are able to influence the market and all of which have perfect market knowledge

peripheral product a secondary product often provided as part of a service, e.g. the complimentary mints at the end of a meal, shampoo at the hairdressers

personal selling an oral presentation, in a conversation with one or more prospective purchasers, for the purpose of making sales

personality a person's distinguishing psychological characteristics that lead them to respond in particular ways

PEST an acronym for the macroenvironment (part of an organisation's external environment): political, economic, social, technological

phenomenological research describes the experiences of individuals concerning some specific phenomena or occurrence

physical distribution the process of moving goods and services between businesses and consumers

physical evidence the tangible aspects of a service, e.g. a bus ticket, shampoo (at the hairdressers); one of the 7Ps of services marketing

piggyback marketing a collective term for a number of joint marketing practices, e.g. co-branding, sharing marketing channels, on-pack promotions, usually for complementary products

piggybacking when one company uses the distribution channels already established by another company, usually, but not always, in an overseas market

pioneer advertising informative advertising, usually for a new product or service

place one of the elements of the marketing mix, concerned with distribution, delivery, supply chain management

PLC most commonly, public limited company but often used in marketing to stand for the product life cycle

point of sale (POS) the place where a product or service is bought

polycentrism polycentric firms have a host country (i.e. the foreign country) focus. They assume that the host country's ways are superior and try to adapt their own business to fit into the other country as perfectly as possible

population a complete group of people, cases or objects which share similarities that can be studied in a survey

portal a website that acts as a gateway to a number of other sites

Porter's five forces model an industry analysis tool

Porter's generic strategies three main competitive strategies: cost leadership, differentiation or focus

portfolio analysis the process of comparing SBUs (strategic business units) or products/services to see which are deserving of further investment and which should be discontinued

position map graphical representation of brand positions resulting from the perceptual mapping process; also called a brand map, perceptual map or space map

positioning the place a product (brand) is perceived to occupy in the minds of customers/consumers of the relevant target market relative to other competing brands

post-purchase dissonance when a consumer is psychologically uncomfortable about a purchase

post-testing evaluating the effectiveness of a proposed marketing communication with its target audience after release

PR   *see* public relations

predatory pricing   also known as destroyer pricing or extinction pricing, it is when a dominant company sells products at a loss with the intention of driving a rival firm out of the market

pre-emptive pricing   setting prices relatively low in order to deter others from entering a market

premium price   a relatively high price

press   the types of media written by journalists, most commonly newspapers, and magazines and directories

press advertisements   adverts placed in printed media such as newspapers and magazines

press conference   a meeting at which journalists are briefed

press release   publicity material sent to editors and journalists

PRESTCOM   an acronym for the marketing environment: political, regulatory, economic, social, technological, competitive, organisational, market

prestige goods   high-status goods, e.g. Rolls-Royce, Rolex

prestige pricing   pricing a product high in order to enhance its status

pre-testing   evaluating the effectiveness of an aspect of marketing communication with its target audience before release

price   how much each product is sold for

price discrimination   charging different prices for the same products/services to different market segments, e.g. off-peak fares

price elastic   when the demand for a good changes significantly after a price change, e.g. price goes up by 10 per cent, demand falls by 20 per cent

price elasticity of demand   a measure of the degree to which demand for a good changes when its price is changed

price followers   firms that set their prices in accordance with others in the market, notably a price leader

price inelastic demand   product sales are not very sensitive to price changes (see also inelasticity)

price leaders   set prices for a market; other firms follow their lead

price makers   another term for price leaders

price premium   a high price charged to give the impression of superior quality

price takers   another name for price followers

price war   two or more firms keep undercutting each other in an attempt to build market share until one or the other backs off or goes out of business

primary data   first-hand data gathered to solve a particular problem or to exploit a current opportunity

primary research (field research)   research carried out specifically for the research task in question

problem children   a category within the Boston Consulting Group portfolio matrix; products or SBUs (strategic business units) with relatively low market share in high-growth markets

process   one of the 7Ps of the services marketing mix; the way in which a service is provided

procurement   buying of goods and services for use within organisations

product adopters model (product diffusion model)   categorises product buyers/users according to their take-up rate of new products

product adoption process   the stages a buyer goes through before purchasing a product

product breadth   the number of product lines a company supports

product depth   the number of items within a product line

product development strategy   developing new products to sell in existing markets (part of Ansoff's growth matrix)

product life cycle   a product analysis tool based on the idea that a product has life stages: introduction, growth, maturity, decline, deletion

product line   a product and all its variants (models, colours, styles, sizes, etc.)

product line pricing   coordinated pricing for a group of related products

product manager   the person responsible for the marketing of a specific product or product line

product orientation   the philosophy of an organisation that focuses on making the best possible product rather than on its customers' needs

product placement   arranging for products to be seen, or referred to, in entertainment media, e.g. during TV or radio programmes, films, plays, video games

product portfolio   all a company's or strategic business unit's products

product portfolio analysis   the process of comparing products/ services to see which are deserving of further investment and which should be discontinued

production orientation   the philosophy of an organisation that focuses on production rather than marketing

profit   the difference between what something costs to make and the price for which it is sold

profit margin   the difference between cost and price, expressed as a percentage

promotion   another name for marketing communications, communication designed and implemented to persuade others to accept ideas, concepts or things; to motivate consumers to action

promotion mix   traditionally, advertising, PR, sales promotion and personal selling

prospecting   looking for prospective customers

prospects   prospective (i.e. possible future) customers

psychographic segmentation   using lifestyles, values and personalities to split up markets

psychological price barrier   the top price a customer is prepared to pay

public relations (PR)   planned activities designed to promote goodwill between an organisation and its publics

public sector   government-owned organisations

publicity   the stimulation of demand for goods or services by generating news about them in the mass media

publicity stunt   an event designed to capture the attention of the media or other publics

publics   PR term for target audiences, the groups of people with whom the organisation communicates

pull   common usage descriptor for part of a pull strategy

pull strategy   a promotional strategy aimed at end customers or consumers

purchase decision   the selection of the preferred product to buy

push   common usage descriptor for part of a push strategy

push strategy   a promotional strategy aimed at distribution channels

qualitative research   investigates people's feelings, opinions and attitudes, often using unstructured, in-depth methods

quantitative research seeks numerical answers, e.g. how many people have similar characteristics and views

question marks an alternative name for problem children, also sometimes called wild cats

questionnaire a set of questions for use during a survey

quota a limit on the amount of foreign goods that can be imported into a country

quota sample picks respondents in proportion to the population's profile, e.g. if 25 per cent of the population are under 25 and female, then researchers set a quota of 25 per cent females under 25 for the sample

random sample a probability sample (*see also* simple random sample)

reach the number (or percentage) of the target audience exposed to an advert or other promotion during a campaign; also referred to as coverage or penetration

recall remembering things (e.g. products, brands, adverts); may be prompted (i.e. aided by stimulus material such as part of an advert) or unprompted (i.e. unaided)

recession when an economy experiences reducing sales and investment; if this continues, it may go into a depression

recognition being aware of something, e.g. a product or an advert, when shown

reference groups the groups to which an individual belongs or aspires to belong

referent power influence over others gained through superior knowledge or expertise

relationship marketing a long-term approach that nurtures customers, employees and business partners

repositioning involves moving existing perceptions to new perceptions relative to competing brands

reseller a business that buys products in order to sell them on to another business further down the marketing channel

response a reaction to a stimulus

retail selling goods to customers for their own use, i.e. not for resale

retail audit a research implement that provides information on retail product sales, e.g. value, volume, market/brand share

retailer a sales outlet that deals with end customers, e.g. a shop

retainers regular, contracted payments for services (fees) provided over a specified time span

return on investment (ROI) profit expressed as a percentage of the capital invested

revenue (sales revenue) the income a firm receives from the sale of goods and services

reward cards similar in appearance to credit cards, used to register points given away with purchases (e.g. Nectar card, Tesco Clubcard)

sales orientation strategic view that focuses on short-term sales

sales promotion short-term special offers and other added-value actitivites, e.g. two for the price of one

sales quota target number (or value) of sales set for a salesperson

sales revenue the income a firm receives from the sale of goods and services

sales volume the quantity of goods sold, expressed in units, e.g. 2 million apples

sample a smaller number of people, or cases, drawn from a population that should be representative of it in every significant characteristic

sampling frame a list of the actual members of a population from which a sample is then chosen

SBUs *see* strategic business unit (SBU)

secondary data data previously collected for other purposes that can be used in the current research task

secondary research (desk research) the search for good-quality data that has been validated and is now published for use by others

segmentation *see* market segmentation

segments distinct parts of a larger market; customers and consumers in each segment share similar characteristics

selective attention the process by which stimuli are assessed and non-meaningful stimuli, or those that are inconsistent with our beliefs or experiences, are screened out

selective distortion occurs when consumers distort or change the information they receive to suit their beliefs and attitude

selective distribution the distribution channel is restricted to a few outlets

selective retention the way consumers retain only a small number of messages in their memory

self-liquidating special offer a sales promotion that pays for itself (usually because the company making the offer has bought the promotional items in vast quantities and so obtained a substantial discount)

self-reference criterion (SRC) a person's own cultural values and experience – reliance on one's SRC is a problem when doing business with people from other cultures

semantic differential scale research subjects are asked to indicate the strength of their views by choosing a point between two extremes, e.g. was the Rosannica Restaurant's service: good – poor?

service convenience a measure of how much time and effort consumers need to expend to use the service offered

service encounter the time during which a customer is the recipient of a service, e.g. the duration of a meal in a restaurant

service recovery trying to retrieve a situation caused by a bad product or poor service encounter

services intangible products

servicescape the total environment in which a service is experienced

shopping agents programs which search the Internet and then display a table of comparative prices for a specified item

shopping goods carry a relatively high risk, perhaps because they are a high price or it may be that the cost of product failure is high

SIC (Standard Industrial Classification) a system of classifying products by allocating numbers (codes) to every product category, industry or business sector

simple random sample the Rolls-Royce of sampling methods, every member of the population has an equal chance of being selected; this can be expensive and often difficult

slump when an economy experiences a severe fall-off in sales, usually accompanied by unemployment, lower prices and low levels of investment, sometimes called a depression

SMART a mnemonic for the setting of objectives, which should be: specific, measurable, achievable, relevant and timed

social costs   the costs incurred by society generally as a result of business processes or decisions, e.g. the clearing up of pollution, the provision of transport infrastructure

social grading   segmentation by occupation of head of household; the typical classifications used are A, B, C1, C2, D and E groups

social responsibility   a sense of duty towards all organisational stakeholders

societal marketing   meeting customers' needs and wants in a way that enhances the long-term well-being of consumers and the society in which they live

space map   *see* position map

spam   electronic junk mail

speciality goods   unusual, probably quite pricey, products

sponsorship   giving financial aid, or other resources, to an individual, organisation or event in return for a positive association with them, e.g. the Coca-Cola Cup

SPSS (Statistical Package for the Social Sciences)   a software program for statistical analysis

stakeholders   individuals or groups who are involved in, or affected by, the organisation's actions and/or performance

standard error   average amount of error introduced through the sampling process

staple goods   essential goods, regularly purchased, perhaps always kept in the cupboard, e.g. coffee, milk, shampoo

stars   a category within the Boston Consulting Group portfolio matrix; products or SBUs (strategic business units) with high market share in a high-growth market

statement stuffers   promotional inserts sent with a statement, e.g. bank statement, credit card statement

stimulus   something that provokes a reaction, activity, interest or enthusiasm

stock out   when a supplier runs out of a particular product

straight rebuy   where the buyer routinely reorders a product or service without any change to the order whatsoever; it may even be an automatic process

strap line   a subheading in a press article or advertisement

strategic alliance   a form of joint venture in which two organisations work together to achieve their goals

strategic business unit (SBU)   a distinct part of an organisation that has an external market for its products and services

subscriptions   regular purchase payments, usually as part of an ongoing contract to buy something, e.g. a monthly magazine

substitutes   other products that might be bought as alternatives; they satisfy the same or similar needs

supply   the quantity of goods that sellers are prepared to put on the market at a certain price

supply chain   the network of businesses and organisations through which goods pass to get to their final destination

supply-led   shortages of goods mean that suppliers can dictate terms of business

survey   direct questioning of market research subjects

SWOT analysis   a situational analysis tool that assesses the organisation's strengths and weaknesses (internal) and opportunities and threats (external)

syndicated data services   combine data from responses to questions on various topics, e.g. the British Market Research Bureau's (BMRB) Target Group Index's (TGI) questionnaire

syndicated research   data consolidated information from various studies

systematic random sampling   uses the whole population as a sampling frame but draws subjects from it at regular intervals, e.g. every 10th name on the list

target audience   the people, or organisations, that are selected to receive communications

target market   a group of buyers and consumers who share common needs/wants or characteristics, and on whom the organisation focuses

target marketing (targeting)   the selection of one or more market segments towards which marketing efforts can be directed; sometimes called market targeting

targeting strategies   used to select a single, or group of, target markets

tariffs   import taxes charged by governments

telesales   making sales calls by telephone

tender (tendering)   where firms bid for a contract and, usually, the lowest-priced bid wins

test market   a subset of a market in which a product offering can be sold for a short period of time in order to predict demand and to try out and refine the marketing mix

top-down approach   senior managers specify objectives, budgets, strategies and plans that are passed down to functions and departments to put into action

total costs   the sum of all costs

total product offering   the total package that makes up, and surrounds, the product, including all supporting features such as branding, packaging, servicing and warranties

tracking   marketing effects are monitored over time

trade trial promotions   sales promotions aimed at members of the supply chain, e.g. a prize for selling 100 cases of wine

trading bloc   a group of countries that work together to promote trade with each other and present a common front to outside nations, e.g. the European Union (EU), NAFTA (North American Free Trade Association)

transactional exchange   a one-off sale or a sale that is conducted as if it were a one-off

transactional marketing   focuses on the immediate sale

triadic comparisons   technique used in perceptual mapping in which three products are compared to each other at a time

turf battles   when individual managers or departments fight for their own interests at the expense of those of other managers/departments

turnover   the monetary value of sales, also called revenue or sales revenue

uncontrollables   events, issues, trends, etc., within the external environment

unconvertible currency   cannot be exchanged for another currency

undifferentiated marketing   where the market is believed to be composed of customers/consumers whose needs and wants from the product are fundamentally the same; in undifferentiated or mass marketing, the same marketing programme is used for all

unique selling proposition (USP)   a clear point of differentiation for a product/service

unit costs   how much it costs to make a single item (usually worked out on average)

unit elasticity price and quantity demanded change at exactly the same rate; as a result, whatever you do to the price, there is no increase in the company's revenue

up-selling persuading a customer to trade up to a more expensive product

variable costs costs that go up as production increases and down when it decreases, e.g. electricity bills

vendor rating a vetting process to help buyers identify where there may be potential benefits or difficulties associated with a particular supplier

vertical communications happen up and down the hierarchical organisation structure, e.g. sales manager to salesperson, and vice versa

vertical integration where a company owns a number of different businesses above or below it in the supply chain

viral marketing modern form of word-of-mouth promotion; it often uses new media, e.g. email and texting

white goods large electrical appliances for domestic use, e.g. fridges, washing machines (traditionally coloured white)

wholesaler a reseller, buying products in bulk to sell on to other businesses in smaller quantities

wild cats an alternative name for problem children, also sometimes called question marks

word of mouth where members of the target audience pass on information or promotional messages to each other; *see also* viral marketing

World Wide Web the graphical user interface to the Internet

write-downs goods reduced for sale

zero elasticity completely inelastic; you can do whatever you like to the price (or other marketing variable), as there will be no change in the quantity demanded

REFERENCES

World Business Council for Sustainable Development (1999) 'Corporate Social Responsibility Meeting Changing Expectations'. Available at: **www.wbcsd.ch** (accessed 13/07/2007).

Index

3M, 220
3Ms approach, 474–5
4Cs approach, 415
4Ps, 199, 202, 270, 396, 398, 415, 478–80
  see also place; price; products; promotion
7Ps, 256–61, 396, 409–12, 415, 478–80
  see also place; price; products; promotion
7S framework, 442–3
Aaker, D.A., 214
Abell, D.F., 465
Abercrombie and Fitch, 260
Aberdeen Journals Ltd, 378
absorption costing (full-cost pricing), 367–8
access convenience, 250
accessories, 211
accountants, 359
accuracy, of information, 193
ACORN (A Classification of Residential
  Neighbourhoods), 129
acquisitions, 67, 468
  see also takeover bids
action stage of AIDA model, 279
adaptation strategy, 470–1
adoption *see* product adoption process
advertising, 281–92, 402
    and AIDA model, 280
    in B2B market, 403
    codes of practice, 53, 103
    defining, 270
    on e-media, 289, 290, 291
    ethics in, xiii, 103
    humour in, 97
    international, 403
    and level of consumer involvement, 95
    pack shots, 408
    and price, 361
    process, 276–8
    regulating, 53, 103, 308, 309, 380, 403
    on television, 95, 182, 282, 290, 291, 292
    test marketing, 182
advertising agencies, 67
Advertising Code of Practice, 103
advertising elasticity of demand, 385
advertising proposition, 288
advertising research, 169–70
Advertising Standards Authority (ASA), 53,
  308, 309
affective attitude, 100
affordable method of budgeting, 309
age-based price discrimination, 375
agencies *see* advertising agencies; research
  agencies
agents, 323
  shopping agents, 386–7
AIDA model, 278–80
AIMRITE framework, 307
Air Miles, 226
airline industry, 226, 314, 341
alcoholic drinks industry, 53, 153, 227, 275,
  360, 380
Amazon, x, 168, 258, 345, 348–9
ambient media, 290

American Marketing Association (AMA),
  5, 162
analysis *see* marketing analysis
Anderson, E., 437
animated advertisements, 288
Ansoff, I., 467
Ansoff's matrix, 465–8
anti-competitive practice, 365, 378
anti-consumerism, 30
anti-globalisation, 30, 52
AOL, 74
Apple, 431–2
arbitrary method of budgeting, 309
area sampling, 188
Arnott, D.C., 60
ASA *see* Advertising Standards Authority
ASDA, 343–4, 427
aspirant (aspirational) groups, 101
asset-led marketing, 40–1
attention stage of AIDA model, 279
attitudes, 99–100, 426
attractiveness *see* market attractiveness
auctions, 364
    see also eBay
audience, 273, 285–7
audience profiles, 285, 286–7
augmented products, 206, 399, 400, 401
Auto-Technic GmbH, 159
automated call handling, 27
autonomic responses, 180, 187
awareness set, 87
awareness stage of buyer readiness, 105, 214
AWOL Recruitment, 473

B2B markets *see* business-to-business markets
B2C markets *see* consumer markets
BA (British Airways), 314, 341
baby boomers, 56, 133
Bagozzi, R.P., 15
BARB (Broadcasters' Audience Research
    Board), 173
barcodes, 173, 328, 345
bargaining power, 458–9
Barnard, N.R., 283
barriers to entry, 457
basic products, 206, 399, 400
Bayliss, Trevor, 223
BBC iPlayer, 216–17
BCG portfolio matrix, 229–32, 402
Bed and Breakfast (B&B) case study, 197
behaviour, 58
    see also buyer behaviour
behavioural segmentation, 132–8
Belen del Rio, A., 217
beliefs, 99–100
benchmarking, 453
benefit convenience, 250–1
Bentley, 39
Berry, L.L., 250
Betamax, 344
Big Brother, 294
binge drinking, 380

biographical research, 176
Bitner, M.J., 256, 260
Bjerke, R., 444
Blackett, T., 418
blueprints, 253
BMRB (British Market Research Bureau), 173
Bonoma, T.V., 139, 140
Booms, B.H., 256, 260
Boots, 217
Boots Advantage Card, 427
Boston Consulting Group (BCG) portfolio
    matrix, 229–32, 402
bottom-up approach, 436, 440–4
Bowers, M.R., 264
brand choices, group influence on, 102
brand communities, 215
brand differentiation, 148–9
brand equity, 214, 419
brand extension, 422–3
brand identity, 208, 213, 353, 407–8, 410,
    417–18, 424
brand image, 208, 403, 412–13, 418–19
brand loyalty, 26, 136–7, 167, 414, 425–8
    loyalty schemes, 172, 426–7
brand managers, 422
brand maps *see* perceptual maps
brand names, 420–1
brand personality, 410, 417, 424
brand portfolios *see* product portfolios
brand positioning, 120, 144, 147–56, 202
    see also competitive position; market
        position; repositioning
brand stretching, 422, 423
brand types, 420
branded content, 295
branding, 11, 202, 208, 416–19
    advantages of, 213–17
    defining, 212–13
    global, 207, 213, 424–5
    lifestyle, 30–1
    and market segments, 124
    and power, 343–4
    role in competitive advantage, 10, 401
    of services, 262–3
    and trust, 330, 426
branding strategies, 422–3
brands
    defining, 212–13
    perceptions of, 147–8, 149–52
    and product life cycle, 227
    product placement of, 295
    top ten, 416
breakeven analysis, 369–72
breakeven point, 369, 370
breaking down, 321
bricks and clicks operations, 27
Bridgewater, S., 60
Brien, R.H., 166
British Airways (BA), 314, 341
British Market Research Bureau
    (BMRB), 173
British Red Cross, 347

broadband, 253
Broadcasters' Audience Research Board (BARB), 173
Broderick, A., 278
Brown, Derren, 204
Brown, S.W., 264
Bryan, L.L., 234
Bucklin, L.P., 211
budgets, 308–10, 451, 474–5
bus market, 141
business mission, 460–3
business objectives, 463
    see also corporate plans
business-to-business (B2B) markets, xi–xii, 65, 106
    characteristics of, 107–9
    customer service in, 400
    impact of e-channels on, 346
    promotion in, 282, 299–300, 403
    push strategies, 274–5
    research, 171
    segmentation in, 126, 138–42
    and strategy, 472
    views of supply chain, 331–2, 333
    see also organisational buying
business-to-business (B2B) products, 211–12
Buttle, F., 301
buyer behaviour, 94
    influences on, 95–104
    see also consumer buyer decision process; organisational buying
buyer readiness, 105
buyers
    bargaining power of, 458–9
    in decision-making units, 104, 110
    partnership with seller, 332
    in retail chains, 333
    in supply chain, 320
    see also consumers; customers
buying centre, 109–10
    see also decision-making units
buying situations, 91–2
buzz marketing, 28
Buzzell, R.D., 476

C2C (customer-to-customer) markets, 348–9
    see also consumer markets
Cadbury, 292, 420
Calkins, T., 428
call centres, 27, 243, 249
camera manufacturers, 136
campaigns, 272
capability analysis, 453
CAPI (computer-assisted personal interviewing), 186, 192
capital goods, 211
Carat International, 132
Carphone Warehouse, 309, 341
cartels, 365
cartoon test, 184
case studies, 177
cash and carry outlets, 331
cash cows, 230, 231
CATI (computer-assisted telephone interviewing), 192
celebrities, xiii, 289
censorship, 51, 262
census surveys, 178, 193
chain stores, 322
Chandra, C., 339

Chandrashekaran, M., 264
change, managing, 443
Channel 4, 204, 294
charities, 347
Chartered Institute of Marketing (CIM), 4, 441
children, 103, 144
China, 51, 262
choice, 205, 415–16
classical conditioning, 96–7
click2procure, 347
climate, 69
clinics, 184
clockwork power, 223
close competition, 63
closed questions, 190, 191
closing techniques, 304
cluster sampling, 188
co-branding, 422
Coca-Cola, 39, 64, 146–7, 207, 215, 216, 320, 425
codes of practice, xii–xiii
    advertising, 52, 53, 103, 308, 309
    alcohol promotion, 380
    market research, 166
coffee market, 421
coffee retail chains, 155
cognitive attitude, 100
cognitive learning, 98
cold calling, 304
collages, 184
Colley, R., 281
commercial research, 171
commercialisation, 222
communication
    as function of supply chain, 345–6
    horizontal and vertical, 441
    telecommunications market, xiii
communications overload, 27
communications process, 276–8
communications technology
    Apple iPhone case study, 431–2
    fast-changing nature of, 28–9
    impact on service providers, 249
    and international marketing, 125
    see also Internet
community relations, 295
competing brands, 148, 149–52
competition
    global, 12
    types of, 63–4
competitive advantage (edge), 10, 122, 244, 460
    and branding, 10, 214–15, 401
    and packaging, 407
competitive environment, 63–4
competitive intelligence (CI), 10, 454
competitive opportunity, 122
competitive parity method of budgeting, 310
competitive position, 232–3
    see also brand positioning; market position
competitive stance, 472–3
competitive strategies, 400–1
    and international trade, 468–9
competitors
    cross-elasticity of demand, 385
    influence on pricing, 363, 364–5
    research and analysis of, 167, 453–60
    rivalry between, 459–60
complaints, 263, 308, 309

complex buying behaviour, 94
components, 211
computer games, 40
computer industry, 143, 155, 319
computer simulations, 221
computer software, 155, 178, 226, 379, 455
computer technology
    and customised marketing, 66–7
    in marketing research, 192
    see also Internet
computer-aided statistical modelling, 181
computer-assisted personal interviewing (CAPI), 186, 192
computer-assisted telephone interviewing (CATI), 192
computer-based research, 175
computerised questionnaires, 192
conative attitude, 100
concentrated marketing, 147
concept stage of product development, 221
concerts, total product model of, 247
conditioning, 96–8
conflict, in supply chain, 342–4
Consignia, 421
consistency of goods and services, 252–3
consolidation, 67
consortiums, 468
conspicuous consumers, 133
conspicuous purchases, 102
consumer buyer behaviour, influences on, 95–104
consumer buyer decision process, 84–91
    level of involvement, 92–5
    for new products, 104–6
    role of packaging, 407
    role of promotion, 278
consumer buying decisions, types of, 91–2
consumer buying roles, 103–4
consumer durables, 168
consumer markets (B2C markets), 106, 348, 472
    segmentation in, 99, 100, 125
        behavioural, 132–8
        demographic, 125–7
        geo-demographic, 129–31
        mediagraphic, 132
        psychographic, 131–2
        social grading, 127–9
    see also C2C markets
consumer models, 84–5
consumer needs, 85–6
    see also customer needs
consumer panels, 173, 185, 186
consumer products, 209–11
consumer promotions, 298–9
consumer protection, 29–30
consumer research, 169
    see also marketing research
consumerism, 29–30
consumers
    compared with customers, 23–4, 65
    and marketing orientation, 22
    as part of service experience, 249–51
    in services marketing mix, 257
    users in DMUs, 104, 110
    views of distribution, 329–30
    see also buyers; customers
Consumers' Association, 29
contingency plans, 475–6

contract agreements, 468
contracting out *see* outsourcing
contribution pricing, 368–9
controllable variables, 42
convenience goods, 210
convenience sampling, 189
convenience stores, 322
core benefits, 205–6, 246–7, 399, 400
corporate brand names, 420–1
corporate coaching, 243
corporate communications, 295
corporate plans, 444–5
    see also business mission
corporate social responsibility (CSR),
    16, 22
cost plus pricing, 365–9
cost-based pricing, 359, 365–72, 391–2
costs, 357
    and pricing, 362–3, 365–72, 391–2
    types of, 366
countertrade, 49
country, and international marketing
    environment, 69
Cox, A., 344
creative execution, 288–9
credit cards, 373, 427
crisis management, 296
Crittenden, V.L., 141
CRM *see* customer relationship
    management
cross-elasticity of demand, 385
cross-selling, 67
culture
    and buyer behaviour, 100
    and international markets, 69–71, 302
    organisational, 20
currency, 69, 376–7, 406
customer complaints, 263
customer contact activities
    outsourcing of, 243, 249, 258
    see also customer service
customer expectations, 203, 261, 411
customer lifetime value, 137
customer needs, 203, 205, 217–18
    see also consumer needs
customer orientation, 19–20, 46, 65
    lifestyle branding, 30–1
customer perceptions, 96, 203, 206–7,
    261, 417–19
customer profiles, 170, 172, 305, 427
    see also audience profiles; databases
customer relationship management (CRM),
    xiv–xv, 26
    impact of Internet, 347
    one-to-one marketing, 123
    in service sector, 249
customer relationships, 14–15, 215, 258
    and outsourcing, 243, 258
    relationship marketing, 25
    service recovery, 263–4
    see also brand loyalty
customer research, 169
    see also marketing research
customer satisfaction, 426
customer service, 243, 249, 258, 324,
    400, 415
customer value pricing, 363
customer-to-customer (C2C) markets,
    348–9
    see also consumer markets

customers
    bargaining power of, 458–9
    compared with consumers, 23–4, 65
    consistency of, 253
    importance of, 23
    influence on pricing, 363, 385–6
    in marketing mix, 257, 412
    product awareness, 214
    promotion and influencing, 275, 278–81
    relationship with brand, 215
        see also brand loyalty
    retaining, 25–6
    as stakeholders, 75
    types, 65
    views of pricing, 358, 360
    see also buyers; consumers
customised marketing, 65–6, 108, 122, 147

DAGMAR model, 280–1
data
    primary, 174, 175
    quality of, 192–4
    secondary, 171–3, 174
data analysis, 165, 455
data collection, 454–5
    see also marketing research
data integration management, 455
data mining, 305
database marketing, xiv, 305–6, 455
databases, 137, 139, 193, 455, 457
Davies, Bruce, 177
Day, G.S., 234
Dean, J., 374
deciders, in DMUs, 104, 110
decision convenience, 250
decision process segments, 141
decision-making units (DMUs), xii, 103–4,
    150, 285
    organisational, 109–10
decline stage of product life cycle, 225,
    414, 422
decoding, 277
Del Monte, 457
deletion stage of product life cycle, 225–6
delivery, 108, 324, 329, 345, 348
Dell Computers, 143
demand, 12–14
    elasticities of, 385
        see also price elasticity of demand
    fluctuations in, 108, 248, 328
    and mark-up pricing, 366–7
    in organisational markets, 107–8
    price, supply and, 359, 360, 381
    push and pull strategies, 274–5
demand-driven markets, 11, 12–13, 122
demographic segmentation, 125–9, 139, 146
demographic trends, 56–7
demonstration advertisements, 288–9
department stores, 322
derived demand, 107
descriptive research, 176
design of supply chain, 334–9
desire stage of AIDA model, 279
desk (secondary) research, 165, 171–3
destroyer (predatory) pricing, 374, 378
Dhalla, N.K., 229
Dibb, S., 124, 132–3, 254
Dichter, E., 169
differentiated marketing, 146–7
differentiation, as purpose of promotion, 283

digital products, distribution of, 349
direct communication, 281
direct competition, 63
direct costs, 366
direct exports, 340, 341
direct mail, 305
direct marketing, 281, 304–7
direct selling, 337
direct-response advertising, 305, 306
disassociative groups, 101
discount stores, 322
discounted prices, 379–80
dissonance-reducing buying behaviour, 94
distortion, 277
distribution, 404–6, 410
    consumer views of, 329–30
    and environment, 62
    evaluation and control of, 480
    importance of, 318–19
    international trade, 339–42
    organisations' views of, 331–2
    and packaging, 408–9
    partnership view of, 332
    place dependency of services, 248
    in product life cycle, 414
    see also supply chain
distribution channels, 319–20
    breadth, depth and length, 336–9,
        404–5, 442
    e-channels, 346–9
    faulty goods in, 333
    intermediaries in, 321
    international, 405–6
    power and conflict in, 342–4
distribution research, 170–1
distributors, trade promotions, 299–300
diversification strategy, 467
DMUs *see* decision-making units
dogs, in BCG matrix, 230, 231
Dolce & Gabbana, 309
Domino Pizza, 273
Donavan, D.T., 264
Dorset Cereals case study, 353
Douglas, S.P., 425
Doyle, Peter, 39
DRIP model, 283
drives, 98
drug users, 183
Dudley College, 193
dumping, xiii
Dupont, 472
durable goods, 209
dyadic comparisons, 151

e-channels, 346–9
    see also Internet
e-mail, 186, 192
e-marketing, x–xi, 26–7
e-media, 289, 290, 291
e-questions, 192
e-tailing, 256, 323, 348
    and conflict, 405
    and distribution, 327, 329, 346, 348
    and pricing, 385–6
    transaction convenience, 250
early adopters, 105, 138, 228
early majority, 106, 138, 224, 228
Easter eggs, 383
eBay, 349, 364, 385
economic cycles, 54–5

economic environment, 53–6
economics, supply and demand, 12–14
economies of scale, 122, 321, 324, 367, 469
economists' views of pricing, 359
EDI (electronic data interchange), 346, 347
effectiveness, 336, 477
efficiency, 336, 477
efficient markets, 386
Ehrenberg, A.S.C., 283
elasticities of demand, 169, 385
    calculating, 384
    see also price elasticity of demand
electoral polling, 188
electric light, 219
electronic data interchange (EDI),
    346, 347
electronic distribution, 346
electronic point of sale systems (EPOS),
    328–9, 345
emergency goods, 210
encoding, 276–7
Enis, B.M., 226, 415
environment
    defining, 38
    see also external environment; internal
        environment; marketing environment
environmental information, 41–4
environmental scanning, 43–4, 455
environmentalism, 44–5, 54, 410
EPOS (electronic point of sale systems),
    328–9, 345
equilibrium point, 13, 14
esteem, 99
ethics, xii-xiii
    of buzz marketing, 28
    customers' views, 330
    in marketing research, 166
    and pricing, 361–2
    privacy, 456
    of products, 204
    and promotion, 309
    and sales, 301
    societal marketing orientation, 22–3
    of targeting children, 103, 144
    see also censorship
Ethiopian coffee, 421
ethnography, 176, 177
European Union (EU), 49, 50, 365
Eurostar, 116
evaluation
    by buyers, 87–9, 90–1, 105
    of marketing research, 166
    see also marketing evaluation and control
events management, 295
evoked sets, 89, 216
excess capacity, 469
exchange, 14–15, 25, 332–4
exchange rates, 377
exchange relationship, 318
exclusive distribution, 336–7
Exel, 328
exhibitions, 111, 403, 404
experimentation, 180–2
expertise, 242
explanatory research, 176
exploratory research, 175
export restrictions, 49
exports, 48, 340, 341
extension strategies, 225
external data, 172, 174

external environment, 41–2, 44–5, 48
    competitive environment, 63–4
    economic environment, 53–6
    impact on buyer behaviour, 100–4
    market environment, 65–7
    natural environment, 61–2
    political environment, 49–52
    regulatory environment, 52–3
    social environment, 56–8
    SWOT analysis of, 72–3
    technological environment, 58–61
external information search, 87
external primary research, 175
external validity, 194
extinction (predatory) pricing, 374, 378
eye movement camera, 179

facilitators, 323–4
factory outlets, 323
FAIRTRADE Mark, 330
fame see celebrities
family, impact on buyer behaviour, 102–3
family life cycle (FLC), 127, 128
family orientation influence, 102
family procreation influence, 102
fantasy advertisements, 288
Farquar, J.D., 251
fast-food restaurants, 252–3
    see also McDonald's
fast-moving consumer goods see FMCG
feedback, 277, 301
    see also tracking
Fernie, J., 328
Fever-Tree, 275
field experiments, 180
field research see primary research
finance department, 47
financers, in DMUs, 104, 110
Firestone Tyre Company, 332
First Direct, 27, 251
first mover advantage, 39
fixed costs, 366, 368
flatpack homes, 362
FLC see family life cycle
flow charts, 253, 259
fluctuating demand, 108, 248, 328
FMCG (fast-moving consumer goods), xi, 168,
    209, 210, 282, 472
focus groups, 183, 186, 193
Ford Explorers, 332
Ford, Henry, 122
Ford Motor Company, 146
forecasting, 194
fragmentation see market fragmentation
franchisees, 253
franchisers, 253
franchises, 67, 323, 468
freedom of speech, 51, 262
Friends of the Earth, 54
Frow, P., 25
full-cost pricing, 367–8
functional plans, 444–5
functional silos, 441

Gale, B.T., 476
garage door case study, 159
gatekeepers, in DMUs, 110
Gay Police Association, 309
GDP (gross domestic product), 54, 241
GE-McKinsey matrix, 232–3

gender, and international sales, 302
gender trends, 57, 58
general need descriptions, 110
general pricing strategies, 374–6
Generation X, 56–7, 133
Generation Y, 133
generic products, 211, 227
geo-demographic segmentation,
    129–31, 193
geographic segmentation, 125, 146
geographic-based price discrimination, 375
geographical concentration in organisational
    markets, 107
geographical diversification, 469
geography, impact on international
    marketing, 69
global branding, 207, 213, 424–5
global competition, 12
global economy, 54
global village, 125
globalisation, xi, 469
    see also international marketing environment
Gluck, F.W., 233
goals, 98
    see also marketing objectives
going-rate pricing, 364–5
Goldsmith, R.E., 67
goods, 202, 240, 245–6
Google, 51, 262
government, as customer, 65
government policy, 49–51
Greenley, G.E., 449
Greenpeace, 462
Gregor, W., 449
Grewal, D., 254
grey importing, 377
Gronroos, C., 260
gross domestic product (GDP), 54, 241
grounded theory, 176
groups see reference groups
growth stage of product life cycle, 224, 414
guarantee advertisements, 288
Guiltinan, J.P., 381
Guiness, 225

habitual buying behaviour, 94
haircare case study, 78–9
Haire, M., 184
Haley, R.I., 136
Hall, Edward, 70
Hanan, M., 437
Handy, C., 242
hard sell, 9, 19
    see also timeshare holiday homes
Harley-Davidson, 101, 423
HDI (Human Development Index), 54
hedonism, and buyer decisions, 92
Heinz, 272, 420
Heitjans, T., 419
Hellmann's mayonnaise, 154
Hennig-Thurau, T., 419
Hewlett Packard, 320
hierarchical management structure, 441
hierarchy of effects models, 278–81, 282
high-context culture, 70
high-involvement purchases, 210
hoaxes, 88
Hocutt, M.A., 264
Hollander, S.C., 324
Hoover, 300

horizontal communications, 441
hospitality, 402
housing
    flatpack homes, 362
    as means of market segmentation, 129
housing market, 323
Houston, M., 419
Howard, J.A., 85
Human Development Index (HDI), 54
human resources, 475
human resources department (HR), 46–7
humour, in advertising, 97

IBM, 319
idea stage of product development, 220–1
IDM (Institute of Direct Marketing), 305
Iglesia, V., 217
IKEA, 321, 362
image
    and price, 357
    see also brand image
import restrictions, 49
imports, parallel importing, 377
impulse goods, 210
impulse purchase, 86
in-depth interviews, 182
income elasticity, 385
incoterms (international commercial
    terms), 335
Ind, N., 444
independent retailers, 322
indirect communication, 281
indirect competition, 64
indirect costs, 366
indirect exports, 340, 341
industrial classifications, 140–2
industrial concentration in organisational
    markets, 107
industrial markets, 65
industrial products, 211–12
industrial research, 171
industrialisation, 11
inelastic demand, 50, 108, 373
influencers, in DMUs, 104, 110
information framing, 96
information gathering function of supply
    chain, 345
information purpose of promotion, 283
information searches, 86–7, 94–5
initiators, in DMUs, 104, 110
Innocent, 410
innovation, 18, 60–1, 217–18, 344
innovative products, 218
innovators, 105, 138, 224, 228
inside-out approach, 440–1
Institute of Direct Marketing (IDM), 305
Institute of Public Relations, 293
Institute of Sales Promotion (ISP), 297
instrumental conditioning, 97
insurance companies, 136
intangibility, of services, 247–8
integrated marketing communication, 281
Intel, 472
intensive distribution, 337
interest stage of AIDA model, 279
interest stage of buyer readiness, 105
intermediaries, 321, 327, 337–8, 471–2
    see also agents; distributors; wholesalers
internal ad hoc data, 455
internal continuous data, 454–5

internal data, 171–2, 174, 454–5
internal environment, 41–2, 45–8, 72–3
    see also organisational environment
internal influences, on buyer behaviour, 95–100
internal information search, 87
internal marketing, 443
internal validity, 194
international agreements, 52–3, 335
international commercial terms
    incoterms), 335
international competition, 12
international distribution, 335, 405–6
international marketing environment
    company development in, 48
    and competitive environment, 64
    and economic environment, 56
    market entry, 48, 339–42
        strategic reasons for, 468–70
    outsourcing, 243, 249
    and political environment, 49–52
    and social environment, 57
    and technological environment, 59
international marketing environment, xi, 51, 65,
    68–71, 125, 302
international packaging, 409
international pricing, 376–8, 406–7
international product decisions, 401–2
international promotion, 273, 403–4
international strategy, standardisation vs.
    adaptation, 470–1
Internet, x–xi, 26–7, 67
    advertising with e-media, 289, 290, 291
    censorship, 51, 262
    consistency of services on, 252
    electronic distribution, 346
    and goods-services distinction, 246
    impact on B2B sector, 346–8
    impact on supply chain, 405
    and international marketing, 125, 403–4
    price comparisons using, 376, 386–7
    pricing on, 385–7
    research using, 186
    self-service using, 249
    shopping see e-tailing
    stealing connections to, 253
Internet auctions, 349, 364, 385–6
Internet banking, 251
Internet Explorer, 39, 379
Internet hoaxes, 88
Internet service providers (ISPs), 74
interviews, 182, 186
intranets, 186
introduction stage of product life cycle,
    223–4, 414
introductory offers, 373
iPhone case study, 431–2
ISP (Institute of Sales Promotion), 297

Jack, Fiona, 177
James, E.S., 166
Jaworski, B., 22
Johnson & Johnson, 154
Johnson, R.M., 152
joint demand, 107
joint promotions, 299
joint ventures, 468
Jones, Ewan, 177
Jones, J.P., 283
judgemental sampling, 189
JVC, 344

K3, 155
Kaur, G., 31
Kellogg's, 309
Kewill, 155
KFC (Kentucky Fried Chicken), 88, 124
Kimiloglu, H., 428
knowledge, and power, 343
knowledge workers, 242–3
knowledge-based economies, 242
Kohli, A.J., 22
Kotler, P., 5, 24, 104, 241, 449, 471, 473
Krugman, H.E., 180
Kumar, S., 339

laboratory research, 180, 184
LaGarce, R., 226, 415
laggards, 106, 138, 228
language, 70–1
late majority, 106, 138, 228
launches, 222–3
law, xii–xiii, 49, 52–3
    and brand identity, 408
    and cartels, 365
    consumer protection, 29–30
    and power, 343
    and pricing, 378
    and sales promotions, 300, 380
    trading hours, 328
    see also codes of practice; regulatory
        environment
LDCs (less developed countries), 57, 59, 183
lead times, 60
learning, and buyer behaviour, 96–8
learning organisation, 208
legitimate power, 343
leisure activities, 243
less developed countries (LDCs),
    57, 59, 183
levels of involvement, 86, 92–5, 255
Lever Fabergé, 289
Levi's, 292, 390
Levitt, T., 18, 228, 246, 415, 425, 462
Levy, S., 5
licence agreements, 468
life cycle see product life cycle
life stage, and market segmentation,
    127, 128
lifestyle branding, 30–1
lifestyle groups, 133–5
lighting, 219
Likert scale, 191
Lindgren Jr., J.H., 146
line extension, 422
Liverpool case study, 34–5
lobbying, 53, 295
location, 325–7
logistics, 328
logistics services, 323–4
loss leaders, 368, 378–9, 383
loss-making customers, 23
low-context culture, 70
Lowenbrau, 153
loyalty see brand loyalty
loyalty schemes, 172, 426–7
Lucozade, 225, 467

McDonald, M., 7
McDonald's, 39, 124, 207, 297, 326, 424, 468
McKinsey's 7S framework, 442–3
McLibel trial, 297

McLuhan, M., 125
macroenvironment, 44–5, 48, 167
   see also external environment
macrosegmentation, 139, 141
Malhotra, A., 262
malredemption, 300
MAM (Multi-attribute Attitude
   Mapping), 149–51
management
   of promotions, 271
   see also marketing planning
manufacturers, 320, 405, 420
margin of safety, 370–1
marginal cost pricing, 369
mark-up pricing, 366–7
market attractiveness, 120–2, 232, 233
market challengers, 39, 472–3
market development strategy, 467
market dynamics, 38–41
market entry
   barriers, 457
   options, 339–42
market environment, 64–7
   see also marketing environment
market followers, 39, 473
market fragmentation, 65–7, 122, 475
market growth, 459
market leaders, 38–40, 459, 472–3
market nichers, 39, 473
market orientation, 7, 15–16, 21–2, 437
market penetration pricing, 373
market penetration strategy, 466–7
market position, 38–40, 472–3
   see also brand positioning
market research, 11, 220, 427–8
   defining, 162, 163
   see also marketing research
Market Research Society (MRS),
   162–3, 166
market screening, 469–70
market segmentation, 66, 120, 121
   approaches
      B2B markets, 126, 138–42
      consumer markets, 99, 100, 125–38
   criteria, 123–5
   defining, 123
   during product life cycle, 224, 225
   reasons for, 122–3
   STP process, 154–6
   see also price discrimination; target
      marketing
market segments, 39, 121, 170
   targeting *see* target marketing
market selection, for international
   trade, 469–70
market sensing, 475, 476
market share, 55, 230–3, 234, 357, 373, 382
market skimming, 373
market targeting *see* target marketing
market traders, 322
market-based pricing, 363–5
market-led companies, 39
marketers, view of pricing, 360
marketing
   changing emphasis of, 24–5
   in context of organisations, 436, 444–5
   defining, 4–10
   importance of, 357
   origins of, 11–12
   twenty-first-century, 26–31

marketing activities, 8
marketing analysis, 44–5
   PRESTCOM model, 45–6, 68,
      72, 143, 453
   situation analysis, 71–4, 445, 446, 448,
      452–60
   SWOT, 72–4, 453
marketing budgets, 308–10, 451, 474–5
marketing channels *see* distribution channels
marketing communications *see* promotion
marketing concept, 7
marketing departments, 5, 436, 442
marketing discipline, 7
marketing environment, 38
   analysis, 450, 452
   international, 68–71
   models, 44–6
   research, 167, 172
   see also external environment; internal
      environment; market environment
marketing evaluation and control, 447, 448,
   451, 476–81
marketing function, 5
marketing information, quality of, 192–4
marketing information systems
   (MkIS), 454–6
marketing intelligence, 453–4
marketing management *see* marketing planning
marketing management tools, 448, 449
marketing metrics, 452, 478
marketing mix, 199, 202, 270, 396, 398–407
   criticisms of, 415–16
   evaluation and control of, 478–80
   extended to 7Ps, 256–61, 396, 409–12, 415,
      478–80
   integrating, 412–13
   objectives, 396–8
   through product life cycle, 413–15
   see also packaging; place; price; products;
      promotion
marketing myopia, 463
marketing objectives, 447, 448, 450, 463
marketing operations and implementation, 447,
   448, 473–5
marketing opportunities, 318–19
marketing organisation, 438–9
marketing philosophy, 7
marketing planning
   business mission, 460–3
   contingency plans, 475–6
   environmental information in, 42–3
   marketing evaluation and control, 476–81
   marketing objectives, 463
   marketing strategy, 463–73
   in new product development, 221–2
   operations and implementation, 473–5
   process, 444–51
   situation analysis, 452–60
   top-down and bottom-up, 440–4
   use of product life cycle in, 226–8
marketing plans, 449–51
marketing programmes, 451
marketing research
   areas of, 167–71
   commercially available research, 173–5
   defining, 162–3
   ethics in, 166
   expenditure on, 164
   and market orientation, 21
   primary (field) research, 175–9

marketing research *cont.*
   methods and techniques, 179–87
   questionnaire design, 189–92
   sampling, 187–9
   process, 164–6
   quality of information, 192–4
   secondary (desk) research, 171–3
   use and value of, 163–4, 455
   see also market research
marketing strategies, 447, 448, 450, 463–73
marketing tactics, 474
markets, 15, 16, 121
   status of Internet, x–xi
Marks and Spencer, 328, 329, 342, 343
Marlboro cigarettes, 154
Mars, 207
Maslow, A.H., 98
mass customisation, 66, 122
mass marketing, 65, 122, 146
mass media, 282, 290
mass production, 11
Masters and Servants, 294
matching process, in SWOT analysis, 74
maturity stage of product life cycle,
   224–5, 414
MDCs (more developed countries),
   57, 59, 242
MDS (Multidimensional Scaling),
   149, 151–3
me-too products, 219
media
   and advertising, 289–292
   mass media, 282, 290
   role in consumer protection, 29
   used for direct marketing, 306–7
   see also television
media classes, 290
media relations, 293–4
media vehicles, 290
mediagraphic segmentation, 132
medical sales, 275
Melewar, T.C., 471
membership groups, 101
merchandisers, 333
merchandising, 299
mergers, 67, 468
messages, 276–7, 288
microenvironment, 45
   see also internal environment
microsegmentation, 139, 141
Microsoft, 39, 40, 319, 379
Miller, 153
Minarik, Andrew, 41
Minitab, 178
misredemption, 300
MkIS (marketing information
   systems), 454–6
mobile phones, 431–2
modified rebuy situation, 109
Monkey Shoulder, 177
Montgomery, D.B., 175
Moore, W.L., 46
Moorthi, Y.L.R., 424
more developed countries (MDCs),
   57, 59, 242
MOSAIC, 129–30
motivation, 98–9, 131, 132
motor industry
   brand positioning, 148–9
   bus market, 141

motor industry *cont.*
  organisational structure, 442, 444
  pricing, 362–3, 376
  product development, 221
  promotion, 274
  Tata case study, 6
mousetrap case study, 237
MRS (Market Research Society),
  162–3, 166
Multi-attribute Attitude Mapping
  (MAM), 149–51
multibranding, 422
multichannel distribution, 337, 338
Multidimensional Scaling (MDS), 149, 151–3
multinational companies, 171, 222
Muniz Jr., A.M., 215
music advertisements, 289
music industry, 387

NAICS (North American Industry
  Classification System), 142
naming
  of products, 213
  renaming organisations, 421
Narver, J., 22, 64
national economies, 54
nationalisation, 49
natural environment, 44–5, 61–2
natural gas, 345
Nectar scheme, 137, 170, 172
need descriptions, 110
needs, 85–6, 98–9, 203, 205, 217–18
nested approach to B2B market segmentation,
  139–40
Netscape, 39, 379
networks, 467
neuro-research, 179
new product development, 168, 218, 219–23
  see also innovation
new product pricing strategies, 372–3
new products, 217–19
  and branding strategies, 422
  branding and success of, 216–17
  consumer buyer decision process, 104–6
new task buying situation, 109
news style advertisements, 288
niche markets, 39, 147, 211, 473
Nike, 52, 214, 337, 461, 462
Nintendo, 40
noise, 277
non-durable goods, 209
North American Industry Classification System
  (NAICS), 142

objective and task method of budgeting, 310
objectives *see* marketing objectives
observation, 179, 187
occupational segmentation, 127, 129
O'Guinn, T.C., 215
Ohmae, K., 425
omnibus surveys, 184–5
one-to-one marketing, 123
OPEC (Organisation of the Petroleum
  Exporting Countries), 365
open-ended questions, 190, 191
operant conditioning, 97–8
operating variables in B2B market
  segmentation, 139
operations *see* marketing operations
operations department, 47

opinion leaders, 105
Oppenheim, A.N., 192
opportunity cost, 358
order routine specification, in buying
  process, 112
organic food, 61
organisational buying, 106–7
  buying centre, 109–10
  buying situations, 109
  process, 108–9, 110–12
  purchase criteria, 112–13
organisational culture, 20
organisational environment, 46–8,
  436, 444–5
  see also internal environment
organisational markets *see* business-to-business
  (B2B) markets
organisations
  objectives, 444–5, 463
  structure of, 436–40, 441, 442
  views of supply chain, 331–2
out-of-town stores, 326, 327
outside-in approach, 440–1
outsourcing, 243, 249, 258, 324, 441
over-redemption, 300
overseas markets *see* international marketing
  environment
overstocks, 328
own-label brands, 420
Oxenfeldt, A.R., 46, 358

pack shots, 408
packaging, 329, 407–9
  and sales promotions, 300–1
packaging design, 62
packaging research, 181
Palmer, A., 240
Pampers, 177
panels, 173, 185, 186
parallel importing, 377
Parasuraman, A., 254, 262
Pareto principle, 26
parody advertisements, 288
participant observation, 179
partners, supply chain as network of, 334
partnership view of supply chain, 332
patents, 248, 343
Pavlov's dogs, 96–7
Payne, A., 25
Pearson, M.M., 349
peer interviewers, 183
people
  in marketing mix, 257, 258, 411–12, 480
  see also consumers; customers; salespeople;
    service providers; staff
Pepsi-Cola, 64, 146, 167, 203
Pepsico, 39, 300
perceived products, 206–7, 399, 400
perceived risk, 92
perceived value, 406
percentage of sales method of
  budgeting, 310
perception, 277
  and buyer behaviour, 96
  impact of branding on, 417–19
  see also customer perceptions
perceptual maps, 149–52
performance reviews, 112
peripheral products, 248, 410
Perlmutter, H.V., 425

personal characteristics, in B2B market
  segmentation, 140
personal selling, 256, 271, 280, 301–4, 403
personalisation, 66–7
personalisation of objects technique, 184
personality
  and buyer behaviour, 95–6, 138
  see also brand personality
persuasion purpose of promotion, 283
PEST model, 44
pester power, 103
petrol crisis, 333
phenomenological research, 176
physical distribution, 350
physical evidence, in marketing mix, 257,
  259–60, 410–11, 480
physiological needs, 98–9
'pick-your-own' fruit farm, 334
Pickton, D., 74, 278
picture associations, 184
Piercy, N., 475, 476
pilfering, 301
pilot production, 221
pilot questionnaires, 190
place, 318, 404–6
  consumer views of, 329–30
  design of supply chain, 334–9
  dimensions of time and space, 324–9
  e-channels, 346–9
  evaluation and control of, 480
  international trade, 339–42
  marketing functions in supply
    chain, 344–6
  organisations' views of, 331–2
  partnership view of, 332
  power and conflict in supply chain, 342–4
  see also distribution; supply chain
place dependency of services, 248
place management, 332–4
planning *see* marketing planning; strategic
  planning
point of sale (POS) promotions, 299
political environment, 49–52
political risk, 470
pollution, 61
population changes, 56–7
populations
  demographic segmentation, 125–9,
    139, 146
  research populations, 178
  sampling, 183, 187–9
Porter, M., 460
  five forces model, 456–60
  generic strategies, 464–5
POS (point of sale) promotions, 299
position maps *see* perceptual maps
positioning, 144, 147–56, 202
  see also market position; repositioning
positioning strategies, 152–3
positive reinforcement, 97–8
post-benefit convenience, 251
post-purchase dissonance, 91
post-purchase evaluations, 90–1
post-testing, 168, 180
postal surveys, 185
power, in supply chain, 342–4
pre-emptive pricing, 374
pre-testing, 168, 180
predatory pricing, 374, 378
Prell, A.E., 226, 415

press advertising, 290
pressure groups, 52, 54, 75
PRESTCOM model, 45–6, 68, 72, 143, 453
prestige goods, 39, 384
prestige pricing, 374
price, 406–7
    and branding, 214
    changing, 380–2
    defining, 358
    evaluation and control of, 479
    importance of, 356–7
    international pricing, 376–8
    on Internet, 385–7
    in marketing mix, 361, 406
    in product life cycle, 385, 414
    and quality, 361, 374, 399, 406
    views of, 358–60
price discrimination, 375, 387
price elasticity of demand, 169, 382–5, 386
price followers, 364
price inelastic demand, 50, 108, 373,
    383–4, 386
price leaders, 364
price makers, 364
price takers, 364
price wars, 381–2
price-offs, 299
pricing methods, 362–72
pricing objectives, 361–2
pricing research, 169, 181
pricing strategies, 362, 372–6
pricing tactics, 362, 368, 378–80
pricing techniques, 362
    see also pricing methods; pricing strategies
primary data, 174, 175
primary (field) research, 165, 175–9
    methods and techniques, 179–87
    questionnaire design, 189–92
    sampling, 187–9
primary motivation, 131, 132
privacy, 456
problem children, in BCG matrix, 230, 231
problem recognition, in buying process,
    85–6, 110
problem solution advertisements, 289
problem solving, and buyer decisions, 91–2
process, in marketing mix, 257, 258,
    412, 480
Procter & Gamble, 484
product adopters model, 138
product adoption process, 105–6, 214–15, 228
product awareness, 105, 214
product benefits, 399
product breadth, 229
product depth, 229
product design, and natural environment, 62
product development, 168, 217–23
    see also innovation
product development strategy, 467
product feature segments, 141
product life cycle, 223
    international trade as means of
        extending, 469
    marketing mix through, 402, 413–16
    planning, 226–9
    and price, 385, 414
    and product portfolio management, 231–2
    stages, 223–6
product line pricing, 374–5
product lines, 229

product orientation, 17–19
product placement, 53, 295, 402
product portfolio analysis, 229–34
product portfolio management, 229–34
product portfolios, 148, 229
product quantities, 108
product research, 167–8, 181
product specifications, 110–11
production orientation, 17
products, 398–402
    defining, 202–3
    evaluation and control of, 479
    goods and services, 202, 240, 245–6
    substitutes, 458
    total product offering, 204–8, 399, 400
    transformed in supply chain, 320
    types of, 208–12
    see also branding; distribution; services
profit, 356–7
    see also target profit pricing
profit margins, 368
projective techniques, 184
promotion (marketing communications), 402–4
    budgets, 308–10
    defining, 9–10, 270, 271
    during recession, 55
    evaluation and control of, 479, 480
    function of supply chain, 346
    influencing customers, 278–81
    managing, 271–2
    objectives, 272–3
    and pricing, 361, 379–80
    process, 276–8
    in product life cycle, 414
    regulations, 307–8, 309
    research, 169–70, 181
    role of packaging, 408
promotion mix, 270–1, 281, 402
    and AIDA model, 279–81
    see also advertising; direct marketing;
        personal selling; public relations; sales
        promotion; sponsorship
promotional strategy, 273–5
proposal solicitation, 111
prospecting, 303–4
prototyping, 221
psycho-galvanometer, 179
psychographic segmentation, 131–2
psychological price barriers, 364
psychological pricing, 378
public affairs, 295
public relations (PR), 270–1, 280,
    293–7, 402
public sector, as customer, 65
public sector research, 171
publications, 294
publicity, 293–4
publics, 293
pull strategy, 139, 274, 471–2
pupilometer, 179
purchase decision process segments, 141
purchase decisions, 89–90, 244
purchasing approach, to B2B market
    segmentation, 140
purposive sampling, 189
push strategy, 139, 274, 471–2

qualitative analysis, 165
qualitative research, 175–6, 178, 193
    survey techniques, 182–4

quality
    of Innocent brand, 410
    and price, 361, 374, 399, 406
    service quality, 261
quantitative analysis, 165
quantitative research, 175, 177–8, 193
    questionnaire design, 189–92
    survey techniques, 184–5
    see also sampling
question marks see problem children
questionnaire design, 189–92
questionnaires, 177–8
quota sampling, 189

random sampling, 188
rank order scale, 191
ranking process, in SWOT analysis, 74
RAP, 155
raw materials, 211
re-targeting, 225
Real Food campaign, 54
recession, 55
recommendation, 27–8
    see also word of mouth
recording devices, 179, 344
recycling, 62
Reebock, 214
Reeves, R., 401
reference groups, 100–2
referent power, 343
regulatory environment, xii–xiii, 43,
    52–3, 343
    and advertising, 53, 103, 308, 309,
        380, 403
    see also law
relationship marketing, 25
relaunched products, 219
reliability, of information, 193
reminder purpose of promotion, 283
renaming organisations, 421
repeat purchases, 216
replacement products, 219
reporting, 455
repositioning, 151, 153–4, 155, 225,
    229, 353
research see market research; marketing
    research
research agencies, 165, 173, 183, 184–5
research briefs and proposals, 165
research and development (R&D),
    47, 60, 220
    see also innovation; product development
research populations, 178
    sampling, 183, 187–9
research problems, 165
resellers, 65, 320, 321
resources
    of buyers, 131, 132
    for marketing, 308–10, 451, 474–5
response, 96
retail audits, 173
retail leverage, 216
retailers
    buyers, 333
    location, 325–7
    loss leaders, 378–9
    stock and timing, 327–9
    in supply chain, 320, 321
    types of, 322–3
    see also supermarkets

retailing, 256
  communication, 345–6
  environment, 260
  mark-up pricing, 366
  online *see* e-tailing
returns, 299
revenue, 356–7
reverse auctions, 364
reward cards, 172, 427–8
Ries, A., 154, 156
risk, 92, 470
risk spreading, 469
rivalry, 459–60
Rock Planet case study, 267
Rocket Science, 193
Rogers, E.M., 106
Rogers, W., 449
Rothschild, M.L., 149, 150
routine problem solving, 91–2
Rowley, J., 251
Royal Mail, 421

Saatchi & Saatchi, 242
safety needs, 98, 99
Sainsbury's, 321
sales contests, 300
sales education, 300
sales orientation, 19
sales promotion, 271, 297–301, 403, 406
  and AIDA model, 280
  and pricing, 361, 379–80
sales research, 170–1
sales revenue (turnover), 357
sales volume, 369
  during product life cycle, 223, 224
  impact of advertising on, 284–5
salesforce promotions, 300
salespeople, 302, 358, 403, 475
samples, 178
sampling, 183, 187–9
sampling frames, 188
SBUs (strategic business units),
    229, 232, 444–5
Schewe, C.D., 91
Schnider, Peter, 159
Schramm, W., 276
Schultz, D.E., 441, 455
Scotland, tourism in, 168
Scriven, J.A., 283
secondary data, 171–2, 174
secondary (desk) research, 165, 171–3
segments *see* market segments
selective attention, 96
selective distortion, 96
selective distribution, 320, 337
selective retention, 96
self-actualisation, 99
self-employment, 243
self-image, 92, 95–6
self-liquidating special offers, 299
self-service, 249
sellers
  partnership with buyer, 332
  in supply chain, 320–3
selling, 9
  direct selling, 337
  see also personal selling; retailing
selling into the pipeline *see* push strategy
selling out of the pipeline *see* pull strategy
semantic differential scale, 191

semi-structured questionnaires, 190
semi-structured questions, 191
sentence completion, 184
service convenience, 250
service economies, 242
service encounters, 250
service environment, 260–1
service products, 202, 210, 212, 399, 415
service providers, 249, 258, 411–12
service recovery, 263–4
service sector
  global figures, 241
  growth of, 242–3
  research, 168
services
  branding of, 262–3
  defining, 240–1
  importance of, 241–4
  and international trade, 340, 341
  nature of, 245–54
  quality of, 261
  types of, 254–6
  see also customer service
services marketing mix, 256–61,
    409–12, 415
servicescapes, 260
SERVQUAL model, 261
Shapiro, B.P., 139, 140
Sharma, R.D., 31
Sheth, J.N., 85, 104, 113
shopping *see* retailing
shopping agents, 386–7
shopping goods, 210
Shostack, G.L., 244, 245
Shrimp, T.A., 146
SIC (Standard Industrial Classification), 140–2
Siemens, 347
simple random sampling, 188
Simply Software Ltd, 181
Simpsons, The, 229
Singh, R., 473
Siren advertising campaign, 289
situation analysis, 71–4, 445, 446,
    448, 452–60
situational factors
  in B2B market segmentation, 140
  see also external environment; internal
    environment; marketing environment
Skoda, 149
Slater, S., 22, 64
slice of life advertisements, 288
Smallwood, J.E., 228, 415
SMART objectives, 397
Smith, W.R., 149
snowballing, 27, 183
social class, 127
social environment, 56–8
social factors, in buyer decisions, 92
social grading, 127, 129, 188
social needs, 98, 99
social networking, 28–9
societal marketing orientation, 22–3
Society of Competitive Intelligence
    Professionals (SCIP), 454
socio-economic segmentation, 127
soft sell, 9
Sony, 40, 344
Souhami, S., 454
space, 324–7

space maps *see* perceptual maps
Sparks, L., 328
speciality goods, 211
sponsorship, 281, 291, 295, 296, 402
spoof advertisements, 288
SPSS (Statistical Package for the Social
    Sciences), 178
staff, 258, 475
  see also salespeople; service providers
stakeholders, xii, 5, 74–5, 441–2
Standard Industrial Classification
    (SIC), 140–2
standardisation strategy, 470–1
standardised products, 401, 402
staple goods, 210
Starbucks, 421
stars, in BCG matrix, 230, 231
statistical analysis, 178
statistical modelling, 181
status, 99
  see also prestige goods
stealth (buzz) marketing, 28
stimulus, 96
stock, 327–9
stock holding function of supply
    chain, 345
stock outs, 328
Storbacka, K., 303
straight rebuy situation, 109
strategic alliances, 467–8
Strategic Business Insights (SBI), 131
strategic business units (SBUs), 229,
    232, 444–5
strategic direction, 464–5
strategic gap analysis, 445, 446
strategic orientations, 15–23
strategic planning, 444–5
  reasons for failure, 443
  see also marketing planning
stratified random sampling, 188
Strauss, J., 386
structured questionnaires, 190
student databases, 193
sub-assemblies, 211
subcultures, 100
substitute competition, 64
substitute products, 169, 458
Sultan, R.G.M., 476
Sun audience profile, 286–7
Supercat case study, 237
supermarket reward cards, 427
supermarkets, 322, 326
  bargaining power, 216, 458–9
  and brands, 216, 326, 343–4,
    353, 390
  data collection by, 169
  loyalty schemes, 170, 172, 427
  online, 329
suppliers
  bargaining power of, 459
  in buying process, 111–12
  relationship with, 25
supplies, 212
supply, 12–14
  price, demand and, 359, 360, 381
supply chain, 319, 320, 404–6
  consumer views of, 329–30
  design of, 334–9
  e-channels, 346–9
  evaluation and control of, 480

international trade, 339–42
issues of space and time, 324–9
marketing functions in, 344–6
members, 319–24
as network of partners, 334
organisations' views of, 331–2
partnership view of, 332
place management, 332–4
power and conflict in, 342–4
research, 170
see also distribution
supply-led markets, 11, 12
surveys, 177–8, 182–5, 186–7
survival, and price, 357
SWOT analysis, 72–4, 453
syndicated surveys, 185
systematic random sampling, 188

tachistoscope, 179
takeover bids, 419
takeovers *see* acquisitions
target audience, 273, 285
Target Group Index (TGI), 173
target marketing, 120, 142–7, 154–6
see also market segmentation
target markets, 143, 272–3, 285, 325, 450
target profit pricing, 369–72
targeting *see* target marketing
targeting strategies, 144–7
Tata motor company, 6
Tate and Lyle, 42
Tax, S.S., 264
taxes, 50
technological environment, 58–61
technological innovation, 60–1, 218, 344
technology
  and growth of service sector, 244
  impact on service providers, 249
  and power, 344
  use in observation, 179–80
  see also communications technology;
    computer technology
teenagers, 134–5
telecommunications market, xiii
  see also communications technology
telephone surveys, 185
television
  advertising on, 95, 182, 282, 290,
    291, 292
  branded content, 295
  level of involvement, 95
  product placement, 53
  ratings and publicity, 294
  research, 173
tenders, 365
Tesco, 169, 216, 329, 390
Tesco Clubcard, 172, 427
test marketing, 182, 222

testimonial advertisements, 288
textile industry, 208
TGI (Target Group Index), 173
third-person techniques, 184
thought bubbles, 184
tickets, 259
time, 324–5, 327–9
time dependency of services, 248–9
Time Warner, 74
time-based price discrimination, 375
timeliness, of marketing information, 192
Times, The, 378
timescales of plans, 475
timeshare holiday homes, 20
tobacco industry, 53
top-down approach, 436, 440–4
Topshop, 342
total costs, 366, 367, 368
total product offering, 203, 204–8,
    399, 400
total service product offering, 246–7
tourism, 168, 197
tracking, 180, 181, 447, 476–7
trade cycle, 54–5
trade promotions, 299–300
trade shows, 111, 403, 404
trademarks, 421
trades unions, 75
trading, 10–11
trading blocs, xi, 49
trading hours, 328
training, 244, 258
transaction convenience, 250
transactional exchange, 25
transactional marketing, 24–5
transportation
  of goods, 12, 324, 329, 345
  see also motor industry
travel case study, 116–17
trend spotting, 194
triadic comparisons, 151
trial stage of buyer readiness, 105
trials, 298, 299
Trout, J., 154, 156
trust, 330, 387, 426
turf battles, 441
turnover (sales revenue), 357
Tybout, A.M., 428

uncontrollable variables, 42
undifferentiated marketing, 144–6
Unilever, 484
unique selling propositions (USPs),
    167, 401
unstructured questionnaires, 190
unstructured research, 175–6
usage rate, 137
user status, 137

users
  in decision-making units, 104, 110
  see also consumers

validity, of marketing information, 194
VALS segmentation, 131–2
value
  added in sales promotion, 297, 406
  added in supply chain, 320–1, 345
  of brands, 419
  customer perception of, 205
  in exchange process, 14, 345
  and pricing, 363–4, 406
values, and buyer behaviour, 98–9
variable costs, 366, 368
variant products, 219
variety-seeking buying behaviour, 94
Vazquez, R., 217
vendor rating, 331
vertical communications, 441
VHS, 344
viral marketing, 27, 292
Virgin, 422
Virgin Wines, 292
VisitScotland, 168
vodka, 227
Volkswagen, 274
voluntary chain stores, 322
Voss, G.B., 254
VW/Audi Group (VAG), 148–9,
    442, 444

Wal-Mart, 340
warehouse clubs, 322
Webster, F.E., 113
Weinberg, C.B., 175
Weitz, B., 437
Wensley, R., 124
Which? magazine, 294
white goods, 15
wholesalers, 12, 321, 331, 405
wild cats *see* problem children
Wind, Y., 113, 425
word associations, 184
word of mouth, 27–8, 90, 292, 332,
    412, 425
World Trade Organisation (WTO), 52
Wright, S., 74

youth lifestyle branding, 31
Yuppies, 133
Yuspeh, S., 229

Zaichkowsky, J.L., 94
Zarali, H., 428
Zeithaml, V.A.I., 262
Zimbabwe, 69
Zopa, 177